AN INTRODUCTION TO
STRESS & HEALTH

Sara Miller McCune founded SAGE Publishing in 1965 to support the dissemination of usable knowledge and educate a global community. SAGE publishes more than 1000 journals and over 800 new books each year, spanning a wide range of subject areas. Our growing selection of library products includes archives, data, case studies and video. SAGE remains majority owned by our founder and after her lifetime will become owned by a charitable trust that secures the company's continued independence.

Los Angeles | London | New Delhi | Singapore | Washington DC | Melbourne

2ND EDITION

AN INTRODUCTION TO STRESS & HEALTH

HYMIE ANISMAN & KIMBERLY MATHESON

$SAGE

Los Angeles | London | New Delhi
Singapore | Washington DC | Melbourne

Los Angeles | London | New Delhi
Singapore | Washington DC | Melbourne

SAGE Publications Ltd
1 Oliver's Yard
55 City Road
London EC1Y 1SP

SAGE Publications Inc.
2455 Teller Road
Thousand Oaks, California 91320

SAGE Publications India Pvt Ltd
B 1/I 1 Mohan Cooperative Industrial Area
Mathura Road
New Delhi 110 044

SAGE Publications Asia-Pacific Pte Ltd
3 Church Street
#10-04 Samsung Hub
Singapore 049483

Editor: Donna Goddard
Editorial assistant: Emma Yuan
Production editor: Sarah Sewell
Copyeditor: Neil Dowden
Proofreader: Derek Markham
Indexer: C&M Digitals (P) Ltd, Chennai, India
Marketing manager: Fauzia Eastwood
Cover design: Wendy Scott
Typeset by C&M Digitals (P) Ltd, Chennai, India

Library of Congress Control Number: 2022938268

British Library Cataloguing in Publication data

A catalogue record for this book is available from
the British Library

ISBN 978-1-5297-7872-4
ISBN 978-1-5297-7871-7 (pbk)

There is a crack in everything.
That's how the light gets in.

Leonard Cohen, *Selected Poems, 1956–1968*

CONTENTS

ABOUT THE AUTHORS

Hymie Anisman received his PhD in 1972 (University of Waterloo), and has been a Professor at Carleton University, Ottawa. Professor Anisman was a Senior Ontario Mental Health Research Fellow (1999–2006) and a Canada Research Chair in Behavioural Neuroscience (2001–2015), and is a Fellow of the Royal Society of Canada. The principal theme of his research concerns the influence of stressors on neurochemical and neuroendocrine systems, and how these affect psychological (anxiety, depression) and immune-related physical disorders. His work has spanned animal models, as well as studies in humans to assess stress, coping, and appraisal processes. In this regard, he has assessed the impact of chronic strain emanating from discrimination and stigmatization on well-being, depression, and posttraumatic stress disorder (PTSD) among refugees from war-torn regions and among Indigenous populations that suffered childhood traumatization, distress associated with abusive relationships and life transitions, as well as the transmission of trauma effects across generations.

In addition to sitting on the editorial boards of several journals, Professor Anisman has published more than 400 peer-reviewed journal papers and book chapters. He has written several books related to stress and pathological conditions, and has edited books dealing with stress processes and psychoneuroimmunology. A mainstay of his research program has been the training of students, graduating more than 25 PhD and 60 MA/MSc students over the years. His research has been funded by the Canadian Institutes of Health Research (CIHR), the Natural Sciences and Engineering Research Council of Canada (NSERC), the Ontario Mental Health Foundation (OMHF), the Canadian Foundation for Innovation (CFI), and the Canada Research Chairs program (CRC).

Kimberly Matheson received her PhD in Psychology in 1988 from the University of Waterloo. She has been on faculty at Carleton University since 1990, is currently a Professor in the Department of Neuroscience, and is the joint Research Chair in Culture and Gender Mental Health at the Royal Ottawa's Institute of Mental Health Research and Carleton University.

Professor Matheson's research addresses cultural identity, collective and individual coping, resilience, and outcomes reflecting well-being, social justice, and social change. She has worked with community groups using multiple methodologies, including qualitative, quantitative, and biological analyses. Her research has been disseminated through academic journals and chapters, as well as to wider audiences through lay publications, videos and podcasts, public talks, and organizing workshops and conferences that engaged community members, youth, and frontline professionals. One of the main groups she has worked with for the past 15 years has been Indigenous Peoples. Professor Matheson is the project co-lead of the Indigenous Youth Futures Partnership that works with First Nations organizations and fly-in communities in Northwestern Ontario to co-develop and evaluate approaches to promoting community and youth resilience.

Professor Matheson has considerable experience with formal and informal cross-sectoral partnerships, developed while serving as Vice-President (Research & International) at Carleton University, as well as through founding the Canadian Health Adaptations, Innovation, and Mobilization (CHAIM) Centre. She has run numerous concurrent research programs relevant to Indigenous youth and communities, and trained over 120 thesis students at different levels. Her work has been funded primarily by the Social Sciences and Humanities Research Council of Canada (SSHRC) and the Canadian Institutes of Health Research (CIHR).

PREFACE

There's a poem by Edward Arlington Robinson about a character, Richard Cory, who was later made much more famous by the captivating rendition sung by Simon and Garfunkel. It seems that Richard was

> Born into society, a banker's only child,
>
> He had everything a man could want: power, grace, and style.

Clearly, he was the type of person that everyone envied, and might have wished that they could trade places with him, until we learn of his fate at the end of the poem:

> So my mind was filled with wonder when the evening headlines read:
>
> 'Richard Cory went home last night and put a bullet through his head'.

Sure, there are those people with seemingly charmed lives, who appear to float from situation to situation untouched by the chaos and distress affecting others. However, look a little deeper and you'll find that they aren't immune from stressors, despite the outward appearances. To turn to an old cliché, 'nobody gets out of this alive', and odds are that there are few, very few, who don't have some scars earned along the way. We're not entirely sure what was ailing Richard Cory. However, it is clear that he was far from 'happy with everything he's got'.

Some of the negative events that we encounter might constitute the usual minor unpleasantries, but some may be traumatic, life-threatening events or experiences that suck the soul right out of your head/body, and leave you shattered. We all know of people who have experienced particularly distressing events or multiple horrible events, and we're left wondering how these people survive and even be cheerful at times, and we shake our heads muttering, 'There but for the grace of God go I'. Most of us also know people who seem to get stressed-out far too often: those people who seem to panic over every minor event, and end up stressing everyone around them. The fact is that there are huge differences in how people react to stressors, who deals well and who deals poorly, who succumbs to the effects of stressors and who becomes stronger in the face of adversity. There's no easy solution to getting rid of stressors, and there's similarly no easy way to make yourself invulnerable; however, there are ways to improve your resilience and to limit the damage that might otherwise be engendered by stressors. This book doesn't describe (or prescribe) some form of anti-kryptonite to help you ward off distressing events, and it isn't a self-help book to make you tough. Instead, it aims to provide information, based on empirical research, about the stress process and the factors that generally facilitate stress resilience. However, along the way, some guidance will also be provided that may (or may not) influence your ways of dealing with bad events, and help you to help others. However, each individual, as you'll see, is very different, and so this book is about stress in general, and not about you in particular. Michelangelo observed that every block of marble has an angel inside it that it is the sculptor's job to set free. We're certainly not at the level of Michelangelo. Nevertheless, with the methods and insights of neuroscience and psychology as our chisel we hope to help you understand how the general processes of stress impact on each of us in different ways, and indeed how our very individuality is a consequence of those processes.

As the reader goes through the chapters of this book it will become clear that there is a simple logic concerning its construction. However, in the hope of the reader getting the most from it, there are some simple considerations on *how to use this book*. The successive chapters build on one another to offer the reader an integrated perspective regarding stress and its relation to well-being and pathology, and the methods that can be used to diminish distress and its pathological consequences. The initial three chapters are meant to inform the reader about the various factors that determine the extent to which stressors might have adverse effects. Among other things, these chapters cover a series of variables that are related to the stressor itself, individual difference factors that govern vulnerability to stressor effects, processes related to appraisal and coping, as well as psychosocial and environmental determinants of health. Having described these multiple contributions to the stress process, the next three chapters outline some of the biological consequences of stressors, focusing on hormones (Chapter 4), neurotransmitters, growth factors (Chapter 5), and immune processes (Chapter 6). In doing so, every effort was made to demonstrate that these systems are interrelated to one another and thus jointly protect us from pathology, and conversely that pathology may involve dysregulation involving multiple systems. In addition, these biological changes are considered in the context of the variables described in Chapters 1–3 that influence the potency of stressors. With an understanding of the biological consequences of stressors and the variables that moderate these outcomes, the next two chapters are concerned with the influence of stressors on physical illnesses, notably immune-related illnesses (Chapter 7) and heart disease (Chapter 8). This is then followed by the analyses of stressors on psychological disturbances, particularly depressive disorders (Chapter 9), anxiety disorders (Chapter 10), and addictions (Chapter 11). In discussing the physical and psychological disorders, the text repeatedly returns to the information concerning what makes stressors more or less potent, our stressor appraisal and coping processes, and the biological sequelae of stressors. Chapter 12 takes a slight detour from the preceding chapters and could well have been included much earlier. This chapter deals with the intergenerational effects of stressors, and includes a consideration of developmental factors, including prenatal and early postnatal stressors, as well as biological processes that might contribute to the effects of adverse experiences being transmitted across generations. Having detailed some of the consequences of stressors, Chapter 13 deals with methods to diminish distress, which go hand-in-hand with methods to diminish psychological disturbances and some features of physical illnesses that might be secondary to the associated distress.

As we all know, learning and remembering complex sets of information are less difficult when they are appropriately contextualized. In writing this text we made a considerable effort to simplify some of the material and make it practically relevant, particularly the sections that were related to biological processes. This was done by repeatedly placing this information in the context of pathology. A case was also made for individualized treatment of psychological disturbances; that is, treating individual patients based on the specific symptoms presented together with biomarkers that might inform treatment strategies and prevention of illness recurrence. Admittedly, this can only be repeated so often before it begins to sound like a seamless GIF loop (in our day, like a broken record), and there were times when we felt this intensely. In reading this book, or for instructors teaching from it, we would encourage returning to the information in the first three chapters when considering the effects of stressors on biological systems, and likewise when dealing with pathologies to put this in the perspective of the information related to behavioral and biological processes. This might sound a bit preachy or patronizing, especially as it's likely being said to many good teachers as well as their students, but this is how we envisioned the book being used as we composed the different chapters. This approach has worked well for us as we taught the material, and we hope it does for you as well.

ACKNOWLEDGMENTS

'We are like dwarfs on the shoulders of giants, so that we can see more than they, and things at a greater distance, not by virtue of any sharpness of sight on our part, or any physical distinction, but because we are carried high and raised up by their giant size.' This comment, which has been attributed to Bernard of Chartres (almost a thousand years ago), was subsequently made more famous by Isaac Newton with his statement, 'If I have seen further, it is by standing on the shoulders of giants'.

Our source for all information, Wikipedia, has told us that a form of this phrase also appeared in the works of Rebbe Isaiah di Trani (c. 1180–c. 1250), a Jewish tosaphist (a highly educated and wise scholar who wrote commentaries on the Talmud), in one of his comments regarding our (his) audacity in contradicting an earlier scholar:

> Should Joshua the son of Nun endorse a mistaken position, I would reject it out of hand, I do not hesitate to express my opinion, regarding such matters in accordance with the modicum of intelligence allotted to me. I was never arrogant claiming 'My Wisdom served me well'. Instead, I applied to myself the parable of the philosophers. For I heard the following from the philosophers. The wisest of the philosophers asked: 'We admit that our predecessors were wiser than we. At the same time we criticize their comments, often rejecting them and claiming that the truth rests with us. How is this possible?' The wise philosopher responded: 'Who sees further a dwarf or a giant? Surely a giant for his eyes are situated at a higher level than those of the dwarf. But if the dwarf is placed on the shoulders of the giant who sees further?... So too we are dwarfs astride the shoulders of giants. We master their wisdom and move beyond it. Due to their wisdom we grow wise and are able to say all that we say, but not because we are greater than they.

In these Acknowledgments we again realized how lucky we've been. There are so many people who hoisted us onto their shoulders to give us a wonderful view. We're grateful, not only for their influence in preparing this book, but also for so many other choices we've made. We've been gifted with many wonderful collaborators who made research fun and offered a shared perspective. The gang included Zul Merali, Alfonso Abizaid, Alex Kusnecov, Robyn McQuaid, Amy Bombay, Paul Villeneuve, Marie-Claude Audet, Katherine Graham, Mindi Foster, Sandy Livnat, Arun Ravindran, Mike Poulter, Steve Ferguson, Alex and Cath Haslam, and Nyla Branscombe. We have also had a bunch of really terrific postdoctoral and doctoral students who've gone on to establish their careers in universities, public sector agencies, medical practices or as clinical psychologists.

We are exceptionally appreciative of Michael Carmichael, Keri Dickens, and Imogen Roome at SAGE who helped us through the first edition of this book. For this second edition, we are especially grateful to Donna Goddard, Esmé Carter, and Emma Yuan who did the heavy work of shepherding this book through its many steps, and for patiently guiding us through this process.

For HA, Shimon and Chana were, without question, most important in every imaginable way. Maida, Simon, Rebecca, Jessica, and Max have been the best. We've taken turns standing on each other's shoulders; I hope the view from my shoulders was a good one.

For KM, Lorelei as well as Bernie and Myrna shaped my worldview and hence the contribution I made to this edition. They modelled curiosity, the quiet confidence to pursue what one believed was right and possible, and to grow from the mistakes that will inevitably be made. But even more important was that they embodied the values of kindness, respect, and connection to all living creatures. Perhaps that's why we had the good fortune to have a great number of dogs and cats who provided unconditional support, affection, and much needed distractions.

Finally, we're particularly indebted to the Canadian Institutes of Health Research (CIHR), the Natural Sciences and Engineering Research Council of Canada (NSERC), the Social Sciences and Humanities Research Council of Canada, and the Canadian Foundation for Innovation (CFI) for providing funding for our research, and to the Canada Research Chairs (CRC) program and the Ontario Mental Health Foundation (OMHF).

1

THE NATURE OF STRESSORS

-Monday morning-

Can hardly get myself out of bed. It's just way too early. Why do they have classes at 8:30? It's inhuman. Well, I better move my butt. I've missed a couple of classes already and I'm pretty far behind, and sometimes I can't even figure out what the prof. is talking about. I borrowed some notes, but I might as well be reading hieroglyphics. I wish I had the time to go through the book, but between working at the restaurant at night and meeting with Jesse on weekends, there don't seem to be enough hours in the day. I can't put Jesse off any longer as I'm sensing annoyance because I'm never around. I really don't want to end up being dumped. Until I met Jesse, I felt pretty alone and didn't have much of a social group to hang with. Aw hell, I can't think about that now. The clock's ticking and those two essays and the class presentation are due soon. I don't even know where to start. It almost seems as if my profs are colluding against me. The exam schedule is nuts. My two toughest exams are on the same day, and then I've got six days to study for that no-brainer course that is easier than what we took in high school. I've also got to get home before the exams to see Dad. He didn't sound good last time I spoke to him and Mom. I really miss them, and I think they're not telling me everything about Dad's heart problems. I don't even know where to begin. I just want to stay in bed and cover my head.

There are certain topics that encourage opinions from everybody and their cousin, and on which people seem willing to make statements with absolute certainty regardless of their knowledge of the subject. It's unlikely you would overhear casual conversations regarding topics in physics, such as quark-gluon-plasma or the space and time continuum. However, you might catch snippets of conversations about how to fix the ailing economy (opposite opinions all being dogmatically pushed), about how badly international affairs have been bungled by this or that political party, and about the stresses of modern life. Here, people often divide into two camps. There are those who view modern life as a grind with a variety of stressors appearing everywhere, exacerbated by work/school and unsupportive friends. Others, in contrast, believe that stressors of modern life are vastly exaggerated and that the daily challenges that people are said to experience are something of a fiction, or perhaps it's something that only others need to endure. In short, stress is something everybody talks about with the view that they have special insights into the topic.

Learning objectives

This chapter will introduce you to some basic concepts, with the goal of familiarizing you with key variables that influence the impact of stressful events. So, if you do get into a conversation regarding the impact of stressors, your opinions will be scientifically based. To this end, we will cover:

- a description of what a stressor comprises and the various forms they come in;
- analyses of the attributes of a stressor that result in it having greater or lesser effects;
- how stressors are assessed in a laboratory or real world contexts, including analyses of stressors that appear to be nothing more than minor inconveniences, or stressors that represent life-changing events;
- the individual differences that influence vulnerability to the effects of stressors, or imbue resilience needed to overcome potential adverse consequences of stressful experiences.

Stressful events are linked to a wide range of mental health conditions and are among the prime suspects in the provocation of several physical illnesses. For this reason, it's important to learn how to recognize and deal with stressful events that entangle us every day (have you noticed that it's a jungle out there?), and major life stressors that most of us will invariably encounter at some time or other.

Did the text in the box at the outset of this chapter sound at all familiar? And if it did, upon finding yourself in a similar situation would you do anything about it or would you just hope everything would get better eventually? As we said in the Preface, this book might not help you solve your specific problems (does anybody ever read a preface?). However, it will provide you with information about stress and coping processes, and insights into a constellation of psychosocial, experiential, and developmental factors and how these relate to a wide variety of illnesses that have been associated with stressful events. You'll learn about various aspects of our biological defense systems, and some of the consequences of not keeping stressful events in check. In essence, the book's core goal is to give you a comprehensive and integrated understanding of stress processes and their relation to health. What we want to emphasize is not only that these various elements are all important facets of human psychology, but that stressful events can have consequences that you might never have considered. Beyond having immediate effects on well-being, stressful experiences can mark you for decades. In fact, the stressors you encounter, depending on when they occurred and how severe they were, can have intergenerational effects.

Some basic definitions and concepts

It's a good idea to begin by defining some key terms so that we're all on the same page. For starters, what do we mean when we use the terms 'stress' and 'stressor'? This sounds fairly mundane, doesn't it? Nevertheless, just humor us, and assume that differentiation of these terms might be useful. A 'stressor' is a stimulus or event that is *appraised* or perceived as being aversive and causes a 'stress response'. This stress response can comprise a series of behavioral, emotional, and biological changes aimed at maintaining well-being. Among other things, the stress response involves changes within the body that occur so that energy resources are directed towards the places they are needed, and away from processes that are not essential at the moment (e.g., reproduction, eating, digestion). Simultaneously, multiple brain regions are activated to help us appraise and then deal with the stressful event.

So, what exactly are these stressors? In fact, there is no easy definition of 'stressor', since appraisals of events may vary with contextual factors and change yet again over time, and they are interpreted differently across individuals. In much the same way, what constitutes a stressor may be highly subjective, and the individual differences that exist can be fairly pronounced. Events or stimuli that are stressful to one individual might not be similarly appraised by a second. In effect, one person's poison is another person's meat. For example, jumping out of a plane (with a parachute, of course) might be exciting for some, whereas it might be exceptionally distressing for others. Even if two people appraise a stressor similarly, they might display different emotional reactions. But even if their emotional reactions were the same, they might use different methods of coping with the stressor. Finally, the fact that individuals' appraisals, coping, and emotional responses are similar doesn't mean that their biological responses will be the same, and hence different psychological outcomes (including pathologies) might evolve over time.

Individual differences in stress responses might come about because of several factors. We'll go through each of these, and revisit them in ensuing chapters, as they have important implications for the development of stressor-induced biological and pathological outcomes. Obviously, assessing the link between stressful encounters and the emergence of psychological or physical disturbances isn't easy, but the research that has been conducted has made significant progress and has resulted in the development of effective strategies for preventing illness and treating pathology.

Characterizing stressors

Even at this very early point you've learned something important about stressors. First, not all stressors have the same impact and, second, individuals differ remarkably with respect to how they appraise stressful events and how they respond to them. You've also learned that there are multiple factors responsible for these individual differences. Figure 1.1 depicts several of the numerous variables that influence the impacts of stressors on psychological and physical disturbances. Some of these factors might reflect characteristics of the stressor itself, whereas others might be related to features of the individual and their experiences, their appraisal and coping methods, and diverse psychosocial influences.

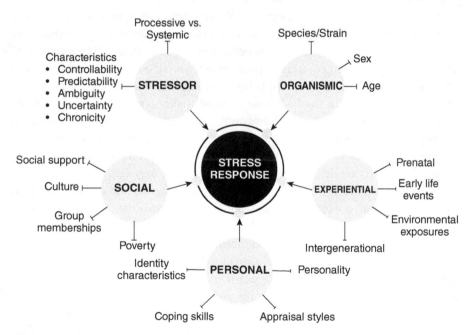

Figure 1.1   Factors that affect the reactions to stressors

Types of stressors

Stressors generally come in multiple forms, and they don't necessarily result in identical outcomes. A stressor that involves information processing (e.g., asking ourselves 'Is that dog drooling and does that glare and posture mean it's dangerous?', or 'Does this guy with the mask covering his face seem like a mugger, or is he protecting himself from catching a virus?') is referred to as a *processive* stressor. Understanding the challenge (stressor) involves several complex cognitive processes that engage numerous brain regions. These include neural circuits responsible for executive functioning to enable appraisals and decision-making (e.g., prefrontal cortex; anterior cingulate cortex), memory processes (e.g., hippocampus and several cortical brain regions), and those involved in anxiety and/or fear responses (e.g., prefrontal cortex, amygdala, bed nucleus of the stria terminalis, and hippocampus). Broadly speaking, processive stressors can be of a purely psychological (psychogenic) nature, or of a physical nature (termed 'neurogenic' stressors), such as those associated with certain illnesses or painful stimuli (e.g., burns). Not surprisingly, psychogenic and neurogenic stressors may elicit similar outcomes in some respects but, as we will see, they can have several very different consequences.

Systemic stressors represent another type of challenge that doesn't involve information processing in the same way, but may nevertheless influence stress-related biological systems. Such stressors might include, but are not limited to, marked changes of glucose concentrations in our blood (as in diabetes), or the presence of inflammation or the production of certain proteins evoked by inflammation (as occurs with heart problems). In these instances, we might not be processing the information with the question 'Is this a threat to my well-being?', as we do when confronted by some processive stressors, but our body might interpret these challenges as threats and send messages to the brain so that certain actions are taken to meet the immediate needs. For instance, the pain associated with a broken bone (a neurogenic processive stressor) might make us more cautious and protective of the injured area, and thus increase the likelihood that it will heal properly. In a similar way, the fatigue and achiness associated with influenza (a systemic stressor) pushes us into bed so that we can rest and thus recuperate more readily. The behavioral changes that occur in response to processive or systemic insults involve the integration of several biological and cognitive systems. It seems that multidirectional communication occurs to coordinate responses between various facets of our brain, peripheral nervous system, hormonal systems, and the immune system.

Psychogenic stressors

Different types of stressors (psychogenic vs. neurogenic vs. systemic) do not necessarily lead to identical outcomes. For example, in rodents, a purely psychogenic stressor, such as being exposed to predator odors, gives rise to neurochemical changes within the brain that are different in several respects from those elicited by a neurogenic stressor (a painful stimulus). In fact, even among psychogenic stressors, marked differences occur as a function of the specific stressor encountered. Those psychological stressors that reflect innate challenges (e.g., predator odors) instigate neurobiological changes that are distinguishable from those elicited by conditioned or learned stressors, such as cues that had previously been associated with a neurogenic stressor. In light of the specific neural circuits activated by these stressful events, it might be expected that they would be associated with the emergence of different behavioral outputs or pathophysiological processes and might require different strategies to attenuate the negative reactions that might occur (Anisman et al., 2018).

At one time scientists thought that we had a 'stress center' in our brain, just as it was mistakenly thought that there was a discrete 'pleasure center'. The neural circuitry associated with stressors is much more complex; we do not have 'a' stress system, but instead there appear to be multiple pathways that respond preferentially to different types of stressors (Merali et al., 2004). When we examine these systems from a perspective relevant to humans, this complexity takes on more tangible meaning and significance. For example, some stress responses reflect outcomes associated with something that has already happened (the loss of a loved one, a business failure, a hurricane, or being ostracized by your friends). In contrast, other challenges might entail future threats (waiting for biopsy results), which might involve the engagement of very different brain pathways.

One can intuitively appreciate that some stressors, particularly those that involve interpersonal events (e.g., the death of a loved one), might favor certain types of responses and lead to depression, but these processes might be distinct from those involving adverse achievement-related events (work-related stress), although these too can favor depressive affect. As we'll see later, varied forms of stigmatization and racism can promote severe psychological and physical disturbances, which might emanate from the activation of other (or additional) processes. Moreover, gender differences appear to exist with respect to the types of stressors that lead to pathological outcomes. In this regard, psychosocial stressors may have more dramatic effects in females than in males, whereas those related to economic problems have more profound effects in males, varying with age (Hu et al., 2021). Other stress responses, especially those that involve uncertainty and are of an anticipatory nature (e.g., imminent surgery, anticipation of an upcoming exam or public speaking, an imminent tax audit, the chance of seeing the bully in the schoolyard), are likely to be accompanied by anxiety (Starcke & Brand, 2016). Still other types of stressors, notably those that are ambiguous in nature (e.g., the 'possibility' of a terrorist attack, or a pilot announcing that 'we have to return to the airport' without further explanation), might be accompanied by disorganized cognitions while the situation plays out.

Some stressors involve an evaluative component (e.g., public speaking or asking questions in class, a job interview), a social component (e.g., a fight with your best friend), one that involves a degree of embarrassment (e.g., certain visits to the doctor), and some that instigate particularly aversive emotional responses (e.g., shame, humiliation). Some psychological stressors may have profound effects, but their actions are fairly transient, whereas others, especially those encountered early in life, may be remarkably powerful, so much so that they can have lifelong effects, even resulting in earlier mortality (Rod et al., 2020). Clearly there are many types of psychogenic stressors, and while they might instigate some common stress responses, their unique features are likely to elicit variations of appraisals, emotions, biological reactions, and psychophysiological outcomes.

Neurogenic stressors

Physical stressors can be brief (stubbing your toe), moderate in duration (e.g., a slight burn, a back strain, or a slightly sprained ankle), they can be persistent (e.g., sustained or recurrent migraine headaches), or they can be both persistent and intense (severe neurological pain, injuries sustained from accidents, or the pain associated with certain diseases, such as rheumatoid arthritis and cancer). There's little question that the more intense stressors call upon an incredible portion of a person's psychological and physiological resources. As well, these neurogenic stressors typically don't appear in isolation of psychogenic challenges. Whether these entail financial difficulties brought about owing to physical illness, repeated trips to doctors or hospitals, loss of employment, having to rely on others, or the anticipation that the distress will continue, it seems that complex multidimensional factors are often at work. As a result, diverse psychological processes might be necessary to cope with these multipronged insults. Often, our abilities may simply be insufficient to deal with events, and external mechanisms that enable us to withstand them (e.g., our social support resources) may become essential.

Systemic stressors

Psychogenic and neurogenic stressors are in some sense tangible (i.e., we can see or feel them), but we can encounter stressors that we might not be conscious of, and hence we might not be aware that we are experiencing strain. Thus, we typically wouldn't think of them as stressors. Nevertheless, surreptitious challenges, such as immune activation, should be considered as stressors given that they elicit a cascade of biological changes that in many ways are akin to those associated with psychogenic and neurogenic insults. Among other things, systemic stressors may affect neuroendocrine functioning, brain neurochemical processes, and could elicit several depression-like behavioral changes (Anisman et al., 2018). However, because we might be unaware that something is happening in our body that might adversely affect us, there is seemingly no opportunity to take steps that might facilitate coping with the challenge. From this perspective, systemic stressors reflect silent, insidious attackers that can have negative repercussions for well-being beyond their potential direct effects. We'll be dealing with this in considerable detail later (see Chapter 6), but for the moment just keep in mind that stressors aren't always obvious but may nevertheless have serious consequences.

Stressor characteristics

Each stressor that we encounter may have unique elements and thus may have very different repercussions. For example, let's consider one broad stressor category, that of being ill, and examine the various elements that make up this type of challenge. An illness can be a brief one (a bad case of the flu, or appendicitis requiring surgery), or one that is less intense, but can still wreak havoc on a person's general well-being owing to the condition lasting for some time, and there are some illnesses that are chronic and/or progressive (get worse over time). Some illnesses might allow individuals to function normally despite the symptoms being exceptionally disturbing (e.g., tinnitus), whereas in other instances (e.g., arthritis, lupus erythematosus, Parkinson's disease) the features of the illness might interfere with multiple aspects of daily life. There are also illnesses, such as type 2 diabetes, that necessitate changes in lifestyle, and can have drastic long-term implications for further diseases, but early on might have few discernible negative effects. Worst of all, for the patient and the family members, are disturbances that rob you of yourself (Alzheimer's Disease), illnesses that might or might not lead to death (cancer, heart disease, HIV), or those that are physically incapacitating (e.g., ALS, paralysis). Some illnesses 'just show up' without any apparent cause, whereas others occur because of traumatic events (a head injury) stemming from one's own behaviors (engaging in certain sports), the actions of others (drunk or incompetent drivers), or acts of nature (flood, hurricane, earthquake). In each instance the illness trajectory may vary over months and years, and the needs of affected individuals might differ accordingly. The psychological aspects related to the illness, attributions regarding the cause of the illness, as well as the extent to which the illness *allows* the engagement of effective coping strategies all differ with the individual's condition.

Severity

Because each stressor has distinct characteristics, it is difficult to compare whether one stressor is more severe and debilitating than another. This is made still more difficult as our perception of stressors may be influenced by the context in which they occur and may vary over time. There are stressors that simply can't be compared to one another in terms of their relative severity (e.g., the death of a child vs. dealing with a severe incapacitating illness) as they are so entirely different on multiple dimensions and are often so severe that comparisons become meaningless. Nevertheless, most people would agree that some stressors are more profound than others (e.g., the loss of a loved one vs. getting a parking ticket), and thus most of us could guess that such stressors are apt to have greater pathophysiological consequences.

Controllability

The notion that control over one's destiny is important in determining psychological health has been around for a long time and there is no question that, under most conditions, uncontrollable stressful events have more profound adverse health consequences than do controllable experiences. Experiments conducted more than 40 years ago documented one of the best-known phenomena in stress research. It was shown that animals exposed to an escapable stressor (a shock to their feet), or that had not been stressed at all, subsequently displayed proficient performance in a test where they were required to escape from a stressor. However, animals that had been exposed to an uncontrollable stressor (a foot shock that they could not escape) later exhibited profound behavioral impairments in an escape test where an active response would have terminated the stressor. In these studies, the animal in the 'uncontrollable' stressor condition received the stressor at the same time and for the same duration as the animal in the escapable shock condition. However, unlike the animals that were exposed to an escapable stressor, those in the uncontrollable condition were unable to control stressor termination. Instead, stressor offset occurred whenever animals in the escape condition made an appropriate response. Thus, animals received the same duration of the stressor, but differed with respect to the psychological dimension of having control over its termination (this is referred to as a 'yoked' paradigm). As only animals in the uncontrollable condition later showed impaired performance, it was concluded that it was not the stressor itself that was responsible for the behavioral impairments. Rather, the animal's inability to exert control over stressor termination resulted in cognitive changes that were crucial in determining whether or not the adverse effects of the treatment would become apparent (Maier & Seligman, 2016).

In describing the characteristics of animals who performed poorly in this paradigm, it was indicated that they did not make overt attempts to avoid or escape the foot shock. Instead, they seemed to passively accept the stressor. Indeed, when an animal made an occasional escape response, this was not predictive of further escape attempts. Cognitive processes were thought to occur whereby they *learned* that their responses were unrelated to outcomes ('nothing I do matters'), and as they had learned that they had no control over the situation they stopped trying to escape. They had learned that they were *helpless*. If animals were initially trained to make an appropriate response and then exposed to the uncontrollable situation, they did not display behavioral disturbances when subsequently exposed to a controllable stressor. Having first learned that they control their destiny, these animals were essentially *immunized* against the effects of the uncontrollable stressor.

NASTY LITTLE CREATURES

For some time it was thought that ulcers were caused by stress. However, it seems that the bacterium *Helicobacter pylori* is responsible for ulcers (Marshall & Warren, 1984), and in recent scientific discussions the contribution of stressful experiences has taken a back seat. To make the point concerning their hypothesis, which most scientists had dismissed, Marshall drank a brew of *H. pylori* to demonstrate that this bacterium would, indeed, cause ulcers. It would, after all, have been tough to get experimental participants for this study or even to get the study through an ethics review panel. For their work in identifying *H. pylori* as the main culprit responsible for peptic ulcer disease, Marshall and Warren received the 2005 Nobel Prize in Physiology or Medicine. Despite strong evidence supporting *H. pylori* in ulcer formation, stressful events and this bacteria may act synergistically

(Continued)

to promote ulceration. Indeed, over the last two decades it has become apparent that the gut is inhabited by trillions of microorganisms that can be beneficial to health. However, factors that cause an imbalance of these microorganisms (called dysbiosis), including stressful experiences and poor nutrition, can promote a wide range of physical and psychological illnesses (Cryan et al., 2019).

The behavioral disturbances elicited by uncontrollable stressors have been seen across a variety of species, but in rodents it is typically seen only in certain situations. It seems that when the stressor is administered to rodents, the high degree of reactivity that is elicited favors an appropriate escape response being emitted (i.e., running from one chamber in which the stressor is administered to an adjacent 'safe' chamber) and thus potential behavioral deficits are obfuscated. However, if the escape response required a motor response that was relatively difficult to accomplish or if an active response had to be maintained for several seconds before successful escape was possible, then performance deficits could be elicited. Such findings gave rise to the suggestion that performance disruption was not a reflection of a cognitive disturbance, such as helplessness, but instead stemmed from brain biochemical changes that hindered the rodents' ability to maintain prolonged or complex active responses (Anisman, 2009).

Failure experiences in humans may have effects vaguely reminiscent of those associated with uncontrollable stressors in animals. For instance, university students exposed to unsolvable problems subsequently displayed impaired performance in a problem-solving task, as did depressed students who had not been exposed to the unsolvable task. Although these outcomes have often been attributed to learned helplessness, there are other explanations that might have little to do with helplessness. For instance, a mismatch between the participant's expectancy regarding their performance and their failure to meet this expectancy might have induced frustration that was responsible for the subsequent impaired performance. As well, an uncontrollable stressor may promote a constellation of hormonal and brain neurochemical changes that undermine effective behavioral responses being initiated and maintained, which can lead to pathological outcomes (Anisman et al., 2018). The differing positions notwithstanding, since these early studies much has been made of the importance of stressor controllability in determining later psychological and physical disturbances.

Stressor predictability, uncertainty, ambiguity, and black swans

The impact of stressors on well-being is influenced by their predictability, uncertainty, and ambiguity. There are occasions when the occurrence of stressors is very predictable, but there are also those when stressors are entirely unpredictable, and our responses in these situations are likely to be quite different. Who among us would have predicted that a pandemic, such as COVID-19, would hit and would have such disruptive effects,[1] or that an earthquake or tsunami would hit a particular region, causing the deaths of thousands upon thousands of people? In contrast, tax time is a stressor, particularly for accountants or those who owe the government a lot of money, and its occurrence is predictable (the behavior of governments may not always be predictable, but you can count on them being systematic when it comes to collecting taxes).

Uncertainty is related to unpredictability, but they can be distinguished from one another. We all will die eventually (that is a certainty), but when this will happen is often unpredictable. Essentially, when we talk about predictability, it is usually in the context of events that will happen; it is simply a matter of knowing when they might happen, whether there will be a warning of their occurrence, and on what schedule they might occur (e.g., a single event, repeated events, events that occur intermittently). Uncertainty, in contrast, deals with events that might or might not occur (e.g., will a new variant of COVID-19 virus end up creating a more destructive pandemic). When there is uncertainty about the occurrence of a stressor, individuals may take on a cavalier attitude that essentially comprises 'whatever happens, happens'. Others, however, seem to have great difficulty dealing with uncertainty, and for these individuals their stress reactions could potentially be pathogenic.

Another similar construct is that of ambiguity. We say that a situation is ambiguous when the stimulus context does not provide sufficient information, or provides multiple but inconsistent bits of information, so that it becomes difficult to determine whether and when the event might occur. For example, ambiguity exists when one has a set of symptoms, but they do not form a coherent pattern that allows for a firm diagnosis.

An old proverb has it that '*mann tracht un gott lacht*', literally translated as 'man thinks (plans) and god laughs'. On a daily basis, most individuals typically behave as if the events in their lives are predictable, that they can reasonably anticipate what the future holds for them, and that they even have some control over their lives. Even though most of us know that this sense of control is an illusion, many of us operate as if we have some say regarding what happens to us: we have expectations for the future, and planning is viewed as necessary given our apparent need for order and predictability. Thus, it shouldn't be surprising that adverse events that are unpredictable are generally viewed as being more unpleasant than predictable events, and are more likely to be associated with disturbed brain neuronal functioning, the excessive activation of some stress hormones, and altered immune functioning (Anisman et al., 2018).

---

[1]To be clear, there had been repeated warnings of an imminent pandemic, and the mantra was frequently repeated that 'it wasn't a matter of if, but when'. Not to pat ourselves on the back, but we were among the many that issued these warnings (see discussion in Anisman, 2021), and based on our research of earlier pandemic responses, we also predicted that vaccine hesitancy would be a major issue that would need to be confronted (Taha et al., 2013). Collectively, we had been preaching to the choir. Political leaders that could have made a difference weren't listening.

So, what is it about the unpredictability and uncertainty regarding bad events that makes them especially aversive? To a significant extent, what differentiates predictable vs. unpredictable events is the anticipatory period. When we know that an event will happen at a particular time, there may be great anxiety about the impending event, and waiting itself, coupled with the probability of events occurring during specified periods, may be stressful. Yet knowing that the event will or is about to happen gives us the opportunity to prepare or adjust our behaviors and expectancies. Unpredictable events, however, don't allow us to prepare in a similar manner, and we may be on edge for extended periods of time. Most people are familiar with the first part of Franklin D. Roosevelt's statement in relation to the Great Depression (1929–1933), but less familiar with the second part; 'the only thing we have to fear is fear itself – nameless, unreasoning, unjustified terror which paralyzes needed efforts to convert retreat into advance'. This very well describes the response to unpredictable, ambiguous, but potentially very stressful situations: irrational, inappropriate, and immobilizing behaviors that reflect our inability to appraise and cope with situations, so that our ability to strategize becomes entirely ineffective.

As with unpredictability, in most situations uncertainty is seen as being more aversive than is certainty. However, there are times when this isn't the case. For instance, some people who are at risk for a genetic disorder, such as Huntington's Disease, might want to know whether they carry the gene for this illness, and hence will invariably be affected. These individuals don't want to live in suspense, essentially with a sword hanging over their heads, and choose to know whether they carry the gene. Others, however, would rather not know and appear to be able to vanquish these thoughts so that their daily routine is not affected. It seems that individuals differ in their *intolerance for uncertainty*. The level of uncertainty that can be tolerated is a trait that individuals bring into situations that involve an ambiguous or uncertain component. High intolerance for uncertainty has been found to be associated with anxiety regarding daily stressors, and the desire to reduce uncertainty predicted elevated information seeking (Rosen et al., 2007).

The co-existence of ambiguity and uncertainty are frequent aspects of our experiences, and they are known to promote anxiety. Consider what your own reactions to ambiguous symptoms of an illness might be (e.g., 'Is this lump something I should worry about?' 'This feeling in my chest seems like indigestion, but it might be a heart attack. What do I do?'). Confirmation of an illness, in turn, might lead to further uncertainties pertaining to the illness and its prognosis ('What are the odds that the treatment will work?'), and the availability of a competent and experienced medical practitioner ('Does this doctor have the experience and skill needed?').

From what has been said to this point, it's clear that unpredictability, uncertainty, and ambiguity can be exceedingly stressful. But there is also a different spin that can be applied regarding the role of uncertainty in the context of serious illnesses. Uncertainty involves two distinct appraisal processes, namely *inference* and *illusion*. If uncertainty exists, then individuals can reconstrue a largely negative situation (inference) to extract a glimmer of hope despite the odds (illusion).

Because uncertain situations are vague and changeable, when events start spiraling downward (e.g., when all treatment efforts to stall the progress of a cancer have failed), individuals can capitalize on uncertainty so that their appraisals take on a positive hue, no matter how limited this might be. Uncertainty, essentially, allows a person to expect the worst, but hope for the best.

Unpredictable and uncertain events obviously have the potential for turning our lives upside down. The death of loved ones, sudden illness, catastrophic natural disasters are all events that we know are possibilities, but we really don't expect them to happen to us. Yet the probability of dying of heart disease is about 31% and that of cancer is about 21–22% (although survival rates have been increasing for several cancers), Type 2 diabetes occurs in about 8.5% of individuals and is climbing, autoimmune disorders occur at 3.1%, and then there's kidney, pancreatic, or liver disease, and serious automobile accidents that lead to severe disability or death occur at a rate of about 1.7% each year. There is also a chance of being hit by lightning or the possibility of being in a plane crash (although these are rare events, for the person hit by lightning or the people on the plane, such probabilities simply don't count). The point of all of this is simple. We might not know how we'll fare in the future but given the number of bad things that can happen to us, and the additive probabilities of these events, we can pretty much count on not getting away untouched. We don't know whether, how, or when we'll encounter these nightmares, but it's almost a certainty that we'll encounter some bad dreams.

ILLUSIONS AND DELUSIONS OF CONTROL

It seems that for many of us, there is a need to maintain a semblance of control over our own destinies. Even when a situation is entirely unpredictable and individuals have absolutely no control over the outcome, those who are self-assured are more likely to choose to exercise their own judgment in determining that outcome. The fact is that when situations are unpredictable and when outcomes are entirely out of our control, our participation in decision-making (e.g., how to treat an illness) is not that far removed from that of engaging in a game of chance (e.g., tossing a coin). For example, when given the opportunity to play a game of chance (say roulette) where individuals either have absolutely no control over outcomes or are allowed to 'pay' a premium to press a button to stop the wheel (in this instance they have a semblance of control insofar as the wheel will stop, but they have no control with respect to where the ball lands), they will more often pick the latter. Similarly, when people buy lottery tickets, they often prefer to choose their own numbers rather than have a series of numbers generated through a computer (as if they have a divine connection with the odds maker in the sky, which the computer, of course, doesn't). It seems that some people feel that they (or others) are endowed with a trait of being lucky ('I'm a lucky person', as opposed to 'This was my lucky day'), and so might get involved in events that involve high risks (e.g., gambling) that they believe don't apply to them because they are, after all, lucky. There are others who develop an 'illusion of control by proxy' wherein they find a 'lucky person' to buy their lottery tickets for them. One wonders whether stock-market players, at least to some extent, are affected by some of these characteristics.

Some time ago Taleb (2007) introduced the 'black swan theory' to explain irrational behaviors that people often endorse in the context of making decisions. Essentially, from Taleb's position, there are events that occur very infrequently and are essentially unpredictable and have a major impact on the individual (or society, or the economy). These events often have people rationalizing, in hindsight, that it might have been predictable if only the right data had been available. For instance, could we have predicted 9/11 and the ensuing stock-market catastrophe; or the earthquake in Japan and resulting tsunami that had the potential to produce a nuclear meltdown? Probably not, but it can be argued that even though any single event is an outlier (a black swan), there are so many possible things that could go wrong that one or more of these will eventually occur. Black swans don't simply refer to 'major' events like a 9/11, a crash in the housing market, or the possibility of another war breaking out somewhere (the latter aren't really black swans given how frequently these occur globally). There are human tragedies that can also occur, such as being diagnosed with a rare disease, sitting at an outdoor cafe and having part of a building suddenly collapse with you as collateral damage, or a piece of space junk re-entering the atmosphere and taking direct aim at your house. We can't know what will befall us, as there are simply too many 'unknown unknowns'; so many that the odds of dodging all of them are slight. However, they can and do occur, and their ramifications can be enormous.

THE BRAIN'S RESPONSE TO KNOWING AND THE UNKNOWABLE

Given that we often find ourselves in situations in which the information available is ambiguous and making decisions entails a degree of risk (e.g., the stock markets), there has been increasing interest in determining which brain regions might be engaged for decision-making under such conditions. For instance, which brain regions are activated under conditions that involve risk (i.e., the outcome probabilities are known), ambiguity (there is a lack of *information* about outcome probabilities), or ignorance (the outcomes were completely unknown and even unknowable)? It was observed that relative to the risk situation, ambiguous information provoked especially marked activation of certain brain regions (inferior frontal gyrus and posterior parietal cortex), and this same outcome was apparent when participants were presented with non-useful information (the ignorance context) (Bach et al., 2009). Using a similar paradigm, marked individual differences could be detected in the neural processes activated in relation to risk and ambiguity (Blankenstein et al., 2017). Perhaps specific cortical brain regions are activated in an effort to make sense of this situation. In essence, the brain doesn't like uncertainty and tries to set things in order. It has been suggested that the individual differences observed in these situations might be related to differences in intolerance for uncertainty, and it is important to consider this variable in assessing neural systems that are involved in decision-making.

Chronicity

There are stressors that, unfortunately, must be endured on a chronic basis: these can be psychosocial or family-related issues, financial impositions, health problems, discrimination or stigma, or a combination of different factors. When stressors are chronic, do not vary much from day to day, and occur on a predictable basis (termed 'homotypic' stressors), we are often able to adapt and perhaps even take charge of our situation. Sometimes, however, the stressors experienced might be chronic, intermittent, unpredictable, ambiguous, and uncontrollable, and vary across days (referred to as 'heterotypic' stressors), making it difficult to establish adequate coping methods, or even to take preparatory steps to enable effective coping. Under such conditions, the usual adaptation that occurs in response to homotypic stressors might be less likely to develop (Anisman et al., 2008). Thus, persistent stressors, such as acting as a caregiver (e.g., for a parent with Alzheimer's or a child with exceptional needs), or dealing with chronic illness or financial problems, each of which involves multiple challenges that might change from one day to the next, might strain an individual's ability to cope effectively and might lead to psychological or physical disturbances (Del-Pino-Casado et al., 2019).

Chronic unpredictable stressors needn't be severe to elicit pathophysiological outcomes. Studies in animals showed that a regimen that comprised a series of mild uncontrollable stressors was effective in this regard (Willner, 2016), although this outcome was not universally observed, tending to appear more readily with somewhat stronger stressors. The chronic mild stress model, perhaps because it has a degree of intuitive appeal (i.e., it 'sounds' right), has received wide recognition and attention, but it seems that the effects of stressor treatments depend on several other factors, such as previous stressor experiences, genetic factors, and the coping styles adopted.

Allostatic overload

In recent years, the concepts of allostasis and allostatic overload have evolved to explain the impact of severe or chronic stressors. Under normal conditions biological changes occur to meet the ebb and flow of environmental demands, thus maintaining stability within the organism. This essentially describes homeostasis. In response to strong or sudden stressful challenges, greater and more rapid biological changes are instigated to restore and maintain stability, which we refer to as allostasis. As adaptable as humans and animals might be, when a strain on the system is excessive, adaptive biological systems might eventually become overly taxed, or specific biological systems excited for excessive periods, resulting in *allostatic overload*. Under these conditions the organism may become ill or more vulnerable to the negative impact of new stressors that might be encountered (McEwen & Akil, 2020).

Measuring stressors

We all seem to know what we mean by a stressor, but for experimental purposes we need to be able to distinguish between different types of stressors and how intense these stressors are perceived to be. Later, we'll be discussing individual differences in how stressors are appraised and perceived, but for the moment we'll examine how stressor experiences are measured, and a few of the limitations of these procedures.

Major life events

Stressful events are known to promote psychological disturbances, and severe stressors are more likely to do so than are relatively mild stressors. In an effort to analyze the impact of stressors, several scales have been developed to predict the relations between stressors and the occurrence of illness or disturbed quality of life. One approach is based on the notion that a stressor ought to be considered in terms of the social adjustment that is required to deal with it (e.g., the Social Readjustment Scale: Holmes & Rahe, 1967). Others simply focus on major life stressors that have been encountered over a set period of time (e.g., six months or one year), basing relative severity on responses from a normative group of participants (Paykel et al., 1971). Other questionnaires focus on particular types of events, such as traumatic experiences that might have occurred at some specific time over the course of the life span (e.g., the Traumatic Life Events Questionnaire; Kubany et al., 2000), or particular emotional-cognitive responses reflective of pathological conditions such as posttraumatic stress disorder (PTSD; the Impact of Events Scale, Weiss & Marmar, 1997). There are scales that deal with specific types of stressors ranging from psychological abuse to breast cancer and other types of challenges.

These scales share certain key attributes (they do, after all, give us an idea of what an individual has experienced), and they share several deficiencies. First, an evaluation of the distress experienced by an individual over some set period of time is implicitly or explicitly based on scaled scores. For instance, in the Social Readjustment Scale, 'death of a child' receives a score of 100, 'trouble with in-laws' gets a score of 29, 'changes in work hours' a score of 20, 'revisions of personal habits' 24, and 'pregnancy' is scored as 40. So the combination of getting pregnant, changing our personal habits, altering our work hours, and having issues with our in-laws is worse than having our own child die. That doesn't make a lot of sense, does it? Furthermore, certain items on the list seem to have a positive valence (e.g., an outstanding personal achievement), others a negative valence (e.g., the death of a close friend), and still others depend on the individual's perspective (e.g., a major change in responsibilities at work, such as a promotion, demotion, or lateral transfer). So, the scale doesn't necessarily reflect adverse events, but instead deals with 'life changes' that might or might not be interpreted as stressors. Of course, the scales don't consider the context in which a stressor had occurred. For instance, the death of a loved one is typically a severe stressor, but it might vary as a function of whether the deceased person had been going through a severe illness or had died suddenly in an accident.

A further problem with each of these approaches is that they ask individuals to report on events that had previously occurred, and hence are subject to 'retrospective bias'. The way individuals interpret or even remember the past may be colored by how they feel at the moment. If an individual is feeling really great, then past negative events might not seem so bad and they might not even recall that certain adverse events had ever occurred. In contrast, if the individual is currently dejected, then all events in their past may be perceived as the slings and arrows of outrageous (mis)fortune and they might even dredge up events that were insignificant at the time. Further to this, when individuals are ill they often want to know why this occurred. Is it something they did, or something that somebody else did? Or is it just bad luck? In the case of people who are depressed they might be looking for causes and might attribute their depression, sometimes inappropriately, to specific past events. In short, as most defense and prosecution lawyers know, we can't be trusted to recall our past experiences accurately.

Daily hassles

One typically presumes that the more intense the stressor the more profound the consequences. To a certain degree this is certainly accurate. But what are the consequences of those day-to-day annoyances that can really bug you, especially when they occur repeatedly or are superimposed on the backdrop of other ongoing stressors (it's not from nowhere that we have expressions such as 'the straw that broke the camel's back')? Most of us know the experience of having to deal with a new stressor when we're in the midst of dealing with an earlier challenge; our immediate response when this occurs is something like 'Oh no! Not now'. It's hard enough to deal with one event, but when coping resources must be redirected to a second, even if it's a trivial one, our abilities to deal with these situations may become stretched. Most of us must deal with multiple concurrent challenges at some time or other. For some, juggling different tasks is so much part of their repertoire that they can't see how anyone would ever have a problem in this respect. For others, however, juggling multiple demands is exceptionally difficult, taxing their resources, and ultimately leading to illness.

Hassles can be a pain and even small increases in these experiences may result in individuals being more prone to illness and mood disturbances. The relations between daily hassles and pathology are evident across a range of illnesses, including depression, irritable bowel syndrome, and diabetes (e.g., Piazza et al., 2019), although this doesn't necessarily mean that the hassles caused the pathology, as those who are already ill may be more sensitive to day-to-day annoyances. Nevertheless, these seemingly inconsequential stressors, when they continue for long enough, can have a cumulative effect.

The formal publication of the Hassles and Uplifts Scale (Kanner et al., 1981) provided an instrument to show that hassles were related to poor well-being. Since the initial publication of this scale, other similar instruments have been developed for specific groups (e.g., caregivers) or circumstances (e.g., transition to university). Investigations using daily hassles scales typically report an overall score, but it may well be that specific types of hassles are more germane to some individuals than to others. Thus, analyses might be considered in terms of the different types of challenges experienced (e.g., partner, friends, and family hassles, as well as those that are related to home, work, health, and financial strains). This hasn't been widely done, but if it was, then we might see that illness varies as a function of both the severity and type of the stressor encountered, and that certain illnesses are more closely related to particular types of hassles.

In their original report, Kanner et al. outlined some of most frequent hassles and uplifts reported. These included concerns about weight, health of family member, too many things to do, misplacing or losing things, and physical appearance. This paper was published about forty years ago, but some of those same hassles are still pertinent. Today, however, we might find that frustration with our computer, loud people talking on cell phones, emails from work when you're at home, junk emails, and misinformation that inundates us on the internet as being especially annoying. Clearly the nature of the daily hassles we encounter has changed over time. In addition, some hassles might be relevant to the population at large, but might not be at the top of the list for individuals dealing with particular issues, such as caregivers, or people dealing with an illness. When hassles are superimposed on major life stressors, then we're dealing with exponentially greater problems.

Prospective analyses

To overcome some of the limitations associated with retrospective analyses, several researchers attempted to obtain confirmation of stressful experiences by interviewing friends and family members. Although, at first blush, this might seem reasonable, such reports can reflect the observers' own spin or bias, and hence can be just as flawed. Besides this, stress, like beauty, is ultimately in the eye of the beholder, and it's hard to know what a particular person feels by asking someone else. Judicial courts don't allow witnesses to testify about what was happening in the mind of someone else, and researchers are equally skeptical of this approach.

Ultimately, the best way to evaluate the relations between stressful events and later outcomes is by *prospectively* assessing stressor experiences and then relating them to specific outcomes, such as aspects of health. This entails following individuals for lengthy periods (often many years) and then determining whether stressful experiences predict later development of an illness. Not unexpectedly, this can be an onerous task that takes an awfully long time to complete, and participant loss (referred to as subject attrition) can be very high. Thus, one might end up with only those participants who are most dedicated to the project, so that the data collected are not representative of individuals in general. If the study is relatively short term, say for a matter of weeks or even a couple of months, a diary approach can be used. This can be conducted using a format in which participants answer a brief set of questions at the end of each day (or week) describing what they've experienced. This requires that the investigator meet with participants and form some sort of relationship with them so that they will be motivated to engage in the study on a daily basis. As useful as this approach might be, its use in long-term studies is obviously limited by logistical considerations.

In addition to assessing perceptions of events that participants had experienced some time earlier, scales have been developed to evaluate overall reactions to more recent stressor experiences (Perceived Stress Scale; Cohen et al., 1983). This scale, which is the most frequently used to evaluate the stress load that individuals are experiencing, has been correlated with various psychopathogies. Shortened forms of this scale have been developed so that it may be useful in tracking people's stress perceptions over the course of persistent stressors, such as during the COVID-19 pandemic (She et al., 2021).

Vulnerability and resilience

To this point, we've focused on the different characteristics of stressors that could potentially influence behavioral or physiological outcomes. Of course, these features are only a few of the many factors that influence how stressors affect us. To a considerable extent, previous life experiences, characteristics of the organism (animal or human), and personality variables determine the nature of the stress responses that occur. In the next section we'll focus on the influence of these variables. In assessing these factors, we will not only think about what makes us vulnerable to pathological outcomes related to stressful experiences, but also what goes into resilience in the face of different challenges.

In the context of illness, vulnerability refers to the susceptibility of a person (or a group, or even a whole society) to increased psychological or physical poor health in response to environmental or social challenges. Resilience, by contrast, refers to factors that limit or prevent these events from having adverse effects or, more often, resilience refers to the ability to recover from illness. Vulnerability and resilience aren't necessarily at opposite ends of a continuum. The absence of factors that increase vulnerability doesn't necessarily imbue resilience. A person can, theoretically, have many factors that engender stressor resilience, but a single catastrophic vulnerability factor might be sufficient to undo all that fitness. For example, how often have you heard of a person being perfectly healthy who suddenly died? It took only one malfunction, an aneurysm or a pulmonary embolism, for instance, to undo all that was 'healthy' about that individual. In this regard, one could take the view that stressors act on weak links within a system. After all, the proverbial chain is only as strong as its weakest link.

For an individual to be resilient, numerous ingredients might have to come together in exactly the right amounts. It was suggested that neural mechanisms related to reward and motivation (hedonia, optimism), responsiveness to fear and fear-related situations, and adaptive social behaviors (altruism, bonding, and teamwork) all acted to influence character traits that affected resilience to severely traumatic events (Southwick & Charney, 2018). Another view has it that resilience increases with greater tenacity, trust in one's instincts, acceptance of change, control, and spirituality. Still another perspective attributes resilience to the ability to adapt and be flexible to changes, the ability to problem solve, and possessing a positive outlook on life. No doubt, other resiliency factors, including early experiences and genetic influences, contribute to the ability to withstand the potential for stressors to create harm. Conversely, certain characteristics might enhance well-being even in the presence of factors that would otherwise increase vulnerability to pathology. For instance, an individual with many factors that make them vulnerable to stress-related pathology may overcome challenges by having an excellent social support network, spending time in nature, or perhaps by espousing a spiritual belief that allows them to endure the worst challenges. Several factors that seem to make individuals resilient in fending off or preventing the adverse effects of stressors have been identified (see Figure 1.2), but it's certainly the case that there are enormous differences across individuals in this regard.

Most studies that assessed the relationship between stressful events and pathology have addressed questions related to what makes us ill and what characteristics of individuals are most likely to favor illness. Much less information is available regarding what makes us resilient. Where we most often encounter this topic is in considering the resilience of some people in coping with illness, and the findings from such studies have been especially informative. There are some who, in the context of serious illnesses, are particularly resilient and can maintain, or regain, their mental health readily. Among individuals who have previously encountered a severe illness, the cognitive restructuring that might have occurred (e.g., finding meaning in their illness, which we'll come back to in Chapter 2) may have facilitated their ability to appraise and cope with the subsequent stressor. In other instances, however, previous stressful experiences might not have served in this capacity, but instead acted against well-being. Having gone through a traumatic experience, individuals might simply be too worn down or they may be sensitized so that later stressors in the form of severe illness might simply be too difficult to handle.

Resilience in relation to illness can be influenced by several personality characteristics, such as self-efficacy, self-esteem, internal locus of control, optimism, mastery, hardiness, hope, self-empowerment, determination, and acceptance of illness. Knowing this, unfortunately, isn't going to be of much help in advising anyone how to deal with illness as we can't easily get people to develop better self-esteem or greater hardiness. However, the way individuals appraise and cope with their illness may have profound repercussions for their well-being. Specifically,

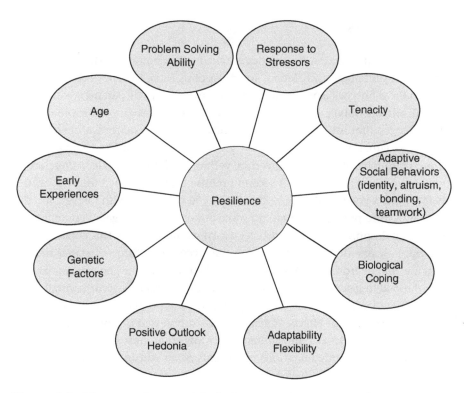

Figure 1.2 Numerous factors might be important in preventing the development of stress-related pathology. These range from personality characteristics, genetic factors, social, cultural, and environmental resources, and a variety of experiences. Some, but certainly not all, of the important ingredients are provided in Figure 1.2. The effectiveness of these resilience factors is likely dependent on the stressor situation, will vary over time as the stressor is experienced, and will also vary across individuals.

positive cognitive appraisal, spirituality, and active coping, which are considered in Chapter 2, were associated with resilience, and these attributes can be promoted with proper training (e.g., using cognitive behavioral therapy or mindfulness training as described in Chapter 12).

In addition to individual difference characteristics, resilience can be attributed to a constellation of processes that reflect a positive social orientation, such as altruism, social bonding, and adaptive social behaviors. In this regard, resilience has been tied to having a strong social identity, being positively connected to others, and having an effective social support network. Socio-ecological frameworks for understanding resilience to some groups, such as Indigenous People, have further emphasized culture, spirituality, and connections to the land. In essence, resilience can entail a relational process involving the interplay of individual, social, cultural, and environmental factors (Liebenberg et al., 2015).

Genetic factors

Years ago, an introduction to genetics entailed a description of Mendelian inheritance (that stuff about pea plants), and most of us came to believe that we inherited certain genotypes (specific genes we received from our parents), which then affected our phenotype (how we looked or behaved). At the same time, it was acknowledged that inheritance could be incomplete, and hence we might not be exactly like either of our parents on any given domain. So, unlike pea plants, people aren't simply tall or short, green or yellow, round or wrinkled: there are all sorts of variations in between. A second premise that was drilled into us was that whatever genes you inherited were those that you were stuck with forever, and that was that. A third premise was that, for some unknown reason, genes could interact with the environment, but nobody ever explained how or why this could happen.

In the past few decades, a revolution has occurred within molecular biology, medicine, and neuroscience. Scientists not only unraveled the genome, they found ways of modifying genes and identifying how genetic changes occur naturally or in response to environmental factors, including stressful events. It is now known that the potential actions or effects of genes can be suppressed by environmental triggers or specific experiences, and consequently might promote (or limit) pathology. In addition, many subtle mutations or variants occur within genes (referred to as 'polymorphisms') that can have profound effects on pathology.

_____ **SO, WHAT'S THIS STUFF ABOUT** _____
GENES CAUSING BEHAVIOR?

There is this notion that genes cause behavioral phenotypes. That seems pretty vague; it's as if you inherit some gene or set of genes, *et voilà* a behavior appears as if by magic. Moreover, it's often thought that the effects of genes are immutable. In fact, however, the job of genes is to produce proteins, including hormones, peptides, enzymes, and receptors that, in turn, influence behaviors. The effects of these genes aren't immutable but are influenced by environmental factors that moderate how they are expressed. So, you might have genes that dispose you to particular characteristics, but whether these characteristics are expressed can be influenced by day-to-day events or those that occurred way back, even when you were just a fetus.

The chromosomes inherited from parents comprise a lengthy DNA strand that comprise many genes. These genes are composed of strings of nucleotides, which in sets of three (a codon) make up amino acids that form lengthy chains. In DNA, these nucleotide bases (guanine, adenine, cytosine, and thymine) reflect the gene playbook. In essence, when strung together the nucleotides, like letters of the alphabet, form words that become paragraphs, which provide the instructions (or blueprints) for the formation of each phenotype expressed by individual humans.

Using the DNA as a template, RNA is formed through a process called *transcription*. The messenger RNA (mRNA) produced through this process is then decoded or *translated* so that a specific amino acid chain, or polypeptide, is created that will produce a protein (e.g., an enzyme, a hormone, or a receptor). When the characteristics of the DNA are altered, as occurs when even a single nucleotide is changed, the message that's delivered can potentially change and have significant consequences.

The genes on a DNA strand are interspaced by a bunch of additional nucleotides, much of which we know little about. But, in this pile of 'junk DNA' we also find strands that precede the gene. These are known as 'promoters' or 'promoter regions' (there are other names used as well, such as 'response elements') that are thought to act as activators or repressors. Essentially, the promoter serves as an instruction manual for the gene that follows it. These promoter regions can tell a gene when to turn on or off, or even when to interact with other genes. Importantly, environmental events, including stressors, influence these promoters by affecting other chemicals present in cells as well as extracellularly, which can then affect the influence of the gene on neurobiological processes that come to affect behavior.

Genes, therefore, have the potential to affect behavior in one way or another (e.g., increasing certain proteins that favor a disposition towards behavioral phenotypes, such as depression or anxiety), but don't directly cause the behaviors. Ultimately, what we do is dictated by much more than just our genes. Face it, whether it's God or Nature, neither fully transcribes our lives before we are born. That would be pretty boring. Instead, we're faced with multiple paths that can be taken, ways to deal with environmental and social challenges, and these affect the way genes get to express themselves.

Approaches in humans

Many studies have shown that genetic factors might be related to various psychopathological states. These studies have included pedigree analysis in which a particular phenotype has been traced through families to identify the presence of particular genes. Other studies compared pathology in monozygotic and dizygotic twins (identical vs. fraternal twins) to determine the degree to which a particular phenotype was inherited or induced by environmental factors. In some cases, comparisons were made between identical twins who were reared together or apart, although as we'll see later these studies were often fraught with difficulties. In more recent years, one of the most common approaches has involved the identification of particular genes or gene polymorphisms in relation to the presence of pathological states. In some instances, this has entailed finding a sample (cohort) of affected and non-affected individuals (who have, or do not have, a particular phenotype or a family history for a particular phenotype), and then doing whole genome analyses to see whether there is a match between the presence of certain genes or mutations and the appearance of a pathology. The idea was that if we could identify the gene associated with an illness, then determining what proteins this gene is responsible for making (e.g., levels of hormones and immune factors) would facilitate the development of treatments to attenuate or prevent pathology.

It sounds simple enough to find a proper cohort and then do the genetic analysis. However, if it were that simple, then many of the problems in the field might already have been solved. First, the diagnosis of an illness needs to be correct, which isn't always a simple matter as different illnesses have overlapping symptoms. Second, just because individuals have similar symptoms doesn't necessarily mean that these stem from the same underlying biological causes (including genetic and biochemical processes). Two individuals can come to have a particular chemical modification, but this might have involved different routes (much in the same way as your bank account can be low either because you're spending too much, not earning enough, a bank error, or unknown to you someone had been removing money from your account). Finally, there are potentially many mutations that can occur across the genome (more than a single mutation can also appear on any given gene), and most of these will be entirely unrelated to the pathology being studied. As a result, a huge number of participants is needed to do the studies appropriately. In retrospect, it is understandable that the data from studies that had been conducted were not particularly reliable, probably because so many mutations occur concurrently and due to the small numbers of participants used. What is clear, however, is that for certain pathologies, as well as the underlying biological processes, the expression of genetic effects was not always evident. However, in many instances, the contribution of genetic factors was apparent in the presence of particular challenges, such as life stressors.

Approaches in animals

Studies conducted using rodents have made it clear that genetic factors are fundamental in determining several stress responses and the pathological outcomes associated with stressors. In this regard, several approaches can be adopted to evaluate these relationships. A first step that is often taken is the use of inbred strains that naturally differ with respect to a given phenotype and genotype. Mice of a given inbred strain are genetically identical to one another and differ from those of other inbred strains. The genetic variation between strains is then related to neurochemical or hormonal differences in response to stressors. Of course, simply because a strain is high (or low) with respect to both a given behavioral outcome and particular biological change doesn't mean that these factors are connected. But as described in the box below, this observation can be followed by further analyses.

━━━━━━━━━ GENETIC ANALYSES IN PAST DECADES ━━━━━━━━━

There are occasions in which it might be suspected that the effect of a stressor is determined by the genetic backdrop upon which it is superimposed; that is, having a particular gene doesn't cause the development of a particular psychological or physical illness, but it might be 'permissive' in that it allows for stressors to have adverse effects. There are some fairly simple, if somewhat tedious, laboratory manipulations that can be conducted to evaluate these possibilities.

When mice of two inbred strains are crossed, the offspring (referred to as the F1 generation) will all be genetically identical to one another. For example, one parent might be dominant for both components of a gene (AA), whereas the other parent may be homozygous recessive (aa). As the offspring inherit one gene from each parent, they will necessarily be Aa. With respect to another gene, both parents may be BB, and so the offspring will necessarily be BB. The same will apply to every gene and hence all F1 animals will be identical to all others. When we cross two F1s, we can then begin to see differences in the genotype: the offspring of an Aa x Aa cross can potentially carry the AA, aa, or Aa combination. Within this F2 generation (also referred to as the 'first segregating generation') we can determine whether a particular genotype and phenotype are linked to one another (either in the absence of a stressor or following exposure to a stressor). For instance, if every mouse that inherited the AA genotype exhibits a particular phenotype, and every mouse with the aa genotype exhibits a different characteristic, then the genotypes and phenotypes might be related. This doesn't mean they are causally linked, as this is once again simply a correlation between variables. However, if those mice that exhibit a given phenotype do not carry a particular genotype, then we would know with a fair degree of certainty that these genotype, and the phenotype are unrelated.

There are occasions where a single gene can have more than a single phenotypic outcome. This is referred to as 'pleiotropy'. Pleiotropy can occur because genes on a chromosome are inherited as a group (termed 'linkage') or because one phenotype (e.g., a biological change) may directly or indirectly lead to a second phenotypic change. Assessing genes across successive crosses allows us to see whether certain characteristics always appear together (e.g., Does a certain chemical always end up being present in conjunction with a particular heart problem? Does having a certain coat color predict the occurrence of epilepsy?). In effect, we could develop 'biomarkers' that predict later disease occurrence.

As well, one could determine whether genetic influences interact with maternal factors in determining outcomes. As we have just learned, all F1s of inbred strains are identical to one another. If a particular trait is entirely due to genetic factors, then it shouldn't matter who their mother is (i.e., from one strain or the other). However, F1 mice can be produced where the dam (mother) is a member of a particular strain, whereas in another cross the dam is of the alternative strain (referred to as a 'diallel cross'). In this instance the F1s will be genetically identical, but if they differ from one another on some phenotype, then we'd likely ascribe this to characteristics of the mother.

With the remarkable advances in our understanding of molecular biological processes and the related technologies, newer and more sophisticated methods have been developed, including those in which the genome of specific strains of mice can be engineered (transgenic mice). Thus, one can assess the effects of stressors on a particular outcome in the presence of a specific genotype. For instance, a gene can be deleted from (knock-out) or added to (knock-in) the genome of a mouse, and then bred so that numerous identical mice are obtained. This allows for analysis of the role of a particular gene or small set of genes in relation to specific pathophysiological outcomes, and how stressors influence vulnerability to pathology. So, if one believes that stressors cause a rise in chemical X, which then promotes depressive-like symptoms, then strains can be developed that lack the gene responsible for producing chemical X and thus determine whether the depressive-like behaviors are prevented. Conversely, mice can be developed that overexpress the gene that determines the presence of chemical X, with the expectation that depressive-like features would be more prominent. In theory, this approach is potentially revealing and might prompt important hints for human pathology. Yet, as most complex human pathologies likely involve many genes, the effectiveness of this approach is necessarily limited, and certainly doesn't reflect the full spectrum of a disorder. Furthermore, in mice born with a particular gene deleted, there is a fair possibility that other genes may compensate for the deleted genes.

With respect to the latter issue, approaches have been developed so that the gene deletion will occur at specific times in life (thereby limiting the adaptations that could occur through early development). The possibility of using this 'conditional knockout' in relation to pathology has been very exciting, and opportunities exist to assess the combined role of more than a single gene.

More recent approaches have entailed the use of CRISPR-Cas9 technology, and variations of this procedure allow for aspects of a gene to be deleted or inserted and then observing changes of pathological conditions (Jinek et al., 2012). This break-through method has met some challenges (e.g., the occurrence of unwanted out-comes, notably 'off target' effects on the genome), but increasingly sophisticated methods are being developed to enhance the accuracy of the procedure.

The key point is that when these genetic approaches are coupled with the analy-sis of stressor effects (and other factors that may favor the provocation of behavioral disturbances) and experiential factors (e.g., early-life experiences), it may be possi-ble to identify the array of variables that contribute to stress-related disturbances. This approach can also be used to identify the relative contribution of different biological processes to specific features (symptoms) of illness and may ultimately provide biomarkers that can be used to predict an individual's vulnerability (or resilience) to disease states.

The data supporting genetic involvement in stress-related pathology are over-whelming and have been fundamental in the development of new targets for the treatment of several illnesses. One can't say, however, to what extent genetic and environmental factors influence pathology as, among other things, their relative contributions likely vary with the specific disease being assessed. Understandably, most of the molecular genetic analyses that have been conducted have involved animals (primarily mice), and studies of the interactive effects of stressors and genes in affecting illness in humans have been more limited. Nevertheless, as we'll see, when these factors were examined concurrently, the results obtained were impressive.

Precision medicine

Before closing off this section one further issue ought to be introduced. Because of the diversity of symptoms associated with most psychiatric disturbances, the var-iability in the effectiveness of pharmacological treatments of such disorders, and the presumed array of neurochemical and hormonal processes that might underlie them, it was suggested that analyses of these illnesses might not be best served by assessing them as syndromes. Instead, it might be more useful to consider specific *symptoms* of a disorder in relation to certain genetic components and neurobiologi-cal processes that might be related to the efficacy of treatment responses. This is not an easy thing to do, but calls for this approach have become more common, and it has led to the idea that rather than treating all individuals diagnosed with a syndrome in a particular way, it would be propitious to identify the biological and behavioral characteristics of each person, and then to apply 'individualized' treatments.

Most often this is referred to as *precision medicine*. This might be expensive in the short run, but more economically sensible over the long term.

Personality

We all know those individuals who, given the least encouragement, seem to turn into Henny-Penny shouting that the sky is falling, whereas others, in contrast, seem stoic even under the worst of conditions. As we've already seen, there are several factors that make us different from one another. An important set of characteristics engendering diversity of responses to stressors concerns personality attributes. There appear to be relatively stable features of individuals that are important in determining whether they will be more or less vulnerable or resilient to the impact of stressors. Certain personality traits might influence the stress process by affecting the way we appraise or cope with stressors. Others might make us more sensitive or reactive to stressors, and there seem to be characteristics that are instrumental in getting us into aversive situations (e.g., high-risk takers). Many of these factors may have evolved through the parenting individuals received, the socialization that occurred in early life including cultural values and expectations, experiences that shaped particular responses, and it is possible that genetic factors also contribute.

One of the best studied views of personality has comprised the analysis of the Big Five or Five Factor Model. This conceptual framework has a lengthy history that culminated (more or less) with the model provided by Costa and McCrae (1992). The Five Factors include Openness, Conscientiousness, Extraversion, Agreeableness, and Neuroticism. One could argue that each of these dimensions could influence stress responses indirectly, but it is Neuroticism (or emotional stability), which reflects a disposition to experience unpleasant emotions readily (anger, anxiety, depression, or vulnerability), that seems most closely related to stressor reactivity. In this regard, some of the questions from the Big Five Factor inventory ('I get stressed out easily'; 'I worry about things'; 'I get irritated easily') tell us this factor is indeed targeted at stress-related reactivity.

Of course, the Big Five represents only one perspective concerning the personality dimensions that might influence the stress response. In fact, because of the broadness of this framework, it isn't clear that it is the best approach to evaluate predictors of stress reactivity, and numerous other factors have been proposed that are viewed as personality-based moderators of the stress response. Of these, *resilience* has received increasing attention, although it is not considered to be a trait. Resilience is seen as a process (or a constellation of factors) leading to changes that make individuals better able to deal with stressors or to bounce back from the adverse effects otherwise elicited by stressful experiences. Based on the many components that influence the stress response, it can be deduced that there are certain characteristics that lead to an individual being more or less resilient, taking into account that stress responses are governed by multiple contextual factors.

Not surprisingly, individuals who approach situations with an upbeat and optimistic outlook will have a very different view of a situation compared to individuals who enter it with a pessimistic perspective. Scheier and Carver (1985) developed the Life Orientation Test (LOT), which was later revised (LOT-R), to measure the attributes of personality that make up optimism/pessimism. Based on studies using this measure it was shown that optimism/pessimism represents a personality trait that was associated with stress reactions and the ability to meet the demands of severe life challenges. Optimism/pessimism influenced how individuals deal with breast cancer in women and radical prostatectomy in men, moderated hormonal changes and immune responses ordinarily elicited by stressors, and was related to stress reactions, such as burnout (e.g., Carver & Connor-Smith, 2010).

As in the case of optimism, an individual's *self-efficacy* (the belief that tasks can be accomplished and difficulties resolved through one's own efforts) can act as a moderator of the stress response, and thus influence well-being. Likewise, *locus of control* may influence how individuals appraise or respond to stressful events. Specifically, those with a high internal locus of control tend to believe that events in life arise primarily because of their own behaviors and actions, whereas individuals with a low internal locus of control generally think that fate, chance, or powerful others determine what events they encounter. These characteristics may influence how individuals interpret or appraise situations and their own abilities to deal with them, and thus will affect psychological stress responses (we'll be coming back to this in Chapter 9, when we discuss depressive illness).

There are many personality factors that play into how we deal with stressors, and only a small number of these have been mentioned to this point. Numerous volumes have been written on this issue and trying to cover this broad field wouldn't do it any justice, certainly not in just a few pages. As we move forward, however, the contribution of several of these many personality traits will emerge, but the important message here is that you should not assume that the things that bother you, and the way you think stressful issues should be dealt with, necessarily apply to everyone.

Age

An individual's age has a lot to do with how they react to stressors emotionally and physically, and whether pathology will arise. In their thoughtful review, Lupien et al. (2009) indicated that regardless of whether stressors occur prenatally, during infancy, childhood, adolescence, adulthood, or in those who are aged, profound brain changes and mental health conditions can emerge. These outcomes, as already mentioned, can reflect the interaction with genetic and psychosocial factors, but the nature of the pathology that emerges may be dependent on the timing of the stressor experience.

Prenatal experiences

Stressors experienced during pregnancy may have effects on the fetus that will be manifested at various times following birth. In humans, the offspring of mothers who experienced chronic or severe stress during pregnancy subsequently exhibited cognitive, behavioral, and emotional problems during both childhood and adulthood. However, studies that evaluated these relations in retrospective analyses were troubled by some of the factors typical of self-report studies. Moreover, prospective analyses of children born following natural disasters were confounded by changes in quality of life that extended well beyond the primary stressful period (e.g., multiple financial and health repercussions). This, however, does not belie the fact that the severity of natural disasters was a strong predictor of mental health conditions among pregnant and postpartum women, which was related to health outcomes in the offspring.

The fetus's intrauterine environment might profoundly influence its brain development, and hence stressful events that influence this prenatal environment may have repercussions that carry through postnatal periods. For example, stressful events give rise to elevated levels of a stress hormone (corticotropin releasing hormone) within the placenta, ultimately affecting the fetal brain. In addition, among rodents, the offspring of mothers that were stressed during pregnancy showed elevated activity of the stress hormone corticosterone when they encountered stressors postnatally (Grundwald & Brunton, 2015). Furthermore, these experiences influenced neurochemical receptors present within the hippocampus, a brain region that is fundamental in regulating biological stress responses and cognitive functioning. It might be particularly relevant that the effects of maternal stressors have profound effects in female offspring and might be an important element responsible for differences between males and females in the development of stress-related pathology. Chapter 12, which largely deals with the intergenerational transmission of trauma effects, provides a lengthier discussion of prenatal stressor effects.

Early postnatal experiences

Stressors can profoundly affect children, and events early in life may subsequently affect biological responses to stressors in adulthood (see Chapters 4–6), and encourage psychological disturbances, such as depressive and anxiety disorders, and substance use disorders (Chapters 9–11), and may even have effects that are manifested across generations (Chapter 12). There are a wide range of stressors that infants and children can experience, ranging from physical, psychological, or sexual abuse, through to neglect or socioeconomic difficulties (poverty). However, children may not appraise specific challenges in the same way that adults do and therefore it is sometimes difficult to discern how they are being affected by adverse events (e.g., Gruhn & Compas, 2020). In addition, the social, cognitive, emotional, and tangible resources to deal with stressors are not as well developed in children as they are in adults. Thus, it can reasonably be expected that stressful events might have marked immediate effects on children's well-being, and the notion is intuitively appealing that stressors experienced early in life would have repercussions on long-term well-being.

Studies conducted by Harlow in the 1950s revealed that monkeys raised in isolated environments later became asocial and had vastly deficient parenting skills. It has likewise been known for decades that raising children in deprived environments, as in the case of hospitals or orphanages where they were not stimulated by touch or caress, gave rise to frequent psychological and physical disturbances and exceptionally high levels of infant mortality. In fact, marked behavioral and biological disturbances are seen even when humans or rodents are brought up in environments that are not nearly as severe as those experienced by children in orphanages or monkeys in Harlow's studies. Early experiences, and in particular maternal care and factors related to socioeconomic status, most certainly influence developmental trajectories and ultimately adult behaviors (Shonkoff et al., 2009). Among other things, children from a nurturing early-life environment were subsequently found to have a hippocampus that was larger (by about 10%) than children from a less nurturing environment (Luby et al., 2012), which could have enormous repercussions for stress responses and mental health, as well as learning and memory processes. Furthermore, stressful early-life experiences have been associated with greater adult anxiety and depression, and have been implicated in the development of a variety of diseases of aging, such as vascular disease and autoimmune disorders, and premature mortality.

Re-programming biological functions and epigenetic processes

To account for why early events might have repercussions many years later, it was proposed that psychological stressors result in the programming of various types of biological signals, including those that involve hormonal and immunological processes. The biological changes driven by adverse early-life experiences give rise to several behavioral and cognitive changes (e.g., high threat vigilance, mistrust of others, disrupted social relations, disturbed self-regulation, and unhealthy lifestyle choices) that might engender further stressors or result in these individuals being highly reactive to threats. These behavioral factors, and the stress reactions they elicit, might exacerbate already disturbed hormonal and immunological functioning associated with the early experiences, and eventually might culminate in pathology (Lautarescu et al., 2020).

In considering the effects of stressful early-life experiences, one should not just focus on severe cases, such as abuse. Indeed, simply having an inattentive or neglectful parent can have profound and lasting repercussions on cognitive functioning and on vulnerability to stress-related disturbances. Studies with rodents indicated that early-life neglect (during the initial ten postnatal days) may engender disturbed adult behavioral and biological functioning, whereas stimulation enhanced an animal's ability to contend with later stressor experiences. In this regard, it seems that if pups had an attentive mother who cared for them well (in the case of rodents, this involves lots of licking and grooming of pups), then these animals grew up to be relatively resilient in the face of stressors (Kaffman & Meaney, 2007). In contrast, stressors experienced early in life, including insufficient maternal attention, was related to the later development of diverse psychological disturbances (Turecki & Meaney, 2016).[2] Essential questions that have emerged have been concerned with which neurobiological processes are involved in these outcomes, and whether the adverse effects of early adverse experiences can be reversed, or if there are variables that may compensate for poor parenting.

In their influential review and commentary, Shonkoff et al. (2009) indicated that numerous diseases that appear in adulthood, including psychiatric disorders, diabetes, heart disease, and various immune-related disorders, might have their roots in childhood stressor experiences. They suggested that the cumulative effects of life stresses contribute to allostatic overload that might eventually lead to pathology or, alternatively, that stressful experiences in childhood may become biologically 'embedded' (either through processes that cause the actions of certain genes to turn off or via sensitized biological responses) so that their consequences might appear years later. These investigators distinguished between 'tolerable' stressors that, with appropriate social support, might allow individuals to learn how to cope with such events, from those described as 'toxic' stressors (extreme poverty, psychological or physical abuse, neglect, maternal depression, parental substance use, and family violence) that are more likely to lead to pathology. In effect, there are challenges that are basically part of growing up that have positive effects as they allow individuals to learn how to appraise and cope with events properly. However, there are also 'toxic' challenges that no one should have to endure.

EPIGENETIC PROCESSES

A fairly hot topic for many years has been the possibility that stressful events (as well as other factors) may affect the expression of genes, without altering the sequence of amino acids that make up these genes. This has been termed 'epigenetics', which essentially refers to changes in gene expression that result in a phenotypic change, but without fundamentally altering the underlying DNA sequence (Szyf et al., 2016). The silencing of genes through epigenetic changes may come about when certain portions of DNA become methylated, which entails a process in which methyl groups are added to genes, thereby modifying their function so that specific phenotypes may be altered. Epigenetic changes can likewise occur through processes related to DNA being wound around histones, which allow a lengthy DNA strand to fit into the nucleus. Should the DNA be wound too tightly, important genes may be less accessible, thereby preventing gene expression. In addition

(Continued)

---

[2]In most species, infant care is conducted by the maternal parent, although there are exceptions in which both parents contribute. In humans, parental responsibilities are often shared, families may comprise same-gender parents, and in some cultures extended families or communities may play a key role in infant care. Under these circumstances, it might be expected that solely considering maternal behaviors may not fully represent the environment of the infant that influences well-being.

to epigenetic changes, after DNA has been transcribed to RNA, gene expression can be influenced through 'post-transcriptional gene regulation' in which small non-coding RNA (microRNAs) can silence RNA thereby affecting phenotypic outcomes. While distinct from epigenetic actions, microRNAs have been related to the development and progression of some diseases.

Epigenetic changes promoted by environmental and experiential factors can occur at any time of life, but the early-life period is especially sensitive in this regard so that the expression of genes are suppressed. This gene suppression could affect whether certain neurochemical processes are operating appropriately, and hence could have effects with respect to how individuals deal with stressors, or they could have effects directly on processes that lead to illness. Importantly, these epigenetic actions could persist over the course of an organism's life and could be transmitted across successive generations (if the epigenetic change occurred within the germline, i.e., the sperm or ova), hence affecting the biological and behavioral processes of the children and grandchildren of the individual that had initially been affected.

Epigenetic changes contribute to some forms of cancer, as well as autoimmune disorders, such as rheumatoid arthritis, and adverse early-life experiences (abuse or neglect) might have long-term consequences owing to epigenetic changes. In this regard, analyses of the brain tissue of depressed individuals who died by suicide revealed epigenetic changes in the genes associated with stress-relevant neurochemical responses among those individuals who had experienced early-life parental neglect (McGowan & Szyf, 2010). Much less studied has been the possibility that epigenetic alterations could have beneficial effects on the offspring by silencing genes whose activation might otherwise produce negative outcomes.

To a certain extent the focus on epigenetic changes associated with early development have overshadowed events that occur in older age, which is also a highly vulnerable period for the development and progression of varied illnesses. As individuals age the accumulation of epigenetic changes, like that of mutations, can have pronounced effects on health. In fact, environmental challenges and stressors may affect biological aging, and an older age may influence the actions of these challenges that can influence stress buffering processes (Barrere-Cain & Allard, 2020). Given the involvement of aging processes in the emergence of so many diseases, much greater attention ought to be devoted to environmentally and experientially determined epigenetic factors that contribute to pathology.

Transitional periods

In addition to prenatal and early postnatal periods, there are other developmental times during which an organism might be especially sensitive to stressors. These include phases of life that are referred to as transitional periods. We all go through events in life that involve change or transitions that call upon our adaptive resources. Entering kindergarten, for instance, is one of these life transitions. You're suddenly a big boy or big girl, having graduated from daycare, but then you find yourself in a new social context, where it's not just you and your family members anymore. Likewise, entering high school, college, university, or the workforce is an exciting major life transition during which we might experience insecurities and may be particularly vulnerable to the adverse effects of stressors. Leaving home, living with someone else, getting married (or divorced), moving cities and retirement, represent life transitions, and at these times responses to stressors might be altered (Rudolph et al., 2021).

In rodents, the juvenile (early adolescent) period spanning postnatal days 28–35, is exquisitely sensitive to stressors and has protracted ramifications on vulnerability to the stressor-provoked neurochemical and behavioral changes that occur in adulthood (Albrecht et al., 2017). The sensitivity of this developmental phase may be related to reorganization of many neurotransmitter systems that occur at this time. As well, it is a developmental phase during which rodents display increased socialization (play) with conspecifics and increased independence from the dam. Stressors in the form of social instability encountered at this age may influence brain development, particularly the hippocampus, and thus may affect some forms of memory in adulthood, including those associated with fear. Moreover, as adults, these rats exhibited elevated levels of the stress hormone corticosterone and reduced numbers of receptors in the hippocampus that are sensitive to corticoids, likely owing to epigenetic variations (Chaby et al., 2020). Interestingly, in both rodents and humans, the adolescent period is one during which fear responses are especially difficult to overcome. Once an anxiety or fear response is established it may persist even after the danger is no longer present, and among adults with fear-related disorders, about 75% of cases have their roots in anxiety that developed at earlier ages. These fear responses are not immutable, as they could be attenuated with appropriate treatment; however, this was more difficult to achieve in adolescent rodents and humans.

Adolescence in humans is a period in which individuals are highly focused on 'fitting in', developing an adult-like identity, finding a peer group that will accept them and with whom they feel comfortable, showing interest in a sexual partner, and even concerns about events that they will be facing some time down the road. These issues become particularly acute as many young people move from secondary school to college or university, as this transition requires considerable adaptation in the face of psychosocial and environmental changes. During this stage of life, particularly if it involves moving out of the family home or to a different city, many individuals leave behind long-standing social networks and form new ones, including changes in their romantic relationships, and efforts to gain social, economic, and emotional independence. In effect, just when young people are expected to establish their independence, they encounter a transition replete with factors that destabilize their support systems. Adolescents may struggle with a collision between expectations of autonomy and contending with a series of novel and stressful experiences that would be best met with the support of others.

Given the distress associated with transitions into adulthood, a considerable number of young people experience clinical levels of major depression, dysthymia (i.e., chronic low-grade depression), and anxiety disorders that were estimated to be as high as 25–40% across many countries. Moreover, many may have undiagnosed or subsyndromal symptoms of depression and anxiety that could reflect the antecedent conditions of major depression. Thus, although the transition into adulthood can be seamless and exciting, for some it is a challenging process that feels overwhelming and every day is filled with hardships. The recognition of this problem has resulted in many universities and colleges instituting programs to diminish distress amongst students, as well as to determine which individuals will be at greatest risk of faring poorly.

Older age

Before starting a discussion of stress and aging, we need to distinguish what we mean by aged or aging. For those born in the mid-portion of the preceding century when the mean life span was somewhere around 75 for females and 70 for males, someone at retirement age (65) was considered to be fairly old. With changes in lifestyle (diet, exercise) and medical treatments, life expectancy has increased appreciably, and 65 is hardly seen as 'old', and certainly not by others who are about that age. Still, being old is no picnic and has significant downsides. With age comes decaying biological systems so that disease states generally become more common: neurodegenerative and cardiovascular illnesses appear; kidney, liver, and lung diseases are on the horizon; and metabolic disorders become much more common. Whether an individual ages 'successfully' or not depends on complex interactions that involve genetic factors, earlier experiences, environmental influences, concurrent morbidities, and the ability to cope with stressors.

Studies in rats point to yet another age-related factor that interferes with well-being in association with stressors. In older rats, the release of several brain neurotransmitters, such as norepinephrine, as well as the stress hormone corticosterone, is elevated under basal conditions (as it is in humans) and increases appreciably in response to acute stressors. However, normalization (the return to basal levels) may take longer to occur than it does in younger animals. It is thought that hormonal and neurochemical responses elicited by stressors are of adaptive value, but once the stressor terminates, things ought to return to normal relatively quickly. The sluggish normalization of neurotransmitter release and corticosterone levels in older individuals might have some unfavorable repercussions.

A good conceptual framework to use regarding stress and aging is that of allostasis and allostatic overload (Goldstein, 2011). Let's face it, the wear and tear on a 70-year-old person (like a 70-year-old car) will be much greater than the load that has been put on a much younger person or car. The greater the strain an individual had encountered previously, and the greater the challenges they are currently undergoing, the more likely it is that the car bumper will fall off. However, as individuals age, vulnerability to pathology might not only stem from decaying biological processes but might be a result of the dwindling availability of resources that lend themselves to effective coping, including the reduced availability of social support from family and from friends who might not be able to help (or who might have predeceased them). Of course, on the other side, with age may come wisdom, including learning better coping strategies, and how to appraise situations and put them into perspective.

─Case study 1.1─

Scamming older people

When Julia A, who had just celebrated her 67th birthday, arrived home from work, her 77-year-old husband, Mel, was giddy with glee. He had received an email indicating that his lost cousin in Russia, Yvegeny A, had died suddenly and he was the only known living relative. He stood to inherit millions and all he had to do was front the legal costs that amounted to $2,000. She told him that this was a scam and that he was behaving foolishly, but he was adamant that it might not be since he had relatives in Russia with whom he hadn't had contact in decades.

The next day, Julia received a similar email but in this case the death was a cousin, Giorgio A, who had lived in a small Italian village. Again, she and Mel could inherit millions and all they had to do was cover legal fees in advance. Upon getting home she presented her still very happy husband with the email she had received assuming this would open his eyes. Instead, he was over the moon delighted, saying, 'How lucky can a guy get. I've won the lottery twice.'

Although elderly, Mel had been functioning perfectly well on a day-to-day basis, even if he seemed to be experiencing mild cognitive decline. Since this gullibility was out of character for Mel, who tended to be on the frugal side and wouldn't send cash to anyone in advance, Julia was concerned and thus consulted with a family friend who was a geron-tologist who specialized in dementia.

She was informed that mild cognitive deficits, or specific components of cognitive functioning that emerge with age, may make older individuals more vulnerable to deceit. Scammers know this and thus older people are often targeted over the phone or internet. The gerontologist had indicated age-related loss of neurons might make some people injudiciously trusting or, phrased differently, that they lost their ability to 'doubt' informa-tion that would ordinarily appear suspicious. It seems that with age, a region in the brain associated with appraisals and decision-making, aspects of the prefrontal cortex, may undergo changes for the worse. Even among otherwise intelligent people, when the brain dysfunctionality occurred, individuals had trouble in the effortful process necessary for disbelief, and hence they were more likely to be the victims of fraud. Being scammed is embarrassing and stressful for anyone, but for the elderly it's yet another slap in the face that highlights their limitations.

Julia was relieved that Mel wasn't necessarily at an early stage of Alzheimer's disease. Of the many illnesses faced by older people, one of the most dreaded is dementia. The loss of self and the indignities that can be experienced in relation to many diseases are often

(Continued)

beyond what anyone envisions for themselves. However, Julia's fears weren't entirely eliminated as she also learned that among the elderly, further cognitive decline could be linked to stressful experiences. A prospective study among elderly individuals conducted over just two and a half years revealed that protracted, highly stressful experiences were associated with increased conversion from individuals exhibiting mild cognitive impairments to moderate levels of dementia. There had been indications that cognitive deficits and 'tau pathology' (a substance implicated in Alzheimer's disease) are influenced by cumulative stressor experiences (Sotiropoulos & Sousa, 2016).

For some 'seniors', particularly those who've aged successfully (healthy in body and mind), this time of life can be wonderful. For many others, however, aging is the pits, and they certainly don't refer to it as 'the golden years'. Besides being accompanied by health problems and repeated visits to different doctors, aging is associated with difficulties getting around, change of life purpose, the loss of friends (through death or translocation), the dispersal of family members, and diminished coping resources. In fact, loneliness, which is stressful for individuals of any age, is often notable in the elderly as their social network might have dissipated, and certain types of stressors produce especially marked physiological changes (e.g., cardiovascular responses) relative to those apparent at earlier ages. Beyond these stressors, older individuals might suffer multiple indignities, including stigmatization and unsupportive interactions (often being patronized, talked down to, dismissed, made to feel invisible, or made to feel like a burden). In light of these factors, it seems that the coping strategies endorsed by older individuals might shift away from those that reflect a sense of control over their own lives, to those that are reliant on others. Is there any wonder that depression rates in older people are as high as they are?

Sex and gender

Certain illnesses, such as mood disorders and autoimmune disorders (those in which the immune system turns on the individual, as in the case of multiple sclerosis, lupus erythematosus, and rheumatoid arthritis), occur more frequently in women than in men. In the case of major depression, the ratio is about 2:1, and posttraumatic stress disorder (PTSD) that develops in response to traumatic events occurs more frequently among females than males. These gender and sex differences might occur for any number of reasons, including differences in the stressors actually experienced, greater stress-relevant neurochemical disturbances in females, the influence of particular sex hormones, socialization processes that promote certain behavioral styles being adopted, the endorsement of less adaptive coping strategies to deal with stressors, or other psychosocial factors that favor the development of illness. To the extent that sensitivity or reactivity to stressors differs between sexes, one might expect to find that the treatment of stress-related disorders would likewise differ. In discussing the neuroendocrine effects of stressors (Chapter 5), we'll see that hormonal responses differ appreciably in relation to sex, which may have significant ramifications for the development and progression of diseases. Despite these inequities, on average, women still outlive men just as they did fifty years ago, although the gap has been closing. This is not simply due to a bias regarding who is in the workforce, as the same statistics are apparent in both industrialized and non-industrialized countries.

HOW COME WOMEN LIVE LONGER THAN MEN?

The greater life span of women relative to men has been observed globally (Ortiz-Ospina & Beltekian, 2018). This difference may be related to sex hormones, notably estrogen and testosterone, that affect immune functioning so that females may be better equipped than males to fend off certain illnesses (e.g., colds and influenza) (Shepherd et al., 2021). Relatedly, the hormonal consequences of women having two XX chromosomes, whereas men have an X chromosome replaced by a Y, may influence vulnerability to non-communicable diseases (Anisman & Kusnecov, 2022), thereby affecting longevity (Sampathkumar et al., 2020). Alternatively, differences in several lifestyle factors may converge to produce the gap, as might the greater disposition of men to engage in risky behaviors. Moreover, men are less likely to seek medical attention in response to signs of non-communicable diseases (e.g., heart disease, cancer) that are highly linked to mortality (Thornton, 2019). There doesn't seem to be a single cause for the sexual dimorphism related to life span; it may be significant, however, that the gender gap has narrowed from 5.2 years to about 3.6 years and it is expected that difference will continue to diminish, especially with the adoption of healthier lifestyles and improved therapeutics.

Previous experiences and sensitization

There is no question, as we've seen in our discussion of early-life events, that an individual's previous experiences may influence responses to later stressor encounters. It's not simply a matter of our memories of previous experiences influencing our responses to stressors, which we hear much about, usually in the context of 'triggering events' that instigate adverse psychological responses. The characteristics of the neurons themselves may have changed, so that the response to later stimulation is enhanced, which is referred to as 'sensitization'.

Studies in animals indicated that the brain's neurochemical changes exerted by acute stressors can be induced more readily if they had previously encountered stressful experiences (Anisman et al., 2008). As we'll see later, stressful events might come to change the characteristics of neurons so that they become more responsive (or, conversely, less responsive, which is termed 'desensitized' or 'down-regulated') to later challenges. There are several ways by which sensitized responses can develop, and many biological systems are subject to this effect. One of these concerns changes of neuronal plasticity, which refers to the ability of the synapses to change, or the connection between neurons to change in strength as a result of experiences. Plasticity is a fundamental feature of the brain that is required for, among other things, learning and memory, and sensitization is an instance of this neural plasticity. However, when we deal with this phenomenon, it should be considered that processes responsible for the sensitization of a given neurotransmitter system may differ from those associated with a second transmitter system. For instance, it is possible that sensitization of some systems may involve altered expression or sensitivity of relevant receptors, whereas in other systems this may involve the synergistic (multiplicative) effects of two or more biological substrates. Importantly, the effects of stressors on these neuronal responses may persist for lengthy times following a stressor event, and it is possible that sensitization processes contribute to the long-term influence of stressors on psychological states.

Based on such findings, it has been maintained that the biological processes that promote depressive illness may evolve over time with repeated stressor experiences and recurrent depressive episodes. With each stressor experience, or with each episode of depression, the stressor severity needed to elicit the depressive mood becomes smaller, until eventually very little is needed to encourage a depressive state. There have, indeed, been numerous reports showing that although the first episode of depression is preceded by fairly strong stressors, less severe stressor experiences may cause illness recurrence. In fact, among individuals who experienced recurrent episodes of depression, very mild stressors were needed to re-induce the depressive state, and even reminders of stressful experiences were sufficient to produce this outcome (Post, 2021).

In addition to sensitization of biological systems, how we appraise (evaluate) the world around us can be influenced by our previous stressor experiences. For example, it isn't hard to imagine that if individuals encounter a stressor that traumatized them, later reminders of these same experiences will have profound psychological and physical repercussions. This also applies to adverse experiences that occurred in early childhood. Children who experience a trauma will, as adults, be much more likely to develop depressive illness (Martínez et al., 2021), and importantly this is apparent even when statistically controlling for the family and contextual factors that have been associated with depressive illness. This effect of early-life adversity is not limited to young children, having similarly been observed in women that had experienced physical or sexual abuse in adolescence. It might be that when certain stressors are encountered, they cause changes in numerous aspects of an individual's life, altering the trajectory of life experiences (friendships and other support networks, coping processes, lifestyles, general world view, and even the propensity for further stress encounters), culminating in a greater vulnerability to psychological and physical illness.

Stress generation

Stress generation refers to occasions wherein individuals, because of their circumstances, may bring stress onto themselves. This doesn't mean that we should blame the victim for finding themselves in adverse situations. Instead, it means that sometimes, through any number of factors, specific events result in a pro-liferation of consequences. For example, a person might lose their job, and as a result can't pay their rent and so lose their home. They might start 'couch-surfing', but slowly their friends no longer respond well to them. Or some people make the wrong decisions or choices in an effort to cope with the event, creating even greater challenges. Depressed individuals, by their behaviors, are thought to be a particularly vulnerable group for stress generation (Liu & Alloy, 2010). For instance, one partner in a romantic relationship may find it challenging to deal with the other person's depressive state (poor mood, negativity, and aggressive behaviors that might occur). This may therefore potentially lead to the dissolution of the relationship because the partner no longer knows how to cope with the situation. Essentially, the depressed partner, by engaging in negative behaviors (often these involve behaviors of a dependent nature), may have contributed to the break-up and the loss of an important relationship that they relied on as a stress buffer. Likewise, the depressed individual, whose symptoms might include apathy and withdrawal, may alienate their co-workers, and ultimately find themselves strug-gling at work. Stress generation is more common among those high in neuroticism (emotional instability), which is not surprising as their emotional sensitivity might provoke interpersonal conflicts. It has been reported that perfectionism contrib-uted to interpersonal stressors, as did sociotropy (a characteristic in which individ-uals exhibit high levels of dependence and an excessive need to please others). This is in line with the perspective that individuals whose self-esteem is based largely on their relationship with others place themselves in a situation where interpersonal conflicts will occur, which might thereby contribute to stress generation.

In a sense, stress breeds stress. In some instances, by their behaviors and atti-tudes, individuals make their worst fears turn into reality. Let's have a look at one example where this appears, namely that of dating abuse, which occurs in about 20% of dating relationships among university-aged individuals (the abuse goes in all directions, as people of all genders report psychological abuse). Significantly, women who had previously been abused were reported to be at increased risk of being in subsequent abusive relationships. Among undergraduate women, about 70% of those who encountered dating abuse reported a previous assaultive expe-rience (childhood assault, assault by a previous partner), whereas only about 25% of those in non-abusive relationships had such a history (Matheson et al., 2007). It was not a matter of women who experienced abuse generally being more likely to encounter traumatic experiences, as other forms of trauma (e.g., accidents, witness-ing violent events, and the death of someone close to them) were not more com-mon among abused women. Instead, it seemed as if an experience of abuse that occurred earlier in life effectively set in motion a cascade of changes that favored later stressor encounters and increased vulnerability *to the effects* of those stress-ors, which provoked depression and PTSD. What exactly this process entails isn't known. It is possible that the initial abusive experience engendered a set of beliefs and learned coping responses that facilitated women's ability to endure or tolerate their abusive situations, or alternatively the experience may have undermined their confidence to leave a bad relationship. Additionally, early abuse experiences may have limited the development of social and emotional skills, which diminished the ability to appraise and respond appropriately to emotionally charged stressor situations. In view of the relations between dating abuse and earlier abusive experiences, increased incidence of stress generation, diminished self-esteem and self-worth, depression, and PTSD, it would be inappropriate to consider an adult experience in isolation from other factors that might be tied to stress generation.

Conclusion

Stressors come in multiple forms and vary across numerous dimensions. The extent to which stressors affect our well-being is related to the nature of the stressor and the psychological attributes of that stressor, such as the controllability, predictability uncertainty, and ambiguity of stressors or threats of impending stressors. As well, the impact of stressors may be governed by the chronicity of stressor experiences as well as stressors that had previously been encountered (e.g., early in life). Individual difference factors are likewise fundamental in determining to what extent a stressor might have severe adverse consequences. In this regard, genetic make-up, age, gender, and personality factors are effective in moderating stress responses.

Stressful events are common life experiences whose effects can be negligible and brushed off readily, or they can be extremely severe, affecting individuals for years and across generations. Numerous factors can contribute to our vulnerability to stressor-elicited illnesses, and likewise being resilient in the face of severe stressors and pathology involves complex interactions between a constellation of variables. To a significant extent, however, the impact of stressors will be determined by how they are viewed or appraised and how individuals cope with them. If there's a single take-home message, it's that stressful events and their effects are not only complex, but that there are marked inter-individual differences in their effects. What might be stressful to you might be a walk in the park for someone else, and conversely someone else's greatest distress may be a mild annoyance for others. Without considerable experience (and perhaps not even then), don't presume to understand another person's stress responses.

Suggested readings

Lupien, S.J., McEwen, B.S., Gunnar, M.R., & Heim, C. (2009). Effects of stress throughout the lifespan on the brain, behaviour and cognition. *Nature Reviews Neuroscience, 10*, 434–445.

Southwick, S.M. & Charney, D.D. (2018). *Resilience: The Science of Mastering Life's Greatest Challenges*. Cambridge, UK: Cambridge University Press.

McEwen, C.A. & McEwen, B.S. (2017). Social structure, adversity, toxic stress, and intergenerational poverty: An early childhood model. *Annual Review of Sociology, 43*, 445–472.

2

APPRAISALS, COPING, AND WELL-BEING

─The ostrich defense─

One strategy that has been used in legal proceedings, often termed the 'ostrich defense', is that of maintaining that the defendant was unaware of certain events that had occurred, even though they ought to have been aware of them. In many scandals that involved corporate fraud, chief executives maintained that their job was to run the company as a whole and leave certain aspects of the corporation to experts in specific sectors. Typically, this defense didn't do much for them.

When little kids see a clown, some of these kids laugh whereas others might find them scary. Obviously, how the clown is perceived is in the eye of the beholder. Of those kids who find the clown scary, some might cover their eyes or put their head under a blanket, and for that moment the stressor doesn't exist. In kids, this ostrich defense might be cute, but comparable behaviors in adults (e.g., don't look or touch that swelling or lump and you can pretend that it's not there; pretend that COVID-19 is not 'really' dangerous) are referred to as avoidance or denial, and are seen to be illogical, not at all cute, and even less useful than the 'ostrich defense' adopted in legal cases.

Learning objectives

We have already learned that stressor features as well as our individual characteristics, regardless of whether they're due to genetic contributions, previous experiences, personality, or age, can influence the extent to which
negative experiences affect our well-being. Relevant to this chapter, these
variables influence how potential stressors are appraised or viewed, and the
coping methods that are used to minimize or eliminate their impact. As we
consider appraisal and coping processes and how they might come to promote negative or positive outcomes, the reader ought to come away with an
understanding of:

- what's meant by stressor appraisal, and how to identify the factors that
  influence the appraisal process and decision-making, as well as how
  misappraisals of events might occur and how illogical thinking might play
  into these;
- how appraisals influence emotions, and how emotions might affect
  appraisals;
- the various ways in which individuals cope with stressors, and some of
  the moderators of a coping response. They should also be able to identify
  how coping strategies might influence the emergence or exacerbation of
  pathological states;
- the extent to which some coping methods can be used to deal with stressors
  more effectively than others, and the circumstances under which this might
  be the case;
- how social support resources can be used to deal with stressors.

Appraisals and coping skills

How we perceive potentially threatening events, and which methods we use to
cope with them, have been linked to both psychological and physical pathologies. For instance, the emergence of depression in the context of specific
illnesses (e.g., cancer, cardiac problems) has been related to the individual's
coping ability. Aspects of coping may be fundamental in dealing with specific
stressors, such as caregiving, the loss of a child, stigma, and discrimination, as
well as in response to severe trauma. As depicted in Figure 2.1, how we perceive
or cognitively appraise (interpret) stressors can influence the coping strategies
we invoke to deal with them (Lazarus & Folkman, 1984), which in turn might
contribute to whether pathological outcomes will emerge. Conversely, the coping methods we use to deal with stressors might come to influence how we
appraise stressors.

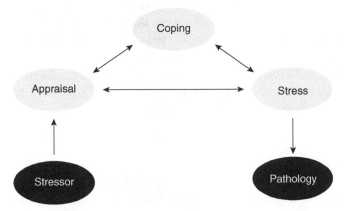

The appraisal-coping-stress triad

Figure 2.1   indicates that our appraisals influence the coping strategies that we use to deal with stressful experiences. Once a stressful event occurs, we make an appraisal of this event, which, in turn, leads to coping strategies being engaged in an effort to attenuate or diminish the impact of the stressor. If the event is seen as aversive, and especially one that is out of our control, then the event will be perceived as stressful and a stress reaction will be engendered, which might provoke or exacerbate a pathological condition.

Appraisals of stressors

Appraisals refer to the evaluations that individuals make in response to a potential stressor. These appraisals comprise the threat or risk associated with the event (i.e., the potential for harm or loss, and the degree of challenge the event represents), as well as an assessment of the severity, controllability, predictability, ambiguity, and the meaning associated with this potential threat. When faced with a potentially stressful event, appraisals ought to be adaptive, as they should enable individuals to distinguish those situations that require action from those that do not, along with the type of action that will most effectively address the stressor. To a considerable extent, appraisals are based on the individual's specific abilities, beliefs, previous experiences in dealing with similar and dissimilar events, and the resources available to contend with the challenge. Thus, appraisals define the extent of the threat that an event imposes and influence the coping methods that are selected to deal with the stressor. Although threat and challenges are similar in so far as they both might promote action, they also have important distinguishing features. Specifically, an appraisal of an event as threatening is often associated with negative emotions (e.g., fear, anxiety, or anger) as it signifies the potential for harm or loss. An event that is viewed as a challenge might similarly be aversive, but might provide the potential for growth or gain and hence might be associated with positive emotions (e.g., exhilaration, eagerness, excitement). For instance, an individual who is sent on a training course to upgrade their skills can see this as being either a challenge ('This will be super. I've always wanted to be able to get the maximum out of the internet and here's my chance to learn') or a chore ('Oh brother. Now I have to leave the comforts of home for two weeks to take a dippy course that I could do on my own'). They can also see it as a cost ('I've got a ton to do and when I get back the pile will have become that much higher') or an investment ('Once I get this under my belt, I'll be able to do searches twice as fast and that'll increase my productivity and give me yet more leisure time').

Primary and secondary appraisals

Potentially stressful events are thought to give rise to two interpretive processes, termed 'primary' and 'secondary' appraisal. Primary appraisal comprises perceptions associated with the impact of a potentially stressful event or stimulus: for example, the impact of an event may be perceived as benign (or even positive), and hence no immediate action might be deemed necessary. Alternatively, the event or stimulus might be construed as a threat and, as such, additional interpretations might be evoked: these include the potential for the event to induce harm, whether it threatens the individual, and to what extent it is a challenge (Lazarus & Folkman, 1984).

Threat might not be easily identified in some situations, but individuals will infer that a threat is present based on experience, previously acquired knowledge, including the positive or negative outcomes associated with earlier experiences. Having identified a threat, individuals ought to engage in behaviors to limit the threat or its impact. Needless to say, remaining in a heightened or repeated state of arousal owing to perceptions of impending threats is hardly adaptive, and might confer increased vulnerability to illness. Indeed, individuals who tend to appraise events as threatening may be at increased risk for greater long-term health problems relative to those who make more positive appraisals.

As we've seen, the response to stressors is governed by numerous factors (e.g., previous experiences, age), and true to this, appraisals of stressful events may be influenced by several antecedent experiences as well as numerous dispositional characteristics. In this regard, general appraisals have been associated with several personality constructs, including hardiness, optimism, hope, hostility, trait negative/positive affectivity, extraversion, and neuroticism. Given the large number of factors that can influence how individuals might appraise a potential threat, it's perfectly predictable that unanimity is often lacking as to how certain stressors are appraised. Certainly, there are stressors that most people will perceive in a similar fashion (e.g., war, natural disasters). However, there are many less intense stressors that are somewhat ambiguous, which will be associated with diverse appraisals.

Whereas primary appraisals are mainly concerned with the perceived impact of a stressful event, secondary appraisals encompass perceptions of the resources available for successfully eliminating or attenuating a stressor. Essentially, the secondary appraisal poses the question, 'Can I cope with this threat?' For example, when confronted with potential unemployment (an occurrence likely to be perceived as threatening or distressing), a secondary appraisal would comprise an assessment of the financial resources available to deal with the stressor (e.g., employment insurance) relative to the demands that will be placed on the individual (e.g., mortgage payments, tuition for kids, gasoline, food), along with other stressors that accompany being 'let go', including diminished self-esteem, anger, or shame. Thus, the apparent stressfulness of the event will depend, in part, on the degree to which the individual's resources are perceived to enable them to meet these demands. Of course, the appraisals that individuals make regarding a threat are influenced by a variety of contextual or experiential factors. For instance, in the case of potential job loss the appraisals might be affected by whether the individual is supporting others, market demand for their skills, whether they're near retirement and would have left the job soon, as well as the extent to which their identity was tied to the job.

Secondary appraisals and control dimensions

One of the most fundamental aspects of secondary appraisals concerns perceived control over the situation. Control can involve several different components or subtypes. *Behavioral control* comprises the ability to influence a stressful situation through the initiation of some sort of action, whereas *cognitive control* can be conceptualized as the ability to influence the situation by using some sort of mental strategy (Cohen et al., 1986). Another aspect of control involves *decisional control*, which entails having a choice over the coping strategies available to deal with a stressor. Finally, *informational control* reflects the degree to which the individual is able to predict and prepare for stressful events. Although each type of control appears to be important in determining strategies to reduce distress, cognitive control likely promotes the most beneficial effects on well-being.

Appraisals, decision-making, and Fast and Slow Thinking

The way we appraise stressors goes a long way in determining the way in which we choose to cope. The model described by Lazarus is, in several respects, reminiscent of a framework that has been adopted in decision-making theory. Individuals frequently make decisions or attributions based on heuristics, which refer to cognitive strategies (or shortcuts) that are made on the basis of information that is easily accessed. These shortcuts might be based on an individual's experiences or rules that were previously established. Thus, rather than going through lengthy processes to make decisions, individuals might simply resort to past practices, educated guesses, or rules of thumb (Tversky & Kahneman, 1974).

When individuals are in stressful situations new learning is often difficult, but well-entrenched performance, memory, and decision-making are not usually impaired. Evidently, in a problem-solving situation that occurs soon after being exposed to a stressor, problem-solving abilities may be compromised, and individuals are more likely to fall back on using heuristics. The initial heuristics or shortcuts considered by Kahneman and Tversky are the *availability heuristics* that refer to how readily decisions come to mind; *representativeness*, entailing specific decisions being made based on their perceived similarity to other situations; and *anchoring or adjustment* in which numerical predictions are based on the initial bits of information encountered (e.g., the asking price for a second-hand car) and then adjusted as additional information is obtained.

To a considerable extent, experiences might prime responses to particular events (Morewedge & Kahneman, 2010). In this regard, decisions may be based on the stimulus or event being consistent with our preconceived 'intuitions' (*associative coherence*). Individuals may engage in *attribute substitution*, such that when making a judgment about a particular stimulus, they might form further unconscious attributes about this stimulus based on what had been learned previously in similar situations. So, if primed to believe that Sarah is a charitable person, they might make further attributions about her, such as Sarah is kind, warm, and even a kindred spirit. Even though virtually nothing is known about Sarah, except for one characteristic (she is charitable), it primes us to believe or accept other features of her personality. In addition to these heuristics, *processing fluency*, or our subjective experience concerning the relative ease/difficulty involved in a given cognitive task, is influential in determining whether particular judgments will be made.

Since Kahneman and Tversky introduced their perspective regarding such heuristics, numerous other shortcuts have been described that in some fashion influence decision-making. It seems that certain emotions and personality variables might influence the way events are appraised and the decisions made. Fearful individuals tend to exhibit pessimistic risk assessments and are risk-averse, whereas angry people seem to be more sure of their assessments and less risk-averse. Unfortunately, these emotions may be associated with a heuristic in which individuals might not select from all the options available to them in a decision-making situation. In discussing the cognitive processes related to decision-making, it was suggested that dual systems are in operation: an automatic operations system (dubbed System 1 or Fast Thinking) and a more cognitively based system, termed System 2 or Slow Thinking. Kahneman (2011) explained that System 1, the automatic, fast-thinking system, is highly influenced by our experiences so that it is *primed* to react in a particular way in response to environmental events, whereas the cognitively oriented slow-thinking System 2 might kick in when more complex decisions need to be made.

DECIDING ON THE FLY

Some decisions that we make are based on lots of thought and reasoning, but sometimes we need to make decisions rapidly and there might not be much time to do so. It seems that although the prefrontal cortex is generally involved in decision-making, some aspects of this cortical region might be responsible for decision-making that occurs on the spur of the moment, whereas others are based on experience and habits that were formed earlier (Jones et al., 2012). It was thought that 'value-based' decisions, such as those that occur when an individual appraises options and potential consequences, involve the functioning of the orbital frontal cortex. Based on studies among individuals that had sustained damage to this region, it was concluded that the orbital cortex is necessary when decisions must be computed quickly. However, other cortical regions likely are involved when the decisions are based on 'cached' values that were determined by previous experiences. This is not far removed from the Fast and Slow Thinking described by Kahneman but ties the processes to specific brain regions. Essentially, when the orbital frontal cortex is disturbed, decision-making 'on the fly' suffers from an impaired ability to base decisions on prior experiences that allow options to be weighed appropriately. This has obvious implications for an individual's ability to learn from their mistakes and may be relevant for the propensity to make bad decisions.

Turning back to primary appraisals, a semi-automatic process might be enacted on the basis of the very same principles described by Kahneman in regard to decision-making. Consider for a moment a sudden stressful occurrence that you encountered. If it was one that you had previously experienced or that was similar to other events, then you might engage in responses that are 'second nature' to you and the resulting actions seem well rehearsed (hence, when going into some situations, a realistic practice run, even cognitively, is well advised). However, if the stressful situation is entirely out of the range of your expectations or experiences, then it may give rise to a confused response and it takes a few seconds for you to 'understand' what is actually happening. It is then that System 2, or secondary appraisals, come into the picture so that appropriate decisions can be made.

There are many situations where decision-making is difficult as we don't have the necessary knowledge or background. For instance, most of us won't have a clue concerning the value of a car or a house when we start out looking to make a purchase. Instead, we look at 'anchors' that help us make a decision (Kahneman, 2011). In this case, the anchor is the asking price (or what other houses in the area have sold for, or advice from an agent who might actually not be on our side, but simply wants to make a sale). After some negotiation, we might come up with a number that is reasonable both to ourselves and to the vendor. However, the seller could have asked for an amount that was 10 or 20% higher (or lower) and we would have gone through the very same process simply because we have no idea what the actual value of the house or car might be. Of course, in some instances the starting point might be so far off the mark that we wouldn't even consider the purchase, but if it is 'in the ball park' then we might proceed with our negotiations none the wiser.

The very same thing holds when it comes to making appraisals regarding threats to our well-being. We need an anchor to tell us what the threat means. When a government agency pronounces that the risk of a pandemic is high, we might ask, 'What's meant by high?' Does 'high' mean that 99% of people will be affected, or is 'high' 30%, and what does this mean when it comes to the risk for me or those close to me? Furthermore, given the past track record of the agencies that inform us about all sorts of threats (e.g., the media, government, or even some celebrity who holds forth on a subject in which s/he hasn't any expertise), to what extent should these anchors be discounted? After all, we've had numerous warnings from government agencies of things that simply haven't materialized. Even though we are able to process a fair amount of information, it is often the case that our appraisals aren't at all sophisticated and might actually be tied to anchors that comprise nothing more than 'what some guy said on Twitter'.

Appraisals and misappraisals

Before we go any further, an important caveat needs to be introduced. We often assume that our appraisals of situations are, in fact, accurate. In part, this is likely correct. This also means that, in part, this conclusion is wrong. How accurate are our appraisals of situations? You probably know that when you're in a slump everything looks bad (this is your appraisal), and when you're riding high, then just about everything looks good, and even obviously bad things look manageable. Essentially, when a person comes into a situation in a poor state of mind, then in dealing with stressors they might not see the world the way it really is, but instead see it from a narrow, dark, and gloomy place. It's under these conditions that we might want to look to our friends to get their reaction to events, as it's often easier for an outside observer to see things 'in perspective'.

Just as we might make appraisals based on our own previous experiences, we do so based on what others tell us or on what we believe that others think. Individuals frequently make social comparisons and then form their appraisals accordingly. Experiments from decades ago illustrated that we tend to conform to what others do when making certain types of appraisals, and it seems that social comparisons are made when it comes to some fairly stressful situations. There are times in which individuals don't make evaluations of events based on their own intuitions but on the basis of social norms. College-aged women who were in psychologically abusive dating relationships and in whom symptoms of depression were elevated were shown a video clip of a young woman describing her steadily increasing abusive relationship (escalating from mild criticism through to verbal and psychological abuse, and finally to clear physical harm). Contrary to expectations, the abused participants were, for the most part, not upset. Indeed, some were upbeat, and even giddy. Further experimental probing suggested that these women seemed to be making social comparisons to justify remaining in their current relationship, as the film clip served to validate their view that their relationship was actually normal. Essentially, some of these women indicated that, 'My relationship isn't all that great. But if my boyfriend treated me that way [referring to the video clip] I'd leave him.' Remarkably, however, when the stress hormone (cortisol) was measured in saliva, it was elevated in comparison to women who were in non-abusive relationships. So, although their *stated* appraisal of the situation was that it did not distress them, their biological stress system seemed to make a different statement; just witnessing the video and answering questions related to their own lives were sufficient to produce this outcome. Their verbal statements might have reflected a social comparison process, but the possibility can't be discounted that their statements concerning their relationship might well have been a cover to avoid admitting that their situation was abusive (Matheson & Anisman, 2012).

At times, a person might find themselves asking for advice from a group of friends on what decisions they ought to make in risky situations. However, the appraisals and actions made by groups might be very different from those that any single individual might make. Specifically, when appraisals and decisions are made by a group, it is more likely that they will engage in greater risk-taking, or greater caution, than might be the case if they do so as individuals. This phenomenon, known as 'group polarization', is more likely to come about when the group comprises like-minded individuals acting on the basis of pre-existing norms or informational biases ('we all agree to take a risk (or not), and so this must be the right response') (Sunstein, 2009). It might be that individuals follow the example of others to gain social acceptance, because contrary opinions aren't expressed, and because one's own pre-existing biases are affirmed by a strong risky (or cautious) response. Regardless of the source of the group's polarized reaction, this tells us that when we, as individuals, make appraisals of situations, the perspectives we come up with alone might differ from those made by a group.

⎯Case Study 2.1⎯

It seemed like a good idea at the time

More than other people Jerome seemed to have a penchant for misappraising situations. He repeatedly made commitments to do things that 'didn't seem like a bad idea at the time'. However, his sense of dread increased as the time for action approached. Although he had experienced extreme discomfort whenever he was required to speak in public forums, he had agreed many months earlier to talk to a large group about the impact of environmental toxicants on gut microbiota and their effects on health. 'I'm a dunce,' he thought. 'When things are far off, I have this "illusion of courage" that makes me less fearful of an event even though I've had lots of experience knowing that I won't deal with this well when the time comes.' Like so many people, Jerome wasn't very good at appraising the distress of distal events (Van Boven et al., 2012). Clearly, what he needed to do at the time of the invitation was to 'fast-forward' to perceive how he would react when the moment of truth came, and importantly, act on these feelings, rather than fool himself into thinking that things will be different next time.

Anxiety produced by immediately threatening stimuli and temporally distal threats involves different brain neuronal processes. Whereas the central nucleus of the amygdala is involved in threat confrontation (i.e., immediate threats), distal events that promote threat anticipation are mediated by the 'extended' amygdala that comprises the bed nucleus of the stria terminalis (Klumpers et al., 2017). Neuronal activity in the latter

(Continued)

brain region is driven by potential future threats that may never actually occur, and this uncertainty allows individuals to make decisions that they might not make if the amygdala was activated (Knight & Depue, 2019). Jerome might have been a victim of a dysfunction within the bed nucleus, or more likely he was just very good at fooling himself, just as most people are.

Related to the fact that experiences influence how we appraise events is the notion that even subtle cues can prime us to perceive events around us in a particular way. We know, for example, that eyewitness testimonies are frequently unreliable, and that our memories of events can be altered through subtle suggestions (Loftus, 2003). Priming, as Kahneman (2011) has indicated, can likewise be based on subtle factors. If our best friend thinks someone is two-faced, and he tells us this, then when we meet this person, we might well be very cautious or even negative. Related to this, stereotypes about certain groups or cultures can influence our appraisals, even if we are not consciously aware that this is occurring. Likewise, if an individual is primed to believe that a certain drug will reduce the pain that they're experiencing, they will report diminished pain after consuming the drug, even if it was only a placebo. A person in a 'uniform' or a relatively tall person is viewed as more authoritative than others, even if there's not a hint that this person is in the least competent. Our appraisals, and our misappraisals, intrude on a huge number of things that we do on a day-to-day basis, and often we might not have a clue about the subtle effects of such priming.

As mentioned earlier, our appraisals concerning the controllability of a stressor may have considerable importance in defining the coping strategies that we use and the behavioral and psychological outcomes that ensue. If we believe that we can influence a situation, then appraisals of that situation obviously ought to differ from those evident when we believe a situation is beyond our control. However, individuals might be motivated to perceive control over their environment, and so frequently overestimate the degree to which they can exert control over otherwise chance events. It goes without saying that these misappraisals might produce difficulties that hadn't been anticipated, but this illusion of control might also have some positive attributes. When we perceive events as controllable, we are generally better able to deal with them through the adoption of problem-focused coping strategies (trying to diminish or eliminate stressors or somehow dealing with them in thoughtful systematic ways), which is usually considered a good way of coping. In a sense, the illusion of control may reflect an adaptive process for dealing with stressors. For instance, cancer patients who believed they had some control over their illness exhibited lower levels of distress than did individuals who did not have these control perceptions (Borgi et al., 2020). Illusory control in this instance might not affect disease progression, but at the very least it allows for lower daily distress.

Appraisals and irrational thinking

There is yet another aspect of uncertainty and ambiguity that is central to our analysis of appraisal processes. This issue also falls into the category of decision-making rather than appraisals, but appraisals of choices and making decisions are (obviously) intricately linked. Kahneman and Tversky had made the point that individuals frequently behave in apparently odd ways, often making seemingly irrational decisions. In one interesting study, students were placed in a situation where they were told to imagine that they had sat a very important exam that would determine their future. They were then asked to imagine that the grades would be posted in two days' time. Some students were told they had passed the exam, whereas others were told they had failed. At this point, they were told that they had the opportunity to take a nice holiday trip and were asked whether they would take this trip. Both students who had passed and those who failed frequently indicated that they would take the trip – presumably those who passed saw it as a reward for their hard efforts, and those who failed saw it as a chance to diminish their despair. Essentially, all the students indicated that they would indeed take the trip, although they would do so for different reasons. Now comes the interesting part. In a second study, students were told that the exam results would be posted in two days, but this time they were given the options of (a) going on the trip immediately (before the results of the exam were released), (b) forgoing the trip, or (c) paying a $5 fee to hold their ticket (delay the trip) until they had received their grades. The students did what you would probably do – they paid the $5 to have the ticket held. Does this decision make any sense at all? In the first experiment, students indicated that they would be making the trip regardless of whether they passed or failed! Yet when offered the option of waiting (and paying $5) they tended to choose this option, even though they would likely take the trip irrespective of their grade. So, what might have motivated this behavior? It seems that uncertainty gives rise to some interesting ways of coping that are understandable, even if they are irrational.

TOO MANY CHOICES

Retailers know that giving the consumer too many choices isn't always the best idea; when faced with too many choices, with varying attributes and prices and confusing information, the potential consumer goes away to 'think about it'. Our friend, a retailer, tells us that when she hears this she wants to scream: 'Think about it? What's there to freakin think about? We're talking about a toaster. A toaster! Not whether you select lumpectomy over mastectomy!' There are numerous instances that we encounter where having too many choices can have serious consequences. Rather than allowing increased opportunities, too many options can produce decision paralysis, also called the 'paradox of choice' (Schwartz, 2004).

Over the past decade, patients and their physicians have been encouraged to jointly decide treatment procedures, which most certainly is appropriate. Many patients prefer the opportunity to share in this decision-making, especially as it allows them agency to

(Continued)

determine their own destiny. At the same time, however, patients offered several options to treat a severe condition, such as cancer, frequently don't have the knowledge to make informed decisions and might simply leave it to the physician. Besides, making these choices may be an excessive burden, especially as patients may be distressed by their illness, which can undermine decision-making ability.

Some individuals have an especially difficult time making decisions, considering their options again and again, seemingly being weighed down by the burden of a better option actually becoming available (Hughes & Scholer, 2017). During the COVID-19 pandemic and the introduction of several vaccines, individuals faced the dilemma of which vaccine to get. 'Do I *settle* for the AstraZeneca vaccine because it's available now, or do I wait until the Pfizer or Moderna vaccines become available?' If the Astra Zeneca vaccine had been the only one developed, then the person would have been more than happy to be vaccinated with this, but in the context of other choices decisions can be an encumbrance.

We can go on with numerous examples of the irrational decisions that people make that often have distressing repercussions. You might recall that stressed individuals seem to get themselves into increasingly distressing situations. They make poor appraisals and then choose the wrong methods of coping, and they do this repeatedly. Let's use a very simple example of this. In our research, we often assess the relationship between coping styles and the emergence of pathological conditions. To this end, we use a coping inventory that asks participants to indicate, on a five-point rating scale, to what extent they use each of the coping behaviors to deal with particular stressors. In some of our experiments we asked participants to indicate how effective they thought these coping strategies would be in dealing with a given stressor. For many people, particularly those who seemed well adjusted, there was a match between the coping method they chose and how effective they thought it might be. However, others, notably individuals with high levels of depressive symptoms, favored particular coping behaviors despite their belief that it wouldn't be effective. One can almost hear them saying, 'I know my coping responses aren't very good, but I just don't know what else to do'.

There are, of course, many factors that go into the irrational behaviors that individuals display. For some, their personality characteristics make it difficult for them to do what's necessary. There are individuals who are so afraid of making wrong decisions, or who can't abide with feelings of regret, that they end up not making any decisions. For others, procrastination might be a way of dealing with the anxiety associated with making decisions (putting off seeing a doctor regarding certain suspicious symptoms), and they continue with these clearly maladaptive behaviors in the full knowledge that their delay in seeking treatment might have terrible consequences (Reece et al., 2021). Not surprisingly, perhaps, the greater the stakes the more difficult it might be for decisions to be made. For instance, decision-making by parents regarding pediatric medical procedures can be an enormous strain, especially when once the decision is made, it can't be unmade. Sometimes the decisions individuals must make are at an entirely different level, such as moral decision-making. In an experimental setting, individuals might be presented with a scenario that entails choices that are difficult to resolve (e.g., in paradigms in which the participant is given the choice of actively sacrificing the life of one person to save the lives of several others). You'd think that such decisions would be based on logic or empathy, but there are actually many factors that influence outcomes. Not unexpectedly, the decisions made in these situations are very much influenced by individuals' recent experiences.

Human behaviors in response to stressors are, in several respects, not all that far removed from the responses that rodents show under adverse conditions. When animals are in stressful situations, their defensive responses narrow to those that are highest in their repertoire, and other response strategies will emerge only as those that are predominant are rejected. However, there are occasions where animals might persist in emitting incorrect responses even though they are never reinforced. In a sense, this is not unlike human behavior when exposed to strong stressors, wherein individuals fall back on those coping strategies that are highest in their repertoires (resorting to the tried and true), even if this approach isn't the most logical or effective. However, humans have a System 2 that kicks in when the reactions of System 1 are not productive, and this serves us well in decision-making even when we find ourselves in some very stressful situations.

TRUSTING YOUR BRAIN AND TRUSTING YOUR GUT

As we learn new things and retain this information, millions of neurons within the hippocampus are firing, and the repeated activation of these neurons is necessary to keep short-term memories in place. Should these neurons stop their systematic vollies, the memory will quickly be lost (think of how quickly you forget a phone number when you're interrupted). Understandably, when stressful events occur, our short-term memory will be disrupted, possibly because some of the neurons that were working to maintain that memory were now engaged with some other task. As memory processes are integral to problem-solving and decision-making, in the face of stressors it's efficient and practical to rely on heuristics that are well entrenched. People working in high-pressure situations (surgeons, air-traffic controllers, soldiers) need to be well trained so that when stressors erupt, as they invariably do, they have the cognitive short-cuts available that allow for rapid and appropriate decision-making.

There are situations that are somewhat ambiguous and making decisions is more difficult. In these instances, we might make decisions based on our intuitions (or trusting our gut). Perhaps not surprisingly, even though the situation was ambiguous, those with expertise fared better with respect to their decisions even though they relied on gut responses compared to those without the same level of expertise. Interestingly, however, when told to ignore their gut instincts and rely on a strictly analytical approach, the experts and non-experts performed equally. It may be that there are heuristics here that kick in when making gut decisions that can take us some way if the gut instincts are based on brain processes (Dane et al., 2012).

Most students, at one time or another, have been faced with the dilemma of whether they should accept their first response in a multiple-choice exam, or rethink it and perhaps

(Continued)

change their initial answer. From the research described here, it seems that if you know your stuff, then go with your first instinct (unless you're fairly certain that an alternative choice is better). If you don't know your stuff, then an analytical process won't help you much, so you might as well go with your gut. However, if you fail the exam don't blame us for giving bad advice. Maybe you should have been attending classes more often ...

Appraisals and personality factors

The meaning that a person constructs about any given situation, as well as their own coping capabilities, might not only be related to events that involved similar experiences but can vary with the individual's global self-constructs that emanate from a lifetime of experiences, including those that occurred during childhood (Carver & Connor-Smith, 2010). In this respect, early-life uncontrollable adverse events may lead to the emergence of dysfunctional beliefs that can distort the individual's evaluation of their own coping capabilities or competency. These evaluations might influence the individual's self-efficacy and the way they appraise the specific characteristics of stressful encounters. Unfortunately, once these negative self-referential attitudes are well entrenched, they're not easily dislodged, and misappraisals of situations might be more common. The ramifications of early-life stressful experiences not only influence mental health but extend to physical health. Early mortality was increased by about a factor of 1.5 among individuals who had experienced episodes of adversity during childhood (43% of children), including poverty or illness in the family. Among children who had experienced prolonged and intense adversity (about 3% of children), early mortality was 4.5 times that of children who had not encountered adverse events (Rod et al., 2020).

As we'll see later in this and in other chapters, methods have been developed to diminish distress, including ways to change the way individuals appraise events. For example, rather than engaging in negative thinking, individuals are taught to appraise events in a more positive or in a more realistic manner, and then to deal with stressors based on these appraisals. Thus, while some aspects of stress management entail effective ways of coping with distress, an important aspect might involve changing an individual's appraisals of the situation.

THE FORECAST

... how many will pass from the earth and how many will be created; who will live and who will die; who will die at his predestined time and who before his time; who by water and who by fire, who by sword, who by beast, who by famine, who by thirst, who by upheaval, who by plague, who by strangling, and who by stoning.

Who will rest and who will wander, who will live in harmony and who will be harried, who will enjoy tranquility and who will suffer, who will be impoverished and who will be enriched, who will be degraded and who will be exalted.

Fans of Leonard Cohen might recognize that this Rosh Hashana prayer of atonement might be at the root of his poem/song 'Who by Fire'. Our take-home message might be that while life isn't all that predictable, most of us don't spend our time worrying about all the 'ifs' and 'maybes'. Although we know we're eventually going to get hit by life-threatening encounters in some form or other, we manage not to think about it. Illnesses are a long way off and might even happen to someone else and not me. Perhaps this is an excellent strategy to deal with uncertainty, since focusing on potential catastrophes likely isn't profitable. What we can do, however, is recognize that there are certain behaviors (or lifestyle factors) that can affect the risk of bad outcomes and we're probably better off dealing with those. Being prepared to deal with adverse events, whether at an individual or a global level, can go a long way in limiting catastrophic outcomes (as we saw in relation to COVID-19 where preparedness was in short supply), especially if it requires collective psychosocial responses (Drury et al., 2019).

Appraisals in relation to learning, memory, automaticity, and habit

Years ago, the view was formulated that as we learn new information the connections between neurons are strengthened, and the assembly of cells involved in recognizing stimuli and responding to them appropriately is both strengthened and widened. Complex learning and memory involve still broader cell assemblies or networks, and once the connections are sufficiently strengthened, stimulating one aspect of the network will result in the entire cell assembly being triggered. So, for example, if we were to tell you that a word in this sentence (the one you are reading at this moment) is spelled incorrectly, you might have to go back again to find the error. Likewise, you won't have any trouble understanding the statement 'a frnd in ned is a frnd indd'. This is because your cell assemblies are in place, and once a component of the cell assembly is activated, you can interpret the sentence appropriately.

According to this formulation, learning occurs via a top-down approach; we learn through associations being made, by being rewarded for certain responses, and generalization (a grizzly bear is a grizzly bear regardless of whether we see it from the front or from the side) and discrimination (grizzly bears are dangerous, but not when we're watching them on a nature show). As topics become more difficult, the networks involved become more complex, but we take advantage of already developed networks so we can build on these. Some perceptions and responses are so deeply ingrained that we respond reflexively to particular stimuli, essentially working on autopilot or using automatic thoughts (Kahneman's Fast Thinking, or Negative Thinking biases displayed by some individuals). In effect, when solving problems, people often use methods that were successful in the past, with the attitude that if the wheel has already been invented, why try to build something new? This axiom has been around for a long time, but it isn't always a correct perspective (for that matter, somebody, somewhere, might well have said that if we already have a perfectly useful abacus, why try something new?). Sometimes, we need novel approaches to old problems.

These same processes are pertinent to how we appraise and cope with stressors. To a certain extent, we are hard-wired to respond to environmental stimuli in a standard manner (fixed action patterns). Young birds, for instance, respond in a stereotypic fashion to a visual image of a hawk moving across their visual field, and animals often respond to warning signals from other animals without having had previous relevant experiences. These automatic responses are essential; an antelope might not get a second chance to discover that a lion running at it is, in fact, a threat. In other cases, factors related to learning (attention, memory) are fundamental in stress processes. Essentially, we are equipped with both top-down (experience-dependent) circuits, and those that develop through a pre-wired bottom-up approach.

Emotional responses

Just about everyone realizes that positive and negative events will give rise to different emotional responses. The nature of these emotional responses will depend on how an individual appraises an event, the context in which the event occurs, as well as previous experiences, personality factors, and motivation. The specific emotions elicited by stressful events can foster the development of varied illnesses, and conversely these illnesses may contribute to emotional changes (Levenson, 2019).

A given event might elicit different emotional responses across individuals owing to their past experiences, various developmental factors, and other socialization processes. As well, damage to certain parts of the brain owing to a stroke or lesions may profoundly influence emotionality, ranging from a loss of emotion and affect through to excessive responses to certain types of stimuli. Just as individuals differ in their intellectual capacity and social intelligence, there are individual differences concerning emotional intelligence (Salovey & Mayer, 1990). Emotional intelligence involves multiple skills related to emotional perception and expression, the emotional facilitation of thinking, emotional understanding, and emotional regulation. Some people are adept in this regard, whereas others seem to express their emotions in odd ways and seem unable to read the emotions of others. An extreme form of this inability to understand emotions is alexithymia, a trait in which individuals seem to have difficulty in identifying their own feelings, describing their feelings, or understanding the feelings of others, and in fact in emotional situations they might look to others to see how they ought to react.

Distinguishing between emotions

There are subtle differences that exist in emotional responses to stressors and our vocabulary is replete with descriptors that reflect these differences. In addition, several emotions can occur concurrently in response to a single event (life transitions, such as leaving home, can bring excitement and joy at the same time as sadness and loss), and sometimes it's difficult for us to even understand the emotion that we are feeling. Indeed, the emotion elicited by an event may vary depending on the context in which it appears. The response to a negative comment will be different when it occurs in a private conversation from when it occurs in public. Some emotions differ from one another in subtle ways that are related to contextual factors. Fear and anxiety are very similar, but fear is thought to be directed to a specific stimulus, whereas anxiety is sometimes thought of as a non-directed emotion. Likewise, shame and humiliation are similar in that they can both be promoted by the behavior of others or in response to one's own socially or professionally unacceptable behaviors that come to the attention or are witnessed by others. However, whereas embarrassment and humiliation are emotions that primarily occur in front of others, shame can occur because of an unacceptable behavior that only the individual knows about.

The emotions mentioned to this point are largely those of a negative nature, but many positive emotions can alter the way we appraise stressful events: desire, ecstasy, excitement, enthusiasm, euphoria, hope, joy, love, lust, passion, pleasure, pride, trust, and zest are just a few of these. They're as complicated as the negative emotions and appear under different conditions. Sometimes these emotions can combine to elicit 'mixed emotions' or those that are 'bittersweet'. Watching adult kids leave home can leave an individual feeling both pride and loss, and having a loved one pass after a lengthy illness can similarly result in both relief and sadness. Of particular relevance to the present discussion is that positive emotions can alter the way we appraise and hence respond to stressful events, and positivity training may be an effective way of precluding the despair and depression that might otherwise be endured in negative situations.

Stress-related emotions

Emotions can involve multiple mechanisms, and because more than a single emotion can occur at the same time, they are often difficult to study, certainly in the context of identifying their biological correlates. While a wide array of emotions emerge under diverse conditions, they serve several common or interrelated functions. Among other things, they provide us with information about events around us. They also let others know how we're feeling (unless we successfully hide our emotions), allowing them to take measures that are corrective (apologize), supportive (empathize), or defensive (aggressive, indignant). There are nuances to emotions that provide the observer more detailed information than simply 'things are bad' or 'everything seems to be okay'.

Different emotions can tell us about the situation we're in and whether defensive actions should be taken, and what these actions should comprise. Anger is an activating emotion, so that in response to some transgression (e.g., a slur against one's group), an individual might want to take a confrontational or aggressive stance toward the perpetrator. At the same time, the person may feel shame, which is an emotion associated with withdrawal or suppression, and as a result they might be less likely to act on the anger they're feeling. This decision might potentially save them from the ill feelings of a group of bystanders who might view aggression as socially unacceptable, although the individual might later experience a period of pervasive rumination about the event and what they should have or could have done differently. Yet it is exactly this experience that provides individuals with critical information, namely that they can't deal with this issue on their own and that collective action by group members will be needed (Matheson & Anisman, 2012).

Just as emotions can influence cognitive processes, cognitions can influence emotions, or the way emotions are expressed. An aggrieved party might become aggressive towards the person who angered them. However, aggression might be more likely if the target was appraised to be smaller and weaker, and less likely when they look strong and able. The 'aggrieved' person may be angry, but in some instances they seem to have executive control regarding behavioral outputs. We often hear the statement 'I just lost control'. This might be true in some instances, but it may also be the case that individuals 'allow' themselves the luxury of losing control when the opponent is viewed as weaker.

As we've already seen, positive or negative moods have a lot to do with how we appraise or interpret events around us. Likewise, being angry or envious will alter appraisals of events related to the person with whom we are angry, or of whom we are envious. More than that, however, our emotions can alter our general disposition to react in particular ways to unrelated events. There's nothing very surprising in this, but even though we all seem to know it, it is remarkable how often we ignore this basic bit of knowledge. We've all heard of the boss who, when in a bad mood, might pick on an employee, or the parent who, having had a rough day, then takes it out on a partner or child. These individuals can't seem to compartmentalize their responses, and their mood increases their own stress reactions, giving rise to stress in others, and in so doing they lose potential sources of support that might otherwise have helped them deal with their own distress. Our emotional responses can affect our decision-making ability, particularly if the situation entails complex and/or stressful aspects. In his 1993 book on negotiating, *Getting Past No*, Ury offers the sound advice that when stress levels are high and emotions are peaking, it's best to 'go to the balcony' (meaning, remove yourself from the situation and see what's going on as an observer, rather than being enmeshed in the turmoil). In this way we can see the scene for what it is, unhampered by our emotional responses. If only we could do that easily.

We've long known that limbic portions of the brain play an integral role in emotions. For instance, fear and anxiety are associated with the central portion of the amygdala and the extended amygdala (a region referred to as the bed nucleus of the stria terminalis), whereas the ventral tegmentum and nucleus accumbens (midbrain regions that we'll talk about much more later) seem to be involved in reward/motivational processes. However, these brain regions do not operate in isolation and instead cooperate with one another to produce organized outputs. Connections exist between the prefrontal cortex and the amygdala, so the brain regions involved in decision-making (the cingulate cortex, prefrontal cortex) can influence those involved in anxiety (the amygdala). Some brain regions, such as the nucleus accumbens, may contribute to more than a single type of stimulus, being activated in stressful as well as rewarding situations. Presumably, complex emotions that entail an amalgam of primary emotions involve multiple brain regions interacting with one another.

It might be expected that different emotions may be tied to diverse peripheral physiological changes. Just as specific events can give rise to different emotional responses, distinct patterns of cardiac and respiratory activity have been associated with fear, anger, sadness, and happiness. Likewise, the release of the classic stress hormone cortisol occurs preferentially if the stressful event elicits shame (Dickerson & Kemeny, 2004) or anger, and the inflammatory immune responses elicited by stressors similarly depend on the specific emotions elicited (Danielson et al., 2011).

Coping with stressors

Appraisal processes are only half the story regarding how stressors can influence well-being. The other half is concerned with how individuals cope with stressors. Some theorists have viewed coping as a *style* (i.e., a dispositional feature that is relatively stable), whereas others have seen this as a *strategy* that varies in response to situational factors, as well as over time as the stressor and its ramifications unfold. There is a middle ground in which coping methods change as a function of the particular situation encountered, but these methods are guided by the particular coping propensities (styles) that individuals bring with them to the situation. In the section that follows we'll go into a fair bit of detail regarding coping processes, but as we do, keep in mind that coping may stem from the way individuals appraise events, but it also may affect appraisals. We're dealing with dynamic processes that are subject to feedback and frequent adjustments.

The stress-appraisal-coping triad

Numerous coping methods can be used to deal with stressful experiences, but they are usually classified into about a dozen different subtypes that fall into three general categories that comprise problem-focused, emotion-focused, and avoidant strategies (disengagement). There have been other names for these overarching strategies, and other classification systems, but these are probably the most widely used. Problem-focused coping, as the name implies, primarily involves coping through problem solving to change the circumstances or situation, or through cognitive processes that can be used to change how we think about stressors, such as cognitive restructuring (re-evaluating the threat, or finding meaning in a bad event). Emotion-focused coping subsumes multiple strategies (e.g., emotional expression, emotional containment, rumination, self- or other-blame, and passive resignation), as does avoidant coping (avoidance, denial). In addition, some coping methods don't fall comfortably into any single class as they can be used in multiple capacities. For instance, emotional expression may signal to others that their help is needed, it may serve in an emotion-focused capacity (a shoulder to cry on), in problem-focused coping ('Help me find a way out of this jam'), or in an avoidant capacity (through distraction). Likewise, active distraction (going to the gym to 'work off' anxiety) and humor can fit into each of the categories, but more often they align most closely with problem-focused coping. Both wishful thinking and rumination are usually viewed as emotion-focused coping methods, but this may depend on what other coping behaviors are used concurrently. Thus, if individuals ruminate and feel sorry for themselves, then this is clearly emotion-focused coping, but some individuals use rumination together with problem solving, in which case it is not part of an emotion-focused strategy. Finally, religion doesn't fit well within any of these categories; it may represent an avoidant strategy, but it can be used as a problem-oriented strategy or one that involves obtaining social support from like-minded people.

COPING THROUGH RELIGION

Religion is potentially a very effective coping strategy, even if it doesn't (necessarily) have healing powers that some have attributed to it. For religious individuals, it may provide comfort when all else fails. Religion can provide a system of beliefs that allows individuals to find meaning in an experience, and to appraise events as predictable and at the very least 'under God's control'. In addition, it often provides a social support network that enables problem-oriented coping, or even emotion-focused strategies that bring about solace, meaning, and peace of mind (Ysseldyk et al., 2010).

Marx disparagingly stated that 'Religion is the sigh of the oppressed creature, the heart of a heartless world, just as it is the spirit of a spiritless situation. It is the opium of the people.' The response to this might be 'Whatever gets you through the night' (Lennon, 1974; this should, of course, be distinguished from the other Lenin), provided, of course, that this is not used as an alternative to potentially more effective coping strategies. Indeed, rather than seeing religion as the opium of the people (masses), it can be argued that among some groups it serves as the SSRI (or the CBT) of the masses.

How to cope

It is often thought that when appraisals and coping strategies are ineffective, then the development of pathology might ensue, whereas effective coping will limit such outcomes. If only it were this simple. Trying to analyze the relations between stressful events, coping strategies, and the emergence of pathological states isn't as straightforward as simply correlating individual coping strategies with particular outcomes. Appraisals and coping strategies not only vary across situations, but they also do so with the passage of time (DeLongis & Holtzman, 2005) and the subjective construal of the stressor. Added to this, individuals won't use a single strategy at a time, but may use several strategies simultaneously, or flip from one to another as the situation demands, as well as because of the opportunities and resources available.

The specific coping strategies that individuals endorse might serve different functions as a stressor evolves over time. For example, when an individual first learns that they have a potentially fatal illness, their first reaction (once the shock has worn off) might be that of seeking support from their partner, children, or close friends. The function of this might simply be to use the support as an emotional-coping method. This might be followed soon after by using this support group to obtain information (e.g., to find out whether alternative treatment strategies are available). Later still, the support may become one of an instrumental nature (taking the person to treatment sessions, supplying food), and finally, in a worst-case scenario, social support may be used to provide social comfort, distraction, and finding peace.

It is often taken as axiomatic that in situations in which the individual has control, problem-focused strategies (e.g., problem solving, cognitive restructuring, or positive growth) that are seen to be adaptive will predominate, whereas those strategies that encourage an undue focus on emotions (e.g., rumination, emotional venting, self-blame) are viewed as counterproductive and maladaptive. This view is intuitively appealing, but is simplistic, especially as emotion-focused coping can comprise either emotion-approach or emotion-avoidant features. In certain situations, the latter coping method (e.g., using avoidance/denial) might be an optimum strategy (e.g., when learning that one has a terminal illness). Avoidance may provide temporary relief from an ongoing stressor, giving someone the opportunity to adopt (or develop) more effective strategies. But it may have terrible repercussions in the long run, as in the case of individuals failing to take action when signs of illness initially appear.

Emotion-focused strategies are often considered to be a poor coping method. Yet, acknowledging the emotions associated with stressors may allow the individual to modify or regulate their emotional responses, which can have positive effects. This coping method can generally be subdivided into emotional processing (attempts at acknowledging, exploring, and understanding emotional responses to events) and emotional expression (reflecting verbal and non-verbal messages conveying their emotions). In emotionally charged situations, emotion-focused coping might be particularly beneficial as it can be an important way to let others know that help is needed. As well, it facilitates the individual's ability to come to terms with their feelings, and in so doing distress may be reduced (Austenfeld & Stanton, 2004). To be sure, emotional expression without coming to an understanding of these emotions can be disruptive, especially when this coping method involves inappropriate rumination or gives rise to negative affect and appraisals.

Table 2.1 provides a description of several coping strategies that individuals might use in dealing with distressing events. As we've seen, any given coping strategy may serve different functions, or operate to facilitate or inhibit other strategies. Despite the frequent discussion of which coping strategies are good and which are bad, keep in mind that individuals do not endorse coping strategies in isolation of one another, and different coping strategies are used concurrently and/or sequentially.

Table 2.1   Coping strategies.

Problem-focused strategies

Problem solving: Finding a solution to limit or eliminate the impact or presence of the stressor.

Cognitive restructuring (positive reframing): Re-assessing the situation or putting a new spin on the situation. This can entail finding a silver lining to a black cloud, e.g., 'My kid flunked out of university, but hey, I save on paying his tuition', through to finding meaning (benefit finding) in adverse experiences.

Avoidant or disengagement strategies

Active distraction: Using active behaviors to distract ourselves from ongoing problems. This can include working out, going to the movies.

Cognitive distraction: Distracting ourselves through thinking about issues unrelated to the stressor, such as immersing ourselves in our work, or engaging in hobbies.

Denial/emotional containment: Not thinking about the issue or simply convincing oneself that it's not particularly serious.

Humor: Engaging in humor to diminish the stress of a given situation, or simply to put on a brave face.

Substance use: Aside from the positive feelings that individuals might obtain from using certain drugs, drugs and alcohol can also serve as a means of dealing with stressors.

Emotion-focused strategies

Emotional expression: Coping with an event through emotions such as crying, anger, and even aggressive behaviors.

Other-blame: Comprises blaming others for adverse events. It can be used in an effort to avoid being the one blamed, or as a way to make sense of some situations.

Self-blame: This comprises blaming ourselves for the events that occurred. Sometimes, of course, we are guilty and should be blaming ourselves, but there will also be instances where we inappropriately lay the blame at our own feet.

Rumination: This comprises continued, sometimes unremitting thoughts about an issue or event; these thoughts often entail self-pity, revenge, or replaying the events and the strategies that could have been used to deal with events. Rumination often accompanies depression, and individuals with certain ruminative styles are at increased risk of depressive illness.

Wishful thinking: This entails thoughts regarding what it would be like if the stressor were gone, or what it was like in happier times when the stressor had not surfaced.

Passive resignation: This comprises acceptance of a situation as it is. It might be a reflection of helplessness when an individual believes that they have no control over the stressor or their own destiny, or it may simply be one of accepting the future without regret or malice ('it is what it is').

Religion

Religiosity (internal): Using a belief in God to deal with adverse events. It can represent the simple belief in a better hereafter, a belief that a merciful God will help attenuate the event, and when things don't work out, falling back onto 'God works in mysterious ways'.

Religiosity (external): Religion may involve a social component where similar-minded people come together (congregate) and serve as supports or buffers for one another to facilitate the individual's ability to cope with a stressor.

Spirituality: Spirituality is often used in reference to religious worship. But it can also refer to other belief systems, such as a search for meaning or purpose in life. For others, it can be realized through connections to music, art, nature, and connections with others.

Social support

Social support seeking: Finding people who can help us cope with stressful experiences is one of the most common methods of dealing with stressors. This is especially the case given that social support may serve multiple functions in relation to stressors. Even pets can provide emotional support.

One would think that if a particular strategy proves ineffective in attenuating the impact of a stressor, then it would be advantageous for an alternative strategy to be adopted. Yet, under certain conditions, cognitive functioning may be impaired, limiting consideration of new responses. In times of distress our behavioral repertoire may be narrowed so that only our prepotent (or well-entrenched) responses will be used, whereas other coping methods, as effective as they might potentially be, fall by the wayside. So, what differentiates individuals who are good at dealing with stressors from those who are not? Being cognitively flexible seems to be fundamental for effective stressor appraisals and may thereby contribute to coping better with negative events (Gabrys et al., 2018), potentially leading to lower depression and anxiety. As well, some forms of psychotherapy benefit from cognitive flexibility as it may promote a shift from negative to positive cognitive sets (Hinton & Kirmayer, 2017).

Assuming that an appropriate appraisal is made, it seems that those individuals who are adept at using a relatively broad range of coping strategies and are prepared to be flexible in their use (i.e., able to shift from one strategy to another as necessary), may be best able to deal with stressors. In contrast, stressors will most negatively affect those individuals with a restricted range of coping methods, or rigidity in the persistent application of ineffective coping strategies. Further to this same point, the functional effectiveness of coping is not simply determined by which strategy is mobilized, but by how various strategies are used in conjunction with one another (Matheson & Anisman, 2003). As a case in point, although rumination is frequently associated with depressive illness (Nolen-Hoeksema, 1998), it typically occurs together with other coping strategies. In fact, in non-depressed individuals, rumination co-occurred with a broad constellation of problem- and emotion-focused strategies, as well as cognitive disengagement (e.g., 'I'm going through some pretty bad times, but if I talk to the guys at work they might have some ideas about what I can do'). In contrast, among dysthymic patients (those with chronic, low-grade depression), rumination was primarily associated with emotion-focused coping, and inversely related to efforts to disengage (e.g., 'I'm going through some pretty bad times, and it's because I'm just a failure at everything I do or ever will do; I just want to lie here and never see the world again') (Kelly et al., 2007). We don't know what came first; the depression might have preceded the narrowed coping methods, but it is equally likely that poor coping could favor the emergence of depression. In either case, poor coping seems to involve the use of rumination in conjunction with emotion-focused coping strategies rather than with an array of other strategies.

There is yet another oddity in the way individuals cope that varies as a function of whether they had previously been stressed. When placed in a problem-solving situation, individuals who had not been stressed tended to consciously take the simplest approach to figure out how things worked, and concurrently their hippocampal activity was high (the hippocampus is involved in memory and its activation serves participants well in this problem-solving situation). Stressed participants, in contrast, tended to use excessively complex strategies, even if they could not verbally express why they chose the strategy that they did (i.e., it seemed to be a subconscious undertaking). In this instance, brain imaging revealed that the problem-solving effort was accompanied by activation of the striatum that might be more aligned with unconscious learning. In effect, stressful events may influence the way we deal with situations, moving us away from purposeful, conscious approaches.

━━━━━━━━━━ **THE GOOD FIGHT** ━━━━━━━━━━

There has been this notion that fighting against an illness might increase survival, whereas feelings of helplessness and hopelessness would have the opposite effect. This is epitomized in movies where the doctor says about the hero that has just undergone some brutal surgery to remove a bullet or a tumor, 'Well, it's up to him/her now. But, I think Matt/Marlene is strong and has a will to live.' It's as if the patient has some control over events. In fact, feelings of helplessness and hopelessness have been negatively related to five- and ten-year survival following breast cancer treatment, although the strength of the relationship was only moderate. But does this imply that having a 'fighting spirit' increases survival? To be sure, several reports indicated that features such as optimism and having a fighting spirit were accompanied by longer survival relative to that of people who had expressed feelings of hopelessness.

The advice that is commonly given to those who are critically ill is 'don't give up', 'be strong', or 'fight against your illness', and obituaries make reference to 'the valiant battle' or 'fought bravely to the end'. Many of us also know the words from Dylan Thomas's famous poem: 'Do not go gentle into that good night, Old age should burn and rage at close of day; Rage, rage against the dying of the light.' There is certainly much to say for putting up the good fight, and there's no doubt that social support, medical treatments, and lifestyle choices can help in this regard. Yet, when raging against the dying of the light has proven to be useless and the person has suffered a long and painful illness, the support a person receives from loved ones can serve as comfort that might help the person let go and die peacefully. In fact, although there are only anecdotal suggestions to support this belief, sometimes a dying person may be waiting for their family to *allow* them to go gently into that good night.

Assessing appraisals and coping

Several instruments have been developed to assess the coping styles or strategies that individuals endorse in stressful situations. In general, measuring appraisals of events is less common than assessments of coping methods. Often, participants are encouraged to think of an event or are provided with a depiction of an event, and then asked how threatening and stressful they perceived it to be, and how much control they think they had over it. There have been scales developed to assess stressor appraisals, with one of the most used being the Stress Appraisal Measure (SAM) (Peacock & Wong, 1990). The SAM is thought to measure different aspects of primary appraisals, including challenge, threat, and centrality, as well as secondary appraisals comprising resources available to contend with the stressor. This widely used instrument has much to offer, especially when used in conjunction with an analysis of the associated coping methods.

Coping has been assessed through various scales. One of the earliest measures was the Ways of Coping Questionnaire, which assesses the degree to which individuals endorse specific coping behaviors in response to a specific stressor that the participant indicates they had recently encountered (Folkman & Lazarus, 1988). Aligning with different theoretical perspectives on stress and coping, alternative scales have been developed. One of these, the Coping Orientation to Problem Experience inventory developed by Carver et al. (1989) assesses how individuals generally deal with stressful events. This measure comprises 15 strategies that are typically organized into problem-focused coping (e.g., planning), adaptive emotion-focused coping (e.g., humor), and maladaptive emotion-focused coping (e.g., denial). Similarly, Matheson and Anisman (2003) developed the Survey of Coping Profile Endorsement (SCOPE) to assess coping styles and strategies and subsequently used this scale to measure appraisals of coping effectiveness (see Table 2.2). This questionnaire asks participants how they would cope with stressors in general (coping styles) or in response to specific events (strategies). The SCOPE comprises 14 subscales aligned with those described in Table 2.1.

The various coping measures have a fair bit in common with one another: there is overlap in some of the items, dimensions of coping, and when factor analyzed (a statistical method to determine which of several items/behaviors link or cluster together to create distinct dimensions), they all provide either the two- or three-dimensional structure already described (e.g., problem-focused, emotion-focused, and avoidant coping). Thus, the choice of instrument an investigator might use depends on the stressor of interest as well as the fit with the researcher's own theoretical approach to understanding the issues at hand, or with how they wish to use the data. There are also other coping scales available that focus on specific situations or variables (e.g., Quality of Social Support Scale), particular illnesses (e.g., Mental Adjustment to HIV Scale; Mental Adjustment to Cancer Scale) or coping within specific subgroups of individuals.

What follows is a sample version of a rendition of the SCOPE as well as the scoring used for this instrument. If you are curious and decide to assess your own coping methods using this questionnaire, bear in mind that you can't use this to self-diagnose (e.g., 'My profile looks like someone who is very unhappy'). The scores provided in the ensuing section are 'group' scores and comparing yourself to these aggregated profiles might not mean much. Further, the scale can be used to measure coping 'styles' or 'strategies' depending on the wording of the question. If the question asks you to respond based on 'stressful events experienced over the past two weeks', then you'll be examining a coping style. If, however, the question is framed as asking about coping with a particular event (e.g., a fight with your spouse, an argument with your boss, distress over not getting things completed), then you'll be looking at coping strategies. If you do each of these assessments, starting with coping styles, and then at later times assess your coping strategies regarding particular stressors, you might find that your coping methods differ across stressor situations, but there will be some similarity to your coping propensities (style). The coping scale is a lengthy one that might not be conducive if researchers wish not to place too great a burden on participants. Shortened versions were developed that were reliable and mapped onto the results obtained with the long version (e.g., Chee et al., 2020).

Coping as a profile of responses

Although a given coping inventory might comprise many subscales, in most studies, factor analysis is conducted to reduce the number of dimensions that need to be dealt with into two or three more manageable units. As indicated earlier, emotion-focused coping comprises several strategies, such as emotion-based strategies, self- and other-blame, rumination, and so forth, and hence these are essentially pooled to represent a single type of coping. Likewise, problem-focused coping might comprise problem solving and cognitive restructuring, and these are combined as a single unit for purposes of analysis.

Table 2.2 A coping scale.

Survey of Coping Profile Endorsement (SCOPE)

The purpose of this questionnaire is to find out how people deal with more general problems or stresses in their lives. The following are activities that you may have done. After each activity, please indicate the extent to which you would use this as a way of dealing with problems or stresses in recent weeks.

Ordinarily, in recent weeks have you:	Never	Seldom	Sometimes	Often	Almost always
1. accepted that there was nothing you could do to change your situation?	0	1	2	3	4
2. tried to just take whatever came your way?	0	1	2	3	4
3. talked with friends or relatives about your problems?	0	1	2	3	4
4. tried to do things which you typically enjoy?	0	1	2	3	4
5. sought out information that would help you resolve your problems?	0	1	2	3	4
6. blamed others for creating your problems or making them worse?	0	1	2	3	4
7. sought the advice of others to resolve your problems?	0	1	2	3	4
8. blamed yourself for your problems?	0	1	2	3	4
9. exercised?	0	1	2	3	4
10. fantasized or thought about unreal things (e.g., the perfect revenge, or winning a million dollars) to feel better?	0	1	2	3	4
11. been very emotional compared to your usual self?	0	1	2	3	4
12. gone over your problem in your mind over and over again?	0	1	2	3	4
13. asked others for help?	0	1	2	3	4
14. thought about your problem a lot?	0	1	2	3	4
15. become involved in recreation or pleasure activities?	0	1	2	3	4
16. worried about your problem a lot?	0	1	2	3	4
17. tried to keep your mind off things that are upsetting you?	0	1	2	3	4
18. tried to distract yourself from your troubles?	0	1	2	3	4
19. avoided thinking about your problems?	0	1	2	3	4
20. made plans to overcome your problems?	0	1	2	3	4
21. told jokes about your situation?	0	1	2	3	4

(Continued)

Table 2.2 (Continued)

Ordinarily, in recent weeks have you:	Never	Seldom	Sometimes	Often	Almost always
22. thought a lot about who is responsible for your problem (besides yourself)?	0	1	2	3	4
23. shared humorous stories, etc. to cheer yourself and others up?	0	1	2	3	4
24. told yourself that other people have dealt with problems such as yours?	0	1	2	3	4
25. thought a lot about how you have brought your problem on yourself?	0	1	2	3	4
26. decided to wait and see how things turn out?	0	1	2	3	4
27. wished the situation would go away or be over with?	0	1	2	3	4
28. decided that your current problems are a result of your own past actions?	0	1	2	3	4
29. gone shopping?	0	1	2	3	4
30. asserted yourself and taken positive action on problems that are getting you down?	0	1	2	3	4
31. sought reassurance and moral support from others?	0	1	2	3	4
32. resigned yourself to your problem?	0	1	2	3	4
33. thought about how your problems have been caused by other people?	0	1	2	3	4
34. daydreamed about how things may turn out?	0	1	2	3	4
35. been very emotional in how you react, even to little things?	0	1	2	3	4
36. decided that you can grow and learn through your problem?	0	1	2	3	4
37. told yourself that other people have problems like your own?	0	1	2	3	4
38. wished you were a stronger person or better at dealing with problems?	0	1	2	3	4
39. looked for how you can learn something out of your bad situation?	0	1	2	3	4
40. asked for God's guidance?	0	1	2	3	4
41. kept your feelings bottled up inside?	0	1	2	3	4
42. found yourself crying more than usual?	0	1	2	3	4
43. tried to act as if you were not upset?	0	1	2	3	4

Ordinarily, in recent weeks have you:	Never	Seldom	Sometimes	Often	Almost always
44. prayed for help?	0	1	2	3	4
45. gone out?	0	1	2	3	4
46. held in your feelings?	0	1	2	3	4
47. tried to act as if you weren't feeling bad?	0	1	2	3	4
48. taken steps to overcome your problems?	0	1	2	3	4
49. made humorous comments or wise cracks?	0	1	2	3	4
50. told others that you were depressed or emotionally upset?	0	1	2	3	4

To determine your score, add up the items for each type of coping method and divide by the number of items (questions) in that category. Below you will find the questions that are relevant for each of the coping methods.

Problem solving: 5, 20, 30, 48

Cognitive restructuring: 24, 36, 37, 39

Avoidance: 17, 18, 19

Active distraction: 4, 8, 15, 29, 45

Rumination: 12, 14, 16

Humor: 21, 23, 49

Social support seeking: 3, 7, 13, 31

Emotional expression: 11, 35, 42, 50

Other-blame: 6, 22, 33

Self-blame: 8, 25, 28

Emotional containment: 41, 43, 46, 47

Passive resignation: 1, 2, 26, 32

Religion: 40, 44

Wishful thinking: 10, 27, 34, 38

Factor analyzing the data and combining different methods with common features may be fine in many situations, but there are occasions where this might not be desirable, and to a certain extent might even be counterproductive. The factor structure evident under one set of conditions (e.g., in a group of individuals who are healthy or non-stressed) might not match that evident under certain stressor conditions or among individuals dealing with a particular experience. In a non-stressed group of individuals, social support may fall into a factor that is aligned with problem-focused coping. However, in response to illness, it might fall into different categories and varies still further over time.

Creating broad categories that combine multiple coping strategies might not allow for the identification of subtle differences that could distinguish groups. However, there may be value in explicitly considering the distinct elements of these categories. For instance, an IQ score provides an overall index of intelligence/ability or separate indices for verbal and performance measures. However, these indices comprise multiple elements that can be particularly informative. Johnny can score comparably across all components of the IQ test, or he might score low in those dealing with language, but high in those that involve creativity. These different profiles might have very different implications. Likewise, the profile of coping responses endorsed may provide important clues as to the subtle differences that exist between groups or between individuals, which might otherwise be obfuscated by pooling data across the several strategies that make up a factor.

When coping styles were assessed among individuals with anxiety, mildly depressed mood (dysphoria), or both, the coping profiles could readily be distinguished from those of individuals who were neither anxious nor dysphoric. The dysphoric individuals used less problem-focused coping and social support seeking than individuals with low or mild symptoms of depression. They also used more rumination, emotional expression, other-blame, self-blame, and emotional containment than non-depressed individuals. Evidently, even in the face of mild depressive symptoms (nowhere near clinical levels), some coping methods were very much like those of individuals with higher levels of depression seen in earlier analyses.

Anxious participants displayed a similar coping profile to dysphoric individuals. However, their problem-focused coping was more like that of asymptomatic individuals, whereas those with dysphoria or dysphoria plus anxiety showed much lower problem-solving efforts. All three of the symptomatic groups reported greater rumination than did those without symptoms, whereas the degree of emotional expression, other-blame, self-blame, and emotional containment varied as a function of the nature of the symptoms presented. It seems that the profiles of coping responses effectively distinguished between individuals with different psychological symptoms, which might not have been detected as readily if the coping methods had been grouped into broad categories.

An important point here is that psychological problems may be accompanied by distinct coping profiles, and may even be apparent when individuals express symptoms that fall below the clinical threshold. Using this profile approach may provide clinicians with information regarding where their focus should lie in helping patients deal with stressors or illnesses. Specifically, if a clinician believes a patient is not coping well, it might be useful to identify which specific aspects of their coping methods are most problematic, and then focus therapy on these particular coping behaviors as well as on associated appraisals.

―――――――――― **EATING TO COPE** ――――――――――

In response to traumatic stressors, as well as severe depression, food consumption typically declines. However, in response to moderate stressors, a fair number of people display increased eating, particularly in the form of junk food rich in carbohydrates (Dallman, 2010). Negative emotions among 'emotional eaters' might elicit this outcome owing to particular hormonal changes. Alternatively, emotional eaters might not accurately recognize bodily sensations when under duress, essentially mistaking arousal for hunger. Yet another view is that distress results in disinhibition which 'allows' for increased eating to occur, and that eating acts as a coping mechanism to alleviate the negative emotions otherwise evoked by stressful events. From this perspective, eating might be a way of coping with adverse events, as either a disengagement strategy or in an effort to 'self-medicate' through increased glucose availability.

Long ago, hominid diets comprised assorted vegetables, fruits, and nuts. But, being omnivores, they also hunted for game. This could be a dangerous activity as the prey could easily become the predator, thus the increased release of a stress hormone, such as cortisol, might have been essential for proper defensive actions. Cortisol ought to have increased food consumption that was necessary for the strength and endurance to partake in the hunt, during which it would readily be burned off. This hormone might contribute to the accumulation of unhealthy belly fat, which likely wasn't a problem for these early hominids. Today, when the hunt comprises a visit to the supermarket and stressors consist of being stuck in traffic or standing in line at the checkout counter, the once functional cortisol release that leads to eating and the accumulation of abdominal fat might be counterproductive.

Finding meaning and personal growth

In some horrific situations, especially those that can't readily be altered (e.g., severe chronic illness; loss of a child), individuals may have no option other than to change themselves (as the Austrian psychiatrist and Holocaust survivor Viktor Frankl put it). To this end, a form of cognitive restructuring may be particularly effective. A common form of this coping method comprises posttraumatic growth, which entails finding meaning from traumatic events. The features of posttraumatic growth were thought to comprise greater appreciation for life, more meaningful interpersonal relationships, greater altruism, compassion, an elevated sense of personal strength, changes in individuals' priorities, richer existential and spiritual life, and creative growth (Kaufman, 2020). Individuals who feel gratitude for having survived traumatic experiences, or in whom gratitude is encouraged during psychotherapy, may be more apt to fare well in finding meaning and are less likely to develop symptoms of PTSD. This said, in response to some traumatic experiences many individuals may feel grateful for having survived but find it very difficult to feel any gratitude for the experience itself. Thus, feelings of gratitude frequently have few health benefits (Dickens et al., 2017) and if they do, it may take considerable time for individuals to feel this way and to gain from these feelings.

Living through traumatic circumstances may result in two independent processes occurring, namely trying to make sense of the event and finding some benefit from the experience. Although severe chronic illnesses, such as cancer can take an enormous physical, psychological, and social toll on individuals, cancer survivors might use their experience as an opportunity to improve their physical and mental health. Some individuals report gaining benefits from living through cancer travails, recognizing the broad positive implications of surviving their experience. Beyond the positive effects of this coping method, it limits negative posttraumatic stress outcomes and the adverse effects of intrusive thoughts on positive affect, life satisfaction, and spiritual well-being (Ochoa Arnedo et al., 2019).

Not unexpectedly, the positive effects associated with finding meaning occur in other venues, such as caregiving for a partner with dementia, family members with cancer, among parents with severely ill children, and in people coming to grips with the loss of a loved one by suicide. The fact is that meaning finding stemming from a severe adverse experience is not at all uncommon. Women treated for breast cancer frequently become engaged in 'walks' to support breast cancer research, and other groups have similarly made heroic efforts to raise funds for certain charities (e.g., the Terry Fox Foundation; Rick Hansen's Man in Motion campaign; the Michael J. Fox Foundation; the Milken Family Foundation). While finding meaning has most often been examined in the context of severe and traumatic stressors, by affecting coping self-efficacy and proactive planning, having meaning in life can diminish the impact of everyday stressors that are encountered (Ward et al., 2022).

It is important to distinguish between two subtle characteristics regarding meaning-making, namely those of searching for meaning ('meaning-making efforts') and arriving at a meaning ('meaning made') (Park, 2010). Simply searching for meaning doesn't necessarily result in appreciable benefits, whereas finding or arriving at some meaning might have positive actions. In fact, seeking meaning can in some instances have adverse effects or might be indicative of a persistent preoccupation with an adverse event. As powerful as finding meaning or posttraumatic growth might be as a coping method, some people simply won't find any meaning. Later, when we deal with methods of stress management, a theme that will be repeated is that there are no treatments that work for everyone. So, too, it seems that finding meaning might be an effective coping method for some individuals but not for others, and it might vary with the situation that culminated in the severe trauma. It is one thing to find meaning in the death of a loved one that can be ascribed to the negligence of others (e.g., legally taking on an automobile company when death was caused by cars bursting into flames upon a moderate back-end collision), it's quite another to find meaning from a person tripping over their coffee table, hitting their head, and subsequently dying.

Several factors may predict which individuals adjust to a severe illness (sometimes referred to as acceptance of the diagnosis and the treatment). These factors include the sustained use of effective coping methods, the ability to manage non-illness related stressors, and a belief system that resulted in an altered meaning of the stressful experience. Thus, the well-being of people in this situation would be best served by providing resources to reduce distress, providing effective support systems that include the opportunity to talk about their experiences, and helping them reframe their beliefs about living with an illness.

Social support

For most people social interactions may be a fundamental need to maintain general well-being, and feelings of loneliness signal the need for social comfort (Cacioppo & Cacioppo, 2014). Much like the cravings for food that are elicited by food deprivation, social craving may occur following periods of social isolation and can trigger brain neurochemical changes that ordinarily are elicited by other forms of reward. The view has been taken that 'social homeostasis' reflects an adaptive response that may have evolved because of the survival advantages obtained through groups (Tomova et al., 2021).

Considerable research pointed to the value of social support in dealing with day-to-day stressors as well as those of a traumatic nature. The benefits of social support have been apparent in relation to stressor-elicited psychological illness, such as depression, and in adjusting to physical illnesses. Support can come from different sources, and social support from family members may have particularly pronounced positive effects on chronic illness outcomes, especially when family cohesion is high and there is an emphasis on self-reliance and personal achievement. In contrast, negative patient outcomes were tied to critical, overprotective, controlling, and distracting family responses to illness management.

Social support as a buffer

Social support might not be effective in eliminating the actions of every stressor (e.g., getting the tax department off your back, unless you're really well connected), but it could serve as a buffer against some of the adverse effects that might otherwise emerge, thereby preventing psychological disturbances (depression, anxiety), improving physical health, and promoting recovery from illness (Anisman et al., 2018). Of course, the positive actions of social support may vary with a great number of factors, and so blanket statements concerning the value of social support need to be somewhat tempered.[1]

Simply having support may not be sufficient to produce health benefits. Instead, the individual's perception of support may be more important as might be their

---

[1]The beneficial effects of social support aren't new. The Talmud, which preceded modern psychology by a fair bit, states that 'whoever visits the sick takes away 1/60th of their illness'. It's unclear where they got this number, and certainly it is not evidence-based. This statement doesn't mean that a tumor will have shrunk by 1.66% with each visitor, but what it implies is that social support lightens the burden (even temporarily) carried by a sick person.

satisfaction with this support. It is known that supportive relations may be important in enhancing quality of life among patients with serious illnesses, but mixed outcomes were reported as to whether illness progression was affected by having social support. Thus, it is especially pertinent that patients who reported satisfaction with their support were more likely to exhibit diminished levels of potentially harmful biological changes (e.g., circulating inflammatory factors) and lower early mortality than among individuals who reported poorer levels of satisfaction with the support. Such effects have been apparent among women following breast cancer surgery (Jutagir et al., 2017) and satisfaction with social support among breast cancer survivors was accompanied by brain activity changes likely signifying diminished anxiety and depression (Muscatell et al., 2016).

Women living alone and who reported poor social support prior to a diagnosis of colorectal cancer were more likely to experience greater overall and cancer-specific mortality (Kroenke et al., 2020), whereas cancer-specific survival was poorer in newly divorced individuals. It seems that married individuals or those having a partner are better able to deal with stressors and more likely to withstand the travails of illnesses. This has been seen in relation to the development of cardiovascular illnesses as well as in the prognosis of individuals with heart disease. Likewise, a large meta-analysis that included the occurrence of metastases in 10 different forms of cancer were diminished in married relative to non-married individuals (Aizer et al., 2013). Such effects are not always evident, which is not unexpected given that not all studies distinguished between relations that were happy from those that were not.

These findings are consistent with the view that social support coming from being married had health benefits. However, it is possible that having a close other may in some fashion result in earlier detection of cancer presence, perhaps reflecting superior adoption of appropriate health behaviors, including regular cancer screening. As well, the biases of oncologists who believe that married people may have the support needed to deal with distress created by cancer therapy may influence the therapies administered and might thereby influence survival (DelFattore, 2019).

POSITIVITY AND SOCIAL SUPPORT

A school of thought, termed 'positive psychology', formed around the concept that positive perspectives and expressions of certain personal characteristics (e.g., optimism) can be essential to foster well-being (Seligman & Csikszentmihalyi, 2000). What this means is that rather than follow the medical model in which attempts are made to diminish the symptoms of illness, the aim of positive psychology is to promote well-being, which can prophylactically prevent the development of health problems. Many clinicians and scientists believe that social support, along with other aspects of positive psychology, may have great benefits for well-being and the healing process (Seligman, 2019). It was suggested that positive attitudes and experiences serve to broaden favorable thought-action patterns, which foster the building of enduring biological and psychosocial resources that support good health (Fredrickson, 2001). Indeed, simply reminiscing about pleasant memories can dampen the behavioral and physiological responses to current stressors (Speer & Delgado, 2017). Positivity could likewise enhance advantageous social relationships and social coping that could favor wellness (Zelenski, 2020). A treatment referred to as positive psychotherapy (or PPT), which comprises a series of exercises to instill positivity, reduces signs of depression in a subclinical population as well as in clinically depressed individuals, and this procedure was alleged to be superior to antidepressant medication (Schueller & Seligman, 2008).

The positive psychology perspective in relation to health outcomes has not been unanimously endorsed. It was, in fact, suggested that the benefits attributable to positive psychology have been over-the-top, being plagued by statistical problems and even conceptual flaws (Wong & Roy, 2018). Moreover, it was maintained that the benefits of positive psychology in relation to illnesses were limited, as the magnitude of the effects observed were modest and could have been influenced by biases inherent in studies with few participants (White et al., 2019). The data related to physiological changes associated with positivity had been taken to provide support for the view that beneficial health outcomes may come about in relation to a positive outlook. However, are the magnitude of the reported effects meaningful with respect to illness attenuation? A 10 to 20% rise in immune functioning may be statistically significant but is this sufficient to translate into a greater ability to fight infection or cancer? Regardless of whether it does or doesn't, positivity and social support may lessen the psychological burden of those in distress.

In addition to diminishing illness related to stressors, social support can limit many stressor-elicited biological changes (hormonal, neurochemical, and immunological) that might have adverse consequences. Social support availability was inversely related to levels of stress hormones (e.g., cortisol) and to variations of oxytocin, both in laboratory stress tests and in natural settings (McQuaid et al., 2014). For instance, women with metastatic breast cancer with a high quality of perceived social support showed lower cortisol levels than those with a lower quality of support. Based on a meta-analysis (see the text box below regarding what is meant by 'meta-analysis'), it was concluded that social support diminished the cortisol response elicited by laboratory stressors. Numerous studies indicated that many other psychosocial and developmental factors (sex, early-life experiences, presence of psychological disorders) influenced the response to stressors and that social support moderated these actions (Anisman et al., 2018). The effects of stressors and social support are not limited to hormonal changes, having been apparent in brain neuronal changes. Specifically, in a stress test where psychosocial support resources were available, brain activity changes ordinarily elicited by stressors were attenuated. Further, individuals who had received social support over several days displayed a blunted cortisol response and elevated neuronal activity within the anterior cingulate cortex in response to a social stressor (Eisenberger et al., 2007).

META-ANALYSES AND SYSTEMATIC REVIEWS

With the proliferation of scientific output, it is desirable to have reviews that synthesize the available empirical evidence. This has become more important in light of the many occasions when the results across studies are inconsistent. The use of meta-analyses has become popular to identify the key variables that determine the processes associated

(Continued)

with various pathologies and the factors that moderate these effects. A meta-analysis is a procedure in which the results of many studies are combined to obtain an unbiased perspective regarding a particular research question. Rather than simply assessing whether studies provided statistically significant effects in relation to a particular condition or treatment, it assesses the 'effect size' in each study (effect size is an index of the strength of associations that exist between variables) and takes into account the number of participants included in each study. Hence this sort of analysis provides a more realistic estimate of how variables are related to one another.

In undertaking a meta-analysis, investigators specify criteria concerning the studies that will be included or excluded. This may be based on the nature of the research approach adopted (e.g., include only studies in which participants experienced an early-life stressor as opposed to stressors encountered at any time in life; alternatively, the analysis could include only prospective studies and not those that were retrospective). By rigorously following predetermined criteria, the reliability and meaningfulness of the results can be evaluated. Clearly, these analyses are only as good as the criteria set out. Inclusion of studies that cover too broad an array of factors (or those that were not especially relevant) can muddy the waters.

A related approach has been that of systematic reviews of the available research. This procedure also comprises detailed analyses of multiple studies to determine the influence of specific variables on specific outcomes. Often, systematic reviews include meta-analyses, as well as both quantitative and qualitative studies. What can make a systematic review especially relevant is if the analysis considers the 'goodness' of the study (e.g., Did it comprise a placebo-controlled, double-blind trial or something less? Did the studies include variables related to gender or ethnicity?).

As important as meta-analyses and systematic reviews can be in deriving evidence-based conclusions, there may be limitations concerning what can be deduced. In the main, these reviews are based on published reports, which typically comprise those that showed significant outcomes (e.g., in relation to a particular treatment having a positive effect in diminishing an illness). However, studies that did not yield significant outcomes are often never published and may not appear in the analysis. As a result, one could readily be misled by a modest number of reports showing that a given treatment is effective when, in fact, there were many more unpublished experiments that indicated that the treatment was ineffective. Far too often, as in the case of SSRIs to treat depression, many years passed before it became apparent that the miracle cure was far less effective than initially claimed. In computer science, the acronym GIGO refers to 'garbage in, garbage out'. This acronym is fully relevant to meta-analyses and systematic reviews.

Conclusion

Adverse events, especially those that occurred during critical periods early in life or possibly during adolescence, result in increased vulnerability to later stressor-induced pathology. However, some individuals can emerge less scathed than others even in the face of the most traumatic events. It is possible that this occurs owing to an inherent biological resilience, the availability of effective coping resources, a sense of mastery, or other psychosocial factors. In fact, stressful events in some cases may imbue individuals with greater resilience (e.g., by putting them in a situation that favors finding meaning or personal growth, or making social resources salient). Individuals may have learned from adverse experiences that with appropriate behaviors and coping methods it is possible to transcend current strife; indeed there might be something to the tiresome cliché, 'That which doesn't kill you makes you stronger'. From a practical research perspective, knowing which behavioral, social, or biological factors distinguish those who succumb to illness in the face of severe trauma and those who do not might prove valuable in defining and mobilizing strategies to immunize or treat individuals so that traumatic events do not have the severe repercussions that might otherwise occur.

It seems that appraisals of events and how we cope with them can be influenced by prior stressful experiences as well as our current affective state. There are some individuals who tend to put a negative spin on events so that others often perceive them as being a negative or pessimistic person (they, in contrast, would say that they are not pessimists, they're realists). Likewise, the coping strategies they typically endorse are stereotypical (fixed), even when the situation might call for a different approach. Breaking well-entrenched behavioral styles (habits) is exceedingly difficult (e.g., emotional rumination in response to stressors), and there are times when these coping methods are entirely inappropriate and hence ineffective. In contrast, an effective way of dealing with stressors is to be flexible in using particular coping strategies and to recognize that this flexibility needs to be maintained over time and across situations. That sounds like good advice, but it doesn't tell you how to do it and might be about as helpful as advising a person to become taller if they want to play in the NBA. However, when we come to Chapter 13 (dealing with treatment and intervention strategies) we'll discuss ways that might help individuals adopt a more flexible pattern of responses to the challenges they encounter.

Suggested readings

Cacioppo, J.T., Cacioppo, S., & Boomsma, D.I. (2014). Evolutionary mechanisms for loneliness. *Cognition & Emotion, 28*, 3–21.

Kahneman, D. (2011). *Thinking, Fast and Slow*. New York: Farrar, Straus and Giroux.

Ysseldyk, R., Matheson, K., & Anisman, H. (2010). Religiosity as identity: Toward an understanding of religion from a social identity perspective. *Personality and Social Psychology Review, 14*, 60–71.

3

PSYCHOSOCIAL AND ENVIRONMENTAL DETERMINANTS OF HEALTH

Traveling the stress-health pathway

'If you want to go fast, walk alone. But, if you want to go far, then walk together.' This old expression is relevant to so many life experiences and our capacity to reach desired goals. We most certainly can accomplish things on our own, and many people take great pride in their individuality, but this doesn't necessarily make this the best strategy for all situations. If a task is large and complex, then many people are needed to make sure that the job is done successfully. Whether we're considering the development of broad health behaviors, diminishing poverty, thwarting pollution and climate change, or limiting the spread of a perilous pandemic, we need to keep in mind that we're all in it together. Our participation and identification with various social groups are fundamental to our well-being. Having others who can be trusted and relied upon can diminish the impact of stressors, encourage the adoption of effective health behaviors, and diminish threats that might otherwise feel insurmountable. This said, even when it seems that we're all in it together, the experiences of individuals can vary dramatically.

When chronic stressors are encountered, biological resources may be overly taxed, leading to allostatic overload that can favor the development of psychological and physical illnesses. In addition, allostatic overload may occur through a more general process. In particular, 'Type 2' allostatic overload occurs because of environmental or societal disturbances, including social conflicts. These threats do not necessarily elicit the same 'corrective' coping responses as do severe or traumatic stressors, and over time their toll might become substantial unless measures are taken to modify the systemic structures that adversely impose themselves on individuals (McEwen & Wingfield, 2003).

Learning objectives

Stressful events may come in diverse forms but some of the most injurious include psychosocial threats, which not only affect day-to-day well-being but can influence a wide range of diseases and life span. These psychosocial factors include poverty, adverse childhood experiences, unsupportive relations, social betrayals and rejection, as well as various forms of discrimination and racism. In addition, environmental factors related to climate change, natural disasters, and exposure to numerous pollutants can profoundly affect health. To a considerable extent, the impacts and ability to contend with these environmental health challenges are tied to psychosocial factors. This chapter is intended to portray:

- several key psychosocial factors that can undermine psychological and physical health and some of the processes contributing to these outcomes;
- the role of psychosocial processes in treatment-seeking for mental health disturbances;
- environmental influences that affect health and approaches that can be adopted to diminish these outcomes;
- how a systems-based strategy is needed to address the complex interplay between social and environmental determinants of health.

PSYCHOSOCIAL INFLUENCES ON WELL-BEING

Numerous factors that affect individuals' social environments influence health span and life span. These factors begin prenatally, are marked during early life, and extend into older age. Socioeconomic and occupational status in humans, and the equivalent in animals, such as being in a low position in social hierarchies (or having lost a position of dominance), have been linked to increased prevalence of multiple illnesses (Snyder-Mackler et al., 2020). Likewise, low social integration (i.e., the capacity of individuals to invest in and maintain affiliative or supportive interactions) and limited social connectivity were accompanied by a 50% increase of earlier mortality, being as powerful as other high-risk variables, such as smoking or poor diet. In this chapter we'll focus on a few of the psychosocial and

(Continued)

environmental determinants that affect health, while in later chapters we'll describe several of the biological changes that are introduced by such challenges and how they come to affect the development of multiple diseases.

Socioeconomic status and poverty

Lower socioeconomic status has long been known to be associated with diminished life span. Simply having a low-income job in which individuals experience high job demands, have little control over their situation, and perceived unfairness was associated with life span being reduced by a decade relative to individuals not in this position (Marmot et al., 1978). The situation is still worse for those living in generational poverty who face a lack of resources to meet basic living needs, such as food insecurity and the threat of homelessness, along with the lack of hope for how to escape or the time or tools to do so given the daily struggle of survival. To be sure, poverty may undermine mental health, which can further affect an individual's ability to obtain and maintain the resources to meet their needs (Ridley et al., 2020).

People living in poverty often encounter multiple challenges that affect physical and psychological health. They often experience poor diets, social violence associated with overcrowding and lack of protective mechanisms, exposure to environmental toxicants is endemic, and in urban settings something as simple as the presence of green space that could have health benefits is rarely a priority. Even when universal health care is available, access to medical care may be lacking due to stigma or trust in the medical system, and preventive care (e.g., screening for various illnesses) is infrequently sought or obtained. Communicable diseases disproportionately affect those sectors of society that are impoverished. These same conditions foster the development and progression of non-communicable diseases, such as type 2 diabetes and heart disease. Despite increases of average life expectancy that have been realized over the past decades, this has been less apparent among economically disadvantaged people (Tetzlaff et al., 2020). As great as these health disparities are within Western countries, they are frequently more pronounced in non-Western nations where the poverty gap may be wider. Although life expectancy has increased in these countries, and maternal and infant mortality has been declining, the gap is still very high (Ortiz-Ospina & Roser, 2016).

POSTAL CODE IS A BETTER PREDICTOR OF HEALTH THAN IS GENETIC CODE

Studies conducted within several North American cities indicated that it was possible to predict a child's destiny based on where they were raised. Those in the lowest (20%) economic sector who lived in poor neighborhoods were six times more likely not to complete school, or to be very young mothers, prenatal care was sought far less often than among those in high economic brackets, and infant death was markedly elevated. Children born in poverty were likely to die 10-15 years before those of the wealthiest 20%. Moreover, among the most disadvantaged groups emergency department visits related to physical conditions were almost double, as were those related to mental health issues (e.g., Belsky et al., 2019).

Those statistics leave us with some daunting conclusions concerning the link between economic factors and health. Now, throw in additional factors to the mix. What are the consequences of families living in impoverished conditions over generations? And what if they had been the victims of historical trauma and rarely had safe spaces to which they could turn to heal? Conditions of poverty may be a vicious cycle carried across generations as individuals might not have the opportunities to extract themselves from the situation in which they find themselves (Matheson, Asokumar & Anisman, 2020).

Adverse childhood experiences

Profound and lasting effects on psychological and physical well-being have frequently been associated with adverse childhood experiences (ACEs), such as abuse or neglect. A systematic review indicated that ACEs were tied to approximately 30% of cases of anxiety and 40% of depression (Bellis et al., 2019). ACEs were similarly associated with harmful alcohol use, smoking, illicit drug use, and interpersonal violence, as well as physical disorders such as type 2 diabetes, cardiovascular disease, stroke, and respiratory disease (Hughes et al., 2021). These physical disorders may be secondary to the promotion of obesity that has been associated with ACEs in conjunction with genetic factors (Read et al., 2022). Figure 3.1 shows a sequence of steps whereby ACEs may influence biological and behavioral processes that culminate in illnesses through the life span.

While not diminishing the importance of research that focused on early-life adversities, it is essential to consider ACEs from a broader perspective, particularly if these experiences are compounded by the challenges created by poverty. Being born into poverty and being raised under these conditions may result in a perpetuation of privation across a life span or even over generations.

Childhood stressors that are tolerable may help children learn to cope and may be an important component of normal development. However, toxic stressors may impair psychosocial development and undermine coping abilities, leading to disturbed physiological processes essential for well-being (Shonkoff et al., 2009). The experiences associated with being raised in lower-income neighborhoods are often (but certainly not always) accompanied by lack of adequate public and school resources, reduced educational attainment, absence of a supportive social safety net, loss of trust, and exposure to harmful environmental toxicants (e.g., Wodtke et al., 2011). These experiences foster poor health outcomes, including stress-related physical disorders that are evident throughout life. Cognitive outcomes, including diminished working memory and executive functioning, are more likely to be present, which have been linked to delayed development of the prefrontal cortex (Hanson et al., 2015). Significantly, self-regulation may be disturbed,

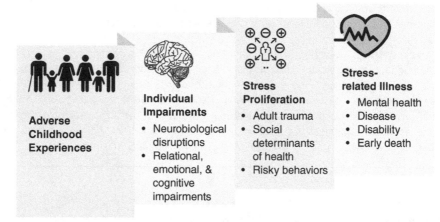

Figure 3.1   Early-life adverse events may influence numerous biological processes as well as emotions, cognitive functioning, and relationships with others. These may form the basis for subsequent poor health-related behaviors and may affect the individuals' encounters with further stressors (stress proliferation). Together, these diverse factors may favor the development of stress-related illnesses and premature death.

reflected by impaired attention and the inability to delay gratification. As well, the prefrontal cortex changes, which are accompanied by alterations of amygdala volume and neuronal reactivity, may influence appraisals of threats and the capacity to engage processes for integrating information needed for problem solving. Together, these many factors subvert social competence and the skills necessary to navigate social stressors and attain goals.

In an informative and thoughtful review, McEwen and McEwen (2017) provided an integrated model that incorporates sociological and neurobiological processes to account for the adverse outcomes of living under economically, socially, and politically disadvantaged conditions. Fundamental to their model is that childhood adversities, including neglect, psychological and physical abuse, household chaos, the lack of adequate parenting, as well as social and community supports, may give rise to stress systems being excessively taxed (allostatic overload). Among other things, these experiences may produce the silencing of certain genes (epigenetic changes), thereby causing the development of brain and peripheral changes that promote impaired cognitive performance and attainment of educational goals as well as risk of varied pathologies.

As much as poverty can have devastating consequences, McEwen and McEwen addressed an essential issue. Specifically, not every child born into poverty suffers, and not every child stays there. Some have the strength to contend with their situation. Some individuals extract themselves from poverty and are exceptionally successful. So, what is it that provides these individuals the resilience to overcome toxic environments and to thrive? In our earlier discussion of resilience, some of these factors were mentioned, but they bear repeating in the context of being raised under disadvantaged conditions. Foremost among these is having strong nurturing parenting, which can be enhanced through support from extended family and the community. As a result, children have an effective social safety net that enables them to cope with stressful experiences, thereby buffering the biological distur- bances that might otherwise evolve. These social dimensions may play a greater role in producing resilience than specific characteristics of the individual, such as the genes they had inherited (Ungar et al., 2013).

In effect, both microlevel and macrolevel factors contribute to well- being, including community, neighborhood, and institutional structures and the resources that they provide. These factors intersect and interact so that disturbances of one component may influence others, pointing to the importance of considering multiple factors to diminish the impact of ACEs rather than try- ing to implement single fixes. As much as events during early life are critically important to later well-being, as are genetic influences, the malleability (plasticity) of the young brain allows for changes to occur so that positive environmental experiences, especially having positive nurturing caregivers, can foster later well-being. As the child continues to develop, a stimulating and supportive envi- ronment further enhances brain development and associated cognitive skills. In this regard, early training programs for young children may ready them to perform well upon entering school and may facilitate their ability to contend with stressful experiences.

When we discuss intergenerational trauma (Chapter 12) it will be seen that poor parenting may beget poor parenting. Thus, children who encountered abuse or neglect from caregivers may in turn adopt poor parenting styles when they have children of their own. Accordingly, there is the question of how to encourage positive and non-punitive behaviors of caregivers to prevent adverse outcomes in the next generation. Enhancing interpersonal dynamics, including parent–child attachment behaviors and relationships with their peers, may provide benefits. Perhaps improving family living conditions may help in this respect, as might parent training programs to develop better skills. This depends on caregivers hav- ing the time, opportunity, and capacity to engage in such programs, which may be relatively unlikely if they are living in poverty and struggling just to survive. Likewise, the programs need to be appropriate and contextualized within the lived experience and cultural norms of caregivers and families, or risk being dismissed as unrealistic or elitist.

Health workers and scientists dealing with the difficulties of attempting to enhance the well-being of children so that their later cognitive and social life, as well as their psychological and physical health are enhanced, realize how many factors feed into this endeavor. Thus, they often ask the question, 'Where do we begin?' In fact, there is no single starting point, and as difficult as this might be, multiple efforts and targets need to be undertaken concurrently (Cadamuro et al., 2021). In their review, Shonkoff et al. (2009) called for changes in public policy to attenuate problems. They suggested that an increased focus be placed on: (a) reducing toxic childhood environments; (b) greater provision of early care and education programs that might not only serve as appropriate learning environments but could foster 'safe, stable and responsive family environments'; (c) evidence-informed interventions and treatments to deal with family mental health conditions; and (d) expanding the role of child welfare services so that they undertake comprehensive developmental assessments in order that professionals can apply appropriate culturally relevant interventions. Such a perspective underlines the notion that individual experiences are shaped considerably by the social environment in which they live.

━━━━━━━ WHEN BAD THINGS HAPPEN... ━━━━━━━

The Adverse Childhood Experiences (ACE) Study is one of the largest public health studies conducted in the United States by the Center for Disease Control. Surveys were administered to over 17,000 participants from 1995 to 1997. Although taken as common knowledge today, the findings were shocking to the researchers who found that about two-thirds of adults had experienced some type of adverse childhood experience and that most of these adults had experienced multiple types. Moreover, there was a direct link between childhood trauma and adult onset of medical, mental, and social problems.

The ACE measure comprises 10 experiences that reflect not just abuse, but also neglect and household dysfunction. These include:

1. physical abuse;
2. sexual abuse;
3. verbal abuse;
4. physical neglect;
5. emotional neglect;
6. a family member who is depressed or diagnosed with other mental illness;
7. a family member who is addicted to alcohol or another substance;
8. a family member who is in prison;
9. witnessing a mother being abused;
10. losing a parent to separation, divorce, or death.

For each type of ACE, one point is added to a person's score. While the effects of encountering more types of ACEs is cumulative, those who score 4 or more are especially likely as adults to have alcohol or drug addictions, attempted suicide, experienced severe depression, be at elevated risk for auto-immune diseases, and engage in riskier health behaviors. The powerful findings of this research and subsequent replications form the basis of a movement towards trauma-informed practices in schools, prisons, hospitals, shelters, and treatment centers.

Demographic determinants of health

Numerous demographic features form the basis for stratifying society into various social groups, including gender, age, and culture. While these features may have biological elements, classifying people into these groups is largely a social construction. The differential status of such groups, the associated stigma, social roles, and even the barriers that exist to transcend group boundaries are pervasive in these key demographics in a way that does not exist for other individual difference features (e.g., eye color). Social stratification renders members of some groups higher in status and others lower, with all the consequences associated with lower social, political, and economic power. At the same time, each of these demographic features has unique elements associated with intergroup relations, as well as biological aspects that come into play. Moreover, although demographic characteristics place some groups into disadvantaged social positions, there is considerable variability among group members in terms of their experiences, coping capacity, and health outcomes.

Gender and sexual difference

Biological differences that exist between men and women play a critical role in determining the sexual dimorphism that has frequently been reported about psychological and many physical illnesses. As well, the neurobiological and immune responses introduced by stressors vary with sex. We'll deal with several of these processes when we consider specific pathologies (depression, anxiety, immune-related disorders, heart disease) in later chapters. Concurrently, many differences exist that are associated with both individuals' adherence to gender norms and gender identification, as well as social constructions that define socialization processes, social experiences (including stressor exposure), and what are deemed appropriate appraisals, coping styles, and emotional reactions.

At times, the focus on understanding biological processes adopted a willful ignorance of social constructions of gender. For example, for a long time, female rodents were relatively infrequently included in experimental research, allegedly because their estrous cycles introduced variability in the data obtained. As well, including both males and females necessarily doubled the size of experiments and hence would be more expensive and time consuming. Research in humans was more democratized, but in many clinical drug trials women were explicitly excluded. It was only in 1993 that the FDA pointed to the absolute need to include women in drug evaluations. The absence of females in many studies was incongruous given that it had long been known that men and women differ in the occurrence of numerous psychological disorders, and it is now well established that pronounced genetic differences are present in tissues of men and women. The absence of females in animal and human studies not only hampered understanding of mechanisms related to illnesses in women, but prevented the identification of specific genetic, hormonal, and immune factors that influenced disease occurrence in both sexes.

Research examining psychosocial predictors of mental health was likewise largely male-dominated for decades, very much shaped by stereotyped conceptions of male–female differences in personality, cognitive abilities, emotionality, and gender-appropriate behavior. Until recently, less consideration was placed on the social context that shapes gender experiences and health outcomes. Gender roles segregated women into caretaking functions in the home. Early in educational streaming, a process of occupational segregation began wherein women were guided into lower-paying but similar discipline occupations (e.g., nurses rather than doctors) or types of occupations (e.g., family vs. corporate law), and were discouraged or excluded from leadership roles (i.e., they reached a 'glass ceiling') or were selected for leadership positions in contexts that were already doomed to failure and an expendable leader was needed ('glass cliff') (Ryan & Haslam, 2005). Women are more likely than men to be single parents and live in poverty, with all of the incumbent stressors and coping strategies associated with being in this position. Women are more likely to experience traumatic stressors, such as sexual assault, domestic violence, and discrimination. Indeed, a report from the United Nations indicated that globally about 30% of women had an experience of physical and/or sexual intimate partner violence, non-partner sexual violence, or both within their life (UN Women, 2022).

Over and above limited social power and resources, gender roles differentially shape coping behaviors of women and men. Whereas men have been encouraged to keep emotions in, women are expected to express their emotions, with the exception of anger and outrage as these latter emotions suggest an externalization of blame for women's situation and the possibility of inciting confrontational actions. Taken together it should not be surprising that women are more likely to be diagnosed with depression and anxiety disorders, PTSD, along with a host of other illnesses associated with trauma and efforts to assert personal control over their lives, such as eating disorders (Hodes & Epperson, 2019).

Largely absent from this conversation is consideration of those individuals who do not identify with the gender assigned to them at birth, including those who are gender-fluid, two-spirit, non-binary or transgender. Yet for many, gender identity in itself becomes a source of stress associated with stigma in a highly gendered world, and is often perceived to be confounded with sexual orientation. It has only been in recent years that the narrative regarding gender identity has moved to one involving a continuum rather than a binary categorization. This said, the dominant culture in most societies continues to adhere to a binary construction of male and female roles and definitions, and while there is a growing research body to understand the effects of stigma and marginalization of those who defy such identities, the normative consideration of gender as a continuum has yet to be incorporated in scientific research.

Ethnoracial identity

While we might be tempted to consider demographic features such as gender as cross-cutting differences, these identities 'intersect' with other characteristics that further shape them. In particular, the experiences of women (or men) who identify with different ethnoracial groups will further vary, as do underlying biological and social processes that link stressor experiences to health outcomes.

WHAT IS RACE?

Though largely viewed as important, consideration of race, ethnicity, or culture in health research is fraught with measurement issues. For example, race is typically interpreted as a biological construct reflecting clear genotypic and phenotypic delineations. And while there may be genetic variation, these are often tied to geographic migratory roots and adaptations over many generations. In addition, particularly in recent decades the notion of any individual being 'purely' of one race or another is highly unlikely, and often identifying racial backgrounds through ancestral tracking is suspect. Indeed, children born to parents allegedly of the same racial background might vary substantially in terms of defining phenotypic characteristics, such as skin color.

As a result, researchers may turn to ethnicity rather than racial categories. Ethnic groups are based on common cultural characteristics rather than physical features. For example, in the US, Hispanic identities are based on identification with Spanish-speaking cultural backgrounds. Thus, two people might identify as white, but be of different 'ethnic' backgrounds; similarly, two people might identify as Black but their ethnic roots might be African American or West Indian. Thus, ethnicity may shape variations of experience, environmental exposures, social processes, health behaviors, and so on, but members of an ethnic group will likely vary considerably in terms of genetic make-up.

Does all this mean that research should ignore ethnoracial identities? Unfortunately, what this typically means is that samples that are homogeneous in terms of ethnoracial status (i.e., white European) become the norm, and important variations that occur in association with ethnoracial status are rendered invisible. Key to good research is thoughtfully considering the variations that exist among a broad range of people from different ethnic groups originating from many geographic regions.

Pronounced ethnic differences exist in relation to a wide variety of illnesses. In part, these may stem from variations of lifestyles, such as diet and physical activity, and may be related to genetic factors. Ethnoracial differences have been observed in type 2 diabetes, hypertension, and many forms of cancer. For instance, the BRCA1 and BRCA2 genes produce proteins that repair DNA damage, but when specific mutations of these inherited genes are present, the accumulation of progressively more DNA damage results in elevated risk of breast and ovarian cancer, and more recently has been tied to pancreatic and prostate cancer. The presence of these mutations does not guarantee that cancer will occur, but the threat of breast cancer (60% in BRCA1 carriers and somewhat lower in those with

BRCA2 mutations) is sufficiently great to prompt some women to undergo double mastectomy (and removal of ovaries) to prevent cancer occurrence. The prevalence of these mutations in the general population is about 0.2–0.3% but is much more frequent (~8%) among Ashkenazi Jews (i.e., primarily those of European descent). It is common among Hispanic American women (3.5%) and is moderately elevated among African American women (1.3%). Other forms of cancer (cervical, colorectal, gastric, lung, and thyroid) also vary with ethnicity and geographical location, which has implications for cancer detection and therapeutic strategies (Bachtiar et al., 2019).

Screening for diseases, such as breast cancer, is linked to socioeconomic status, which might be tied to ethnoracial factors. In this regard, the diagnoses of breast cancer occurred later among Black and South Asian women in the US than among white people of European descent. Similarly, in the case of illnesses, such as systemic lupus erythematosus, the general profiles, severity, and the course of the disease were related to ethnicity, as well as to socioeconomic status, education, environmental and occupational factors, social support resources, and the availability of health insurance (Carter et al., 2016).

Chronic pain is a powerful stressor that can have profound psychological consequences and may influence the emergence of physical diseases. In addition to the link between ethnoracial status and pain perception, in recent years there has been increasing attention devoted to the role of gender (Mogil, 2020). In most Western countries the prevalence of chronic pain is typically 17–20%, being somewhat higher in women than in men, and occurring in almost one of three individuals 65 or older. Similar prevalence rates have been reported in countries within Africa and the Middle East. Be this as it may, sensitivity to, and perception of pain varied with ethnoracial status, as did pain associated with illness conditions. For instance, African American and Hispanic patients reported greater postoperative pain than did white patients (Perry et al., 2019). Disparities likewise exist in the treatment of chronic pain patients with Black and Hispanic patients being less likely to receive opioid medications than were white patients (Morales & Yong, 2021). The disparities that exist concerning access to pain medications is pronounced when examined across countries, despite the modest cost of some of these treatments. To some extent, this is due to the over-regulation of opioid-acting agents but given the need for these treatments to manage the pain associated with some disorders, such as cancer, policy changes ought to be enacted to be more equitable.

Race has frequently been included in algorithms to determine best treatment strategies, often working on the assumption that genetic differences associated with race are critical to diagnosis and therapies. There has, however, been debate as to whether race should be considered in the diagnoses and treatments of illness. Consideration of race has been useful in some instances (e.g., in the case of some treatments of cardiovascular disease) but could be misleading as was reported in diagnosing and treating kidney disease among Black males. The simple fact is that skin color is not a good proxy for underlying genetic factors that may be related to diseases and their treatment, and relying on such a characteristic as a biological marker could have fairly serious negative repercussions (Vyas et al., 2020).

In light of genetic factors potentially being linked to various diseases, whole genome analyses have been conducted to evaluate the associations between multiple genes and disease occurrence. As many diseases are determined by multiple genes (polygenicity), gene signatures for them have been sought. These studies necessarily require analyses of many people across diverse groups. While some studies included individuals of different ethnoracial status, their representation has been infrequent and restricted to limited geographical locations (Uffelmann et al., 2021). For instance, studies conducted within China largely comprised individuals from that region, while most studies conducted in Western countries largely assessed individuals of white European descent (Gurdasani et al., 2019). Such analyses have been uncommon across Africa even though many genes and gene polymorphisms may have had their origins across the continent several hundred thousand years ago. Indeed, analyses that have been conducted in regions of Africa showed an enormous number of previously unreported gene variants related to viral immunity, DNA repair, and metabolic processes (Choudhury et al., 2020). Analyses conducted with participants from disparate regions around the world might permit the identification of genetic factors that contribute to varied specific illnesses and in doing so could potentially facilitate equitable health care across diverse populations. Moreover, variations might be linked to differences in lifestyles, nutrition, health access, stressor exposures, and other psychosocial and environmental determinants of health. Once more, one can't but wonder about the information that has not been gleaned by restricting demographic diversity in so many studies.

AGEISM AS A GLOBAL PLAGUE

There are several versions of the statement 'the true measure of any society can be found in how it treats its most vulnerable members'. In some societies, elders are relied upon for their wisdom, and they are treated with great respect. However, it is shocking that the treatment of older people is so often as poor as it is, particularly given that, with a little luck, we will all join the ranks of the aged. Coping methods of older individuals, particularly social support from spouses or peers who may have died, may be diminished, and as a result already elevated health risks may be exacerbated. And when they have lost their capacity to fend for themselves, older individuals are frequently shuffled off to old people's homes that may not be properly staffed, organized, or regulated. While the challenges of ageism have long been recognized, this became particularly notable during the COVID-19 pandemic.

The poor treatment received by older people is not limited to residential homes, and ageism reflected in stereotypes and discrimination has been identified in numerous other situations. Many reports have pointed to elderly adults being subjected to abuse because of frustrations experienced by caregivers, especially among older people with

(Continued)

severe neurological problems, such as Alzheimer's disease or Parkinson's disease, and those who had experienced a stroke. A position statement by the American Academy of Neurology had called on clinical neurologists to screen elder patients for signs of abusive experiences.

Predictably, stigma directed at older individuals may impair their health, hinder recovery from illnesses, promote loneliness, depression, and cognitive decline, as well as reducing life span. The World Health Organization (WHO) and other organizations have repeatedly indicated that ageism seeps into diverse aspects of institutions, including those that are supposed to ensure the health of all members of society. The time has certainly come for issues related to ageism not just to be talked about but to be acted upon (Mikton et al., 2021).

Social homeostasis and social identity

Demographic characteristics are not simply organizing constructs, as they form the basis of the creation of social groups. We have considered how such groups are often characterized by variations in social, political, and economic power, and as a result members of disadvantaged groups may come together to form an identity that enables them to find meaning and affirmation in shared experiences, and to establish solidarity to bring about change. Likewise, advantaged group members may use their collective power to diminish threats to their tangible and self-defined moral superiority. The notion of 'social homeostasis' conveys how participating in social collectives comprises an adaptive response that may have evolved because of the survival advantages obtained through groups (Tomova et al., 2021). In contrast, social isolation or loneliness instigates multiple biological changes that result in the development of numerous illnesses. Loneliness may act as a signal, just as hunger and thirst signal the need for food and water. In essence, feelings of loneliness may inform individuals that they are lacking a fundamental survival resource, and they need to take steps to address social deprivation (Cacioppo et al., 2014).

Integrated approaches that include both psychosocial and pharmacological interventions have been developed that could diminish feelings of loneliness and hence could have wide-ranging health benefits (Cacioppo et al., 2015). However, these do not address the fundamental need to belong. Alleviating loneliness is not simply a matter of immersing oneself in a social environment. One can 'feel lonely in a crowd'. The social contexts that individuals identify with and hence benefit from may depend on their prior social interactions (e.g., encounters of betrayal may diminish social trust), their personal characteristics (e.g., introverts vs. extraverts), and their feelings of connection to others.

In the absence of being able to connect with members of meaningful groups, social adversity and rejection have been linked to disadvantages (e.g., lower economic levels, access to healthy foods, limited access to preventive health care) that can favor the occurrence of both communicable and non-communicable diseases.

Studies across species, including humans, have indicated that inequities related to holding low social rank, as well as other social adversities, instigated broad biological alterations that negatively impacted health and interfered with recovery from illness. Among many other actions, these experiences were accompanied by faster biological aging reflected by cellular senescence (i.e., new cells are not being produced), excessive activation of stress-related hormonal processes, disturbed immune functioning, and the increased presence of inflammatory factors that can directly affect various diseases.

Consistent with the notion of social homeostasis, belonging to groups with whom individuals share meaningful identities (i.e., they see themselves as being part of a collective, ranging from families to nations), even those that are socially disadvantaged, has been associated with reduced disease occurrence (Berkman et al., 2000). In the face of stressors, benefits might be derived from social support from ingroup members who share relevant experiences. These benefits are apparent in diverse situations but are particularly profound in mutual support groups, such as among parents of children with cancer or family members of those who died by suicide. In these circumstances, individuals share an identity that might permit meaningful support that is not readily obtained from others ('they share their pain').

It has been maintained that shared social identities can be sufficiently powerful to provide a 'social cure' in illness prevention and treatments (Haslam et al., 2018). Even simple social group supports (e.g., engaging in arts-based groups, exercise groups) can diminish levels of depression and recurrence of illness over and above the activity itself (Dingle et al., 2020). The subjective psychological bonds that people feel toward one another and to social groups, which defines social connectedness, results in a sense of belonging and enhanced well-being. Predictably, social connectedness can be instrumental in diminishing distress, thereby limiting depressive episodes and enhancing well-being (Haslam et al., 2016). Having even a single close connection was accompanied by illness resilience and multiple group memberships had still more potent effects in this regard (Cruwys et al., 2014).

Obtaining support and elevated social connectedness may be accompanied by increased neuronal activity in brain regions that have been linked to reward processes, and can diminish biological changes, such as immune and inflammatory alterations that are otherwise provoked by social stressors (Leschak & Eisenberger, 2019). Paralleling these findings, participation in community activities, attending religious services, and greater frequency of contacts with family and friends were accompanied by an appreciable decline of early all-cause mortality among breast cancer survivors. Similarly, among women who had been diagnosed with stage I/II breast cancer, their prognosis was better if they had a relatively large social network, which varied further based on the quality of these relationships (Kroenke et al., 2017).

Aside from affecting the course of diseases, identifying with social groups may be instrumental in having people engage in beneficial health behaviors, such as reduced smoking and regular screening for diseases that allow for early disease detection, as such groups may establish behavioral norms that promote wellness. Further to this, following cancer therapy, social support and connectedness may encourage the adoption of positive health behaviors and could be instrumental in the promotion of psychological growth through shared meaning-making (Thong et al., 2018).

These are only a few of the many benefits of identifying with social groups, and it was maintained that the value of social connection may be so broad and pronounced it ought to be a public health priority (Holt-Lunstad et al., 2017). Thus, it is significant that programs have been developed to foster meaningful social connectedness (e.g., Groups 4 Health), which could diminish health-related disturbances (C. Haslam et al., 2016).

BENEFITS OF ALTRUISM

Typically, when the influence of social support is considered, the focus is on the benefits obtained by the support recipient, rather than the benefits to the support provider. For some individuals, acting as a support provider (e.g., a caregiver) can be meaningful and rewarding, and it seems that charitable giving and volunteer work can have a similar impact. Day-to-day enactments of prosocial behaviors can influence coping processes and diminish the effects of stressors on emotional well-being (Raposa et al., 2016). Evidently, giving support elicits positive outcomes in the support giver, and in some instances diminishes their distress (Aknin et al., 2011).

Prosocial behaviors, such as charitable giving, have been associated with specific brain activity changes, including increased neuronal activity in the ventral striatum and nucleus accumbens, brain regions involved in reward processes, as well as activation of prefrontal cortical regions associated with executive functioning (Fede et al., 2021). Even making a commitment to charitable giving over the ensuing month was associated with elevated happiness and changes of brain connectivity related to reward networks that pointed to top-down control of reward functioning. The brain regions activated in these studies mapped on to those that are associated with cravings for food and sex, as well as those that accompany substance use disorders, indicating the fundamental nature of altruistic behaviors – whether it's to gain social approval or because they're intrinsically driven, they make us feel good.

It has been said that altruism is a hard-wired feature of humans that may have evolved through natural selection since group cooperation provided survival advantages. Various social processes (e.g., loyalty, reciprocity, love, heroism, deference to superiors or elders, fairness, property rights) can combine in multiple ways to determine moral behaviors and those that are socially acceptable and those that are not. In the end, these all boil down to respecting others and facilitating the well-being of one's group as well as that of others (Curry et al., 2021). This, of course, raises the obvious question as to the factors that overwhelm these 'instinctive behaviors' so that individuals and groups engage in selfish behaviors or even behave with malice. Perhaps, evolution didn't simply favor the development of altruism but promoted parochial altruism in which members favor their group with whom they share ethnic, cultural, or religious identities, and in doing so defend against outgroup members.

Forgiveness and trust

Among the most common stressors experienced are those that entail conflicts in interpersonal relationships. These can take the form of betrayals, let-downs, disputes between family members, close friends, and authority figures, bullying, as well as conflicts between social groups. There are many instances in which a victimized individual or group is asked to forgive (or might choose to forgive) the behaviors of the transgressor. Apologies can be offered by one party in the hope that forgiveness can be obtained from the other. In a best-case scenario, one individual sees that they behaved poorly and values the relationship, and hence apologizes. If the recipient of the apology views this as sincere then they may forgive the other party. However, it is not uncommon for transgressions within intimate relationships to be the hardest to forgive. Depending on the severity and chronicity of the offenses (e.g., abuse or partner dissolution or betrayal), the consequences may comprise shame, anger, anxiety, depression, and considerable rumination that can be exceedingly damaging, making it hard to forgive (Ysseldyk et al., 2019). Of course, numerous other factors might come into play that could undermine reconciliation (e.g., ego, trust, self-righteousness, financial concerns).

So who benefits from forgiveness? Both parties may gain but it may be particularly beneficial for the forgiver. Forgiveness of interpersonal transgressions might limit the adverse impact of these events on well-being, primarily by limiting the ruminations that go with them (e.g., McCullough, 2000). Forgiving the transgressor allows the victim freedom to move on. As a result, forgiving someone for their behaviors might be, as is often said, 'a gift to the forgiver' (Brown & Phillips, 2005).[1]

As difficult as apologies and forgiveness might be to achieve between two individuals, intergroup transgressions can often be so pervasive and damaging, emanating from one group's perceived superiority and feelings of threat, that the consequences may be just too great and the hurt too strong for forgiveness to be possible. However, there are notable cases in which apologies have been offered with the expectation of forgiveness. For example, the Australian government, and later the Canadian government, via their respective prime ministers, apologized to Indigenous Peoples for wrongdoings related to the treatment of children who had been forcibly removed from their homes and sent to 'residential schools' where they were subjected to many forms of abuse and the eradication of their culture and family bonds. The apology was intended to ask Indigenous people to forgive the respective national governments (and by extension their citizens) for past wrongs. It seems as if this should have been an easy thing to do, but it took years for such

---

[1]As many transgressions cannot be fully forgiven, and may never actually be forgotten, it might be more appropriate in many situations to regard forgiving behaviors as 'forbearance'. This implies, 'I'll let it go for the moment, but you're not off the hook'. The forbearer might be cautious waiting for a recurrence of the transgression, which could end the relationship forever.

apologies to be enacted (see Chapter 12 for a discussion regarding intergenerational trauma effects).

One might wonder what sort of effect this apology could have as it didn't come from those who committed the atrocities, and sometimes the apology came with considerable reluctance given the implications for reparations for wrongdoing. If nothing else, however, it's a message that says, 'We don't condone the past egregious behaviors, and we would like better relations with you'. Often, the response from groups that receive an apology is a positive one, but with caveats attached: 'Your apology will be meaningful *if it comes with actions that achieve justice and improve quality of life for our group.*' In effect, the apology serves as vindication for the oppressed group's experiences, and a first step toward reconciliation. Thus, an apology, whether at the level of the individual or group, is not an end in itself; but it might influence cognitive, behavioral, and affective responses of the parties involved. There is a downside to this, of course, as equity for the aggrieved group may not occur (indeed, it frequently hasn't). Thus, the apology becomes yet another betrayal especially if members of the perpetrator group convey the attitude of, 'We gave them an apology, now what do they want?'

Although forgiveness is typically associated with positive psychological outcomes, in certain situations a forgiving response can have the opposite effect. In the case of an abusive relationship, forgiveness might serve to perpetuate the victim's illusion of long-term safety and well-being, and thus reinforce remaining in an unhealthy relationship. Forgiveness of a currently abusive partner might act to diminish the perceived severity of the transgression (e.g., 'Oh, maybe I'm being a bit too sensitive'), which might undermine an individual's well-being in the long run (e.g., through self-blame, avoidance and social isolation, and continued experiences of abuse). As a result, rather than serving as a buffer against distress, in some situations forgiveness may alter appraisals and coping efforts, culminating in a greater probability of stress-related outcomes evolving.

This brings us to another component of the apology–forgiveness relationship. For genuine forgiveness to occur it is essential that the behavior of the perpetrator be trustworthy. Trust is essential in conflict resolution as forgiveness requires trust that the other person or group will not subsequently repeat their offense. 'Trustworthiness' is frequently taken to reflect the benevolence, integrity, and ability of a trustee (person or organization or group), and 'trust' as comprising an intention or willingness to accept (or allow oneself) to become vulnerable with the faith that the trustee will behave appropriately. When we trust another person, we are essentially leaving ourselves uncloaked and unprotected, believing that no harm will come to us.

While trust makes for good relationships, a breach of trust may create exceptionally distressing and damaging effects. This is frequently evident in the dissolution of a relationship (separation/divorce) in which an individual may feel that 'I trusted you, and you have betrayed my trust in the worst possible way'. Often, this type of situation is accompanied by rumination, bitterness, and thoughts of retribution. Rumination can have positive attributes when it's used in combination with problem solving or cognitive restructuring. Negative rumination, in contrast, is unhealthy and may be linked to future depression. Ultimately, when trust has been violated, individuals may ruminate more and enact counterproductive coping behaviors. It may not be immediately satisfying, but sometimes walking away is the only way to achieve peace of mind.

Trust comes into our lives in various ways. Trust in the workplace (in this case, trust in the organization and trusting other employees) influences our well-being and our job satisfaction. Helliwell et al. (2009) indicated that one unit of trust (on a 10-point scale) was associated with improved well-being that is comparable to a 30% salary increase. In effect, offering people the equivalent of an extra 20% of their salary (i.e., some amount less than 30%) or the opportunity to work in a trusting environment, they would likely pick the latter.

The violation of trust may be at the root of intractable group conflicts, which are conflicts that elude resolution not only because the stakes are high and complex (and often intangible, such as core values and moral beliefs), but there is a lack of trust in the motives of the parties involved. After all, are those living in poverty going to trust the motives of the rich to achieve equity – just look at the battles over the right to a living wage. When history provides much evidence of repeated conflict, no matter if an apology (or simple solution) has been offered, numerous psychosocial processes make it difficult to achieve trust. Whether it entails close interpersonal relationships, workplace situations, or intergroup conflicts, an essential factor concerns the view that talk is cheap: trust will be dependent not on what is said, but on what is done.

Trust is also foundational when we look to others for information about our health and wellness, irrespective of whether it comes from scientific research, health professionals, or media coverage of health issues. Vaccine hesitancy has been around as long as vaccines have existed. It had been apparent in response to smallpox, polio, the 2009 H1N1 pandemic, along with the COVID-19 pandemic. As in previous public health interventions, anti-vaccination attitudes in the face of COVID-19 stemmed from multiple factors. For example, among disadvantaged ethnoracial groups distrust of health systems generally, and vaccinations more specifically, may have come about based on the belief that their well-being was not considered equally to that of white people of European descent. In some instances, this distrust has been linked to historical instances of such groups (African Americans, Indigenous Peoples) being used for medical experiments.

Political influences, feelings that individual rights were being abridged, and safety concerns were among the most prominent factors associated with vaccine hesitancy. At their core, a lack of trust may prevail, including in pharmaceutical firms that manufacture vaccines, scientists involved in the creation and testing of vaccines, as well as governments and media organizations that had been encouraging vaccination. Mistrust was abetted by the perverse false information spread through the media by political figures who had their own malign agenda. Some anti-vaxxer groups expressed great criticism of COVID-19 vaccinations (e.g., on Facebook) even before vaccines had been developed (Kalichman et al., 2022). Some individuals, particularly those with pre-existing depressive moods were especially susceptible to accepting misinformation (Perlis et al., 2022), which raises the question of whether people who generally see the world negatively are more ready to accept false information. Indeed, embittered individuals were more likely to hold COVID-19 conspiracy beliefs and were especially likely to be vaccine-hesitant (Koroma et al., 2022).

We had indicated years ago that lack of trust in the media, pharmaceuticals, and public health was an essential component that fostered vaccine hesitancy (Taha et al., 2013). But we hadn't imagined the potential tsunami created by the anti-vaxxer movement, nor did we predict that this movement would have so many zealots who not only chose not to be vaccinated but took active steps to prevent others from exercising their rights to be vaccinated. In contrast, within countries in which there was a consensus concerning the trustworthiness of science, vaccine confidence and vaccination rates were elevated (Sturgis et al., 2021). It seems that for trust to evolve, it is necessary to promote greater community engagement to build vaccine acceptability and confidence in their safety, and to eliminate barriers related to cultural, socioeconomic, and political influences (Burgess et al., 2021).

THE ULTIMATE VIOLATION OF TRUST

For some people, religious affiliation and beliefs represent a powerful coping resource. After the September 11 attack on the World Trade Center in the United States, 90% of Americans allegedly turned to religion to cope (Schuster et al., 2001). Religion enables followers to find meaning in their experience, and to believe that what happened was destined by a higher order, thereby providing a sense that everything 'is under control'. Spiritual and religious worldviews can satisfy the need for belonging and offer confidence in the midst of uncertainty.

This said, severe trauma can undermine beliefs in a higher power, as victims feel that the God or spiritual entity they believe in has abandoned them. This might be especially the case when confronted with a 'morally injurious' event, which essentially involves an experience that damages a person's conscience or moral compass because of perpetrating or failing to prevent acts that transgress deeply held moral beliefs. Moral injury has been referred to as a 'deep soul wound that pierces a person's identity, sense of morality, and relationship to society' (Silver, 2011). Although primarily studied among military personnel exposed to combat, such events are also encountered by refugees, journalists, frontline personnel in a natural disaster, or even among hospital staff forced to weigh decisions about the provision of treatment (Barnes et al., 2019).

When such events happen, individuals may come to question their moral worth, goodness in the world, and spiritual faith. While moral injury might co-occur with PTSD, the latter is more likely to be fear-based (Barnes et al., 2019), and the functional brain connectivity changes associated with moral injury compared to PTSD could be distinguished (Sun et al., 2019). Moral injury is more strongly associated with post-event emotions (shame, guilt, (self-)contempt, fear of judgment), rather than the emotions experienced during the event (Barnes et al., 2019). Healing moral injury might entail re-establishing human trust through compassion and resolving spiritual struggles through forgiveness and repentance.

When social support isn't supportive

We have talked a lot about the importance of perceived social support as a buffer against the negative impacts of stressors. However, actually receiving support can, in some circumstances, be a mixed blessing. While such support is often helpful, it could undermine self-esteem if individuals feel less competent in contending with the situation without assistance. In addition, individuals might feel indebted to the support provider, which may serve as an additional stressor for an already distressed person.

Even more detrimental to well-being is when an individual approaches others, such as friends, for support with the expectation that it will be forthcoming, only to have that support fall through. Such experiences, referred to as 'unsupportive relations' or 'unsupportive interactions', can have marked negative repercussions (Ingram et al., 2001) that far exceed those of not anticipating assistance in the first place. Unsupportive responses may come in several forms, including minimizing (e.g., 'felt that I was overreacting'), blame (e.g., 'I told you so'), bumbling (e.g., 'did not seem to know what to say, or seemed afraid of saying or doing the *wrong* thing', as well as forced optimism, more recently referred to as toxic positivity), or distancing and disconnecting (e.g., 'did not seem to want to hear about it'). Think of a time when you counted on your two best friends to help you out, but both had more important commitments or said things that were just plain thoughtless ('well, you know, there are two sides to every story'), or worse still, blamed you for the situation in which you found yourself ('well, maybe you brought it on yourself'). How long was it before you were able to overcome this rebuff? Of course, when help is requested, friends may unintentionally cause harm simply because they may be uncertain about how to act and what to say due to a lack of experience. Nonetheless, their responses can feel unsupportive, effectively undermining trust that they will 'be there' when needed.

While our friends might occasionally fail to support us properly, there are times when we misinterpret what can be done or we have unreasonable expectations concerning what our friends ought to do. When a person is diagnosed with a severe chronic illness, such as cancer, friends might rally to support them. However, there may be a time limit on this behavior, as people are able or willing to provide support for only so long before they tire or need to get on with their own lives. Unfortunately, the ill person might see this withdrawal of support as a betrayal or unsupport ('you know who your friends are when the chips are down'), which can exacerbate the distress associated with illness.

Unsupportive interactions have been linked to reduced psychological well-being, over and above the perceived unavailability of social support, or the effects of the stressor experience itself (Ingram et al., 2001). These actions can be much more devastating when they occur in conjunction with stigmatization. Many of us have heard of cases where family members distance themselves from one of their own who has been diagnosed with HIV/AIDS. The stigma of this illness, which is often confounded with prejudicial attitudes toward gay men or sub-stance users, is enormous and having family members turn on a patient is obvi-ously counterproductive. Remarkably, the stigma associated with HIV/AIDS is so profound that even children who contracted the disease prenatally or through transfusions are victimized by stigma and unsupportive reactions. Specifically, the families of children with HIV/AIDS and those with cancer exhibited comparable family functioning and both groups tended to seek support from family mem-bers. However, the parents of children with HIV/AIDS were more reluctant to seek support from outside the family, reflecting their anticipation of stigmatizing social reactions.

Yet another example of how unsupport affects outcomes is based on research with young women in abusive relationships. The problems for abused women, as enormous as they are, may be compounded by unsupportive relations. When abused women disclose information regarding their situation, family and friends may initially be very supportive, offering all sorts of advice. Some might suggest that she 'work things out', whereas others may encourage her to 'get out'. If the advice isn't acted upon (e.g., leaving the relationship), supporters may become frus-trated and blame her for her predicament. Either way, these women may feel that they can no longer rely on their social network for support, and will stop confiding in them, thus further isolating themselves. With no one to turn to, their partner may become their sole source of support, despite the abuse. These women could be said to have transitioned from 'soul mate' to 'cell mate'.

In addition to direct effects on well-being, unsupportive relationships may undermine the use of effective coping methods. Perceived distancing and the dis-interested responses of others predicted greater use of disengagement and denial coping strategies, which, in turn, were associated with greater mood disturbances. The net result of unsupportive interactions is that individuals become reluctant to seek support and may limit or re-orient their help-seeking in an ineffective manner.

Sitting on the fence

There are times when oppressed groups might expect support, even if they don't explicitly seek it. When group members encounter threats of genocide, or are victims of discrimi-nation, but do not receive support from other groups in the face of such adversity, these unsupportive actions can have profound and lasting ramifications. It has been said that 'In the end we will remember not the words of our enemies, but the silence of our friends' (Martin Luther King; Nobel laureate, 1964) and 'to remain silent and indifferent is the greatest sin of all' (Elie Wiesel; Nobel laureate, 1986).

This said, there are cases when others might intervene without sufficient under-standing or knowledge, basing their behaviors on instinctive gut responses, media manipulation, well-orchestrated political campaigns, or simply by taking the side of the perceived underdog. Ideologies may become confused with realities, and without 'on the ground' context, discerning what is true and what reflects bias becomes exceedingly difficult. Such decisions likely follow the heuristics described by Kahneman and Tversky as opposed to well thought-out, reasoned decisions. And the actions that follow can serve more to perpetuate the differential status and experience of disadvantaged groups than to alleviate it. For this reason, even in their efforts to serve as allies, the unanticipated negative repercussions that emanate from the misinformed or misguided support from members of other (often more powerful) groups can contribute to the mistrust experienced.

Social rejection

A particularly potent stressor entails social rejection, as in many respects, it is the essence of betrayal and violation of trust. Social rejection can be experienced both personally and collectively, including discrimination related to physical appearance, gender, sexual orientation, ethnicity, or religion. Some adolescents will know the feeling of having their friends turn on them, leaving them out of social events and generally making them feel diminished. Such targeted rejection can be especially damaging, often promoting or exacerbating depressive feelings. No matter the age, the impact of social rejection can be intense and undermine individuals' abilities to contend with ongoing stressors, just as unsupportive relations act in this capacity. One might think that online social exclusion might not be as bad as it is when it occurs in person, but it can be equally devastating, especially when everybody can witness the social diminishment or 'defriending'.

Fear of social rejection is in itself a very powerful negative emotion that can create other social barriers and insecurities, such as social anxiety, imposter syndrome, and evaluation apprehension. It has been linked to elevations of the stress hormone cortisol, and if sufficiently pervasive and protracted, the overall biological profile observed is not unlike that characteristic of other chronic stressors and those that accompany PTSD. Essentially, fear of social rejection reflects a state that is accompanied by chronic distress, leading to an adaptation to limit the excessive physiological activation that might culminate in allostatic overload.

Given the powerful effects of social rejection on psychological well-being, several paradigms have been developed to assess it in a laboratory context. One approach involves a computer game referred to as cyberball, in which a virtual ball is tossed between three characters (Blackhart et al., 2007). One of the icons is controlled by the experimental participant who assumes that the other two players are similarly controlled by participants like themselves. But the other players' responses are predetermined by the experimenter. Initially, the ball is tossed evenly between players, but shortly afterward it is passed between the other two virtual participants and the actual participant is excluded. This has the effect of eliciting negative ruminative thoughts, altered mood, hostility, and elevated cortisol levels (McQuaid et al., 2015). In addition, social rejection in the cyberball paradigm markedly influences brain processes (notably, neuronal activity within the dorsal anterior cingulate cortex) associated with appraisals and decision-making as well as with depressed mood.

What makes these findings particularly interesting is that a very similar brain activation profile has been seen in studies assessing the effects of physical pain, leading to the suggestion that the anterior cingulate cortex is fundamental in the neural circuitry that supports both physical and social pain and may be part of a broader 'neural alarm system' (Lieberman & Eisenberger, 2015). Similar effects were observed in adolescents and were accompanied by decreased neuronal activity in the ventral striatum, supporting the position that the rewarding experience that could accompany a game with others had lost its luster. Furthermore, the way in which an adolescent's anterior cingulate cortex responded to social rejection was predictive of their risk of later depression (Masten et al., 2011). It was maintained that social rejection may give rise to negative self-referential cognitions ('people just don't like me') and emotions stemming from these beliefs, especially shame and humiliation. These emotions, in turn, activate brain regions that are involved in regulating mood and may affect certain aspects of the immune system (inducing inflammatory effects) that might further contribute to depressive-like states (Slavich et al., 2010). This said, it is of particular significance that social support during adolescence, reflected by the time spent with friends, diminished the brain changes associated with peer rejection that were subsequently evident in the ball-tossing game. This would suggest that social supports earlier in life can serve as a buffer against sensitivity to rejection encountered at a later time.

Social rejection can occur simply because an individual is singled out as different from their peers, or they may be viewed as behaving in a way that is contrary to the group's public image. Essentially, members of the ingroup don't want their group identity tarnished by a member who doesn't fit with their values, self-values, or norms. The more unified or cohesive the group is, the more likely that perceived outliers who don't fit the image will be denigrated and rejected to preserve the standing of the group as a whole (Lewis & Sherman, 2010). In fact, an unfavorable ingroup member will be diminished to a greater extent than an unsavory outgroup member. This targeted derogation may serve as a protective strategy that limits the threat of being associatively miscast ('He's not one of us, and I'm not like him at all') (Eidelman & Biernat, 2003). It further serves to maintain the solidarity among ingroup members who typically wish to remain in good standing to derive the social benefits associated with belonging to a valued group identity.

Navigating stigma and discrimination

Of the stressors we encounter, many have effects that are so strong as to scorch us permanently. Some affect us personally and some collectively, giving rise to emotions ranging from shame to outrage. Some of these stressors are so far beyond our coping abilities as to induce feelings of helplessness or hopelessness. While for some individuals, support is derived by sharing the experience with their support networks, others remain silent to suppress reminders and the emotions they elicit.

Discrimination in its many guises (ethnoracial, religious, gender, or in relation to mental illness, obesity, or physical challenges) often represents an exceptionally powerful stressor. At the least, when injustices are perceived, they affect an individual's worldview concerning fairness and meaning, and prejudices against a group can be a profound threat to self-identity. At its most severe it comes in the form of many groups experiencing persecution that has continued over generations. Underlying discriminatory actions and policies are the stigmatizing stereotypes (beliefs) and attitudes (emotional reactions) toward particular social groups. Such stigma marks individuals (or groups) so that they might be singled out, but not in any good way. They stand apart, they're different, and they're 'not one of us'.

At times discrimination is severe and unmistakable, but it may be manifested in more ambiguous ways as microaggressions that comprise seemingly innocuous remarks. In a liberal society, individuals have learned how to express their views without appearing overtly bigoted or insensitive. Unfortunately, such ambiguity makes it difficult for the target to be certain whether they are over-interpreting the meaning intended: 'Was that a racist remark? Were they joking? Was the remark aimed at me, or at my group? How do I respond? Should I challenge them at the risk of appearing aggressive, or do I "just let it go" and ruminate for days afterward (sky-high levels of stress hormones notwithstanding)?'

Some individuals may be especially likely to encounter discrimination because their membership in targeted groups is visible to others (e.g., based on skin color, language, etc.), whereas for others it can be concealed (e.g., religion, mental health issues). Relationships to the advantaged outgroup differ, for example, due to a capacity to 'pass', or because of social norms and roles that promote day-to-day integration (e.g., gendered relationships). Belonging in some groups is acquired (e.g., at birth), whereas in others it is achieved, or more accurately is perceived as reflecting the non-exertion of effort, control, or hard work (e.g., poverty, obesity). And still others represent a threat because people simply don't want to acknowledge the fact that one day they too might belong to a stigmatized group (e.g., older adults, accident victims). Many factors shape the experience of stigma and discrimination, how it is appraised by targeted individuals, how it can be coped with, and its emotional toll.

Even after adjusting for age or socioeconomic status, members of disadvantaged groups express disproportionately high levels of psychological and physiological disruptions (e.g., immune disturbances, oxidative stress in red blood cells, type 2 diabetes, cardiovascular problems, physical disabilities, infant mortality) (Paradies et al., 2015). Structural conditions can place various groups and individuals at even greater risk, and because stressors proliferate over an individual's life and across generations, health gaps between the advantaged and disadvantaged groups might widen. The American Heart Association acknowledged that the occurrence of cardiovascular illnesses not only stems from individual experiences of racism but reflects a wider problem that is associated with structural racism (Churchwell et al., 2020). Ultimately, greater attention needs to be placed on programs and policies to diminish psychosocial and economic stressors, and programs ought to target children who, because of poverty and other factors that promote stressful family occurrences, may be at particular risk of poor well-being (Thoits, 2010).

Despite the considerable negative effects of discrimination, not all groups who are targeted show the same profile of poorer outcomes and, under some conditions, enhanced well-being may be evident. Likewise, not all members of stigmatized groups are equally vulnerable or affected by the negative social attitudes and discrimination they encounter. But no matter what the basis, stigma and discrimination can have powerful effects, and when these occur on a pervasive and systematic basis, they represent a strong precipitating factor for the development of anxiety, depression, PTSD, substance use disorders, and a constellation of physical illnesses.

SHAME AND ANGER

One of the most cogent and destructive outcomes of stigma is the negative emotional experience, such as shame, among those who are targeted (Rüsch et al., 2009). Shame is a particularly powerful emotion that makes people shrink into themselves and feel diminished and worthless in the eyes of others and even in their own eyes. Given the profound brain neurochemical effects induced, the shame associated with stigma might promote illness and limit recovery, as well as increase vulnerability to the impact of further stressor encounters (Matheson & Anisman, 2012). Added to this, the pervasive stigma and constant efforts to remain invisible might be traumatizing and hence serve to exacerbate mental health conditions. The Czech novelist, playwright, and poet Milan Kundera indicated that, 'The basis of shame is not some personal mistake of ours, but the ignominy, the humiliation we feel that we must be what we are without any choice in the matter, and that this humiliation is seen by everyone'.

In contrast, when group members perceive that an injustice has been committed against them, they may feel a sense of anger and outrage. Anger, which is the predominant emotion when discrimination has been experienced, can catalyze action, particularly when group members interpret the situation as one that they have the collective strength to control and resolve and work collectively to do so. However, anger and especially feelings of hostility have a downside, particularly in relation to an increased risk of coronary heart disease.

Social identity as a stress buffer

Stigma can come in several forms; it can be expressed by other people (public stigma), can be internalized by the individual (self-stigma), and may be reflected as inequities that occur through procedures and policies adopted by organizations and societies (structural stigma). At the same time, identifying with a group can buffer against the negative effects of stigma and discrimination. Individuals who highly identified with a stigmatized group were least likely to experience a loss of esteem or fall into depression when their identity was threatened. Essentially, group identification may provide a cognitive framework that diminishes appraisals of threat and facilitates effective coping. Individuals who identify strongly with their group are more likely to acknowledge discrimination when it occurs, yet they may be the most likely to perceive that they have appreciable coping resources in the form of ingroup support. Such support might act as a buffer so that individuals will not perceive themselves as the distinct target of stigmatizing stereotypes, and hence prevent feelings of internalization and personal rejection. With the support of other group members, discrimination may enhance features of identity, including self-concept (centrality), ingroup affect or pride, and a sense of belonging or attachment with other group members (ingroup ties). In effect, adversity from the outside might promote greater ingroup cohesion, give individuals purpose, enhance social support, and engender collective action that encourages systemic change and resilience to the insidious effects of discrimination.

The Last of the Just

As bad as severe discrimination and bullying are in adults, it can have more profound effects on children who don't yet have the resources or coping skills to deal with these insults, and who day after day face their oppressor's malicious behaviors. Among children and youth, bullying and cyberbullying have been associated with self-harm, suicidal ideation, and death by suicide (John et al., 2018). These occurrences vary with factors such as previous depressive illness, earlier trauma experiences, family dynamics, and other psychosocial factors. Not surprisingly, being targeted because of a stigmatized identity, such as being of a gender or ethnoracial minority group was accompanied by elevated suicide risk (Poštuvan et al., 2019; Rudes & Fantuzzi, 2021).

A quote in *The Last of the Just* (Schwarz-Bart, 1959) speaks loudly, even if such comments are now more often spoken in whispers. His comment refers to events in Germany in 1934, which was soon after the campaign against the Jews began, and was prevalent in schools, but preceded the mass killings that occurred subsequently. He stated:

> Statistics show that the percentage of suicides among the German Jews was practically nil during the years before the end. So it was in the prisons, in the ghettos, in all the caves of darkness where the beast's muzzle sniffed up from the abyss, and even at the entrance of the crematoriums - 'anus of the world' in the words of a learned Nazi eyewitness. But back in 1934, hundreds and hundreds of little German-Jewish schoolboys came up for their examinations in suicide, and hundreds of them passed. (p. 255)

Of course, the situation today, at least in the West, is unlike the situation in 1934, but the distress and the most severe consequences of bullying have persisted worldwide.

(Continued)

Suicide in youth is the second most common cause of death (accidents are the greatest cause of death) (Orri et al., 2020), and the incidence of suicide is particularly high among Indigenous youth. This has not been averted by common methods to prevent suicide, but may be diminished by cultural revitalization, essentially pointing to 'culture as treatment' (Barker et al., 2017).

Coping with discrimination

The coping styles of women, as well as several ethnoracial minority group members who experienced discrimination but reported not feeling distressed, often maintained effective cognitive restructuring combined with emotional expression ('This was upsetting, but I'll know better next time') (Matheson & Anisman, 2012). In contrast, among those who acknowledged discrimination and were distressed by it, cognitive restructuring was highly related to self-blame. These group members were construing the experience as one that they should have been able to control but had failed to do so ('If only I had taken precautions, this might not have happened'). It was similarly observed that when women were angered by a discriminatory situation, the inclination to use problem-focused coping was associated with a greater propensity to want to confront the perpetrator. Both problem-focused and avoidant coping styles were associated with lower feelings of shame and diminished cortisol reactions following discrimination. Thus, although anger is usually frowned upon as being 'inappropriate', and is often unfairly frowned upon for women or members of socially marginalized groups, it may be associated with (or perhaps promote) a greater range of coping methods and diminished internalization, which might foster action-oriented methods for dealing with the situation.

It is not only the support from ingroup members that is crucial for coping, but outgroup support may be particularly effective when social groups are highly integrated (as in the case of gender or age). For example, males and females often work together and may be in intimate relationships. Thus, male support may be forthcoming, but when women are the victims of gender discrimination (by men) the implications of such support may be altered. Of course, outgroup support in socially and politically sensitive situations might be appreciated, and in fact support from a powerful outgroup sometimes has more credibility and impact than support from ingroup members as it reinforces the idea that 'my cause is just and is widely recognized' (witness the role of allies of the Black Lives Matter movement). This said, as disadvantaged groups establish their agency and self-determination for change, there is an expectation that outgroup members follow, 'don't act for us without us', and use their positions of power to change oppressive attitudes, policies, and systems.

The coping strategies used concerning discrimination have implications for biological responses to stressors that, as noted earlier, may render individuals more vulnerable to health problems. For example, sexism in a laboratory context where an equally qualified woman was rejected for a position by a man in preference for another man elicited elevated cortisol levels. However, those participants with a propensity to problem solve reported greater appraisals of control, a more optimistic mood, and limited cortisol reactivity following the discrimination challenge. In contrast, individuals who distanced themselves from their group identity following discrimination showed increased cortisol reactivity. It might be that in the latter instance, individuals found the situation especially aversive, and thus engaged in distancing to alleviate such feelings.

How does racism occur?

Reflections on history make us wonder how large groups of people might come to feel hatred of others, and then behave in unspeakable ways toward them. Why, for instance, were so many people (not all, but certainly very many) seduced by the attitudes of the Nazi regime? And why were specific groups such as the Jewish and Roma communities and other marginalized groups so negatively targeted? Times were tough and a scapegoat might have been needed so that individuals would coalesce around a common cause. However, the people of Germany and Austria were intelligent, civilized, and understanding; so, one wonders, what were the catalysts that allowed national racism to flourish? Perhaps it's a matter of individuals being highly identified with their group so that they are more vulnerable to propaganda that suggests that a particular line of thought and action is better for the homeland (i.e., for the group itself). In defending the actions against gay people, Himmler, a leading member of the Nazi Party, commented that the actions were for the common good.

It had been known for decades that in a laboratory situation many people will engage in deplorable acts when asked to do so by an authority figure with whom they identified (Milgram, 1963). Thus, the abhorrent behavior seen in numerous contexts is not simply a matter of 'following orders' but reflected 'the endeavor of a committed subject' (Haslam & Reicher, 2012). If participants behave this way in a contrived context, then how much more powerful will the influence be on an individual when a whole society appears to be marching in the same footfalls? When everyone else in a group displays racist behaviors, individuals may feel emboldened to openly express despicable, repugnant, and immoral attitudes that would otherwise have remained covert. In this context, Primo Levi, a Holocaust survivor, chemist, and remarkable writer, stated: 'Monsters exist, but they are too few in number to be truly dangerous. More dangerous are the common men, the functionaries ready to believe and to act without asking questions.'

Stigma related to mental illness

In the case of ethnoracial, religious, and gender identities, individuals can often turn to other ingroup members in the face of stigma and discrimination. However, if the ingroup comprises features that are socially stigmatized, these stigmatizing beliefs may become internalized. In some instances a support network within the group might offset the impact of stigma, but this is less likely to occur with certain mental health conditions (e.g., schizophrenia, bipolar disorder). To be sure, there are many patient-advocate groups focused on mental health, and there has been increasing societal recognition of the importance of dealing respectfully and sup- portively with people who have these conditions. Nevertheless, the stigma associ- ated with mental health conditions continues to be enormous, and the buffers that protect individuals from other forms of discrimination aren't there.

Just as many other group identities can affect anyone (and indeed, age-based identities affect us all), mental health conditions aren't confined to particular sec- tors within society. They appear in all genders across cultures, in rich and poor, in movie stars, sports figures, children, adolescents, and in older people – and some forms of mental illness are exceptionally common in university-aged individuals. The prevalence of depression and anxiety in university students was estimated to be about 33–44% and many students display subclinical symptoms that could be of concern, especially as these symptoms can be a forerunner of a major depressive disorder. Too often, however, those with clinically relevant symptomatology failed to receive professional attention for their depression and/or anxiety. One hears from these students 'I don't need help (denial)', 'I don't believe in seeing psychia- trists', or 'I don't want foreign substances in my body'. Left untreated these symp- toms may flourish, culminating in more severe illness.

So why don't people with mental health conditions seek help? Some individuals might not recognize or appraise their distress appropriately, thinking that their mood was simply a transient 'down' that everybody goes through. Alternatively, they may recognize their situation for what it is, but are unable to mobilize personal coping or social support resources to seek help, or they might fear that if they do so, then this would be a sign of weakness and they will be diminished in the eyes of others (public stigma). Stigma has been recognized as *the* fundamental barrier to mental health. Stigma not only impacts those with mental health issues, but it can also mark fami- lies across generations. There is little question that the stigma of mental illness, and the potential lifetime labeling, may have much to do with the reluctance to acknowl- edge mental health difficulties and seek help. There is a critical need to bring those living with mental illnesses 'out of the shadows', create a positive social environment for affected individuals, enhance trust in our medical and social systems, and provide the resources necessary to facilitate help-seeking (Kirby, 2006).

Barriers to help-seeking due to stigma

Part of the stigma associated with mental health disorders is that those experienc- ing them may be perceived to be at fault for their illness, as if they could change if they chose to ('Come on, just snap out of it'). For the individual who has inter- nalized stigmatizing beliefs, including feelings of shame associated with the notion that they must be 'weak, lacking self-control, malingering, or irresponsible', having to 'out themselves' to seek help may simply be too difficult. Even when help was sought, self-stigma was reported to erode morale and undermine the commitment to treatment. Predictably, under these conditions, individuals might prematurely discontinue the treatment that they might be receiving and turn to inappropriate help sources (e.g., internet chat rooms) where they may perhaps receive inadequate or counterproductive advice. The stigma of obtaining mental health treatment among children and youth may have negative ramifications that can even manifest in adulthood (Kaushik et al., 2016). This is particularly relevant given that mental health issues frequently begin to appear during adolescence.

The stigma associated with mental health issues may be so powerful as to cause families to conspire to 'protect' their loved ones by not acknowledging the problem, both out of a sincere concern for the individual, and to avoid the stigma and blame that may generalize from the individual to the family (Larson & Corrigan, 2008). Perceived parental disapproval of seeking help from professional services, at least in some families or cultures, further promotes young people's perceptions of stigma associated with emotional problems and the reluctance to seek help. In large measure, these familial responses unintentionally serve as a potent form of unsupport that may be damaging to the interests of the young person experiencing distress.

Changing attitudes within the general population, either through education or increased contact with individuals with mental health issues, should be enacted to diminish stigma-related health disturbances. It has been surmised that if people understood that mental illness had a biological basis, like heart disease or cancer, then they might not engage in stigmatizing behaviors. However, educating people about the biological basis for these disorders did not reduce avoidant behaviors, even among health professionals. Although short-term benefits were apparent with increased social contact, the lasting effects of this approach are uncertain (Thornicroft et al., 2016). However, it is especially encouraging that there are mutual help groups, led by some very courageous people, who have come out to indicate that they have suffered a mental illness, and they have made efforts to organize others to work toward destigmatizing mental illness. Mutual help programs (social support networks) may be effective in attenuating the self-stigma associated with mental illness (Corrigan et al., 2011).

Structural stigma related to mental health is manifested in (a) the very long waits for treatment for mental illness, (b) lower-quality treatment for concurrent physical illnesses, (c) professional biases when patients seek help, and (d) an over-attribution of mental illness as a causal factor among patients presenting with other health problems. The life span of those with mental illness is reduced by several years because their physical illnesses are often misattributed to being a manifestation of their mental illness.

Even as mental health professionals advocate for the eradication of stigma, many of them share these stigmatizing views. Health professionals may even self-stigmatize when they experience symptoms and combined with their concerns about exposing themselves to the judgment of their peers, they might avoid self-disclosure and treatment-seeking. The unfortunate communication by health-care professionals (by word, facial expression, or gesture) of low expectations of those with a mental health issue figures prominently in the reluctance of people to seek services (Lyons et al., 2009). Predictably, such biases do little to engender trust in key sources of help for mental distress. Trust in the health system may be particularly relevant to mental health issues, especially given that the need for confidentiality may be essential. Indeed, reaching out to a psychiatrist or mental health counselor means exposing some of the individual's most private issues at a time when they are most vulnerable. Thus, when individuals or agencies entrusted with one's mental well-being are perceived as letting an individual down, regaining this trust may be especially difficult.

THE PERILS OF THE INTERNET

Online social networks have become prominent in the day-to-day lives of many people, and there has been a proliferation of internet support groups. Increased social isolation and loneliness, as well as greater stress experiences, were linked to using the internet for emotional support, in many instances with considerable success (Pretorius et al., 2019). Internet support groups provide an anonymous forum where non-verbal rejection is less evident, and where individuals can feel relatively comfortable disclosing their innermost feelings, including suicidal ideation. Compared with face-to-face communications, online interactions demonstrate higher levels of self-disclosure and intimacy, as well as greater openness about personal trauma.

Although young people may turn to the internet seeking support, they frequently act as support providers. Such reciprocity may have positive benefits, but these interactions can reinforce pre-existing emotional difficulties. Because of this, shared feelings and behaviors among like-minded individuals can become the norm, including the encouragement of self-injurious behaviors. Unfortunately, many of these sites are not supervised by trained professionals. Thus, vulnerability to exploitation or the ill effects of online relationships may be especially high for young people who have troubled offline lives.

Environmental determinants of health

Let's start with climate change

Once upon a time in places near and far away, streams and lakes were pristine, the air was clean, and the land verdant. It had been naively assumed that oceans and the atmosphere were too large to be threatened by human behaviors. Provided that the rains came down and the sun shone, we could count on the seeds sown inch by inch and row by row would make the garden grow.

Of course, we now know better.[2] Drought, flooding, extreme heat, pests, and an increasing number of hurricanes, tsunamis, and forest fires have assailed us in recent years. These events give rise to crop failure, wildlife loss, rising water temperatures, and less robust ecosystems, resulting in greater global water and food

---

[2]It isn't our intent to recount all the scary possibilities that will evolve if measures aren't taken immediately. As indicated by Wallace-Wells (2019) in a remarkable treatise, we might not be able to predict precisely what we can expect in the future, but it can reasonably be predicted that it will be horrid.

insecurities. As human behavior contributes extensively to climate change the solutions to prevent the degradation of our environments would do well to obtain input from social scientists. They might not be able to identify strategies to curb global warming, but they could provide guidance on how to deal with human behaviors and the humanitarian crises that will inevitably evolve (e.g., Drury et al., 2019).

Environmental experts and advocates frequently paint a doomsday scenario that will occur by 2040 if preventive steps aren't taken immediately. To be sure, there is increasing understanding of the environmental agents that need to be controlled to prevent worst-case scenarios, assuming we haven't already passed that point. But let's get real about this. We don't have to look to some far-off date and wonder what will occur. Natural disasters that are described as 'once in a hundred-year events or once in a thousand-year events' are already happening regularly, and the frequency of numerous diseases (e.g., heart disease, some forms of cancer, and illnesses in children, such as asthma) have been progressively on the rise. While we can't attribute the emergence of these illnesses solely to environmental factors as they are often tied to lifestyle choices coupled with the increasing reliance on unhealthy foods, environmental factors may directly or indirectly contribute to the cumulative loads that foster diseases.

Needless to say, in the wake of natural disasters related to climate change millions of animals are killed (for example the devastation of the 2019–2020 Australian 'black summer'), and the mental health of local victims may be severely undermined. Most people are aware of the impact of sudden catastrophic environmental events, but risks to human and animal health typically stem from more insidious changes. Fine particulate matter in the air (air particles smaller than 2.5 microns in width: PM2.5) has progressively increased, leading to inflammatory airway diseases, and heat waves will continue to appear more frequently resulting in a large number of deaths in vulnerable populations. When wildfires occur at the same time as extreme heat, the elevated fine particulate matter is accompanied by increased ground-level ozone which promotes greater health risks. The fine particulate matter in smoke from forest fires can travel hundreds of kilometers, thereby creating health risks across vast regions.

It is more than a little ironic that much of the world responded immediately and forcefully when COVID-19 first emerged in early 2020 and enormous resources were mobilized to curb the growing death toll, which reached 6 million by the end of 2021 (this is likely a vast underestimate). While this was entirely appropriate, one must wonder about the less enthusiastic reponses to the far more deadly effects of the many pollutants that affect us every day. According to the WHO, about 7 million people die prematurely each year owing to indoor and outdoor pollution, whereas others have suggested that the figure is closer to 8.7 million (Vohra et al., 2021). Perhaps these numbers are so great that they strain credulity, or maybe people are unable to fathom or register the risks imposed, or they might believe that these events won't affect them – it's more of a problem in faraway places or for future times. The fact is that pollutants affect the health of people in all industrialized countries. Pollutants, such as fine particulate matter, alter every cell in the human body and thus disturb every organ, thereby instigating a wide assortment of illnesses, particularly cardiovascular illnesses, stroke, chronic obstructive pulmonary disease, and several forms of cancer. Aside from increased deaths, health span is diminished so that the last years of people's lives are less likely to be comfortable. Diminished life span is especially acute in India and China but air pollution also kills many people yearly in the US (60,000), UK (40,000), Canada (14,500), and Australia (5,000), although these numbers have declined over the past 20 years as measures had been taken to decrease indoor and outdoor pollutants.

Excessive heat and pollutants have been implicated in stillbirths, preterm births, and low birth weights (Bekkar et al., 2020). Indeed, prenatal exposure to ambient particulate matter, as well as exposure during the early postnatal period may affect postnatal development, including accelerated biological aging and increased incidence of illness in later life. These actions may be brought about by epigenetic changes that affect multiple processes, such as mitochondrial function and inflammation, that are tied to health risks (Isaevska et al., 2021). Of course, these adverse effects to the fetus or during early development are compounded by exposure to chemicals that disrupt hormonal processes (i.e., endocrine-disrupting chemicals), such as phthalates, bisphenol A, and perfluoroalkyl substances (the latter are used commercially to make products that are heat resistant and repel grease and oil).

Changing climatic conditions have altered the migration and spread of disease-carrying insects that pose health risks to humans and other animals. Ticks carrying Lyme disease that had been infrequent in southern portions of Canada have now become endemic to these regions. Dengue fever transmitted by certain mosquitos in tropical and subtropical regions has likewise been increasing over the years. With greater access to ports in the Antarctic region, several invasive species (e.g., algae, barnacles, crabs, mussels) that attach themselves to the hulls of ships from much of the world have been 'biofouling' the regional waters, altering ecosystems, and potentially influencing fisheries (McCarthy et al., 2022).

Climate change has promoted gradual shifts in agricultural practices, including an increase in insecticide and pesticide use, resulting in their accumulation in aquatic systems. With the development of resistance to pesticides (owing either to characteristics of insects changing through epigenetic processes or the effectiveness of pesticides being altered by environmental conditions), greater amounts of these agents will be needed to achieve their effects (Matzrafi, 2019). Moreover, these pesticides are often non-specific, killing off many beneficial insects, with negative repercussions on plant systems (reduced pollination) and other species that are critical to the food chain.

Our diet has often been implicated in the development and progression of numerous illnesses. For example, it has been maintained that the adoption of an anti-inflammatory diet, such as the Mediterranean diet, could have health benefits. At the same time, the fact that these foods may be contaminated with insecticides

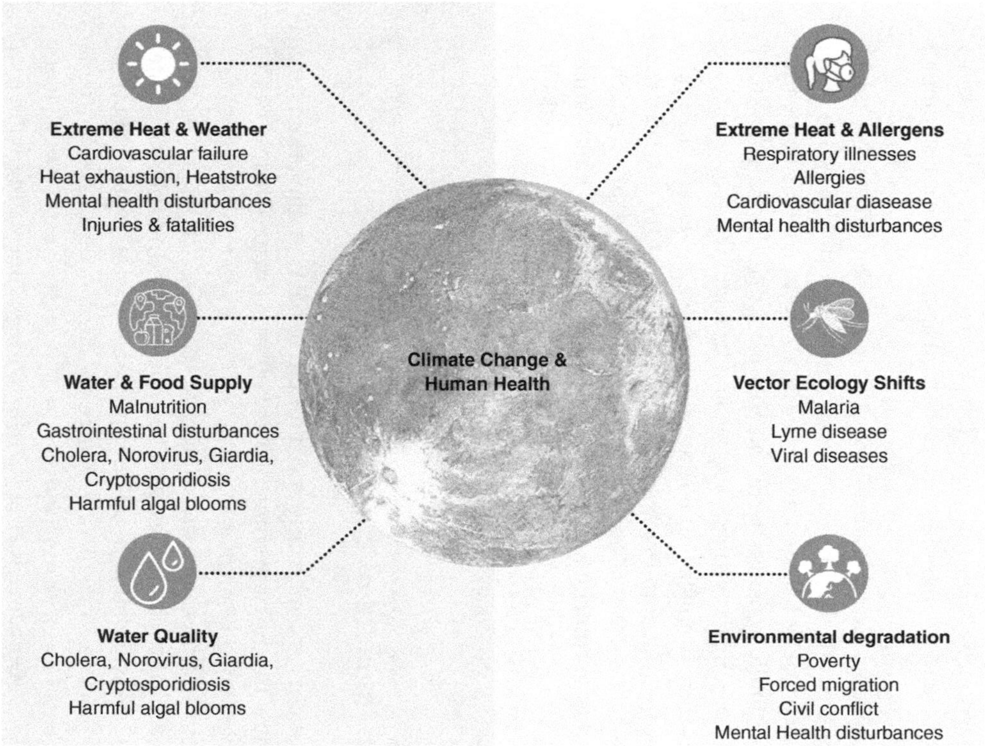
Extreme Heat & Weather
Cardiovascular failure
Heat exhaustion, Heatstroke
Mental health disturbances
Injuries & fatalities
Water & Food Supply
Malnutrition
Gastrointestinal disturbances
Cholera, Norovirus, Giardia,
Cryptosporidiosis
Harmful algal blooms
Water Quality
Cholera, Norovirus, Giardia,
Cryptosporidiosis
Harmful algal blooms
Climate Change &
Human Health
Extreme Heat & Allergens
Respiratory illnesses
Allergies
Cardiovascular diasease
Mental health disturbances
Vector Ecology Shifts
Malaria
Lyme disease
Viral diseases
Environmental degradation
Poverty
Forced migration
Civil conflict
Mental Health disturbances

Figure 3.2 Climate change, which promises to become increasingly more pronounced, has already been affecting human health. As depicted on the left side of the figure, increasing heat and altered weather conditions, water and food scarcity, and water contamination have increased the appearance of diverse illnesses, including non-communicable disorders as well as those related to bacterial and viral infection. Likewise, as shown in the right side of the figure, climate change has promoted air pollution and the presence of allergens, shifts in the ecology so that vector-borne diseases are becoming more apparent, and environmental degradation has affected psychosocial and intergroup processes that affect mental and physical health.

and pesticides could negatively affect human health (Nicolopoulou-Stamati et al., 2016). When diet is obtained from organic food (i.e., grown without the use of pesticides) consumers' urinary pesticide residue excretion was lower than it was following a Mediterranean diet that was not free of pesticides, which has a bearing on disease occurrence (Rempelos et al., 2021).

The fact is that climate change has wide-ranging effects on multiple components of the environment, which independently or in combination engender numerous health risks. Figure 3.2 shows how some of these come about, but the extent of the damage that has already been created and forecasted for the future has taken a toll on mental health and feelings of hopelessness and apathy concerning human abilities to limit disaster.

The Lancet Countdown provided a detailed set of recommendations that ought to be adopted to prevent the health consequences of climate change (Watts et al., 2021). But will policy makers be listening? A Lancet report in 2009 had raised the same red flags, but limited changes were initiated after that. Perhaps it will be different this time. Dealing with climate change and its sequelae needs to succeed based on Plan A as there is no Plan(et) B through which we can escape. This said, a report released by the American Psychological Association in 2019 indicated that 56% of individuals believed that climate change is the most important issue facing society. Yet, only 40% of individuals had engaged in behaviors to limit climate change, frequently saying that they simply didn't know where to start. Remarkably, almost a third of those who responded to the survey indicated that they had no interest or intention to alter their behaviors.

Mental health impacts of climate change

In its depressing summary concerning the multiple impacts of climate change, the UN report from the Intergovernmental Panel on Climate Change (IPCC) highlighted the likelihood of mental illnesses, such as anxiety, depression, and PTSD, increasing still further over the coming years (IPCC, 2022). Those with underlying mental health conditions will be especially vulnerable to mental health conditions, as will children, adolescents, and elderly people. Many of the mental health issues tied to climate change are already with us. As extreme climate-related events have increased in frequency in recent years so have mental health conditions (Obradovich et al., 2018). With the increasing burden of climate change, including food and water insecurity together with social and cultural instability, allostatic load may increase and hence lead to further mental health deterioration.

Relatively recent reports indicated that young people (16–25 years of age) overwhelmingly felt sad, anxious, angry, powerless, helpless, and guilty regarding the impacts of climate change, and they frequently expressed feelings of betrayal by government responses to the impending disasters (Hickman et al., 2021). Some groups are being especially hard hit by climate change. For instance, Indigenous Peoples who are witnessing the lands to which they are connected being harmed are experiencing 'ecological grief' (Cunsolo & Ellis, 2018).

The diverse mental health symptoms that have been dubbed 'eco-anxiety' have become increasingly concerning. Most often, the mental health issues associated with eco-anxiety do not reach clinically significant levels. Yet, the worry created in some individuals has been sufficiently intense to make them rethink whether they wish to have children. As well, given what we know about the long-term consequences of stress and anxiety in children and youth, it's possible that persistent emotional disturbances associated with eco-anxiety may prevail for lengthy periods and may have further downstream consequences on physical and mental health.

Beyond their physical effects, pollutants may contribute to the development of dementia, as well as substance use disorders, anxiety, depression, and suicide. It was surmised that particulate matter together with ozone influences brain processes (e.g., HPA functioning) that contribute to these disorders, possibly interacting with genetic factors (Z. Li et al., 2021). To a considerable extent, physical and psychological disorders may arise owing to elevated levels of inflammatory factors, and while genetic influences and epigenetic changes moderate the effects of pollutants, the effects of air pollution are more pronounced in the absence of psychosocial buffers (Schraufnagel et al., 2019). Findings such as these have led to the suggestion that amelioration of symptoms could be attained through social support (Baudon & Jachens, 2021) and expression of agency by taking collective actions.

An often overlooked factor that influences the risk of health disturbances concerns urbanization. An analysis that included 191 countries revealed that mental health conditions were elevated most in countries where urbanization was greatest. Given the potential interactions between multiple environmental and social factors, identifying the specific aspects of the urban environment contributing to mental health challenges is difficult, and may include crowding, pollution, lack of green spaces, and even lack of wildlife such as bird diversity. Still, analyses that consider multiple inputs, including those that change over time, may ultimately provide the information necessary to establish preventive strategies. For the moment, it should be acknowledged that there are instances in which relatively small environmental manipulations can have very great effects. Simply having more green spaces in cities has been associated with diminished depression among middle-aged and older individuals, and children who had greater access to green spaces exhibited lower levels of oxidative stress that could diminish later health risks. These relations were particularly marked among lower-income individuals who may lack green spaces in their neighborhood (Cottagiri et al., 2022). Growing up in the presence of usable green spaces was associated with a marked difference in the later occurrence of a wide assortment of psychiatric disturbances even after adjusting for socioeconomic factors, parental age, and history of mental health issues (Engemann et al., 2019).

Environmental racism

It is no coincidence that environmentally toxic human activities, including industrial plants that deposit pollutants into the environment, are located in areas proximal to people living in poverty or socially marginalized groups. Referred to as 'sacrifice zones', these regions with sometimes enormous numbers of petrochemical plants, and the resulting pollutants have been linked to cancer occurrence being 50 times greater among residents compared to the national average. In some underserved northern Indigenous communities in Canada, drinkable water has been unavailable for decades; mercury-polluted waters from mining and other industries have affected Indigenous communities in Canada and beyond (e.g., Amazon forests), damaging entire ecosystems, including the fish and wildlife that humans rely on as sources of food.

Other forms of environmental racism, such as the location of busy highway corridors or flight paths disproportionately expose low-income ethnoracial populations to greater levels of air, light, and noise pollution. In a report from the National Center for Environmental Assessment in the US, it was indicated that particulate matter exposure among Black people exceeded that associated with poverty itself. Socially marginalized communities don't have the resources to tackle government policies, and the disparities that exist concerning regulatory standards have become progressively more prominent (Jbaily et al., 2022). To escape stringent regulations when they are successfully implemented, numerous high-polluting industries have moved to low-income countries where their environmental abuses are not closely monitored. This issue has been discussed in the scientific literature for more than two decades; an editorial published in *The Lancet Planetary Health* (2018) suggested that it's time for these inequalities to change.

Nature and land-based healing

While those who spend much of their time outdoors or who rely on the land to meet life needs are acutely aware of climate change, at the same time the healing properties of spending time outdoors and in nature can promote resilience and wellness. Several reviews have concluded that immersive nature experiences are associated with positive well-being, cognitive and social functioning, and lower levels of stress and other risk factors associated with diminished health and mental health (Bratman et al., 2019). Nature experiences might involve a range of outdoor activities, including simply sitting on a park bench, gardening, outings in natural settings, fishing, hunting, or being in the wilderness. These activities may serve to reduce stress and relieve mental fatigue, increase physical activity and social connections, expose people to improved air quality, and enhance immune function. At the same time, there is little clarity on the kinds of experiences that contribute most to well-being, how much time in nature is needed to feel a sense of connection, or for whom such contact or connection is most beneficial (Frumkin et al., 2017).

Public health as precision medicine

Just as precision medicine has been at the forefront of approaches to treat diseases based on specific biomarkers and symptoms, there has been a movement towards precision public health in dealing with broad health threats (Arnold, 2022). This approach asserts that targeted applications be endorsed. If a disease, such as cholera, breaks out in a limited portion of a city, then it would be best to track down affected people and determine the common denominator that might have led to the disease, just as John Snow did in the Soho region of London, UK, in 1854.

With greater capabilities thanks to sophisticated machine learning techniques (as opposed to a pencil and paper map available to Snow), it is possible to more readily identify the epicenter of disease spread and take appropriate actions. Likewise, it should be possible to determine where vaccines, masks, and testing are needed most (assuming that vaccine hesitancy won't be an issue). Furthermore, why indiscriminately spray insecticide throughout a city if the problem can be localized to one region? Targeted spraying with insecticides to kill mosquito larvae reduced the occurrence of malaria within Central and South America, and this might be possible within the continent of Africa. The very same procedures can be adopted to identify regions of the world most in need of certain remedies and to deliver therapies accordingly (e.g., for childhood diseases). A one-size-fits-all approach has often been less than ideal in treating various diseases, including those that involve strong genetic influences, hence encouraging the adoption of precision medicine. A precision public health approach might similarly provide benefits for environmentally linked diseases.

One planet, one health, one cure

Increasingly greater attention has been dedicated to the adoption of a 'One Health' approach to enhance well-being and disease prevention. A One Health approach entails working across multiple disciplines to address global health issues at the intersection of human and animal health, with the natural and built environments contributing to, and transforming this relationship. Many One Health initiatives are driven by socioeconomic issues that include, but are not limited to: population growth; nutritional, agricultural, and trade practices; technological advances; poverty; globalization; land use and resource development; urbanization and migration; social justice and conflict; and climate change. Problem identification and solution-seeking from a One Health perspective requires not only an understanding of the fundamental biological mechanisms underlying health risks and the transmission of disease but also an astute awareness of the cultural and technological contexts in which humans interact with each other and their environments. In effect, One Health entails a recognition that the health of the planet is tied to the intricate and complex relationships that exist between humans, animals, and their shared environment.

The One Health approach began with a focus on limiting the occurrence of bacterial and viral diseases, vector-borne and parasitic infections. Diverse factors associated with the environment (including climate change), exposure to animals and wildlife, and human behavior all influence bacterial and viral infections, as well as non-communicable diseases, and have implications for both prevention and therapies (Destoumieux-Garzón et al., 2018). A One Health solution recognizes the need to involve diverse systems at the local and the global level to mobilize efforts to identify markers that facilitate the detection and monitoring of exposures that have health implications. This would allow the establishment of comprehensive and integrated policies and regulations to mitigate risk and build resilience, and ultimately to manage and effectively respond to global crises (from pandemics to climate change).

Fundamental to the One Health approach is the integration of diverse methodologies from different fields of social, natural, and data sciences, human and veterinary medicine, engineering, public policy, and so on. In essence, it is recommended that existing research and implementation silos that typically operate independently of one another be dismantled and then reintegrated. By promoting cross-fertilization of diverse approaches, it is more likely that complex 'wicked' health and environmental problems can be tackled effectively.

To better understand what One Health is about, it may be useful to use a concrete example to illustrate how this perspective considers disease occurrence and intervention. Prior to the introduction of antibiotics, humans were at the mercy of bacterial infections that could occur with minor cuts and abrasions, dental and surgical procedures that could lead to sepsis, septic shock, and death. The introduction of antibiotics largely reduced the risk of these conditions and were effective in the treatment of numerous infectious conditions. With the realization of the benefits of antibiotics, their use increased dramatically.

Unfortunately, bacteria find ways of defending themselves through processes like natural selection. When bacteria in a petri dish are challenged by an antibiotic virtually all of them are destroyed. But a few hardy survivors can produce equally hardy bacteria. When this new group of bacteria is again challenged by an antibiotic, the majority will once more be eliminated, but again a few will survive – these are the hardiest of the hardy (Al Mamun et al., 2012). Eventually, with repeated antibiotic exposure, bacteria evolved that were entirely resistant to antibiotics so that the ability to treat bacterial infections was severely disturbed. For instance, infection with staphylococcus aureus (Staph infection) that contributes to post-surgical infection and sepsis could be treated with methicillin, preventing millions of deaths worldwide. However, a bacterial strain eventually evolved that was resistant to methicillin (termed methicillin-resistant *Staphylococcus aureus* (MRSA)) (Lee et al.,

2018). For a while, bacteria such as MRSA were primarily found within hospitals where antibiotics were used most frequently. However, MRSA has been appearing in the population and has had particularly nasty effects among high-risk individuals, such as those with diabetes, cancer patients receiving chemotherapy, patients with HIV/AIDS, or individuals with compromised immune system functioning that developed for other reasons. In 2019, antimicrobial resistance was associated with 4.95 million deaths worldwide and 1.27 million deaths were directly attributable to resistance to antibiotics.

So, how did we reach this point? Well, there isn't a single cause and we can point fingers in multiple directions. Physicians began to use antibiotics relatively indiscriminately (on a just-in-case basis), sometimes prescribing antibiotics for illnesses that would resolve on their own in a few days and for symptoms that were virally produced, such as sore throat, colds, or flu, and are not eliminated by antibiotics. Patients were also guilty of fostering antibiotic resistance. Contrary to the instructions they received, patients often stopped taking the full course of the antibiotic treatment once symptoms disappeared, thereby allowing relatively hardy bacteria to survive. Patients stored antibiotics in case they were needed, and then used them inappropriately. Aside from this form of misuse, animals on farms were frequently given antibiotics to treat bacterial infections and, for a while, these agents were used routinely in a preventative capacity. Animals develop bacteria that are resistant to antibiotics, and these can be passed on to humans when we consume red meat or chicken. Moreover, antibiotics in these animals influence soil through urine and feces, which can contaminate vegetables and fruits, and they can be washed into water systems, which ultimately affect us (McEwen & Collignon, 2018). In effect, human behavior, animals, and the environment function cooperatively to create conditions that promote antibacterial resistance.

We're now down to our last effective drugs, such as vancomycin, the so-called antibiotic of last resort, and even though it has been used relatively sparingly, signs of resistance to it have been appearing. Many pharmaceutical companies have been reluctant to develop new antibiotics given that these would likely encounter the same fate as current antibiotics. Novel approaches are in development to replace antibiotic remedies. For instance, attention has been devoted to the development of viruses (we are replete with these just as commensal bacteria are present within us) that can attack and destroy bacteria (these are referred to as bacteriophages, or phages). These phages can potentially target harmful bacteria, rather than having broad indiscriminate effects, and thus may be especially advantageous (Brives & Pourraz, 2020). The recognition that excessive use of antibiotics had become problematic led to changes of recommended behaviors and policies, including those related to agriculture and veterinary medicine, and the development of better technologies to deal with diseases.

Similar relationships between human, animal, and environmental health are evident regarding viral pandemics, particularly viruses that affect humans that originated in other species. Thus, the WHO has advocated for a 'pandemic treaty' whereby member organizations would commit to establishing enhanced capacity to prevent and predict the emergence of pandemics. Among other things, this entails monitoring and limiting the encroachment of humans into the natural habitats of animals, as well as better integration of multiple sectors (e.g., medical, educational, environmental, computer sciences) that could play a pivotal role in pandemic preparedness. The One Health notion asserts that as a global society we need to take ownership and stewardship to assure that these elements are well managed (Amuasi et al., 2020).

Conclusion

Psychological and physical health is influenced by diverse psychosocial and environmental determinants. Psychosocial factors can occur across the life span, ranging from adverse early-life experiences to elder abuse. These experiences occur within a social context that can exacerbate negative outcomes, including the effects of poverty, racism, social rejection, and discrimination. However, social factors can be fundamental to the capacity to cope with life stressors, including having a supportive and trustworthy social safety net. It has been maintained that social support and connection may be a basic need for individuals and may be relevant to enhancing health. These actions may come about by buffering against behavioral and emotional stress reactions, including the biological disturbances that emanate from chronic stressful experiences.

Environmental factors at both the micro and macro level are known to profoundly affect psychological and physical health. The sequelae of climate change and elevated levels of pollutants globally are already being felt and will no doubt have further ramifications. The influence of environmental challenges affects all individuals, but some groups are more likely to be affected (e.g., environmental racism). Ultimately, limiting the damaging effects of environmental abuse will require coordinated actions, such as those that are advocated based on a One Health approach.

Suggested readings

Destoumieux-Garzón, D., Mavingui, P., Boetsch, G., Boissier, J., & Darriet, F. (2018). The one health concept: 10 years old and a long road ahead. *Frontiers in Veterinary Science, 5*, 14.

Drury, J., Carter, H., Cocking, C., Ntontis, E., & Guven, S.K. (2019). Facilitating collective psychosocial resilience in the public in emergencies: Twelve recommendations based on the social identity approach. *Frontiers in Public Health, 7*, 141.

Wallace-Wells, D. (2019). *The uninhabitable earth.* New York: Tim Guggan Books.

4

HORMONAL CHANGES ASSOCIATED WITH STRESSORS

─────Searching for the source of illness─────

When people think of scientists, they often think of nerdy people standing at a lab bench and throwing around big words. In contrast, someone who works as a CSI or NCIS agent, or as a behavioral profiler, seems pretty cool. Likewise, archeologists and anthropologists all seem, at least in the last few decades, to be stereotyped as Indiana Jones. Scientists working in health-related disciplines are more like detectives who are hunting down culprits that cause the brain or other organs to act in particular ways. They find clues related to a disease, rule out those that are either simply bystanders, but not directly involved in its provocation (i.e., dismiss those with alibis), and then once they have a very good suspect, they tie the behavior of that variable (person) of interest to the pathology (crime). Among other things, they try to simulate the crime by administering drugs (or other treatments, including creating mice with or without a certain biological makeup) to determine whether a pathological state emerges (recreating the crime scene), assess whether this happens all the time or only under certain circumstances (serial killer or a unique event), and finally evaluate whether the pathological state can be reversed by eliminating or blocking certain chemical systems. As we go through the next sections, keep in mind that the basic approaches to evaluating the role of different hormonal and neurochemical systems in the stress process or identifying the cause of

(Continued)

pathology involve some keen detective work and, in the end, any judgment comes from a jury of peers (journal or grant reviewers).

Learning objectives

Stressors influence hormonal systems, which may be related to the provocation and exacerbation of pathophysiological outcomes. These comprise many psychological, immunological, cardiovascular, muscular, or gastrointestinal illnesses – you name it, and stressors affect them. The trick is defining which specific stressor-related biological processes, or sets of biological processes, are responsible for specific pathologies. In this chapter, we'll consider hormonal processes activated in response to stressors that may have adaptive consequences and maintain our well-being but can also contribute to pathological outcomes. By the end of this chapter, you should appreciate that:

• Multiple hormonal systems exist that interact with one another, and each of the hormones has multiple actions.
• Some systems, such as one that leads to an elevation of the prototypical stress hormone cortisol, have received particular attention. However, stressful events influence numerous hormones and their receptors, each of which plays a fundamental adaptive role to meet the organism's needs in response to a variety of challenges.
• Several hormones are often considered in the context of stressors and have profound effects on mood states, such as anxiety and depression. Other hormones are associated with eating and energy balances or promote prosocial behaviors. In each instance, the hormones are nonetheless influenced by stressful events, and coordination exists so that appropriate defensive actions can be initiated, whereas processes that are not essential at the moment are suppressed.
• Pathological outcomes can arise because of the dysfunction of one or another hormonal process or the interactions of hormones with other biological systems and these actions are often moderated by psychosocial factors.

Hormones and behavior

The stress responses that comprise varied hormonal changes are determined by a constellation of factors related to stressor characteristics and various individual difference factors, as well as how we appraise and cope with threats and challenges. Many of these biological changes might act in an adaptive capacity, but when stressors are too intense or long-lasting, aspects of these systems may ultimately fail, thereby leading to the emergence of pathological states. Alternatively, pathology may reflect the side effects or secondary consequences of the adaptive system's efforts to respond effectively. In theory, each of us has a weak link(s), and when the load becomes too heavy this link might break and lead to pathology. The specific link(s) that breaks will presumably contribute to the specific illness that is elicited.

To understand how stressful events come to affect our health, it's necessary to appreciate that stressors might do so by virtue of their actions on multiple biological systems. This chapter will primarily consider the hormonal processes related to stressors, and in Figure 4.1 you can see where these hormones originate. In the

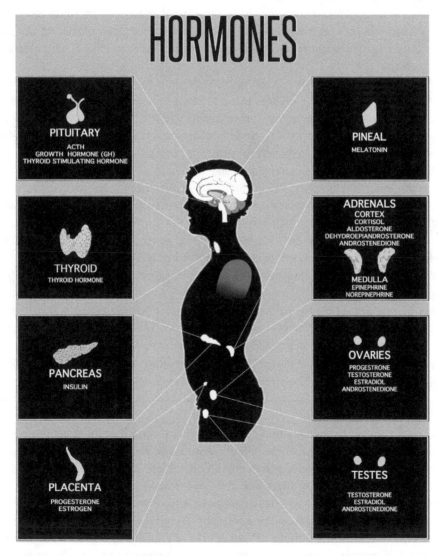

Figure 4.1 Several sites within the body from which particular hormones are released.

Source: Illustration created by Lucas J. Wareing.

ensuing two chapters we'll be considering neurotransmitters and growth factors as well as immune and microbial changes, all of which may in some fashion interact with hormonal processes.

What's a hormone?

A hormone is a chemical released by a cell or gland in response to external or internal signals (e.g., stressors, altered sugar levels), which then travels to a distal site where it affects other cells of the body. Typically, hormones are transported in the blood, and cells respond when a hormone triggers specific receptors that are present, which then provoke a series of changes that culminate in a cellular response. Several different types of receptors may be present for any given hormone, each of which may trigger different outcomes.

Hormone molecules that are released directly into the bloodstream are referred to as 'endocrine' hormones, whereas those secreted directly into a duct and then flow either into the bloodstream or from cell to cell by diffusion are referred to as 'exocrine' hormones (this process is known as 'paracrine signaling'). When the hormone stimulates the very cell that released it (yes, this happens, and there are reasons for this as we'll see later) this is referred to as 'autocrine signaling'.

Hormones come in several flavors. Some are derived from lipids and phospholipids (i.e., naturally produced substances, such as fats, sterols, mono-, di- and triglycerides, and an assortment of vitamins). The hormones that are of particular interest to us are the steroid hormones, such as corticoids and sex hormones (e.g., estrogen). Glucocorticoids refer to a class of hormones that bind to the glucocorticoid receptor, which is present in virtually every cell, with cortisol being the prototypical stress hormone.

A second class of hormones made up of lengthy amino acid chains are peptide hormones (usually referred to simply as peptides). These comprise vasopressin, growth hormone, insulin, ghrelin and the heart hormone atrial natriuretic peptide, as well as several others. Certain hormones, such as adrenaline (also called epinephrine), are manufactured (synthesized) and released in the periphery and by neurons in the brain, and in the latter capacity they are referred to as neurotransmitters (see Chapter 5).

Tables 4.1 and 4.2 provide a broad overview concerning the functions of several hormones that are found in the hypothalamus and the pituitary gland, respectively. The hormones released from the adrenal gland are provided in Table 4.3. Many of these hormones affect our ability to contend with stressful events by influencing our readiness to make appropriate behavioral or emotional responses, modify cognitive processes, and promote physiological changes (e.g., variations in immune and heart functioning, as well as energy regulation) that are essential for survival. Hormones have functions beyond that of stress regulation, being fundamental to our basic functioning, metabolic processes, the initiation and cessation of eating, regulating immune activity, reproductive processes, preparing the body for transitional phases of life (puberty, parenting, bonding, the menopause), and the production and release of yet other hormones. Moreover, they contribute to cell death (apoptosis) and the stimulation or inhibition of cell growth, they influence our mood states and cognitive functioning, and play a pivotal role in the development of a wide range of physical diseases.

Table 4.1 Hypothalamic hormones and their effects.

Secreted hormone	Biological effect
Corticotropin-releasing hormone (CRH)	Released from paraventricular nucleus of hypothalamus: stimulates adrenocorticotropic hormone (ACTH) release from anterior pituitary
Dopamine (DA)	Released from the arcuate nucleus: inhibits prolactin secretion from anterior pituitary
Growth hormone-releasing hormone (GHRH)	Released from the arcuate nucleus: stimulates growth hormone (GH) release from anterior pituitary
Somatostatin (SS)	Released from the periventricular nucleus: inhibits growth hormone (GH) and thyroid-stimulating hormone (TSH) release from anterior pituitary
Gonadotropin-releasing hormone (GnRH)	Released from the preoptic area: stimulates the release of follicle-stimulating hormone (FSH) and luteinizing hormone (LH) from anterior pituitary
Oxytocin (OXT)	Released from both the supraoptic and paraventricular nucleus: promotes uterine contraction, milk ejection
Melanocyte-stimulating hormone (MSH)	Produced in the lateral hypothalamus: associated with feeding, motivation
Vasopressin (VP)	Released by both the paraventricular and supraoptic nucleus: promotes water reabsorption and increased blood volume
Orexin (hypocretin)	Produced within the hypothalamus, but orexin receptors are found throughout the brain: involved in arousal, wakefulness, and appetite

Table 4.2 Pituitary hormones and their effects.

Secreted hormone	Biological effect
Anterior portion	
Growth hormone (GH)	Stimulates growth and cell reproduction, and insulin-like growth factor (IGF-1) secretion from liver
Thyroid-stimulating hormone (TSH)	Stimulates thyroxine (T4) and triiodothyronine (T3) synthesis and release from thyroid gland, and stimulates iodine absorption by thyroid gland

(Continued)

Table 4.2 (Continued)

Secreted hormone	Biological effect
Adrenocorticotropic hormone (ACTH)	Stimulates corticosteroid (glucocorticoid and mineralcorticoid) release from adrenocortical cells and promotes androgen synthesis
Beta-endorphin	Inhibits perception of pain
Follicle-stimulating hormone (FSH)	In females: stimulates maturation of ovarian follicles in ovary. In males: stimulates spermatogenesis, production of androgen-binding protein
Luteinizing hormone (LH)	In females: stimulates ovulation and formation of corpus luteum; In males: stimulates testosterone synthesis
Prolactin (PRL)	Stimulates milk synthesis and release from mammary glands; involved in sexual gratification
Melanocyte-stimulating hormone (MSH)	Stimulates melanin synthesis and release
Posterior portion	
Oxytocin (OXT)	Elicits uterine contraction; lactation
Vasopressin (AVP)	Water reabsorption and increased blood volume

Table 4.3 Adrenal hormones and their effects.

Secreted hormone	Biological effect
Adrenal cortex	
Cortisol (corticosterone in rodents)	Stimulates gluconeogenesis and fat breakdown in adipose tissue; inhibits protein synthesis; inhibits glucose uptake in muscle and adipose tissue, promotes immune suppression and acts as an anti-inflammatory
Mineralocorticoids (e.g., aldosterone)	Stimulate active sodium reabsorption and passive water reabsorption, thus increasing blood volume and blood pressure
Androgens (e.g., DHEA and testosterone)	Masculinization (limited compared to effects of androgens from testes); in females this has masculinizing effects
Adrenal medulla	
Epinephrine (adrenaline) and norepinephrine (noradrenaline) (Epi and NE)	Elicits flight or flight response; increase oxygen and glucose in the brain and muscles; promotes vasodilation, increases catalysis of glycogen in liver and the breakdown of lipids in fat cells; suppresses bodily processes (e.g., digestion) during emergency responses; influences immune system activity
Dopamine (DA)	Increased heart rate and blood pressure
Enkephalin (Enk)	Involved in pain regulation

Assessing the relationship between hormones and behaviors

Several approaches can be used to assess the relationship between hormones and behaviors. This is fairly simple in animals, but a bit more complicated in humans. In animals, the effects of the hormone can be assessed by administering it (by injection or in their food or water), and, conversely, treatments can be given to block the receptor or block the source of the hormone through surgical interventions (e.g., by adrenalectomy to reduce adrenal hormones, or ovariectomy to reduce female sex hormones). Alternatively, mice can be genetically engineered so that the hormone or its receptors are diminished. Once the hormone is reduced and the consequences assessed, one can then determine whether these effects are reversed by the exogenous administration of that hormone (i.e., a replacement therapy). Things can become a bit complicated as hormones may interact with one another, as well as with other biological processes and life experiences, so it often requires sophisticated experimentation to determine how and when this occurs.

In humans, the analyses of hormones in relation to behavior and pathology require different approaches. One can assess individuals with diseases that involve hormonal disturbances. For instance, it is possible to study those with Addison's disease in which an adrenal insufficiency exists. Alternatively, pituitary adenoma and adrenal adenoma are accompanied by high cortisol levels, and thus the influence of hypercortisolemia can be assessed. An adenoma refers to a benign tumor of glandular origin; it can eventually become malignant, and the term 'adenocarcinoma' is then applied. The same types of procedures could be used to assess the behavioral influence of sex hormones, thyroid hormones, and other hormone secreting glands. In some instances, hormones are administered clinically (corticoids, estrogen, progesterone) or experimentally, and in these conditions the potential behavioral effects can be deduced. Yet another approach is to rely on individual differences in hormonal levels and simply determine whether individuals with high (or low) levels of a given hormone exhibit differences of certain behaviors, reactivity to stressors, or the development of specific pathologies.

Another frequent approach to assess the connection between hormones and behaviors has been to determine whether a variant of a gene is associated with reduced levels of a hormone or disturbances of a hormone receptor and then relate this to behavioral phenotypes. It will be recalled that variants of a gene (polymorphism) can arise that can alter hormone levels or the functioning of specific receptors. If a nucleotide is altered at an important place on the gene, then this polymorphism can have dramatic effects (just as a letter in a word, or a word in a sentence, can alter the meaning of an entire sentence). Often, the polymorphism can involve just a single nucleotide, in which case it is referred to as a single nucleotide polymorphism (SNP, pronounced 'snip'), or it can involve multiple nucleotides. The greater the number of mutations (it might be better to call them 'variants', since mutation is often used as a pejorative, and not all mutations have negative consequences), the more likely one or more will appear at critical sites on a gene, and hence the greater the risk of a bad outcome. There are all sorts of factors that could influence the appearance of mutations. For instance, the polymorphisms can be inherited, they can be produced by environmental factors, or they may appear in a newborn, possibly being tied to the age of the mother or the father.

Biological stress responses

The brain and peripheral nervous system, as well as many other organs, contain numerous hormones and receptors that influence every aspect of our functioning. As we'll see, too little or too much of any hormone creates its own characteristic set of problems. As one would expect from well-regulated processes, there are many checks and balances within and between the systems in our body and brain, but when these are sufficiently disturbed, pathophysiological outcomes might appear. Unfortunately, because there are so many biological changes that occur concurrently and interact with one another, it's sometimes difficult to determine where the problem lies, which biological systems contributed to the imbalance, and how to repair the problem or at least patch it up for the moment.

When we encounter a stressor, a series of biological changes occur that reflect adaptive responses to deal with the stressor or its repercussions. These might be important for appraisal processes, serve to diminish the physical or emotional pain associated with the stressor, prepare the individual to deal with ongoing or impending insults (e.g., enhancing arousal, vigilance, and the cognitive processes necessary for effective coping), increase energy substrates that may be needed for survival, and limit potential adverse effects that might otherwise be provoked. When hormonal processes don't function as they should, they serve to inform us that something is amiss. We'll deal with how and why this occurs later, but for the moment we can use the analogy of pain perception, and the obvious questions of 'What's it good for?' and 'Wouldn't we be better off if there were no such thing?' Pain gives us a clear message that something is wrong, and that actions need to be taken to avoid further problems. Individuals with a congenital lack of pain receptors wouldn't know if they had their hand on a hot stove, and thus would suffer severe tissue damage. In the same fashion, the biological changes associated with stressors send out the message that we ought to be doing something about the situation we're in.

The hypothalamic-pituitary-adrenal (HPA) axis and glucocorticoids

Several hormones play essential regulatory roles to make sure that the body's needs are being met. Some of these are fundamental to the stress process, including behavioral responses, such as fighting or fleeing, and are activated very soon after an adverse event is experienced. Others seem to kick in a little later, but they too have important actions in dealing with the stressors that might be encountered.

Cortisol response to an acute stressor

Within seconds of a stressor being encountered, several neuronal changes occur in cortical brain regions that are involved in appraisal processes and those associated with decision-making (e.g., the prefrontal, including the anterior cingulate cortex) as well as in brain regions that govern emotional responses (amygdala, bed nucleus of the stria teminalis, hippocampus). At roughly the same time the sympathetic portion of the autonomic nervous system is activated, which entails the release of epinephrine and norepinephrine that stimulate several organs in the body (e.g., causing increased cardiovascular functioning). As illustrated in Figure 4.2, stressor-provoked activation of neurons within the prefrontal cortex and amygdala lead to a series of biological changes that culminate in the release of cortisol (corticosterone in rodents) from the adrenal gland into the bloodstream. Once in circulation cortisol reaches the brain where it stimulates neurons in the hypothalamus and hippocampus, which will have the effect of stemming further release of the hormone. This self-regulating HPA loop (referred to as a negative feedback loop) is of fundamental importance as a persistent glucocorticoid increase may have damaging effects. Specifically, if the glucocorticoid receptors on hippocampal cells (where the receptors appear in high densities) are excessively stimulated, they may be damaged, and thus a component of the shut-down mechanisms will not operate properly. As a result, cortisol will continue to be released, leading to still greater hippocampal cell loss. If this continues unabated, then disturbances of cognitive functioning will ultimately ensue. During normal aging neurons are typically lost, but this could be exacerbated by experiences or treatments that cause sustained cortisol elevations (McEwen & Gianaros, 2011).

It's essential to have a well-regulated corticoid response to stressors, so that mild stressors elicit a moderate cortisol release from the adrenal gland, whereas stronger stressors elicit a greater release. In addition, as in the case of most stress systems, the release of the hormone should diminish relatively quickly after the stressor has terminated. Indeed, the magnitude of the cortisol rise, as well as the time needed for normalization to occur, varies as a function of factors related to the stressor itself, such as its nature and severity, although it seems that there are some stressors (e.g., social defeat) that result in the duration of the corticosterone rise in rodents being relatively persistent (Audet et al., 2011). As well, in animals, these neuroendocrine changes vary as a function of the strain of animal examined, its sex (female rodents ordinarily exhibit a greater response), and age (older animals take longer to normalize following stressor termination), as well as the constellation of variables listed in Figure 4.3 that were discussed in Chapters 1 and 2.

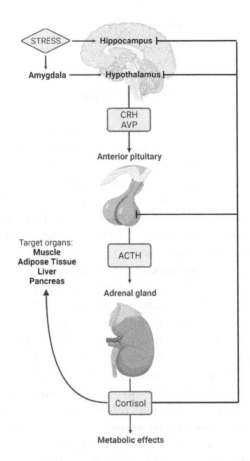

Figure 4.2   Stressors influence hypothalamic–pituitary–adrenal (HPA) functioning and regulation. Neuronal activation within the prefrontal cortex and aspects of the amygdala are elicited by stressors, which cause activation of neurons within the hypothalamus, resulting in corticotropin-releasing hormone (CRH) and arginine vasopressin (AVP) release. The CRH stimulates adrenocorticotropic hormone (ACTH) release from the anterior (front) portion of the pituitary gland, which enters the bloodstream. Upon reaching the adrenal glands (located just above the kidneys) the ACTH stimulates cortisol release into the bloodstream. Once in circulation, cortisol influences various target tissue, including muscles, adipose (fat) tissue, liver, and pancreas, and may also interact with other hormones. Upon reaching the brain, cortisol influences the hypothalamus and the hippocampus, so that CRH release is inhibited, and hence HPA activation is turned down. In essence, this reflects a self-regulating loop, wherein cortisol, the final product of the HPA activation, inhibits the functioning of CRH initiated the HPA cascade. The extent to which hormonal changes occur is determined by the type and characteristics of the stressor, a series of organismic variables, as well as the organism's previous experiences, including those that occurred prenatally and early in life. Lines with arrows denote excitatory processes; lines with blunted ends signify inhibitory processes.

Source: Created using BioRender.com.

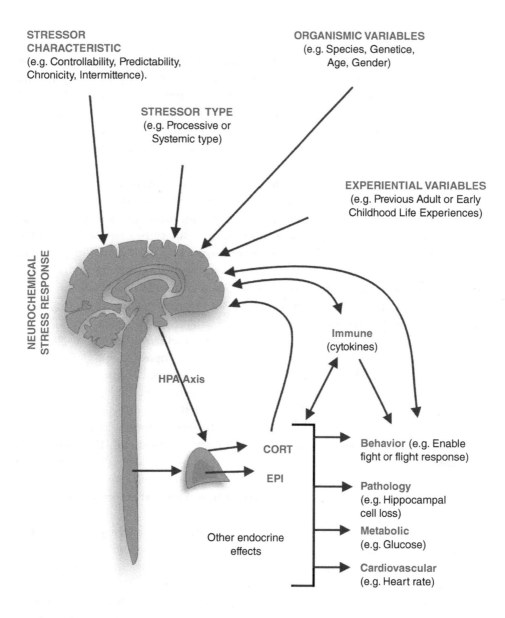

Figure 4.3 Activation of the HPA axis is associated with hormonal changes that can influence the multiple biological systems, body organs, and brain regions that will ultimately affect well-being. The extent to which hormonal changes occur is determined by the type and characteristics of the stressor, a series of organismic variables, as well as the organism's previous experiences, including those that occurred prenatally and early in life.

What cortisol does for us

Cortisol has numerous positive actions, many of which are not evident for some time following the stressor (e.g., an hour or so). Among its many regulatory actions, cortisol increases blood sugar through gluconeogenesis in the liver and in muscle (this simply means the production of glucose from substrates such as lactate and glycogen). In addition, cortisol aids in the metabolism of fats, carbohydrates, and proteins, and limits immune over-activation that might otherwise occur in response to stressors. Owing to some of these actions, glucocorticoid-acting agents are widely used clinically (e.g., hydrocortisone, prednisone, prednisolone, and dexamethasone). In low doses they are used to treat Addison's disease (a condition, as we saw earlier, where the adrenal glands do not make sufficient cortisol), and because of its immunosuppressive effects at high doses, they are used to suppress inflammatory responses. Cortisol is also utilized to manage disorders in which the immune system attacks certain parts of the self (rheumatoid arthritis is an example of one of these autoimmune disorders) as well as to prevent tissue rejection following an organ transplant and in graft-versus-host disease (where the transplanted tissue, the graft, attacks the recipient or host).

Although cortisol is often thought of uniquely in terms of the HPA axis, it affects neuronal functioning in several brain regions. For example, chronic glucocorticoid elevation increased the release of peptides (bombesin and corticotrophin releasing hormone) in stress-sensitive brain regions, such as the prefrontal cortex and amygdala (Merali et al., 2008). Corticosterone activation of neuronal activity at the amygdala has diverse effects, including changes in visceral and somatic pain sensitivity among female rodents, and these effects varied with the estrus cycle, possibly owing to interactions with ovarian hormones. Glucocorticoid stimulation of the prefrontal cortex can enhance memory consolidation (Shields et al., 2016), a process in which short-term memories are firmed up so that they become part of our long-term memory.

Glucocorticoids have been described as having several primary actions tied to stressful experiences (Sapolsky et al., 2000). They may allow for the effects of other stressor-provoked hormonal changes to occur or be amplified (permissive actions). Specifically, glucocorticoids may permit the effects of other hormones (e.g., epinephrine and norepinephrine) to be expressed. Likewise, this combination of hormones may be involved in the release of free fatty acids and hence energy availability, or in allowing certain types of immunological factors to affect cells in our body. In addition to the permissive actions, glucocorticoid release in response to stressors may suppress the actions of other hormones. Glucocorticoids may limit or suppress the actions of still other systems, such as immune functioning, to prevent adverse effects that might develop with excessive immune activity. Importantly, it seems that the function of corticosterone under normal conditions (in the absence of a stressor) and that associated with a response to a stressor might differ.

Not only are glucocorticoids essential during a stress reaction, but they act to set the stage so that the organism is prepared to deal with an impending stressor (preparative changes). In a sense, this points to the plasticity or malleability of this system, as it implies that the basal state may be altered in anticipation of forthcoming events. We know that these types of changes can occur in animals that had previously encountered stressors, including those experienced during early life, and it seems that when encountered repeatedly, corticoid functioning may be diminished (suppressive).

In animals, the corticosterone changes are exquisitely sensitive to stressors, and various characteristics regarding the glucocorticoid changes have been described in remarkable detail, including the short- and long-term benefits that are derived (Joëls et al., 2018). Although factors related to the appraisal of stressors are fundamental in determining the corticosterone response, the contribution of variables, such as stressor controllability, in governing this response, is more complex. When an animal is first confronted by a novel stressor, there is uncertainty as to whether this stressor will be brief or prolonged, and controllable or uncontrollable. Adaptive biological systems can't sit around idly waiting for the brain to figure out all the contingencies of the situation, and often must react rapidly to deal with threats. It would be advantageous to mount a strong defensive response to maintain well-being, and then, as information is acquired regarding the characteristics of the stressor, it might be appropriate for this neuroendocrine response to be adjusted accordingly.

Mineralocorticoids

In addition to glucocorticoids, another class of corticoid exists, referred to as mineralocorticoids, which have their own receptors (MR). The MRs were historically linked to the retention of sodium in the body and were not typically associated with stress responses, although we now know that they are influenced by stressful events and have implications for stress-related pathology. For instance, MRs are present within the hippocampus, where they temper (or balance) the effects of glucocorticoid receptor activation and may also affect hippocampal neuronal activity. Likewise, early in a stress response, when corticosterone levels are at their peak, MR activation occurs, resulting in hippocampal neuronal excitation that could potentially be important for other stress responses (ter Heegde et al., 2015). Illnesses that have been associated with stressors, such as metabolic syndrome (characterized by obesity and insulin resistance) and diabetes, are tied to the elevated production and release of aldosterone (a hormone that is part of the mineralocorticoid family) from the adrenal gland, which contributes to sodium levels, water retention, and blood pressure (Faught & Vijayan, 2018). As a result, MR stimulation may be associated with cardiac problems (heart failure and hypertension).

Chronic stressors

Adaptation-like effects may occur in response to chronic stressors so that the corticosterone response is less pronounced. Ordinarily, the adaptation occurs fairly readily if the stressor is the same on each occasion, whereas the adaptation occurs slowly, if at all, when the stressor occurs on an intermittent, unpredictable basis, and when the nature of the stressor varies (Anisman et al., 2008). Although the corticosterone response diminished with repeated exposure to a given stressor, if animals were then exposed to a novel stressor the increased corticosterone response was again evident, and in some instances was even exaggerated. It seems that the adaptation that occurs is specific to certain events or stimuli and might not reflect the diminished biological processes associated with corticosterone release, but instead represents an adaptation that is unique to specific events or cues. What these findings tell us is that even if it appears as if the organism has 'adapted' to stressor experiences, this is not fully accurate and vulnerability to exaggerated neuroendocrine changes, as well as behavioral disturbances, may be elevated.

In considering the influence of glucocorticoids on behavioral and physical well-being, it is not enough to simply examine levels of this hormone but also to determine the effects on the glucocorticoid receptors that are ordinarily stimulated. The receptors are present on virtually all organs and tissues, and if their sensitivity is altered, the effects of cortisol will be altered accordingly. As it happens, in response to chronic stressors glucocorticoid receptors are 'down-regulated', meaning that they are less responsive to the effects of cortisol. Thus, the beneficial actions that would ordinarily be produced by the hormone may be lost. For instance, following chronic stressor experiences, vulnerability to the common cold may be elevated, seemingly because the immune response has been altered. Under normal conditions, cortisol limits immune activity as well as inflammatory responses. With the down-regulated glucocorticoid response, immune activation may be unleashed to a degree, which could potentially influence infection after exposure to the cold virus (Cohen et al., 2012). However, with sustained stressor experiences chronic inflammation may also be provoked, which may contribute to numerous serious diseases, such as type 2 diabetes and heart disease. Thus, the down-regulation of glucocorticoid receptors may promote broad health risks. It should be added that glucocorticoids interact with many other hormonal and brain neurochemical processes that may influence multiple diseases.

Tracing the past through your hair

The release of cortisol following stressor exposure, typically determined in blood or saliva, persists for a matter of minutes, and in some cases hours. But hair can be used to measure more distal stressor experiences or to track stressful periods over weeks or months. Cortisol accumulates in hair, and as hair grows at about 1 cm a month, by assessing cortisol in snippets of hair a diary of cortisol (and hence stressor experiences) can be determined (Khoury et al., 2019). This is a relatively novel approach that holds promise for studies assessing the link between cortisol and a variety of stress-related pathologies. Even after controlling for several other pertinent factors, elevated levels of hair cortisol predicted the risk of acute myocardial infarction and were linked to prenatal stressful experiences.

Prenatal and early postnatal events influence the corticosterone response

Stressful events experienced by a pregnant female rodent or human can have multiple effects on the offspring. In Chapter 12 we'll be discussing the intergenerational effects of stressors, including corticosterone variations introduced by prenatal stressors, so we won't cover this topic here. However, consider that stressing a rat while she is pregnant results in elevated levels of corticosterone in both the mother and the fetus. This, in turn, results in further downstream effects, including structural changes within stress-sensitive brain regions. Given the fundamental involvement of these areas in cognitive and behavioral processes, a variety of disorders may be observed in the offspring, such as attention and learning deficits, as well as a disposition toward anxiety and depression, and it has been suggested that the risk for schizophrenia is elevated. Essentially, by promoting excessive prenatal levels of glucocorticoids, the programming of fetal neurons may be altered, thereby affecting behavior throughout the life span. As we'll see, these effects are subject to moderation by genetic factors and the postnatal environment, including the care that pups receive from their mother.

Stressors encountered early in life may have profound long-term ramifications on well-being in response to later challenges. These early experiences can change the developmental trajectory of stress-relevant processes so that biological reactivity, including corticosterone changes elicited by subsequently encountered stressors, is altered in adulthood. Glucocorticoid receptor functioning may be influenced by epigenetic processes so that adult responses to stressors are affected (e.g., Szyf, 2011) and cognitive and emotional disturbances may be promoted (Chen & Baram, 2016).

Like early life, the juvenile (adolescent) period in rodents is highly stress-sensitive. Stressors experienced during this period have protracted ramifications on vulnerability to stressor-provoked neurochemical and behavioral changes in adulthood. The adolescent phase in rodents is exquisitely sensitive to stressors that involve social instability (e.g., changing cage mates on successive days) and may have more enduring effects than similar stressors experienced in adulthood.

Stressor-induced glucocorticoid effects in humans

Based on studies in animals, one would think that stressor-provoked corticoid elevations would be readily apparent in humans but this is not the case at all. In rodents, 200–300% increases of corticosterone are introduced simply by placing the animal in a novel environment, and 400–800% increases occur in response to relatively strong stressors. In humans, by contrast, the effects of stressors are far less marked. The anticipation of heart surgery, for instance, only caused a cortisol increase of about 30–50%, academic exams typically were not associated with cortisol elevations or the elevations were limited, and only half the graduate students assessed immediately before their thesis oral exams showed elevated cortisol levels, even though virtually all reported high levels of anxiety. The effects of other naturally occurring stressors have likewise been associated with limited cortisol changes (Michaud et al., 2008). Yet, cortisol levels can be elevated in association with certain types of stressors, including a threat to an individual's social identity, such as sexism or racial discrimination (Matheson et al., 2019), and under conditions where shame (or anger) was elicited (Dickerson & Kemeny, 2004).

Cortisol changes associated with laboratory stressors

Several basic approaches have been used to determine cortisol changes elicited by stressors in humans within a laboratory context. These entail responses to a challenge that may or may not include reminders of previous stressor experiences (auditory or visual representations, or written scripts). Such paradigms may be associated with cortisol variations, but the magnitude of these effects is typically modest. The most common stressor paradigm is one that involves public speaking in front of a small panel of judges followed by a verbal arithmetic test. This paradigm, known as the Trier Social Stress Test, or the TSST (Kirschbaum et al., 1993), promotes an increase of cortisol in blood or saliva within 10–15 minutes and returns to basal levels in less than one hour. The extent of the reported rise varies across studies, ranging from 40 to 100%, although increases of high as 200–300% have been reported. Predictably, the extent of the cortisol rise varied with several factors known to influence stress responses, such as previous stressful experiences, and among women it can be moderated by whether they were using oral contraceptives, and as a function of their menstrual cycle (Foley & Kirschbaum, 2010).

It might seem curious that this relatively contrived laboratory stressor would promote greater cortisol elevations than the anticipation of real-life stressors, such as open-heart surgery or the distress among students preceding their thesis oral exam. So, what does this mean? It is hardly likely that open heart surgery is appraised as being less stressful than the TSST (even though public speaking can be terrifying), but these findings suggest that there's more to the cortisol response than just the potential threat associated with the stressor. Multiple differences exist between the TSST and a stressor such as impending surgery. Participants in the TSST are typically unaware of what the test will be like before they get to the experimental setting and hence have no opportunity to prepare themselves, whereas surgery patients will usually have been forewarned about the procedures and some degree of 'adaptation' may have occurred. Importantly, cortisol levels in the TSST were determined in blood (or saliva) taken *after* the stressor test, whereas in the case of heart surgery or an academic oral examination, blood samples were taken before (i.e., in anticipation of) the primary stressor. Predictably, the cortisol response may depend on an individual's anticipation that an expected stressor would not be overly aversive and that they could deal with it (Pulopulos et al., 2020).

It seems that the cortisol response in the TSST may be tied to particular emotions that were elicited. It was suggested that social-evaluative threats (e.g., when there is an audience appraising the person being stressed) may give rise to emotions, such as shame, that is particularly effective in provoking cortisol elevations (Dickerson & Kemeny, 2004). Elevated cortisol levels occur in other situations that elicited shame and/or anger (e.g., when women who had been abused were provided with reminders of the abuse). In the latter case, however, only anger accounted for the unique variance; shame was related to the anger, but once the influence of anger was accounted for statistically, the contribution of shame was negligible (Matheson & Anisman, 2012). This doesn't mean that shame was not involved, as it might have promoted the self-directed anger ('I'm so embarrassed I can't stand myself – I'd like to just kick myself around the block') that was ultimately responsible for the cortisol response.

Previous experiences influence the cortisol changes elicited by laboratory challenges

As many serious stressors involve a chronic component as well as worry or rumination secondary to the threat, it is necessary to consider whether acute and chronic stressors have different effects. Although the cortisol rise associated with acute stressors has multiple adaptive attributes, sustained release of the hormone, as we discussed earlier, may have adverse consequences. Therefore, it might be a good thing that some of the neuroendocrine responses elicited by acute stressors are limited or diminished following chronic challenges (Michaud et al., 2008).

The down-regulated HPA response associated with certain stressor experiences was evident in response to certain pharmacological challenges in previously traumatized individuals. It turns out that these studies are exceptionally informative from a broad perspective concerning how stressors operate. Ordinarily, when a person is injected with CRH, a rise of ACTH is evident in blood. However, the ACTH release in response to a CRH challenge was less evident among depressed women who had been abused when they were young, indicating that their HPA functioning was down-regulated. Of particular significance, when these women were placed in a situation that elicited a social evaluative threat (the Trier Social Stress test), their HPA response was exaggerated (Heim et al., 2008). It was likewise observed that among women who had experienced psychological and/or physical abuse in a dating relationship, cortisol levels were low if they exhibited posttraumatic stress disorder (PTSD) symptoms. However, when these women were presented with reminders of their abuse, their cortisol levels increased markedly, particularly among those who exhibited the highest PTSD scores (Matheson & Anisman, 2012). In effect, despite down-regulated HPA functioning, in the presence of a *meaningful* stressor, an exaggerated cortisol response occurs.

Intuitively, these data make sense. Following trauma, individuals might become hyper-reactive to environmental cues that were potentially stressful, but if HPA activation was engendered by every aversive stimulus encountered, then the system would become overly taxed (allostatic overload), and pathology would be more likely to occur. Thus, it would be advantageous for HPA down-regulation to occur to prevent excessive cortisol release. Yet it would be counterproductive for the HPA system to be down-regulated all of the time, as activation of this system might occasionally be necessary. Thus, the cues that are particularly relevant or those that elicit strong emotional responses might effectively promote the activation of the brain regions (e.g., the prefrontal cortex or amygdala) involved in stressor-appraisal processes, which would then influence HPA functioning, essentially overriding the down-regulation that would otherwise occur.

Cortisol as a marker of illness vulnerability

The cortisol rise (or that of other hormones) observed in response to stressors brings up another issue. Specifically, if one wanted to predict the potential for illness based on hormone levels, it might be sufficient simply to measure the basal levels of a hormone and use this to predict who might (or might not) develop a pathology. However, what hormone levels are like under basal conditions might be very different from those evident in response to a challenge. As a result, it would be propitious to measure the basal levels of a hormone, and then apply a challenge and determine (a) the extent to which the hormone level changed, and (b) how long it took for the hormone level to normalize (i.e., return to basal levels). Presumably, the hormonal release should drop off quickly once a threat is no longer present, and thus sustained activation might be indicative of a system that is not working optimally and might thus be predictive of the potential for pathological outcomes.

Let's examine this in another context to illustrate why biological responses should be measured after a challenge. In assessing heart health, a doctor can simply examine an individual's heart rate and blood pressure, which will provide some good information (e.g., do they have hypertension). Better information can be obtained when an electrocardiogram (ECG) is used in conjunction with an index of blood pressure. Even more revealing information can be derived when a load or challenge is placed on the system, for instance by having the patient run on a treadmill (termed a 'stress test') during which measures are taken when the system is being strained and how long it takes for heart rate and blood pressure to normalize. Essentially, when a load (strain) is placed on the system a better index can be obtained concerning how the organ (or specific biochemical) is doing and perhaps how it will function in the near future.

The morning cortisol response in relation to stressful experiences

Like other hormones, cortisol levels vary over a 24-hour period (circadian rhythm). Levels are relatively high in the morning and then decline over the day, eventually reaching their nadir around midnight, before climbing to the high levels seen on awakening. Superimposed on this rhythm is an interesting change that is relevant to the influence of stressors. Circulating cortisol levels typically rise over the first

30 minutes following awakening (a 40% increase is typical when measured in saliva) and will then decline rapidly. The early morning cortisol rise is particularly great among individuals dealing with ongoing or recent stressors (Schmidt-Reinwald et al., 1999), such as job strain, or among those individuals who perceive their life circumstances as being hopeless (Schlotz et al., 2004).

In contrast to the cortisol profile associated with moderate stressors, among individuals who had experienced a traumatic stressor that led to PTSD, as well as under conditions of excessive or prolonged strain (e.g., job-related burnout or fatigue, exhaustion related to distress), the diurnal hormone profile might be flattened (i.e., the morning cortisol levels are reduced, and evening levels are elevated). As described earlier, excessive cortisol release over extended periods could have adverse effects, including hippocampal cell loss, and the down-regulated morning HPA response might be adaptive, limiting the negative outcomes that might otherwise occur.

─Case study 4.1─

Probing in the dark

Rebecca was a young researcher interested in determining the biological processes by which stressful events might come to favor the development of diseases. Unfortunately, it was the 1970s, and the existing data concerning neurochemical changes induced by stressors were sparse, leaving her perplexed as to where she should begin her research. She had heard that physicists facing such dilemmas sometimes engaged in 'thought experiments'. Physicists, she believed, were very smart and if thought experiments worked for them, perhaps she could do the same.

The strategy she adopted to guide her work was to imagine how adaptive biological systems ought to act and how these would change across situations. Or to put this another way, if she was Nature or God, how would she develop a system so that it would be most effective in dealing with challenges? At the time, this seemed like a nifty idea ('nifty' is a word from that era), although it was doomed from the beginning for many reasons, least of all that limited knowledge was available about how the brain worked, as well as about how chemical messengers were produced, what receptors entailed, and there was exceptionally little knowledge about the many other components that were fundamental for brain functioning. She devised numerous evolutionary models as to how adaptive systems ought to work and then determined whether the existent data fit the models. At every turn, she discovered that nature was, in fact, much more inventive, intuitive, and thoughtful in creating ways of protecting animals and humans relative to her best plans. The down-regulated HPA system at baseline and the hyper-reactivity in response to relevant stimuli are examples of processes that she hadn't even considered.

The notion that multiple systems might act cooperatively with one another was part of her thinking and she had even figured that communication might occur between the brain

(Continued)

and the immune system, but she had no clue as to what mechanisms might be involved. At that time the notion that the brain and immune system interacted was considered heretical and she was reluctant to wade into waters whose currents were uncertain. Her colleagues had cautioned her that if she supported this view, she would be seen as conducting 'soft science' and her research wouldn't be supported by granting institutions. In the end, she opted to play it safe and conducted traditional basic science that moved forward in increments, but she deeply felt that her earlier thinking had been on the right track. Surely, events in nature didn't happen by chance as she knew from research related to evolution, so there had to be ways to predict the course of adaptive stress responses. She took solace when she read a comment made by Einstein in which he suggested that things in nature don't just happen by accident. He had famously said that 'God doesn't play dice with the universe'. Then again, she thought that her colleagues were not unreasonable in suggesting the corollary that 'only an idiot would try to play God'.

Corticotropin releasing-hormone (CRH)

Stressor effects on CRH functioning

In addition to being a fundamental regulator of the HPA system, CRH has actions beyond those involving the hypothalamus. Indeed, CRH and its receptors are key players in the stress response at several other brain sites, including the prefrontal cortex and amygdala, regions that are associated with cognitive and emotional responses. The extrahypothalamic activity of CRH may directly influence behavioral outputs or may do so by influencing still other neurochemical processes. CRH may regulate a subpopulation of neurons within the raphe nucleus, a region in the hindbrain that is the site of cell bodies for neurons that send their trajectories to the hippocampus and frontal cortex. This promotes the release of the neurotransmitter serotonin at terminal regions, which can influence behavioral disturbances. Likewise, the infusion of CRH into the locus coeruleus (a site of norepinephrine cell bodies within the brainstem) increases forebrain norepinephrine neuronal activity, whereas drugs that block CRH receptors (antagonists) attenuated these effects. These data raise the possibility that CRH has notable effects beyond its involvement in HPA functioning, and that the effect of CRH on behavior might involve a series of diverse biochemical changes. The prefrontal cortical regions and the hippocampus play an essential role in appraisals, decision-making, and memory, and one might suspect that stressors might have some effects by altering CRH and other neurotransmitters at these sites.

What does mRNA expression mean?

Analyses of hormones, such as corticosterone and CRH and their receptors, have often relied on analyses of the activity of genes that code for these substances. You'll recall that genes comprise lengthy stretches of DNA that contain the code for the eventual production of an individual's many phenotypes. The DNA serves as a template or blueprint to produce RNA, which occurs through a process called transcription. In a series of steps, a type of RNA (messenger RNA or mRNA) is formed that carries the code for the production of specific proteins, such as CRH. In theory, the more mRNA that code for a particular protein, the more of that protein is synthesized. However, this isn't always the case and thus it is often not sufficient simply to measure mRNA expression, but needs to be backed up by a demonstration that the protein levels have actually changed. Statements such as 'expression of CRH mRNA is increased' mean that an experimental treatment has the *potential* of increasing the synthesis of the CRH protein. Some genes are continually transcribed (constitutive genes), whereas others are transcribed as needed (facultative genes), for example, in response to environmental change. The stressor-induced changes of CRH mRNA expression are an example of an environmental event triggering the transcription of a specific gene.

Fear and anxiety

Fear and anxiety related to activation of the amygdala are often thought of as negative emotions, especially if these emotions are strong. However, in many instances in which fear and anxiety are moderate, they may have important survival functions, keeping individuals alert and apprehensive in the face of potential threats. Fear and anxiety are essential parts of the defensive or survival repertoire, and events or brain changes that impede these processes may have severe negative repercussions on an organism's ability to survive.

Although the terms 'fear' and 'anxiety' are frequently used interchangeably, they are distinct from one another. Fear is a directed emotion that is elicited in response to stimuli that have been paired with an aversive experience (i.e., when individuals fear some things or places). Anxiety, in contrast, is usually elicited by diffuse stimuli (e.g., a general environmental context, but anxiety can be independent of prior experiences) or it can reflect a free-floating emotion, or one that is felt in anticipation of a threatening event. Stressors increase CRH production and release within the amygdala leading to such stressor-provoked emotions. In this respect, different aspects of the amygdala, notably the central, medial, and basolateral portions may be differentially involved in the acquisition, expression, or extinction of a fear response (LeDoux, 2000). Moreover, although psychogenic and systemic stressors (the presence of inflammation) induce many similar effects, their actions on amygdala functioning are not identical as they seem to engage different aspects of this region. Whereas systemic stressors markedly influence central amygdala activity, psychogenic stressors have more potent effects on the medial amygdala.

It also seems that fear and anxiety involve the activation of CRH neurons within different aspects of the amygdala and related regions. Whereas fear-eliciting stimuli increase CRH expression within the various portions of the amygdala, diffuse stimuli that promote general anxiety are more closely aligned with CRH variations that occur within extended aspects of the amygdala, such as the bed nucleus of the stria terminalis (BNST), which is a major output pathway that runs from the amygdala to the hypothalamus. The activity of neurons within the BNST may be particularly important in governing responses to spatially or temporally distant challenges (Klumpers et al., 2017).

Finally, the mechanisms involved in fear/anxiety reactions might depend on the presence of particular environmental triggers. Specifically, numerous psychogenic (e.g., learned fear cues) and neurogenic (physical) stressors provoke CRH release from amygdala neurons and, conversely, the anxiety associated with these treatments can be attenuated by agents that antagonize CRH receptors. However, anxiety elicited by a naturalistic stressor (e.g., exposure to an unfamiliar environment), which might involve pre-wired neural circuits, was not altered by CRH antagonists. It was thus suggested that anxiety associated with a naturalistic stressor might involve processes other than, or in addition to, CRH (Merali et al., 2004). Evidently, while the amygdala contributes to stressor-elicited emotions, not all aspects of the amygdala act in the same way in response to varied challenges and may have different implications for the behavioral and emotional responses that emerge. Moreover, fear and anxiety may be moderated by frontocortical regions that are responsive to uncertain threats (Hur et al., 2020). These findings, and others like them, raise the possibility that anxiety disorders may involve diverse mechanisms and that treatment strategies to diminish anxiety ought to consider the nature of the stressor encountered – is it a learned stress response or one that engages pre-wired systems?

CRH receptors

Correspondence might be expected between the amount of hormone or neurotransmitter present and specific emotional or behavioral outcomes, as we described in discussing cortisol. However, the functional effectiveness of hormones and neurotransmitters depends upon whether they successfully trigger specific receptors that instigate downstream biological effects. In this regard, a given hormone can stimulate several receptors and their activation may have consequences that might be very different from one another. Moreover, stressors can promote hormonal changes that preferentially activate certain receptor subtypes. Analyzing the effects of various treatments on behavioral outcomes is not only a matter of measuring the levels, synthesis, or release of a neurochemical but necessitates the examination of which receptors were stimulated. If this weren't difficult enough, the behavior of the receptors may be influenced by the presence of still other receptor types (i.e., receptor–receptor interactions may occur) or the actions of other neurotransmitters.

Consistent with the view that CRH activation was directly linked to elevated anxiety, administration of a CRH receptor antagonist attenuated the depression-like behavior provoked by an uncontrollable stressor (Dedic et al., 2018). Moreover, in mice that had been genetically engineered so that the expression of CRH receptors was altered (elevated or reduced), changes of anxiety and depressive-like behaviors were apparent, but this varied with which of the primary CRH receptors, CRH_1 and

CRH_2, was influenced. Mice that overproduced CRH had higher levels of anxiety, whereas reduced anxiety was seen in mice with the CRH_1 receptors deleted, and diminished anxiety was elicited when the CRH_1 receptor was antagonized pharmacologically (Lu et al., 2008). Such findings suggested that CRH_1 receptor expression in limbic forebrain regions may be especially pertinent to the development of anxiety states.

Evidence regarding the involvement of CRH_2 receptors in anxiety is less extensive than that associated with CRH_1 receptors. It initially appeared that the contribution of CRH_2 to the promotion of anxiety was limited, but it has since been shown that when CRH_2 receptors were knocked out, elevated anxiety was apparent, particularly among males. Studies in double mutants (where both the CRH_1 and CRH_2 were knocked out) indicated that both receptors may influence anxiety, and that early experiences, especially those related to maternal care, moderated the actions of these receptors. As seen with numerous other hormone responses, the effects observed in males and females were different from one another, suggesting that anxiety was mediated by more than just specific CRH receptor subtypes.

The involvement or interactions between CRH_1 and CRH_2 in anxiety has yet to be fully deduced and is further complicated by the actions of CRH in diverse brain regions that contribute to anxiety (Dedic et al., 2018), as well as the involvement of other neurotransmitters. This caveat notwithstanding, the two CRH receptor subtypes might influence different components of anxiety. For instance, CRH_1 may be fundamental in regulating explicit processes, including attention, executive functions, the conscious experience of emotions, and even learning about these emotions. In contrast, CRH_2 might contribute mainly to the implicit processes necessary for survival, largely involving motivated behaviors such as eating, reproduction, and defense. In this regard, CRH and downstream effects that are provoked are intricately related to both anxiety and eating processes (Sominsky & Spencer, 2014), and it has been considered that patients presenting with anxiety and depression might benefit most from drug treatments that antagonize CRH_1 receptors, whereas patients with eating disorders would be best served by drugs targeted at CRH_2.

It is typically thought that basic emotional responses are dictated by subcortical circuits that are innately driven. In an intriguing discussion of consciousness related to emotional experiences, it was maintained that higher cortical structures interpret unconscious feelings into conscious emotional experiences and memories of these experiences (LeDoux & Brown, 2017). In response to an immediate threat, activation of innate fear and defensive survival circuits involving the amygdala are instantly activated. Concurrently, processing of the threat occurs through several cortical circuits, including the visual cortex, those related to memory processes, and the complex systems that govern cognitive processes associated with appraisals (e.g., anterior cingulate cortex and aspects of the orbital frontal cortex and prefrontal cortex). The model presented by LeDoux and Brown is far more complex and detailed than we have provided here. Suffice for the moment that by incorporating diverse processes in relation to unconscious and conscious experiences of fear (and other emotions) it becomes possible to make sense of different forms of fear, anxiety, and the dread that may be experienced in response to existential threats.

Stress, energy balances, and eating to cope

A great number of hormonal and environmental factors influence eating-related behaviors. The circadian cycle plays a prominent role in this regard; eating tends to occur at prescribed times, in part prompted by various hormonal changes that occur over the course of the day. Added to this, specific environmental stimuli, such as the smell of freshly baked bread or a smoked meat sandwich, will rouse appetite, and some good-looking carbohydrate rich foods are tempting even when a large meal has just been eaten. The presence of danger will have the opposite effect on the inclination to eat. Whether it's elk, deer, rodents, or even grasshoppers,

Table 4.4 Hormones related to energy regulation and eating.

Secreted hormone	Biological effect
Corticotropin-releasing hormone (CRH)	Formed in the paraventricular nucleus of the hypothalamus. In addition to being fundamental to stress responses, it diminishes food intake and increases metabolic rate.
Cortisol (Corticosterone)	Released from the adrenal gland it is the prototypical stress hormone; also stimulates caloric intake and may promote a preference for high calorie foods under stressful circumstances (stimulates the consumption of comfort foods).
Leptin	Produced by fat cells: reduces food intake, and is involved in changes in brain cytokines.
Ghrelin	Produced in gut: serves to stimulate increased eating; may affect reward processes; modulates stress responses.
Insulin	Produced in the pancreas: involved in getting glucose from the blood into various body cells and storing it as glycogen; regulates fat and carbohydrate metabolism.
Bombesin (in humans neuromedin B [NMB] and gastrin-releasing peptide [GRP])	Produced in gut and in several brain regions: acts as a satiety peptide (signals when an individual is full) and promotes anxiety.
Neuropeptide Y (NPY)	Hypothalamic hormone: increases food intake and reduces physical activity; increases energy stored in the form of fat; blocks nociceptive (noxious) signals to the brain; increases vasoconstrictor actions of norepinephrine.

when a predator is in the vicinity, the search for food diminishes and animals tend to eat less. For that matter, for nocturnal eaters, such as rodents, the amount of food consumed is lower on clear moon-lit than on dark nights, possibly reflecting the danger of exposing themselves to predators. Apparently, hard-wired biological processes might exist across species so that the danger cues that elicit vigilance and anxiety/fear diminish the search for food, with the result that it's less likely that these animals will become some other critter's supper.

There's good reason to suppose that appetitive and aversive systems act in opposition to one another so that when an individual is stressed, the resulting CRH release that encourages defensive behaviors might also inhibit eating or other processes related to reward systems, but this depends on the nature or severity of the stressor. In the next chapter, we'll be covering the actions of neurotransmitters, such as dopamine (DA), which are integral to feelings of reward and pleasure. It seems that in response to an acute moderate stressor the release of CRH and the excitation of CRH_1 and CRH_2 receptors promote the release of DA at the nucleus accumbens, possibly making rewards more salient, and could thus lead to increased consumption of tasty foods. However, if the stressor was relatively intense, the effect on DA was abolished. This switch in the CRH–DA relationship was accompanied by a shift in reaction to CRH from one that was associated with appetitive responses to one that was in line with more common emotional responses to aversive stimuli (Abizaid, 2019).

Given the intersection between eating and stress processes, the section that follows describes some of the hormones implicated in energy regulation and stress responses (see Table 4.4). Moreover, in Chapter 11, we will be discussing the possibility that eating can be a coping mechanism among some individuals, and it appears that in many ways eating shares some of the characteristics related to substance use disorders.

I eat when I'm stressed

We've likely all heard someone say, 'I eat when I'm stressed', sometimes mumbled through a mouthful of cake or slobber of ice cream. There's selectivity, however, as to what's eaten when a person is stressed. You'll just never hear anyone say, 'I'm really stressed out. I think I'll have a nice celery stick.' What we're looking for in response to moderate distress are comfort foods. It could be that these make us feel better, and in this sense, such foods act as a way of coping. Alternatively, there may be chemical changes in the brain and body that are activated by stressors that drive us to crave comfort foods. It is equally possible that the fast caloric fix provided by sugars and carbohydrates, and the ensuing biological changes instigated by these comfort foods, are responsible for providing sufficient energy to keep animals one step ahead of predators and may facilitate coping with psychological stressors. It seems that eating comfort foods essentially reflects the brain's attempt to reduce the activity of a chronic stress-response network that would otherwise promote anxiety.

It had been suggested that with continued distress, the persistently high concentrations of glucocorticoids contribute to eating changes (Dallman, 2010), which may be tied

(Continued)

to an individual's disposition to eat when stressed. Specifically, the glucocorticoid eleva-tions cause an increase of CRH activity within the central amygdala, promoting strong emotional responses, thereby setting other stress systems in play. Glucocorticoids are also important in stimulating caloric intake, and in the presence of insulin may contrib-ute to the preference for high calorie foods, especially under stressful circumstances. Essentially, the glucocorticoid increase elevates the salience of pleasurable or compulsive activities (ingesting sucrose, fat, drugs), so that comfort foods promote greater hedonic responses than they would otherwise. While that might sound appealing, glucocorticoids are involved in the redistribution of stored energy (fat) so that it appears as abdominal fat depots, which contain inflammatory factors whose release promote a variety of illnesses. In fact, given the link between stress, cortisol, eating, and metabolic processes, these fac-tors might contribute to the current obesity epidemic and the many health disturbances that follow.

Leptin, ghrelin, insulin, bombesin, and neuropeptide Y involvement in eating

The discovery of the hormone leptin has been considered among the most sig-nificant research findings in the field of energy balance. Produced primarily by adipocytes (fat cells), this hormone enters circulation following a meal, and then, by affecting the brain and peripheral organs, reduces further food intake. Multiple efforts were made to use leptin manipulations to reduce obesity, but these have largely been unsuccessful. Yet, with new approaches that are being developed the promise for leptin-based strategies in curbing obesity and related diseases may be rejuvenated (Zhao et al., 2019).

As well as affecting metabolic processes, leptin influences HPA axis activity and the release of neurotransmitters such as serotonin (5-HT) and dopamine (Fulton et al., 2006) and might thereby influence the effects of stressors on processes related to reward and mood. In fact, by virtue of effects on neurochemical systems, leptin influences reward-seeking behaviors and may influence affective tone related to feeding.

Several hormones have been found to promote the initiation of eating. When elevated, both ghrelin and neuropeptide Y are associated with increased food con-sumption (Abizaid & Horvath, 2008). Ordinarily, the levels of ghrelin increase just before mealtime, presumably signaling us to eat (or act as a preparatory response for the food we're about to eat), and then decline after we've eaten. A disturbance of ghrelin functioning can have adverse effects related to energy and feeding pro-cesses. For instance, ghrelin levels are altered among women with clinical levels of eating disorders, being elevated in anorexia and bulimia nervosa, whereas binge eating is associated with decreased ghrelin. This doesn't necessarily mean that these hormones cause eating disorders, although they might be contributors.

As with other eating-related peptides, ghrelin activates dopamine neurons that are involved in reward processes and could thus be an intermediate step for the rewarding feelings derived from food (Abizaid, 2009). Eating was increased when ghrelin was injected directly into the ventral tegmental region of the brain, which is known to be involved in reward processes, whereas ghrelin antagonists had the opposite effect. Ghrelin also directly stimulates orexin cells in the lateral hypothalamus (orexin is a hormone that has been associated with food craving), as well as cells in several other hypothalamic nuclei. In humans, ghrelin administration increases food-related imagery and stimulates reward pathways, thereby implicating ghrelin in appetitive responses to incentive cues (i.e., the secondary stimuli that have been associated with reward) as well as the visual and olfactory stimuli that promote food cravings. Much like other hormones associated with eating processes, ghrelin may be an important factor that regulates stress responses and the connection between stressful experiences and obesity may be mediated by ghrelin changes (Abizaid, 2019).

In addition to leptin and ghrelin, mammalian analogues of the amphibian hormone bombesin (BB), namely neuromedin B (NMB) and gastrin-releasing peptide (GRP), contribute to the regulation of eating, essentially serving as a satiety signal just as leptin acts in this capacity. Several other peptides, notably glucagon-like peptide-1 (GLP-1), have similarly been tied to eating and energy regulation. Agents that stimulate GLP-1 activity (termed GLP-1 agonists) are most often used in the treatment of type-2 diabetes and have potent actions in facilitating weight loss (Zanchi et al., 2017).

Few readers don't know at least a little bit about insulin (e.g., it has something to do with diabetes). This hormone, like others we've discussed, is involved in the regulation of energy balances. Ordinarily, insulin's main job is one of regulating fat and carbohydrate metabolism, and it is necessary for various cells in the body to take up glucose from the blood, and to then store it as glycogen inside these tissues. In addition to these vital peripheral actions, insulin inhibits neuropeptide Y release from the arcuate nucleus of the hypothalamus, which has the effect of reducing food intake. Insulin interacts with glucocorticoids, as well as leptin and other regulatory hormones that have been implicated in the development of obesity and metabolic disturbances associated with chronic stressors (Zanchi et al., 2017).

There's no good news for those with metabolic syndrome

It's startling how little most people know about metabolic syndrome even though it increases the risk of numerous illnesses. Metabolic syndrome is characterized by increased fasting glucose, elevated blood pressure, high triglycerides, low levels of high-density lipoprotein cholesterol (HDL), and abdominal obesity. The syndrome has been progressively increasing over the past decades, now being present in more than 30% of people in the US and UK, but somewhat lower in most EU countries.

Metabolic syndrome, which is promoted by poor lifestyle habits (poor diet choices and limited exercise) and chronic stressful encounters, is accompanied by elevated visceral fat. The fat cells (adipocytes) release chemicals, such as those related to inflammatory

(Continued)

processes, that can have numerous adverse health consequences, including later development of type 2 diabetes, heart disease, and depression. If all this weren't bad enough, type 2 diabetes is accompanied by a doubling in the occurrence of Alzheimer's disease. Although this could just be a correlation and the two aren't causally related, it seems that insulin signaling might be relevant to the tau tangles and beta amyloid plaques that are characteristic of Alzheimer's disease.

Leptin, ghrelin, insulin, bombesin, and neuropeptide Y involvement in stress processes

Stressful events influence each of the peptides involved in feeding and energy regulation. In particular, leptin and ghrelin might be related to stress responses and contribute to stress-related pathologies, such as depression, or certain eating-related symptoms associated with depressive illness. The data from animal studies have shown that depressive-like behavioral disturbances provoked by a chronic stressor regimen could be antagonized by leptin administration. In contrast to these animal-based studies, leptin variations in relation to depression in humans have not been entirely consistent, and the factors that determine leptin levels in mood disorders have yet to be determined. Nonetheless, as leptin and ghrelin are tied to eating processes, it is possible that the neurovegetative features of depression, particularly the altered eating behaviors, might be linked to these hormones as well as inflammatory processes (Abizaid et al., 2013).

Paralleling the effects of leptin, it seems that bombesin-like peptides (neuromedin B and gastrin-releasing peptide) that act to trigger satiety can promote anxiety, whereas receptor antagonists had the opposite effect. These two peptides have not been examined as extensively as other stress and feeding hormones, but the changes associated with them and the conditions in which they are altered suggest that they are part of complex circuits that link appetitive and stress processes to one another (Moody & Merali, 2004). It also seems that bombesin influences the neurotransmitter serotonin in brain regions associated with emotional responses, including both anxiety and depression. Moreover, stressors provoked the release of bombesin-like peptides from the central amygdala leading to elevated ACTH release, which was attenuated by pretreatment with a CRH antagonist (Merali et al., 2013). As well, stressor exposure may increase 5-HT activity, but this outcome was absent in mice genetically engineered so that a form of the bombesin receptor was absent, supporting the view that bombesin processes are involved in this particular stress response.

Insulin is critical in energy-related processes and plays an essential role in response to acute stressors, acting to promote the mobilization of energy stores and uptake of glucose into cells that are necessary to deal with environmental challenges. However, with chronic exposure to stressors, insulin insensitivity may develop, possibly through glucocorticoid and inflammatory actions (Black, 2006).

This means that following sufficiently protracted stressor experiences, the effectiveness of insulin may be undermined (insulin resistance), thereby contributing to type 2 diabetes (Sharma & Singh, 2020).

When insulin changes are considered in the context of stress responses, the focus is typically placed on its secretion from the pancreas, which can account for the eating and obesity changes that occur. However, there's more to insulin's actions than just that. Dopamine neurons in the ventral tegmental area express insulin receptors, making it possible that insulin could thus affect the hedonic or pleasurable component of eating (Baik, 2021). Moreover, problematic over-eating might represent an altered balance (or a disconnect) between hypothalamic regulatory functioning and midbrain reward circuits that involve dopamine activity. Indeed, for problematic eating to persist, hormones that provide satiety signals, such as leptin and insulin, might have lost their ability to regulate the circuits that engender pleasure (Egecioglu et al., 2011).

Multiple processes regulate eating and energy balances

So why do we have so many systems involved in feeding initiation and feeding cessation? Wouldn't one have been enough? The fact is that each of the peptides has multiple functions, and their actions go beyond feeding or processes associated with stressors. Furthermore, simply because two peptides might be involved in initiating eating doesn't mean that their actions are identical. Feeding is more complex than knowing that you're hungry, putting stuff in your mouth, chewing for a while, and then swallowing. There are anticipatory responses that get the juices going so that eating will be facilitated, certain eating responses are tied to environmental cues that tell us it's time to eat (circadian clocks work in this capacity), and there are processes that coordinate eating responses with those involved in decision-making and stress. Of course, the actions of these various processes aren't perfect as many eating-related disturbances can occur, including anorexia, bulimia, emotional eating, binge eating, and the recent epidemic of other obesity-related conditions, such as metabolic disorder and diabetes.

Estrogen and testosterone

The greater prevalence of depression and anxiety disorders in women than in men might simply mean that women are 'more sensitive' to life experiences, and generally more likely to express these emotions, possibly owing to factors related to socialization. Alternatively, it might be that relative to men, women encounter more and greater stressors or life restrictions that favor the development of illness. Women tend to use emotion-focused coping to a greater degree (although not necessarily at the expense of problem-focused efforts), and some hormonal and neurochemical responses to stressors may be greater in women than in men. Particular attention has been devoted to the analysis of the impact of ovarian hormones in depression and anxiety (see Table 4.5). Studies in animals have shown that estradiol (the primary sex hormone present in women) can have a range of effects, including the modulation of several neurotransmitters within limbic brain regions (many of which are associated with emotion), and may influence HPA activity. Further, over the estrus cycle, several hormonal changes occur that can influence brain neuronal growth factors that have been implicated in depressive illness.

Table 4.5   Sex hormones and their effects.

Secreted hormone	Biological effect
Testosterone	Male steroid hormone produced in the testis in males and ovaries in females. Involved in the development and sexual differentiation of brain and reproductive organs, and is fundamental in secondary sexual features developing, including body hair, muscle, and bone mass.
Dehydroepiandrosterone (DHEA)	In males, produced in adrenals, gonads, and brain, and is involved in the production of androgens and estrogens. Has been implicated in maintaining youth.
Estrogens (estrone, estradiol, estriol)	Estradiol is predominant of the three estrogens produced in the ovaries; involved in female reproductive processes, sexual development; affects bone density, liver, arterial blood flow, and has multiple functions in brain; involved in protein synthesis, fluid balances, gastrointestinal functioning and coagulation, cholesterol levels, and fat depositions.
Progesterone	Formed in the ovary; precursor for several hormones; involved in triggering menstruation, and for maintaining pregnancy (e.g., inhibits immune response directed at embryo; reduces uterine smooth muscle contraction; inhibits lactation and the onset of labor); influences the resilience of various tissues (bones, joints, tendons, ligaments, skin).
Luteinizing hormone (LH)	Produced in the anterior pituitary gland. In females, an 'LH surge' triggers ovulation and development of the corpus luteum, an endocrine structure that develops from an ovarian follicle during the luteal phase of the estrous cycle. In males, LH stimulates leydig cells to produce testosterone.
Follicle-stimulating hormone (FSH)	Secreted by gonadotrophs of the anterior pituitary gland; regulates development, growth, pubertal maturation, and reproductive processes. With LH it acts synergistically in reproduction and ovulation.

Stress responses in males and females

In animal studies, sexual dimorphisms (differences in phenotypes as a function of sex) are apparent in neurobiological responses to stressors. Females were generally more behaviorally reactive to stressors than males, typically accompanied by greater stressor-related neuroendocrine changes, such as corticosterone, as well as differential activity of stress-relevant genes (Brivio et al., 2020). Moreover, neuronal activity is increased in numerous brain regions that govern behavioral and cognitive responses to stressors (e.g., frontal, cingulate, and piriform cortices, and the hippocampus, hypothalamic paraventricular nucleus, medial amygdala, and lateral septum), and the extent of the activation varies over the estrous cycle, implicating a role for sex hormones in determining these outcomes (Oyola & Handa, 2017).

In humans, the effects of stressors on hormonal processes vary in men and women, and sex-specific periods have been identified (e.g., during the decline of sex hormones following menopause) that were linked to increased occurrence of illnesses in women (Bale & Epperson, 2015). It similarly appears that the cortisol variations elicited by stressors vary over the estrous cycle, with the greatest responses in women occurring during the luteal phase (the latter part of the menstrual cycle during which the hormone progesterone is very high). As well, the effects of social stressors on cortisol levels in women are blunted among those using oral contraceptives, indicating interactions between stressors and estrogen in provoking the stress response. When estrogen levels are high (or following the administration of estradiol), stress responsiveness is reduced (Juster et al., 2016). Based on fMRI analyses of women, stress-arousing stimuli provoked especially marked neuronal activity in stress-relevant brain regions (amygdala, orbitofrontal cortex). These effects were more pronounced during the early follicular phase (prior to ovulation during which the follicles in the ovary mature and estrogen levels climb) compared with mid-cycle. It seems that estradiol acts as a brake on HPA axis functioning, whereas progesterone may result in disturbed negative glucocorticoid feedback. In effect, sex hormones in women influence the biological processes that govern stress responses and may thereby affect mood states (Dan et al., 2019). Immune responses elicited by stressors similarly vary, likely through actions of estrogen (Finnell et al., 2018), which might contribute to the huge female over-representation in the occurrence of most autoimmune disorders (e.g., multiple sclerosis, systemic lupus erythematosus).

No doubt numerous factors could account for the difference between cortisol responses in human males and females, including those related to the nature of the stressor encountered (intrapersonal stressors might have greater effects in females, whereas performance pressures have greater effects in males), earlier stressor experiences, and the appraisal/coping processes that might be instigated by the stressor in particular situations (Moisan, 2021).

Testosterone's bad rap

Testosterone is important for male development and several behaviors, but it has received a bad rap in other respects. Occasionally, macho guys are referred to derisively as 'Mr. Testosterone', and the link to aggression is usually used as a put-down. But of all of the nasty things said about testosterone, what cuts to the quick most are reports that testosterone disrupts collaborative behaviors and causes males to be egocentric (Wright et al., 2012). Specifically, it was reported that treatments that increased testosterone promoted behaviors that reduced the benefits that would be accrued by operating collaboratively with others. This seemed to be a result of individuals giving greater weight to their judgments relative to those of others (egocentric choices) during joint decision-making.

As you read this, you likely saw the term 'egocentric' as a pejorative. But this is how our biology works, possibly because there might be some benefit to it. There may be times when collaborative behaviors need to be balanced against those that are self-oriented, depending on the social environment. In a sense, this egocentrism may have high survival value for the individual, and under some circumstances may be beneficial for the group as a whole. As a result, testosterone-driven guys might be getting a bad rap, even though what they do might sometimes have positive attributes.

The primary sex hormone in males, testosterone, is formed in the testes, and to a limited extent is produced in the adrenal glands. As with HPA hormones, testosterone is influenced by hypothalamic and pituitary processes through a negative feedback mechanism. Testosterone is known to play a pivotal role in the production of male reproductive tissues and is involved in the development of secondary features, such as the growth of body hair, as well as muscle growth and bone density, and it is for the latter reasons that it has been abused by athletes. In addition, this hormone has been deemed important in dominance challenges and aggressive behaviors, as well as cognitive processes. The effects of stressors on testosterone have been inconsistent, but it does seem that levels of this hormone are particularly elevated in animals that had won in competitions or were higher in a dominance hierarchy.

Anabolic-androgenic steroids aren't a great bet in relation to health

Anabolic (tissue building) androgenic steroids (more commonly referred to as anabolic steroids) have become relatively popular in some circles, especially among some professional athletes. These agents have medical uses in low doses, but at higher doses have masculinizing effects, building greater muscles and hence improved strength and athletic performance. Of course, they don't only affect muscles in the arms and legs, they may also affect the heart muscles. Indeed, at one time it was maintained that these steroids could promote heart disease, but several systematic reviews indicated that exogenous use of testosterone in relatively young individuals did not increase the risk for myocardial infarction or stroke. However, other reviews suggested that the data, in general, were not compelling and subgroup analyses suggested adverse effects on cardiovascular disease in older individuals (Onasanya et al., 2016). Anabolic steroids may promote immune system problems, hypogonadism, and they don't do any favors for users' complexions.

It's not often talked about, but anabolic steroids affect the brain, as do virtually all hormones. These hormones interact with neurotransmitters and can influence brain connectivity related to emotions (particularly anxiety) and could potentially affect cognitive functioning (e.g., Votinov et al., 2020). Increasingly, the use of anabolic steroids has filtered down to adolescents, where these agents can have permanent, or at least very long-lasting, effects on brain neurons and behaviors. Given the balance between health risks on the one side and potential sports stardom on the other, it's not altogether surprising which way individuals will move, especially young people who by nature are risk-takers.

It's not just anabolic steroids that have adverse effects on mood and behavior, but these have received the most attention. What's less known is that certain drugs that affect hormones, like those that are used to minimize hair loss and enlarged prostate, can create problems. Propecia and Proscar (that contain finasteride) are the commonly used treatments for this condition. Finasteride can have several negative side effects, such as impotence, abnormal ejaculation, abnormal sexual function, gynecomastia (developing breasts), erectile dysfunction, and testicular pain, and may be associated with high-grade prostate cancer. Ordinarily, finasteride inhibits the enzyme 5-alpha-reductase, which is involved in the conversion of testosterone into the potent androgen dihydrotestosterone, and thus may result in testosterone levels being elevated. It also contributes to the conversion of progesterone to dihydroprogesterone and then to allopregnanolone. This, in turn, modulates GABAA receptors and might thereby cause the anxiety and depression that have been reported among finasteride users. When the treatment is discontinued, vulnerability to depression, including suicidal thoughts, is elevated. So, it might be an ego-boost to diminish hair loss, but in some individuals this comes with a greater cost than what they bargained for.

Stress and reproduction

When a person is distressed their sexual desires may be altered. Females may be less likely to engage in the behaviors that lead to sex (proceptive behaviors), and less inclined to respond to male overtures (receptivity). Male sexual behavior is often altered as well (although it might take a bit more distress for males to lose interest). Essentially, the person may be anxious and distracted and they may experience anhedonia ('I just don't feel like it').

In general, ongoing stressors can have a suppressive effect on reproduction itself. In females this comes about because stressors disrupt ovulation, disturb the uterine changes that are necessary for implantation, and proceptive and receptive behaviors are inhibited (Wingfield & Sapolsky, 2003). Added to this, the corticoids released in response to stressors influence the ovaries so that responsiveness to luteinizing hormone is reduced (Joseph & Whirledge, 2017). The net result of this complex set of hormonal changes is that the reproductive cycle lengthens and becomes irregular. Not surprisingly, the decline in receptivity among female rodents can be reversed by treatment with the female hormone progesterone. In males, stressors diminish gonadal hormone production and may impair erectile functioning. Among the hormonal changes elicited by stressors is the secretion of β-endorphin (an opioid peptide that is produced in the pituitary and hypothalamus), which inhibits the release of gonadotropin-releasing hormone coupled with diminished sensitivity of pituitary gonadotropes (the cells in the anterior pituitary that produce luteinizing hormone, which is involved in provoking ovulation).

Among free-living wild animals, the presence of predators can produce a reduction of prey owing to fewer offspring being born (or hatched) as well as altered patterns of parental behaviors, including diminished search for food that affects offspring survival (Allen et al., 2022). It is not just stressors in mature adults that influence sexual behavior. It seems that stressors at various earlier times of life may influence later adult sexual responsiveness. For instance, among juvenile mice, even a stressor such as being shipped from the breeder to the laboratory, or being exposed to mild infection, reduces receptivity among females, and diminishes behavioral responsiveness to estradiol and progesterone in adulthood, possibly owing to an enduring reduction of estrogen receptors in several brain regions. As well, in rodents, stressful events encountered during the prenatal period can affect the behavior of pups when they were subsequently assessed as adults, and these outcomes could be attenuated by neonatal administration of testosterone (Valsamakis et al., 2019). Prenatal stressors, including infection in the pregnant dam, resulted in later maternal behaviors being disturbed, and as adults the male pups exhibited disrupted sexual behavior. Clearly, stressful events can have enduring behavioral repercussions, some of which might be related to estrogen and testosterone variations.

Prolactin

Prolactin is a hormone that is released from the anterior pituitary following stimulation by thyrotropin-releasing hormone. It was initially thought that the prime function of prolactin was that of promoting lactation (secretion of milk from the mammary glands), but it also contributes to several other essential biological processes, including sexual behavior and sexual pleasure, eating-related processes, pain perception, and responses to emotional stressors. Indeed, prolactin receptors are present in several stress-sensitive brain regions, such as the central amygdala, the bed nucleus of the stria terminalis, and the nucleus accumbens, so that this peptide can activate neurons in these brain regions. The stressors that ordinarily affect neuronal activity within these regions appear to affect prolactin functioning and might contribute to HPA activation (Marano & Ben-Jonathan, 2014).

The finding that lactation and stressors are associated with prolactin processes, and that prolactin influences other stress-endocrine mechanisms, has resulted in an interesting perspective regarding the stress responses that occur during pregnancy and subsequently during lactation. Although HPA activity is very responsive to stressors in rodents, it is blunted during the last trimester of pregnancy and during the lactation period. Presumably, this suppression is essential so that excessive corticosterone does not reach the fetus or pups (postnatally through the mother's milk). Any of several factors could be responsible for this outcome, including alterations in the function of hormones such as prolactin, as well as oxytocin, opioid peptides, and the diminished ability of norepinephrine to elicit the hypothalamic responses that promote CRH and arginine vasopressin release. Whatever the process, it seems that during this period moms are protected from biological changes ordinarily associated with anxiety (although postpartum depression is an obvious deviation from this pattern). However, a critical feature for this was that the mother and her pups had to have been in contact with one another within the preceding few hours. In the absence of this contact, the effects of stressors on HPA functioning in the moms were not attenuated (Walker, 2010).

There is likely an important evolutionary need for stress hormone responses to be inhibited during the lactation period. However, there seems to be a degree of selectivity regarding the effects of different stressors. Unlike stressors directed at the mom, the corticosterone release is marked when the threat is aimed at the pups. In effect, while caring for their young, animals distinguish between or 'filter' relevant from irrelevant stimuli, as well as different types of relevant stressors. In this regard, when the threat is directed at offspring, the HPA response in the mother is particularly activated, presumably to offer the resources needed to protect the well-being of the young (Walker et al., 2010).

Oxytocin

A prosocial hormone

Oxytocin is a particularly interesting hormone that has been associated with a variety of prosocial behaviors, such as attachment, maternal behaviors and bonding, love, generosity, altruism, empathy, the motivation to be with others, and even the ability to infer the emotions of others based on their facial cues. Moreover, oxytocin is one of several hormones (together with vasopressin, dopamine, and serotonin) that contributes to various facets of love, such as trust, pleasure, and reward, and when the oxytocin receptors are altered (through a gene variant), individuals may see the world as more threatening and have a tendency to be less generous (McQuaid et al., 2014).

One of the early views concerning the influence of oxytocin on behavior distinguished between its actions in males and females. It was maintained that in females oxytocin strengthened their 'tend and befriend' characteristics, which included nurturing behaviors and the development and maintenance of social connections. As well, along with opioid peptides and gonadal hormones, oxytocin fostered altruism (i.e., helping fellow group members even at a cost to oneself) (Taylor et al., 2000). Expanding on this view, it was maintained that oxytocin could promote similar behaviors in males, but they would display 'tend and defend' character-istics. This *parochial altruism* not only entails support for group members but also involves defense against other groups (De Dreu, 2012).

Another face of oxytocin

While not dismissing the prosocial actions of oxytocin, another perspective was offered. Specifically, elevated levels of this hormone may increase the salience of or sensitivity to social stimuli irrespective of whether these were positive or nega-tive (McQuaid et al., 2013). Thus, in the context of positive effects, elevated oxy-tocin could promote prosocial behaviors and enhance well-being. In contrast, in the presence of high oxytocin levels, negative events (e.g., early-life mistreatment) could promote more damaging actions than would otherwise occur. However, in the presence of a polymorphism of the gene coding for oxytocin, the negative consequences of these same abusive events were less notable (McQuaid et al., 2013). Relatedly, in response to a breach of trust, women who had been treated with oxytocin were less forgiving relative to participants that had been treated with a placebo, suggesting that in the presence of high oxytocin levels the betrayal was perceived as more profound or caused these women to become less tolerant of betrayals (Yao et al., 2014). Findings such as these raise the possibility that using oxytocin to reduce the effects of stressors or to treat depression could be risky. If oxytocin was not diminished in a depressed individual, then the high oxytocin levels resulting from its exogenous administration might cause them to become overly sensitive to negative social cues. As appraisals among depressed individu-als might already be dysfunctional, ordinarily benign stimuli may be negatively misinterpreted.

The importance of oxytocin cannot be overstated, particularly as so much of our lives are dictated by social interactions and our social identity, and is an essential element in intergroup, intragroup, and interindividual relationships. Trust is also a fundamental element needed for coping with certain types of stressors, includ-ing those associated with conflict resolution, and oxytocin may help us reach out to others to gain their support. As we saw in Chapter 2, to end a social conflict we might accept an apology from another person by offering forgiveness. This might come about if we *trust* that the other person will not repeat their duplicitous behavior, but for this to occur oxytocin functioning might need to be adequate. There is evidence that the administration of oxytocin (through a nasal spray) can enhance trust. However, this outcome was not always apparent, and it may be that this might only occur among individuals who tended to be mistrustful (Declerck et al., 2020).

To a certain extent, the emotions and behaviors linked to oxytocin might be thought to be uniquely human. However, interactions with animals of diverse spe-cies (e.g., petting), including primates, dogs, rodents, and lambs were associated with increased oxytocin levels, and these interactions could limit the cortisol rise that might otherwise occur in response to social isolation (e.g., Coulon et al., 2013). In this regard, some of the initial studies that evaluated the role of oxytocin in bonding found that in certain rodent species (e.g., prairie voles) strong pair bonds developed, and social interaction was accompanied by changes of oxytocin (Insel & Young, 2001). Moreover, when prairie voles were socially isolated, they exhibited depressive-like behavioral disturbances that could be attenuated by the administration of oxytocin.

Furthermore, positive social interactions between dogs and their human companions are associated with increased oxytocin levels and it appears that mutual gaze between the two may have similar effects. When dogs received intranasal oxytocin treatment their gaze towards a friendly face increased, but this did not occur in response to an angry face. The dog's gaze further increased oxytocin activity in the human, supporting the contention that this hormone is fundamental in maintaining the social connection that exists between the two (Nagasawa et al., 2015).

Moderation of the stress response

Beyond promoting varied prosocial behaviors, oxytocin may diminish the effects of stressors by encouraging social coping. When oxytocin was administered to humans the stressor-provoked cortisol response was diminished (Cardoso et al., 2014) as was anxiety elicited by an interpersonal stressor. This treatment attenuated the negative cognitive appraisals otherwise evident in trait anxious individuals, and together with the hormone vasopressin, oxytocin appeared to be a key regulator for stress coping, anxiety, and depression.

Paralleling the adverse effects of early-life stressors in rodents, childhood maltreatment in humans (particularly emotional abuse) has enduring effects in the form of reduced oxytocin levels measured in cerebrospinal fluid. Moreover, this outcome was inversely related to the number of different types of stressors the individual had experienced, the severity and duration of the maltreatment, and current anxiety ratings (Opacka-Juffry & Mohiyeddini, 2012). Of particular significance was the finding that it wasn't just any childhood stressor that elicited the oxytocin variations in response to subsequent adult challenges. Specifically, in the Trier Social Stress test oxytocin levels were altered to a greater extent among women who had experienced childhood abuse than in those that had experienced childhood cancer (Pierrehumbert et al., 2010), although, of course, the experience of childhood cancer will have other stress-related consequences. Evidently, early experiences involving social challenges have protracted actions on adult stress responses that might not be evident among individuals who had experienced childhood medically related stressors. These negative social or parental early experiences may have long-term consequences on behaviors (e.g., bonding, trust) that are mediated by oxytocin.

Conclusion

Numerous hormones are necessary for day-to-day functioning, being essential for energy regulatory processes and eating, characteristics related to sex-based phenotypes, growth and maturation, as well as adaptation to the effects of stressors. Stressful events have marked effects on numerous hormonal processes. Some reflect adaptive responses to help the organism deal with potential or actual challenges, whereas others may contribute to the adverse effects of the stressor. In this chapter we've only touched on some of the hormones affected by stressors, focusing on those that are best known. Indeed, stressors also affect various other hormones (e.g., thyrotropin-releasing hormone, growth hormone, β-endorphin, melanocyte-stimulating hormone, as well as somatostatin and histamine), all of which have been implicated in various stress-related pathologies. Yet, given the complex interactions that occur between hormones, neurotransmitters, and other processes, understanding the immediate and long-term impact of stressors will ultimately require analyses that focus on the synergistic and antagonistic effects of stressors, and how these change over the course of a stressor experience.

Suggested readings

LeDoux, J.E. & Brown, R. (2017). A higher-order theory of emotional consciousness. *Proceedings of the National Academy of Sciences, 114*, E2016–E2025.

McEwen, B.S. & Akil, H. (2020). Revisiting the stress concept: Implications for affective disorders. *Journal of Neuroscience, 40*, 12–21.

Sapolsky, R.M. (2017). *Behave: The Biology of Humans at Our Best and Worst*. New York: Penguin Press.

5

NEUROTRANSMITTER PROCESSES AND GROWTH FACTOR CHANGES

─**Grandma gets a neuroscience lesson**─

'The brain is amazing, Grandma. There are billions of cells in it; these neurons have long tentacles coming off them and each of these tentacles has a bunch of branch-like projections – thousands upon thousands of them. And on each of these branches there are little connectors through which messages can be received. These messages come in different forms so that they can receive information of various types – sort of like someone working at the UN and being able to understand different languages. OK, that's a bad example; those people at the UN don't understand each other and never will. Anyway, Grandma, if all that isn't enough, these neurons also have a long projection through which they can send messages to other neurons. It's like an electric cord, but once you get to the end, chemicals come out of it and send messages to other neurons. They call these chemicals neurotransmitters because they're transmitting information from one neuron to another. And, Grandma, inside each of these neurons are little factories churning out a whole bunch of these chemicals so that messages keep going down the track. The amazing thing is that all these neurons, and their little connectors work in coordination with one another, otherwise we wouldn't know what we're doing.'

(Continued)

Sagely and thoughtfully, and with the hint of a frown, she says 'Very interesting... But it seems to me these little neurons aren't always working so good. Some days I go to the kitchen to get something, and once I'm there, I don't remember what I went there for.'

Learning objectives

Behavioral and cognitive responses to stressors are largely governed by the efficiency of brain neurons in communicating with one another as well as the presence of growth factors that influence the synaptic plasticity that is essential for this process. In this chapter, we will explore the effects of stressors on brain neurotransmitter functioning as well as on several growth factors. Readers should come away with a fundamental understanding of:

- how individual neurons work and the contribution of particular neural circuits to cognitive, emotional, and motivational processes;
- the effects of stressors on various neurotransmitters and their interactions with one another and hormones that have been linked to anxiety disorders, depression, drug addiction, and schizophrenia;
- how stressors can undermine neurotrophic (growth) factors essential for synaptic plasticity and keeping neurons viable. These processes are essential for memory and psychological functioning.

Neuronal and glial processes in relation to stressors

The billions of cells within the brain, and the still greater number of synaptic connections, must operate in a coordinated fashion. This essentially involves different cells speaking to one another in a way that is clear, fast, and precise. This means that there ought to be the capacity for neurons not only to be activated but also to be inhibited when appropriate. The dance that goes on between neurons is remarkably elegant, and the integration that exists between neuronal systems is awesome. Occasionally, when we consider the complexity of the brain, and even the complexity of a single cell and its immense and coordinated machinery, we must wonder how natural selection was involved in achieving this.

Glial cells

The brain has two basic types of cells: neurons and glial cells. While neurons act to communicate information, it was thought that glial cells primarily served as support cells for neurons. However, glial cells do much more than that. Several types of glial cells exist, but those of particular interest to us here are astrocytes and microglia (oligodendrocytes are also a type of glial cell in the brain, being involved in the myelination of neurons; in the periphery, Schwann cells serve in this capacity). Astrocytes provide nutrients to neurons, maintain the ion balances within fluid outside of the brain cells, and are important in the repair of cells within the brain and spinal cord. Astrocytes can communicate with neurons in that they respond to and release particular neurotransmitters (e.g., GABA). Microglia, like certain immune cells in the periphery (e.g., macrophages), are essential for the functioning of the central nervous system (CNS), acting as the primary form of active immune defense. Microglia constantly search for potential CNS damage, as well as plaque and infectious agents, and ordinarily respond quickly to destroy agents that pose a risk to neurons (Colonna & Butovsky, 2017) and may play a fundamental role in the stress response. As we'll see when we discuss immune and inflammatory processes (Chapters 6 and 7), even though activated microglia ought to provide benefits to neuronal functioning, they can introduce adverse effects. Among other things, by promoting strong inflammatory responses and excessive levels of free oxygen radicals, neurodestruction may be engendered, possibly contributing to neurodegenerative disorders (e.g., Alzheimer's and Parkinson's disease). Thus, despite having some positive effects, microglia or some of their products end up as the bad guys, and it was even suggested that their presence might serve as a biomarker for neurodegenerative processes (Guo et al., 2021).

Neurons

The response to environmental stimuli, including stressors, is governed, to a considerable extent, by the activity of neurons in higher brain centers. Brain neurons communicate with one another by releasing a neurotransmitter that stimulates (or inhibits) adjacent cells. Once this neurotransmitter is released from vesicles (located at the terminals of axons) into the space between two cells (synaptic cleft) it influences the adjacent neuron by triggering the receptors that are present. Some of the released transmitter is degraded by enzymes present in the synaptic cleft, and in the case of many transmitters, some may be transported back into the cell to be recycled. The longer the neurotransmitter stays in the synaptic cleft, the greater the opportunity for that neurotransmitter to activate the receptors. Thus, the efficiency of the neurotransmitter can be increased by extending its time in the synaptic cleft either by inhibiting enzymes that ordinarily destroy the transmitter or by inhibiting the reuptake into the neuron. In addition to this, exogenous agents (e.g., drugs) can simulate a neurotransmitter and go directly to the receptor and stimulate it (agonists), whereas other agents can block the receptor (antagonists) thus diminishing neuronal functioning.

Eco-friendly neurons

Neurotransmitter systems are the poster boys (or girls) for going green. When more transmitter is needed, rather than just making a bunch more, some of it stays in the synaptic cleft to make maximal use of what's already there. Furthermore, after it has done its job, it's taken back up into the neuron to be used again (recycling) through a process called 'reuptake'. Our neurons, it seems, recognize the importance of recycling, even if some of us don't.

As indicated when we discussed hormones, different types of receptors exist that promote varied effects upon being stimulated. Receptors are also present on the cell that released the neurotransmitter (presynaptic receptors or autoreceptors) that, upon being triggered, have the effect of reducing the rate of transmitter production. When large amounts of a neurotransmitter are present in the synaptic cleft, the neuron is informed to stop producing further transmitters. In essence, these processes represent an efficient system in which products of neurotransmitters are recycled, and when sufficient neurotransmitter is present, resources aren't unnecessarily wasted making more.

Neurotransmitter production, release, and reuptake are reminiscent of industrial processes: The factory sends cars to the dealers, however, if the lot fills with unsold cars, the dealer might contact the plant to ask for production and delivery to slow down to avoid flooding the market and using up the resources to make further products. (Incidentally, this car lot example has nothing to do with the word 'auto'receptor.)

It wasn't all that long ago that we thought of a transmitter and a receptor as a lock and key arrangement in which little key-like chemicals floated across the synaptic cleft and fitted into little locks that resided on the dendrites or cell bodies of neurons. There have been many changes to this conceptualization. Receptors are not considered as locks that (semi)permanently reside on the cell surface, but as chemical attachment sites that are continuously synthesized (and thus the number of receptors present can change as a function of numerous variables) and can be internalized (essentially being sucked into the cell), so that at a given time the complement of receptors present on the cell surface can vary. Moreover, for a given transmitter several types of receptors may be present that upon being triggered might have different downstream effects. For instance, certain types of dopamine (DA) receptors have been implicated in schizophrenia, whereas other DA receptors subtypes might be more closely aligned with depressive disorders (Belujon & Grace, 2017). Once again, when assessing the effects of stressors on neuronal functioning, it is not enough to consider only the amount of transmitter available and released, but to take into account the impact of the transmitter on specific types of receptors.

There is a common misconception that certain neurotransmitters are responsible for specific behavioral processes. For instance, it might be thought that serotonin (5-HT) is involved in depressive illness, norepinephrine (NE) and 5-HT are involved in anxiety, DA is responsible for reward processes, and so on. To an extent this type of formulation is accurate, and treatments that affect one or another neurotransmitter might influence specific behaviors. However, this is an overly simplistic perspective, as the neurons triggered by different neurotransmitters might have conjoint actions with several other transmitters, eliciting additive or synergistic actions. Furthermore, multiple brain regions and many neurochemical processes are involved in any given behavior. In the ensuing sections we will consider the actions of several neurotransmitters, each in turn, but keep in mind that we're dealing with a community of neurons, involving several brain regions that do things in synchrony with one another.

Neurotransmitter changes elicited by stressors

As in the case of stressor-induced hormonal changes, the sections that follow rely heavily on data from animal studies that pertain to stressor-provoked neurochemical alterations. There's no doubt that studies of this sort have enhanced our understanding of the stressor effects on mood, cognitive processes, mental disorders, and illnesses involving neurodegenerative processes, as well as those that involve immune functioning. At the same time, it can be difficult to generalize animal-based findings to human pathologies given the fundamental role of cognitive processes (e.g., appraisals) in accounting for the reaction to stressors. Furthermore, in humans, certain types of stressors (e.g., those dealing with social threats or ostracism) may engage neuronal processes that differ from those involving other forms of distress, such as shame, loss, and rumination. Unlike hormones that can be detected in blood, analyzing brain neurotransmitters in humans is difficult. Analyses using positron emission tomography (PET) can offer some clues regarding neurotransmitter and receptor changes in the brain, and the combination of PET and functional magnetic resonance imaging (fMRI) analyses can provide information concerning some moment-to-moment changes attributable to specific emotional or cognitive alterations that occur during stressful events. These approaches are impressive but don't allow for analyses of the multiple neurotransmitters that occur across brain regions that contribute to normal behaviors or those that accompany psychopathology.

Reading facial expressions

As useful as studies in rodents might be, there are limitations regarding the possibility of gauging emotional responses in these critters and how these might be related to specific neurotransmitter or endocrine changes. Attempts were made to determine whether facial gestures in mice can tell us something about what they are feeling. For instance, a mouse grimace scale was developed that entails a standardized behavioral coding system to assess the facial responses elicited by noxious (painful) stimuli of moderate duration (Langford et al., 2010). It seemed that mouse facial expressions were reliable and could

(Continued)

potentially be used to assess the efficacy of treatments meant to act as analgesics. It's less certain whether this would be possible for complex emotions such as shame. For that matter, what would humiliate or shame a mouse, and what would they look like if they did feel shame?

Those with pets, typically cats and dogs, will tell you that they communicate with them readily and can read their expressions with little difficulty. Many people have known cats that when let into the house would rub against their leg, and they did the same thing when a can of food was being opened. Those who have experienced this might think this was a smart cat, and the person might politely say 'you're welcome' in response to the cat's apparent leg-rubbing that signified 'thank you'. It seems, however, that the cat was actually 'marking' you as if you were part of its territory. Hearing this may be a bit disappointing but be thankful that the cat hadn't chosen another method to mark you.

Stressful events in rodents influences central neurochemical processes that may be fundamental to psychological well-being. In fact, of the more than 60 different molecules that can act as neurotransmitters, including a variety of amines, peptides, and gases, a fair number are affected by stressful events. These neurochemical changes, as indicated earlier, likely serve in an adaptive capacity, being fundamental in maintaining allostasis. Among other things, the neurochemical alterations that are elicited might prepare the organism to deal (cope) with the stressor, blunt its psychological impact, and engage appropriate cognitive appraisals systems and those necessary for effective coping (Anisman et al., 2008).

Although stressors have ubiquitous consequences, studies in animals indicated that not all stressors have the same effects, as different neural circuits may be engaged, depending on the nature of the stressor encountered. For example, processive stressors (those that involve higher-order processing) that entail physically aversive properties (neurogenic stressors), and those of a psychological origin (psychogenic stressors, including learned as well as innate threats) might engage different neural circuits, just as we saw in the case of CRH. It is difficult to compare the influence of different types of stressors, given that they might not be appraised similarly, or they may not be equally aversive. Nevertheless, given that psychogenic and neurogenic insults differentially influence several neurotransmitters within varied brain regions, these challenges might also have different behavioral consequences (Merali et al., 2006).

Biogenic amines: norepinephrine, dopamine, and serotonin

Acute stressor effects on utilization and levels

Of the large number of neurotransmitters and their receptors, treatments for psychiatric disorders have often targeted some of the earliest neurotransmitters identified, specifically NE, 5-HT, and DA, which are collectively referred to as biogenic amines. These neurotransmitters and their receptors are rich in limbic and forebrain regions (e.g., hippocampus, amygdala, and prefrontal cortex) that are associated with executive functioning (appraisals, decision-making), emotions, and memory processes, and contribute to several forms of psychopathology. These amines are also present in hypothalamic nuclei (e.g., paraventricular nucleus, arcuate nucleus) and are essential for hormonal functioning, including HPA and hypothalamic-pituitary-gonadal (HPG) activation, as well as basic biological responses such as energy regulation, feeding, and sexual behaviors.

As depicted in Figure 5.1, the rate at which a neurotransmitter is used (released from the neuron) is ordinarily met by an equivalent rate at which it is manufactured (synthesized), and so the level of the neurotransmitter doesn't change. This is the 'steady state' of the transmitter. In response to stressful stimuli, the rate at which neurotransmitters are used increases, presumably to set in motion the processes that maintain well-being. Ordinarily, the increased neurotransmitter utilization is accompanied by increased synthesis (production) so that levels remain stable. In response to sufficiently severe challenges, particularly those that are uncontrollable, the amine release increases still further so that the rate of utilization may exceed the rate of synthesis, and consequently the transmitter levels will decline. The reduced neurotransmitter reserves, in theory, would render the organism less able to contend with further insults, and thus it would be more vulnerable to pathology.

As we saw earlier, when an animal first encounters a stressor, it is uncertain whether the stressor is controllable or uncontrollable, and it ought to respond strongly irrespective of stressor controllability. After all, when a potential threat emerges, a rapid response is needed given that there might not be any second chances. Only when the stressor is appraised as being controllable can the organism afford to temper the biological responses that would otherwise be provoked. It would seem reasonable to expect that those brain regions involved in appraisal/coping processes ought to be more sensitive to this differentiation relative to those brain regions that are more fundamental to vegetative or basic life processes. Consistent with this view, inescapable stressors are likely to cause excessive utilization of NE and 5-HT and promote a reduction in the levels of these neurotransmitters. Furthermore, if rats were first trained in an escapable test (a treatment that protects [immunizes] animals against the behavioral disturbances elicited by an uncontrollable stressor), the increased 5-HT release ordinarily elicited by an inescapable stressor was prevented in frontal brain regions associated with cognitive appraisals (Maier & Seligman, 2016). Despite control over a stressor being fundamental to brain neurochemical changes and the provocation of behavioral disturbances, the prefrontal cortical neuronal changes associated with stressors are sex-dependent (Baratta et al., 2019), which may be relevant to their differential vulnerability to psychological disturbances.

Stressors influence the release of DA, but these stressor-provoked changes seem to be less widespread than those of NE and 5-HT. Of particular significance, however, was that the DA changes were evident within the arcuate nucleus of the hypothalamus, a region that is involved in the regulation of several hormones, as well as the nucleus accumbens, which is important in mediating reward processes. It has been speculated that the DA changes elicited by stressors might be responsible for the anhedonia (the diminished reward gained from otherwise positive stimuli) that occurs in response to stressors and might thus contribute to syndromes, such as depressive disorder, in which anhedonia is a key feature. In Chapters 9 and 11 we'll be discussing the impact of stressors on DA systems in relation to depression and addiction, respectively. At that point, it will become clear that the stressor-elicited changes of some DA systems might play a fundamental role in the instigation and maintenance of these psychological disturbances.

Impact of chronic stressors: adaptation and allostatic overload

Do we adapt to adverse experiences, or are the effects of stressors more and more damaging the longer we endure them? From a behavioral and a neurochemical perspective, both could be correct, but this would largely depend on many of the factors described earlier concerning previous experiences, genetic disposition, and stressor characteristics. Moreover, there is no reason to believe that all biological systems will operate in the same way. An adaptation-like effect can evolve concerning the actions of a particular neurotransmitter in a specific brain region, whereas changes in the levels or utilization of other transmitters (or even the same transmitter in other brain regions) may become more pronounced with repeated stressor experiences.

Reductions of a neurotransmitter's levels for extended periods may render the organism vulnerable to pathology and multiple adaptive biological mechanisms act to limit the sustained reductions of a neurotransmitter. Typically, the reduced levels of biogenic amines associated with strong acute stressors are not evident after protracted or repeated insults. As described earlier, this appears to result from a compensatory enhancement of synthesis in the case of NE and 5-HT (see Figure 5.1). This can only go on for so long; eventually, the excessive release of neurotransmitters will have negative health consequences.

With repeated stressful experiences, or with a prolonged stressor, we might manage in some fashion to gain the biological (and psychological) resources that are needed to meet the demands encountered. But ultimately the burden may become too great and our adaptive systems may fail. In effect, there seem to be several checks and counterchecks to maintain allostasis in response to chronic stressors. However, we should not be misled into thinking that things are 'back to normal'. Our transmitter levels might have been re-established, but this occurred through increased neurochemical production, elevated utilization, and receptor activation which could potentially take a toll on the neurotransmitter system. Indeed, if a stressor experience is sufficiently severe and/or long-lasting, the load placed on critical systems may be excessive, and the resulting allostatic overload might ultimately result in increased vulnerability to pathology (McEwen & Akil, 2020).

There's more to this adaptation than just a moderate change of synthesis or use of a transmitter. In chronically stressed animals, amine levels sometimes don't simply return to pre-stress levels, but might come to exceed basal levels. Ordinarily, when animals are exposed to a stressor, the synthesis and utilization of NE and 5-HT increase, and then normalize quickly when the stressor terminates. That is, once the threat or stressor is gone, neuronal activity quickly reverts to the prestress state. However, when an animal is stressed day after day, and the risk of utilization exceeding synthesis is persistent, yet another adaptive change occurs. In this case, it seems that when the stressor terminates, the utilization of the transmitter normalizes readily as it should, whereas the elevated synthesis of the transmitter does not, but instead continues for some time. The elevated production, in the absence of heightened utilization, results in transmitter levels being elevated above the initial baseline (perhaps owing to autoreceptors being down-regulated), potentially rendering animals better prepared to deal with subsequent stressors. This represents a fairly elegant adaptive mechanism. If the stressor occurs predictably, day after day, then the right thing for the system might be to build up a reserve of neurotransmitters that would be available for use when the stressor reoccurs the next day. At a certain point too much neuronal activation may be counterproductive (e.g., leading to sustained anxiety, or causing peripheral effects, such as excessive immune activation), and so further adaptive changes occur to diminish NE and 5-HT receptor activity and the processes activated by these receptors (Anisman et al., 2008).

Certain chronic stressor conditions don't lend themselves to adaptation at all or are less likely to do so. Specifically, if the chronic stressor varies over time, occurs unpredictably, is uncontrollable, and involves a series of different types of challenges, the pressure on biological systems might be especially marked and risk exists that this overloaded system might collapse. In this regard, the 'adaptation' of biogenic amine functioning ordinarily associated with a predictable stressor may be absent or less pronounced following an intermittent chronic stressor regimen (Anisman et al., 2018). Moreover, chronic exposure to variable stressors may set the stage so that exaggerated neurochemical responses are elicited when the organism encounters yet another adverse experience long after the original stressor. Of course, genetic or other experiential factors (e.g., early-life events) might influence the organism's adaptive capacity (or resilience) in dealing with such insults, and it is likely that these factors, among others, moderate the stress response that accompanies a chronic variable stressor regimen.

INCOME AND EXPENSES: BALANCING THE BOOKS

The behavior of neurons in response to stressors is reminiscent of how we deal with our financial expenditures. Ordinarily, if the amount we spend is met with equivalent earnings, then the account will be stable. In times of emergency (e.g., paying off old school loans, repairing the roof), the amount that leaves our bank account might exceed our earnings,

(Continued)

and so our account balance drops. To compensate for this, we might take on part-time work in order that our balance returns to what it was before. Should other expenses come along, then we might have to sell a few possessions or put off holiday plans. So, for the moment we seem to be getting by, but simply because our balance has been reinstated doesn't mean everything is back to normal. Things have changed and the pressures on us have increased, the good times may be gone, and we have less room to maneuver. Not only does the possibility exist that we might be unable to maintain this heavy workload but should yet another emergency arise, the strain will have become too heavy and we might be less able to contend with the challenge.

Amine receptor changes associated with stressors

Various receptor subtypes can be differentially affected by stressors, depending on the brain region examined. In this regard, receptors can be up-regulated or down-regulated in their number (density) or sensitivity to agonists (agents that directly stimulate receptors). For instance, 24 hours following a forced swim stressor, 5-HT_{1A} receptor density was down-regulated in the dorsal raphe nucleus (where the serotonin cell bodies reside, and where this type of receptor acts as an autoreceptor) and in the hippocampus, but was elevated in the thalamus, hypothalamus, and amygdala. It also appeared that behavioral impairments following stressor expo-sure were related to yet other receptor changes. For example, a stressor regimen that engendered behavioral impairments was associated with an increase of mRNA expression of 5-HT_{1B} receptors within the dorsal raphe nucleus, without producing such effects within the hippocampus or prefrontal cortex (Anisman et al., 2018).

At first blush, this diversity of effects might seem a bit puzzling. Then again, why should the neurotransmitter or receptor changes be the same in all brain regions, particularly as neurons at various brain sites might serve in different capacities? Some may be involved in appraisals, others in mediating either psychological or physical coping responses, or they might contribute to energy regulation, and still others might be involved in the regulation of neurotransmitter synthesis (as occurs when autoreceptors are altered). From an adaptive perspective, selectivity as to which transmitters and receptors are altered may be highly advantageous.

Stressor characteristics influence amine changes

Many studies that evaluated the impact of stressors focused on physical stressors, demonstrating that the severity and predictability of these challenges influenced the nature and magnitude of the neurochemical changes elicited. It was similarly demonstrated that psychogenic insults that are ethologically significant (e.g., social defeat or similar threats) are particularly effective in promoting NE and 5-HT release from neurons within limbic brain regions. Even vicarious stressor experiences (wit-nessing another mouse encounter social defeat) can have pronounced anxiety and depressive-like actions (Iñiguez et al., 2018).

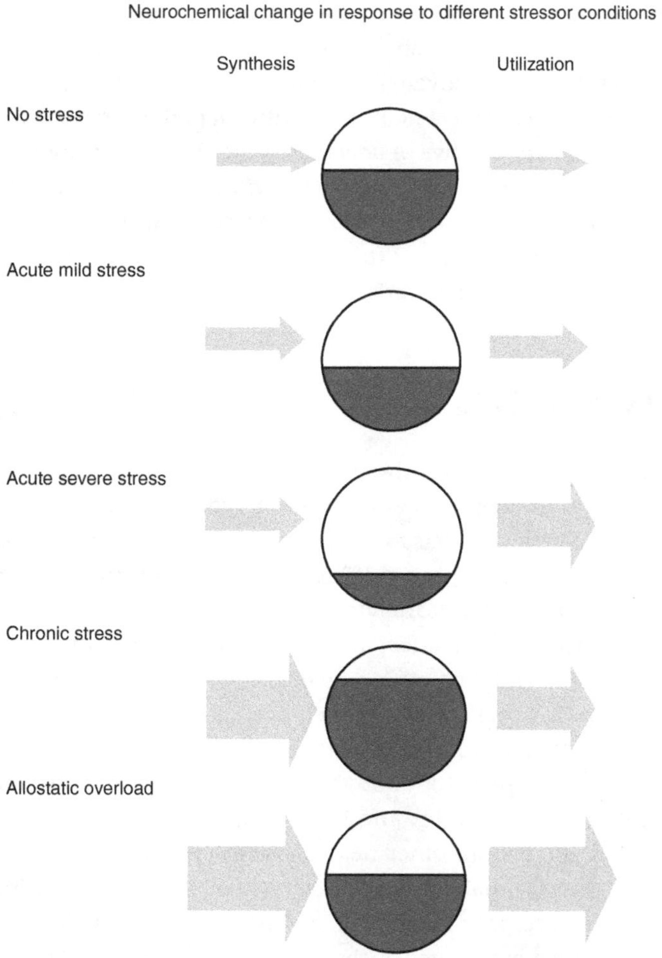

Figure 5.1 The changes of monoamine synthesis, utilization, and consequently the levels, vary with the nature of the stressor. Under nonstress conditions the synthesis and utilization of a transmitter are comparable and the levels thus remain stable. When a stressor is administered that is mild/moderate the utilization of the transmitter occurs for the organism to deal with the stressor. This is met by increased synthesis, and thus once more the level of the transmitter remains stable. As the stressor severity increases, or if the stressor is uncontrollable, the burden of coping rests on biological systems, and in this case utilization of the transmitter may increase sufficiently, outstripping synthesis, and hence the transmitter levels will decline. If the stressor continues, a compensatory increase in utilization occurs, possibly because of down-regulation in autoreceptors, and consequently the levels may again revert to their usual state. However, the increased synthesis and utilization under these conditions can go on for only so long, and eventually the adaptive processes may be overwhelmed (allostatic overload), thus favoring the development of pathology. There are multiple processes affected by stressors simultaneously, and this represents only one way in which pathology might arise in response to stressors.

To some extent, the circuitry associated with certain stressful experiences may be hard-wired, and how threats are appraised likely influences to what extent the neuronal processes will be activated. Of course, the brain's neuroplasticity allows for the development of adaptive neurotransmitter variations in response to specific stressful experiences. Irrespective of how they come about, behavioral or emotional changes may accompany stressor-provoked neurotransmitter variations (e.g., anxiety). The anxiety itself may be an adaptive response to prepare the organism, to deal with imminent or ongoing threats, and provided that these are not long-lasting serious pathology will not arise.

Acetylcholine (ACh)

Acetylcholine (ACh), which was the very first neurotransmitter discovered, plays a fundamental role in peripheral and central nervous system functioning. In the peripheral nervous system, it acts as a countervailing force to the excitatory effects of epinephrine and norepinephrine. Whereas epinephrine stimulates sympathetic functioning (e.g., increasing heart rate), ACh promotes parasympathetic activity that has the opposite effect. In effect, there is a system to get things going, and one to calm things down, and these systems ought to work cooperatively.

Despite ACh having been studied for decades, analyses of the effects of stressors on this neurotransmitter within the brain have been sparse. Nevertheless, psychogenic stressors, such as predator odor and immobilization, increase the release of ACh within the prefrontal cortex and hippocampus, and cholinergic functioning was regulated by input from other neurotransmitters, such as GABA, glutamate, CRH, and DA. It was maintained that the elevated ACh release in the frontal cortex and hippocampus is responsible for the modulation of neuronal activity in other stress-sensitive brain regions, such as the amygdala and prefrontal cortex, and may strengthen the connection between stressful events and other environmental cues. In this way, excessive levels of ACh may contribute to the emergence of depressive features that often accompany stressor experiences (Mineur & Picciotto, 2021).

In addition to influencing ACh levels, aversive stimuli promote changes in the density of certain ACh receptors, notably the muscarinic receptors (this is one of the two types of ACh receptors, the other being nicotinic receptors). Activation of muscarinic receptors may be necessary for fear reactions to be learned and could potentially contribute to the emergence of PTSD (Hersman et al., 2019). It similarly appeared that the effects of stressors on behavior may be mediated by the nicotinic receptors as blocking the actions of this receptor altered some behavioral effects of stressors (Javadi et al., 2017).

As in the case of other neurotransmitters, the effects of stressors on ACh release varied with different organismic and experiential variables. Specifically, vulnerability to stressor-induced ACh changes was increased appreciably if rats had experienced an early-life stressor, whereas the effects of stressors on ACh activity were attenuated if rats had been raised in an enriched environment (Segovia et al., 2009).

Furthermore, the ACh variations were more pronounced in females than in males, particularly during the diestrus and proestrus phases of the estrus cycle (during the first half of the estrus cycle). While the involvement of estrogen (or related factors) in determining the impact of stressors on behavioral disturbances seems likely, it is uncertain to what extent these actions are related to ACh changes.

What else is there to know about acetylcholine?

During the first few months of 2013, reports from Syria had indicated that chemical weapons (primarily choline gas, sulfur mustard gas, and sarin) were being made available to the Assad regime and had been used against civilians. There had been reports that Assad transferred chemical weapons to Hezbollah in Lebanon, raising concerns that such weapons might fall into the hands of al-Qaeda operatives who had mingled with anti-Assad forces. The situation had reached new levels of immorality.

ACh has a tainted history as several of the gases used in World War I involved effects on this transmitter. These gases were the type that blocked the enzyme acetylcholinesterase, which normally degrades ACh, resulting in excessive levels of this transmitter, culminating in death. Today, there are more than 70 agents that can be used as war gases to either kill or incapacitate. Some of the more infamous agents are sarin, soman, and tabun, which were made in secrecy in Germany both before and during World War I and II for use as chemical weapons through their effects on ACh. Other war gases include mustard gas, chlorine, hydrogen cyanide, and several that have scary names, such as VX, VR, and Agent 15. One can add ricin and botulinum toxin to this list, although they are not technically 'gases'. Zyklon B, developed by the Nazi regime, was not used on battlefields, but instead was used to kill noncombatants in concentration camps.

Most countries have prohibited the use of poison gas in warfare. The 1925 Geneva Protocol for the Prohibition of Poisonous Gases and Bacteriological Methods of Warfare stated that 'the use in war of asphyxiating, poisonous or other gases, and of all analogous liquids, materials or devices, has been justly condemned by the general opinion of the civilized world'. Of course, this hasn't stopped the development of new poison agents, and it didn't stop its use in the Sino-Japanese war, the Iran–Iraq war, World War II, the North Yemen civil war, and Iraq's war on the Kurds, as well as its alleged use in Chechnya. It seems that several countries still maintain appreciable stockpiles of chemical weapons.

The Conference on Disarmament (1992) submitted the Chemical Weapons Convention to the UN General Assembly (although it was not signed for about five years), which banned chemical weapons (but, oddly, it didn't include biological weapons). Given the 'politics' of the UN, did anyone possibly believe that the results of that agreement would be any more credible than the Geneva Protocol almost seventy years earlier?

γ-Aminobutyric acid (GABA)

GABA, the most abundant neurotransmitter in the brain, acts as the principal inhibitory neurotransmitter within the mammalian CNS, essentially acting as a brake so that neuronal functioning is properly regulated. It's all well and good to have a powerful engine that gets a car moving from 0 to 60 in seven seconds, but at the end of the road, brakes can come in pretty handy, and GABA serves in this capacity in brain processes.

The view that GABA is important in the stress response, particularly anxiety and depression, has come from multiple sources of evidence. In rodents, chronic stressor treatments reduced GABA in several brain regions, and consistent with a role for GABA in depressive illness, these stressor effects were attenuated by anti-depressant treatment (Shalaby & Kamal, 2012). As in the case of several hormones, stressors experienced in early life provoked long-lasting changes of GABA$_A$ receptor activity, especially among animals that were again exposed to the stressor in adult-hood (Skilbeck et al., 2010). Moreover, rat pups that had been repeatedly separated from their moms later displayed behavioral disturbances (reminiscent of 'learned helplessness') that appeared to be mediated by GABA variations within the pre-frontal cortex and amygdala (Lukkes et al., 2018). Variations of GABA and GABA receptors are among many neurochemical changes that are introduced by early-life stressful experiences (e.g., Mumtaz et al., 2018), any of which alone or in combina-tion might be responsible for the later emergence of psychopathology.

It is generally thought that GABA may influence anxiety by inhibiting the actions of excitatory neurons that might contribute to this condition. It was postulated that in response to chronic stressors disturbances of inhibitory neurotransmission occurred within prefrontal cortical neural circuits. If this was not matched by excit-atory neurotransmission, then the development of anxiety and depressive disorders could occur as might other stress-related illnesses (Fogaça & Duman, 2019). Indeed, many anti-anxiety medications act through certain types of GABA receptors, notably the GABA$_A$ receptor subtype. The influence of GABA on anxiety may involve sev-eral brain regions, but alterations of amygdala functioning may be especially cogent (Nuss, 2015). GABA levels were also frequently found to be reduced in depressed patients and in conjunction with anhedonia (Gabbay et al., 2017).

The nature of the GABA receptor is different from most other receptors. The GABA$_A$ receptor (a second form is the GABA$_B$ receptor) is made up of five sub-units (or components) that basically 'hold hands' with one another, forming a ring, where the central region comprises the channel through which ions can pass. The five-unit receptor may comprise any of 19 subunits, so an enormous variety of permutations are possible. The conformations of the receptor are differentially sensitive to treatments, such that some are sensitive to anti-anxiety agents (e.g., benzodiazepines), whereas others are preferentially sensitive to other GABA acting agents, such as neurosteroids (e.g., estrogen) and alcohol.

Stressors can affect the characteristics of the GABA receptor in that certain types become more abundant, whereas others are less prominent. Rats that had been stressed as juveniles (the equivalent of adolescence in humans) more readily exhib-ited GABA subunit and opioid receptor variations in response to later stressors, and were more sensitive to the anti-anxiety agent diazepam, indicating that the early stressor experience had functional outcomes stemming from the altered GABA$_A$ subunit expression (Horovitz et al., 2020). The characteristics of the GABA$_A$ receptors within stress-sensitive brain regions were similarly elevated in response to stressors, an outcome that was particularly strong when the stressor involved a series of different challenges administered over several weeks. These effects varied with the basal anxiety that mice displayed, being more pronounced in a very anxious strain than in a hardy, stress-resilient mouse strain (Poulter et al., 2010). Findings such as these have led to the view that by influencing the trajectory of biological processes related to GABA functioning, early-life stressful experiences determine the basal and stressor elicited levels of anxiety in adulthood and old age (Wang et al., 2019).

Studies in humans have shown that stressful experiences that are tied to anxiety are associated with altered GABA neuronal functioning. In the face of a threat, GABA activity decreased relative to levels evident during a safe period (Hasler et al., 2010). Likewise, in depressed humans who died by suicide, GABA$_A$ subunit expression was disturbed relative to that of individuals who died of factors unrelated to suicide (Merali, Du et al., 2004). The latter findings don't necessarily causally tie GABA functioning to depression (or to suicide), but these data are certainly in line with the suppositions offered concerning stress, depression, and GABA functioning (Schür et al., 2016). It has similarly been reported that regional GABA specificity occurs in association with PTSD and was differentially present with different symptoms of this disorder (Rosso et al., 2021). These neurochemical signatures could potentially be used to predict the efficacy of treatments for different forms of PTSD.

Interactions of GABA and other neurobiological factors

GABA's capacity to inhibit the influence of excitatory transmitters has been implicated as being fundamental in determining the occurrence of pathological conditions. For instance, GABA$_A$ and 5-HT processes affect one another (reciprocal innervation) within the prefrontal cortex and hippocampus (both of which have been associated with depression). In view of the fundamental inhibitory role of GABA in prefrontal cortex functioning, coupled with its interactions with 5-HT, antidepressant treatments (as well as those related to anxiety) might ultimately have their therapeutic effects through actions on GABA processes.

The interactions involving GABA are not limited to 5-HT, as intimate relations exist between GABA and CRH functioning (Dedic et al., 2019). In this regard, GABA might serve as an essential mediator by which CRH (and possibly stressors) come to influence 5-HT functioning, and such relationships again may be reciprocal. If this weren't sufficiently complex, GABA$_A$ subunit expression may be altered by ovarian hormones, such as progesterone and its metabolite allopregnanolone, which might thereby contribute to the sex differences that exist concerning depression and anxiety (Mody & Maguire, 2012). As well, this interaction may contribute to the development of postpartum depression, which has led to specific therapeutics to alleviate symptoms.

The specific role that GABA plays in depression may seem somewhat confusing considering its interaction with many other neurotransmitters, but there's a simple way of thinking about this that may be useful for the moment. Specifically, several neurotransmitters, including 5-HT and CRH, influence one another and may thereby influence behavioral outputs. To make sure that this mutual regulation functions smoothly, GABA acts as a coordinator (much like an orchestra conductor) to make sure that these transmitters are working together, hushing (inhibiting) one or the other as the situation requires. But when we say 'as the situation requires', this doesn't just mean the presence or absence of a stressor, but also the broad context concerning what else may be happening in the body or brain. Changes in the hormonal milieu that accompanies the estrus cycle, for example, may influence how the conductor behaves.

Glutamate

Glutamate is the most abundant excitatory neurotransmitter within the CNS, stimulating N-methyl-D-aspartate (NMDA) and α-amino-3-hydroxy-5-methyl-4-isoxazolepropionic acid (AMPA) receptors on adjacent cells. Glutamate transporters present in neuronal and glial membranes remove glutamate after it has been released. However, under certain conditions, such as brain injury (e.g., a stroke), glutamate can accumulate in extracellular space, which can promote cell damage and cell death, referred to as 'excitotoxicity'.

The increased glucocorticoids elicited in response to acute stressors augment the release of glutamate at the prefrontal cortex, amygdala, and hippocampus. As well, prenatal or early-life stressors that induce anxiety in adulthood might be due to persistent variations of glutamate functioning (Musazzi et al., 2015). Beyond the changes of glutamate release, acute stressors can increase the expression of NMDA and AMPA receptors, thereby increasing synaptic transmission. These effects occur rapidly in the hippocampus but are generally not immediately apparent in the prefrontal cortex. Instead, they appear more than one hour after stressor termination, but persist up to and beyond 24 hours. Given the temporal changes that were observed, the possibility exists that glutamate in some brain regions (e.g., the rapid changes in the hippocampus) might be fundamental for defensive responses, including those that involve experience-based (learned) behaviors.

Among other things, glutamate is fundamental to synaptic plasticity (i.e., the moldability or changeability of synapses), and is therefore important for learning and memory processes. It seems that acute stressors inhibit plasticity within limbic and cortical brain regions, and this outcome can be attenuated by antidepressant treatment or by glucocorticoid receptor antagonism. Interestingly, impaired neuroplasticity could influence fear memories. It similarly appeared that in response to chronic stressors neuronal plasticity might be disrupted within the prefrontal cortex and hippocampus and could thus disrupt behavioral flexibility and working memory, possibly being mediated by glucocorticoid functioning (Popoli et al., 2011). The impact of chronic stressors on glutamate release has not been extensively assessed, although it appears that a degree of adaptation occurs in the prefrontal cortex but is less notable in other brain regions. The implications of these brain region-specific changes on behavioral outcomes are not fully understood given the paucity of data that have been collected.

As a variety of stressors affect glutamate transmission in limbic and cortical brain regions and promote dendritic remodeling as well as diminished synapses and reductions of brain volume, it is conceivable that the glutamatergic system is involved in the evolution of stress-related psychopathology. It had been suggested that glutamate may be a component of a final common pathway underlying the therapeutic action of antidepressant agents (Duman et al., 2016). Consistent with this, repeated treatments with antidepressants attenuated the glutamate changes otherwise induced by an uncontrollable stressor, just as antidepressants had the effect of attenuating behavioral disturbances. It is of particular significance that chronic stressors may promote depression by affecting glutamate receptors and conversely, the fast-acting antidepressant ketamine may have its beneficial actions by diminishing excessive glutamatergic neuronal functioning (Elhussiny et al., 2021).

Cannabinoids

We can't leave this section without some comment on the endocannabinoid system, especially in light of its broad actions that play a prominent role in moderating the response to endogenous and environmental insults (Lu & Mackie, 2016). Naturally occurring substances, endocannabinoids, notably anandanine (AEA) and 2-arachodonoylglycerol (2-AG) can bind with two types of receptors. While the CB_1 receptors are present in abundance within the brain, the CB_2 receptors are primarily present in the periphery although they also appear within the brain.

Endocannabinoids have been implicated in modulating basal anxiety and that provoked by stressors (Hill & Tasker, 2012). Excitatory neurotransmitters released by some neurons stimulate receptors present on the postsynaptic site. This results in endocannabinoid release from the postsynaptic neuron (this is quite different from the usual case in which neurotransmitters are released from the presynaptic neuron). The released endocannabinoid causes activation of the presynaptic CB_1 receptor, which results in the suppression of other neurotransmitters that would ordinarily have an excitatory action on arousal, thereby assuring that the organism will remain calm. Like CB_1, it seems that CB_2 has important actions, playing a role in immunomodulation and is prominent in the inhibition of inflammatory responses and is thus important in dealing with physical injuries, and through inflammatory processes could influence mood states.

Through its actions on the endocannabinoid system, the psychoactive component of cannabis, Δ9-tetrahydrocannabinol (THC), can bind to CB_1 receptors situated at the paraventricular nucleus of the hypothalamus, hippocampus, prefrontal cortex, and amygdala. Thus, cannabis may have potent effects on anxiety, fear, and stress coping processes (Lutz et al., 2015). At low doses, cannabis reduces anxiety but may have the opposite effect at high doses. As well, individual differences exist in the effects of cannabis so that in some people cannabis tends to promote anxiety (Sharpe et al., 2020). In addition to Δ^9-THC, cannabidiol present in cannabis plants has lower binding to CB receptors but can nevertheless produce many effects like those of Δ^9-THC but without producing a high.

AEA may act to maintain stable HPA functioning under nonstress conditions, which can be disturbed by stressors. As we've already seen, in response to acute stressors CRH is released at the amygdala, which comes to promote HPA activation and the ultimate release of corticosterone from the adrenal gland. At the same time, the CRH changes result in levels of AEA declining in brain regions associated with fear and anxiety (amygdala, hippocampus, as well as the prefrontal cortex). These effects are still more pronounced following a chronic stressor and consequently might be responsible for exacerbated and persistent anxiety.

The mechanisms by which endocannabinoids affect stress responses (e.g., anxiety, fear memories, pain perception and regulation, synaptic plasticity) involve more than just variations of HPA functioning, being regulated by several intersecting systems (Morena et al., 2016). It appears that eCB signaling of CB_1 receptors is key in affecting stress reactions, and pharmacological blockade of CB_1 receptors increases HPA activity both under basal conditions and in response to acute psychogenic stressors. More than this, the corticosterone release in response to stressors stimulates endocannabinoid release that binds to CB_1 receptors present on GABAergic terminals, thereby limiting GABA activity. Because GABA ordinarily inhibits norepinephrine release, diminishing GABA functioning promotes norepinephrine activity that can favor the consolidation of emotionally aversive memories (Hill & McEwen, 2010).

Stimulation of CB_1 within the amygdala may play an important role in determining stress responses through actions on glutamate functioning and by influencing stressor-induced activation of the HPA axis. Indeed, changes of glucocorticoids, which have been implicated in mediating emotional responses associated with a stressor may contribute to the consolidation of emotionally arousing memories (Hill et al., 2018). In line with this view, soon after animals were trained to avoid a stressor, administration of a CB_1 receptor agonist enhanced the retention of this avoidant response, as did glucocorticoids administered soon after initial training. It had provisionally been suggested that endocannabinoid deficiency among some individuals may increase vulnerability to PTSD and other pathologies stemming from intense stressors. As a result, in an effort at self-medication, these individuals might be more likely to use cannabis to deal with trauma-related disorders.

Aside from AEA alterations, stressors promote an increase of 2-AG in several brain regions. The rise of 2-AG is delayed relative to the effects on AEA, and these actions are amplified in response to a chronic stressor. Elevated cortisol release provoked by stressors may cause 2-AG production, which then promotes normalization of amygdala activity, hence reducing anxiety. In effect, once the 2-AG system kicks in, it turns off stress reactivity. From this perspective, the stress response is not something that simply fades with time, but instead its decline entails active 2-AG functioning. Hence, chronic anxiety might involve persistent AEA activity or the absence (or failure) of a 2-AG response.

What can cannabis really do for health?

Cannabis has taken on mythic status in the alleged health benefits that can be produced. For instance, it was maintained that cannabis or cannabidiol (CBD) can promote weight loss, act against diabetes, reduce acne, enhance bone healing, diminish symptoms of ADHD, autism, and multiple sclerosis, and reduce Parkinsonian tremors. In the main, however, these claims have not been accompanied by supportive data.

Only a few health conditions were reliably affected by cannabinoids. Treatment-resistant epilepsy could be diminished and nausea resulting from cancer treatments was attenuated through cannabis (Parker, 2017). Given that more than 20% of adults experience chronic pain, it is important that cannabis and CBD can produce reductions of pain, although this may not reflect a decline in the intensity of the pain as much as its unpleasantness (De Vita et al., 2021). Unfortunately, cannabis was largely ineffective in diminishing cancer-related pain, although animal studies suggested that cannabis and CBD may be useful as an adjunctive cancer therapy and might diminish chemotherapy-provoked sleep problems and gastrointestinal disturbances, and perhaps diminish cancer cachexia and anorexia (Bar-Sela et al., 2019). As CB_2 plays a role in immunomodulation and is prominent in the inhibition of inflammatory responses it could potentially be important in dealing with physical injuries. As well, there is reason to believe that CBD can enhance the effects of antibiotics. This may allow for lower doses of antibiotics to be used, thereby diminishing bacterial resistance (Wassmann et al., 2020).

Contrary to some claims regarding the psychological benefits of cannabis, a meta-analysis indicated that it was ineffective in the treatment of most psychological disorders (Black et al., 2019). For that matter, cannabis can instigate cognitive disturbances, persistent functional brain changes, impaired neuronal plasticity and organization, especially in the adolescent brain. Moreover, in highly vulnerable individuals, powerful strains of cannabis could favor the development of schizophrenia or alter the disease trajectory (Renard et al., 2018), and early chronic cannabis use may stunt the development of brain white matter. Still, the value of cannabis has continued to be advanced for the alleviation of symptoms associated with an ever-growing number of illnesses through its actions on CB1 and CB2 receptors present in many organs and thus can have wide-ranging consequences.

For years legal restrictions limited research to uncover the benefits or harms that could be created by cannabis (Mechoulam et al., 2014). In some countries, cannabis use has been legalized, which might allow greater research to determine its value for diverse illnesses. This may be a bit of a Pollyanish perspective as cannabis-related health research remains difficult to accomplish, certainly in humans (Haney, 2020). This is doubly unfortunate since health-care providers need to have the correct information that would allow them to counsel their patients appropriately.

Growth factors

For the longest time, researchers focused exclusively on hormonal and neuro-transmitter functioning in determining behavioral outcomes. However, it became clear that growth factors support the survival of cells, and promote cellular growth and proliferation, as well as cellular differentiation (the latter refers to the processes where cells become more specialized). While this may have been a fresh perspective concerning brain functioning, growth factors were discovered by Rita Levi-Montalcini and Stanley Cohen years earlier and were subsequently found to have important ramifications in cancer processes.[1] A lengthy list of growth factors has since been identified, but in this section, we'll focus on neurotrophins that primarily influence brain functioning. Another class of molecules, termed 'cytokines', are also classic growth factors, but as they are heavily involved in immune functioning, we'll cover these in Chapter 6, which deals with immunity.

It had been believed at one time that whatever neurons you were endowed with at birth were what you were stuck with and that invariably cell loss would occur as you age. We now know that this isn't entirely correct. Although most of our neurons might have been formed prenatally, in some parts of the adult brain new neurons can be formed from neural stem cells through a process termed 'neurogen-esis'. Furthermore, dendritic arborization (increase in the length and branching of dendrites) and increased appearance of synapses and synaptic plasticity occur at a rapid pace after birth and increase with experiences.

The growth factors that have been of most interest in relation to stress-ors have been brain-derived neurotrophic factor (BDNF) and others that are structurally similar, including basic fibroblast growth factor (FGF-2), glial cell line-derived neurotrophic factor (GDNF), nerve growth factor (NGF), neurotro-phin-3 (NT-3), and neurotrophin-4 (NT-4). As these growth factors influence neurons and their neurotransmitters, it was suggested that they might contrib-ute to depression, anxiety, and substance use disorders. Furthermore, because of their fundamental role in neuronal development, plasticity, and maintain-ing the well-being of individual cells, there has been a prominent focus on the relationship between growth factors and learning/memory, as well as neurode-generative disorders.

---

[1]The early studies conducted by Rita Levi-Montalcini began while she was at the University of Turin in Italy. However, in 1938 Mussolini's Fascist government forbade Jewish scientists from holding academic positions. She was resourceful, determined, and passionate about her research and so she conducted her experiments in a makeshift laboratory within her bedroom at home. Years later, she and her associate Stanley Cohen discovered nerve growth factor (NGF), which had enormous implications for health processes. For their remarkable work they shared the 1986 Nobel Prize in Physiology and Medicine.

Brain-derived neurotrophic factor (BDNF)

In rodents, acute stressors reduced BDNF in limbic brain regions that are associated with mood states and were particularly notable within the hippocampus (Duman & Monteggia, 2006). These effects were not only provoked by neurogenic or psychogenic stressors but could be elicited by reminder stimuli that comprised cues that had been associated with a stressor (Chang et al., 2021). Following exposure to the same stressor on successive days, the magnitude of the BDNF reduction in the hippocampus was less pronounced than after acute treatment, but if the chronic stressor involved a series of different challenges administered over several weeks, the BDNF reductions were marked and persistent (Grønli et al., 2006). The BDNF changes, which were associated with a depressive-like state, were readily instigated by the powerful stressor that comprises social defeat (Koo et al., 2019). Moreover, with chronic stressor experiences, epigenetic changes occurred in the BDNF promoter gene leading to its diminished presence (Miao et al., 2020). Overall, the data were in keeping with the view that chronic or sufficiently powerful aversive events led to disturbed BDNF levels and functioning that can foster the development of a depressive-like state.

Although both the prefrontal cortex and hippocampus are likely involved in depressive illness, stressors do not consistently induce comparable effects on BDNF in these brain regions. Rather, stressor treatments were frequently found to increase BDNF mRNA expression in several aspects of the prefrontal cortex (the anterior cingulate, prelimbic, and infralimbic). Further, the appearance of stressor-provoked behavioral disturbances, which have been used to model depression, aren't always accompanied by BDNF reductions, nor are reduced levels of BDNF necessarily accompanied by behavioral impairments. Findings such as these point to the importance of distinguishing between the hippocampus and aspects of the prefrontal cortex in determining stress responses, even though these regions are considered stress-sensitive, and both have been implicated in stressor-related psychological disorders. It is conceivable that reduced BDNF and neurogenesis in the hippocampus may be aligned with some attributes of reduced mood, whereas altered BDNF within aspects of the prefrontal cortex might serve to strengthen the cognitive and behavioral responses that support the negative thinking and poor appraisals that are apparent in depressive illness. Furthermore, the frontal cortex has many sub-regions, often with very distinct functions regarding cognitive processes, and hence differentiating the changes of BDNF at discrete cortical sites may be central to understanding the processes underlying psychopathological conditions.

Despite the many studies that have assessed the impact of stressors on BDNF at diverse brain sites, the findings have been inconsistent. Determining why differences occur between studies has been complicated by the use of different stressors (the type, severity, and predictability), characteristics of the animals being tested (species, strain), the time of life at which stressors were administered, as well as sex differences that have not been assessed as thoroughly as they should have (Miao et al., 2020). Stressor effects on BDNF in various brain regions aren't nearly as uniform as one would like in order to provide a simple explanation concerning the relation between stressors, BDNF, and the emergence of pathology. Furthermore, while many reports have pointed to reduced BDNF being involved in depression, other factors likely interact with the BDNF changes elicited by stressors.

BDNF variations associated with early-life experiences

Prenatal and early postnatal stressors (e.g., separating pups from their mom) have long-lasting effects on the cortical expression of BDNF, particularly if mice were exposed to a stressor during subsequent adulthood (Sun et al., 2021). Such persistent effects of early-life stressors may be related to epigenetic factors, as repeated periods of separation from the mother resulted in reduced mRNA expression of BDNF, accompanied by elevated methylation of genes on the BDNF promoter region that would have resulted in BDNF production being shut down (Roth et al., 2009). Evidently, adverse early experiences might have lasting (perhaps permanent) suppressive effects on the regulatory genes that permit BDNF activation, and hence these early experiences may profoundly influence adult responses to stressors, and the development of pathologies, such as a major depressive illness.

Early adversity can have pronounced negative consequences on later neuronal function but, as indicated earlier, experiences with manageable stressors might have the effect of augmenting the ability to respond effectively to subsequent stressors, including through compensatory elevations in the release of neurotrophic factors. As well, mild or moderate stressors might prime neurotrophin processes so that when stressors are subsequently encountered, these systems will be ready to respond appropriately.

Basic fibroblast growth factor (FGF-2)

Like BDNF, the FGF-2 system contributes to cell proliferation, differentiation, and survival involving neurons and glial cells. Of particular significance to behavior is that FGF-2 appears to be associated with hippocampal neurogenesis, and the expression of FGF-2 is influenced by stressful events. In response to an acute stressor, the levels of FGF-2 were transiently reduced in some brain regions (prefrontal cortex) but increased in others (the entorhinal cortex, hippocampus, hypothalamus). As in the case of BDNF, a stressor experience could increase FGF-2 mRNA expression in several parts of the prefrontal cortex and hippocampus, and these effects occurred more rapidly and were more pronounced following an escapable stressor than after an inescapable stressor (Bland et al., 2007). As a result, having the ability to control (cope with) a stressor, rather than simply experiencing it, may be more pertinent in altering FGF-2 production. Unlike the effects of acute stressors, FGF-2 declined among mice exposed to a chronic stressor (Turner et al., 2012), which may influence the organism's capacity to deal with further challenges and can influence the development of psychopathology.

Stressors that occur during early life or the prenatal period markedly influence childhood anxiety and depression, which were tied to circulating FGF-2 (Lebowitz et al., 2021). As well, stressors experienced during late gestation may reduce adult hippocampal FGF-2 and the adult behavioral responses to a stressor were disturbed. Essentially, stressors in a pregnant dam had the effect of altering the trajectory of the developmental changes of FGF-2 in the offspring, thereby potentially rendering them less prepared to deal with stressors during adulthood (Fumagalli et al., 2005). Conversely, treatments that alleviate depression increased FGF-2 in cortical and hippocampal sites. This outcome was observed in response to chronic antidepressant or anxiolytic medications, as well as repeated (noninjurious) electroconvulsive shock. As might be expected if FGF-2 disturbances play a causal role in promoting depressive-like states, FGF-2 administered directly into the brain of rodents enhanced behavioral performance in tests that modeled depression.

Glial cell line-derived neurotrophic factor (GDNF)

Relatively limited research has been conducted concerning the contribution of GDNF to stressor-related behavioral outcomes, but this growth factor has been linked to depressive features stemming from stressor encounters. Using a chronic stress model of depression in rats, hippocampal GDNF was reduced in parallel with several behavioral impairments, and treatment with an antidepressant reversed these effects. Not unexpectedly, the influence of stressors and GDNF on depressive-like states varied with genetic factors. Stress reactive versus resilient strains of mice, for instance, behaved differently in response to chronic stressors, and this was matched by the differential epigenetic status of the GDNF gene in the ventral striatum (Uchida et al., 2011). Likewise, in rat pups separated from their mother for extended periods, epigenetic changes related to GDNF genes within the ventral striatum were accompanied by depressive-like behaviors in adulthhood (Zhang et al., 2019). It seems that epigenetic modifications of GDNF might influence the behavioral responses that follow stressor treatments, which can manifest throughout life.

Sensitized neuronal responses

The psychological effects of stressors may be profound and the repercussions may last for many years. Childhood trauma can have especially persistent effects even if we don't remember having been traumatized. So how can traumatic events have such effects, especially as some of these could have occurred before a child can remember events as a cohesive and understandable narrative (i.e., before they had acquired language) as opposed to one that existed simply in symbolic form? The Freudians would have told us that these memories were buried as unconscious thoughts that fought to emerge in some manner. Maybe so, but other explanations are more parsimonious or at least testable.

The past influences the future

There is a very interesting aspect about stressors that ought to be considered from both a psychological as well as a neuronal perspective. Many of the hormonal and neurotransmitter changes elicited by stressors are relatively transient, typically being present for minutes or hours, although there are instances in which the effects can be lasting. Stressor-elicited neuronal activity returning to normal doesn't mean that the reactivity of neuronal systems had returned to their original state. Neuronal functioning might have become 'sensitized' so that if a stressor was encountered at a later time, stress processes might be more readily activated, reflected by brain neurotransmitter changes being greater and more readily provoked (Anisman et al., 2003). Exaggerated changes in NE, DA, and 5-HT neuronal activity and HPA functioning occur upon stressor (or cue) re-exposure among animals that had initially encountered either acute or chronic stressors. It appears that the nature of the changes observed may be brain region-specific and may vary over time following the initial stressor experience. Hence, even though the emotional and biological effects of a relatively severe stressor may have subsided with the passage of time, the recurrence of the stressor (or even reminders of the event, i.e., triggering stimuli) may have pronounced repercussions on some neurotransmitters and neurotrophic factors and thus influence the later emergence of pathology. So, with apologies to Yogi Berra, it ain't over *even* when it's over.

─── Case study 5.1 ──────────────────────────

Carrying an enormous burden

Jenny didn't have it easy growing up. She had been born into poverty and her parents weren't prepared to have a child. They seemed unaware of how to be proper parents and they generally neglected her, infrequently providing physical or emotional comfort. She had seen other kids being pampered by their parents and she envied their closeness but felt that the coolness she experienced from her parents was a result of something she had done – she was undeserving and consequently didn't obtain affection from them, or anyone else. Over time she became increasingly more withdrawn and experienced clear signs of depression and anxiety, and she seemed to be afflicted by every viral illness that came around.

   She had multiple difficulties at school. She had no friends, she was lonely, she was frequently bullied, and her academic performance was abysmal. After high school, which seemed to last forever, she obtained a job at a fast-food joint, and she felt lucky to have that after being turned down at every other job for which she had applied. It was at her job where she met her first boyfriend, who turned out to be abusive. Nevertheless, she stayed in this toxic relationship, believing that she provoked him and that his behaviors were her fault. She used every imaginable ineffective method of coping with her horrible situation. Self-medicating with alcohol and other drugs, and excessive consumption of comfort food resulted in her appearance deteriorating, her weight progressively increased, and she developed skin conditions. She felt ashamed of her appearance and often skipped going to work, eventually losing her job, and ending up living on the street. Her health deteriorated and she developed pneumonia which caused her early death. After she had died her few acquaintances commented that she was simply one of those people who were unlucky, not realizing that her earliest experiences created the trajectory she had been on. She wasn't unlucky, she was a victim of a lifelong domino effect that began in early life.

Cross-sensitization: drugs and stress are a bad mix

The sensitization of neuronal systems is apparent when the second stressor exposure involves a different type of insult (cross-sensitization) (Belda et al., 2016). The earlier trauma resulted in later stressor encounters promoting greater activation of cortical and limbic brain regions fundamental for both reward and emotional processing (Hermes et al., 2021). The cross-sensitization is even evident in response to some pharmacological treatments (e.g., amphetamine, cocaine) that act on these same neurotransmitter systems (Anisman et al., 2003), and stressor experiences can influence the analgesic effects provoked by later exposure to morphine (Charmchi et al., 2016). The implications of this cross-sensitization are fairly broad. Among other things, this means that a stressor might not only influence responses when this or similar insults are later encountered, but may have ramifications regarding the impact of virtually any life stressor that might subsequently be experienced. Furthermore, the way certain drug treatments affect us might be altered by our previous stressor experiences, leading to the possibility of some particularly adverse effects occurring. Given that stressors influence the response to later amphetamine and cocaine treatment, is it the case that these agents similarly affect reactions to stressors that are subsequently to be encountered? Several reports showed that this occurs with both behavioral changes and neurochemical functioning. Using these substances may alter neuronal processes so that later stressor responses are exaggerated and might thus favor the emergence of pathology. As we'll see when we discuss the use of illicit drugs, early-life stressful experiences can have profound ramifications on substance use disorders in adulthood.

The sensitization associated with stressor experiences is not restricted to biogenic amines. There is ample reason to believe that early-life experiences influence adult BDNF responses to later stressors, as well as in response to drugs such as cocaine. In this regard, BDNF may be instrumental in modifying (or controlling) the responsivity of neurons to transmitters, such as DA, and might thus influence pathologies that have been associated with this transmitter, including drug addiction, schizophrenia, depression, and Parkinson's disease. Impressive evidence similarly indicated that FGF-2 may be fundamental for the neuronal plasticity associated with the protracted effects elicited by stressors and by amine stimulants. It is thought that this growth factor might be particularly crucial for the reinstatement of drug addiction by relevant cues among individuals who had ceased their drug intake (e.g., Flores & Stewart, 2000).

Sensitized responses are apparent following exposure to repeated stressors. When animals are exposed to a series of stressors that involve the same insult, an adaptation may develop so that monoamine utilization becomes less pronounced. However, if chronically stressed animals are later exposed to a novel stressor (termed a 'heterotypic' stressor), then the diminished stress response is not seen, and instead exaggerated monoamine changes may be elicited. As depicted in Figure 5.2, it is almost as if a chronic treatment provokes two distinct actions that are antagonistic to one another. Specifically, in relation to a stressor, the processes that give rise to the release of the transmitter become increasingly more pronounced (essentially a sensitization response), but at the same time antagonistic (or countervailing) processes may be set in motion, which might be tied to the contextual cues associated with the initial stressor, making it appear 'as if' an adaptation had developed (i.e., counter-conditioning occurs to diminish the stress response). As a result, when a new stressor is encountered, the sensitized processes burst into action

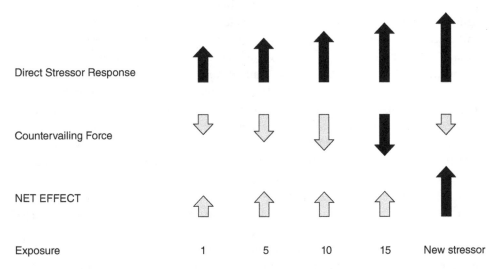

Figure 5.2 Hypothetical responses to repeated exposure to the same stressor over successive days, after which a novel stressor is introduced. On successive days the direct stressor actions become progressively stronger owing to a sensitization of the processes that promote these effects, as do the countervailing responses, leading to modest changes in the net response. However, when a new stressor is encountered the direct, sensitized responses are instigated, but the countervailing actions, which are determined through their association with the stress cues (likely through classical conditioning processes), are limited, resulting in an exaggerated response

(a cross-sensitization) so that the neurochemical changes are elevated. However, as the stressor is a new one, the compensatory countervailing response typically triggered by cues associated with the earlier stressor no longer occurs, thereby allowing the full measure of the sensitization to become evident. This view isn't all that novel, as similar explanations, based on 'opponent process theory', were used to describe several stress-related emotional responses, and a similar conditioning model was proposed to explain processes related to drug addiction and overdose (Siegel & Ramos, 2002; see Chapter 11).

It is of clinical interest that although anxiolytics (drugs that act to reduce anxiety), such as diazepam, limit the NE and DA release elicited by acute stressors, this was less apparent in rats that had been chronically stressed previously. It seems that once the neurochemical changes are pronounced, such as those associated with stressor re-exposure, these are less well managed by anxiolytics. In effect, chronic, unpredictable stressors might not only promote greater vulnerability to psychological problems but might instigate treatment resistance. It likewise seems that once the neuronal systems have become sensitized so that further stressors provoke greater responses, drug treatments are less effective in antagonizing these outcomes.

In summary, although stressful events may have short-lasting neurochemical effects, these experiences may have long-lasting repercussions. If neuronal systems can be programmed by stressful events, then these events may influence responses to later adverse experiences. One needn't even remember having had these encounters, such as if they occurred during infancy, they may nevertheless shape subsequent behaviors. In a sense, biological systems are preprogrammed to be flexible and molded by experiences. In an ideal world, these sensitized responses might help in dealing quickly and efficiently with later stressors. However, depending on the severity of the initial challenge or vulnerability factors that influence responses to a challenge, aversive events might instigate excessive neuronal sensitivity or reactivity to further challenges, thereby favoring the development of certain pathologies.

Conclusion

Stressful events induce multiple neurochemical changes, many of which occur across several brain regions. Although activation of these neurochemical processes might have adaptive value, the capacity for these variations to be sustained may be limited, and when biological systems are overworked (which can happen after severe acute or chronic stressors), behavioral and physical disturbances might ensue. Furthermore, if sufficiently intense, stressful events can alter the characteristics of neurons so that later stressor experiences are more likely to engender neurochemical changes, increasing the likelihood of allostatic overload and hence the development of pathological outcomes.

The point was made earlier that vulnerability to pathology could come about because of dysfunction in any of numerous systems, especially when stressors were unremitting, uncontrollable, and unpredictable. Several questions come to mind when considering the association between stressor-related biological changes and threats to mental or physical health. Significantly, which of the many changes elicited by stressors are helpful, acting to attenuate the psychological or physiological disturbances that might otherwise occur, and which changes are involved in the provocation of damaging effects?

As complicated as this might appear, consider that many neurotransmitters that we haven't touched upon could be affected by stressors. Currently, more than 50 peptides have been identified, many of which can act as neurotransmitters (e.g., neuropeptides such as β-endorphin, dynorphin, enkephalin), and could be influenced by stressful events. In the same way, other monoamine neurotransmitters can be affected by stressors (histamine, melatonin, octopamine, and tyramine). Gaseous substances, such as nitric oxide, can also act like neurotransmitters, and these can likewise be affected by stressors. As we learn more about the effects of stressors on varied processes, it won't be surprising to find that these contribute to the emergence of mental and physical disturbances.

A second aspect of the stress response that needs to be considered is that many of the central actions of stressors can have effects on peripheral processes. Accordingly, it needs to be asked whether any of these, as well as hormonal variations, can serve as biomarkers of illness. That is, can they tell us about pathologies that are imminent, and can they be useful in predicting which treatments might be best? A stressor may give rise to the peripheral release of factors such as cortisol, epinephrine, norepinephrine, and cytokines (immune messengers), together with brain neurotransmitter responses. Other biological alterations may occur, possibly reflecting compensatory effects comprising the under- or over-production of primary neurotransmitter and endocrine changes. Among others, these include variations in insulin, glucose, high-density lipoprotein cholesterol, and triglycerides, as well as inflammatory markers, such as acute phase proteins (e.g., C-reactive protein) that might contribute to a variety of pathologies. Given that these factors vary with stressor experiences, it might be possible to use the changes of neuroendocrine, immune, and metabolic alterations as indices of allostatic overload. Essentially, these might be biomarkers for the stress systems becoming overly taxed and indicative of which systems would be apt to fail, and hence, the types of pathology that might ensue. It's still a bit too early to determine how these multiple biological substrates will be used to predict the development of diseases. For instance, do they have additive predictive power or are some factors redundant with one another so that we don't need all of them to make a prognosis? Likewise, are some more pertinent to certain pathologies and not others? Whatever the case, it seems that the search for stress-related biomarkers is a reasonable approach to determine the predictors of impending illness and the treatments that might be most efficacious.

Suggested readings

Duman, R.S., Aghajanian, G.K., Sanacora, G., & Krystal, J.H. (2016). Synaptic plasticity and depression: New insights from stress and rapid-acting antidepressants. *Nature Medicine*, *22*, 238–249.

McEwen, B.S., Bowles, N.P., Gray, J.D., Hill, M.N., & Hunter, R.G. (2015). Mechanisms of stress in the brain. *Nature Neuroscience*, *18*, 1353–1363.

Parker, L., (2017). *Cannabinoids and the Brain*. Cambridge, MA: MIT Press.

6

THE IMMUNOLOGICAL AND MICROBIAL EFFECTS OF STRESSORS

Science, non-science, and nonsense

There's something to be said about folk wisdom or what some people dismissively refer to as old wives' tales or grandmother tales. These can seem quaint and typically aren't considered seriously. There are also all sorts of superstitious behaviors that seem to be inherited across generations (squashing a spider will cause it to rain; you only use 10% of your brain; don't swim too soon after eating; the five-second rule about food that's fallen onto a filthy floor). Others, however, emerged because they have so frequently been found to be at least partially true, such as it's probably not a great idea to walk beneath a ladder, and for some people pains in their joints mean that the weather is about to change. There is also considerable benefit that can be derived from Indigenous wisdom based on many years of experience passed down across generations of knowledge keepers.

It's also widely thought that if you're sufficiently stressed, you'll end up with any one of several immunologically based illnesses. Over the years there have been repeated suggestions that stress is associated with vulnerability to the common cold or fatigue-related syndromes. In fact, when your doctor can't figure out what's causing your ailment, they may resort to suggesting that stress might be the causative agent for what's been ailing you. Stress is also thought to make you old before your years and since cancer is often a disease of aging, the link between stress and cancer, according to some grandmas and grandpas, is undeniable. There is certainly a lot of folk wisdom that fits into the baloney category, but that doesn't mean all of it is delicatessen grade.

Learning objectives

The immune system is essential for our survival, serving to fend off the challenges that we encounter every day in the form of bacteria, viruses, and other microscopic creatures that seem to be determined to cause us harm. In this chapter you'll come to understand:

- the function of the immune system and the various different cell types and processes that make up this system;
- how hormonal systems interact with the immune system;
- the effects of stressors on immune functioning and some of the moderating variables that affect immunocompetence;
- that immune cells communicate with one another through chemicals referred to as cytokines, which can also affect brain processes and the development of psychological disorders;
- the mechanisms by which inflammation develops, and how stressors promote inflammation that can increase disease susceptibility;
- that many microorganisms (microbiota) ordinarily exist within our bodies that can have either beneficial or harmful effects on health. The actions of these organisms can affect well-being through their effects on hormones, brain functioning, and immune processes.

What the immune system is supposed to do

Most people have some familiarity with the functions of the immune system, including that it's supposed to protect us from all manner of foreign microscopic invaders. Knowing this, you might wonder why we ever get ill. Is the system not very effective? Does it fail us only on a few unique occasions? Are some of us more vulnerable to illness than others? Are there factors that cause our immune systems to malfunction, thereby leaving us vulnerable to the ravages of all sorts of microorganisms that are hanging around? Alternatively, are some threats that we encounter, such as the development of cancer cells, sufficiently adept to outwit our immune system?

Many individuals seem to believe that stressful events increase vulnerability to illnesses, simply because this idea is intuitively appealing. Indeed, you might have noticed that stressful events sometimes precede becoming ill. Of course, if you've made this observation it doesn't qualify as a valid scientific inquiry, nor does it suggest causality. However, numerous studies confirmed that elevated life stressors in the recent past were associated with an increased likelihood of developing respiratory symptoms and clinical colds or influenza. Conversely, having effective ways of coping limited the adverse effects of stressors on immune functioning and the emergence of illnesses.

In line with the findings that stressful events are associated with illness, stressors can influence several aspects of immune functioning. Not unexpectedly, many variables that influence the nature of the immune system changes elicited by chronic stressors also affect the development of physical and psychological disorders. Moreover, it has become ever-more certain that the inflammatory response elicited by stressors can have serious ramifications on both psychological and physical pathologies (Anisman et al., 2018).

Most psychology and neuroscience students will have covered material related to hormones and neurotransmitters, and so in Chapters 4 and 5, some shortcuts were taken in describing these systems. It's less likely that these students will have dealt with the immune system in much detail. Thus, before delving into immune–stress relations, a brief primer concerning the immune system is provided.

The immune system (a very brief primer)

Most analogies of immune processes describe this system as an army that is intent on defending individuals from invading pathogens. This army, like any other armed force, has lots of needs and functions. First, an essential component of any army is to recognize the enemy forces, and concurrently to recognize what comprises the self since it's obviously undesirable for the immune system to cause the death of its own cells by 'friendly fire' (what an oxymoron!). Second, an effective communication system needs to be present so that different functions can be carried out in synchrony and at the right time, including getting new recruits into the battle. Third, there need to be troops who engage the enemy at the front line, those that make up the heavy artillery companies, units that search and destroy (the latter is referred to as 'cell trafficking' in the immune system), and combatants that are in hiding, waiting to ambush the enemy. Fourth, there need to be mechanisms by which soldiers are called off, especially if they become too voracious in their appetite for killing, eventually turning on their own. Finally, the soldiers need to have a memory of the enemy and be able to mount a fast and strong defense should that enemy decide to re-engage at some future date.

Another way of viewing the immune system is through the lens of ecosystems in which the diversity of plants, animals, and microorganisms operate in a coordinated fashion to create harmony and avoid chaos, as described in Chapter 3 where the One Health perspective was introduced. If changes come about within this ecosystem, the organisms present either adapt over generations (through natural selection), operate in a symbiotic manner to enhance survival, or they disappear.

If the challenge to the ecosystem occurs suddenly, essentially acting as a powerful stressor, then adaptation is more challenging to its inhabitants. To an extent, our biological systems operate in a similar manner. Balances ordinarily exist so that our intrinsic environment remains within certain bounds (homeostasis is an example of this). We saw this in the context of hormonal and neurotransmitter systems where checks and balances are present to maintain effective functioning. This also holds for immune functioning in which systematic, coordinated changes occur so that the integrity of the organism is maintained. This is typically achieved, although any number of challenges can be encountered so that the immune system is less able to contend with threats, and as a result illnesses may develop. Strong, unremitting stressors may undermine immune functioning, resulting in elevated vulnerability to illnesses brought about by extrinsic factors (viruses, bacteria) as well as those that stem from intrinsic processes (e.g., the development of excessive inflammation).

Components of the immune system

The immune system constantly monitors the organism's internal environment for indications of tissue damage and the presence of bacteria and viruses. This entails knowing what the 'self' comprises, and then anything that isn't 'self' can be treated as foreign. Much of this information is established in the developing fetus, during which the immune cells are 'learning' what's you and what's not. We term this aspect of the immune system 'innate immunity'. Postnatally, certain immune cells acquire further information about foreign particles, which is referred to as 'adaptive' or 'acquired' immunity.

Ordinarily, after immune cells are exposed to an antigen (i.e., foreign particles or molecules from damaged tissues), an exquisitely orchestrated immune response occurs. To a considerable extent, this is achieved by leukocytes, a type of white blood cell, that circulate throughout the body to provide immunological protection against microbial antigens (essentially engaging in surveillance and search-and-destroy missions). The other type of blood cells that are present comprise red blood cells (erythrocytes) that carry oxygen to body tissues.

Innate immune cells

Myeloid and lymphoid cells are the primary classes of immune cells. The myeloid cells, which are derived from bone marrow, comprise granulocytes (primarily neutrophils), monocytes, macrophages, and dendritic cells. The macrophages and dendritic cells are key players during the early stages of an immune response being mounted. These cells act in a nonspecific fashion to phagocytose (literally 'eat up') microbes and necrotic (dead) tissue, digest and process these, and then display parts of them on their surface. These immune cells are referred to as antigen presenting cells (APCs) as a main part of their job is to present an antigen (a molecule or molecular structure present on the outer surface of a foreign substance that can trigger an immune response) to certain types of T cells that make decisions about whether these cells belong to the individual (self) or are foreign. In addition, natural killer (NK) cells play a fundamental role in innate immunity, but it has characteristics of cells of the adaptive immune system, including a rudimentary memory capacity.

Antigen presenting cells

In 1973 Ralph Steinman and Zanvil Cohn described dendritic cells that turned out to be a type of antigen presenting cell. It was a while before immunologists started paying attention to the importance of this cell type (in fact, this didn't occur until the 1990s), and in 2011 Steinman won the Nobel Prize in Physiology or Medicine for his discovery. Although the Nobel Prize isn't given posthumously (Cohn died in 1993), an exception was made in the case of Steinman, who died three days before the announcement of the prize. The committee members were unaware of his death, and once announced, retracting the prize would have been a pretty miserable thing to do.

Natural killer cells

Of the innate immune cells, appreciable attention was devoted to the actions of natural killer (NK) cells because of their ability to attack and destroy viruses and some types of cancers. Once an NK cell encounters a suspected tumor cell or one that contains a virus, it searches for a marker or switch that will inform it whether the cell is safe or dangerous. If the marker is present (signaling that it is not a threat), then the NK cell will back off and go on its way. However, if this marker is not found, the NK cell will attack the target cell, penetrating its outer shell and injecting chemicals into it (e.g., *perforin* and *granzyme*), causing its death and disintegration, along with the viruses that reside inside the cell. From their name, NK cells sound as if they're the tough guys of the immune world. In fact, they're not all that tough compared to other types of immune cells and serve primarily to contain an invading enemy, giving the adaptive immune system the opportunity to mount stronger cytotoxic T and B cell responses to deal with the virus. Scenes such as this play out again and again, day after day, and represent part of the surveillance system that protects us from intruders. But under certain conditions this system may fail, and the result can be disastrous.

The actions of NK cells can be directed by specific signaling molecules released by immune cells. These signaling molecules, referred to as cytokines, include interferons (IFN) and several interleukins (ILs) that can act to keep NK cells active and alive (Abel et al., 2018). Typically, NK cells serve in a protective capacity, but they can have deleterious actions by causing tissue damage. Moreover, NK cell subtypes can promote the release of certain growth factors (e.g., transforming growth factor-β; TGF-β), which can suppress antitumor responses so that cancer growth can be promoted.

The sword cuts both ways

While neutrophils and macrophages are essential to eliminate foreign particles, they can promote negative outcomes. These cells are among the first to migrate to sites of injury where they phagocytose bacteria or viruses and release cytotoxic particles that act against infection. The cytokines released by these immune cells contribute to the production of an inflammatory microenvironment. Ordinarily, inflammation is beneficial, but when it is excessive and persistent it may promote a variety of disease conditions, including clinical levels of depressive illness, metabolic disorders (e.g., type 2 diabetes), heart disease, and the exacerbation of cancer progression.

Innate immune cells that promote an inflammatory response also produce reactive oxygen species (ROS), such as peroxide and superoxide, together with nitric oxide that in combination produce the highly damaging radical, peroxynitrite, which serves to destroy invading pathogens. However, as with so many other biological processes, the 'Goldilocks principle' applies so that the benefit of ROS occurs when maintained within circumscribed limits: neither too high nor too low. When ROS levels are too high, genomic instability may develop and DNA mutations may contribute to the transformation of healthy cells into tumors. In effect, when inflammation occurs chronically, the production of oxygen free radicals that hadn't been neutralized by antioxidants may promote age-related diseases, including heart disease and the development of cancer. This has given rise to the view that elevated intake of foods rich in antioxidants (e.g., some fruits, and vegetables, as well as resveratrol obtained through red wine) reduce the risk of some diseases. It has also fostered large business ventures to peddle over-the-counter pharmaceutical supplements that act as antioxidants even if their medicinal value hadn't consistently been experimentally confirmed.

Adaptive (acquired) immunity

The primary lymphoid organs, namely, the thymus and bone marrow, are the sites for the generation of lymphocytes that comprise T and B cells, respectively, that serve to implement adaptive immunity. In addition, *secondary* lymphoid organs, such as the lymph nodes as well as the spleen and lungs, are essential as immune responses can be amplified at these sites. As lymphocytes divide and multiply during infection, this is often reflected by a swelling of the lymph nodes.

While T and B cells deal with pathogens in different ways, they share several essential characteristics: (a) *Specificity*: any given B or T cell can respond to only a single antigen. Both T and B cells can respond to the same antigen. (b) *Diversity*: multiple antigenic markers may be present on the surface of foreign particles; with the great diversity of immune cells present, different targets located on a foreign molecule can be attacked. (c) *Discrimination between self and non-self*: After developing into specific types of immune cells, self-recognition mechanisms need to be in place to prevent attacks and damage to self-tissues. (d) *Proliferation and elimination*: Once the adaptive immune response is activated, the effector arm of the immune response promotes the elimination of microbial antigens. Among other things, this entails the production of antibodies by B cells as well as cell-signaling molecules, such as cytokines that promote immune cell proliferation and differentiation of lymphocytes. The resulting elevated number and range of lymphocytes provide a quantitative advantage over microbial intruders. (e) *Memory*: after being prompted to multiply by an antigen, the T and B cells clones will maintain a memory of the antigen, so that when they encounter it again they will respond more rapidly and robustly. Consequently, the foreign particle will be eliminated before a disease can develop. Until recently it was thought that NK cells do not have 'memory' abilities, but it seems that they may have a short-lived 'trained memory' making them stronger and more efficient in dealing with the same (or very similar) challenges (Nikzad et al., 2019). (f) *Self-limitation*: memory cells ought to limit their attack to previously encountered antigens.

Lymphocytes: T and B cells

Having captured a foreign particle, APCs present a component of these to lymphocytes, thereby promoting their activation, ultimately leading to cytotoxicity (the destruction of infected cells). T and B lymphocytes eliminate pathogens in different ways.

B cells

B cells neutralize foreign products by attacking them when they're traveling within the body. The B lymphocytes produce antibodies that recognize and indirectly destroy foreign matter. The actions of B cells are termed *humoral* immune responses, since antibodies or immunoglobulin molecules (abbreviated as Ig) appear within bodily fluids (humors), such as blood, where they mark invaders for destruction.

Following their activation, B cells differentiate into either (1) memory cells that can survive in the body for years and whose function is that of remembering an antigen and responding quickly when that antigen is encountered again, or (2) antibody-producing cells (also referred to as plasma cells) that secrete soluble antibody. There are five classes (isotypes) of antibody molecules: IgA, IgD, IgE, IgM, and IgG. The general make-up of all antibodies is very similar, comprising a Y-shaped structure composed of two light and two heavy polypeptide chains (depicted in Figure 6.1). The ends of the two arms of the Y of this protein are variable, meaning that their composition can differ from other antibodies. This part of an antibody is essential for recognizing a foreign particle. As there are millions of these antibodies, each with slightly different tip or end structures (referred to as antigen binding sites), they can recognize a very wide range of foreign antigens. These recognition sites don't need to identify the entire antigen, they only need to see a part of it to promote an immune response (you don't need to see every element of your friends to recognize them, just seeing their face is enough). Once an antigen is recognized as being foreign it is 'tagged' to signal its removal by other immune cells. As well, antibodies can neutralize targets directly by binding to a part of a pathogen and activating the 'complement pathway' (several small proteins present in the blood), which contributes to the formation of a complex that helps antibodies kill the pathogen. As described in Figure 6.1, the classes of antibodies serve somewhat different functions and are concentrated at different points in our bodies.

At the outset of this chapter, a primary function of certain immune cells was said to be that of learning about the enemy as there is a possibility that this force will return later, and we would be well served if our immune cells recognized the enemy as soon as they returned. In fact, 'immunological memory' (also referred to as acquired characteristics) is the hallmark of some immune cells, so that a rapid and powerful response is mounted to an antigen that the immune system had previously encountered.

During the primary immune response, which occurs the first time a particular antigen is met, a memory of it is established so that when these memory B cells subsequently encounter the antigen again (or something that looks sufficiently similar to it), a rapid immune response occurs during which the IgG isotype predominates. Because of the magnitude and speed of the secondary immune response being mounted, the illness is not likely to reappear. Thus, for instance, when exposed to the chickenpox virus for the first time, we might end up with a bunch of sores and feel poorly for days. However, when we again encounter this virus years later, the immune system mounts a strong secondary response, and the virus is destroyed before it can make us ill. In the case of some illnesses, such as chickenpox, a related illness, shingles (also known as Herpes Zoster, which is very different from Herpes Simplex that some readers might be more familiar with) can occur because the virus was not fully eliminated from the body, hiding in nerve cells or other places, and may subsequently re-emerge to create considerable discomfort. Most viruses don't act in this way, and once we've seen an end to their initial assault, we likely won't be *plagued* by them again. But, as we've seen with COVID-19, antibodies can decline over time following infection or vaccination so that reinfection is possible.

T cells

The T cells have regulatory and direct cytotoxic functions in which they directly destroy foreign cells, thus the responses of T cells are referred to as *cellular* immune responses. Ordinarily, a virus gets into a cell and then into the nucleus where it uses the cell's own DNA machinery to replicate itself (as these crafty little devils don't have their own capacity to multiply, they hijack host cells to do their dirty work). T cells have evolved to attack cells that have been infected by a virus, and in doing so they destroy whole factories that would otherwise be making the virus.

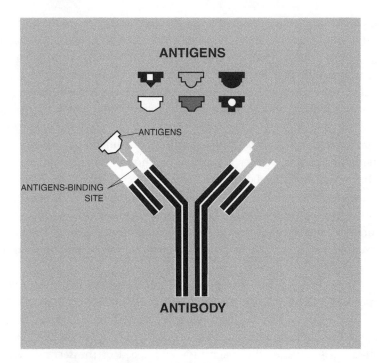

Figure 6.1   Antigens have external characteristics which can bind with the end parts of an antibody, provided that the antigen binding site is compatible with the antigenic features. The five types of immunoglobulins appear during different periods of infection and are not equally distributed in different parts of an individual.

IgA is present in mucosal areas, such as the respiratory tract, urogenital tract and the gut, as well as in saliva and tears, and thus might be the first to encounter foreign substances that enter the body.

IgE binds to antigens that provoke parasitic infections, but in some individuals, it binds to environmental substances that can elicit allergies (allergens). When this occurs, histamine is released from mast cells and basophils, resulting in the common symptoms of allergies.

IgD appears on the surface of naïve B cells (i.e., those that have not previously been stimulated), serving as receptors for antigens. IgD activates aspects of the immune system, including mast cells and basophils that are involved in actions that enhance immune functioning.

IgG contributes to antibody-based immunity against previously encountered invading pathogens. As IgG can pass into the placenta it can also provide passive immunity to the developing fetus.

IgM is involved in eliminating pathogens upon initial encounters with them. This antibody is activated during the early phase of a B cell mediated response, acting as the first line of defense.

Source: Illustration created by Lucas J. Wareing.

Several types of T cells exist that fall into distinct classes with different functions. We can tell them apart by their name tags. In this case, the name tags are made up of molecules present on the cell surface that can be identified (e.g., terms such as CD4 and CD8, as well as CD16 and CD56, among others, are used to signify the T-cell type). One type of T cell referred to as a cytotoxic T cell (CD8+), can directly lyse virally infected cells (lysis occurs when the T cell attaches itself to the target and ruptures the cellular membrane, thereby causing the viral contents to be destroyed). A second type of T cell is the T helper (T_h) cell (designated as CD4+ cells) that doesn't kill infected cells as cytotoxic T cells do, nor do they remove debris like macrophages do. Instead, they serve as information couriers that direct and stimulate the actions of other cells. Upon being presented with a portion of an antigen (this is termed an *epitope*) a type of T_h cell (the T_h1 cell) may recognize it as being foreign and then promote the multiplication of cytotoxic T and B cells to attack the enemy.

It is essential that regulatory processes exist so that immune cells don't attack the self. *Immune tolerance* develops through the down-regulation of immune cell functioning, which is an essential self-regulatory feature to limit the risk of autoimmunity (i.e., diseases in which the immune system turns against the self, thus provoking an autoimmune disorder). Certain immune cells have multiple functions serving to deal with challenges while concurrently acting in a regulatory capacity. Specifically, T_h2 cells play a particularly important role in promoting immune responses targeting bacteria, extracellular parasites, allergens, and toxins as well as regulation of antibody functioning. Significantly, T_h2 cells serve in an anti-inflammatory capacity, thereby countering the actions of T_h1 cells. Fundamental to the inhibitory immune process are T regulatory (T_{reg}) cells that inhibit cytotoxic cells from attacking self-tissue and they simultaneously provoke metabolic changes that influence energy production and can thereby limit immune functioning.

For the complex set of events involved in an immune response being mounted, as described in Figure 6.2, a fair bit of cross-talk occurs between different types of cells. Messages are sent from one immune cell to another through chemical signals (cytokines) that, in some respects, are reminiscent of how neurons in the brain communicate with one another. These cytokines are synthesized and released by various immune cells (macrophages and lymphocytes in the periphery, and by astrocytes and microglia in the brain). Within the periphery, these cytokines act as signals for growth and the differentiation of lymphocytes and act in a paracrine or autocrine fashion (stimulation of cells that are close or by self-regulation, respectively). Certain cytokines, such as interleukin (IL)-1β, IL-6, IL-18, tumor necrosis factor-α (TNF-α), and interferons (IFN), are classified as proinflammatory (largely produced by macrophages and T_h1 cells) as they encourage inflammation. Others, such as IL-4 and IL-10 that are produced by T_h2 cells, act against the proinflammatory cytokines and hence are referred to as anti-inflammatory cytokines. The T_{reg} cells similarly release IL-10 and several other factors that are essential in preventing attacks on the self. Ideally, the pro- and anti-inflammatory cytokines are 'in balance' with one another.

In response to viral or bacterial challenges the proinflammatory cytokines go into action, and when the job is done the anti-inflammatory cytokines kick in to have immune attacks cease. There are many other cytokines, but these players will be introduced as we get to them.

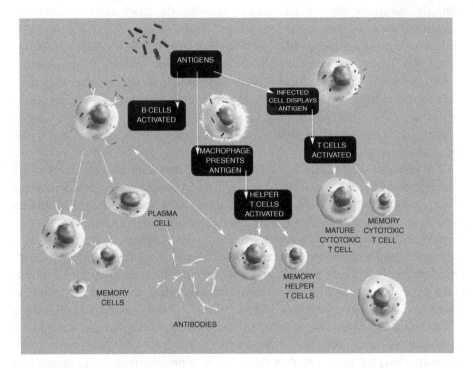

Figure 6.2   Upon exposure to an antigen, macrophages engulf the foreign particle and then display aspects of it to T and B cells that may either be naïve or have a memory of the foreign substance. By influencing B cells and antibody production, as well as affecting different types of T cells, a strong immune response is mounted to eliminate the foreign matter. If the antigen had previously been encountered, sensitized B cells and antibodies, as well as memory T cells, react quickly and strongly, thereby dispatching the threat (modified from J.W. Bastien (www.uta.edu/chagas/html/biolImS1.html).

Source: Illustration modified by Lucas J. Wareing.

Chemokines

Like cytokines, chemokines play an important role in immune processes. Chemokines comprise several families of small cytokines that attract immune cells through their *chemoattractant* capacity to sites of tissue infection and inflammation. Chemokine receptors are expressed on all leukocytes, being especially prominent on T cells, so that these circulating lymphocytes are directed to sites of injury and inflammation. As well, during the normal course of immune surveillance, chemokines direct lymphocytes to the lymph nodes where pathogen screening occurs through interactions with antigen-presenting cells. In addition to these functions, chemokines contribute to nervous system development by affecting axonal guidance and may be involved in the growth of new blood vessels (angiogenesis), which, unfortunately, can facilitate cancer growth.

T cell memory

The process by which T cells gain memory abilities is not as well described as those related to B cells. It is thought that after exposure to an antigen, naïve T cells form into effector T cells that target specific antigens. After the pathogen is eliminated, most effector cells die off through apoptosis, the process by which 'programmed' cell death occurs so that old cells or ineffectual cells are removed. However, a subset of these T cells remain and clones are produced. The change from effector T cells to memory T cells may be related to the heterogeneity that exists between CD8 cell subsets so that some are programmed to become memory cells (e.g., Martin & Badovinac, 2018). Other T cells will become memory cells simply because of their enhanced longevity, or through epigenetic changes (Youngblood et al., 2017). Prior to the COVID-19 pandemic, most people were likely poorly educated concerning immune processes and the development of acquired immunity. Since then, the frequent discussion of vaccines has educated some people about the role of B cells and antibodies in immune memory, but too often the importance of T cell memory has not received much attention. However, it is certain that vaccines operate in producing memory T cells that can act against viruses (Akondy et al., 2017) and the capacity of these cells may be more lasting than that of B cells.

———Oh heck, wear a mask and keep away from me———

Well before the discipline of immunology came about, or even before much was understood about viruses and bacteria, at a time when bloodletting and leeches were used as cures, there was clearly a rudimentary understanding of some immunological concepts. For instance, the history of diseases is replete with examples where affected individuals were isolated (and even shipped off to islands) for fear of the illness spreading (think of the poor lepers). During times when the Black Death rampaged through Europe, ships that had reached port on the Italian coast were kept at sea for a period to make sure that the silent killer wasn't brought on to shore, thus infecting the populace. Typically, ships were kept away for 40 days, referred to as 'quarantena', and it is from this that we've got our word 'quarantine'. The duration of this quarantine ought to vary with the disease being considered as infectious periods can vary depending on the virus.

Despite these common-sense precautions, as we've seen during the COVID-19 pandemic, there are large segments of society that have vigorously opposed these measures, indicating that they violate their individual rights. Unfortunately, their behaviors violate the rights of the rest of us not to become infected.

Changes in immune competence

In assessing the effects of stressors on the capabilities of the immune system, several aspects of competence are frequently measured. Analyses of various treatments on immune functioning can be conducted through *in vitro* procedures (in parts of an organism, or in a test tube or petri dish) and *in vivo* (in the living organism). Analyses of immune functioning can include counting the number of specific types of immune cells that are present (per a fixed volume of blood). But this doesn't provide a *functional* index of immune competence, such as the extent to which immune cells are doing what they were programmed to do, namely multiply, search out and identify invaders, and then kill them.

It is necessary to determine, among other things, whether a treatment such as a stressor influences the 'cell trafficking pattern'. For example, where are lymphocytes actually residing? Are they in circulation looking for potential pathogens or are they just hanging out at secondary immune organs, such as the spleen? In addition, it is essential to determine the rate of T or B cell proliferation (i.e., their multiplication in blood or in secondary immune organs) in response to specific stimulants (called mitogens), as well as the antibody responses evident upon exposure to foreign substances (antigenic stimuli). In concert with measuring immune cell multiplication, it is important to know the killing ability of specific immune cells upon being challenged. Of course, in the end, what we really want to know is whether a treatment has positive or negative effects on the organism's well-being in the face of an infectious challenge (i.e., has their vulnerability to pathology been altered?). This question is typically examined by assessing the vulnerability to viral or bacterial insults, recovery from illnesses or rate of wound healing, and the development or exacerbation of pathological symptoms.

Inflammasomes

The *inflammasomes* are key immune sensors that are involved in the promotion of inflammation in response to infectious microbes as well as specific host proteins. Inflammasomes comprise multiprotein complexes that serve as a way through which changes of cellular integrity and biological threats are detected by endogenous processes. Specialized detection receptors are present within and on the surface of immune cells. These 'pattern recognition receptors' (PRRs) can recognize molecules that are broadly shared by pathogens, collectively dubbed 'pathogen-associated molecular patterns' (PAMPs) (Riera Romo et al., 2016). Activation of PRRs on immune cells stimulate an innate immune response accompanied by inflammation, as well as activation of adaptive immunity, which eventually results in infection being resolved. Activation of inflammasomes is not only influenced by microorganisms, but can be instigated by diverse environmental irritants, toxicants, and by molecules associated with cellular damage (Levy et al., 2015). When cells are distressed, they release danger-associated molecular patterns (DAMPS) that stimulate PRRs. Important components of the PRRs are toll-like receptors (TLRs) and NOD-like receptors (NLRs) that can detect a variety of signals, which may contribute to inflammation. The inflammatory response, as we've seen, can be beneficial to health, but when it is excessive and persistent, multiple health problems can ensue, such as diabetes, heart disease, inflammatory bowel disease, and some cancers, as well as psychological disorders, such as depression and anxiety (Iwata et al., 2013).

Sterile inflammation

Inflammation can be engendered by non-infectious agents, such as diverse toxicants, tissue damage, ischemia (low oxygen levels), necrotic cells (dying cells in which membrane rupture has occurred), and by psychological stressors, and is thus referred to as *sterile inflammation* (Fleshner & Crane, 2017). Danger signals that prompt sterile inflammation may come from intracellular molecules that function as DAMPs. These actions can occur owing to elevated levels of certain types of proteins (heat shock proteins) that can be promoted when cells are stressed, as well as by fragments of degraded proteins that are required for tissue repair. Furthermore, when released into the extracellular fluid (fluid outside the cell) in response to cellular distress, the body's primary cellular energy source, adenosine triphosphate (ATP), can act as a DAMP. As well, high-mobility group box 1 (HMGB1), a protein that is ordinarily present within cells can be released into the extracellular space where it can likewise serve as a DAMP. This protein has been implicated in several forms of cancer and may undermine the effectiveness of chemotherapy, and HMBG1 within the brain can provoke neuronal changes that favor the development of neurological and psychiatric illnesses. Thus, targeting HMBG1 could potentially be a way of acting against some forms of cancer and inflammation associated with some viral illnesses.

The occurrence of sterile inflammation can wreak havoc in association with several medical conditions. The overwhelming inflammatory response is frequently seen in patients with an acute lung injury or acute respiratory distress syndrome that occurs in severely ill patients or after patients have been placed on a ventilator. The interaction between DAMPs and dendritic cells is thought to play a key role in tumor immunity, autoimmunity, and chronic inflammatory conditions. Sterile inflammation has likewise been implicated in the provocation of peripheral inflammatory-related diseases and can provoke cytokine changes that occur within the brain owing to activation of glial cells, including astrocytes and microglia, thereby instigating psychological and neurological disorders.

While immune processes are typically considered in the context of invading microbes, considerable evidence has accumulated showing that physical, chemical, and metabolic stimuli can trigger sterile inflammation that can have enormous health repercussions. It is significant that psychological stressors can promote sterile inflammation (Fleshner & Crane, 2017), but the adoption of healthy lifestyle factors, such as exercise and proper diets, can limit its promotion or progression.

Immune-hormone interactions

The regulation of hormones, neurotransmitters, and growth factors are obviously essential for well-being, and this holds for immune functioning as well. Once again, the Goldilocks analogy seems to be particularly applicable, especially as different pathological outcomes may occur when our immune activity goes off the rails in one direction or another. Fine reciprocal balances exist between and within different aspects of the immune system, and regulatory factors that are external to the immune system are essential in determining the effective functioning of our defensive systems.

Glucocorticoids and other hormones

Glucocorticoids (such as cortisol) are not only activated by stressors, but by inflammatory immune stimuli. At physiological levels (i.e., those that naturally occur in the body in response to a challenge) this hormone modulates immune functioning, preventing excessive immune activity. At pharmacological doses (high levels engendered by administration of a compound at doses exceeding those that ordinarily appear in the body) glucocorticoids can have more pronounced effects acting as potent immunosuppressants rather than simply preventing a rise of immune activity. Given the pronounced effects of stressors on glucocorticoid release, it is reasonable to assume that stressors will affect immune functioning (Cain & Cidlowski, 2017). However, it is necessary to bear in mind that the corticoid changes might be dependent on whether the stressor is acute or chronic, and whether it is a moderate stressor versus one that is traumatizing, as well as in relation to previous stressor experiences. In response to chronic stressors, for instance, the actions of glucocorticoids can be down-regulated so that the regulatory actions of hormones on components of the immune system may diminish.

The interactions with the immune system are not limited to glucocorticoids, and several other hormonal processes act in this capacity. Sex hormones, such as estrogen and progesterone, as well as epinephrine, thyroid hormones, melanocortin, and many others, may influence immune activity and hence the emergence of pathological states (e.g., Anisman & Kusnecov, 2022). As stressful events affect many of these neuroendocrine processes, the identification of unique environmental factors that interact with multiple hormonal and immunological processes has garnered increasing interest.

Interactions between the immune system and the brain

At one time, it had been maintained that the immune system and the brain were independent of one another. Immunological activity was thought to be restricted to peripheral domains and was not influenced by psychological events. This position was eventually abandoned and replaced with the view that multi-directional communication occurs between the immune, endocrine, autonomic, microbial, and central nervous systems. Recognition that hormones could affect immune functioning came early but figuring out how the immune system communicated with the brain (and vice versa) had proven to be another matter entirely.

The brain was held to be 'an immunologically privileged organ' (i.e., not affected by peripheral immune functioning), but it was thought that messages could get to the brain through the molecules by which immune cells communicated with one another (i.e., cytokines). Although cytokines are large molecules that have only limited access to brain neurons owing to the tight junctions of capillary endothelial cells (cells that line blood vessels) that comprise the blood–brain barrier, under some conditions this semipermeable membrane may be compromised allowing greater access to the brain. For instance, this may occur with head injury and in the presence of high fever, and even metabolites of gut microbiota can affect the blood-brain barrier, resulting in greater access to the brain by relatively large molecules. Even in the absence of these factors, cytokines can be ferried into the brain through active transport systems (Banks, 2019), thereby influencing neuronal functioning. Moreover, cytokines can influence neurons within regions at the edge of the brain or where the barriers to the brain are less efficient, including around the ventricles (termed 'circumventricular organs', such as the organum vasculosum of the lamina terminalis and the area postrema), the posterior pituitary, and the median eminence.

Regardless of the route, activation of the inflammatory immune system can influence HPA activity and affect neurotransmitter functioning in several forebrain regions that are associated with mood processes and decision-making. To an appreciable extent, the neurochemical changes elicited by inflammatory factors are reminiscent of those elicited by psychogenic and neurogenic stressors, which led to the suggestion that the brain interpreted peripheral immune challenges as if they were stressors. Essentially, the immune system may be part of a regulatory loop that, through its actions on neuroendocrine, neurochemical, and growth factors, might contribute to the symptoms of mood and anxiety-related disorders as well as several neurological disturbances (Anisman et al., 2018).

Microglia

Microglia are present in the brain in enormous numbers, making up about 15% of cells within the brain. As described in Chapter 5, contrary to beliefs maintained several decades ago, they aren't simply 'the help'. Under certain conditions, including in response to chronic stressors, they may have a lot to do with the development of psychological pathology. Microglia communicate with neurons, are involved in synaptic pruning (i.e., eliminating synapses that have not been used) and in neurogenesis, and might play a role in memory formation (Matejuk & Ransohoff, 2020).

An important feature of microglia is that they serve in a macrophage-like capacity in the brain, acting as the brain's immune sentinels, orchestrating powerful inflammatory responses. Activation of microglia occurs in response to systemic or central challenges by bacteria or viruses, and cytokine synthesis and release are generated by brain microglia in response to physical and chemical insults (e.g., brain injury, concussive injury, seizure, cerebral ischemia, chemically induced brain lesions). Moreover, stressors increase the production and levels of cytokines within the brain, which influence hormonal and neurotransmitter activity. The increase of cytokines stemming from brain insults might reflect their involvement in a reparatory capacity; however, when the concentration of these cytokines is too high, they might act in a destructive manner leading to psychopathology and neurodegenerative disorders (Bachiller et al., 2018).

Stress, central processes, and immunological alterations

In describing the effects of stressors on immune functioning, we've been painting with a very broad brush, and understanding how stressors affect illnesses requires analyses of the diverse ways by which immune functioning is altered. Many of the elements that make up the immune system could be disrupted by stressful events and it may not be productive to consider these in isolation of one another. Even if NK cytotoxicity in any given individual is strong, it may be that the B cell or T cell responses are weak, or these lymphocytes don't proliferate as they should, or maybe they simply don't recognize invaders properly. While the immune system is very powerful and protects us fairly well, it isn't perfect, and by disturbing immune functioning stressors can favor the development of diverse illnesses.

As much as one would like to make some very simple and straightforward conclusions concerning the impact of stressors on immunity and our vulnerability to pathology, we still don't have a complete picture of how stressors lead to immune-related disorders. Numerous factors seem to influence the way in which stressors affect immune functioning, and stressors might not affect all the components of immune processes in the same way. Besides, as most of us know, viruses and bacteria are not simple little critters that just hang around waiting to be destroyed by the immune system, but instead they evolve and engage in strategies to evade detection and destruction. Cancer cells are similarly able to adopt strategies to evade our immune system and therapeutic agents that ought to destroy them. Just when our immune system seems to have learned how to deal with a virus, bacteria, or type of cancer cell, new variants can emerge so that our protective arsenal could be evaded.

Moreover, stressful experiences might limit the adaptability of the immune system to deal with these ever-changing challenges.

Studies in animals

Stressful events influence immune functioning across a range of different species, including laboratory animals (mice, rats) and domesticated farm animals (fowl, pigs, cattle). The immune changes are dependent on the stressor severity and chronicity, and are influenced by experiential, developmental, and organismic factors, such as those described in Chapter 1. Altered immune functioning is frequently seen in response to neurogenic (physical) challenges, but stressor effects on immune activity are not attributable simply to tissue damage, as they are provoked by psychological stressors and by cues that had been associated with stressors, as well as by variations in social stability.

Strong and weak stressors

Much attention has focused on the effects of stressors on first-line immune defenders comprising macrophages and dendritic cells that are drawn to sites of inflammation to neutralize invaders before further adaptive responses are engaged. As such, it is meaningful that stressors undermine the functioning of these cells (Maslanik et al., 2012). As well, stressors cause altered trafficking of these first-line defenders to tissues where they are likely to encounter potential pathogens.

The actions of stressors on immune functioning can be moderated by individual difference factors (e.g., sex, age, previous stressor experiences) as well as by features of the stressor, thereby influencing susceptibility or resilience to diseases (Hodes et al., 2014). For instance, among mice that experienced social defeat, dendritic cells were diminished within the spleen (a secondary lymphoid organ involved in filtering out and destroying pathogens). Significantly, in a social aggression paradigm more pronounced immune effects were noted in submissive than in dominant animals (Hodes et al., 2014) accompanied by greater and more persistent inflammatory changes. These mice displayed elevated neutrophils, monocytes, and spleen cells that produced and released proinflammatory cytokines. Such actions may have resulted from hormonal alterations through epigenetic changes that were provoked.

Stressors' effects on immune functioning, circulating cytokines, and the production of cytokines within the brain vary with the timing of the stressor relative to an immune challenge. If animals are exposed to a stressor and they then encounter an antigenic challenge not long afterward (say, within 24 hours), the immune response and certain cytokines may be elevated. In contrast, if animals were first exposed to an immunogenic challenge and then exposed to the stressor, immune suppression might be apparent. It likewise appears that corticoid treatment administered hours prior to an immune challenge may lead to immunoenhancement, whereas this does not occur if the corticoid treatment and the immune challenge occur together. It seems that the stressor (or corticoid) serves as a priming stimulus so that the immune system is ready to respond if necessary. It is as if the initial stressor might have caused the deployment of essential immune cells, but once the emergency has abated and the immune cells were again 'relaxed', a sneak attack in the form of an immunogenic challenge was particularly effective in getting around the protective capacity of immune cells.

Acute versus chronic challenges

It generally appears that mild stressors may augment immunity, whereas severe or protracted stressors have the opposite effect (Dhabhar, 2014). For instance, exposing animals to a predator enhanced the proliferative response of B cells, but this did not occur if mice had been exposed to the stressor on a chronic basis. An acute stressor ought to result in a surge of immune functioning to deal with the challenges, and at the same time those functions that aren't essential at the moment, such as digestion or reproduction, should be shut down. But as the stressor continues, the availability of biological resources may decline, thus rendering the organism more vulnerable to immunological disturbances. Moreover, having dealt with an initial challenge the capacity of the immune system to deal with a second stressor that comes along may be diminished, either because of hormonal activation that elicits immune suppression or because the immune system has, in a sense, become fatigued by the first experience. With still further stressors these negative immunological reactions might become more pronounced.

The immunological disturbances associated with chronic stressors have been observed in various paradigms and in relation to diverse aspects of the immune system. In this respect, lengthy stressor periods could promote apoptotic death of macrophages (Y. Xiang et al., 2015) and following a chronic stressor experience T_{reg} cells, as well as tumor-associated macrophages were increased, which could diminish the actions of CD8+ T cells (Antoni & Dhabhar, 2019).

One of the most potent stressors for social animals, as in the case of humans, concerns social disruption (or social defeat), and this insult may have marked effects on immune functioning and susceptibility to infectious disease. This is especially the case as social stressors likely don't occur on an occasional basis but represent the norm among communal animals. A chronic social stressor suppressed CD8+ T cell proliferation and macrophage-derived IFN-γ (Muthuswamy et al., 2017), and increased monocyte trafficking to the brain, thereby affecting microglia (Ramirez et al., 2017).

Ordinarily, corticoids inhibit immune functioning and could potentially regulate (limit) the actions of stressors on immunity. However, after sustained social disruption, resistance was evident to the immunosuppressive effects of glucocorticoids

(Kempter et al., 2021). Although this should enhance the ability of the immune system to fight off invaders, the absence of the suppressive effects of glucocorticoids would allow for excessive cytokine production that might result in increased autoimmune responses as well as mortality in response to inflammatory immune challenges. Once more, these findings point to the limits of adaptive changes that might be associated with stressors, and persistent or repeated social stressor experiences may give rise to immune alterations that could promote or exacerbate serious health complications. Effects such as these were not only observed in response to a pathogenic stimulus encountered for the first time but can disturb the very powerful secondary immune response (Dhabhar, 2009). This may have implications for the ability of our immune system to fend off previously encountered microbes and may be relevant to the efficacy of vaccines to protect us from viruses.

It won't be the least surprising to learn that there are many variables that could influence the impact of social stressors (as well as other psychogenic and neurogenic stressors) on immune functioning, as well as vulnerability to disease. Table 6.1 provides a general overview of the effects of acute and chronic stressors on immune functioning and the hypothesized impact on various pathological conditions. The immunosuppression associated with chronic stressors might be taken to signify the failure of an adaptive response being sustained, which might culminate in elevated illness susceptibility (Dhabhar, 2018).

The differential effects of acute and chronic stressors might appear to be straightforward, but it needs to be kept in mind that immune processes comprise a dynamic system and hence the influence of a given manipulation can vary over time. As well, the outcomes observed are dependent on individual differences (e.g., between highly stress-reactive and nonreactive mouse strains) and with the specific immune compartment being examined (e.g., reflected by measures taken in blood versus the spleen). In fact, the cytokine variations in the periphery were not necessarily paralleled by those appearing in the brain (Gibb et al., 2011).

Sex differences in response to stressors

Males and females differ in the occurrence of numerous diseases, including a female bias in relation to autoimmune disorders. However, vulnerability to infectious disease pathogenesis is generally diminished in females, including viral and bacterial illnesses as well as parasitic and fungal infections. Paralleling these findings, immune functioning was generally greater in females than in males, although males exhibited greater NK cell functioning (Klein & Flanagan, 2016). Sex dimorphisms have been tied to sex hormones that can stimulate receptors on immune cells and may be related to differences in the production of inflammatory damage, apoptosis, and oxidative stress (Bhatia et al., 2014).

Given the sex differences in hormonal responses to stressors, it would be reasonable to surmise that corresponding sex dimorphisms would occur in the immune responses elicited by stressors. Somewhat surprisingly, the effects of stressors on

Table 6.1   Acute and chronic stressors may have pronounced effects on immune functioning and disease outcomes. Moderately intense acute stressors most often enhance immune functioning and promote a modest, beneficial increase of circulating inflammatory factors. With intense acute stressors immune functioning may be disturbed and inflammation may become excessive. Chronic stressors instigate still more pronounced immune disturbances and both excessive and prolonged elevation of inflammation, which can increase the occurrence of communicable diseases and the production and progression of several non-communicable diseases. These actions are moderated by varied features of the stressor, and a constellation of genetic and epigenetic factors, as well as age, sex, and earlier experience.

	Acute moderate stressor	Acute strong stressor	Chronic stressor
Immune functioning NK and CD8 cells	↑	↓	↓↓
Inflammatory response	↑	↑↑	↑↑↑
Sterile inflammation	—	↑	↑↑↑
Infection and wound healing	↑	↓	↓↓
Infection susceptibility	—	↑↑	↑↑↑
Cancer progression and metastasis	—	←→	↑↑↑

Source: Modified from Anisman & Kusnecov (2022).

male–female differences on immune functioning have not been widely studied in animals. Nonetheless, neuroinflammatory responses elicited by stressors were reported to be more pronounced in females, which may contribute to the greater physical and psychological disturbances that occur in females (Martinez-Muniz & Wood, 2020). Aside from the influence of sex hormones in promoting immune alteration, processes related to the microbiota–immune–brain axis may contribute to the actions of stressors in response to infection (Audet, 2019).

Conclusions concerning the sex differences in humans are still more daunting than in animals. To be sure, a more robust immune response is elicited by acute stressors in females than in males, whereas chronic stressors produced more pronounced immunosuppression in women, especially with respect to indices of innate immune responses (Bekhbat & Neigh, 2018). At the same time, it needs to be acknowledged that the stressors encountered by women may differ from those experienced by men, and women may experience more frequent and chronic stressors. Moreover, coping methods and emotional responses can differ between the sexes, which may interact with the effects of stressors on immune functioning (Dich et al., 2020). Thus, while sex differences in the development of illnesses may well be tied to stressor experiences, it probably does not involve a single factor and it is more reasonable to attribute these outcomes to a concatenation of influences that occur throughout life.

Surgery as a challenge

Many people will undergo some form of surgery during their lifetime and multiple surgical procedures will be required for some people. These may be undertaken for cosmetic rea-sons or in emergency situations, and they may be necessary to alleviate pain, or as part of treatment for severe illnesses. As much as surgical procedures are often vital, they reflect complex stressors to body tissues and to psychological well-being. The psychological dimension may stem from the anticipation of not having control when in an anesthetized state, or it may stem from uncertainties about the outcomes, as well as the pain expected during recovery. There is ample cause for concern regarding the risks inherent in surgery. Globally, about 7.7% of deaths occur within a relatively brief time span after surgical pro-cedures (about 30 days). In older individuals, a moderate decline of cognitive functioning may occur following surgery (possibly related to the effects of the anesthetic or to effects related to activation of inflammatory cytokines released by microglia) and approximately 7% of patients older than 65 experienced a silent stroke during the ensuing year (e.g., Mrkobrada et al., 2019).

Surgery may have effects like other intense stressors, inducing the suppression of immune activity, and may be associated with postoperative complications related to sep-sis leading to multiple organ dysfunction that likely involves excessive proinflammatory cytokine activity. Owing to effects on various hormones (cortisol, prostaglandins, norep-inephrine), growth factors, and the functioning of immune cells, cancer recurrence, and metastasis is more likely to occur (e.g., Ananth et al., 2016). In fact, even dermal wound-ing associated with surgery was sufficient to provoke elevated tumor inflammatory gene expression and the subsequent increase of the tumor mass at a site distal from the surgi-cal wound (Pyter et al., 2018).

Many of the effects associated with surgical stress could be attenuated by treat-ments that affect immune functioning or by blocking peripheral norepinephrine activ-ity and by reducing inflammatory responses (Ricon et al., 2019). In the case of surgery for gastrointestinal cancers, maintaining a preoperative immune-modulating diet (e.g., a Mediterannean diet) was accompanied by fewer infection-related surgical complications and reduced stay in hospital (Adiamah et al., 2019).

The nature of surgery has been changing over the years. Some procedures that required opening the body cavity have been replaced with keyhole surgery in which a small cut allows access to organs. As a result, some forms of surgery are less traumatic and recovery is much faster. There will come a day when tiny robots the size of just a few cells (nanobots) will be doing essential work so that extensive surgery won't be necessary at all. When we look back in history, we perceive procedures, such as bloodletting, as an odd and counterproductive practice. Well, in the future people might be saying, 'Oh yuckers! Can you believe it! In the twentieth century and the first part of the twenty-first century they used to cut people open!'

Stressor effects on immune functioning in humans

Insofar as studies in rodents have been informative in demonstrating the influence of diverse physical and social stressors on immune activity, the data obtained are limited in several important ways. Among other things, the intensity and chronicity of stressors in animals come nowhere near those too often experienced by humans. Thus, they don't speak to the immunological actions of severe chronic experiences. Likewise, they cannot address the influence of stressors that are uniquely human, such as shame and humiliation, discrimination, and stigmatization.

Studies in humans have resolved some of these questions even if they were conducted in laboratory settings. Stressors administered within such a context alter various facets of immune and cytokine activity allowing for causal connections to be established between specific attributes of stressors and immune and cytokine changes. For instance, in response to the Trier Social Stress Test (public speaking combined with an arithmetic challenge) the expression of genes that code for inflammatory and antiviral responses was elevated and this action could be attenuated by pretreatment with the norepinephrine β-blocker propranolol (MacCormack et al., 2021). It was similarly reported that stress in the Trier test was accompanied by elevated numbers of circulating granulocytes and monocytes that were influenced by treatments that affected norepinephrine levels (Beis et al., 2018). Prior studies had indicated that the effects of this stressor were affected by earlier adverse experiences. Specifically, the level of IL-6 in blood, as well as that of NK cells, was elevated among depressed individuals that had experienced an early-life stressor, potentially pointing to the influence of these combined experiences (Pace et al., 2006). Interestingly, among individuals who practiced a form of meditation (compassion meditation) the IL-6 changes introduced by this stress test were diminished.

Consistent with the effects provoked by the Trier test, social rejection within a laboratory context, which was found to increase neuronal activity within the anterior cingulate cortex, increased TNF-α and IL-6 receptor availability (Slavich, Way et al., 2010). Remarkably, when taken for three weeks, the anti-inflammatory acetaminophen, which ordinarily reduces physical pain, similarly reduced the pain of social rejection as well as the brain neural responses associated with rejection (Dewall et al., 2010). Moreover, acetaminophen could ameliorate social pain over time (20 days) and this action was most prominent among individuals who expressed forgiveness (Slavich et al., 2019). It seems that the inflammatory actions of social stressors can be exceptionally powerful, and the mood states elicited by rejection might be causally related to the inflammatory effects provoked. Of course, these laboratory studies do not speak to the impact of intense chronic stressors that arguably are most potent in promoting pathology.

Powerful stressors experienced in real-world settings were associated with disturbed immune functioning, including diminished T cell proliferation and antibody responses to influenza vaccines (Glaser & Kiecolt-Glaser, 2005). With prolonged stressors, such as those created by stressful jobs, pronounced disturbances of immune functioning have frequently been reported. Likewise, lengthy periods of unemployment were accompanied by marked reductions of NK cytotoxicity that reverted to normal levels once employment was obtained (F. Cohen et al., 2007). Paralleling these findings, antibody production in response to immunization (i.e., vaccines) showed that humoral immune responses can be modulated by stressors and chronic adverse experiences influenced the secondary immune response (Cohen et al., 2001). Challenges in the form of chronic pain and chronic illness are accompanied by disturbed immune functioning and elevated inflammation. It is difficult to determine to what extent these immune alterations are directly related to the distress of the condition relative to that produced by the illness itself. In fact, inflammation may contribute to the illness or the pain experienced (e.g., Grace et al., 2021).

The influence of stressful life experiences and related diseases have been linked to emotional responses that were introduced and varied with the way individuals appraised and coped with these challenges. It has long been known that caregiving (e.g., for a partner with a neurodegenerative disorder such as Alzheimer's disease) can be a profoundly distressing experience not only because individuals helplessly witness the decay of loved ones, but because the task can be unrelenting. This issue has become especially important given that yesterday's baby boomers have reached older age and increasingly more attention will need to be devoted to 'caring for the caregiver'.

The strain created by caregiving was accompanied by disturbed immune functioning together with impaired wound healing. As well, the distress of caregiving was accompanied by poor responses to vaccines, accelerated cellular aging, elevated levels of inflammatory cytokines, disturbed NK cell functioning, slower recovery of immune dysfunction, and delays of restorative processes being produced (e.g., Gouin et al., 2008). Reduced immune responses were similarly evident among dementia caregivers in response to the Herpes simplex virus-1 antigen (HSV-1; this is the form associated with cold sores, whereas HSV-2 is associated with genital herpes). Together, such findings illustrate the importance of diminishing the distress of caregiving. However, a meta-analysis indicated that the relationship between caregiving for a family member and compromised immune functioning and elevated inflammation was modest (Roth et al., 2019). This is not overly surprising as the distress of caregiving varies appreciably across individuals, and it is necessary to dig deeper to understand such variation. While some individuals might view the caregiver role as a hardship foisted upon them, others are intrinsically motivated to serve in this capacity and find a sense of purpose in this role. Accordingly, they would be less likely to experience immune disturbances and elevated health risks.

The actions of stressors in undermining immune functioning was particularly notable among older people (Fali et al., 2018) and a prospective analysis of individuals of 64–92 years of age indicated that stressors promoted immunological aging, thereby increasing disease susceptibility (Reed et al., 2019). In this population, markers of inflammation were evident in association with stressors, whereas engagement in positive social behaviors was accompanied by diminished levels of the inflammatory marker C-reactive protein (Walker et al., 2019).

Just as stressors have especially pronounced actions in older individuals, adverse early-life experiences profoundly affect immune functioning and illness vulnerability and may affect well-being throughout the life span. Early-life stressful experiences may result in immune and hormone alterations persisting (or reoccurring), thereby rendering individuals at increased risk for immune-related disorders and those promoted by elevated inflammatory factors. For instance, among women raised in a harsh family environment, the cytokine response was markedly increased in response to an antigenic challenge. This outcome was accompanied by a reduction in the sensitivity of glucocorticoid receptors, possibly resulting in diminished immunoregulatory responses (Miller et al., 2011).

Stressors and cytokine changes

Chronically elevated levels of proinflammatory cytokines have been implicated in psychiatric, neuropathological, and cardiovascular disorders, and hence there has been increasing emphasis on the assessment of circulating cytokines in response to stressors. Cytokines are particularly sensitive to neuroendocrine changes, and thus the stressor-induced alterations by immune cells might be moderated by hormonal alterations. This view is certainly the simplest explanation for the effects of stressors on cytokine levels and activity and the one that makes the fewest new assumptions. However, in the case of stressor effects on biological processes we've seen again and again that the simplest explanations often fall by the wayside. Science has a way of humbling us. Often, we think that we've got a handle on the characteristics of a stress-related biological outcome, only to be disappointed by the data. Instead of the law of parsimony (Occam's razor; the simplest solution is likely the correct one), we're reminded of Gilbert and Sullivan's *HMS Pinafore*:

> Things are seldom what they seem,
>
> Skim milk masquerades as cream

To understand how stressors and cytokine changes contribute to the development of illnesses we have to evaluate these links more extensively, including consideration of the many moderating forces that shape the development of pathology.

T_h1 and T_h2 derived cytokines

T_h1 and T_h2 cells, as we've seen, have different functions, as do the cytokines produced by them. These cells and the cytokines they release need to act cooperatively. Shifts in the balance towards T_h1 creates a bias towards proinflammatory processes, whereas a shift toward T_h2 reflects the opposite effect. Excessive and prolonged skewing in either direction may have adverse consequences and effective functioning of T_{reg} cells are critical to maintaining balances between proinflammatory and anti-inflammatory actions. Early in an immune response to a pathogen, the increased macrophage activity and the ensuing predominance of T_h1 cell function promote stimulation of antibodies and the release of proinflammatory cytokines. These actions are subsequently down-regulated by T_h2 and T_{reg} cytokines, particularly IL-10. These actions essentially shift the immune response away from an unnecessarily protracted and potentially damaging impact on tissue function.

Stressors modify the production of T_h1 and T_h2 cytokines and may provoke imbalances in their functional relationship. As stressors influence several cytokines, it might not be enough to simply determine which cytokines go up or which go down. Instead, as in the case of other biological systems, it is pertinent to concurrently evaluate the relationships between multiple cytokine perturbations in relation to the emergence of stressor-elicited challenges to well-being. Furthermore, stressor effects on cytokines may vary over time, and not every cytokine follows the same temporal trajectory. In fact, if one were to examine the effects of a stressor at a single point in time, the impression might be that the treatment elicited enhanced inflammation, whereas analyses at a different time, just a few hours later, might suggest that the stressor inhibited inflammation. Stressors and immune challenges both set in motion dynamic processes and finding a single rule that predicts what would happen at different times is complicated.

Impact of stressors on proinflammatory cytokines

Analyses of the effects of stressors on cytokine production in animals have involved measurement of circulating cytokines, or their *in vitro* production in the blood, spleen, or other lymphoid organs (i.e., in analyses undertaken outside the body). *In vitro* analyses can tell us how certain cells behave in response to specific stimuli and can thus provide essential information regarding the capacity of these cells to produce cytokines. But what happens in a petri dish may not actually be representative of what happens in the body, especially as the influence of other factors, such as hormones, are no longer present in these *in vitro* studies. This is often dealt with in animal research through *in vivo* analyses using challenges with immune-activating agents, such as lipopolysaccharide (LPS; this is the outer coat for E. coli bacteria) that reliably produces both *in vitro* and *in vivo* actions. Using this approach, it was determined that the production of proinflammatory cytokines, such as IL-1β, were elevated after stressor exposure, and after several days of social disruption, mice exhibited greater amounts of IL-1β and TNF-α in lymphoid regions (e.g., spleen and lung) and in the brain. Typically, these changes were matched or followed by variations of IL-10 so that the proinflammatory effects of the stressor were appropriately regulated, but this was not always apparent, especially when stressors were sustained and unremitting (Gibb et al., 2013).

For some time, analyses of IL-1β and TNF-α had been predominant in animal studies that assessed the impact of stressful events. Research in humans made it clear that IL-6, which promotes cell growth, differentiation of B cells, and neuronal functioning, may be tied to psychological disturbances. For instance, elevated levels of IL-6 were frequently associated with depressed mood, and life stressors could affect IL-6 production, depending on the intensity and chronicity of the stressor. Among older women who had been experiencing chronic loneliness, a laboratory challenge altered IL-6 and cortisol (Hackett et al., 2012). Intense stressors, such as those experienced by parents of young cancer patients, were accompanied by dysregulation of the coordination between IL-6 and cortisol functioning. Although IL-6 has often been taken simply as a marker of inflammation, it may actually be causally involved in harm created by pathogens (Del Giudice & Gangestad, 2018).

It shouldn't be surprising to learn that personality factors may influence cytokine functioning. For instance, the effect of an acute stressor on IL-6 levels was moderated among optimistic individuals. Thus, the improved health reported among optimists might be due to this trait counteracting stress-induced increases in inflammation that could potentially be harmful (Brydon et al., 2009). Likewise, higher self-esteem was accompanied by limited TNF-α elevations in response to an acute stressor relative to that observed among individuals with lower self-esteem (O'Donnell et al., 2008), prompting the suggestion that this might be one way in which self-esteem protects against the development of disease. The effects of stressors on cytokine levels were also linked to emotional responses that were observed. In particular, among women who had been in an abusive relationship, reading a relevant script pertaining to abuse was accompanied by the rise of IL-6 and IL-10 in blood samples in direct relation to self-reported shame or anger (Danielson et al., 2011).

Aside from these cytokines, IL-18, a member of the IL-1 family, which influences T_h1 functioning, can be affected by stressors, and thus might contribute to stress-related pathology (Wedervang-Resell et al., 2020), including infectious illness, cancer, autoimmune disorders, diabetes, and atherosclerosis. Yet another cytokine class that has received considerable attention is that of interferons (IFN), so named because they interfere with viral replication. Interferons come in different forms (e.g., IFN-α, IFN-β, IFN-γ, and several others), each of which has a somewhat different function, although they all influence viral replication and can fight tumors. In mice, stressor exposure reduced IFN-γ production in spleen lymphocytes, and following repeated daily restraint the production of IFN-γ was diminished in response to tetanus toxin, herpes simplex virus, influenza virus, or tumor antigens, suggesting that chronic strain might be associated with greater vulnerability to the effects of pathogens.

Although IFN-α administration has powerful biological actions, its behavioral effects in rodents, as well as the corticosterone response was far less pronounced than that elicited by other cytokines, such as IL-1β. Yet, as we'll see when we discuss depressive illnesses, when IFN-α was used to treat certain forms of cancer and hepatitis C, it provoked intense depressive mood. Thus, it was interesting that when mice had been moderately stressed (through social disruption), the effects of IFN-α administration were greatly increased as were signs of sickness produced by the cytokine. In effect, the adverse behavioral actions of IFN-α are exaggerated when administered on a stressful background (Anisman et al., 2007). This may be clinically significant as humans undergoing immunotherapy are typically experiencing considerable distress. Accordingly, it may be helpful to provide patients with interventions to diminish distress prior to the initiation of cytokine therapy.

Despite the many studies that assessed the influence of stressors on cytokine (and immune) functioning in humans, there is still much that we don't know concerning the impact of stressors on these processes. Among other things, it remains to be determined whether stressors differentially influence cytokine activity within different immune compartments in humans (e.g., spleen vs. blood), whether the effects observed are unique to certain types of stressor regimens, and to what extent their actions vary with the constellation of individual factors described earlier. As more studies are conducted that consider individual difference factors and various stressor characteristics, interpretations may arise that will provide a uniform picture of how stressors affect T_h1 and T_h2 cytokine functioning and their balances. For the moment it does appear that acute stressful events of moderate severity may increase immune and cytokine functioning. Given a strong enough stressor, however, the immune enhancement might not be evident, but inflammation is increased thereby favoring the development of assorted illnesses. The immune and cytokine variations associated with stressors likely vary dynamically over time, which may be influenced by many hormonal changes introduced by stressors. Ultimately, to understand the effects of stressors on immune and cytokine functioning as well as their effects on well-being, it will be necessary to conduct large-scale studies that prospectively evaluate changes that occur with time and consider individual difference factors that could influence stress responses.

Sensitization

When we discussed the impact of stressors on neuroendocrine and neurotransmitter functioning, the point was made that a stressful event typically had short-lasting neurochemical effects. Upon subsequent exposure to a stressor, exaggerated biological changes could be promoted. Commensurate with these reports, stressful events sensitize inflammatory processes so that amplified responses can be re-induced by later stressors (Anisman et al., 2003). Likewise, among animals that had been exposed to a chronic stressor, a later challenge with an immune activating treatment elicited marked changes of IL-1β, IL-6, and other inflammatory factors within the hypothalamus and prefrontal cortex. As early life is a period that is exceptionally sensitive to the actions of stressors and immune challenges, it is significant that among rat pups that experienced a strong immunological challenge, the subsequent hormonal, brain neurochemical, and immune response to stressors was altered during adulthood.

The transience of neuronal and inflammatory responses might be highly adaptive since our defense systems ought to be engaged only so long as the stressor is present, and then terminated when the stressor disappears or is dealt with effectively. The sensitized response may likewise provide advantages to well-being by facilitating a swift reaction to further stressor encounters. However, this process might contribute to the emergence or re-emergence of psychological pathologies.

─Case study 6.1─

The benefits of old friends

Maria was beside herself. She was always sick with something or other. She had numerous allergies and developed asthma as a child. In recent years she had developed inflammatory bowel disease and then psoriasis that undermined her self-esteem. She had been so careful in taking care of herself, eating all the 'right' foods, exercising routinely, and taking precautions to avoid infectious illness, but she nevertheless seemed to catch every bug around. Her parents had likewise been especially diligent in protecting her as a child, making sure that she didn't come into contact with potentially harmful bacteria. In fact, she would chide them as true blue germaphobes. Yet it seemed that every illness had it in for her.

With the development of psoriasis, she went to see a skin doctor who upon learning of her history indicated that she may well have been experiencing the consequences of having an environment that was *too* clean. The physician informed her that exposure to a diversity of bacteria during childhood may be important for the development of effective immune functioning ('hygiene hypothesis'). Having been protected from every bug as a child, her immune system may have become less well-versed in combatting infection. As a result, later encounters with ordinarily harmless stimuli could promote responses that led to allergies and asthma (Strachan, 2000).

She also later discovered that a modest refinement of this notion, the 'old friends' hypothesis, suggested that experience with bacteria was necessary for the development of functionally effective immunoregulatory processes that could interfere with the development of self-tolerance (the capacity of the immune system to recognize self-antigens). Basically, because she hadn't encountered a sufficient variety of microorganisms when young her immune capacity may have been undermined, making her vulnerable to physical diseases associated with excessive inflammatory immune responses, including autoimmune disorders (Rook et al., 2013). Critical to this was that her T_{reg} cell functioning wasn't regulating her immune inflammatory response as needed. She began worrying about what other diseases she might develop in the future. In fact, she became concerned that she might be in a group that was highly vulnerable to SARS-CoV-2 infection. She wondered whether all those little kids that had been isolated during the preceding two years to protect them from the disease might have been deprived of 'old friends' that they would need for the development of effective immune functioning.

Microbiota and health

Microorganisms, including bacteria, viruses, fungi, and archaea (the latter are single-celled organisms without a defined nucleus) are present in and on all parts of the human body, being particularly abundant in the gut and to a lesser extent in the mouth, adipose (fat) tissue, skin, vagina, uterus, and lungs. The human gut contains trillions of *commensal* bacteria (i.e., those that derive benefits from other bacteria or from the host) along with harmful bacteria. Ordinarily, they live in harmony with one another (*eubiosis*) for their mutual well-being. Should the balance between diverse bacteria be disturbed (*dysbiosis*), an exceptionally broad range of illnesses can be produced, including inflammatory bowel diseases, obesity, metabolic syndrome, type 2 diabetes, cardiovascular disease, and the risk for the occurrence of some types of cancer may be elevated. Moreover, dysbiosis was associated with the efficacy of cancer therapies being diminished (Gentile & Weir, 2018). Indeed, a longitudinal study conducted over a 15-year period indicated that the presence of harmful microbiota was associated with earlier mortality independent of the contribution of obesity and smoking (Salosensaari et al., 2021). As stressors can profoundly affect microbiota, which can influence inflammatory processes, dysbiosis and the alterations of specific gut bacteria have been implicated in varied physical and psychological disorders (Anisman & Kusnecov, 2022). While the focus on the actions of the microbiome and health concerned the involvement of bacteria within the gut, the substantial presence of microorganisms at multiple sites offers ample opportunity for bacterial interactions between different parts of the body. For instance, bacteria in the mouth affect those present in the gut, and those situated in the gut can affect microbiota in the lungs.

For the most part, mechanistic approaches to determine the contribution of gut bacteria to brain functioning or physical health have primarily been conducted in animal studies. To this end, diverse challenges on the microbial community, including the impact of poor diets or antibiotic challenges that deplete microbiota, could engender negative health outcomes. Likewise, when fecal bacteria from an unhealthy mouse or from an ill person were transferred to recipient mice, they develop some of the symptoms evident in the donor. Moreover, the transfer of fecal microbiota from stressed organisms could promote activation of inflammatory processes in the recipient, thereby promoting disease (Levy et al., 2015). While causal links have been observed between microorganism presence and the promotion of diseases, illnesses may well cause alterations in the abundance and diversity of microbiota.

The influence of evolutionary processes

Like all living organisms, the development of the microbiome (referring to the genetic characteristics of all microbes) was subject to selection pressures that shaped the suitability of microbiota to specific environments. The diet of our ancient ancestors was likely plant-based, and probably meat when it could be obtained. Dental remains and archeological finds dating back more than 100,000 years revealed that, contrary to myths that led to the paleo diet, our forebears were likely consuming numerous starch-rich foods (Fellows Yates et al., 2021). They likely had fewer opportunities to engage in unhealthy lifestyles that favored poor well-being, and consequently their microbiota was well adapted to the environment. Diet-related microbiota may well have provided Sapiens with advantages over Neanderthals, including cognitive abilities, ultimately resulting in Neanderthals becoming extinct. With the slow migration out of Africa about 70,000 years ago, diets would have progressively changed, resulting in alterations of the microbial community.

Over time, especially with industrialization, the symbiotic relationship among microorganisms was subject to new evolutionary pressures, especially when humans migrated from rural to urban environments. In recent years, these moves led to the consumption of unhealthy foods, including those that were ultra-processed, which may have disturbed microbiota abundance and diversity. Dysbiosis was exacerbated by environmental toxicants and new medications (e.g., antibiotics that indiscriminately eliminate gut microbiota). The result has been a decline of certain commensal bacteria and elevated presence of less beneficial or harmful bacteria, which may have contributed to the progressive increase of diverse illnesses (Sonnenburg & Sonnenburg, 2019). It has been maintained that diet itself might have had a more profound impact on the quality of microbiota than host genetics, but many other factors, such as chronic stressors, sedentary behaviors, fad diets, and lack of exercise, have also been prime contributors to poor microbial health.

Vast interindividual differences exist in the composition of the gut microbiome of healthy people even when their diets are similar. Appreciable microbiota differences similarly occur across cultures, countries, and specific locales within countries (Dhakan et al., 2019). Accordingly, both culture and geography, as well as related features (e.g., diet) ought to be considered in analyses to determine factors that are linked to disease occurrence and progression as well as in treatment approaches. The development of culture-specific microbial communities likely reflects the actions of evolutionary pressures. For example, despite the high consumption of a fatty seafood diet, Greenland Inuit were at low risk of heart disease possibly owing to the evolution of genes that protected against the actions of elevated levels of cholesterol and triglycerides (Fumagalli et al., 2015). Likewise, illnesses such as type 2 diabetes occur infrequently among Inuit within Northern Canada owing to the actions of genes that facilitate muscles being sustained by a diet rich in fat and protein but lacking in glucose. However, with continued changes in the Inuit diet, these well-adapted genes might no longer provide the benefits that they had previously so diabetes has been increasing progressively. Given the microbial diversity that occurs within and between cultures, it is difficult to identify what a 'healthy' microbial community comprises, although over- or under-abundance of some microorganisms have been tied to poor or good health.

BEYOND BACTERIA: THE INFLUENCE OF GUT VIRUSES

It is certainly reasonable that scientific attention focused on bacterial eubiosis and dysbiosis in relation to health and disease. Yet, it is somewhat curious that relatively limited attention has been devoted to the role of intestinal viruses given that about 33,000 unique viral populations have been identified in the human gut (the gut virome). Like bacteria, viral particles are absent at birth and then progressively increase through the intake of breast milk and by other environmental contributions (G. Liang et al., 2020). The virome differs markedly across individuals, often remaining stable over time, although it may vary in parallel with gut bacteria.

Viruses typically reside in a symbiotic relationship with gut bacteria, although they could act as pathogens that infect host bacteria. Viruses that infect bacteria, referred to as bacteriophages (or simply 'phages'), insert genetic material into the host bacterium thereby altering its metabolism. They can replicate within bacterial hosts, releasing virus particles that are bactericidal (Tetz & Tetz, 2018). These phage-mediated effects have not been extensively examined but interest in them has increased because they can potentially be used in a therapeutic capacity. Specifically, numerous harmful bacteria have developed antibiotic resistance, thereby creating a considerable risk in our ability to fight bacterial infections. New antibiotics have been slow in coming, in part owing to the inevitable fate of these becoming ineffective as bacteria develop resistance. As an alternative to antibiotics, efforts have been ongoing to use phages to attack harmful bacteria. Because phages can more directly target specific bacteria, rather than produce broad actions that include elimination of beneficial bacteria as antibiotics do, this form of therapy may turn out to be advantageous.

Developmental changes of microbiota

Although the placenta had been considered to be a sterile environment, this view has been vigorously debated. Bacterial DNA has been detected in placental tissue, possibly reflecting their intrauterine origin. Furthermore, the amniotic fluid of women about to undergo Caesarean section (C-section) indicated the presence of bacterial DNA, and the first feces of newborns contained bacteria (Stinson et al., 2019). It was suggested that the presence of certain bacteria, such as *Mycoplasma* and *Ureaplasma*, might contribute to preterm labor and spontaneous preterm delivery (Leon et al., 2018).

The makeup of a mom's microbiota may vary during pregnancy, and it was maintained that bacterial challenges during this time could be involved in educating the immune system, including activation of memory T cells (Mishra et al., 2021). In fact, among pregnant mice that had been colonized with a form of *E. coli* that does not survive postnatally, multiple microbial and immune changes were apparent in pups relative to that evident in offspring whose mothers had not been prenatally colonized with bacteria (de Agüero et al., 2016). These findings do not speak to whether the fetus acquired bacteria but nonetheless indicate that prenatal events can markedly influence later immune development. Further to this, gut microbiota diversity was diminished among pregnant women who had obesity or had been consuming poor-quality diets, leading to metabolic disturbances that could affect the fetus and contribute to postnatal diseases (Younge et al., 2019). Ample evidence revealed that gut bacteria may influence postnatal immune functioning and that the presence of specific bacteria during the perinatal period (i.e., shortly before or after birth) may contribute to susceptibility to the later emergence of diseases, including psychological and neurological disorders.

During the birth process, the neonate obtains beneficial vaginal microorganisms that can have health ramifications throughout life (McDonald & McCoy, 2019). As infants born through C-section would not obtain these beneficial microorganisms, the possibility was considered that they might be more vulnerable to later inflammatory and metabolic diseases (Chu et al., 2017). To offset the disadvantages of C-section there had been attempts to create a positive microbiome for these infants by vaginal seeding, which entailed vaginal swabs being applied to the neonate. While there had been reports supporting the benefits of this procedure, the findings were inconsistent. Coupled with concerns that seeding could transmit pathogens to the infant, the American College of Obstetricians and Gynecologists ultimately did not recommend this procedure being adopted. Since then, however, larger observational studies have confirmed that vaginal swabbing of C-section babies resulted in normalization of their microbiome, prompting a call for greater evaluation as to whether this procedure has health benefits (Song, 2021).

Breastfeeding contributes to microbiota diversity and richness in infants and might thereby enhance infant health. Of course, other components of a mother's milk are beneficial for the infant, including simple and complex carbohydrates that influence microbiota and immune functioning. Complex sugars (oligosaccharides) present in breast milk serve as prebiotics that feed bacteria, and infants obtain immunoglobulins that can protect them from harmful microbes. Consequently, breast-fed infants subsequently experienced fewer respiratory illnesses, and asthma occurrence was diminished as were problems associated with the gastrointestinal tract, obesity, diabetes, and there have even been reports that the occurrence of childhood leukemia and lymphoma were diminished (e.g., Amitay & Keinan-Boker, 2015). Breastfeeding may provide benefits in comparison to that evident in bottle-fed infants, including that obtained from stored pumped milk. Thus, it was surmised that aside from the breast milk itself, contact of the infant's mouth and the mother's breast might transfer microorganisms that affect the child's microbiome.

The benefits of breastfeeding were thought to be exceptional to the extent that its practice could diminish global annual childhood mortality by 800,000 (Victora et al., 2016). Both the World Health Organization and American Academy of Pediatrics recommended that exclusive breastfeeding be adopted over the infant's first 6 months of life, and combined breast and formula feeding be used until the infant reached 1–2 years of age. For a variety of reasons, breastfeeding tends to be much less common in industrialized than in developing countries; breastfeeding is infrequently adopted in the UK, France, and the Netherlands (30–40%), but is more common in Scandinavian countries (70–80%). While breastfeeding is initially high in the US (75%), by the time infants are 6 months of age only about 13% are breastfed. In Canada, 91% of mothers initially breastfeed infants, but by 6 months of age, this declined to 34%. Rates of breastfeeding are still lower among socially and economically disadvantaged mothers.

By one year of age, a distinct microbial profile is apparent among children, and by 2–5 years of age, it resembles that of adults, although further variations may subsequently develop depending on numerous lifestyles and other experiences. Should microbiota disturbances occur during this early stage of development, adverse effects may subsequently arise. To the point, depletion of microbiota created by antibiotics among young children was associated with increased occurrence of later metabolic diseases (such as obesity) as well as several immune-related disorders, including food allergies and asthma (Aversa et al., 2021).

Stressors experienced in early-life influence microbiota

Being a stage of life during which stressful events can have pronounced immediate and long-term repercussions, it isn't surprising that stressors experienced during early life can affect the composition of gut bacteria (De Palma et al., 2015). The microbial changes, in turn, can influence later responses to stressors, including neuronal functioning within stress-sensitive brain regions. Separating pups from their mom, which affects stress hormones, similarly produced gut bacterial alterations, and even relatively innocuous challenges, such as disturbing a rodent's nest may reduce microbial diversity in pups, perhaps secondary to erratic maternal behaviors elicited in the mother. Predictably, if pups had experienced multiple stressors, more pronounced microbial changes were introduced, which were associated with behavioral perturbations and altered brain neurochemical activity that varied with sex (Rincel et al., 2019). The impact of early-life challenges on hormonal and behavioral alterations could be precluded if young animals were treated with specific dietary supplements (O'Mahony et al., 2020) and microbiota manipulations similarly reversed the neuroendocrine and immune disturbances and diminished the level of anxiety (De Palma et al., 2015). Micronutrient supplements during early life similarly limited later stressor-provoked corticosterone changes and affected serotonin in critical brain regions, and prevented behavioral disturbances that might otherwise have been apparent (Mika et al., 2017).

Microbiota and aging

Just as early life is sensitive to the effects of stressors, aging is a period that for numerous reasons can be exceptionally distressing and may be accompanied by diverse biological changes that favor the development of illnesses. With age, the abundance of several bacterial species diminishes, whereas others become more abundant, and gut dysbiosis is more likely to occur, especially in response to stressors. It generally seems that aging is accompanied by a microbial shift that fosters a proinflammatory profile that favors the occurrence of inflammatory diseases, which can instigate affective and neurocognitive disturbances. Yet, disadvantageous bacterial genera declined with age in some individuals and their metabolomic signatures were linked to diminished inflammatory processes (Wilmanski et al., 2021). It may be telling that in centenarians (individuals who lived beyond 100) who were in good health, their microbiota profile was not unlike that of healthy younger people (Bian et al., 2017).

Much like many physiological processes that are affected by stressors, chronic challenges can promote marked microbial alterations in aging rodents and humans, which could favor inflammatory dysregulation, hence influencing neurodegenerative processes (Cui et al., 2018). As numerous age-related processes may be associated with inflammatory changes and cognitive decline, it is uncertain to what extent microbiota contribute to this. Thus, it is notable that in young rodents that received gut bacteria transplants from old mice, greater vulnerability to inflammation was elicited as was leakage of inflammatory bacterial factors into circulation (Fransen et al., 2017). As described to this point, numerous lifestyle factors and experiences can affect gut microbiota, which could influence the development and the course of illnesses. Among these are adverse early experiences that can affect microbiota throughout life and owing to the neuronal consequences imparted, neurodegenerative conditions could potentially be promoted (Dinan & Cryan, 2017). Whether or not these experiences have such effects through microbial changes hasn't been conclusively demonstrated, but the possibility ought to be considered that the adoption of lifestyles that enhance microbiota diversity and abundance as well as limit chronic inflammation, could enhance well-being and limit age-related infirmities.

Microbiota and immune functioning

The foods we eat can affect our microbiome, which can influence immune functioning. To this end, diets with adequate food-derived fatty acids, monounsaturated fats, and numerous essential vitamins and minerals (e.g., zinc, selenium, iron, copper, and folic acid) are beneficial. Food high in fiber, such as whole grains, vegetables, fresh fruits, nuts, and seeds, reach the large intestine largely undigested where certain microbiota use them to create short chain fatty acids (SCFAs), comprising butyrate, acetate, and propionate. These SCFAs are essential for maintaining gut health and affect numerous other health-related conditions by influencing the development and functioning of immune processes. Commensal bacteria and their metabolites promote effects on several components of the immune system, such as innate lymphoid cells, B cell receptor diversity, modulation of varied T cell subsets, and NK cell functioning (Geva-Zatorsky et al., 2017). Like dietary factors, as described in Figure 6.3, stressful experiences through brain changes can affect hormonal, immune, and inflammatory processes that affect microbiota. The microbial changes can likewise affect innate and adaptive immune responses, and these cumulative actions can affect communicable and non-communicable illnesses. As well, gut microbiota and inflammatory immune changes may feedback to alter brain functioning, potentially leading to varied psychological disturbances.

Ordinarily, eubiosis is accompanied by effective immune and inflammatory activity, maintaining self-tolerance, and acting against autoimmune disorders. However, when dysbiosis occurs or when certain harmful bacteria are present, immune functioning can be disturbed and excessive inflammation may be produced that promotes the development of illnesses. In essence, under some conditions, pathogenic stimuli overwhelm the positive actions of beneficial bacteria and the immune system is affected accordingly (Wiles & Guillemin, 2019). Aside from promoting inflammation, microbiota can produce DNA-damaging toxins and carcinogenic metabolites and could thus promote diverse types of cancer and cause them to become resistant to chemotherapeutic agents.

Through their actions on multiple facets of the immune system, microbiota may affect several disease conditions (Ost & Round, 2018). The gut mucosal barrier produced by epithelial cells (the thin outer layer that surrounds organs), which separates microbiota from innate immune cells, can be disturbed by pathogenic bacteria, creating a 'leaky gut' condition that precipitates inflammatory-related pathologies. Leaky gut syndrome has only recently received experimental or clinical attention but has been implicated in the promotion of varied medical conditions, especially those in which inflammatory factors are prominent, including Crohn's and celiac disease.

Just as microbiota affect immune functioning, the immune system plays an essential role in assuring that microbial communities remain in a balanced state (Hooper et al., 2015). Moreover, like some immune cells, it appears that microbiota can 'learn' from previous experiences in the sense that bacterial infection may result in commensal microbes regrouping to deal with subsequent encounters with the same pathogenic bacteria (Kendall & Sperandio, 2021). Paralleling these findings, bacterial infection can promote beneficial actions so that gut macrophage activation is readily engendered upon further infection, thereby protecting the vast array of enteric (gut) neurons and limiting intestinal disorders, such as irritable bowel syndrome (Ahrends et al., 2021).

Microbiota and illness comorbidities

It is not unusual for an illness to be comorbid with one or more other health conditions. For instance, depressive symptoms have been associated with the occurrence of heart disease, stroke, and cancer. This was not simply a matter of depression occurring because of the strain created by these physical illnesses, as depressive disorders frequently preceded these conditions, often by many years. As well, the

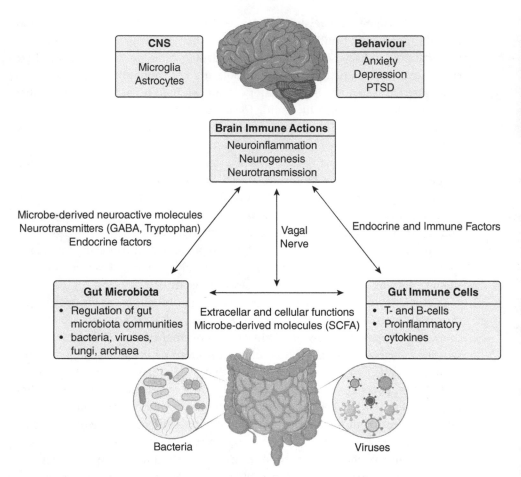

Figure 6.3   Stressful experiences promote neuronal and microglial functioning, including variations of neurotransmitters and neurotrophins, and variations of microglial functioning. The brain changes elicit diverse effects on hormonal processes that can affect immune functioning and can thereby influence gut microbiota. The microbes present in the gut likewise influence innate and adaptive immune functioning and affect inflammatory factors. These processes can affect brain functioning directly or through activation of the vagal nerve. As a result, mood states, such as anxiety and depression, can be provoked.

Source: Created using BioRender.

prognosis for individuals who had been depressed (or experienced substance use disorders) was worse than for others and they died earlier because of heart disease, cancer, and other illnesses than did individuals who had not experienced depressive illness. Comorbid conditions may occur because one illness sets in motion biological changes that promote the occurrence of a second condition. Alternatively, common denominators, such as inflammatory factors, can independently favor diverse illnesses (Anisman et al., 2018). For instance, disturbed microbial balances can engender inflammation, which then increases the occurrence of a broad set of illnesses. These actions may be more cogent in the context of specific genetic factors or the adoption of poor lifestyles, such as eating the wrong foods (e.g., refined carbohydrates), not getting sufficient sleep, adopting sedentary behaviors, and not being able to cope effectively with stressors.

Conclusion

Stressors affect immune, cytokine, and microbiota functioning, which may influence vulnerability to an array of communicable and non-communicable diseases. The impact of stressful events varies with psychosocial influences and individual difference factors. Of course, there is still much that we don't know concerning the impact of stressors on these processes and how they come to affect disease conditions. Among other things, it is uncertain whether the effects that have been observed are unique to certain types of stressor regimens or certain types of immune challenges (e.g., being unique to bacterial or viral challenges, or for that matter whether the effects differ in relation to different types of viral challenges). Moreover, under what circumstances do stressor-provoked immune changes translate to specific pathological conditions, including those of a physical nature and those that involve brain processes?

In contrast to acute stressors of moderate severity that may increase immune and cytokine functioning, if a given stressor is strong enough and occurs on a chronic basis, immune capacity may be impaired, whereas inflammatory process may be activated (e.g., reflecting a chronic sterile immune response). The effects of stressors on immune functioning in the periphery as well as cytokine changes in the brain are influenced by a constellation of hormonal factors, which could affect vulnerability to physical illnesses and may have neuropathological consequences.

The many specific attributes of stressors, and the moderating influence of experiential, social, developmental, and genetic factors in determining immunocompetence and central cytokine functioning, have not been fully worked out. Nevertheless, it is certain that chronic stressors, irrespective of whether they entail sustained illnesses, chronic pain, or purely psychological challenges, can disturb biological processes, thereby increasing the development of diverse illnesses. Immune functioning can be influenced by multiple processes, including various lifestyles, especially if they influence microbiota. Considerable evidence has been amassed showing that microorganisms can be altered by stressful events, diet, sleep quality, and exercise, which can influence hormonal processes as well as microbiota. Accordingly, the possibility has been entertained that altering microbiota may have health benefits, operating as both a preventative and therapeutic strategy in relation to diseases.

Stressor effects on immune and cytokine disturbances, as well as recovery of immune functioning, may vary across individuals and might be fundamental in determining the emergence of pathological conditions. Ultimately, to understand the effects of stressors on immune and cytokine functioning, as well as their effects on illnesses, large-scale prospective studies are needed to evaluate the changes that occur over time, and how individual difference factors moderate these actions.

Suggested readings

Cryan, J.F., O'Riordan, K.J., Cowan, C.S.M., Sandhu, K.V., & Bastiaanssen, T.F.S. (2019). The microbiota–gut–brain axis. *Physiological Reviews*, *99*, 1877–2013.

Punt, J., Stanford, D.S.A., Jones, P.P., & Owen, J.A. (2019). *Kuby Immunology*, 8th edition. New York: Macmillan.

Sonnenburg, E.D. & Sonnenburg, J.L. (2019). The ancestral and industrialized gut microbiota and implications for human health. *Nature Reviews in Microbiology*, *17*, 383–390.

7

STRESS, IMMUNITY, AND DISEASE

—The dreaded diseases—

Factors that disturb hormonal and immune functioning may influence our ability to fend off bacterial infection and viral illnesses as well as aggravate the symptoms associated with autoimmune disorders. Many of the same processes have likewise been associated with the development of an array of inflammatory-related diseases, including metabolic syndrome, type 2 diabetes, and heart disease. But cancer holds a special place in our worst dreads. The very words 'You have cancer' or 'The tests came back positive', or even that horribly ambiguous statement that has lots of undertones, 'Can you come back in as the tests showed an anomaly?', send a fright through most individuals. Even though heart disease is responsible for more deaths than cancer, it seems that cancer instigates horror beyond that of other diseases. We have special names for cancer, such as 'the big C', as if saying it this way will ward off the evil eye.

The suggestion that diseases may be associated with stressful events or that they occur more frequently among individuals with mood disorders has been around for centuries. We still don't have definitive answers concerning how stressors might favor the development and progression of many illnesses. Nonetheless, it is believed that stressful events and lifestyles can influence the course of various diseases by operating through multiple processes, such as immune and hormonal changes, growth factors, microbial and inflammatory processes.

Learning objectives

The fact that stressful events might compromise immune functioning is interesting, but the bottom line that needs to be considered is whether stressful events actually cause immune-related diseases or promote the worsening of diseases. Furthermore, if stressors act in this way, then what can be done to deter these outcomes? This question is simple enough, but the answers are complicated. Humans are afflicted by numerous immune-related diseases, and although some individuals might succumb to one disease or another, many individuals seem to travel through life unmolested by these illnesses, despite numerous stressful experiences. Moreover, some individuals without extraordinarily stressful lives succumb to immunological disturbances, likely owing to other risk factors related to sex, diet, environmental toxicants, or the genes that they had inherited. We'll assess the evidence that stressful events play a role in the provocation or exacerbation of disease states, keeping in mind interactions with other factors. In this chapter you will learn about:

- infectious diseases and how they come about, as well as the contribution of stressful events in affecting these illnesses;
- a class of illnesses, termed autoimmune disorders, in which the immune system turns on the self;
- the cancer processes, and the possibility that the course of this illness can be exacerbated by stressors. Cancer can come about through factors unrelated to immune disturbances, and thus this chapter will also deal with the stressor effects that involve processes related to hormones and growth factors;
- the effects of stressors on diseases and the influence of a constellation of non-modifiable factors (e.g., age, sex) and those that are modifiable (stress management, diet, sleep, exercise).

Immunity and disease

Immune-related illnesses can come about for any number of reasons. They could occur because of disturbances within the immune system itself, or they may develop because of alterations of processes that ordinarily regulate immune activity (e.g., neuroendocrine factors). The nature of the illness itself might also vary with the specific component of the immune system affected. For instance, reduced T and B cell activity has been associated with human immunodeficiency syndromes, whereas diminished NK cell activity has been related to viral illnesses and cancer. Disease states may also arise because the recognition abilities of immune cells may be compromised. In addition, if suppressor cells (or inhibitory cytokines) do not operate efficiently, then the immune system may attack the self, leading to the development of autoimmune disorders.

In the early days of psychoneuroimmunology (the 1970s and 1980s), most of the work on stress and pathology was prompted by clinical reports showing relationships between stressful life events and autoimmune disorders, as well as infectious illnesses, and cancer. Animal models for some of these illnesses were still limited, and the data from human studies came from retrospective analyses that have many limitations, and the findings that had been reported were often inconsistent. Considerable progress has since been made, although the processes through which stressors influence pathology aren't thoroughly understood. Furthermore, while stressful events might not *cause* some of these illnesses they can exacerbate symptoms once the disease state is present. Conversely, does maintaining a healthy lifestyle, keeping fit, eating well, sleeping properly, and dealing with stressors properly extend life span? To this we can provide a very definite maybe. Maybe you can, if you have the right genes, if you don't do anything really foolish, and if you're lucky.

Weak links and vulnerability

At the funeral of a close friend, one of our buddies turned to us saying, 'David worked out every day, ate properly, got plenty of rest, balanced his home and work life ... he died a healthy man'. There are several messages embedded in that statement, including the philosophical and practical. The philosophical side isn't new, and can seem a bit hokey (e.g., live every day as if it were your last), but the practical view is that it takes only one weak link in our physiology to bring down even the toughest individual. In studying the stress–pathology relationship it is good to take a holistic approach, but not at the expense of ignoring molecular analyses that could potentially pinpoint the specific weak links that make individuals vulnerable to pathological outcomes. If a stressful experience is sufficiently intense and lasting, most individuals will succumb to some form of pathology. The specific pathology that evolves will likely be determined by their specific weak link that could be inherited or promoted by earlier psychosocial experiences or environmental influences.

Infectious illness

Infectious diseases arise when pathogenic biological agents (e.g., viruses or bacteria) are transmitted from a carrier to a host in which the foreign substance can flourish. Infectious agents responsible for diseases can be transmitted through foods, bodily fluids, contact with an infected person or infected surfaces, or via an airborne route. In addition, infectious diseases can be transmitted through a vector, which refers to an intermediate that is responsible for the transfer of a disease, as in the case of mosquitoes or ticks that transmit malaria or Lyme disease to humans, respectively.

Bubonic plague (Black Death) that traversed the globe during the fourteenth century caused the death of between 75 and 200 million people, which represented about one-fifth of the population at that time. This zoonotic disease appeared in rodents through bacterial infection with Yersinia pestis. Fleas that had contracted the bacteria from rats could transmit it to humans, usually through the skin. The disease continued to spread, killing about 65% of infected individuals. There had been no protection to avert the disease other than quarantine, although it was suggested that the end of the bubonic plague may have been helped along because the bacterium evolved so that it was less deadly. There had been outbreaks of the Black Death in subsequent centuries that were less intense killing *only* about 12 million people. We've been fortunate over the past eight decades as bacterial infections could readily be treated through antibiotics. Unfortunately, because of the indiscriminate use of these agents, bacterial resistance has become much more common, and we're down to our last effective treatments. In a sense, the makings of the next bacterial pandemic are already here.

Viral infections have, of course, been a continuing threat to humans, and many viral pandemics have been a scourge that decimated populations. COVID-19 was only the latest of many such diseases. The route by which SARS-CoV-2 reached humans is uncertain. It may have been transmitted from bats to civet cats and then to humans. Then with a few well-placed mutations of the virus, the infected human could transmit the virus to other humans, although other hypotheses have been offered, including the possibility of accidental viral release through a research lab in Wuhan.

As bad as the COVID-19 death toll has been, this disease doesn't hold a candle to that produced by smallpox that has been around for centuries. Currently, smallpox is largely eradicated, but this disease, which is spread by the variola virus, is estimated to have killed up to 300 million people in the twentieth century, and as recently as the 1960s, millions of deaths occurred yearly.

Influenza pandemics are a constant threat, although in recent times none has been as pervasive or deadly as the 1918 pandemic that originated in birds and ultimately killed about 50 million people worldwide. Unlike other viral illnesses that primarily affect the very young or those who are old, about half the deaths occurred in those who were 20–40 years of age. It is believed that contracting the influenza virus when young may act against later infection stemming from viruses like those previously encountered, a phenomenon referred to as 'original antigenic sin'. The possibility was raised that the deadly effects of the 1918 pandemic among 20–40-year-old individuals might have occurred because they had not gained immunity from a flu virus contracted decades earlier (Gostic et al., 2016). There was evidence that prior coronavirus infection may have influenced the later response to the H1N1 virus during the 2009 pandemic and a similar scenario may be playing out in response to SARS-CoV-2 (Aydillo et al., 2021). Specifically, earlier infection with some form of coronavirus could be responsible for asymptomatic COVID-19 rather than severe infection. This has become somewhat controversial as a previously imprinted memory of infection can also interfere with the antibody response mounted against a new virus, leading to more severe illness. Whatever the case, imagine how different the response to COVID-19 might have been had the deadly effects of SARS-CoV-2 appeared in the 20–40-year-old age group as it had during the 1918 influenza pandemic.

In recent times, Ebola virus that originated in Central Africa, which was transmitted from bats (and possibly infected non-human primates) has been contained to a significant extent, but there had been fears of its spread beyond Africa. One of the most studied viruses that were transmitted from animals to humans in recent decades had been HIV. This virus was passed to humans through the Simian immunodeficiency virus (SIV), which is frequent in some species of non-human primates. It was probably transmitted to human hunters through eating the meat of their primate neighbors or having had the blood of these critters get onto their hands and into wounds that might have been present. Once in the human, SIV mutated into HIV and then transmitted to other people. There is no cure for HIV/AIDs, but antiretroviral therapies can control the virus.

The past two decades have witnessed still other infectious viral diseases, such as SARS, West Nile Virus, and H1N1. Given our previous encounters with such threats, individuals ought to have been aware that the COVID-19 pandemic wasn't a rare event. Of course, we hadn't been certain when we would experience a pandemic or the form it would take, but it was almost a certainty that this would occur. You might have heard the statement, 'It's not a matter of if, but when'. Warnings to this effect had been issued repeatedly. However, government officials entrusted with our safety weren't listening and, remarkably, they were caught unprepared.

We were exceptionally fortunate in vaccines having been developed as quickly as they had. While most people in developed countries have eagerly lined up to be vaccinated, a large number of individuals have been vaccine-hesitant. Frankly, this isn't at all surprising, although the scope of this resistance is astonishing. Vaccine hesitancy had initially been encountered to smallpox vaccination and this also occurred when a polio vaccine was first introduced. When we were threatened by H1N1 during 2009–2010, only about 40% of people (varying slightly across countries) were inoculated, despite the World Health Organization (WHO) and various government agencies and the media encouraging us to take preventive measures. Several factors contributed to this low level of inoculation: a lack of trust in media and government agencies, ineffective communication, and apathy on the part of the population owing to 'flu fatigue' (in part stemming from the frequent false alarms issued by health agencies), as well as a strange sense of invulnerability ('Relative to others, it's less likely that I'll get sick, and if I do get sick the symptoms will also be less pronounced than my neighbors' symptoms') (Taha et al., 2013). Fortunately, H1N1 turned out to be less of a danger than originally feared, although the CDC estimated that worldwide between 150,000 and 575,000 people had died owing to that pandemic. COVID-19 has been far more infectious and lethal, but it has encountered vaccine hesitancy for some of the same reasons.

The SARS-CoV-19 virus has been enormously successful in its evolution, but human behavior has largely been resistant to the necessary changes needed to protect us, particularly concerning vaccine hesitancy. Over the past decade, the anti-vaxxer movement has gained strength, which may have contributed to vaccine hesitancy. The scourge of misinformation circulating through social media has also facilitated the adoption of counterproductive attitudes concerning vaccination. In some countries, political considerations have also played a signif-icant role in people refusing vaccination. But, as indicated earlier, lack of trust in those responsible for vaccine promotion is likely the greatest deterrent to appro-priate health behaviors.

Thanks to vaccines and preventive behavioral measures the frequency of SARS-CoV-2 virus infection initially declined in developed countries, and the hope had been that it might, at worst, only become a treatable endemic condition. However, given that vaccines had not been readily available in many countries, COVID-19 spread rampantly, and new variants emerged. We saw the emergence of mutations of COVID-19, such as the delta variant that was more transmissible and produced more severe symptoms, followed by the omicrom variant and the BA.2, BA.4, and BA.5 form of this variant that was still more transmissible but generally produced less severe symptoms, although it has been having greater effects in children than earlier variants. Having a booster shot could to some extent protect against hospi-talization and death, but the omicron variant could break through these defenses. It has been maintained that we are only a few mutations away from some variant entirely escaping the benefits of vaccination, and a well-placed mutation could also make it more deadly. This may or not turn out to be the case, but it needs to be considered that the occurrence of such variants (or new viruses) will be encouraged further by the lack of vaccines in some countries (e.g., within Africa) and among non-vaccinated people in developed countries who chose not to be vaccinated.

We were fortunate in other pandemics (e.g., the 2009 H1N1 pandemic) burning out as quickly as they had – we dodged a bullet! We obviously weren't as lucky with the COVID-19 pandemic, even though the rapid roll-out of vaccines was miracu-lous. But this doesn't mean that we will always be so fortunate. Making specific predictions of the future is risky, but certain eventualities seem inevitable. Even if COVID-19 is tamed to an appreciable extent, we will eventually encounter another novel virus that could potentially be still more virulent and perhaps we won't be prepared to deal with it (again) and a vaccine won't be created as readily. Pandemics and attacks by terrorists share a crucial and common feature: We can be successful a whole lot of the time in our preventive measures, but all these successes will be forgotten if we're unsuccessful even once.[1]

What's a vaccine?

Vaccines against illnesses are based on the same principles that are involved in memory in immune cells. Vaccination comprises the administration of dead or weakened virus, but because the agent is not alive (or is weakened) the individual won't get the disease

---

[1] In our earlier writing, we were accurate in our predictions regarding pandemics and vaccine hesitancy. In part, our perspective of vaccine hesitancy was based on our previous research concerning the response to the 2009 H1N1 pandemic (Taha et al., 2013). Anyone who knew anything about pandemics often made identical predictions in relation to a pandemic occurring and the vaccine hesitancy that could be expected. But it seems that we were collectively screaming into the ether.

because of the treatment. Yet the dead virus is recognized as being foreign, leading to an immune response being mounted, and memory cells will retain the information about this virus. Thus, when the viral threat is encountered, the immune system will recognize and destroy the virus quickly and therefore sickness will not occur.

In some cases (e.g., seasonal flu bugs) the virus might mutate (change its recognition characteristics), and thereby evade detection, and so we're stuck being unprotected unless new vaccines are made. It's no easy trick to predict these mutations, and sometimes the makers of vaccines can be inaccurate in predicting the nature of expected influenza epidemics so these vaccines are not particularly effective. Even under the best conditions, the influenza vaccine is only effective in about 60-70% of individuals. This contrasts with the efficacy of the childhood vaccine for measles, mumps, and rubella (MMR) that is about 97% effective after a booster shot (and, no, MMR vaccines absolutely do not lead to autism despite the claims of the anti-vaxxer group).

Vaccines based on mRNA operate on a somewhat similar principle, but rather than administering a weakened form of a virus, a harmless section of the mRNA is administered that corresponds to a viral protein, such as that present on the outer surface of the virus. Cells are thus prompted to create antibodies to this protein so that when they encounter the virus that carries the recognizable protein, an immune response will be mounted to attack the virus before the illness can be caused.

Ordinarily, high antibody titers ought to be present following vaccination, but unfortunately, natural immunity and the response to vaccines, as we're aware, wanes over time. As varied forms of distress in humans (loneliness, partnership dissolution, employment loss, as well as altered lifestyle factors) can diminish the effectiveness of vaccines, the possibility was raised that psychosocial influences, including distress, could potentially diminish the efficacy of vaccines for COVID-19 (Madison et al., 2021).

Stressor effects on infectious illnesses

Numerous studies have evaluated the factors that influence the *incidence* of viral illness (i.e., the proportion of people who develop an illness during a set period) as well as the *prevalence* of illness (i.e., the proportion of people who have a specific illness). Whether or not an individual will contract a virus or encounter other infectious agents depends on several factors. Some are related to extraneous influences or personal habits (e.g., hand washing, crowded workspaces, or encountering infected individuals who heroically (but thoughtlessly) decide to come to work), whereas others are related to the nature of the contagious agent. Having an appropriate antibody or T cell response is fundamental in preventing or attenuating illness. As we know, however, our immune system may not be prepared to deal with new viruses, and factors that further compromise our immune system may render us still more vulnerable to pathology. Some toxins, including bacteria such as anthrax lethal factor and C. difficile, may disturb glucocorticoid receptors and hence disrupt our immune capacity. As well, sex differences associated with the occurrence of bacterial or parasitic infection might be tied to corticoid and progesterone variations, and sex differences in antibody production have been linked to viral clearance as observed in SARS-CoV-2 infection (Gabriele et al., 2021).

Given the marked effects of stressors on immune functioning and the hormones that act on immune processes, it is reasonable to expect that stressors would influence vulnerability to infection or the ability of a host organism to fight off an ongoing infection. Consistent with this hypothesis, negative life experiences similarly predicted the appearance of the common cold and diminished the immune response to influenza vaccination (Cohen et al., 2001). A one-year prospective study revealed that negative affect, stressful life events, and perceived stress were tied to the occurrence of the common cold (Takkouche et al., 2001). Moreover, experimental administration of a cold virus was more likely to produce infection in individuals who reported greater stressor experiences (Cohen et al., 1991). As expected, elevated job strain that comprised high job demands and limited control, coupled with low levels of social support, were associated with increased occurrences of the common cold, more so in males than in females. Conversely, fewer incidents of the common cold and absent days were related to job satisfaction. Differential symptoms were likewise observed between individuals with high versus low negative (or positive) trait affect, varying with the availability of social support (Janicki Deverts et al., 2017).

WET HEAD, GO TO BED

Have you ever wondered why going out with your hair wet in the winter might lead to you getting a cold? One possibility is that viruses communicate with one another and are attracted to people with wet heads ('Hey, there's Murray, he's got wet hair. Get him!'). Since this isn't likely, another possibility is that your body temperature declines, making for a comfortable environment for viruses. Perhaps the heat loss associated with going out with wet hair when it's -10°C reduces your immune capacity, resulting in a cold if the virus happens to be around. However, your core body temperature would have to drop quite a bit before this would happen, making this unlikely.

It's also possible that the premise is wrong and that we aren't more likely to get sick because of going out with a wet head in the winter. It might simply be the case that we're more likely to get a cold in the winter than in the summer, wet head or not, because we spend more time indoors and thus are more likely to come into close contact with people who are sick. The wet-head notion, however, has been passed down from mothers and grandmothers (and fathers and grandfathers) for years, and it would be pointless to try to dissuade them of this well-entrenched myth. Besides, it wouldn't hurt to listen to your mother and wear a hat when it's cold.

The link between stressful experiences and infection is not restricted to cold or influenza. Herpes Simplex and Epstein Barr Virus are present in most people, but their actions are typically kept in check by the cell-mediated immune responses. This restraint, however, can be undermined by intense life stressors (Glaser & Kiecolt-Glaser, 2005). Furthermore, individuals who experienced elevated feelings of distress, anxiety, and depression at the start of the COVID-19 pandemic were more likely to subsequently self-report SARS-CoV-2 infection together with more intense symptoms (Ayling et al., 2022). A large-scale investigation similarly indicated that occurrence of life-threatening infectious illnesses occurred more frequently among people with stress-related disorders, such as acute stress disorder and PTSD (Song et al., 2019). In general, studies that attempted to relate naturally occurring viral illness to stressful experiences have indicated that such events were associated with elevated susceptibility and the frequency of illnesses, delay in recovery from illness, and more frequent complications related to infection.

Stressful events may promote the loss of helper T cells, and hence promote the onset of AIDS symptoms in HIV positive individuals. Of particular interest, in this regard, was the finding that certain aspects of psychosocial events appeared to be particularly tied to HIV progression. Both personality type and ineffective coping styles were more closely aligned with HIV progression than were the specific stress stimuli encountered. Results like those associated with HIV were also observed in relation to herpes simplex virus recurrence. Essentially, perceptions of stressors or the coping methods used to deal with these challenges were particularly important in determining the response to existent infection.

─Immunological foresight─

The presence of infection influences neuronal functioning and hormonal outputs, culminating in mood changes. Indeed, altered brain neuronal activity may occur even before the full symptoms of an illness have emerged. Have you ever noticed that you're a bit more lethargic just before showing the symptoms of a cold? In fact, your friends might seem to notice this with comments such as, 'You seem to be a bit off today. Maybe you're coming down with something?' It might be that in response to a viral insult the immune response that is being mounted gives your brain a message to slow down to conserve energy to deal with the cold that is about to be experienced.

Research in animals has provided important information concerning the conditions under which stressors favor the development of viral and bacterial infections and the processes by which this occurs. In mice that had been infected with the influenza virus, a stressor reduced IL-1β and NK cell activity, thereby increasing vulnerability to illness. Using a herpes simplex virus type 1 infection model, stressors applied early in infection reduced viral clearance and worsened the course of the illness, and this outcome was tied to the immunosuppressive effects of increased corticoids elicited by the stressor (Elftman et al., 2010). In addition to affecting the response to a newly encountered virus, stressors can produce other lasting effects. For instance, herpes simplex virus type 1 (HSV-1) can be a recurrent disorder that stems from the reactivation of a latent virus that might have migrated to the trigeminal ganglia but is usually inactive (the trigeminal nerve is involved in facial sensations and movement). Stressful events may promote virus reactivation by undermining certain cells of the immune system, namely CD8+ T cells, leading to the reappearance of the cold sores associated with HSV-1. Interestingly, the effects of stressors on HSV-1 infection were less pronounced in female rodents than in males, but the susceptibility of females after ovariectomy was like that of males.

So, something about the ovaries might be imbuing females with resistance; however, as the stressor effects were not modified by administration of estradiol, the reduced susceptibility in females was likely due to ovarian factors other than that of estrogen.

Summarizing, chronic stressors can disturb various facets of immune functioning, thereby allowing viral and bacterial infections to occur, and may cause illnesses to be longer lasting. The actions of stressors are, predictably, related to nonmodifiable factors, such as age and sex. Likewise, an individual's ability to contend with stressors may have considerable bearing on immune functioning and hence disease occurrence and progression. We would be delinquent in not saying that numerous modifiable factors, including specific diets, obtaining proper sleep, and engaging in moderate levels of exercise, may enhance immune functioning, thereby increasing disease resistance and could offset the effects of stressors (Anisman & Kusnecov, 2022).

Trauma and sepsis

Sepsis refers to an extreme immune response to infection in which tissues and organs can be severely damaged. This condition can develop owing to major trauma, serious burns, pneumonia, and abdominal infection, but any infection can cause this outcome, including bacterial infection that might develop following surgical procedures. The development of sepsis is more prominent in individuals with a weakened immune system, those with diabetes or other medical conditions, as well as in the very young and in older patients. Given that chronic stressors undermine immune functioning and increase proinflammatory cytokines, possibly involving the NLRP3 inflammasome, psychosocial stressors and ongoing depression were suggested as being a risk factor for the occurrence and worsening of sepsis (Ojard et al., 2015).

Sepsis can evolve into septic shock that is lethal in more than 40% of patients. In about 50% of survivors, post-sepsis syndrome may develop that is characterized by numerous physical ailments, such as fatigue, sleep disorders, limb swelling, joint and muscle pain, and disturbed functioning of several organs. As well, numerous psychological disturbances may occur, such as depression, panic attacks, and PTSD. It was estimated that about 48.9 million cases occur globally, leading to 11 million deaths (Rudd et al., 2020). Sepsis currently kills more people than does cancer, and with annual cases increasing as they are, it will outstrip heart disease by 2050.

Autoimmune disorders

When regulatory processes do not operate effectively, the immune system may attack self-tissues, causing autoimmune disorders. There are about 80 such disorders that affect different organs and systems. Most of these disorders are infrequent but as a group their prevalence is substantial. Worldwide, about 4% of people have some form of autoimmune disorder, but the prevalence is particularly high in developed countries in which 4–7% of people are affected. The regional differences, coupled with the rise of these disorders in recent years, suggests the involvement of environmental factors or lifestyles to these conditions emerging.

Varied explanations have been offered to account for the development of auto-immune disorders. Ineffective functioning of T_{reg} cells that ought to inhibit cyto-toxic T cell functioning have often been assumed to be responsible for the attack on self-tissue. It has likewise been suggested that activation of innate myeloid cells (e.g., macrophages and dendritic cells) by memory Th1 cells may produce excessive levels of proinflammatory cytokines that contribute to these disorders (McDaniel et al., 2022). There have also been indications that certain enzymes (e.g., KAT7) are critical in the training of immune cells so that they selectively identify and attack foreign particles while not responding to self tissue. When KAT7 was inhibited, the expression of particular genes was turned on, resulting in immune cells becoming excessively activated and attacking body tissues, thereby promoting autoimmune disorders. Other enzymes or genetic factors may likewise contribute to the devel-opment of autoimmune disorders, and it is exciting that in a mouse model manip-ulation of KAT7 could alter disease occurrence (Heinlein et al., 2022). Still, these explanations alone do not address the question of how (or why) selective targeting of certain tissues occurs thereby leading to varied autoimmune disorders or why the incidence of these diseases has been increasing over the past few decades.

Some of the most frequent and serious autoimmune diseases are type 1 diabetes, rheumatoid arthritis, multiple sclerosis, systemic lupus erythematosus, and inflam-matory bowel disorder. Other common forms of autoimmune disorders, such as psoriasis and celiac disease are less threatening but can seriously undermine quality of life. In the main, autoimmune disorders occur much more frequently in women than in men (about 75–90% are women), except for type 1 diabetes and psoriasis that occur equally often in men and women. Stressful events have been associated with an exacerbation of autoimmune disorders, and there have been suspicions that such events may contribute to the occurrence of such disorders, but there has been limited evidence supporting the latter proposition. We'll now have a brief look at some of the more common and damaging autoimmune conditions and what factors moderate their occurrence or progression.

Multiple sclerosis (MS)

Characteristics of the illness

Multiple sclerosis (MS) is a disease wherein immune responses are directed toward the sheath (myelin) that surrounds axons within the brain and spinal cord. Myelin is necessary for the rapid propagation of an action potential down an axon, and when demyelination occurs, conduction speed is slowed, leading to compromised signals between neurons within the brain and between the brain and periphery.

The disease, which typically first appears among individuals 20–30 years of age, is characterized by an extensive set of symptoms that can initially make it difficult to diagnose. Symptoms of MS may include changes in physical sensation, such as loss of sensitivity or tingling, prickling or numbness, muscle weakness, muscle spasms, or difficulty in moving. Moreover, symptoms may comprise problems with coordination and balance, or speech and swallowing, as well as visual problems. Cognitive impairments are common as the disease progresses, and depression is a frequent comorbid condition.

Generally, MS can appear in a form in which new symptoms occur as discrete attacks followed by months or years without further incidents (relapsing-remitting MS). Although symptoms may disappear entirely between episodes, the underlying neurological disturbances may persist and even progress. Secondary progressive MS is diagnosed in patients who initially presented with signs consistent with relapsing-remitting MS and subsequently experienced progressive neurologic decline where definite periods of remission were not apparent, although false signs of abatement may appear. Still another form of the disease, primary progressive MS that affects about 15% of patients, is not accompanied by remission following the initial symptoms. In both latter forms, the progressive phase commonly occurs when individuals are about 40 years old, but the prognosis for the disease is difficult to predict.

There is no known cure for MS, and at present there are only 'disease-modifying treatments' (DMTs) that limit the course of the relapsing-remitting form of the illness, and in the progressive-remitting form, even these treatments are largely ineffective. Treatments comprise those that affect immune functioning, comprising forms of IFN-β, immunosuppressive agents, or a monoclonal antibody immunomodulator (monoclonal refers to antibodies that are clones of a single ancestral cell). In addition to DMTs that operate by altering immune functioning, it is believed that lifestyles can influence symptoms of the disease, including those that affect microbiota and the ensuing variations of inflammation (Adamczyk-Sowa et al., 2017).

Impact of stressors

Although there had been reports that major stressful life events were associated with the subsequent occurrence of MS, in many other studies neither severe life stressors nor socioeconomic status was linked to MS. Most studies that assessed the relationship between MS and stress were of a retrospective nature that involved self-reports of stress (which could be biased), and the variance accounted for was small.

Unlike the effects of stressful experiences on the production of MS, a detailed meta-analysis indicated that stressor duration, severity, and frequency contributed to the *progression* of MS symptoms as well as the presence of new brain lesions, whereas these effects were diminished in conjunction with social support received (Briones-Buixassa et al., 2015). Predictably, new brain lesions were most prominent among individuals that focused on their illness through emotion-based coping and were least evident in patients who used avoidance/distraction to cope (Mohr et al., 2007). Consistent with the role of stressful experiences in aggravating MS features, distressing events were more likely to occur during the period prior to relapse of MS symptoms relative to well periods (Bufill et al., 2015). As expected, non-pharmacological stress reducing therapies, such as mindfulness-based approaches influenced features secondary to MS, but these effects were small (Senders et al., 2019).

The processes responsible for MS remain to be fully identified, although it has been shown that rogue T cells may steal proteins from the surface of B cells that make them more harmful to self tissue. Moreover, astrocyte functioning may play a key role in this regard, possibly through effects on cytokines and chemokines, impaired regulation of oxidative stress, and disturbances related to blood–brain–barrier integrity. As these mechanisms can be influenced by stressor experiences, the possibility exists that stressors might affect MS through such processes, but at this time this is mostly conjecture.

It has been suggested that MS might be triggered by a viral infection, and in this respect a longitudinal analysis indicated that Epstein-virus infection, a form of herpesvirus, was associated with a 32-fold increase in MS occurrence (Bjornevik et al., 2022). It is interesting as well that gastrointestinal problems, such as intestinal inflammation and intestinal hyperpermeability, have been associated with many autoimmune disorders. Moreover, MS was associated with a disturbed relationship between the microbiome and immune functioning that was linked to the amount of meat consumed (Cantoni et al., 2022). Further to this, MS was accompanied by variations of gut microbiota and their SCFA metabolites, possibly being tied to the effects of stressors on microbial dysbiosis (Ilchmann-Diounou & Menard, 2020). As manipulations that affected microbiota and SCFAs may alter features of MS in an animal model, greater focus on the intestinal microbiome and microbial metabolites may ultimately produce an effective disease-modifying strategy.

Given the distress created by MS, this condition is frequently comorbid with depressive illness. Beyond this, however, depressive disorders frequently precede MS, and depression in MS patients is more common than would be expected in illnesses of a chronic nature. Thus, it is possible that MS and depression may share some common underlying features. These can be related to antecedent stressful events and/or the involvement of common mechanisms, including neuroendocrine factors or cytokine variations, both of which may be connected to stressful experiences. Not unexpectedly, having a potent coping strategy, particularly social support, predicted better psychological adjustment among those diagnosed with MS; however, it did not appear that social support was related to the effects of stressful experiences on symptom remission. Thus, social support may help individuals deal with their situation, but once present the illness is not abated by having this support.

Lupus erythematosus

Characteristics of the illness

Systemic lupus erythematosus (SLE) is a disease wherein the immune system attacks any of several parts of the body, such as the heart, nervous system, liver, kidneys, skin, lungs, and blood vessels, promoting inflammation and damage to these tissues. The disease usually manifests between 15 and 35 years of age. The symptoms of the disease vary appreciably but typically include joint pains, fatigue, myalgia (muscle pain), and fever, which may appear and disappear on an unpredictable basis. Because this pattern of symptoms is evident in other illnesses, it may initially be difficult for a firm diagnosis to be made. As with so many other illnesses, particularly immunologically related conditions, with disease progression increased risk occurs for cardiovascular disease and infections. It is possible that inflammatory factors, notably cytokines such as IFNs and neutrophil functioning, contribute to pathological outcomes (Tumurkhuu et al., 2019).

The neurological and psychiatric manifestations of SLE are characterized by periventricular white matter hyperintensities (brain lesions that appear as increased brightness on certain types of MRI scans). As well, hemorrhages, and infarcts (lesions that stem from cell death brought on by a lack of oxygen) may occur, as may cell loss in several brain regions together with cerebral atrophy. Microstructural abnormalities may be present that affect processing speed and executive functioning, which could influence memory impairments that sometimes occur in association with SLE.

The marked brain disturbances associated with SLE have been attributed to antibodies that are directed against proteins in the brain (brain reactive autoantibodies). These autoantibodies could potentially disturb the blood–brain–barrier, and their subsequent access to different aspects of the brain might cause damage. As well, cytokine access to the brain can be increased under these conditions so that when their levels are sufficiently great, neuronal disturbances can be engendered leading to the neurocognitive and neuropsychiatric features of MS (Deijns et al., 2020). A related accounting of the central actions associated with SLE is that lupus autoantibodies can cross-react with particular subunits of NMDA glutamate receptors, which might cause cell death (Chan et al., 2020) and might thereby contribute to depressive features often observed in this disease.

Another line of inquiry related to SLE concerns the possibility that viruses might in some way promote or exacerbate the disorder. Support for this view has come from reports indicating SLE was associated with the presence of endogenous retroviruses, Epstein–Barr virus, and parvovirus B19, as well as specific bacteria that can stimulate immune and inflammatory processes (Quaglia et al., 2021). This outcome is probably not just due to the provocation of inflammation as other viruses (e.g., cytomegalovirus) have not been reliably related to SLE. Thus, it is more likely the disease may be related to interactions between immune functioning and virus-specific proteins.

At the moment, SLE is incurable, and the available treatments are essentially used to manage (rather than eliminate) the illness. Typically, when symptoms are mild or remittent, treatment is limited to nonsteroidal anti-inflammatory drugs (e.g., prednisone). In more severe cases, drugs that affect immune functioning are used, such as corticosteroids and immunosuppressants such as cyclophosphamide, even though these agents can have marked adverse effects. In addition, antimalarial drugs, such as hydroxychloroquine (Plaquenil) and chloroquine phosphate (Aralen), can diminish signs of lupus and limit the occurrence of flares (these agents do not have any positive effects on COVID-19 as claimed early in the pandemic). As much as this disease has been difficult to manage, the therapeutic landscape concerning SLE has finally been changing. Drug development has focused on targeting B cells rather than treatments that affect the immune system broadly. A human monoclonal antibody, Benlysta, which blocks the actions of B cell stimulation and reduces autoantibodies, has received FDA approval, the first drug in 50 years to have achieved this milestone. Several other agents are in the pipeline, which may have similar positive effects on aspects of SLE, although failures in clinical trials were not unusual (Liossis & Staveri, 2021).

Impact of stressors

The fact that SLE occurs primarily in women points to the possibility that sex hormones might be a fundamental feature in this illness. Estrogen enhances autoantibody production, whereas testosterone has the opposite effect. Whether such factors are responsible for the observed difference between males and females warrants further assessment, but it should also be considered that other factors, including elevated stress reactivity in females, might also contribute to this. To be sure, estrogen and other hormones may have profound effects on immune functioning, and as stressful events influence these hormones, the course of the illness may be altered.

An enormous number of environmental factors have been associated with the occurrence of SLE, with some of the most prominent being cigarette smoking, oral contraceptive use, and postmenopausal hormone therapy. Suspicions have also arisen that silica dust in agricultural or industrial settings, pesticides, and air pollution might contribute to the progression of the disease, although in most studies the number of patients assessed was relatively small. It was nonetheless suggested that environmental exposures might provoke SLE through their effects on inflammatory and hormonal factors (Barbhaiya et al., 2016).

Beyond environmental challenges, psychosocial factors such as elevated perceived stress, negative emotions, as well as anxiety and depression, together with various sex hormones have been linked to SLE (Pan et al., 2019). The symptoms of SLE can be aggravated by day-to-day irritations, particularly those associated with social relationships but symptom exacerbation was more often associated with strong or chronic stressors. A 24-year follow-up study indicated that strong stressors that promoted PTSD-like symptoms were associated with increased risk of SLE (Roberts et al., 2017). Furthermore, allostatic overload that stemmed from habitually being exposed to societal stressors, including poverty and the challenges that come with this, notably insecurity related to food, housing, and medical care, were accompanied by increased incidence of SLE flares.

It is understandable that a diagnosis of SLE can be devastating to the individual and may promote other stress-related disorders, such as depressive illness, varying with how individuals cope. Depressive illness and diminished quality of life among SLE patients was prominent in those who used disengagement or emotion-focused coping strategies and low levels of problem-focused strategies (Farhat et al., 2020), whereas quality of life was enhanced among individuals who used coping that entailed positive reinterpretation and growth. As expected, depressive symptoms and quality of life could be improved to some extent through cognitive behavioral therapy, but these procedures do not generally limit organ damage.

Rheumatoid arthritis

Characteristics of the illness

Rheumatoid arthritis is a chronic inflammatory disease that affects the synovial joints (the movable joints surrounded by a capsule containing a lubricating synovial fluid), including the membrane that lines joints and tendon sheaths as well as cartilage, primarily in the fingers, wrists, knees, and elbows, and cervical spine. As a result, affected individuals may experience joint pain, difficulty using the hands, moving joints, or even walking. Patients often experience muscle aches and pains, general malaise or feelings of fatigue, weight loss, and poor sleep. Several forms of arthritis may occur in children or young adolescents (under the age of 16), with juvenile idiopathic arthritis (juvenile rheumatoid arthritis) being the most common.

The occurrence of rheumatoid arthritis has been associated with autoantibodies (RF; rheumatoid factors) directed at portions of the IgG molecule and other proteins. These factors may be apparent in advance of clinical signs of rheumatoid arthritis, implicating them as possible causal agents or they may be useful as biomarkers. Cytokines, such as IL-1β and TNF-α, have also been implicated as culprits in the rheumatoid arthritis process, and dysregulation of a form of T helper cells, the Th17 regulatory cells that produce the inflammatory cytokine IL-17, may influence the progression of this disease (McInnis et al., 2016).

Treatments to diminish symptoms of the illness can include physiotherapy, lifestyle changes, and exercise, but primarily comprise drug treatments like anti-inflammatories, corticosteroids, and monoclonal antibodies, as well as analgesics. There have also been promising outcomes using disease-modifying antirheumatic drugs (DMARDs), which slow down disease progression. Within this group are TNF-α inhibitors and drugs that inhibit both IL-1β and TNF-α. Unfortunately, the disease is often refractory to treatments and many patients do not reach sustained remission. Given the potential involvement of microbiota in inflammation and the promotion of arthritis, it was suggested that anti-inflammatory diets (e.g., Mediterranean diet) might be an effective adjuvant therapy (Dourado et al., 2020).

Impact of stressors

As in other chronic illnesses, a sizeable portion (22%) of patients with rheumatoid arthritis attributed their illness to stressful experiences, and 45% believed that these exacerbated their illness or provoked flares. Consistent with patient perspectives, a review of autoimmune disorders, including rheumatoid arthritis, indicated that day-to-day stressful events exacerbated pathology and that social support was fundamental in attenuating these adverse effects. In line with this, chronic interpersonal stress among rheumatoid arthritis patients was associated with greater production of IL-6, coupled with impaired ability of glucocorticoids to inhibit this cellular inflammatory response. As stressful events may influence peripheral cytokine activity, and chronic stressful events may lead to glucocorticoid resistance, thereby limiting the inhibition of cytokines otherwise provoked by corticoids, it is tempting to surmise that arthritic flares may involve these processes (Sharif et al., 2018).

Arthritis is associated with distress that can worsen inflammation that is already present, thereby exacerbating illness symptoms and could likewise cause intensification of depressive symptoms. Thus, being able to diminish mental health challenges may be an important component in managing arthritis symptoms. It seems that CBT can diminish some features of rheumatoid arthritis, especially fatigue, and some beneficial outcomes were realized through a mindfulness-based intervention (DiRenzo et al., 2018).

Inflammatory factors influence neurodegenerative disorders

Alzheimer's disease (AD) is usually characterized by neuropathological hallmarks, such as increased β-amyloid plaques, neurofibrillary tangles, and misfolded tau protein. It seems that variations of inflammatory and anti-inflammatory processes, secondary to the misfolded tau or to other brain anomalies might contribute to AD (Heneka et al., 2015). The view has been adopted that the development of AD may stem from chronic viral, bacterial, or fungal infections, and gut microbiota may also contribute to inflammation that promotes the disease (Sochocka et al., 2019). Indeed, markers of inflammation present in the brain may appear years before symptoms of Alzheimer's disease are present (Brosseron et al., 2022).

Astrocytes and microglia that can promote inflammation may contribute to the development of Alzheimer's disease. The plaques associated with AD are surrounded by microglia, which ought to be involved in eliminating these plaques and dead neurons, but the release of IL-1β by microglia might produce neuronal damage. Traumatic brain injury can serve as a risk factor for the later development of AD, possibly through apoptotic or epigenetic mechanisms, or instigation of the inflammatory processes that influence

(Continued)

cell death. Over-expression of multiple proinflammatory cytokines and diminished anti-inflammatory cytokines were associated with AD (Ransohoff, 2016). As chronic stressors influence microglia activation and the excessive release of cytokines and alterations of neurotrophins, under certain conditions these experiences may be a precipitating factor in AD (Bisht et al., 2018). Conversely, epidemiological studies suggested that continued intake of nonsteroidal anti-inflammatory drugs (NSAIDs) reduced the risk of developing AD. However, once frank symptoms were present, NSAIDs did not yield impressive outcomes, although a suppressor of proinflammatory cytokine upregulation had positive effects in a mouse model of AD.

It has been maintained that the combination of a healthy (non-inflammatory) diet and exercise may slow down age-related cognitive decline and the development of AD (Vasefi et al., 2019). These actions could come about by limiting chronic microbiota dysbiosis and in randomized controlled trials probiotics seemed to enhance cognitive performance, probably through actions on inflammatory processes. However, the few trials that had been conducted were deemed insufficient for firm conclusions to be drawn concerning the efficacy of this procedure in diminishing cognitive impairments (Den et al., 2020). There were indications that omega-3 supplements could limit mild cognitive decline that precedes the development of AD (La Rosa et al., 2018), but better outcomes might have emerged through specific diets rather than supplements, which had likewise been found to be more effective in treating numerous other conditions.

Cancer

As indicated at the outset of this chapter, the notion has been tossed around for years that stressful events or stress-related illnesses, such as depression, might contribute to the emergence or exacerbation of certain types of cancer. This isn't the place to try to provide extensive information on the cancer process, but some basic concepts must be explained before we enter a discussion of how stress might influence the growth of cancer cells (see Anisman & Kusnecov, 2022, for a more extensive description).

The cancer process

Although 'cancer' is frequently mentioned as if it was a single entity, there are about 200 forms of cancer, and even cancers of a particular organ can be very different from one another. Types of cancer can generally be classified within several broad categories and with their stage of development as described in Table 6.1. Cancer cells can differ based on genetic and epigenetic characteristics, as well as whether they are influenced by specific hormones, growth factors, or inflammatory processes. Forms of cancer can also be distinguished from one another based on the tumor microenvironment (the environment surrounding a tumor comprising immune cells, blood vessels, fibroblasts, and the extracellular matrix that provides structural and biochemical support) and the presence of specific markers on their surface. Owing to the vast heterogeneity of cancer types, therapies differ with varied types and characteristics of the disease.

Cancer comprises diseases in which certain cells undergo uncontrolled growth. These cells can leave a place of origin (i.e., from the primary tumor site), acquire the ability to get into blood vessels or penetrate the lymphatic walls, travel through the blood or lymphatic system, our body's superhighways, and then find a comfortable home to establish a new cancer colony. This process, referred to as metastasis, distinguishes malignant from benign tumors, as the latter typically do not metastasize.

A cancer's development is typically described based on the size of the tumor and whether it may have spread. Stage 0 (carcinoma in situ) refers to an early form of cancer characterized by these cells being present only in the location where they had initially formed. Stage I cancers are localized to a single part of the body and have not grown deeply into nearby tissues. Stage II cancers are also local, but more advanced. Stage III cancers are locally advanced but may involve lymph nodes being affected. Stage IV cancers are those that have metastasized or spread to other organs.

Table 7.1 Cancer subtypes.

Carcinoma: involves epithelial cells that comprise tissues that line surfaces and cavities within the body, including the skin. Cancers that affect the breast, prostate, colon, and lung are typically carcinomas.

Sarcoma: cancer that affects connective tissues that largely comprise blood, cartilage, bone, tendons, adipose tissue, as well as lymphatic tissue.

Myeloma: cancer that originates in the plasma cells of bone marrow.

Lymphoma: develop in the nodes or glands of the lymphatic system, which serve to purify bodily fluids and produce lymphocytes to fight infection. Lymphomas are broadly categorized as Hodgkin lymphoma and non-Hodgkin lymphoma, as well as multiple myeloma and immunoproliferative diseases.

Leukemia: cancer of blood-forming (or hematopoietic) cells that originate in the bone marrow, culminating in abnormal white blood cells appearing in excessively high numbers.

Blastoma: a type of cancer that stems from precursor cells (referred to as blasts) that are essentially primitive and incompletely differentiated cells. Several types of blastoma exist, one of which is a cancer type that is seen in children.

Melanoma: a form of cancer that originates in melanin-containing cells (melanocytes) primarily found on the skin, but can be found elsewhere (pigmented tissue, including the eye).

Germ cell tumor: derived from pluripotent cells (i.e., those that come from a stem cell and thus can differentiate into several different germlines). This type of cancer is also seen in children and babies.

Brain and spinal cord tumors: involve different types of cells and are named on this basis. The varied brain cancers comprise gliomas, oligodendroglial tumors, astrocytic tumors, medulloblastomas, ependymal tumors, meningeal tumors, and craniopharyngioma.

So, how does cancer come about? How do first cancer cells occur, and why do they multiply without apparent restraint? And why is it so difficult to eliminate cancer once it has developed? There is little question that genetic factors, gene mutations, and epigenetic changes contribute to cancer occurrence and progression. Earlier, in discussing DNA and its replication, it was indicated that gene mutations occur frequently and could potentially appear in daughter cells of the initially mutated cell. Fortunately, during replication, proofreading and editing occur so that the errors in the transcribed code are repaired. Even if the errors get by this editing process, the mutation may show up at a point in the DNA strand where its effects are not meaningful – then again, they can also show up in genes that influence pathological outcomes. For instance, genes contain a section that, when activated or uncovered, causes cell death or suicide, which is referred to as apoptosis. If a cell is damaged or could cause harmful effects, it would be advantageous for it to die off. However, changes can occur that affect the segment of a gene containing these apoptotic messages so that these cells would not die. In the absence of this regulatory mechanism, this cell would multiply again and again, ultimately creating a tumor mass.

Mutated genes that favor cancer occurrence can be passed down from a parent to their offspring, making them especially vulnerable to certain types of cancer. Many such genes have been discovered, but among the best known are mutations of BRCA1 and BRCA2. These genes ordinarily contribute to processes responsible for DNA repair, but if they are mutated, then the risk of breast cancer (and to a lesser extent ovarian cancer) increases appreciably. The risk (>60%) is sufficiently great that some women who inherited the BRCA1 mutation have opted for double mastectomy (and sometimes ovariectomy) to be assured that they would not develop cancer. Many other genes have been identified that favor cancer development and several gene mutations (e.g., the KRAS mutation and that of the TP53 gene) have been associated with the development of multiple forms of cancer. The TP53 gene codes for a protein p53 that serves as a tumor suppressor by orchestrating DNA damage control. When mutations occur on the gene responsible for p53, sometimes referred to as the guardian of the genome, vulnerability to many cancers is elevated.

The presence of a gene mutation, such as on BRCA1, doesn't guarantee that cancer will develop, and other factors might contribute to whether cancer will develop. The presence of certain hormones or immune factors or environmental toxicants that affect these hormones could trigger the development of cancer in those with the BRCA1 mutation. This 'second hit' hypothesis has understandably encouraged a search for the factors that could enable cancer-related mutations to become expressed as tumors, or conversely the factors that might hinder the development of cancer. Basically, the presence of oncogenes (a gene that has the potential to cause cancer) or carcinogens that produce oncogenes may serve as a first hit. The occurrence of a second hit, such as depressive illness or poor diets, could culminate in tumorigenesis (Bandinelli et al., 2017).

Certain chemicals or environmental stimuli may be carcinogenic by instigating DNA mutations, more so if DNA repair processes are ineffective. We've heard a lot about cigarettes and sun rays, but there are a vast number of agents that have carcinogenic properties, including many that are found in the workplace. As well, poor lifestyles, including lack of exercise, alcohol consumption, choosing a poor diet, and having obesity were associated with the development of cancers and might be responsible for the differences in the occurrence of certain types of cancer seen across countries, regions, and cultures.

In addition to environmental carcinogens, cancer can be provoked by viruses, such as the human papillomavirus, which has received a lot of press because of efforts to have young people immunized against this virus. In the presence of a compromised immune system, as in the case of individuals with HIV/AIDS, vulnerability to Kaposi's sarcoma herpes virus is elevated. Other viruses, such as hepatitis B and C can promote liver cancer, but with treatments of hepatitis having become available, cancer prevention has been possible. As well, Epstein–Barr virus, a form of herpes virus that is found in most people (90–95% of the population), when present for extended times have been related to Burkitt's lymphoma, Hodgkin's lymphoma, post-transplant lymphoproliferative disease, nasopharyngeal carcinoma, and some forms of stomach cancer. Certain Epstein–Barr virus strains can produce mutations that could engender cancers, particularly among individuals with immune disturbances. As well, this virus can interact with genetic, environmental, and dietary influences, although these have not been identified (Bakkalci et al., 2020). While stressors can influence virally related processes, including the reactivation of Epstein–Barr virus, the evidence suggesting a role for stressors on these viral cancers hasn't been determined.

The immune system and cancer

One of the early views concerning the cancer process, the immunosurveillance hypothesis, held that lymphocytes served as sentinels responsible for recognizing and eliminating cancer cells (Burnett, 1970). This view was modestly altered later (Lussier & Schreiber, 2016), but the basic tenets were maintained. When cancer cells first appear, immune cells (e.g., cytotoxic T cells and NK cells) ought to sense their presence and destroy them (the *elimination phase*). The functioning of these immune cells is enhanced by tumor-disrupting chemical mediators and genetic processes that suppress tumor proliferation. During the subsequent *equilibrium phase*, additional immune cells are called upon to engage the cancerous cells. In some instances, they may be successful, whereas the two sides might battle to a stalemate. Thus, a tumor would not immediately develop (tumor dormancy), but may instead develop some time afterward, even decades later. During the final phase of this process, the *escape phase*, cancer cells can infiltrate the epithelium, which comprises the cellular layer lining the outer surface of blood vessels, organs, and varied body cavities. Thereafter, they can overrun the body's defenses and find novel ways of evading attacks by the immune system, ultimately expanding into an uncontrolled mass. Although cancer development typically occurs in older people, in the case of childhood brain cancers, the culprit cells might originally appear during the embryonic stage of development during which the immune system is still immature, and then appear as cancer early in life (Vladoiu et al., 2019).

In essence, tumor development may occur owing to immune cells not being able to dispatch cancerous cells, which can occur for a variety of reasons. Even if the immune system is operating the way it should be, wily cancer cells can find numerous ways of escaping detection and thus flourish. Being mutated forms of our own cells, surface markers (checkpoints) on cancer cells make them appear as if they belong to the self, basically expressing a 'don't eat me' signal, so that immune cells won't attack them. The cancer cells are also able to co-opt immune cells so that they actually favor tumor growth. As the tumor continues to grow it may also have multiple ways of obtaining the energy that cancer cells need to proliferate and grow. This includes a process in which cancer cells can attract their own blood supply (angiogenesis) and by diverting nutrients so that cancer cells have an advantage over healthy cells.

Almost a century ago, Otto Warburg had observed that cancer cells could obtain energy in a manner unlike that of other cells. The Warburg effect (Warburg, 1956) as it came to be known, was proposed as a way by which cancer cells could flourish and multiply prodigiously. Ordinarily, cells in the body obtain energy through a process, glycolysis, in which glucose is turned into pyruvate in the presence of oxygen. Cancer cells need considerable energy to maintain their rapid multiplication and, unlike other cells, they can do so even in the absence of oxygen (anaerobic metabolism). They are particularly fond of sugars (glucose), taking up large amounts of glucose that is converted to pyruvate, which then forms lactate that serves as a fuel to meet their energy needs (Boroughs & DeBerardinis, 2015). As it happens, lactate is converted into lactic acid, and the resulting pH reduction also favors tumor growth and invasion while concurrently limiting immune functioning that might otherwise attack cancer cells. For a while, the views offered by Warburg fell off the map but have since received increasing attention and have been used to develop cancer treatment strategies.

Repeated attempts have been made to starve cancer cells of energy sources, such as by depriving them of amino acids or by finding ways to limit angiogenesis so that blood vessels would not be available to nurture them. However, cancer cells have been ruthless in finding alternative ways of obtaining nourishment, even going so far as to cannibalize their neighbors, including cancer cells that aren't effectively doing their job. Indeed, in response to some efforts to destroy them, they appear to become more aggressive. Thus, strategies to eliminate cancer by depriving them of nutrients have largely proven to be ineffective. However, better outcomes could be obtained by combining these efforts with standard therapies as well as by immunotherapies.

Implications for cancer treatment

Cancer therapies have evolved considerably over the decades so that many types of cancer can now be treated more successfully than in the past, although admittedly several cancer types have not been treatable or the therapies added only a few months or years to survival. Cancer therapy (or management) includes better and more focused chemotherapy, radiation therapy, surgery, and a newer arsenal of treatments that comprise various forms of immunotherapy. Despite the promising advances in the treatment of cancers, the therapies are arduous, with numerous obstacles, stumbles, and backward steps sometimes being encountered. As well, the long-term ramifications of the treatments can be a heavy load to carry, and the resulting distress could potentially influence the course of the illness and can certainly influence individuals' quality of life.

Therapeutic approaches

As cancer types are genetically diverse, differentially sensitive to certain hormones as well as manipulations by growth factors and immune alterations, it is unlikely that any single treatment will emerge to treat all cancers. The effectiveness of individual therapies varies with the type of tumor being dealt with, its aggressiveness, stage, location, as well as the genetic and epigenetic characteristics of that cancer. To a considerable extent, therapeutic approaches to deal with cancer have relied on surgery to eliminate the main tumor mass, together with chemotherapy and radiation therapy. Chemotherapeutic agents damage the cancer cell DNA and inhibit enzymes needed to repair the damage. Radiation therapy, which is a component of treatment in approximately 50% of patients, similarly damages the DNA of cancer cells resulting in their demise. This procedure is generally adopted when the cancer is localized to a particular site, and the type of radiotherapy used varies with the nature and stage of the cancer, how close the tumor is to other sensitive tissues, and features of the patient (general health, age). Radiation treatments may be administered to shrink the size of a tumor, thereby making it more manageable by other types of treatment. Alternatively, it may be used after surgery or chemotherapy to reduce the odds of cancer recurrence. Increasingly sophisticated methods of radiotherapy have been developed so that tumor cells can be targeted with limited effects on nearby non-cancerous cells.

Chemotherapy may be the primary method of treating cancer or as in the case of radiation therapy, it may be used as a *neoadjuvant* therapy to diminish the size of tumors so that they are more amenable to being eliminated through surgery or radiation therapy. Chemotherapy is also used as an *adjuvant* therapy after surgery to eliminate cancer cells that might remain. While these treatments are often successful in increasing life span and health span, many cancers do not respond to these treatments, especially if the cancer was difficult to detect until it was advanced, as in the case of ovarian and brain cancers. Moreover, resistance to therapeutic agents may develop, which is among the greatest challenges to effective treatment. To be sure, novel techniques have been developed to detect cancers earlier, such as detecting cancer cells in the blood that had been shed by tumors. Until such screening procedures are found to be sufficiently sensitive and specific as well as widely used, better treatment methods will be necessary.

Several new approaches had been developed to treat cancers, including some that had been thought to be untreatable. Nanotechnologies were created in which minute drug doses can be delivered to target sites, thereby increasing attacks on specific cancer cells. This can diminish resistance developing to the treatments and, at the same time, the small doses are less likely to produce severe side effects. Other approaches entailed ways of strengthening the immune cells or eliminating the ability of cancer cells to avoid detection and attack by immune cells. These have included ways of targeting cancer cells using viruses that directly attack tumors or increase the presence of immune cells that can do so (oncolytic viral therapy). Nonspecific therapies have also been adopted in which cytokines (e.g., interferon-α) are used to eliminate certain forms of cancer. An approach that has received a great deal of attention to deal with several blood cancers comprised CAR T therapy. This entails immune cells being taken from patients (typically cytotoxic T cells, but the procedure can be used with NK cells and macrophages), modified to attack certain types of cancer cells based on an antigen present, grow them, and then readminister them to patients. The procedure may be successful in some patients, but it can lead to very serious side effects, including cytokine storm in which excessive cytokine levels lead to severe respiratory problems and death.[2] There are indications that variations of standard CAR T therapy with diminished toxic actions might be in the offing (e.g., Ying et al., 2019).

An immunotherapeutic approach to deal with solid tumors that proved to be effective involves the use of *checkpoint inhibitors* (Demaria et al., 2019). As already mentioned, checkpoint proteins (e.g., PD-1 or CTLA-4) are present on immune cells that act as an 'off-switch' when they bind to markers present on healthy cells, such as a programmed death-ligand 1 (PD-L1). Cancer cells, being derived from our cells, may also have the PD-L1 marker present, thereby avoiding attack by the immune system. Thus, antibodies were created that bind with PD-1 or PD-L1 (or both) or with CTLA-4, thereby eliminating this aspect of the cancer's defenses so that the immune system is able to attack them. These procedures have been remarkably effective in otherwise difficult to treat cancers, although success is only achieved in 20–30% of patients. By using several immunotherapeutic approaches concurrently or combining immunotherapies with other treatments, success was somewhat elevated.

Even under the best conditions, treating cancer cells may run into obstacles that limit their effectiveness. A major stumbling block has been the development of side effects, sometimes being sufficiently severe as to cause patient death, although this was less pronounced using checkpoint inhibitors. Some of the treatments can produce organ damage, such as cardiotoxicity (heart problems) that can affect subsequent well-being and quality of life. In fact, in response to some chemotherapies

---

[2]Cytokine storm can also be provoked by COVID-19, which led to death in many people who had been infected.

(e.g., among women treated with anthracyclines to treat breast cancer) cardiovascular disorders caused more fatalities than did the cancer itself, particularly among those women who had obesity or who were smokers. Likewise, in strengthening the immune response or by inhibiting checkpoints, autoimmune disorders could be engendered. A fine balance exists wherein therapies ought to enhance immune functioning or diminish the cancer's defensive mechanisms, yet not cause untoward outcomes.

Treatment resistance and metastasis

As mentioned earlier, among the greatest therapeutic challenges is that even when cancer treatments initially appeared to be effective, resistance to the treatment's effectiveness often develops. This might occur because individuals are inherently resistant to specific agents (*intrinsic resistance*) but typically develops with continued treatment (*acquired resistance*). Cancer cells are unstable in that gene mutations and epigenetic changes are common, increasing their growth. Moreover, the attacking immune system and the therapies themselves place selection pressures on tumor cells, thereby increasing the propensity for gene mutations to occur. With the changing features of the cancer, it may be more difficult for them to be recognized by the immune system and the effectiveness of treatments in destroying the cancer cells decline (e.g., Russo et al., 2019). Furthermore, with ongoing chemotherapy, drug inactivation may be provoked, and efflux of the drug is increased (i.e., it is more readily pumped out of the cell). While drug resistance has continued to be problematic, clever combinations of treatments, including the co-administration of agents to enhance DNA repair processes, have yielded positive early signs (Cipponi et al., 2020).

Cancer therapy through natural selection

The objective of cancer therapies has been to eliminate cancer cells - every last one - so that the disease doesn't return in a more aggressive form. In theory, this could be achieved with sufficiently high treatment doses, but the consequences to the patient, including side effects and damage to body organs can be extensive. Selecting the right dose for patients requires consideration of the patient's general health and age, the potency of the treatment, and the potential side effects of the chemotherapeutic agent. But, as good as a therapeutic agent may be in destroying cancer cells, the development of treatment resistance has been a prominent roadblock for effective cancer treatment. Even therapeutic agents that had been heralded as breakthroughs in the treatment of untreatable cancers turned out to be stymied by the development of treatment resistance.

Given the repeated failures that had been encountered in developing strategies to get around treatment resistance, new ways of thinking about cancer were adopted. This entailed considering tumors as being an ecological system in which the rules of

(Continued)

Darwinian evolution applied, including how adaptation evolved in response to chemo-therapeutic challenges (Gatenby & Brown, 2018). Specifically, with continued chemo-therapy an increasing number of mutations emerge so that cancer cells may become hardier, giving rise to stronger clones that are progressively more resistant to therapeu-tic agents. Accordingly, instead of attempting to eliminate cancer cells entirely using high-intensity, high-dose treatments, it was considered that it might be more profitable to employ less intense therapies that would not kill all cancer cells but would be less likely to produce treatment resistance. To this end, different therapies would be admin-istered sequentially, altering them before treatment resistance developed (Gatenby et al., 2019). While the cancer might not be fully eliminated, it could be controlled. In essence, the disease would persist and patients would have to learn to live with their illness – but they would survive.

This approach morphed somewhat since its initial inception and has been considered on the basis of 'game theory' that had been popular in both economics and psychology in predicting human behavior in competitive situations. From this vantage, an oncologist can behave rationally and flexibly in response to the behaviors of cancer cells so that they can be assaulted by therapeutic agents, and using sophisticated algorithms it may be possible to predict how cancer cells will respond as they meet new challenges. As duplicitous and ruthless as cancer cells are, they respond solely to the ongoing condi-tions and lack the capacity to see into the future. Thus, it becomes possible to stay steps ahead of the cancer cells so that therapies can be switched before the cancer cells are able to adapt.

Being antithetical to the position that it was necessary to fully eradicate cancer, this approach wasn't initially embraced fervently (in fact, the evolutionary perspective was initially advanced in 1991), but has been gaining increasing interest.

Unlike most cells in the body that seem content to stay where they are and do the work they were genetically engineered to do, these same characteristics do not apply to cancer cells that can metastasize to distant sites. Genetic differences may exist among individuals prior to cancer occurrence that may influence the proba-bility of metastasis occurring. More than this, the features of cancer cells vary over time (or with therapies) so that metastasized cells typically differ from the original cancer cells in numerous ways. Their genetic features could have changed, and multiple epigenetic alterations may have developed, making them more difficult to eliminate. Furthermore, the transitions across phases of cancer development (e.g., from tumor initiation, invasion, and eventual metastasis) might involve diverse processes that entail distinguishable gene regulatory networks and microenviron-ments (i.e., the environment around the tumor, comprising blood vessels, immune cells that may be present, and inflammatory factors). The mutated cells may leave their initial site, enter the blood system, and then lodge at distal sites. This jour-ney can be arduous for cancer cells, and not every environment that they reach is hospitable. Nonetheless, numerous factors can facilitate their ability to lodge and obtain a supply of nutrients (e.g., angiogenesis can be enhanced by specific growth factors). Because of the changes in metastasized tumors, therapies that might have been effective in treating the initial cancer will have lost their potency. Ultimately, identifying the multiple features of cancer cells will likely be needed, facilitated by artificial intelligence approaches (e.g., machine learning) to establish a precision medicine method to provide the best treatments for individual patients.

Influence of lifestyles

Cancers may be a preventable condition in more than 40% of cases, being influenced by lifestyles, such as diet, sedentary behaviors, sleep, and circadian factors. As well, lifestyles and various sociological factors may influence the efficacy of many treatment approaches as well as diminishing side effects that would otherwise develop (e.g., Deshpande, 2020).

Research related to the benefits attributable to specific foods and diets is fraught with inconsistencies and the legitimacy of many findings has been questioned (Ioannidis, 2013). This critique was entirely warranted; at the same time, it may be premature to dismiss all the available data, provided that the findings were based on rigorous experimentation and are replicable. In fact, in animal models diets high in fat and sugar were accompanied by greater gastrointestinal cancer progression. Conversely, anti-inflammatory diets (e.g., Mediterannean diets) were found to provide health benefits and could aid cancer treatments and limit treatment resistance. This was similarly reported for foods high in the polyphenol, quercetin, which is present in cruciferous vegetables and many fruits. Curcumin, an ingredient of turmeric, can inhibit glucose uptake, thereby acting against the growth of some forms of cancer. Fasting diets (intermittent fasting) or a ketogenic diet can also have positive effects (Turbitt et al., 2019), perhaps by depriving cancer cells of nutrients and by reducing inflammation. This said, such diets can sap the energy of patients who may already be weakened, especially if cachexia had developed (a wasting syndrome characterized by anorexia, weight loss, anemia, weakness, and lack of energy), as it does in about 50% of patients. It is also possible to starve cancer cells selectively by depriving them of amino acids, such as methionine, serine, asparagine, and histidine, which can enhance the effects of immunotherapy (Leone et al., 2019). Aside from these diet-related manipulations, the drug metformin that is primarily used in the treatment of diabetes owing to its ability to reduce sugar formed by the liver, can also be useful in depriving cancer cells of an energy source as well as by altering microbial processes (Verdura et al., 2019).

Appreciable data have amassed indicating that microbiota can provoke either beneficial or harmful effects on cancer occurrence in mice and that the diversity of gut bacteria enhanced the response to radiation and chemotherapy, as well as immunotherapy. These positive effects might be due to the actions of bacterial metabolites on oncogenic mechanisms, as well as by affecting the tumor microenvironment (Zitvogel et al., 2017). Specifically, SCFAs, such as butyrate, derived from microbiota can cause reprogramming of CD8 T cells so that the effects of cancer immunotherapies can be enhanced (Luu et al., 2021). A good number of studies have shown that the effectiveness of immunotherapies can be enhanced in the presence of specific microbiota and diets rich in fiber that facilitate the production of SCFAs by gut microbiota enhanced the ability to treat melanoma using immuno-therapy (Spencer et al., 2021). Microbiota can also affect monocytes/macrophages and NK cells that can recognize PAMPs and limit inflammatory changes elicited by the therapies administered (e.g., Negi et al., 2019). Demonstrations such as these have fostered increasing attention on the possibility of targeting specific microbes to enhance the actions of anti-cancer treatments.

Influence of stress on cancer progression

Stress stemming from cancer

Following the initial shock of a cancer diagnosis comes a series of tests, some of which may be invasive and dehumanizing. Therapies themselves reflect yet another series of stressors as these can include amputation or the removal of certain organs or parts of organs, as well as damage to other functions secondary to the surgical procedures. In the case of chemotherapy or radiation, patients often experience sickness, nausea, vomiting, chemo brain (cognitive disturbances associated with chemotherapy), extreme fatigue, and because of the multiple stressors, depression or PTSD may evolve.

Even if the therapy is effective doesn't mean that the stress has been fully alle-viated. After treatment, the patient may have to spend time in physical or occupa-tional rehabilitation, and this too can be demanding. And added to this, patients often require regular medical testing to see if the cancer has returned or whether other illnesses associated with the disease or its treatment need attention. Then there's the issue of survival beyond one year, beyond two years, and beyond five years, as well as the possibility that another form of cancer might show up (the risks of this are increased appreciably in cancer patients who carry a KRAS mutation). There are many anticipatory stressors that persist well after the initial treatment. Accordingly, being a 'cancer survivor' doesn't mean back to life as it was before. Cancer survivors may develop a better appreciation for the good aspects of life (finding meaning), but they may also be subject to enormous strain and uncer-tainty about the future.

—Case study 7.1—

Social support following cancer treatment

Patients undergoing cancer treatment need lots of social support, which frequently needs to go on for a considerable time aftre the treatment ends. Mary had been treated for breast cancer, seemingly successfully, but she was nevertheless dismayed. She said, 'To this point, I've been kept alive by the chemo. Now, I'm on my own. And I'm scared.' She said that she had received a lot of support from friends when she was first diagnosed and during treatment. Once her chemotherapy and radiation therapy were completed, her friends seemed to feel she was 'cured', and so they became relatively scarce. They did, after all, have their own problems and commitments and they could only spend so much time supporting Mary. Unfortunately, she also experienced unsupportive responses when she expressed her fears about the cancer coming back. These included comments such as, 'I'd think you'd be a little less neurotic about this' or 'Why don't you just thank God for getting this far, instead of always being such a downer'. She was thankful that she had made it as far as she had, but she was always on edge waiting for the other shoe to drop. She commented that, 'My friends were great, and I appreciate all they've done for me. But they've never been there, and they just don't get it.'

A stress-cancer link

Studies in animals

Let's have a look at the possibility that stressful events might influence the cancer process itself. Studies in animals indicated that stressors could influence the growth of induced, transplanted, and carcinogen-induced tumors. The cancers exacerbated by chronic stressors involved a wide variety of different organs, and metastatic spread was also observed (Zhang, Pan et al., 2020).

Aside from physical stressors, cancer progression was affected by psychosocial disturbances. Among communal animals, being housed in isolation increased the progression of mammary cancer (Budiu et al., 2017), especially if they were genetically disposed to developing tumors. These actions varied with the way mice dealt with stressors. Specifically, a social stressor and later re-exposure to this stressor shortly after tumor cell transplantation, resulted in pulmonary metastases being increased five-fold. However, this was most pronounced in mice that responded to the stressor with a passive coping style compared to those that engaged in active coping. Moreover, early-life social isolation was associated with increased growth of subsequent carcinogen-induced tumors. As epigenetic changes might readily be induced during the early postnatal period, challenges encountered at this time may have especially pronounced effects on later neuroendocrine functioning that influence carcinogen-induced tumor growth.

Many processes might have contributed to these outcomes, such as genomic instability, promotion of angiogenesis (growth of new blood vessels to feed tumor cells), enhanced immune evasion, elevated inflammation, metabolic changes, and actions on autophagy in which damaged cells are eliminated. Considerable evidence similarly pointed to the actions of stressors on immune functioning in promoting tumor growth, including changes in the phenotypic expression of NK cells, and by disturbing CD8+ T cell functioning, as well as the maturation of dendritic cells (Sommershof et al., 2017). Additionally, stressors can interfere with cancer cell apoptosis so that cancer cell survival is enhanced, and DNA repair can be disturbed, thereby allowing mutated cells to multiply.

Several hormones have been implicated in stressor-elicited cancer progression. By promoting the release of corticosterone, stressors could disturb immune functioning, thus resulting in less restrained tumor growth. The NE release and the consequent β-NE receptor signaling promoted by stressors can affect cancer cell migration and invasion. It also seems that increased tumor growth elicited by stressors could come about through angiogenesis, just as stress-related hormones have such effects (Kim-Fuchs et al., 2014). Aside from affecting tumor progression, social stressors can increase vulnerability to metastasis of colon carcinoma cells (Zhao et al., 2015), likely operating through hormones (e.g., cortisol) or by stimulation of norepinephrine receptors. Indeed, chronic stressors and the change of norepinephrine can affect the response to therapies that ordinarily diminish cancer growth. The hormonal changes induced by chronic stressful encounters can also promote cancer progression by affecting cancer cell proliferation, chromosomal instability, immune evasion, and by promoting metabolic disorders (Cui et al., 2021).

Retrospective studies in humans

In many respects, the data from studies in humans mapped on well to those witnessed in rodents. Retrospective studies in humans indicated that stressful life events were associated with increased cancer progression and greater cancer-related mortality, whereas this was not evident concerning cancer development (Tian et al., 2021). Childhood adversity was associated with increased adult cancer incidence accompanied by elevated levels of proinflammatory cytokines as well as poorer survival if cancer subsequently developed (Steel et al., 2020). Among individuals that experienced a major life stressor in the preceding year and who also reported poor early-life maternal or paternal care, immune responses were impaired, and the recurrence of a form of skin cancer was increased. Consistent with the long-term consequences of stressors, a nationwide study conducted in Israel had revealed that the incidence of colon cancer and lung cancer years later was elevated among survivors of the Holocaust, being particularly prominent among individuals who reported the most distressing experiences (Sadetzki et al., 2017). This relationship could have been linked to biological effects associated with the trauma experienced but could just as readily have been secondary to events that followed the trauma, including the adoption of counterproductive lifestyles (e.g., increased smoking), and the development of depressive states.

The links between stressful experiences and cancer progression were associated with diminished NK cell activity and immune-related epigenetic changes within peripheral blood mononuclear cells. Conversely, effective coping abilities, benefit finding, social support, and optimism were related to enhanced NK cell activity and lymphocyte proliferative responses among individuals being treated for diverse malignancies. In line with such reports, high levels of psychological stress among breast cancer patients were accompanied by impaired NK cell function-ing relative to that seen in patients with lower stress levels. For instance, among women monitored for 18 months following surgery, those who indicated greater levels of distress exhibited diminished NK cell activity and reduced lymphocyte proliferative responses (Andersen et al., 2017). Conversely, providing cancer patients with stress-management tools enhanced postoperative mood together with augmented immune functioning. Predictably, the most rapid decline of distress following surgery was accompanied by comparable recovery of NK cell activity.

In addition to affecting the progression of cancer, the possibility was considered that recurrence of cancer was associated with stressor experiences or the ability to cope effectively. Studies that evaluated the link between major life events and can-cer recurrence failed to show consistent effects. But assessments of the influence of major life stressors on cancer recurrence have often ignored one of the most potent stressors experienced by patients who had previously been treated, notably the persistent distress and anxiety experienced related to concerns of 'it coming back again'. Consistent with this, breast cancer recurrence as well as cancer-specific and all-cause mortality, were more prominent among individuals experiencing high levels of anxiety and depression (Wang et al., 2020). Thus, the frequent post-treatment distress expressed among some cancer survivors has fostered repeated calls for psychosocial and psychotherapeutic interventions, which frequently were accompanied by longer survival.

The studies in humans that assessed the stress–cancer relationship have largely been correlational, often relying on retrospective analyses that attempted to tie a current cancer state to past stressful events. Aside from the usual shortcomings of retrospective studies described earlier, with a few exceptions these studies focused on stressors (or life changes) encountered during the preceding 6–24 months. Moreover, the effects of earlier stressor encounters, including those experienced in childhood, were often not considered even though these expe-riences could profoundly influence neurobiological processes throughout life. Many retrospective studies also failed to consider both the cumulative effects of chronic stressors as well as the dynamics related to cancer development. One of the few studies that considered this indicated that work-related stress over 15–30 years was accompanied by elevated cancer occurrence (Blanc-Lapierre et al., 2017).

The deficiencies of retrospective studies are even more problematic given that the cancer process is typically lengthy, such that malignant cells can remain in a stalemate with protective immune processes for many years before entering the escape phase and rapid cancer cell multiplication. Thus, searching for links between cancer occurrence and recent (6–24 months) stressors may simply be looking at the wrong time. It may be more germane to evaluate whether stressors influenced cancer multiplication during the elimination or equilibrium phase of the immune surveillance phase.

───**Oh, why me?**───────────────────────────

When women with breast cancer were questioned regarding factors that might have been responsible for their illness, 58% attributed it to stress, whereas the next two leading attributions concerned previous hormone therapy (17%) and genetic factors (10%). Patients believed that stress was an important etiological factor for their illness, but this doesn't necessarily make it so. Often, when distressed or ill, individuals feel the need to know why this happened to them. Were they responsible for their destiny, or did someone or something cause it? Sometimes there simply isn't an answer; it might just be a matter of bad luck, or it might be because of environmental agents to which they had unwittingly been exposed.

Sometimes people afflicted with severe illnesses make the statement 'Why me?', and the answer, while not pleasant or comforting, simply amounts to 'Why not you?' As we saw earlier, people often have beliefs that don't align well with reality; one was that of a 'just world', in which individuals believe that the world is fundamentally just and thus when things go wrong there must be a reason for it. As individuals believe that they are basically good, then their misfortune needs to be due to external forces, possibly stressful experiences. The sad fact, however, is that sometimes 'bad things happen to good people' (Kushner, 1981).

───

Prospective studies in humans

Few studies prospectively assessed the stress–cancer relationship and those conducted yielded inconsistent findings. An analysis based on the pooled data of 16 prospective cohort studies indicated that distressed individuals free of cancer at the start of the investigations subsequently exhibited increased mortality related to a variety of cancers among those individuals that had been most distressed (Batty et al., 2017). Likewise, in the Nurses' Health Study, which included a 26-year follow-up, the presence of PTSD symptoms associated with multiple stressor experiences predicted the doubling of ovarian cancer almost a decade later (Roberts et al., 2019).

A detailed review that included 38 prospective studies suggested that no single stressor or psychosocial factor was convincingly tied to cancer occurrence, although it appeared that the lack of social support and having a personality that favored feelings of 'helplessness' was accompanied by moderately greater cancer progression (Garssen, 2004). Social connectedness may likewise have positive effects in limiting cancer progression, but these benefits were restricted to an early cancer stage and only for some cancer types and were most prominent in younger patients (Pinquart & Duberstein, 2010).

A similarly inconclusive analysis of the stress–cancer relationship was gleaned from a systematic analysis that included both retrospective and prospective analyses. This review identified 26 independent studies in which personality traits and stressful events were linked to breast cancer; however, contrary findings were reported in 18 studies, and eight were inconclusive (Chiriac et al., 2018). The complexity concerning the link between stressful experiences also came from a report showing that among individuals who experienced chronic high stressor levels cancer occurrence was elevated by 11%, but this relationship was most prominent if other poor health behaviors had been adopted. As such, cancer development or progression might not be directly related to stressor experiences, instead coming about owing to the influence of factors secondary to the stressor.

Taken together, the evidence related to the influence of stressors on cancer has been inconsistent and somewhat confusing. This is not overly surprising given that different stress measures were used across studies, and differences were common with respect to the chronicity of stressors and their timing. As well, in some cases limited attention was devoted to analyses in different types of cancer. Finally, the interactive effects of other risk factors that could have affected cancer often received insufficient attention.

To overcome some of these shortcomings, another approach was used to assess the stress–cancer relationship. This entailed the assessment of patients' stressor history when a tumor was first suspected and a biopsy performed, but before the biopsy results had been received. If distress was a factor in the cancer process, then it would be expected that greater stressor reports would be apparent in those individuals later found with malignant tumors than in those with benign tumors. In contrast, if reported stressor experiences stemmed from biased appraisals, then elevated negative life events would be evident in both the malignant and benign groups relative to that apparent in control individuals. It turned out that women diagnosed with malignant cancer had experienced greater life stressors than did healthy controls or women that were found to have a benign condition. As well, among women with suspected ovarian cancer, nocturnal cortisol levels were higher among those who had malignant tumors than among those with benign tumors. Furthermore, patients awaiting assessment for ovarian cancer reported elevated vegetative and affective depressive symptoms and exhibited greater plasma IL-6 and cortisol relative to women with tumors that were of low malignant potential (Lutgendorf et al., 2008).

Findings such as these lend credence to the view that distress, aspects of depression, and cancer might be linked, and that neuroendocrine factors and cytokines mediate these relationships. However, one shouldn't be misled that the case supporting a link between stress and cancer progression is a done deal. Cancer is a complex molecular biological disease, and it would be overly simplistic to attempt to boil it down to the simple notion that stressful events are the primary contributors to disease progression. If anything, stressors might be one of a constellation of factors that come together to influence the course of the disease.

Stress and metastasis

Can stressors influence metastasis, and if so how would this come about? One way we could think of answering this question is to examine the characteristics of the tumor cells that have metastasized or are attempting to do so. Have they become stronger? Do they have some sort of protective coating or cloak that protects them from destruction by immune cells or by specialized proteins (e.g., metastasis suppressors) that are on the lookout for cancer cells? Or is it that stressors result in the general environment being more hospitable so that tumor cells can thrive more readily? It is also conceivable that chronic stressors cause epithelial cells to gain the ability to migrate and gain invasive characteristics. Cancer metastasis, as described earlier, is accompanied by the growth of a new network of blood vessels (angiogenesis) that feed the tumor cells, and stress hormones could contribute to this process as might changes of growth factors, such as VEGF, that are elevated in depressive illnesses. Related to this, stressful events might favor the survival and growth of cancer cells that have migrated through their action on sympathetic nervous system activity. Specifically, sympathetic activation and the release of norepinephrine might result in an environment conducive for cancer cells to flourish. It has indeed been shown that blocking β-adrenergic receptors using propranolol diminished cancer progression and metastasis in mice. It's premature to say whether these data will be relevant to metastasis in humans, but the possibility that anti-stress treatments could have positive effects on cancer processes is an exciting proposition (Antoni & Dhabhar, 2019).

Psycho-oncology

At one time, the notion that stressful events might influence the cancer process was viewed as wacky stuff. Today, it is not unusual to find health-care workers accepting the notion that stressful events, lifestyle, and patient comfort could influence cancer progression and the efficacy of treatments. As well, even if these variables didn't affect cancer progression, considering them as part of the treatment regimen may have positive effects on the patient's psychological well-being.

Some clinicians and researchers might see the link between psychosocial factors and cancer as an interesting phenomenon to which they give lip service, but they might not believe that it is as important as patient advocates would have us believe. This is not to say that oncologists are not concerned with patients' psychological well-being, but they might think that they should focus on what they do best, namely treating the cancer, whereas other aspects of the patient's well-being should be someone else's job. Framed that way, maybe they're right, particularly as they may be ill-equipped to deal with psychological interventions. Thus, cancer patients might be best treated by medical teams rather than any single individual. Yet patients typically pin their greatest hope for a positive treatment outcome on the oncologist, and thus this person may have the greatest sway on a patient's psychological state.

Stress and its implications for cancer treatment

As often happens with severe adverse events, such as cancer, some individuals find especially effective methods of coping and may even be able to find something positive in bad experiences (finding meaning). This may amount to appreciating life more, and for others it may involve devoting themselves to a cause to improve the lives of others. This 'benefit finding' or 'posttraumatic growth' has repeatedly been associated with reduced stress and reduced psychological disturbances. But as indicated earlier, only some patients are able to find meaning from adverse events, and one can't push people in this regard. Nonetheless, teaching individuals about their disease and facilitating meaning-making, especially if this is incorporated with other approaches to diminish cancer-related distress (such as CBT or mindfulness), might prove useful.

While amid the distress associated with cancer and its treatment, it may be difficult to find meaning from the experience and may primarily appear afterward. Accordingly, psychotherapeutic approaches have been used to attenuate patient distress during treatment. Indeed, psychological interventions may not only affect subjective indices of the disease (fatigue, sleep loss), but might also affect neuroendocrine functioning, lymphocyte proliferation, and proinflammatory cytokine production that ordinarily favor cancer progression.

Several stress-management procedures have been used to diminish distress associated with cancer. Traditional stress-reducing therapies, such as cognitive behavioral therapy (CBT) alone or in combination with pharmacological interventions could reduce cancer-related anxiety and depression as well as the fear of cancer recurrence. Aside from diminishing anxiety and depression, in some patients, CBT attenuated cognitive dysfunctions associated with cancer, notably memory and attention disturbances, as well as concentration difficulties. Paralleling the antidepressant effects that have been observed, CBT could diminish fatigue and sleep disturbances that are often related to cancer (Johnson et al., 2016). Moreover, as psychological factors (e.g., catastrophizing) have been associated with cancer-related pain, efforts were made to diminish psychological distress to reduce pain stemming from cancer.

Mindfulness interventions could similarly diminish distress in cancer patients, although these positive effects may be modest and wane over time. An overview of 30 studies indicated that the outcomes observed were highly variable (Shaw et al., 2018), and produced only small benefits among breast cancer patients (Schell et al., 2019). Ordinarily, in the absence of cancer, CBT and mindfulness are only effective in a subset of patients, thus it is not surprising that limited and inconsistent effects would be apparent in cancer patients.

A systematic review and meta-analysis confirmed that diverse psychotherapies, including CBT, mindfulness, acceptance-based interventions, and relaxation training could modestly reduce cancer pain although the outcomes were variable across patients (Warth et al., 2020). Typically, for most diseases, no treatment is effective in all patients, and cancer-related depression, anxiety, and pain are no exception. It may be productive to tailor procedures to individual patients, and optimal actions might be obtained through multimodal strategies (several approaches combined systematically) that have been effective in alleviating distress in other situations. This might comprise commonly used treatments together with moderate excercise, yoga, and music therapy. Each of these could have limited effects on its own but could have more pronounced actions when applied together in a therapeutic program.

Beyond the benefits of CBT to diminish distress, this procedure was associated with lower breast cancer and all-cause mortality (Stagl et al., 2015). Other stress-reduction treatments (e.g., supportive group therapy) similarly enhanced survival time among women with metastatic and gastrointestinal cancer, and a combination of psychotherapy and drug treatments enhanced NK cell functioning. While these interventions enhanced survival assessed one year later, this outcome was largely absent at lengthier times (Fu et al., 2016).

Not unexpectedly, while some reports pointed to psychological therapies affecting the course of cancer progression, many reports indicated that psychological intervention did not have such effects on the course of the illness. It would have been nice to see consistent results in such studies, but frankly it is not surprising that this wasn't the case, particularly given the variable effects produced by these interventions in diminishing distress, anxiety, and depression. Besides, as much as stressful events could exacerbate tumor growth, this by no means implies that stress reduction would diminish cancer growth. Once present, cancer cells engage multiple processes to ensure their survival and psychological interventions might simply lack the power to overcome these. Nevertheless, as indicated repeatedly, even if the de-stressing treatment doesn't impact tumor progression, if it helps the individual cope with day-to-day burdens and instigates benefit finding, then this treatment ought to be viewed as being highly beneficial.

Conclusion

The immune system plays a fundamental role in protecting us from foreign pathogens, and in the main it does a fairly good job. However, as effective as immune functioning is in protecting us from several diseases, it obviously has limitations in dealing with novel viral and bacterial threats. Moreover, there are occasions wherein the immune system turns on the self, producing autoimmune disorders.

Immune functioning does not operate independently of other systems, reciprocally interacting with peripheral and central nervous system functions. Thus, stressful events that affect hormones, growth factors, and neurotransmitter functioning also affect immune activity. Activation of inflammatory factors can have profound repercussions on CNS and behavioral processes as well as on the progression of diseases, such as cancer. The questions that need to be answered concern which factors moderate these relationships. What makes individuals more or less vulnerable to stress-related biological disturbances, or conversely which factors create resilience, and given this knowledge what can we do to mitigate these stressor effects?

Suggested readings

Anisman, H., Hayley, S., & Kusnecov, A. (2018). *The Immune System and Mental Health*. London: Academic Press.

Cohen, S., Gianaros, P.J., & Manuck, S.B. (2016). A stage model of stress and disease. *Perspectives in Psychological Science, 11*, 456–463.

Zitvogel, L., Daillère, R., Roberti, M.P., Routy, B., & Kroemer, G. (2017). Anticancer effects of the microbiome and its products. *Nature Review in Microbiology, 15*, 465–478.

8

CARDIOVASCULAR DISEASE

The heart: you gotta ♡ it

Most people don't think much about their heart or heart problems, and certainly not when they're fairly young, but as we age its functioning (or, more appropriately, its malfunctioning) comes to mind more often. It's an amazing little organ made up of 'involuntary' muscle and connective tissue, regulated by various hormones and receptors. The heart is not all that large, about the size of a fist, typically weighing 250–300 gm in females and 300–350 gm in males, but it's got a big job.

The human heartbeat can be detected at about five weeks after conception. The embryonic heart beats at a very rapid rate, reaching 165–185 beats per minute (BPM) at about seven weeks of gestation, and then begins to slow down, eventually reaching about 70 BPM after birth. Ordinarily, this heart rate ought to be sustained for our entire lives. Think about it. That's about 2.94 billion beats over an 80-year life span. With all the technology available, no car motor or virtually any other type of machine could last that long without breaking down, even with maintenance every 20,000 km.

The human heart has one main function, and that's to pump blood, which occurs with every beat. To do this, those billions of cells that make up the heart must be coordinated. You can't very well have one cell doing one thing, and another cell doing something else. Think of what would happen if some cells decided to pump, while others decided to rest. It turns out that there's a natural pacemaker present in the human heart (the sinoatrial node) that sets the rate and timing for all the cardiac muscle cells to contract. What a cooperative organ the heart is.

It's smart too, or at least it seems to know what it's doing. The right atrium of the heart in mammals collects de-oxygenated blood from the body (via the superior and inferior vena cavae), pumps it into the right ventricle and then to the lungs, where carbon dioxide is removed and oxygen obtained. The left atrium then receives the oxygenated blood from the lungs, pumps it into the left ventricle, which then drives it to the body through the aorta, so that nice clean, oxygenated blood serves all those other organs that depend on it.

So, take care of your heart, and it'll take care of you.

Learning objectives

As good as the heart might be, there are limits to its durability and eventually problems can arise. Illnesses that involve the heart, arteries, or veins, referred to as 'cardiovascular' or 'circulatory' diseases, represent the greatest causes of death worldwide, typically being 20–30% in most Western countries. There are several types of heart disease and a great number of factors that might contribute to some of them. In this chapter we obviously can't deal with all of these, and so we'll focus on only a few issues that might be especially pertinent to stress processes. The messages that you should come away with from this chapter concern:

- how coronary heart disease comes about;
- how psychosocial factors and stressful events might come to influence coronary heart disease;
- the common finding that depression is a comorbid feature of heart disease, which has significant implications concerning its cause and treatment;
- the possibility that personality factors might contribute to heart disease;
- several stressor-induced biological changes contribute to heart disease, and of these inflammatory processes might be particularly relevant.

Diseases of the heart

Chronic illnesses are powerful stressors that diminish quality of life, promote the appearance of other illnesses, and lead to earlier death. An editorial in *The Lancet* published in 2009 indicated that 133 million people within the US experienced a chronic illness, and it was predicted that by 2020 the prevalence of chronic illnesses would reach 157 million, including many individuals who would be plagued by multiple chronic conditions. These predictions were vast underestimates. According to the CDC, in 2019 almost 60% of the US population suffered a chronic disease (e.g., coronary heart disease, pulmonary disease, type 2 diabetes, cancer, Alzheimer's disease, chronic kidney disease, autoimmune disorders) and nearly 40% of these people had more than one chronic condition. With an aging population, chronic illnesses will need to receive more attention, and greater efforts will be required to curb the lifestyles that favor their development.

In general, cardiac illnesses are the leading cause of death worldwide, and while the incidence of cardiac disturbances has been declining in Western countries over the past few decades, they have continued to rise in developing nations. Cardiovascular diseases come in several forms as described in Table 8.1. In this chapter we will primarily be concerned with hypertension, coronary artery disease (CAD), and heart failure. We will also consider some of the psychosocial and biological factors that are associated with these illnesses and their comorbid conditions.

Table 8.1   Types of heart disease.

- **Coronary artery disease** (CAD) encompasses illnesses that involve diminished blood flow to the heart so that ischemia (lack of oxygen) occurs
- **Hypertensive heart disease** comprises cardiac illness that arises due to elevated blood pressure
- **Heart failure or congestive heart failure** refers to instances in which the heart is unable to pump enough blood to meet the needs of the body and organs
- **Cardiomyopathy** comprise diseases of the cardiac muscle that makes it more difficult to pump blood to the rest of the body
- **Cardiac arrhythmia** entails abnormal electrical activity of the heart so that it beats irregularly; too slowly (*bradycardia*) or too quickly (*tachycardia*)
- **Inflammatory heart disease** includes endocarditis (inflammation of the inner layer of the heart), myocarditis (inflammation of the muscle portion of the heart), and inflammatory cardiomegaly associated with enlargement of the heart

The heart's typical response to a stressor

In times of distress, one of the first biological responses elicited is that of the autonomic nervous system being activated. This initially involves the sympathetic nerve fibers stimulating the heart, which entails the release of epinephrine (adrenaline) that promotes increased heart rate (from 60–80 beats per minute to 100–140, depending on fitness). Once the stress has passed, the heart begins to slow down through the help of the parasympathetic nervous system's inhibitory influence that involves the release of the transmitter, acetylcholine. There are occasions following a stressor in which the parasympathetic response may predominate, leading to a lowered heart rate that in some instances can be fairly dangerous owing to insufficient blood flow. Sufficiently reduced heart rate may result in fainting, feeling dizzy, light-headed, nauseous, sweating, weakness, or heart palpitations. Many of us might have experienced these symptoms after a sudden stressful experience, such as a near-miss in a car, or receiving some very bad news.

Hypertension

Heart rate and blood pressure are controlled by a set of hormones, including epinephrine, norepinephrine, acetylcholine as well as hormones, such as atrial-natriuretic peptide and brain natriuretic peptide that affect vasodilation and sodium expulsion. As heart rate goes up, more pressure is required so that the blood is pushed with sufficient strength or pressure. Thus, in association with distress, increased blood pressure accompanies the elevated heart rate. When a block exists somewhere in the arterial circulatory system, such as a narrowing of the arteries due to plaque formation, the pressure will also rise (as occurs when you place your thumb at the end of a hose to get more distance when watering the garden). Therefore, elevated resting blood pressure is a sign of something being amiss, and these signs are more pronounced under conditions (e.g., distress) that increase heart rate. Blood pressure is usually expressed as systolic blood pressure and diastolic blood pressure. Systolic pressure refers to the peak pressure in the arteries when the ventricles are contracting, pushing blood to the rest of the body, whereas diastolic pressure reflects the minimum pressure present once the ventricles are filled with blood, just before the pressure of the heart is applied. It is currently recommended that systolic pressure should be about or below 120 and diastolic pressure below 80. Should blood pressure reach 140–159 over 90–99 (the upper number reflects systolic pressure, and the lower diastolic pressure), individuals are said to have Stage 1 hypertension, and when it exceeds 160 over 100, Stage 2 hypertension is diagnosed. If it is any higher, then a hypertensive crisis exists.

When the development of hypertension occurs owing to medical conditions, such as kidney or thyroid disease, it is referred to as secondary hypertension. When the cause of the condition is unknown, it is referred to as essential hypertension. These cases are usually attributed to genetic influences and poor lifestyle choices, including short sleep duration as well as obesity. There is ample evidence indicating that diverse stressors (e.g., at the workplace), especially when coupled with a lack of social support, give rise to hormonal and inflammatory changes that influence the development of essential hypertension, and will be more likely to occur among individuals who had maintained sedentary behaviors for extended times (Ushakov et al., 2016).

Individual characteristics, such as anger and hostility, were likewise related to hypertension. Moreover, marked ethnic differences exist in the occurrence of hypertension, being especially high in African Americans, possibly owing to genetic factors, diet, and persistent racism (Hill & Thayer, 2019). Social stigmatization is an exceptionally powerful stressor, and its negative effects on heart health have not only been reported in relation to ethnicity but also to stigma related to body weight/obesity and sexual orientation (Panza et al., 2019).

There is little question that diet influences the development of hypertension, being particularly notable when the foods consumed contribute to inflammation, whereas diets that limit inflammation (e.g., Mediterannean or ketogenic diets) have the opposite effect. The DASH diet (Dietary Approaches to Stop Hypertension) has been especially effective in limiting hypertension (Sukhato et al., 2020). This diet comprises foods rich in potassium, magnesium, fiber, and protein, low in sodium and saturated fats. It entails the consumption of lots of vegetables, fruits, whole grains, beans, and nuts, fat-free or low levels of dairy products, poultry, fish, and very limited amounts of saturated fats (e.g., fatty meats). The actions of diet on heart health may come about through multiple processes that increase inflammation and the development of cholesterol that can influence plaque formation, and microbiota alterations have been implicated in the development of hypertension (Katsi et al., 2019). Given the pronounced effects of stressors and lifestyles on microbiota, it is reasonable to hypothesize that the link between these life experiences and hypertension is mediated by microbial changes. Moreover, drugs to treat heart problems have been related to the development of a healthier microbiome, varying with the specific drug combinations that had been used (Forslund et al., 2021).

Hypertension is more likely to develop as we age, but it is concerning that it has become more common in young people, including children. The sources for this likely include poor diet, especially foods containing high levels of fat and sodium coupled with low levels of potassium, abetted by the increased presence of obesity and type 2 diabetes that had previously been uncommon in children. The incidence of elevated blood pressure in youth has likewise been attributed to increased adoption of sedentary behaviors that come with greater screen time. Particular attention has focused on the contribution of sugar sweetened drinks and ultra-processed foods, lack of nutrients that can have anti-inflammatory actions (Mediterannean diet and high-fiber foods), and those that contain trans fat (P. Song et al., 2019).

Factors associated with coronary artery disease

Coronary artery disease (CAD) evolves because of a buildup of plaque within the coronary arteries. The plaque comprises fat, calcium, cholesterol, waste products that come from cells, as well as fibrin that ordinarily acts as a clotting factor. The plaque that builds on the endothelium (the cell layer inside veins that comes into direct contact with blood) is typically covered by a thin fibrous layer made up of collagen and smooth muscle cells. The accumulation of plaque over time might eventually restrict the flow of oxygen-rich blood to the heart muscle (i.e., atherosclerosis), which culminates in CAD. With the first signs of endothelial damage, macrophages and T cells are recruited to this site. These immune cells release cytokines that promote inflammation and the formation of plaque, as well as further lesions to the inner layers of the vascular cell wall. At this stage, damage to the vessel wall is still primarily at the level of the innermost layer of arteries and veins (referred to as 'intima'), but the accumulation of potentially hazardous factors continues so that plaque formation is increased (Gimbrone et al., 2016).

Coronary artery disease is most often diagnosed in men in their fifties and in women who are somewhat older, most often in their sixties. Plaque buildup begins years earlier, but for most people CAD is asymptomatic until things get very bad, and they run into a life-threatening coronary event or syndrome. It seems that symptoms of CAD don't show up until the blood flow is highly constricted, typically when it is reduced by more than 75%. Ordinarily, acute ischemic episodes come about when the supply of blood to the heart doesn't keep pace with the demands placed on it (e.g., in response to physical exertion that increases the heart rate and blood pressure), leading to the pain of angina pectoris (chest pain). The term 'stable angina' refers to a condition in which myocardial ischemia is transient and resolves upon the discontinuation of behaviors that place a load on the heart (e.g., exercise).

As heart disease progresses, ischemia may become more persistent and last longer (more than ten minutes) and can cause unstable angina (i.e., angina is present with minimal energy output or even when individuals are at rest), MI, arrhythmias, and sudden cardiac death. Other symptoms may signal that something is amiss (e.g., shortness of breath, fatigue related to exertion, or pain in places other than the chest), which need to be considered seriously, especially in high-risk groups (e.g., in those with a family history of the illness). Coping strategies that comprise avoidance or denial are not feasible options, although it isn't unusual for these to be adopted. A stressor or heavy exercise, which increase blood flow (referred to as 'hemodynamic stress') can result in a piece of plaque breaking off and an embolus (blood clot) may occur that could lead to MI, or the clot can lodge in the brain, causing ischemic stroke. When an MI occurs, the ability of the heart to pump blood is impaired, which culminates in damage to the heart muscle.

The widow maker

The name itself tells you a lot. If the left main coronary artery or proximal left anterior descending coronary artery of the heart is abruptly and completely blocked (occluded), then a massive heart attack occurs that results in 'sudden death'. For instance, when a cholesterol plaque ruptures, for whatever reason, platelets flow to the site of the rupture, forming a blockage, and hence a myocardial infarction (MI; a heart attack) ensues.

Once a widow maker occurs, a person might last for only a few minutes, but it can extend to a couple of hours. Certain symptoms may precede the full attack, although they progress rapidly, and sometimes there may be little warning at all. These signs include shortness of breath, nausea, pain in the head, jaw, arms, or chest, or numbness in the fingers. It's not uncommon for these early signs to be mistaken for flu, indigestion, or food poisoning, and individuals might prefer to believe that 'it's nothing', but the symptoms may intensify rapidly.

We might prefer to believe that a person experienced 'sudden death', and we have all sorts of expressions, such as 's/he was dead before s/he hit the ground', so that we believe that the person was unaware of their imminent death. In fact, when a widow maker hits, a person can stay alive for several minutes. There is, after all, some oxygen stored in the blood that keeps organs functioning. Thus, with very fast action it is possible to have individuals survive but having the right equipment (e.g., automated external defibrillator) and a trained individual available to act often isn't an option.

Many risk factors of heart disease are well known, such as high blood pressure, large waist circumference or waist–hip ratio, high levels of low-density lipoprotein (LDL) cholesterol and low levels of high-density lipoprotein (HDL) cholesterol. The importance of elevated LDL cholesterol in promoting heart disease has largely been accepted, reinforced by the repeated reports that statins that reduce LDL by inhibiting a liver enzyme that produces cholesterol diminished heart disease and the occurrence of a heart attack. Curiously, some types of cholesterol-lowering drugs did not induce these positive effects, raising the possibility that the benefits of statins may come about owing to factors other than those comprising diminished cholesterol levels. Be this as it may, even if statins have beneficial effects, it may be productive to look to the multiple factors that influence heart disease and to take steps that limit their development (Healey, 2021).

Some of these reflect poor lifestyle choices that are modifiable, whereas other premorbid factors, such as certain stressor experiences and coming from a lower socioeconomic class, might not be of the individual's own making. A large prospective cohort study conducted over an 11-year period across 21 countries revealed that cardiovascular disease varied with economic levels, education attained, household air pollution, presence of depression, hypertension, and several metabolic disorders, such as diabetes. Significantly, many of the between-country differences were related to several modifiable risk factors associated with diet quality, physical activity, and smoking (Yusuf et al., 2020). Beyond these contributors, social stressors and responses to them have been implicated in the development of CAD. Specifically, the social environment, including social isolation, loneliness, low social support, early-life negative experiences, and stress-related emotional responses, such as anxiety, anger, and hostility, has been implicated in the development and progression of hypertension and CAD. As expected, the risk cumulatively increases with the presence of multiple risk factors (Bu et al., 2020).

Stressful experiences influence heart disease

In evaluating the processes responsible for the development of chronic illnesses, such as heart disease, it is important to consider that these conditions frequently take many years to reach the point of being serious threats to life. Thus, many young people and those at early middle age frequently pay scant attention to the risky behaviors in which they engage. Yet, the impact of diverse factors that contribute to disease is cumulative and stressful experiences may be a key ingredient for poor future well-being.

Prospective studies indicated that the risk for new diagnoses of CAD and CAD-related mortality was increased by more than 25% among individuals who reported high levels of distress. The influence of chronic stressful events is related to several biological processes, such as disturbed autonomic and hormonal homeostasis, metabolic abnormalities, and elevated inflammation. Aversive events that are chronic (e.g., emotional disturbances and depression), even if they resolve after a few months or years, can render individuals more likely to develop CAD at a later time. Several psychosocial stressors (e.g., job strain, marital discord, caregiving) have been linked to cardiovascular problems. As well, stressors could indirectly contribute to risk of heart disease by affecting the lifestyles that individuals endorse, such as smoking, alcohol consumption, reduced sleep, and non-compliance with medications and other self-destructive behaviors.

The nature of the stressors that promote CAD can vary appreciably as can events that promote MI. A study that comprised over 24,000 patients and age- and sex-matched controls across several continents (the INTERHEART study), indicated that the risk of MI was associated with elevated levels of perceived stress, depression, and lower levels of internal locus of control, work and home distress, and a constellation of lifestyle factors (Teo et al., 2021). Among individuals already at risk, acute emotional events or emotional upset can serve as a trigger to elicit MI. The occurrence of MI produced by mental stress or physical challenges is not uncommon, estimated to be linked to about 20% of occurrences and did not occur exclusively in those with known underlying heart problems. One of the important factors found to elicit such events was the expression of anger, which likely encourages autonomic changes that comprise an imbalance between blood flow to the heart relative to that needed by other organs to maintain proper functioning.

The risk for heart disease and MI increases with chronic stressful experiences, but intense acute stressors may also have such effects. In some instances, especially among older people, the loss of a close significant other can promote death. In the first month of bereavement, for example, the incidence of mortality associated with cardiac events increased two- and three-fold in men and women, respectively. Even among young or early middle-aged people, loss can have disastrous effects, particularly if this entails the loss of a child. The occurrence of MI is most prominent during the days following the loss, but increased MI risk may go on for years afterward. These effects were evident in parents whose children had been ill for some time as well as when the loss was sudden and unexpected. Thus, in some instances the occurrence of MI might not have stemmed from cumulative distress, instead occurring with intense challenges, although this does not rule out a role for premorbid conditions contributing to the severe outcomes that emerged (Wei et al., 2021).

Because of sensitized biological systems, an emotionally significant event can instigate the neurobiological changes that increase blood pressure, thereby facilitating a clot being thrown from a plaque. Establishing this relationship may be complicated given the identification of specific triggering factors that might contribute to MI is difficult due to the problems inherent in attempting to follow individuals for extended periods. As a result, most studies that assessed stress–MI relations comprised retrospective analyses, and when asked about potential triggering events, as discussed earlier, individuals might try to make sense of their situation and thus make unwarranted appraisals of events (or an emotional state) that preceded their MI. This said, when patients reported on potential triggers that occurred in the period that immediately preceded the MI versus a period of comparable duration that had been encountered somewhat earlier, anger was associated with increased

MI occurrence, as was 'emotional upset'. The chance of MI occurring in association with these triggers was elevated still further if individuals had encountered major life changes in the preceding four-week period. Hence, the effect of acute events can be influenced by the psychological backdrop against which these occur.

Given the ties between stressful experiences and poor mood and increased risk of heart disease, it has been considered that positive events and mood might be accompanied by improved heart functioning. High life satisfaction was linked to a modest decline in the risk of CAD even after controlling for other risks related to heart disease (Boehm et al., 2016). Moreover, optimistic individuals tended to have relatively healthy hearts, and individuals high in dispositional mindfulness and hence less likely to be distressed by daily setbacks, were less likely to experience heart disease (Loucks et al., 2015). A prospective study that spanned about 15 years likewise indicated that those individuals who reported greater positive well-being were at lower risk for chronic heart disease. Studies that assessed individuals before they had signs of illness as well as individuals who had an already established illness, supported the view that positive well-being was associated with lower levels of mortality (Sin, 2016). The protective actions of positive mood in regard to CAD exceeded the contribution of simply not encountering emotional distress. In effect, the incidence of heart disease is not only diminished by lowering negative mood states, but also by enhancing positive affect, and positive affect among CAD patients was accompanied by increased survival (Hoen et al., 2013). Such effects may come about by buffering against the effects of stressors, or because a sense of well-being may encourage the adoption of better health behaviors. Indeed, feelings of optimism, happiness, and gratitude were tied to improved health behaviors, and the prognosis related to cardiovascular problems was enhanced (Huffman et al., 2017). In this regard, it is well established that moderate exercise undertaken on a regular basis can act against the development of heart disease. This may occur for a variety of reasons, including the taming of inflammation, and be reducing depressed mood and diminishing the impact of stressors.

Case study 8.1

Can you die of a broken heart?

After recovering from a compound fracture that required months of healing, Shirley found herself alone when her husband of 27 years, seemingly going through an existential crisis, decided to leave her. She was upset, but more than this she was terribly lonely. Things became worse when she suddenly showed signs of a heart attack, including chest tightness. She was rushed to the emergency unit of the hospital. On the trip there she ruminated about all those poems and plays that portrayed characters who died of a broken heart, which made her wonder, 'Can this be happening to me? I thought that dying of a broken heart was an urban myth.'

A series of tests were quickly conducted. Blood was drawn, an electrocardiogram (ECG) was performed, as were all sorts of body and brain scans. The kind attending physician came to see her, saying she had good news. Shirley hadn't had a heart attack after all, although there were ECG changes detected and levels of cardiac enzymes were modestly elevated. It seems that she had experienced Takotsubo cardiomyopathy, which Shirley learned was known as 'broken heart syndrome' or 'stress-induced cardiomyopathy', frequently mistaken to be a heart attack. Most of these cases, like her own, were preceded by intense emotional or physiological stress. She was relieved but not fully mollified by this seemingly good news. The physician explained that unlike what they would have seen if Shirley had experienced a heart attack, her coronary arteries were normal. However, as usually observed with this syndrome, ballooning of certain aspects of the left ventricle was apparent thus limiting the heart's ability to pump blood properly. In addition, parts of Shirley's brain, notably her amygdala, were overly active, which was in line with a recent report concerning Takotsubo cardiomyopathy.

Upon asking for more information, the physician informed her that they knew a lot about this syndrome, but there were still significant gaps. It seemed that this condition might occur owing to coronary artery vasospasm, microcirculation dysfunction, transient obstruction of the left ventricular outflow, and excessive epinephrine activation. The physician told her that the syndrome typically occurred among individuals who had encountered chronic stressor experiences, as she had, which had been aggravated by her marriage dissolution. As the syndrome occurred most often in postmenopausal women, it was suspected that low levels of estrogen may be a contributing factor.

Not long afterward she was discharged. Because of the uncertain cause of the disorder, there was no formalized approach to managing the condition. But thankfully, the symptoms typically resolved on their own. Aside from taking the meds provided to manage hypertension, Shirley was smart and chose to enroll in a program to help her manage feelings of distress and how to cope effectively with life challenges.

Socioeconomic status (SES)

Low SES has been linked to increased occurrence of CAD, which could be mediated by multiple factors, including job strain and lifestyle factors (smoking, alcohol consumption, food choices). Moreover, low SES may be associated with greater aversive experiences, including psychosocial stressors, as well as elevated threat or actual loss/harm, and these, in turn, might promote greater negative emotions and cognitions. They might also have poorer access to medical care, fewer resources for preventive care, and insufficient health knowledge. Even in young and middle-aged individuals, the racial disparities that have been associated with CAD were largely mediated by socioeconomic factors (Garcia et al., 2021). Individuals from less affluent communities are typically treated with standard procedures, but prevention and treatment likely require broader approaches, including individual, community, and population-level considerations (Schultz et al., 2018).

As we discussed earlier, stressful events give rise to neurochemical and hormonal changes that might come to affect heart functioning, and these effects can be influenced by coping methods used and the availability of social support. However, when multiple adverse processes conspire to limit an individual's ability to cope, and when multiple stressors are encountered across different domains, biological limits can be reached. This could be the case in low SES individuals who might maintain a smaller arsenal or 'resource capacity' of interpersonal and intrapersonal ways of coping with stressors. Essentially, in response to stressors, those of low SES may be relatively prone to allostatic overload that favors atherosclerosis and CAD. In Chapter 12 we'll talk about the influence of early life and prenatal stressors on illness that occurs over the life span and across generations. Suffice it for the moment that being born into poverty (or simply low SES) can affect individuals' general well-being and vulnerability to heart disease throughout their lives.

Job strain

Given the enormous portion of our lives that directly involves our jobs, this could be an important source of distress or joy that could affect well-being. Indeed, some jobs are aligned with heart disease to a greater extent than are others. The largest study to assess the relationship between socioeconomic status, rank (pecking order) within an organization, and numerous indices of health and well-being was the Whitehall study that involved more than 18,000 British civil servants, with the ensuing Whitehall II study covering more than 10,000 participants. These studies indicated that early mortality among individuals in more senior ranks was lower than in those in lower ranks. Early mortality was associated with a variety of illness conditions but was especially notable regarding heart disease (Marmot et al., 1978). Given the enormous implications of the Whitehall findings, similar studies were conducted in other countries that largely confirmed the contribution of work-related stressors to cardiovascular and other disturbances.

Several factors influenced the relationship between health risk and job rank, including lifestyle factors; however, these variables accounted for only a modest amount of the health risk. One factor that seemed to be particularly pertinent to the increased health risk in the lower job grades was that workers were experiencing greater levels of psychological distress, which then influenced their well-being. Individuals with low decision latitude (essentially, not being in charge) but high job demands, a combination that is often referred to as 'job strain', were at the greatest risk of heart disease. If chronic job strain was accompanied by the perception of unfairness or injustice within the workplace, the risk of metabolic syndrome was increased (a constellation of conditions that collectively increase the risk of developing Type 2 diabetes) as was coronary heart disease.

In line with these findings, a meta-analysis of 14 prospective studies indicated that after adjusting for age and gender, a combination of high work efforts and low rewards was associated with a 50% increase in CAD. Individual records of about

197,000 participants from 13 European cohort studies confirmed these findings in both males and females, several age groups, and socioeconomic strata (Kivimäki et al., 2012). As well, increased risk for CAD was associated with distress that promoted anxiety, irritability, and poor sleep in the preceding years. Not surprisingly, marital problems were accompanied by increased heart-related mortality (more so among men than women), and the double whammy of poor work life and poor home life had particularly adverse outcomes. Conversely, having a good home life could buffer against the adverse consequences of job strain. When the influence of social inequalities related to occupation are combined with behavioral risk factors (e.g., smoking and poor diet) as well as biological changes that develop (e.g., elevated circulating inflammatory factors) the development of heart disease is still more predictable (Marmot et al., 2008).

Depressive illness in relation to heart disease

One of the most consistent findings has been that depressive illness was highly predictive of the occurrence of CAD and that the risk of heart disease was directly proportional to depression severity, especially given the presence of hopelessness and pessimism, and these relations were mediated by the presence of circulating inflammatory factors (Halaris, 2017). In fact, CAD occurred about twice as often in those with depression than in the remainder of the population, and mortality risk was appreciably increased. As in the case of depression, anxiety has been associated with sudden cardiac death, and anxiety-related disorders (e.g., panic disorder) have been associated with increased CAD. Significantly, social support diminishes stress and acts against the adverse effects of depression related to heart disease.

Speaking to the long-term ramifications of mood disorders, depression evident in young people predicted the development of heart disease that occurred years later (Rottenberg et al., 2014). Among individuals between 17 and 39 years of age, the presence of depression was highly predictive of later heart disease, to the extent that antecedent depression was associated with a 3 and 2.4 (women and men) times greater risk of dying from cardiovascular disease. The results observed in other studies were not as dramatic but still revealed that, over a 19-year period, individuals with a history of depression were more likely to experience MI mortality than did individuals who had not been depressed.

It is not uncommon for anxiety, depression, and PTSD to develop following an MI. Individuals who experienced such psychological changes were at elevated risk of further cardiac events and were more likely to die early relative to those who did not experience these psychological disturbances. Likewise, depression that occurs following stroke (post-stroke depression; PSD) is predictive of subsequent early mortality. The depression that occurs may be due to numerous factors, such as the extent and location of the stroke, as well as elevated levels of inflammatory factors, cell death generated by excessive glutamate levels, disturbed neurotrophin functioning, and HPA dysregulation. While psychotherapeutic and pharmacological treatments have been helpful in diminishing and treating PSD, it continues to be a serious problem (Guo et al., 2021).

Beyond these links, other mental illnesses, such as schizophrenia and bipolar disorder, were associated with a markedly elevated risk of subsequent heart disease and stroke (De Hert et al., 2018). The relations between these diseases might well reflect common underlying biological processes, but this does not preclude indirect effects of these psychological conditions. Specifically, mental illnesses may be accompanied by counterproductive lifestyle habits, such as elevated use of tobacco and alcohol, poor diet, and physical inactivity. As well, some drugs prescribed for several mental illnesses promote substantial weight gain that could impact heart health. Furthermore, it is not unusual for individuals with psychiatric disturbances not to seek medical attention related to physical illness symptoms, and even when care is sought, physicians might incorrectly attribute patient self-reported cardiac symptoms to their mental health.

Vital exhaustion

When the resources to deal with stressors have been depleted, vital exhaustion (often referred to as burnout) may ensue. This syndrome comprises feelings of excessive fatigue and a lack of energy, increased irritability, and feeling demoralized. The syndrome is also reminiscent of the features of depressive disorder, and indices of depression and vital exhaustion were found to be highly correlated.

A systematic review and meta-analysis indicated that vital exhaustion was linked to incident and recurrent CAD (Frestad & Prescott, 2017). Moreover, among middle-aged men who were free of CAD, vital exhaustion predicted later angina, MI, and sudden cardiac death, even after controlling for other variables associated with heart disease, such as blood pressure, cholesterol levels, and smoking. A similar meta-analysis indicated a moderate relationship between vital exhaustion and the occurrence of stroke (Cohen et al., 2017). Other studies confirmed the fundamental predictive nature of vital exhaustion in age, gender, and ethnic adjusted analyses, and controlling for blood pressure, body-mass index, and diabetes.

Although vital exhaustion and depression are related, the link between vital exhaustion and heart disease went beyond that of depression, anxiety, and hostility (Balog & Konkolÿ Thege, 2019). This said, in considering the ties to heart disease, features of the illness need to be dissociated from one another as some features of depression that occur with vital exhaustion may be especially pertinent. The presence of 'somatic depressive symptoms', which comprise fatigability, sleep problems, appetite changes, and psychomotor alterations, was predictive of elevated post-myocardial infarction mortality, whereas this was not apparent in relation to the cognitive-affective depressive symptoms (depressed mood, anhedonia, negative feelings about self, concentration problems, and suicidal ideation) (Hwang et al., 2015). It may be that the physical symptoms of depression, like that of vital exhaustion, are more closely aligned with the presence of inflammatory factors that influence CAD.

Numerous biological factors were tied to vital exhaustion, including reduced basal cortisol levels, and imbalance between proinflammatory (IL-6 and TNF-α) and anti-inflammatory cytokines (IL-10). Moreover, vital exhaustion was related to elevated leukocytes and C-reactive protein, and an overall increase of viral load. Together, these data point to the possibility that vital exhaustion might be influenced by inflammatory processes, just as CAD was linked to inflammation.

The finding that depression and heart disease are comorbid conditions is interest-ing from several perspectives, but the fundamental question is why this comor-bidity occurs at all? It might be thought that depression itself is very stressful, and hence may place excessive strain on the heart. Indeed, there is good reason to believe that the combination of chronic stressors (particularly in women), cou-pled with an internalizing coping style, might instigate the physiological pro-cesses (alterations in the HPA axis and autonomic nervous system functioning) that promote heart disease. A related position, the cardiovascular reactivity view, is that vascular alterations might arise in depressed individuals because they are highly reactive to stressful stimuli. Thus, depression itself might not promote heart disease, but rather the high stress reactivity in these individuals might be responsible. While not dismissing these possibilities, as we'll see shortly, it is more likely that stressful experiences that accompany or lead to depression give rise to elevated circulating inflammatory factors that increase vulnerability to heart disease.

Despite the strong relations between depression and heart disease, interven-tions to reduce depression frequently did not diminish the risk for CAD and had only limited effects in preventing mortality related to heart disease. Mortality was only modestly influenced by antidepressant medications prior to indi-viduals experiencing MI. Psychological interventions that reduced depressive symptoms were not accompanied by diminished occurrence of subsequent MI but were associated with reduced mortality specifically related to heart disease (Richards et al., 2018).

It needs to be underscored that CAD is a chronic condition compromising mul-tiple physical changes that evolved with depression being a fundamental chronic stressor that contributes to this. By the time depressed patients sought medical attention, significant damage to the heart may already have been underway and might not be reversible, although this doesn't imply that the treatment would not be effective in preventing further damage. Treatment of depression that occurs following cardiac events may be associated with improved prognosis related to further cardiac events. As we'll see in Chapter 9, the effectiveness of antidepres-sant treatments varies considerably across patients, although it remains to be determined whether the strategies to reduce depression were uniquely suited for individuals with specific features of depression. Either better treatments to deal with depression need to be developed or the choice of depression therapy needs to be based on individual features that could predict best outcomes (Carney & Freedland, 2017).

The drag of loneliness

Our social groups and networks have multiple important health benefits and feeling connected to other people are essential to diminish feelings of loneliness (Haslam et al., 2022). Although loneliness had been considered to be a component of depression, to some degree they are distinguishable from one another and loneliness may be involved in the promotion of depressive illness (Cacioppo et al., 2015) and can have negative effects above and beyond those associated with depression. Loneliness may comprise distinct components that entail intimate or emotional loneliness (i.e., not having a close other who can be relied upon), relational or social loneliness (not having core social or family connections), and collective loneliness (i.e., not having networks of connections that can be contacted, even distally).

Isolation and loneliness can be exceptionally powerful stressors that are associated with multiple psychological disturbances, including a three-fold increase of dementia, and has been associated with greater occurrence of CAD and stroke (Valtorta et al., 2016). The damaging effects of loneliness are particularly profound in older people in whom a functional decline may be prominent, and risk of death was elevated.

Loneliness was long known to be an exceptionally distressing stressor among young people, which has markedly increased globally over the past decade. Numerous factors could play into this increase, but it seemed that to a considerable extent this was related to increased use of smart phones, rather than face contact with others (Twenge et al., 2021). This is especially concerning as these relatively early experiences can predict later behaviors and emotions that may have serious health ramifications. While social support from close others is certainly important for those feeling lonely, community-based interventions that foster community identification have been associated with improved well-being (McNamara et al., 2021), which speaks to the importance of social connectedness in accounting for enhanced health.

The development of illnesses have been assessed in connection with individuals' living situations. A four-year prospective study comprising nearly 45,000 participants at risk for heart disease indicated that those who lived alone were more likely to die from heart attack, stroke, or other vascular-related problems relative to those who lived with others. This said, living alone should not be taken to imply loneliness, nor does living with others preclude loneliness – as the saying goes, 'One can be lonely in a crowded room'. In fact, living alone increased the risk of early death by 24% in 45- to 65-year-old individuals, whereas this difference was less pronounced (12%) in people aged 66 to 80, and was very infrequent in the 80+ age group. Any number of factors could account for these age-related effects. Living alone is unusual in those aged 45–65 years and could be indicative of other problems. Conversely, living alone in older individuals may be an index of independence and may reflect hardiness and good health that allows them to live on their own. It seems that the impact of living alone is not the critical feature accounting for findings such as these. Rather, feeling lonely, regardless of living conditions, may have been fundamental in the relationship with heart disease.

Diabetes and heart disease

Diabetes is among the most common diseases worldwide, affecting more than 200 million people, and is a major risk factor for the development of heart disease.

Type 1 diabetes is a metabolic autoimmune disorder in which blood sugar levels are elevated owing to insufficient insulin being produced by beta cells within the pancreas so that glucose is not taken up into cells (insulin is needed for this process). Type 2 diabetes is usually attributed to cells having become resistant to the effects of insulin and hence do not respond. In both cases, elevated circulating glucose levels can result in tissue damage and provoke numerous illnesses. A third form of the disorder, gestational diabetes, may occur among pregnant women even if they had not previously shown indications of the illness. This form of diabetes usually disappears after delivery, but it may be a precursor to type 2 diabetes.

The symptoms of untreated diabetes typically comprise weight loss, polyuria (frequent urination), polydipsia (increased thirst), and polyphagia (increased hunger), and when the illness is left untreated for a prolonged time numerous complications may occur, particularly those that involve damage to blood vessels, which leads to peripheral vascular disease, atherosclerosis, ischemic heart disease (angina and myocardial infarction), and stroke. Furthermore, because of the vascular disturbances engendered by the illness, wound healing may be diminished, and difficult-to-treat foot problems (e.g., ulcers) may develop that can result in amputation. If this weren't bad enough, diabetes can lead to eye damage and blindness, neuropathy (tingling, numbness, or weakness in the hands and feet owing to the disorder of nerves that connect to the spinal cord), and kidney disease that requires dialysis (in fact, diabetes is the leading cause of kidney failure). As well, diabetes is accompanied by elevated levels of beta amyloid and tau protein in brain cells that surround blood vessels and might contribute to Alzheimer's disease.

The prevalence of type 2 diabetes varies considerably across developed countries, ranging from 5 to 15%. Many more people are prediabetic (meaning high glucose levels, but not yet reaching the diagnostic level), and many people have certainly gone undiagnosed. It affects men and women equally, but appears earlier in men. Abdominal fat has been linked to elevated presence of inflammatory factors and the occurrence of type 2 diabetes; however, in men fat it is more prominent around organs (referred to as visceral fat), whereas in women fat it is stored just beneath the skin. It seems that estrogen may serve to protect women from elevated development of subcutaneous fat but with menopause and the accompanying reduction of estrogen this protection is lost. As a result, women ultimately develop diabetes at rates comparable to that of men. By the age of 65+, more than 25% have been diagnosed with diabetes

Much like the differences in the prevalence of heart disease, diabetes varies greatly across ethnic groups. Within the US the prevalence of type 2 diabetes in Hispanic Americans and Asian Americans was almost twice that of non-Hispanic whites. Diabetes in Native Americans was much higher, just as this was apparent among First Nations people in Canada. Importantly, the diabetes in ethnic groups also varied with the place in which they lived. For instance, the prevalence of diabetes in Africa is much lower than among African Americans in the US, which may be tied to lifestyles, including the amount and types of foods consumed.

The frequency of type 2 diabetes has increased remarkably over the past few decades across all Western countries as well as in China and India. A heredity component makes some individuals more prone to the disorder, but the increased incidence of type 2 diabetes likely stems from greater consumption of unhealthy foods, limited exercise, and obesity. Of relevance in the present context, chronic stressful experiences, including those encountered when young, have been linked to the appearance of diabetes (Hackett & Steptoe, 2017). For that matter, stressors encountered by the mother while she was pregnant could also influence the propensity for diabetes in her offspring. Predictably, factors that diminish the impact of stressors, including the availability of effective coping resources, may limit the development of this disorder.

Diabetes is associated with a change in which nutrients are used so that there is a tendency for fat to be used as the fuel for cells. This results in marked changes of mitochondria within cells, which ordinarily serve as the energy producers, which can then disturb heart functioning. Furthermore, type 2 diabetes is accompanied by indications of inflammation, including the presence of elevated inflammatory factors TNF-α and IL-6, as well as C-reactive protein and fibrinogen. The elevated levels of these inflammatory factors are evident within the liver and adipose (fat) tissue and could act as mediators between obesity and both diabetes and heart disease. Indeed, elevated levels of adipokines (cytokines and related factors derived from fat cells) exacerbate insulin resistance and promote the formation of fatty plaques within arteries. As stressful events increase levels of these cytokines, including their release from fat cells, it is likely that the ravages attributable to stressors in obese individuals might occur through inflammatory mediators (Furman et al., 2019).

Given the influence of type 2 diabetes in the promotion of heart disease, coupled with the greater incidence of diabetes in minority and economically disadvantaged groups, it is predictable that deaths stemming from heart disease associated with diabetes are far greater in these communities (Zuma et al., 2021). Obviously, greater social equality is needed to minimize the development of type 2 diabetes and physicians ought to be more atuned to the importance of social and cultural practices tied to diseases.

Genetic processes associated with heart disease

Genetic and epigenetic influences

Many heart conditions run in families, suggesting the presence of inherited risk factors. Genome-wide association studies have revealed numerous genes that were in some fashion linked to heart disease (Khera & Kathiresan, 2017), accounting for almost 30% of the variance associated with CAD. Interactions occur between specific genes and lifestyle factors, and adherence to healthy lifestyles can diminish the risk of CAD by as much as 50% among high-risk individuals (Khera & Kathiresan, 2017).

Epigenetic changes, including altered microRNAs, were associated with several types of heart disease and ischemic stroke (e.g., Colpaert & Calore, 2021). The influence of epigenetic factors on heart disease was, predictably, elevated in the presence of other high-risk factors, such as metabolic disorders and type 2 diabetes. These epigenetic changes may have arisen owing to stressor experiences, early-life adverse events, nutrients consumed, sedentary behaviors, as well as microbial changes. Together, these factors may promote allostatic overload that could lead to the emergence of heart disease. The diverse heart conditions related to genetic and epigenetic influences may involve identifiable biological mechanisms that might allow for the development of specific treatment strategies. This will likely be dependent on the capacity to interpret polygenic risk scores coupled with diverse experiential and lifestyle factors based on algorithms that focus on different components of risk.

Ethnic and cultural factors

Pronounced differences exist across ethnic and cultural groups concerning genetic factors and various lifestyles, which may contribute to differences of multiple illnesses, including heart disease, as well as the efficacy of various therapies. For instance, relative to white males of European descent, African American men were considerably more likely to die from heart disease, especially as they were more apt to express elevated blood pressure, more frequent type 2 diabetes, and vascular injuries (Flack et al., 2014). These outcomes have been linked to multiple factors, including lifetime stressor experiences, including racial discrimination, and these effects were more prominent in males than in females (Sims et al., 2020). Similar differences were apparent between white and African American women and other ethnic minority women, possibly being tied to diet, physical activity, and being overweight. While the risk of heart disease is relatively low among people from East Asian countries, in the children of people who migrated to developed countries, the risk of heart disease was elevated, likely owing to the adoption of diets that favored obesity (Muncan, 2018).

Sex differences in heart disease and stressor responses

Chronic heart disease is the leading cause of death in women and is generally more closely linked to psychosocial stressors and depression relative to that evident in men. Ordinarily, premenopausal women are far less prone to heart disease than are men of the same age, but thereafter the rate of illness equals that of men. There is reason to believe that estrogen levels play a role in the 'female protection' against heart disease in premenopausal women. With the decline of estrogen levels following menopause, vulnerability to CAD emerges (Regitz-Zagrosek & Kararigas, 2017). As well, menstrual irregularities and abnormalities in the production of estrogen accelerate atherosclerosis in premenopausal women, consequently increasing their vulnerability to CAD.

In addition to sex hormones, low socioeconomic status is a stronger predictor of heart disease among women than men. Likewise, CAD in both sexes was lower in those who were employed, and women in higher administrative positions had lower rates of CAD than did women in the lower ranks. However, in women dealing with the double load of working and taking care of a family, the positive effects of working were eliminated, and the risk of CAD increased. Although work can provide a way of coping with other stressors, when the load becomes excessive, the very factors that serve as buffers can become stressors (Albert et al., 2017). Not unexpectedly, when further loads were placed on women the risk of CAD increased accordingly (e.g., in the case of women who were Black, divorced or separated, or who had obesity, diabetes, depression, or anxiety).

Often, surviving a heart attack is dependent on how quickly an individual can get to hospital so that emergency measures can be undertaken. Delays in seeking treatment can occur for a variety of reasons but can be especially problematic among women, often because they hadn't recognized their symptoms as reflecting a heart attack. Certain symptoms appear in both sexes, such as shortness of breath, nausea and vomiting, chest pain, as well as jaw, neck, and back pain. However, women are more likely to experience fainting, extreme fatigue, throat discomfort, pressing on the lower chest or upper abdomen, and indigestion, which can be misinterpreted as reflecting something other than MI. Women need to be closely acquainted with the signals of heart attack, which could be achieved by improved education concerning this issue, as well as by information provided by physicians.

Personality factors associated with heart disease

Type A personality and hostility

It had been maintained that people with certain personality types might be at particular risk for heart disease. Most people will have heard that the Type A personality, characterized as a person who is ambitious, competitive, impatient, hostile, and rushed, will be at increased risk of heart disease (e.g., Rosenman et al., 1975). The initial reports suggesting this created considerable excitement, but studies conducted since then have not fully supported this contention. However, one element of this personality type, namely that of hostility, might be predictive of heart disease. Despite some negative findings in the latter regard, based on a meta-analysis, it seemed that anger and hostility were related to heart disease, particularly in men, and that hostility was associated with more severe CAD as well as an increased risk of a subsequent MI (Chida & Steptoe, 2010). Rather than considering anger and hostility alone, a composite stress score that included anxiety, perceived stress, depression, and posttraumatic stress was predictive of heart disease, particularly among women (Pimple et al., 2019). As much as anger/hostility may be an important consideration in the promotion of heart disease, it is important to distinguish between anger/hostility that is outwardly directed and that directed at the self (anger-in). There is reason to believe that individuals who exhibit this anger-in characteristic or those who do not overtly express their anger are more prone to CAD than those who express their anger.

Type D personality

Another personality construct has been described that may be relevant to CAD. Individuals with a Type D or 'distressed' personality were deemed to be at high risk for heart disease. This personality type is characterized by the tendency to experience negative emotions (e.g., depressed mood, anxiety, anger, and hostile feelings) and to be particularly attentive to negative stimuli. As well, these individuals tend to be worriers who generally had limited personal ties with other people, and displayed inhibition of self-expression in social interactions. They are typically uncomfortable with strangers, generally feeling inhibited, tense, and insecure when they encounter other people (Kupper & Denollet, 2018). As a result, they may lack social supports that could diminish the impact of stressors. It seemed that the link between the Type D personality and the occurrence of depression was linked to cortisol dysregulation.

Among patients undergoing cardiac rehabilitation, those characterized as having a Type D personality were markedly more likely to experience further heart problems (MI, angina, ischemic heart disease) and to die of cardiac-related causes, even when controlling for other risk factors, such as depression (Denollet et al., 2010). Consistent with a role of the Type D personality in the promotion of heart disease, these individuals displayed greater cardiovascular reactivity in response to repeated stressors, and in a community sample ventricular arrhythmias were more common (Einvik et al., 2014). This is not to say that other psychological factors are unimportant, but that many such factors (including depression, anxiety, anger and hostility, and the avoidance of social contact and hence social support) often cluster together, with the Type D personality being a root factor in this regard. Despite support for the position that the Type D personality was linked to heart disease, having a Type D personality might be accompanied by more unhealthy lifestyles and a lack of social support that promoted heart disease (Ginting et al., 2014).

Physiological stress responses that affect heart disease

Acute laboratory stressor effects

Stressors applied within a laboratory context produce elevated heart rate and blood pressure and could potentially be used to predict cardiac events. Among CAD patients in whom myocardial ischemia could be induced by exercise, about one-half displayed ischemia in response to psychological stressors applied in a lab-oratory setting, varying with the nature of the mental stressor encountered (Zhang, Bao et al., 2020). Emotionally laden and/or personally relevant stressors, such as a speaking assignment concerning personal faults, provoked greater frequency and magnitude of inducible left ventricular wall motion abnormalities than did rela-tively non-specific mental stressors. More than this, psychological stressors applied within a laboratory were predictive of later cardiovascular disturbances (Liao & Carey, 2015) and among patients with stable CAD, the ischemic response to a psy-chological challenge was predictive of subsequent MI and cardiovascular-related death (Vaccarino et al., 2021).

In addition to considering heart rate and blood pressure, interest has focused on the significance of heart rate variability (HRV) in predicting pathology. HRV refers to the variation in time between heart beats that is controlled by sympathetic and parasympathetic nervous system functioning. In addition to the fundamental role of these autonomic responses, HRV elicited by certain stressors (e.g., uncertainty) was accompanied by both cortical and subcortical brain neuronal changes, point-ing to the top-down modulation of heart activity (Thayer et al., 2012). It gener-ally appears that in response to stressors HRV is diminished (along with increased heart rate), whereas methods to diminish stress responses are accompanied by increased HRV. The diminished HRV associated with stressors in a laboratory test is particularly pronounced among individuals experiencing depression or PTSD. When combined with other risk factors, HRV enhanced the prediction of later CAD as well as MI. Significantly, altered HRV was associated with stressful expe-riences, such as those related to discrimination experienced by ethnic minorities (Hill & Thayer, 2019).

Sympathetic nervous system hyper-responsivity

Stressors promote activation of sympathetic component of the autonomic nerv-ous system and if sufficiently chronic may contribute to endothelial disturbances, hypertension, left ventricular hypertrophy (thickening of the left ventricle that can be indicative of further cardiac problems, including enlargement of the heart), arrhythmia, and atherosclerosis. As norepinephrine and epinephrine are the funda-mental neurotransmitters associated with sympathetic functioning, treatments to diminish excessive pressure brought about by sympathetic activation have involved blocking β-norepinephrine receptors. While β-blockers reduce blood pressure, they don't get to the root of the problem responsible for the elevated blood pressure and might thus leave individuals with a false sense that their heart problem has been resolved. In fact, contrary to the original beliefs concerning these agents, they were not especially effective in deterring the risk of heart attacks, deaths from heart attacks, or stroke (Wiysonge et al., 2017). This said, in patients younger than 75 who experienced an MI but without heart failure occurring, β-blockers reduced the risk of further MI and reduced all-cause mortality (Safi et al., 2022). It is troubling, however, that in some individuals, these agents increased the occurrence of cardiac events, and worse still, among individuals who had been using β-blockers, death following non-cardiac surgery was appreciably increased.

Fortunately, more effective treatments have been developed to reduce hypertension. These have included *calcium channel blockers* to dilate coronary arteries, thereby enhancing blood flow to the heart. Still other compounds, notably angiotensin-converting enzyme (ACE) inhibitors that block the production of the hormone *angiotensin II* or those that serve as angiotensin II receptor blockers (ARBs) were found to be particularly effective. These agents limit blood vessel constriction, thereby allowing improved flow of blood being pumped by the heart, leading to lowered blood pressure, and they can diminish the cardiovascular effects of stressors. Unfortunately, these agents, particularly ARB inhibitors, have been associated with mood disturbances as well as increased suicide risk (Mamdani et al., 2019).

Brain influences on cardiac functioning and disease

Sympathetic hyperreactivity in response to various challenges occurs in some individuals, and these 'hot reactors' are more prone to atherosclerosis than are 'cold reactors' who tend to exhibit less sympathetic activity activation. The factors that make some individuals either hot or cold responders aren't certain, but they likely involve brain processes that are tied to appraisals of stressors, and potentially involve genetic factors and earlier stressor experiences.

The sympathetic nervous system is influenced by neuronal activity within the central nervous system (CNS). When β-NE antagonists are administered directly to the hypothalamus of rodents, sympathetic nervous system activity is diminished and may thereby influence cardiovascular functioning. Other processes, such as those related to glutamate activity similarly influence sympathetic nervous system activity. Beyond the involvement of the hypothalamus, heart functioning and cardiac disturbances involve several brain regions that are involved in emotional processing and decision-making. In this regard, individual differences in stressor-evoked blood pressure reactivity were accompanied by unique activation patterns in cortical and limbic brain areas that are involved in the processing of information relevant to stressors. These brain regions are responsible for the hemodynamic and metabolic changes that accompany behavioral responses elicited by stressors (Ginty et al., 2017).

Just as the brain influences heart functioning, it seems that heart health influences brain-related diseases, and factors that influence heart health similarly influence the brain. The development of cognitive impairments was five times greater among individuals who developed hypertension during midlife and was accompanied by the doubling of subsequent dementia and Alzheimer's disease. Likewise, a two-fold increase in the risk of Alzheimer's disease was evident among individuals who experienced heart failure, and a 40% increase was apparent among individuals with CAD (Tsao et al., 2022).

Stress-related coagulation

Fibrinogen that is made in the liver is a blood plasma coagulant that contributes to blood clotting, and elevated levels of fibrinogen are a risk factor for CAD in healthy people but more so among individuals with a history of heart problems. Elevated fibrinogen can be promoted by stressful events and depression and could thus be a common denominator for the stress/depression connection to heart disease. Ordinarily, in response to psychological stressors fibrinogen and inflammatory responses were elevated, possibly being fundamental in producing hypertension (Steptoe et al., 2016). These actions may be dependent on heart health as an acute mental stressor ordinarily activates coagulation to a moderate extent, but among individuals with atherosclerosis a hypercoagulable state was provoked.

Inflammatory processes in heart disease

Although the inflammatory immune system is meant to protect us from invading pathogens, as we've learned, prolonged inflammation can have unfortunate adverse actions. This is apparent regarding psychological disturbances, such as depression and may also influence cardiac problems. By promoting sterile inflammation, persistent stressor experiences could promote atherosclerosis (Fioranelli et al., 2018). Furthermore, following an MI an inflammatory cascade is set in motion that results in a further increase of atherosclerotic plaques as well as enzymes that could cause the rupture of a plaque (Prabhu & Frangogiannis, 2016).

Evidence that inflammatory factors might be related to heart disease has come from various sources. Among other things, several immune-related disorders, including rheumatoid arthritis, were associated with cardiovascular disturbances, and following a splenectomy (a major warehouse for immune cells), patients were at increased risk of myocardial infarction. Furthermore, over the course of CAD, immune factors (macrophages and cytokines) infiltrate the endothelium to facilitate healing, but they may also create more damage that leads to still further cytokine changes.

In the presence of some challenges, notably pathogens or in response to tissue injury, receptors sensitive to immune-related agents may be activated. As described in our discussion of immune processes (Chapter 7), several types of toll-like receptors (TLRs) can be stimulated in response to diverse challenges, including stressors. Once stimulated, these TLRs cause the release of cytokines that promote an inflammatory response. The TLRs most common in cells that make up heart muscle (cardiomyocytes) comprise TLR3, TLR4, and TLR9. If activated on a sustained basis they can produce adverse cardiac consequences (Jaén et al., 2020).

C-reactive protein

C-reactive protein (CRP) and fibrinogen are released from the liver and are readily measured in blood. Both rise remarkably in response to inflammation, with CRP elevations being evident within two hours and persisting for several days. Because of its sensitivity, it is used to determine whether inflammation is present, and longitudinal epidemiological studies revealed that CRP was associated with increased risk for cardiovascular events. Thus, CRP is frequently used as a biomarker to predict subsequent cardiovascular problems.

Like the rise of CRP following stressors, elevated levels of this protein was associated with major depressive disorder, whereas positive mood was accompanied by lower CRP levels. The data concerning the relationship between CRP and stress reactions and depression have been taken to be indicative of a link between mood disorders and inflammatory factors and has been considered as evidence that the comorbidity that exists between depression and heart disease involves such processes. To be clear, however, the link between CRP and depression has been based on correlational analyses. CRP is an index of inflammation being present but is not necessarily a factor that promotes inflammation or heart disease. That said, recent clinical studies provisionally suggested that reducing CRP may diminish the incidence of heart disease (Fu et al., 2020).

Cytokines and stressors

Coronary artery disease is not simply a passive process that develops with the accumulation of cholesterol and plaque formation. Instead, active participation of proinflammatory cytokines, such as TNF-α, IL-1β, IL-6, and IL-18, may contribute to cardiac disorders, irrespective of the levels of circulating cholesterol. The presence of inflammatory factors and elevated C-reactive protein in blood can predict the development of heart failure (Fioranelli et al., 2018).

The development of heart disease is a lengthy process that involves different cytokines from diverse sites, such as the gut or lymphoid organs, as well as those that originate from tissues within the heart. In addition to favoring atherosclerosis, the evolution of different inflammatory cytokines may contribute to different forms of heart disease, and the effects on cardiac pathology depend on the level and duration of the cytokine elevation, as well as on the precise mix of proinflammatory cytokines that are present, as they can act synergistically with one another. It is particularly significant that in a four-year double-blind randomized controlled trial with more than 10,000 patients that had previously experienced an MI, treatment with an anti-inflammatory agent that targeted IL-1β led to fewer cardiac events (Ridker et al., 2017).

Another immune-related component, caspases, may be relevant to inflammation-elicited cardiovascular disturbances. Caspases play a fundamental role in apoptosis (programmed cell death), necrosis, the maturation of lymphocytes, and inflammation. One of the caspases, namely caspase-1, which could readily be induced by a stressor (Frank et al., 2020), was implicated in several non-communicable illnesses, including heart disease, through its effects on inflammatory processes and by affecting apoptosis in the myocardium (Molla et al., 2020).

As depicted in Figure 8.1., beyond local events, stressors are intimately related to heart disease by virtue of the effects of brain processes in modulating sympathetic nervous system activity. Indeed, the infusion of IL-1β or TNF-α directly into the brain of rodents increases sympathetic activity and arterial blood pressure as well as

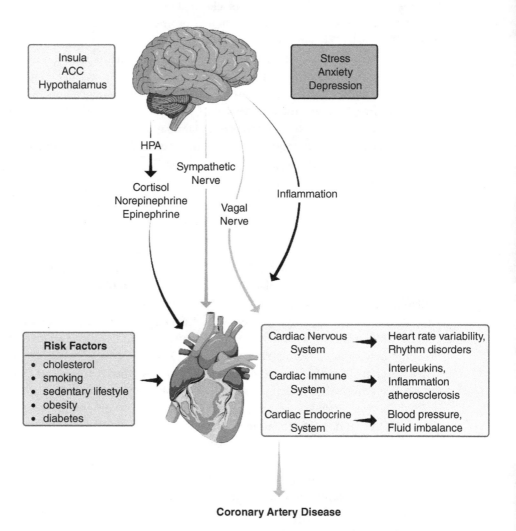

Coronary Artery Disease

Figure 8.1 Atherosclerosis is often considered to be a systemic inflammatory disease. Chronic stressors and depressive illness are among the most potent predictors of cardiovascular diseases and for poor prognosis following myocardial infarction. Psychological distress can precipitate heart function through a dysregulated neuroendocrine and autonomic response, as well as the promotion of inflammatory processes. ACC, anterior cingulate cortex; HPA, hypothalamic–pituitary–adrenal axis.

Source: Created using BioRender. Modified from Fioranelli et al. (2018).

the synthesis of several hormones that have been implicated in heart disease. Such findings speak to the role of brain processes in mediating the relation between both stressors and depressive disorders in the promotion of heart disease. These relationships are multidirectional so that CAD has been related to the later development of age-related cognitive decline (Xie et al., 2019).

The source and course of chronic inflammatory effects

Exogenous factors, such as pathogens, can trigger immune molecules that eventually culminate in heart disease. Elevated levels of antibodies indicative of pathogen presence have been found in CAD patients, and chronic infection was associated with increased risk of cardiac illness, as were other pathogens, including Helicobacter pylori (also associated with ulcers), Chlamydia pneumoniae (which is associated with pneumonia), and cytomegalovirus (which is associated with forms of herpes) (Kop & Mommersteeg, 2013). It is unlikely that any single bacterial challenge is uniquely responsible for cardiovascular outcomes, but the total number of infections experienced ('pathogen burden') was aligned with CAD. Likewise, through the actions of gut microbiota metabolites, inflammation could be induced that might come to affect atherosclerosis, hypertension, and heart failure. Beyond the strain provoked by these bacterial challenges, other types of insults, such as tissue damage originating from chemical or physical trauma can also create an inflammatory environment that contributes to CAD. Moreover, when stressors and immune activating agents are present concurrently, they can synergistically influence several hormones and brain processes that could potentially affect cardiovascular functioning. In response to a combined stressor and immune activating agent, a notable rise of plasma atrial natriuretic peptide (ANP) was evident as were left ventricular ANP levels (Wann et al., 2010). Along with brain natriuretic peptide (BNP), these heart hormones affect vasodilation and sodium expulsion that can affect heart functioning and have frequently been used to predict cardiovascular disturbance.

Influenza and heart disease

On a yearly basis, 300,000–550,000 deaths are attributable to respiratory effects related to influenza, and it has become clear that influenza can precipitate acute myocardial infarction. The latter actions may stem from the release of cytokines, as well as disturbances of atherosclerotic plaques that result in artery occlusion. Of relevance is that treating patients with an influenza vaccine could diminish the occurrence of MI, perhaps by as much as 45%, which is equal or better than that of other treatments to manage CAD and prevent MI (MacIntyre et al., 2016). As well, over a 12-month period following MI (or in high-risk CAD patients) mortality was diminished by influenza vaccination relative to placebo treatment (Frøbert et al., 2021).

Gut bacteria and the heart

When gut dysbiosis occurs, bacterial metabolites promote inflammatory processes that favor the development and progression of cardiovascular disturbances (Tang et al., 2019). Many risk factors associated with heart disease, such as aging, obesity, maintaining unhealthy diets, and engaging in a sedentary lifestyle, promote gut dysbiosis and inflammation that favors heart disease. Conversely, the heart benefits promoted by exercise, diet, and stress reduction procedures, may come about, in part, through their actions on microbiota (Jia et al., 2019). Importantly, disturbances of gut microbiota were noted among people who were overweight or had type 2 diabetes well before various forms of subsequent heart disease developed (Fromentin et al., 2022). The use of probiotics may help limit heart disease, but as we indicated earlier it may be better to obtain these through specific diets rather than the use of supplements. Incidentally, a glass of red wine has been offered as a protective strategy to prevent CAD. This may occur either because of the presence of polyphenolic compounds present in red wine, such as resveratrol, the antioxidant actions of red wine, and by diminishing gut dysbiosis that developed owing to a poor diet.

Adiposity and cytokines in relation to heart disease

Among individuals who had obesity at middle age, life span was reduced by 5.8 and 7.1 years in men and women, respectively, and health span (disease-free years) was similarly reduced. Being overweight may be a risk factor for heart disease among both men and women, and increased risk may even be evident with a moderate elevation of body mass index. But how does this come about? Is being heavy a strain that wears down the heart? Or is being heavy associated with less exercise that could potentially improve heart functioning?

Obesity encourages a variety of biological disturbances that could lead to heart disease. It is related to metabolic syndrome, impaired glucose tolerance, insulin resistance and diabetes, hypertension, and elevated LDL cholesterol levels, all of which are associated with CAD. Importantly, white fat cells that appear around the belly are replete with cytokines that can promote inflammation, and their sustained release might contribute to heart disease. As atherosclerosis and obesity are associated with inflammatory changes, this form of heart disease is often thought of as an inflammatory disease.

Even though the ties between being overweight or having obesity were broadly accepted, it has been argued that this conclusion may not have been fully warranted. Having severe obesity was tied to earlier death, but this was not necessarily evident in overweight individuals or those with moderate obesity (Flegal et al., 2013). For that matter, having obesity was primarily linked to heart disease and mortality among individuals who were considered to be physically unfit (McAuley et al., 2012). These findings led to the perspective that 'metabolically healthy obesity' may occur in some individuals who present with cardiorespiratory fitness, low liver and visceral fat, adequate insulin sensitivity, and low levels of inflammatory markers. While such studies supported a 'fat-but-fit' perspective, they ignored important factors that could negate this conclusion. Having obesity and still being metabolically fit at a given time, does not preclude the subsequent development of illnesses (Blüher, 2020). Among individuals who had obesity and appeared to be healthy based on their blood pressure, fasting blood sugar, cholesterol, and insulin resistance, upon subsequent assessment 10 years later, 40% of these 'healthy obese' people were no longer characterized as being healthy, and after 20 years more than 50% were deemed to be at risk for heart disease (Bell et al., 2015). Clearly, it is essential not simply to assess whether obesity is present but to determine how long it had been present.

Consistent with this, among individuals who had been followed for as long as 43 years, being obese when young and continuing to gain weight was accompanied by progressively greater risk for health problems (Zheng et al., 2021). It seems that chronic obesity is accompanied by multiple biological outcomes that are reminiscent of aging so that health span and life span are abbreviated (Salvestrini et al., 2019). It seems that chronic obesity is accompanied by multiple biological outcomes that are reminiscent of aging so that health span and life span are abbreviated (Salvestrini et al., 2019). In contrast, several studies indicated that mortality was diminished in some individuals who had only gained weight later in life, which has been referred to as the 'obesity paradox'. This 'paradox', however, may not be as paradoxical as it might seem. The assumption that late life obesity is causally linked to longer survival is unwarranted (Banack & Stokes, 2017). In fact, it may be more a reflection of their earlier moderate weight than factors that were subsequently assessed. Furthermore, studies assessing the link between obesity often had not considered the influence of other factors (e.g., smoking, lifelong sedentary behavior) that may be more prominent in those with lifelong obesity relative to individuals who gained weight late in life. It is also possible that individuals who lost weight may have been experiencing illnesses or had been using medications that reduced weight, as in the case of diabetic patients using GLP-1 agonists. These individuals would then be classified as not being obese, hence biasing the results showing that survival was shorter than in those with late-life obesity.

Implications of inflammation for treatment of heart disease

One would think that if inflammatory factors contribute to CAD, then manipulating these processes would influence heart disease. However, the effects of nonsteroidal anti-inflammatory drugs (NSAIDs) on CAD have not been encouraging (Raggi et al., 2018). Despite the data suggesting TNF-α involvement in heart disease, the anti-TNF-α agents etanercept and infliximab were not effective treatments for CAD and even caused further problems. As with so many other pathologies, multiple processes are likely involved in heart disease, and thus altering only one component might not be sufficient. Furthermore, as not all cases of heart disease stem from excessive inflammation, NSAIDs or other inflammatory treatments would only be effective for a subset of patients. Importantly, once frank signs of heart problems appear the window for modifying problems may have passed and hence NSAIDs will be ineffective in remedying cardiovascular disturbances. These agents may offer their positive effects in preventing the development of illness, rather than reversing already existent damage. In the end, selecting appropriate treatments for CAD ought to be based on the multiple features that might be associated with illness (Lawler et al., 2020).

It had been maintained for decades that daily low-dose aspirin (baby aspirin) could diminish the risk of heart disease and stroke, especially among individuals that had previously experienced a cardiac event. This view was challenged based on reports indicating that baby aspirin produced limited benefits, which were offset by the risk for intestinal bleeding. Thus, the American Heart Association recommended against its use. This caution has been reinforced by the finding that aspirin use was associated with a 26% increase in the incidence of heart failure. Yet, some individuals may benefit from aspirin use, which could be predicted based on genetic markers related to blood platelets that are associated with blood clotting. Once again, such findings point to the possible adoption of anti-inflammatory agents on an individualized basis (Selak et al., 2019).

The introduction of any medication always needs to weigh the benefits against the potential harms that can be created. Overall, in the case of heart disease, it seems that the benefits of aspirin are small relative to the possibility of gastrointestinal bleeding. However, this doesn't necessarily imply that the benefits for other illnesses don't exceed the risks. The case has been made that the anti-inflammatory effects of aspirin to deter the occurrence of cancer can be fairly substantial (Anisman & Kusnecov, 2022). It isn't certain, however, whether these outweigh the risks created.

Conclusion

The development of heart disease, which is the greatest cause of death worldwide, may come about through a variety of factors, such as those related to diet, lack of exercise, and some heart conditions have been linked to genetic influences. Chronic psychosocial stressors seem to exert negative effects on cardiovascular health and may account for about 30% of the risk for MI. Both retrospective and prospective analyses indicated that hostility, depression, and anxiety, together with personality features, were associated with an increased risk of coronary heart disease and mortality. Furthermore, strong negative emotional responses (e.g., anger) can act as a trigger for MI in those with existent cardiovascular problems, even if they had previously been undetected.

Increasingly, the view has been adopted that stressful events can instigate cytokine changes peripherally and in the brain, which can favor the development of heart disease. The inflammatory changes can promote altered levels and turnover of neurotransmitters such as 5-HT, elevated levels of CRH, and lowered neurotrophins (e.g., BDNF). These biological changes favor the development of depression and could affect heart disease, raising the possibility that cytokines (or cytokine–stressor combinations) serve as a link between these different pathologies. That said, both depression and CAD are complex illnesses that involve multiple factors, and therefore this perspective is likely a bit simplistic. Ultimately there will no doubt be other processes identified that link these pathological conditions. Accordingly, the most effective preventive and therapeutic strategies will need to be based on individually tailored treatment that includes biological considerations together with psychosocial factors.

Suggested reading

Carney, R.M. & Freedland, K.E. (2017). Depression and coronary heart disease. *Nature Reviews in Cardiology, 14*, 145–155.

Healey, N. (2021). Is there more to a healthy-heart diet than cholesterol? *Nature, 594*, S12–S13.

Khera, A.V. & Kathiresan, S. (2017). Genetics of coronary artery disease: Discovery, biology and clinical translation. *Nature Review in Genetics, 18*, 331–344.

9

DEPRESSIVE ILLNESSES

Depressive illnesses are the most common mental disorders and together with anxiety disorders are among those that carry the greatest burden of disease. Estimates of its prevalence have varied widely but it is generally thought that depressive illnesses occur in about 20% of individuals at some time (some say it is as high as 30%), and the recurrence rate is very high, exceeding 50%. It manifests across socioeconomic, educational, and cultural backgrounds; it doesn't discriminate. Depression frequently begins relatively early in life, often presenting in teenage years, and among university students the incidence of depression and anxiety appear at about 33%, with more than 50% of these individuals reporting suicidal ideation and 15% acted on these ideations. In fact, suicide is the second leading cause of death in youth (after automobile accidents). In the US, 47,000 people died by suicide in each of the past few years, and in Canada, ~4,000 individuals died by suicide, with ~750 being under the age of 29. Given these estimates, it should not be surprising that antidepressants are the most prevalent prescription drugs used on university and college campuses. The prevalence of depression in the elderly population is also exceptionally high, with over 45% of seniors in residential care homes being affected to some extent.

Aside from its emotional cost on individuals and their families, mental illness has staggering economic costs on health-care systems and contributes greatly to a substantial loss of potential labour supply (e.g., through sick leave and reduced work productivity). Upwards of 50% of new disability benefit claims in some countries are for reasons of poor mental health, with depression being the fastest-growing category of disability costs.

The financial cost attributed to depression exceeded that of lung, colorectal, breast, and prostate cancer combined. With depression being forecasted to become the no. 1 burden of disease worldwide by 2030, the days ahead could be pretty gloomy unless a concerted effort is made to change approaches to prevention and treatment and to diminish the stigmatization of individuals with this illness.

Learning objectives

Depressive disorders have become the plague of the twenty-first century and attempted cures have had limited success, although this may be changing. This chapter will deal with several aspects of depression that provide the following take-home messages:

- Depressive disorders comprise a combination of different symptoms that vary across individuals.
- Subtypes of depression exist that differ in their behavioral presentation and likely differ in the underlying mechanisms, and hence may require different therapeutic approaches.
- Depressive disorders may come about through cognitive disturbances, such as the development of feelings of helplessness or hopelessness.
- Brain neurochemical changes elicited by stressors, including neurotransmitters, neurotrophins, hormones, inflammatory factors, have been implicated in depressive disorders.
- Manipulations that affect cognitive stress processes and stressor-provoked biological changes can be used to treat depressive disorders.
- Treatment for depressive disorders might call for an individualized approach based on the specific symptoms and biomarkers individuals present.

What is depression?

Most people experience periods when they feel down, possibly because things aren't going right, or because they're overworked, or maybe because they woke up cranky. 'Depression' would be the wrong term for this type of mood, and 'down' or 'sort of sad' would be more appropriate. However, in some individuals, poor mood may be more intense or persistent and could reflect a depressive disorder. Several subtypes of the illness exist and the symptoms may vary across individuals, and these features can change over time. Overall, depressive disorders are twice as frequent in women compared to men, and in certain subtypes of depression, the ratio is closer to 3:1 and may begin relatively early in life. Some individuals may exhibit one or more episodes of mania (or hypomania where manic symptoms are not excessive), in which case a diagnosis of bipolar depression is made.

Given the frequency of mental illnesses, there's a high likelihood that one or more of your family members might suffer from some sort of mental health disturbance at some time. As we noted in Chapter 3, the stigma that accompanies mental illness is considerable so that very few people talk about it – a veritable conspiracy of silence. What is particularly alarming is the large number of individuals with a full set of symptoms of depressive disorders (or other mental health disorders) who fail to seek help and even reject help when it is offered, preferring to suffer in silence.

Diagnosing depression

The *Diagnostic and Statistical Manual – 5th edition* (*DSM-5*) provides detailed symptoms of depressive disorders and other mental illnesses (see Table 9.1). The *DSM* is a source that provides standard criteria for the classification of mental disorders so that clinicians will define syndromes using the same criteria. The World Health Organization's *International Statistical Classification of Diseases and Related Health Problems* (*ICD-11*) is a similar instrument that is more commonly used in Europe. As we'll see shortly, as much as having clear diagnostic criteria for depression is important, as it is for any other illness, this can also create problems in treating the disorder, which has led to other approaches being considered in the assessment and treatment of mental illnesses.

Table 9.1 Symptoms of depression.

Based on the DSM criteria, major depressive disorder (MDD) is diagnosed when an individual presents with the following symptoms for two weeks:

(a) Depressed mood

OR

(b) anhedonia (i.e., no longer receiving from pleasure from events or stimuli that had previously been rewarding)

And at least four of the following symptoms must be present:

(a) significant weight loss or weight gain

(b) insomnia or hypersomnia almost every day

(c) psychomotor agitation or retardation that is observable by others

(d) fatigue or loss of energy

(e) feelings of worthlessness or excessive, inappropriate guilt

(f) diminished cognitive abilities (impaired concentration, difficulty making decisions)

(g) recurrent thoughts of death, recurrent suicidal ideation.

In addition, individuals who are affected with MDD may display feelings of helplessness, hopelessness, and even self-hatred, as well as impaired concentration and/or memory, social withdrawal, and especially low self-esteem and high levels of rumination.

Is there a problem with diagnosing depression?

With a bit of insight, you'll recognize that there's a problem inherent in the diagnostic features associated with depression. Let's change the framework for a moment. Imagine that you go to a doctor and present with a certain set of symptoms; say, a runny nose, muscle fatigue, and fever. The doctor tells you that you've developed a viral infection, a cold or flu, and tells you to get bed rest and recommends you take ibuprofen. Imagine that a month later you go to the doctor presenting with headache, loss of appetite, and difficulty swallowing. The doctor suggests that your symptoms are consistent with a viral infection and again prescribes ibuprofen. Does this sound suspicious? Do such different symptoms reflect the same illness? Well, that's what is faced when it comes to diagnosing depression, only it's still more puzzling; two individuals can have entirely different symptoms (opposites in some instances) and still be said to be suffering from depression. Alternatively, they may have identical symptoms but respond very differently to a particular therapeutic agent. So, what is it that's being treated? Is it the specific symptoms or is it the amorphous concept 'depression'? Should individuals with different symptoms get the same treatment or is there something fishy in the way depressive illnesses are conceptualized and treated?

Some clinicians and researchers believe that a classification system that applies labels to illnesses may be counterproductive, especially as it might dictate standard treatments for all the individuals placed in a particular category. As we've already seen, it may be more appropriate to treat individuals based on the specific symptoms they express, their social, cultural, and environmental context, along with the presence of biochemical and genetic markers.

Depressive subtypes

Subtypes of depression have been identified, as described in Table 9.2, that share several common features, but can nonetheless be distinguished from one another. Given that these subtypes differ from each other, one might question whether they are, in fact, part of the same syndrome and whether they might have very different etiologies. Despite the different illness features, it is not unusual for the same treatment to be prescribed to all individuals considered to be depressed, and in many research studies these illnesses are thrown into a single category. The need for personalized (individualized) treatment strategies has repeatedly been advanced since different underlying processes might be involved in depression across patients and consequently, they might not be equally responsive to a given treatment. Identifying the mechanisms responsible for an illness might lead to more effective treatment strategies.

Table 9.2   Subtypes of depression.

Major depressive disorder, Typical: Involves mood changes and/or anhedonia, and a constellation of other symptoms, such as reduced eating, weight loss, and sleep disturbances (e.g., early morning awakening).

Major depressive disorder, Atypical: Comprises mood changes and/or anhedonia. It is characterized by reversed neurovegetative features (increased eating, weight gain, and increased sleep) as well as a tendency towards persistent rejection sensitivity and mood reactivity (mood enhancement in response to positive stimuli).

Melancholic depression: Characterized by a severely depressed mood that exceeds that of grief or loss. Individuals display pronounced anhedonia, with symptoms being worst in the early mornings, early morning awakening, excessive weight loss, or excessive guilt. The atypical features of depression are not evident in melancholia.

Dysthymia: Chronic low-grade depressive symptoms present for at least two years, although symptoms wax and wane. Symptoms can take on typical or atypical features. If not effectively treated, major depression may develop, superimposed on a dysthymia background (termed 'double depression'), wherein symptoms are much more difficult to treat.

Seasonal affective disorder (SAD): This form of depression is tied to the seasons (or the duration of light over the day), coming on in the autumn or winter, and then resolving in the spring. This diagnosis is made if, over two years, two (or more) episodes have occurred in months with less light, but without episodes occurring at other times.

Recurrent brief depression: Characterized by intermittent depressive episodes that occur, on average, at least once a month over at least one year, but are not tied to any particular cycles (e.g., the menstrual cycle). The diagnostic criteria for recurrent brief depression are the same as those for major depressive disorder; however, as the name implies, it occurs for brief periods (typically two-four days). These episodes can be particularly severe and may be accompanied by suicidal ideation and suicide attempts.

Minor depression: This diagnosis is made when a mood disorder does not fully meet the criteria for major depressive disorder, but individuals present with at least two depressive symptoms for two weeks.

Postpartum depression: This form of depression occurs after childbirth and affects about 5-10% of women. Symptoms are much like those of major depression. The depression may be linked to the hormonal changes that accompany pregnancy, or those that occur in association with childbirth, but hormonal therapy has not been found to be an effective treatment strategy.

Treatment-resistant depression: Many patients, as high as 30%, are not helped by antidepressant treatments, even after repeated efforts. Treatment resistance is usually defined as the failure of two (or three) medications from different classes.

Illness comorbidity

Depressive disorders, as we've seen, may be comorbid with a variety of other illnesses occurring at some time, and they potentially might involve common environmental triggers (e.g., stressors) or underlying processes (such as activation of the inflammatory immune system). We saw this when we discussed cardiovascular illness as well as inflammatory disorders, but there's a much broader range of comorbidities that ought to be considered. Figure 9.1 shows some of the conditions that have been reported to be comorbid with depression, and if nothing else points to the need for greater attention being devoted not only to research to cure depression but also to greater public awareness. In fact, depression may be a marker that forewarns physicians about the potential for other illnesses subsequently emerging (Anisman & Hayley, 2012).

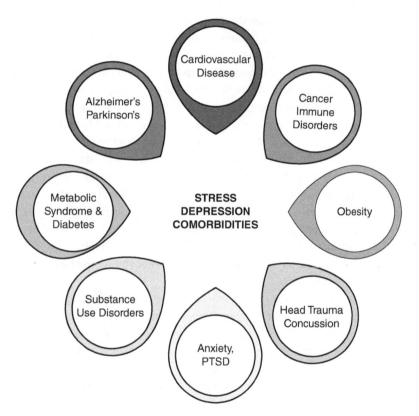

Figure 9.1 Depressive illnesses, frequently brought on by stressful experiences, are often comorbid with a large variety of other psychological and physical disorders. As well, many of these illnesses, such as diabetes and heart disease, are highly comorbid with one another. Just as depression is associated with heart disease, it is often seen following stroke, and in these patients, recovery is poorer than it is among those who had not been depressed. Furthermore, depression was accompanied by increased cancer progression and a poorer response to chemotherapy relative to the effectiveness evident among those individuals who were less depressed. There is also reason to believe that depressive illness may be causally related to Alzheimer's disease, possibly because they share certain genes acting through inflammatory processes. In effect, depressive illness is not only related to the development of other illnesses, but also the course of these illnesses and the response to therapies.

Case study 9.1

One too many losses

By all accounts, Susan was a typical young woman who moved from home to attend university in a city about 400 km away. Although she was excited at finally taking this big step, she was fairly distressed, experienced a fair bit of homesickness, and seemed to have trouble with the transition to university. She met many other kids in university; happy kids, friends with each other, partying, going out, and studying. However, she didn't feel like one of them, even though they frequently came by and invited her to all sorts of events. Instead, she felt at the margins of the group, largely isolated and lonely. Her distress became progressively more pronounced as the term continued, and she had a great deal of trouble studying. Reading through the tears, neither her class notes nor texts seemed to sink in. She read the same paragraph over and over, usually in automatic mode, but each time nothing seemed to stick in her head. She ruminated between sentences, ruminated as she fell asleep, and ruminated still more early in the mornings. She read sad books and listened to sadder music. She had lost her appetite, her weight had plummeted, her shoulders had become boney, and she hated looking at herself in the mirror; she especially hated her sallow, pale, tired-looking skin. Finally, the Christmas break came, and she went home. Her family knew something was wrong with her, but she wouldn't speak to them about it. Instead, she hid away in her room. She didn't interact with her parents or her younger sister and avoided all her high school friends. Following the Christmas break, her symptoms and social withdrawal became more profound, and she felt guilty for being such a wretch toward her family during the break. She felt that she was just a loser and that nothing would ever change.

Several weeks later Susan disappeared from her residence. It was not until the spring ice had broken that her body was found along the shore of a nearby lake. It seems she had walked out on the lake, and eventually the ice gave way. Her friends and family were devastated, wondering why she hadn't turned to them for her help. Her friends described her behavior before her disappearance as stressed and withdrawn, but not desperate or extreme. As far as they could tell there had been no outward signs that she had reached the depths of hopelessness and despair. She had not relied on the caring and concerned support of those around her. Instead, it seems that she had shared her distress with an online 'friend', who turned out to be a viperous predator that over several weeks had encouraged her to take her life, even offering to join her in a shared suicide. Those who loved her are still trying to comprehend how such a thing could have happened, how they missed all the signs, whether anything could have been done to prevent it, and why in the world she reached out to an internet stranger while shutting them out.

Perhaps the question shouldn't be one of why *didn't* she reach out for help, but more aptly why *couldn't* she reach out for help?

Theoretical constructs related to depressive illness: cognitive perspectives

Several theoretical positions have been adopted concerning the factors that provoke and maintain depressive disorders, as well as the most appropriate treatment strategies. In a broad sense, these have included perspectives that focused on medical models (the illness is a result of disturbed biological processes and can be remedied by pharmacotherapy) and those that involved cognitive processes (depression arises because of disturbed ways of thinking of oneself). These views are not exclusive of one another and efforts have been made to tie specific biological disturbances to aberrant cognitive functioning. As indicated earlier and revisited in Chapter 13, increasing attention has focused on the influence of psychosocial factors in moderating the response to stressors and the development of depression. Cultural factors are similarly important in affecting stress responses and in the development of depressive disorders (Kessler & Bromet, 2013), but insufficient attention has been given to cultural differences in the treatment of this condition.

Hopelessness

One of the most influential views of depression suggested that 'hopelessness' was a primary characteristic of depressed individuals (Beck, 2008). Fundamental to this cognitive model of depression is that individuals develop schemas (or perspectives) based on experiences that subsequently influence the way events are appraised and interpreted. With repeated negative experiences the schemas become more entrenched, resulting in biased information processing, memories of past events take on a more negative tone, and individuals develop pervasive negative perspectives of the future. Adverse events, including those experienced early in life (e.g., abuse and neglect) might be involved in the development of dysfunctional perspectives of the self, which may have repercussions that carry through to adulthood. This state is particularly apt to develop if individuals lack experiences that allow them to develop affirming self-concepts and effective coping skills to negotiate stressful encounters.

As depressed mood becomes more prominent, individuals experience pronounced streams of negative thoughts that tend to emerge spontaneously. These individuals develop a negative triad in which they see the past negatively, the present as being fraught with unassailable threats, and the future as hopeless. The perspectives they have of themselves often comprise themes such as inadequacy, worthlessness (poor self-esteem and self-worth), and failure, and they tend to form dysfunctional attitudes that influence how they perceive external events and their value in relation to others. Further to this, individuals may selectively attend to those stimuli that are consistent with their negative perspectives, while concurrently filtering out or ignoring positive events (or evidence inconsistent with their negative perspectives), thereby strengthening their detrimental cognitive views and further aggravating their depression (Beck & Dozois, 2011).

Brain perspective of hopelessness

The first scent of an illness may begin with one or two disturbed thoughts or processes, which subsequently give rise to still other cognitive changes. The concatenation of symptoms that eventually emerges likely involves multiple biological and experiential factors. Neither depression nor anxiety disorders are static conditions, but instead the characteristics of the illnesses change over time (increase or decrease and involve the incorporation of new symptoms), and even the symptom severity may ebb and wane. Moreover, although depression is often considered a 'passive' state (e.g., characterized by increased sleep, increased lethargy and fatigue, avoidance of social encounters), it is a very active process in other respects. The specific biological processes that underlie these dynamic affective and cognitive variations remain to be fully defined, although it is certain that multiple brain regions are involved in subserving the varied symptoms of depressive disorders.

Elaborating on Beck's theorizing, Disner and colleagues (2011) offered a cognitive model wherein the different attributes of depression involve diverse biological networks. As depressive symptoms are reinforced by negative ruminative thoughts that are associated with altered emotion and memory processing, biased self-referential cognitions, and a diminished ability to inhibit these cognitions, those brain regions involved in each of these elements of depression were considered.

The model described by Disner and colleagues has two major components. One involves limbic brain regions that regulate emotionality (bottom-up components), and the other involves the inhibition of cognitive processes through a top-down process that involves cortical regions. It is particularly important to this model that depression is most likely to occur under conditions where inhibitory control is limited, thus permitting unrestrained neuronal activation in the brain regions that govern emotional responses, including rumination. For instance, rumination often involves negative thoughts that feed on themselves to such an extent that they appear compulsive. Ordinarily, cognitive processes operate to keep excessive, negative rumination in check, but in individuals (or under those conditions) in whom these inhibitory control systems are not operating properly, ruminative behaviors may proceed unabated. This type of negative rumination (termed 'depressive rumination') is a good predictor of later depression, as well as the deteriorating and chronic course of physical illnesses (Nolen-Hoeksema, 2000). Essentially, depression might be viewed as a dysfunction in limiting the automatic responses (e.g., rumination) that propagate depression, coupled with a focus or bias on negative appraisals of events. It was especially interesting that among depressed individuals, processing of issues related to the self was accompanied by a distinct electrophysiological frontal brain profile relative to that associated with non-self-related cognitions or those apparent in non-depressed individuals engaged in self-related thoughts (Hsu et al., 2021).

Different aspects of the prefrontal cortex may contribute to the evolution and maintenance of depression-related cognitive dysfunctions. Disturbed medial prefrontal cortex functioning was seen as being fundamental for control of self-referential schemas, whereas the dorsolateral prefrontal cortex was important for rumination and biased processing, and ventrolateral prefrontal cortex disturbances could be responsible for biased attention. As well, the lateral orbitofrontal cortex may contribute to the development of a negative sense of self and the accompanying poor self-esteem. Ordinarily, the prefrontal cortex (and adjacent cortical regions) influences amygdala functioning so that disturbed prefrontal cortical activity results in the control over subcortical regions being abdicated (i.e., its influence on the amygdala will be diminished) so that the impact of disturbed bottom-up processing persists. The resulting enhanced amygdala reactivity will encourage biased attention and processing, thereby allowing for negative appraisals, attributions, and anxiety to progress undisturbed. In addition, nucleus accumbens responses will be blunted affecting the recognition of and/or the response to positive stimuli or events.

A key aspect of the cognitive model of depression was that individuals who were depressed (or at risk of depression) tended to react strongly to negative events and to exhibit memory biases of a negative nature. Indeed, among depressed individuals engaged in a task to suppress memories, neuronal disturbances were observed that comprised altered amygdala and hippocampal functioning as well as greater activity in brain regions that are involved in attention processing. As negative memories might be tied to attentional biases and the negative processing of information, the memory disturbances in depression might be related to each of these processes (Sacchet et al., 2017).

Aspects of the amygdala might contribute to emotional memory, and the hippocampus may be involved in episodic memory (memory of autobiographical events, including times, places, and contextual knowledge), and together these regions might be involved in the memory biases associated with depression. The presence of hyperactivity in the right amygdala among depressed individuals may be tied to the superior encoding of negative stimuli (i.e., the stimuli are converted into a construct, stored, and then potentially recalled later), which through increased connectivity with the hippocampus promotes enhanced memory of affective stimuli and events.

Predicting recurrence of depression

Given its high rate of recurrence, depression has been considered to be a lifelong disorder. In both currently depressed patients and those in remission, a sad mood induction, in which individuals are exposed to autobiographical memory scripts, was accompanied by reduced cerebral blood flow in the medial orbitofrontal cortex, but this was not evident in never-depressed controls. In addition, in the remitted group, mood provocation decreased blood flow in the anterior cingulate cortex (Liotti et al., 2002). Likewise, when

(Continued)

previously depressed patients were presented with words relevant to specific personality traits that encouraged self-referential thoughts, neuronal activity within the anterior cingulate cortex and dorsal medial prefrontal cortex were markedly elevated in association with the propensity toward rumination (Nejad et al., 2019). It seems that when patients were in remission, a mood challenge 'unmasked' a depression marker that could potentially predict who might be most likely to fall back into depression given further stressor encounters.

The perspective advanced by Beck was instrumental in the development of cognitive behavioral therapy (CBT) as well as variants of this procedure, one of the most widely endorsed therapeutic strategies to deal with depression (Beck et al., 1979). We will consider CBT and other treatment strategies in Chapter 13. However, as we deal with other pathologies, we'll see that beyond its use in treating depression, CBT is used in the treatment of anxiety disorders, such as obsessive-compulsive disorder (OCD), as well as posttraumatic stress disorder (PTSD) and eating disorders.

In some respects, there is considerable similarity between the views expressed by Beck, Disner, and their associates concerning the negative thoughts and schemas associated with depressive illness, and the involvement of System 1 and System 2 in determining the decision-making processes outlined by Kahneman (2011). In both instances there is automaticity of thought based on previous experiences (priming) that influences the way individuals see the world. In a sense, among depressed individuals, negative perspectives and appraisals associated with automatic thoughts (System 1) have hijacked the more logical System 2 processes. Ultimately, the job of cognitive behavioral therapy is to reestablish more appropriate System 1 (automatic) responses and reshape the schemas (System 2) that have been established regarding perceived self-worth and negative views of the future.

Helplessness

To explain how depression comes about, a hypothesis was advanced that was somewhat related to the hopelessness position (Maier & Seligman, 2016). This perspective, which came to be known as 'learned helplessness', was initially developed in animal experiments, and then extended to humans. It will be recalled that when animals were exposed to a controllable stressor regimen or had not been stressed, they subsequently exhibited proficient performance in a test where they were required to escape from a stressor. However, animals that had been exposed to an uncontrollable stressor subsequently exhibited profound behavioral impairments in a test where an active response could terminate the stressor. These animals often did not make overt attempts to avoid or escape, but instead appeared to passively accept the stressor, which was interpreted as animals having 'learned' to be helpless, and consequently gave up further attempts to escape. The effects of uncontrollable stressors are not limited to situations that involve aversive situations but were evident in tasks that entail responding to acquire rewards, such as obtaining favored foods (e.g., sucrose or cookies), rewarding brain stimulation, or social rewards (Anisman et al., 2018; Daniels et al., 2021).

The results of animal experiments led to studies that considered how uncontrollable events affected human behavior. If participants were initially tested in problem-solving tasks that were rigged so they would fail, then their subsequent performance in legitimate tasks was impaired. The participants' expectancy regarding their performance and their failure to meet this expectancy was seen as being fundamental in provoking the impaired performance. Extending such findings to real-world situations, it was suggested that if individuals encounter uncontrollable situations in everyday life, this could lead to feelings of helplessness that would then lead to depression among some individuals. One would think that animals exposed to uncontrollable neurogenic stressors and college students who fail in some tests in a contrived laboratory setting don't have much in common with one another. Nor does it seem that the effects pertaining to perceived controllability map on to the complex cognitive disturbances associated with depressive disorders, to say nothing of the implications (and responses to) of some of the severe, chronic, unremitting stressors that humans might encounter. However, the idea that these students (or dogs and rats) learned to be helpless seemed to fit the zeitgeist and thus the helplessness perspective was widely accepted.

Individual difference factors related to attributional style

Not all individuals who encounter a given stressor respond in the same way, and only some individuals that experienced stressful events succumb to depression. To account for these individual differences, it was suggested that attributions concerning failure were fundamental in determining the development of helplessness, and hence the ensuing depression (Abramson et al., 1978). Individuals were seen as differing on three appraisal dimensions related to *locus of control* so that helplessness would emerge as a response to particular appraisal combinations. When individuals fail in reaching their goals, they frequently ask themselves why this occurred. They make appraisals of the situation and then form attributions concerning their failure. These attributions can be internal ('I'm not very good at writing exams') or external ('Professors ask the dumbest questions, and so I don't do well on exams'), they can be stable or unstable ('I'm never any good at writing exams' versus 'At times, I'm not very good at writing exams'), and they can be specific or global ('I'm not very good at writing math exams' versus 'I'm not good at writing any exams'). Individuals who make internal, stable, global attributions regarding their failure will have negative expectations of the future and may have broad feelings of inadequacy and poor self-esteem, which culminate in feelings of helplessness that favor the evolution of depressive disorders.

Most cognitive perspectives of depression have taken the view that depressive disorders stem from negative appraisals and dysfunctional patterns of thinking about life events. Many factors may contribute to the evolution of dysfunctional ways of thinking, including early experiences that shape cognitive styles. For instance, emotional maltreatment and negative inferential feedback (i.e., the tendency to attribute negative events to stable and widespread causes) can create schemas that influence how individuals respond to stressful events (Alloy et al., 2008). These responses lead to inappropriate inferences being drawn regarding the causes of events, attributes of the self (e.g., self-worth), and the consequences of these events on an individual's future. A meta-analysis of prospective studies indicated that factors related to cognitive theories of depression, notably dysfunctional attitudes and negative emotionality, predicted the onset of major depressive disorder (Fu et al., 2021).

Perhaps because depressed patients often describe themselves as feeling helpless and their situation as hopeless, the learned helplessness model was widely adopted in the psychological and psychiatric literature as being fundamental to the emergence of depression. The alternative, specifically that feeling helpless was a symptom of depression but did not necessarily act as a causal agent, seemed to receive only limited attention. To be sure, stressful events of an uncontrollable nature could lead to helplessness and hence promote depressive illness, but it is equally likely that feelings of helplessness represent one of the early symptoms associated with depression or that helplessness was more readily induced by stressors among depressed individuals or those with subclinical levels of depression.

Neurochemical perspectives on stressor-provoked behavioral disturbances

Depression is a complex mood state that we sometimes think of as being a uniquely human condition, and so one might wonder whether it is possible to have an animal model of such a disorder, and if so, then what are the requirements for such a model? It can be argued that mice and rats don't have the same feelings that humans do, and if they did, then they wouldn't necessarily be governed by cognitions like those associated with depression in humans. At the same time, are these complex processes really necessary for depression to occur? Isn't it possible that certain symptoms or biological processes related to depression can readily be recapitulated in animal models? When piglets are separated from their moms, they become exceptionally distressed, and they seem to show signs of depression; the momma pig likewise undergoes considerable distress, and she too shows behavioral changes that look a lot like depression. The same thing seems to happen in rodents, but it might seem a bit less obvious as their vocalizations are ultrasonic and so we don't hear their distress. Although we can't be certain whether the behavior of these critters is akin to our own, several animal models were developed that seemed to recapitulate many of the characteristics of human depression and were affected by antidepressant drugs.

Animal models of psychopathology

It has frequently been acknowledged that human psychological disorders are not fully captured through animal models. Do animals feel shame and humiliation as humans do? Is there self-stigma among animals with certain illnesses? Are animals ever hopeful about the future (and do they even know there is a future)? Despite these questions, most researchers agree on the minimum criteria for an animal model to be considered valid. Of course, just because criteria have been provided to ensure a model's validity doesn't necessarily mean that the model is valid. In an odd sort of way, it's like a jury trial. Because a jury finds a defendant not guilty, this doesn't mean that that defendant is actually innocent. It's not perfect, but it's the best we've got.

Animal models must resemble the human condition in several respects (Anisman & Matheson, 2005): (a) there should be similarity in the symptom profile presented (face validity); (b) treatments effective in the amelioration or attenuation of symptoms in humans should be effective in animal models, and conversely those treatments that are ineffective in attenuating the human disorder should not be effective in an animal model (predictive validity); (c) those events or stimuli that provoke the pathology in humans should be effective in eliciting the symptoms in animals (etiological validity); and finally, (d) the human and animal models ought to involve similar biological processes (construct validity).

These fundamental principles are certainly straightforward. However, numerous obstacles need to be overcome to meet these criteria. For example, in some instances, such as autism spectrum disorder, we don't know which brain processes are involved or what treatments might be effective, and hence meeting these criteria may be near impossible. Thus, creating a sufficiently good animal model for some disorders has proven to be difficult, and having these accepted broadly has not been easy.

A neurochemical alternative to learned helplessness

An alternative explanation for the behavioral interference induced by an uncontrollable stressor came from studies showing that stressful events provoke several brain neurochemical changes, some of which are aligned with the processes that are thought to subserve depression. When confronted by a stressor, animals ordinarily emit species-specific defensive responses to contend with this challenge. Concurrently, as described earlier, a sequence of neurochemical changes is provoked (e.g., including the altered activity of several neurotransmitters, hormones, neurotrophins, and inflammatory factors) to facilitate adaptive behavioral responses, or to maintain the integrity of the biological processes necessary for survival. Essentially, coping with stressors is shared between behavioral, cognitive, and neurochemical processes. However, when behavioral and cognitive methods to deal with stressors are unavailable or ineffective (i.e., in response to an uncontrollable stressor), then the burden of coping rests on neurochemical processes. This may result in excessive utilization of certain neurotransmitters (e.g., serotonin), ultimately provoking a decline of the levels and altered receptor functioning, rendering animals less able to deal with further stressors, and favoring the emergence of behavioral disturbances. Concurrently, neurotrophin levels may be diminished and inflammatory processes elevated, which could promote depressive features. In essence, the behavioral interference elicited by uncontrollable stressors was attributed to disturbed brain processes that, in turn, affect behavioral and cognitive functioning (Anisman et al., 2018).

In line with this perspective, pharmacological treatments that reduced NE, DA, and/or 5-HT functioning mimicked the behavioral effects of inescapable stressors among animals that had not been stressed (i.e., these drugs disrupted escape performance, just as an uncontrollable stressor had this effect). Furthermore, drug treatments that were effective in treating human depression (e.g., SSRIs) were effective in attenuating the pharmacologically induced behavioral disturbances (Anisman et al., 2008). Although this is certainly consistent with an animal model and speaks to their validity, several drugs known to be *in*effective as antidepressants (e.g., the anticholinergic, scopolamine, and the dopamine precursor, l-DOPA) diminished the adverse effects of uncontrollable stressors. What these data tell us is that assessing rats or mice in an escape test after exposure to an uncontrollable stressor might, in fact, not be a valid model of depression. Instead, the procedure might be useful to *screen* which drugs could potentially (although not necessarily) be effective as antidepressant agents and which might be ineffective to this end. Essentially, drugs that eliminate the behavioral disturbance might turn out to be effective antidepressants, whereas those that do not attenuate the behavioral disturbance will be ineffective. Other behavioral tests, however, may be more useful to assess the influence of uncontrollable stressors. For instance, the anhedonic effects of stressors can be assessed by evaluating whether animals will engage in rewarding behaviors after they have been stressed (consuming ordinarily preferred snacks or responding for rewarding electrical brain stimulation), and one can evaluate an animal's cognitive abilities in different types of problem-solving tests. Responding to otherwise rewarding stimuli is more in line with human depression than is escaping from an aversive stimulus. That said, there's really no way to get around the fact that what we assume reflects depression in animals might not actually be akin to that seen in humans. Accordingly, these paradigms may be informative with respect to the actions of stressors, but they might not reflect the processes aligned with depressive disorders. Nonetheless, when the data from animal and human studies line up with one another, they can provide essential clues regarding the processes by which illnesses emerge and how they can potentially be treated.

The effects of acute and chronic stressors, as we saw earlier, yield very different outcomes, depending on the characteristics of the stressor. Although severe events can promote depression (e.g., in response to the loss of a child or an intimate partner), chronic stressor experiences are more aligned with most diseases in humans. Studies in rodents indicated that relatively mild stressors that varied over days promoted a depressive-like condition. Numerous studies have supported this contention and it was maintained that this approach met the conditions necessary for a valid animal model of depression (Willner, 2016). The effectiveness of chronic unpredictable mild stress in promoting a depressive profile varies with the strain of animal used and is subject to between-laboratory differences based on the specific test protocols used (Antoniuk et al., 2019). As a result, the reliability of the procedure is highly variable across laboratories and there have been reports maintaining that this effect was not especially reliable. However, exposure to a series of different stressors that were more intense generally produced greater behavioral disturbances.

When a stressor persists for too long, and especially if the stressor experiences vary over days, the demands placed on adaptive biological systems may become excessive, and as a result the effectiveness of several neurobiological systems may be compromised, or secondary neurobiological changes might develop (allostatic overload). Consequently, adverse effects may develop, including the provocation of mood disorders, neurodegenerative processes, inflammatory immune-related pathologies, diabetes, cardiovascular disease, and the progression of certain types of cancer (Anisman & Kusnecov, 2022).

Neurochemical explanations of depressive disorders

Basic perspectives and difficulties

As stressors elicit numerous neurobiological changes, any of which might contribute to pathology, uncovering the specific neurochemical mechanisms subserving stress-related illnesses is challenging. This is particularly the case in clinical depression as it involves numerous brain regions and biochemical factors that vary with sex (Labonté et al., 2017). As described at the outset of this chapter, even among individuals diagnosed with a particular form of depression, vastly different symptoms might be present, and the efficacy of treatment strategies can vary appreciably, potentially signaling the involvement of diverse neurobiological processes. One gets the sense that we're dealing with several disorders that share common features, namely that the individual is unhappy or doesn't find life as pleasurable as it once was. Diverse forms of depression or the individual differences that are often apparent may involve varied mechanisms, and the specific features of the illness might provide indications that point to the possible efficacy of therapeutic strategies.

Determining the biological substrates of mental illness

The research methods used to define the biological processes associated with depression have included:

1. animal models in which the biochemical effects of stressors are determined, coupled with analyses of the effects of pharmacological treatments in attenuating stressor-induced behaviors reminiscent of depression;

2.   pharmacological studies in humans that assessed the effectiveness of antidepressant drugs with presumed neurochemical actions, or those that compared the relative effectiveness of different treatments;

3.   evaluation of the hormone and neurochemical factors in blood and cerebrospinal fluid in depressed versus nondepressed individuals;

4.   imaging studies (e.g., PET, fMRI) to determine functional changes in specific brain regions in patients versus healthy controls (by assessing either blood flow indicative of cellular activity in certain brain regions, or the activity or density of particular neurotransmitter receptors);

5.   analyses of brain chemicals and receptors in postmortem tissues obtained from depressed individuals who had died by suicide in comparison to those that had not been depressed and had died through causes other than suicide;

6.   genetic analyses related to depression that comprise whole genome or epigenome analyses to determine multiple genes (or altered gene expression) associated with illness or identification of the polymorphisms that might be uniquely associated with the illness.

Remarkable elegance has been brought to many studies, and each approach has merit, especially when this body of research is considered as a whole. These studies have made it clear that several organismic variables (age, sex, genetic factors) and experiential factors (ongoing stressors, previous stressful experiences) contribute to the provocation and maintenance of depression, as well as its frequent recurrence following successful treatment. Likewise, stressor-provoked neurochemical changes, some of which may be aligned with depression, might vary across individuals, possibly accounting for the diversity reported concerning the efficacy of treatments.

Monoamine variations associated with depression

To varying degrees, NE, DA, and 5-HT had been implicated in the etiology of depression or the treatment of this disorder, and for some time 5-HT functioning was the most widely studied. In large measure, the focus on these neurotransmitters came about because antidepressant medications that seemed to provide some benefits acted on these neurotransmitters as well as because of the effects of stressors on their functioning.

Serotonin

Stressors provoke marked changes of 5-HT levels and turnover, as well as various 5-HT receptor subtypes that seem to be linked to behavioral impairments in rodents that are thought to reflect depressive symptoms. Moreover, SSRIs are effective in eliminating many stressor-induced behavioral disturbances in animal models and in some human patients. The effectiveness of SSRIs may be derived, at least in part, by the increase of 5-HT at the synapse that is promoted by reuptake being inhibited, and owing to effects on specific 5-HT receptor subtypes. But as we'll see, SSRIs affect other biological processes, such as neurotrophins, which may be responsible for the benefits of the drug treatment. The neurotrophin changes occur gradually, thus accounting for the need to treat patients over several weeks before therapeutic actions are obtained (Duman et al., 2016).

Effectiveness of pharmacotherapy in treating depression

Despite the many advances that have been made in determining which factors cause depressive symptoms, we're still a long way from developing effective treatment strategies. In the late 1980s, with the broad introduction of SSRIs, the media were littered with reports of this new class of miracle drugs. But their effectiveness hasn't been all that it was cracked up to be. At present, about 50-60% of patients are successfully treated with these drugs, which is not all that impressive considering that there is about a 20-30% placebo response. Moreover, even when a positive response is obtained, depression may not be entirely ameliorated as residual symptoms frequently persist, and the recurrence of illness is exceptionally high (exceeding 50% over five years).

The limited effectiveness of these compounds and others like them does not speak well for a model of depression that focuses exclusively on 5-HT, nor on the success of 'big pharma' in bringing effective treatments to market. These limitations, coupled with the realization that depressive disorders likely involve numerous biological factors, prompted multi-targeted approaches in the treatment of depressive disorders. Contrary to earlier approaches that focused on increasingly more 'specific' treatments hoping to limit side effects, greater beneficial effects could be obtained from drug combinations that affected several neurotransmitters. Indeed, the assiduous use of drug combinations can lead to markedly improved treatment responses, so much so that the positive outcomes in treating depression could be doubled (Blier, 2016).

5-HT receptors in humans: imaging, binding, and postmortem analyses

In assessing the relation between neurotransmitter and pathological states it is important not only to assess the turnover and utilization of transmitters but also to determine receptor functioning. Of the 5-HT receptors that have been identified, several have been implicated in mediating depressive disorders (Yohn et al., 2017). While there have been some inconsistencies across studies, molecular, imaging, postmortem analyses, and pharmacological studies indicated that depressive illness was accompanied by elevated 5-HT1A and 5-HT1B *autoreceptors* in various brain regions, thereby causing diminished 5-HT release (Nautiyal & Hen, 2017). The functioning of these receptors was subject to genetic influences (Albert et al., 2019) and might be instigated by epigenetic changes related to stressor experiences.

It similarly appeared that 5-HT2A receptors may be altered in depression, and the functions of these receptors in depression might be functionally distinguishable from those of others. Some of these receptors may be more aligned with anxiety or they may be linked to neurovegetative features of the illness. Still others may be fundamental in providing the plasticity and flexibility needed to overcome the impact of adversity (Carhart-Harris & Nutt, 2017). Several studies had suggested that increased 5-HT2A binding in the dorsolateral prefrontal cortex was particularly evident among patients with strong feelings of pessimism and hopelessness.

Differences in receptor subtypes have been reported with other behavioral variables associated with depression, such as hostility or aggressiveness. It was similarly suggested that dysfunctional connectivity profiles that were apparent in several brain regions (insula, orbitofrontal cortex, ventromedial prefrontal cortex, and several subcortical areas) were related to specific clinical symptoms, such as feelings of sadness, hopelessness, helplessness, anhedonia, and fatigue or low energy (Drysdale et al., 2017). At the same time, it ought to be kept in mind that 5-HT interacts with other neurotransmitters that could affect specific symptoms of depression, which may be why it is so difficult to identify a one-to-one correspondence between 5-HT receptors and the diverse characteristics of depressive disorders.

What do studies of brains from depressed suicides really tell us?

Several studies assessed differences in brain chemistry or morphology in depressed individuals who died by suicide and that of non-depressed individuals who died of causes other than suicide. Among other things, these studies revealed that the individuals who had been depressed displayed altered 5-HT and CRH receptor subtypes and epigenetic changes may have contributed to some of these outcomes. Such studies have been difficult to conduct, and in some instances the value of the data might have been compromised by procedural factors. In considering the findings from these postmortem analyses several questions need to be addressed. (1) Were the depressed individuals who died by suicide really depressed or did they suffer from something else? Although depression and suicide have been linked, numerous other factors have been associated with suicide. These include alcohol/drug use, schizophrenia, incurable illness, relationship issues, financial stressors, bullying at school or work, severe loss (e.g., of a partner or child), and shame (related, for instance, to job loss or relationship dissolution). (2) What drugs had the person been taking that could have contaminated the biochemical analyses? (3) Were the non-depressed controls really not depressed, especially as depression often goes undiagnosed? (4) What was life like for individuals prior to death (was death prolonged or painful), and could these factors have affected brain functioning? (5) Was the tissue obtained viable, especially if the postmortem delay in getting tissue may have been lengthy? (6) Was the depressed person who died by suicide generally representative of depressed patients (e.g., did they exhibit impulsiveness that might not be evident in others)? (7) Could thoughts or emotions immediately preceding the actual suicide have affected neurochemical and/or receptor functioning? So, what do studies of this sort tell us? They certainly have the potential to be informative but restricting analyses to a history of depression without considering a broad set of other factors limits the usefulness of this approach.

The 5-HT transporter

Let's now turn to yet another aspect of 5-HT functioning that might be pivotal in the depressive process. Following its release, 5-HT is taken up into the presynaptic neuron through a reuptake process that involves the 5-HT transporter (5-HTT). The serotonin reuptake inhibitors, as the name indicates, have the effect of inhibiting reuptake, thereby allowing 5-HT to remain in the synaptic cleft longer. It was maintained that depression might be caused by the dysfunction of endogenous processes associated with reuptake of this transmitter.

Genetic links between serotonin functioning and depression in humans

Animal models have increasingly focused on the analysis of stressor effects on behavioral outputs in vulnerable strains of mice or those with a genetic deletion (knockout) or insertion (transgenic) of genes. Using these approaches it was observed that the benefits of antidepressant drugs were absent in mice genetically engineered to lack the serotonin transporter (Nackenoff et al., 2016). Aside from the 5-HTT transporter, a polymorphism was found on the gene controlling the enzyme tryptophan hydroxylase-2, which is fundamental in 5-HT synthesis. If, as a result of a genetic mutation, this enzyme wasn't working properly, then the availability of 5-HT would be reduced and depression might ensue, and could also diminish SSRI responsiveness.

Much excitement had been generated with reports that depression and suicidality were more frequent among individuals carrying particular alleles of the 5-HTT gene. The alleles in this case can be either short or long (a gene can be shortened because part of it has been deleted, or it can be long because nucleotides have been added). Those individuals carrying the short form of the 5-HTT promoter on one or both alleles were at greater risk of depression than those individuals who were homozygous for the long allele (i.e., they have long form of the gene on both alleles) provided that they had encountered major life stressors, early-life trauma, or experienced a stressful family environment (Caspi et al., 2003). In effect, genetic constitution might dispose individuals to depression because of greater sensitivity or reactivity to environmental stressors, but simply having a particular gene doesn't necessarily condemn an individual to depressive illnesses unless experiential triggers are present.

Unfortunately, following the initial reports of this 5-HTT gene x environment interaction, many studies failed to replicate these findings consistently. A report that included 31 independent data sets did not support the position that carrying the short 5-HTT allele conferred increased vulnerability to depression in the context of stressor experiences irrespective of when these were encountered (Culverhouse et al., 2018). This doesn't imply that other aspects of the 5-HTT gene (unrelated to the short and long alleles) do not interact with stressors in promoting depression. For instance, early-life adverse experiences could cause epigenetic changes of the

5-HTT gene thereby favoring later depression, but as so often occurs, when findings in one domain appear not to have been productive, further efforts may be abandoned (the proverbial baby being thrown out with the bathwater).

Dopamine

As DA plays an integral role in reward processes and depressive disorders are frequently characterized by anhedonia, it was reasonable to hypothesize that DA would be intimately related to this illness. Perhaps because drugs that affect DA (e.g., l-DOPA) did not act as an effective antidepressant, or because DA was overshadowed by 5-HT being presumed to be the main culprit of depression, analyses of DA in depression were sidelined. Relatively recent therapeutic strategies that incorporated DA functioning in the treatment of this disorder have yielded positive outcomes, thus the presumed involvement of DA in depression has been rejuvenated (see Chapter 13). Indeed, stressors influence DA functioning in brain regions associated with reward processes, notably those that involve the midbrain circuitry consisting of the ventral tegmental (VTA) and nucleus accumbens. Moreover, manipulations that increased DA functioning diminished the impact of stressors on depressive-like behaviors in animal models, and such stressor effects could potentially have epigenetic effects that affected reward pathways (e.g., Koo et al., 2019).

The neural circuits that include the ventral tegmentum and nucleus accumbens may be involved in eliciting depressive behaviors that vary with the nature of the environmental triggers encountered. While anhedonia may stem from dysfunction of the ventral tegmental – nucleus accumbens pathway, coping responses elicited in response to stressors may be related to the pathway between the ventral tegmentum and the prefrontal cortex (Bai et al., 2017). Speaking to the complexity of dopamine involvement in depressive disorders, variations within these pathways may be modulated by CRH, glucocorticoid functioning, opioid receptors, and BDNF, and may be related to the programming of sex hormones during prenatal development.

Although the mesolimbic dopamine circuit was most often tied to reward processes, a somewhat different view was generated by the finding that both stressors and rewarding stimuli affected nucleus accumbens DA release. Specifically, the view was offered that the nucleus accumbens responds to changes in environmental stimuli, irrespective of the valence of this change. Dopamine activity within this pathway might make stimuli more salient, thereby readying other systems for something important that is happening or is about to happen. Moreover, in considering the actions of dopamine it is important to distinguish between its action on liking (i.e., the pleasurable derived from reward) and wanting (incentive salience, which refers to the motivation for reward that is driven by learned associations) (Berridge & Robinson, 2016). Thus, appreciation of the role of dopamine in depressive disorders requires broad analyses of the many factors that encompass the promotion of diseases (Douma & de Kloet, 2020).

Corticotropin-releasing hormone (CRH) and cortisol

Depressive disorders have been associated with variations of several aspects of HPA functioning. Glucocorticoid-related polymorphisms have been identified that are germane to depressive disorders. Individuals with a polymorphism related to glucocorticoid resistance (i.e., diminished responsiveness to cortisol) were at increased risk of developing a depressive disorder and a diminished clinical response to antidepressant medication. As well, prior to the presentation of clinical symptoms, HPA abnormalities were present among genetic relatives of depressed patients (Holsboer & Ising, 2010). As a result, basal cortisol functioning or the glucocorticoid responses to pharmacological challenges could potentially serve as biomarkers for increased risk of illness. In addition, adverse events, especially those encountered in early life, can promote epigenetic changes of the FKBP5 gene that result in altered glucocorticoid signaling and the later development of depression. The FKBP5 epigenetic changes were not alone in predicting depression and changes on a gene coding for the serotonin transporter and for BDNF were also linked to depressive disorders (Park et al., 2019).

Like glucocorticoids, CRH might play a prominent role in depression. In this regard, stressors not only promote CRH variations associated with HPA functioning but affect CRH in limbic and cortical regions (Merali, Khan et al., 2004). In rodents, a CRH1 receptor antagonist could attenuate depressive signs stemming from a chronic mild stressor regimen (X.B. Wang et al., 2020), and in humans, elevated CRH was observed in the cerebrospinal fluid of depressed patients and in the frontopolar and the dorsomedial prefrontal cortex of depressed individuals who had died by suicide. The elevated CRH levels were accompanied by reduced mRNA expression of CRH1 receptors, possibly reflecting a compensatory down-regulation secondary to the sustained CRH elevation (Merali, Du et al., 2004). Although CRH2 receptor mRNA expression was not affected in this study, this receptor has been implicated in depression as well as in PTSD and anxiety disorders, possibly operating in conjunction with the functioning of 5-HT1A receptors (Neufeld-Cohen et al., 2012).

Several SNPs were identified involving the CRH1 gene that might be relevant to depression. One of these was associated with a diminished therapeutic response to SSRI treatment among anxious depressed patients (O'Connell et al., 2018). Thus, CRH and glucocorticoid receptor gene polymorphisms seem to be risk factors for depression and might predict the response to treatment. Given the integral role of these hormones in the stress response, it would be reasonable to predict that such interactions are intimately involved in depressive outcomes.

Pharmacological studies

Manipulations that increase CRH functioning can influence behavioral outputs reminiscent of anxiety and depression in animals, but progress regarding CRH as a pharmaceutical target for depression in humans has been limited (e.g., Holsboer & Ising, 2010). Administration of a CRH1 antagonist reduced the symptoms of depression in a relatively small study of depressed patients, and this treatment altered the depressive EEG sleep profile, with few side effects or disturbances of neuroendocrine functioning being evident. Several subsequent reports, however, did not reveal prominent effects of such treatments. It is probably short-sighted to assume that CRH manipulations would not affect depressive and anxiety states, or the development of substance use disorders, especially considering the many actions of this peptide in several brain regions (Spierling & Zorrilla, 2017). Indeed, CRH serves to integrate information from internal and external sources, which then instigate neurobiological and behavioral stress responses. Novel CRH processes have been identified that may be pertinent to the integration of biological systems that culminate in depression and anxiety and CRH may be a fundamental component that affects inflammatory processes implicated in the development of these disorders (Silberstein et al., 2021). Given the biochemical heterogeneity of depressive illnesses, it can be expected that not all patients would show a positive response to CRH manipulations. As such, the usefulness of this type of therapy may come down to finding biomarkers that reflect the nature of the biochemical disturbances in each individual and then tailoring treatment strategies accordingly.

CRH-AVP interactions

Arginine vasopressin (AVP), also referred to as vasopressin, is present in various brain regions in addition to the hypothalamus, where it can influence social behaviors and memory processes. The role of AVP in depression has largely been overshadowed by that of CRH, but the level of this hormone was reported to be elevated in the cerebrospinal fluid of depressed patients, in the plasma of melancholic (severe) depressed patients, and in several brain regions (e.g., the locus coeruleus and dorsomedial prefrontal cortex) of depressed individuals who died by suicide (Merali et al., 2006). Early-life adversity that favors the development of depression and anxiety was accompanied by disturbed social behaviors together with epigenetic changes of a gene coding for AVP (Bodden et al., 2017), and disturbed AVP and oxytocin functioning could align with social disturbances that might contribute to depression. There has been interest in assessing the effects of blocking AVP receptors in the treatment of depression. In rodents, this treatment had both anti-anxiety and antidepressant-like effects. Large-scale trials of AVP antagonists in humans have yet to be reported, although in small trials a positive effect was obtained with such a treatment, most prominently among individuals with high cortisol levels (Chaki, 2021).

An interesting perspective regarding the role of AVP in depression has come from studies in animals that assessed AVP changes that occurred in response to chronic stressors or with the passage of time following acute stressors (or challenge with a proinflammatory cytokine). Ordinarily, CRH is abundant within specific regions of the hypothalamus (the median eminence that rests at the base of the hypothalamus).

With the stressor or cytokine treatments, the storage of AVP increases greatly at this site. As a result, in response to subsequent stressors CRH and AVP are co-released, which synergistically stimulate ACTH release from the pituitary, and hence an exaggerated increase of adrenal corticosterone secretion (Tilders & Schmidt, 1999). In essence, neurosecretory neurons within the hypothalamus have the capacity to change for extended periods, and may consequently have long-term behavioral ramifications. This could explain how stressful events prime neural circuits so that later stressful experiences lead to depression. It isn't known whether the co-expression of these hormones normalizes after successful pharmacotherapy. However, if this normalization doesn't occur, it might account for why individuals tend to fall back into their depressive state upon later stressful encounters.

γ-aminobutyric acid (GABA) and glutamate

In rodents, chronic stressors have been associated with disturbed GABA activity within prefrontal cortex neural circuits (Czéh et al., 2018), being especially prominent in females. Dysfunction of this inhibitory neurotransmitter has been associated with numerous cognitive disturbances evident in depression and in other psychiatric disorders (Prévot & Sibille, 2021). Furthermore, variations of an enzyme involved in GABA synthesis, glutamic acid decarboxylase (GAD), were observed in the hippocampus and aspects of the prefrontal cortex of depressed suicidal patients.

It might be recalled that GABAA receptors comprise five subunits from a set of 19 subunits, and the specific combination of subunits determines how they behave in response to drug treatments such as benzodiazepines or alcohol. The possibility was raised that anxiety and depression elicited by stressors occurred owing to variations of these subunits and hence the composition of the GABAA receptors. Consistent with this perspective, in some brain regions the mRNA expression of GABAA subunits may be up-regulated in association with major depression (Poulter, Du, et al., 2010). Furthermore, GABA-related genes in those who died by suicide were altered in several cortical and subcortical brain regions, including the prefrontal cortex and hippocampus. As these effects were evident among individuals who died by suicide irrespective of whether they had been depressed, they raise the possibility that GABA changes were related to suicide (or antecedents of suicide) rather than to depression itself (Sequeira et al., 2009).

Beyond differences of GABA subunit expression in depression, it appeared that GABAA subunit expression 'patterns' were disturbed among depressed individuals who died by suicide (Poulter, Du et al., 2010). Among non-depressed individuals who had died suddenly of causes unrelated to suicide, the expression of the different GABAA subunits was highly correlated in several brain regions, such as the frontopolar cortex, hippocampus, and amygdala. That is, changes of mRNA expression of a particular subunit were matched by similar changes in the expression of other subunits. It seems as if some process orchestrates these subunits to react synchronously. In contrast, among the depressed individuals who died by suicide, the inter-relationships between the GABAA subunits were considerably altered, seeming to be in disarray. It was provisionally suggested that coordination between these subunits might be essential for the behaviour of neural networks and for the neuronal rhythms that ordinarily occur in various brain regions (Poulter et al., 2010; Anisman et al., 2012).

Another perspective of depression: the inflexible brain

An interesting perspective was offered in which depression was thought to be associated with increased connections between many brain regions (Leuchter et al., 2012). It could be argued that for efficient brain functioning, including proper appraisals, decision-making, coping responses, and the emergence of mood changes, synchronous activity across brain regions is necessary. At the same time, selectivity is necessary concerning the interconnections that are formed. What this means is that it might not always be advantageous to have too many associations in our memory circuits, since the resulting cognitive and emotional associations might be counterproductive. In a sense, this is what one sees with symptoms such as rumination, where the person persists in negative thinking, each cognitive association takes them to a distressing place, and the repetition consolidates the pathway.

Central to appraisal and coping was the ability to maintain flexibility and to be able to move from one strategy to another as the situation demands. Essentially, the depressed individuals' brain networks, particularly within the prefrontal cortex, may have lost their selectivity and their flexibility in altering connections, and are consequently less able to adapt to changes that are necessary to deal with stressors. Since GABA plays a pivotal role in inhibiting the messages between neurons, variations of the subunit coordination might be intricately involved in limiting unwanted connections and in maintaining flexibility.

As much as the data in animals have supported the involvement of GABA and its receptors in stressor-provoked depression, it may be more appropriate to consider inhibitory actions of GABA conjointly with the excitatory functions of glutamate (Fogaça & Duman, 2019). It has become apparent that dysfunction of this excitatory neurotransmitter may contribute to the production of depressive disorders brought about by stressor experiences. These actions may arise because elevated glutamate release may affect synaptic plasticity and dendritic remodeling within both limbic and cortical brain regions (Duman et al., 2019), and glutamate variations in the prefrontal and anterior cingulate cortex were tied to the severity of depression (Li et al., 2019). In fact, early-life stressors that induce depression in adulthood might stem from persistent variations of glutamate functioning (Averill et al., 2020).

Consistent with the involvement of glutamate in depressive disorders, repeated antidepressant treatments limited the glutamate changes ordinarily elicited by an uncontrollable stressor. It is especially significant that the NMDA glutamate receptor antagonist ketamine rapidly diminishes depression and suicidality even among treatment-resistant patients. In Chapter 13 we'll discuss ketamine effects on depression in greater detail along with the recent use of other psychedelic agents (e.g., LSD, psilocybin) in the treatment of severe depressive disorder.

Neurotrophins in depression

While the search for neurotransmitters associated with depression was at center stage for decades, the fact that drug treatments had limited effects in alleviating the disorder didn't sit right with these traditional perspectives. This was reinforced by repeated reports that structural and functional brain changes, including reduced hippocampal and amygdala volume, were associated with depressive illness. The extent of the reductions was particularly marked among patients who experienced repeated or lengthy depressive episodes and was lower in non-remitted patients than among those in remission (Nolan et al., 2020). Moreover, just as depressive illness could be influenced by early-life stressful experiences, grey matter volume (reflecting neural cell bodies) within cortical brain regions was associated with such events, depending on the nature of the maltreatment experienced (physical vs. emotional neglect vs. both). Genetic influences, previous distressing events, or corticoid variations in response to chronic strain contribute to this outcome, although the possibility cannot be excluded that pre-existing hippocampal disturbances can act as a risk factor for depression. Significantly, reduced hippocampal volume was not unique to depression, having been reported in patients with schizophrenia. Thus, the hippocampal changes might represent a risk factor for a variety of mental illnesses, which is not surprising given the fundamental role of the hippocampus in numerous psychological processes. With this knowledge, research turned to the processes that might contribute to the altered brain features.

Brain-derived neurotrophic factor (BDNF)

Factors that undermine the survival of neurons and limit the growth of new neurons and synapses (neurogenesis) might be fundamental in depressive illnesses. Neurotrophins, such as BDNF, fibroblast growth factor-2 (FGF-2), and vascular endothelial growth factor (VEGF) were reduced in several limbic brain regions of stressed rodents. Likewise, BDNF expression and protein levels and those of its receptor (tyrosine kinase B; TrkB) were lower within the hippocampus and prefrontal cortex of individuals who died by suicide than in age- and sex-matched controls. The effects of stressors in reducing hippocampal BDNF in rodents were linked to epigenetic changes, and major depression in humans was similarly linked to epigenetic factors involving genes that code for BDNF (Park et al., 2019).

Consistent with the perspective linking BDNF and depression, the positive effects of several antidepressants (and electroconvulsive shock) in animal models were accompanied by elevated hippocampal neurogenesis and prevention of the reduced hippocampal cell proliferation ordinarily induced by stressors. Added to this, antidepressants provoked elevated levels of BDNF at several brain sites, whereas the positive effects of an antidepressant were diminished among mice with targeted deletion of genes for BDNF (Monteggia et al., 2007). Based on such findings the view emerged that antidepressants had their beneficial effects by increasing BDNF. These changes could take several days or weeks to develop, which could account for the lag between antidepressant treatments and the eventual decline of depressive symptoms. The effects of the glutamate antagonist ketamine in alleviating depression may similarly come about by altering synaptic plasticity and by attenuating the synaptic disturbances ordinarily provoked by stressors but these actions occur rapidly so that a lag does not occur between treatment and the antidepressant action (Duman et al., 2016).

In addition to the brain BDNF variations, concentrations of BDNF in blood serum were reduced in depressed patients and were inversely related to the degree of clinical impairment (Emon et al., 2020). The lower BDNF levels were particularly notable in depressed patients who presented with anxiety, those with recurrent depressive episodes, and in patients who were the most suicidal. Predictably, serum BDNF levels increased with clinical improvement following antidepressant treatment, but not in patients who did not show clinical improvement (Lee & Kim, 2008). While BDNF present in blood may not reflect BDNF functioning in the brain, it was hoped that it could represent a biomarker for depression. To some extent, this relationship was observed, although reduced BDNF in blood was not reliably associated with depression, did not always vary as a function of depression severity, and was unrelated to certain depressive symptoms. As well, when antidepressant treatment (e.g., using the SSRI sertraline) yielded positive effects, these were not consistently accompanied by elevated BDNF levels. So, while changes of hippocampal BDNF may be associated with depression, it is less certain whether circulating BDNF is useful as a marker of depressive illnesses.

BDNF polymorphisms

Supporting BDNF involvement in depression, a meta-analysis that included 31 studies revealed that the link between stressful events and depression was moderated by the presence of a BDNF polymorphism (Zhao et al., 2018). As well, a prospective study of at-risk adolescents indicated that depression was elevated among those with the polymorphism who also displayed elevated morning cortisol levels (Goodyer et al., 2010). Moreover, the presence of a polymorphism related to genes for BDNF and 5-HT reuptake in young people was accompanied by elevated rumination following life stressor experiences and greater incidence of depression (Scaini et al., 2021). These actions may come about because these polymorphisms moderate the actions of stressors. The presence of the BDNF mutation not only predicted the occurrence of depression in relation to general life stressors but was accompanied by increased vulnerability to depression following a stroke. It seems that the presence of genetic dispositions related to BDNF may increase the risk of depressive illness associated with a variety of challenges.

Links between early-life events, SNPs, and depression

Adverse childhood experiences (ACEs) are associated with the increased occurrence of adult depression, which might be related to BDNF variations. Maternal deprivation in female rhesus macaques was associated with reduced plasma BDNF levels, accompanied by behavioral passivity, possibly reflecting a depressive profile. These effects could be attenuated if monkeys were reared by peers, but this positive outcome was least apparent if they carried the BDNF polymorphism. Consistent with these findings, extended separation of rat pups from their mother resulted in signs of depression that were accompanied by growth factor changes, including reduced BDNF in the amygdala and the hippocampus. There is evidence indicating that early-life adverse experiences in humans, especially in the presence of the BDNF polymorphism, have important implications for depression in adulthood. The negative consequences of early-life adversities in relation to depression were greater among individuals carrying the BDNF polymorphism (Zhao et al., 2018), as was the tendency toward negative affectivity and biases towards recalling negative stimuli. Paralleling some of the behavioral changes, the presence of childhood adversity coupled with this polymorphism was associated with low grey matter within the subgenual anterior cingulate cortex, but not in other brain regions that have been implicated in depression (the hippocampus, prefrontal cortex). This raised the possibility that this region might serve as a mechanistic link between stressful early-life experiences, the BDNF polymorphism, and adult depression (Gerritsen et al., 2011). Since the same interactions were apparent among individuals with schizophrenia, this combination may be aligned with general psychological dysfunction rather than being uniquely tied to depression.

Fibroblast growth factor-2

Of the various growth factors, BDNF has been the most studied link to depression, but fibroblast growth factor-2 (FGF-2) may also play a role in this condition. Stressors disturb FGF-2 functioning, and in depressed individuals, FGF-2 and its receptors are reduced in limbic brain regions, including the prefrontal cortex (Turner et al., 2012). It seems that the FGF system might contribute to the actions of SSRIs, as the reduction of FGF transcripts was attenuated in those individuals who had been receiving antidepressant medication.

Commensurate with a role for FGF-2 in depression, antidepressant treatments effectively increased the levels of this growth factor in both animals and humans. In addition, the administration of FGF-2 directly into the brain of rodents attenuated behavioral disturbances that were associated with stressors, whereas an FGF-2 antagonist abolished the positive behavioral effects of antidepressant treatment in attenuating the effects of stressors (Elsayed et al., 2012). Indeed, the presence of FGF-2 is necessary for the beneficial effects of antidepressants to emerge (Simard et al., 2018). It remains to be determined how FGF-2 comes to produce its antidepressant effects, although it could involve changes in glutamate or the excitatory synapses in brain regions such as the prefrontal cortex, and there is reason to suppose that FGF-2 influences hippocampal microglia that contribute to inflammatory processes linked to depression (e.g., Tang et al., 2018).

Vascular endothelial growth factor (VEGF)

Like other growth factors, VEGF serves in multiple capacities, being best known for its role in the creation of new blood vessels during embryonic development, as well as in response to injury. This growth factor is influenced by stressors and may promote the development of depressive illnesses. Chronic social instability in rodents provoked depressive-like behaviors that were accompanied by alterations of VEGF mRNA in the amygdala and hypothalamus, and these actions could be attenuated by antidepressant treatments (Nowacka-Chmielewska et al., 2017). Likewise, in both animal models and depressed humans, VEGF was diminished in the hippocampus and prefrontal cortex. The reduced VEGF, like BDNF, could be reversed by standard antidepressant treatments. These growth factors are dependent on one another so that the presence of VEGF is needed for BDNF to provide antidepressant actions and BDNF is needed for VEGF to have its positive effects (Deyama et al., 2019). Similarly, VEGF reductions may cooperate with inflammatory cytokines in promoting depressive behaviors in rodents. Overall, these findings are consistent with a role for VEGF in stressor-provoked depression, but this neurotrophin has not been assessed extensively, thus the influence of other factors (e.g., early-life experiences, coping) on these actions is uncertain.

Inflammatory processes associated with depression

Immune activation and immune signaling molecules (cytokines) significantly increased HPA activity and affected the turnover of brain monoamines. As the effects of these cytokines on central neuroendocrine and neurotransmitter processes are remarkably like those elicited by stressors, the view was advanced that the brain translates inflammatory activation much as it interprets psychological and physical stressors. As such, activation of the inflammatory immune system may contribute to the development of depressive illness, as well as other neurological conditions (Miller & Raison, 2016). The cytokine alterations that affect depression may be of peripheral origin, although their entry to the brain may be somewhat limited. Microglia within the brain can likewise release cytokines that could influence depression and other disorders.

Promotion of depression in animal models

Cytokines had primarily been thought of as signaling molecules of the immune system and attempts to link cytokines and depression had typically considered the impact of peripheral inflammatory changes. However, as we've seen, cytokines are endogenously expressed in the brain, where they are synthesized by microglia. These brain cytokines are increased following traumatic head injury, stroke, seizure, bacterial endotoxins, and stressors (Anisman et al., 2018). Repeated social defeat likewise increased immune receptors (TLR2 and TLR4) within the brain, but when these receptors were deleted, anxiety otherwise elicited by the stressor was not apparent and when this occurred in the prefrontal cortex, depression features were also diminished (Nie et al., 2021). Predictably, the depressive-like behaviors elicited by a chronic stressor were enhanced by cytokine challenges, whereas these outcomes were attenuated in mice in which IL-1 receptors in the hippocampus were knocked out (Goshen et al., 2008).

In addition to the stressor-like neurochemical changes elicited by cytokines, animals treated with proinflammatory cytokines or immune activating agents display a depressive-like behavioral profile, including anhedonia and disrupted social interaction. These treatments give rise to a constellation of symptoms, collectively referred to as 'sickness behaviors' (e.g., anorexia, fatigue, reduced motor activity), that in some respects are reminiscent of the neurovegetative features comprising atypical depression, which could be attenuated by chronic antidepressant treatments (Dantzer et al., 2011). These behavioral changes can be exacerbated by stressors, raising the possibility that stressors and inflammatory immune activation synergistically promote depressive disorders (Anisman et al., 2018). It seems, however, that the sickness behavior and the depressive-like outcomes can be distinguished from one another in several respects, and antidepressants preferentially influence the affective impact of cytokines relative to the sickness symptoms.

Promotion of depression in humans

Several lines of research pointed to a role for the inflammatory immune system in the provocation of depressive disorders in humans. Some of the findings came from studies showing that immune-related disorders, viruses, and common parasites were associated with increased levels of depressive illness. Furthermore, depressive illness was accompanied by an inflammatory response being mounted, reflected by elevated acute phase proteins, such as C-reactive protein. The data concerning brain cytokines in humans in relation to depression are limited, but it was reported that among teenage individuals who died by suicide, mRNA and protein expression levels of IL-1β, IL-6, and TNF-α were increased in the frontopolar cortex relative to normal controls. However, some individuals who died by suicide had been diagnosed with conditions other than depression, and so the cytokine variations likely were related to suicide rather than depression alone (Pandey et al., 2011).

It is particularly significant that major depressive disorder was associated with elevated levels of inflammation and reduced volume of the hippocampus and prefrontal cortex, which became progressively more pronounced with repeated depressive episodes (Belleau et al., 2019). These findings speak to the fact that stressors can interact with inflammatory factors in provoking damaging outcomes, and that these effects are manifested in the brain, just as they are within the peripheral immune system.

There have been reports that depression was accompanied by elevated blood levels of IL-6, TNF-α, and IFN-γ, and that levels normalized with antidepressant treatment, although this was not always observed. The failure of normalization might suggest that peripheral cytokine elevations could serve as markers for a disposition toward depressive disorders recurring. Essentially, the sustained cytokine elevations might be indicative of something still being amiss that could promote a further depressive episode. Therefore, it would be informative to know whether those with the continued cytokine elevations were the most likely to fall back into depression once pharmacological treatment for the illness was discontinued. The possibility shouldn't be ruled out that factors secondary to depressive illness (e.g., drug use, disturbed sleep and circadian rhythms, sleep, poor health-related behaviors, and weight changes) were responsible for the cytokine alterations, but otherwise have little to do with the provocation of the disorder.

Obesity can affect health through inflammatory processes

Typically, when we think of inflammatory factors we might have in mind infection, viral or bacterial insults, or various forms of injury. Numerous other factors that aren't immediately considered may be relevant to inflammatory processes. Aside from being linked to type 2 diabetes, heart disease, and some forms of cancer, obesity is a risk factor that was related to inflammation and depressive illness. Individuals with obesity were more likely to be depressed than average-weight people, possibly owing to issues related to stigma, shame, and bullying. As well, adipose tissue, particularly belly fat, is an exceptionally rich source of several cytokines and related factors. As a result, depression in overweight people might have to do with the greater release of cytokines from fat deposits. In this regard, a vicious cycle may exist in which adiposity contributes to depression, and this depression, in turn, may promote elevated eating (Shelton & Miller, 2011). Given the wide actions of inflammatory factors, it has been suggested that inflammatory factors related to adiposity may contribute to the high comorbidity that exists between depression and several physical illnesses.

Cytokines associated with depression under challenge conditions

Cytokines elevations within the brain may be promoted to facilitate healing of micro-damage, and depression is an unfortunate by-product of these processes. In response to head injury or strong stressors, an injury repair response may be initiated that comprises the release of neuroinflammatory factors from microglia. However, in high concentrations, these molecules could instigate other neurochemical effects or cytotoxicity that might provoke psychological disturbances, such as depression. Numerous studies have indeed linked the presence of inflammation and depression in adults, and an extensive systematic review indicated similar relations in youth (Toenders et al., 2021). Moreover, among depressed individuals, reduced functioning of brain reward systems and diminished anticipation of pleasure were accompanied by excessive activation of immune activity in peripheral blood cells (Costi et al., 2021).

Beyond the data indicating a correlation between inflammatory factors and depression, several studies in humans assessed the causal connection between immune activation and mood states. For instance, treatment with a low dose of a bacterial endotoxin (a component of certain forms of bacteria) that increased plasma TNF-α and IL-6 levels elicited a mildly depressed mood and a feeling of social disconnection. Likewise, triggering an inflammatory response using vaccines (e.g., for typhoid) promoted a depressive-like mood, lassitude, as well as fatigue, confusion, and impaired concentration that may have been related to altered neuronal activity within the anterior cingulate cortex (Harrison et al., 2009). Although the mild depressive-like symptoms elicited by an endotoxin were attenuated by subchronic pretreatment with the SSRI citalopram, the peripheral cytokine changes were not altered, suggesting that these cytokine variations were markers of depression, but were not direct modulators of mood state. Of course, this does not exclude the influence of antidepressant agents on brain inflammatory processes that can ameliorate mood disorders (Tomaz et al., 2020).

Inflammatory processes could influence features of depressive states that extend beyond cognitive and neurovegetative symptoms. The mild depressed mood and social disconnection and elevated IL-6 produced by a low dose of an endotoxin were exaggerated in participants who were put through a challenge that entailed social rejection (Eisenberger et al., 2010). These data are consistent with the view that the activation of inflammatory processes increases threat-related neural sensitivity to negative social experiences, which could favor the development of depressive features. Social stressors can increase proinflammatory cytokine activity, especially among individuals already experiencing social challenges (e.g., loneliness), hence exacerbating feelings of depression (Eisenberger et al., 2017).

Treatments for depression based on inflammatory processes

The relevance of inflammatory processes to depression may have implications for treatment strategies. Among individuals being treated for rheumatoid arthritis or psoriasis using the TNF-α antagonist etanercept, anxiety and depressive symptoms that were often present were diminished (A. Yang et al., 2019). Moreover, among depressed patients, a TNF-α antagonist engendered beneficial effects, provided that these individuals displayed elevated levels of inflammation reflected by high C-reactive protein before treatment (Raison et al., 2013).

Less powerful, non-steroidal anti-inflammatory drugs (NSAIDs), such as ibuprofen, naproxen, celecoxib, or aspirin, reduced depression and suicidal ideation relative to that produced by the non-NSAID acetaminophen (Lehrer & Rheinstein, 2019). NSAIDs similarly enhanced the effectiveness of antidepressant medication in treating depression, and when coupled with the SSRI fluoxetine, the production of proinflammatory cytokines was reduced, and the antidepressant actions were superior to those elicited by fluoxetine alone. Several meta-analyses supported the contention that NSAIDs may be useful in alleviating depressive symptoms in some, but not all depressed individuals. Reconciling these different outcomes might be possible by considering the effects of these treatments in subtypes of illness, or better still among individuals presenting with particular symptoms together with biomarkers related to inflammation (e.g., Kohler et al., 2016). If patients exhibit high levels of inflammatory markers, potentially pointing to inflammation as contributing to depressive symptoms in particular patients, then the NSAIDs are more likely to serve in a positive capacity. In the absence of elevated inflammation among depressed patients, the anti-inflammatory treatments will be of little value.

Depression associated with immunotherapy: the case of IFN-α

Telling findings concerning inflammatory effects on mood states have come from studies of patients receiving IFN-α immunotherapy in the treatment of some forms of cancer or hepatitis C. Treatment with IFN-α had been adopted for these conditions because of its immunological and its antiviral effects, but over the course of being treated, a large percentage of patients (30–50%) develop depressive-like states that required treatment discontinuation (Miller et al., 2009). The severity of depression was particularly pronounced among individuals with higher levels of depressive symptoms prior to immunotherapy and in those with poor social support. Depression was most readily produced among individuals with low levels of tryptophan, which is necessary for the production of 5-HT, and with relatively high pretreatment levels of IL-6. These risk factors for cytokine-induced depression are very much like those related to stressor provoked depressive states, and treatment with antidepressants reduced the depressive symptoms provoked by IFN-α (Miller & Raison, 2016).

The finding that drugs such as IFN-α can elicit a depressive state may be due to this compound generating a cascade of biological changes that culminate in 5-HT reductions together with CRH and neurotrophin changes that could promote depressive illness. It is more likely the depressive symptoms may evolve because it causes increased production of a substance, kynurenine, through increased activity of an enzyme indoleamine 2,3-dioxygenase (IDO). This, in turn, results in the formation of oxidative metabolites, 3-hydroxykynurenine and quinolinic acid, which promote neurotoxic actions that can disturb anterior cingulate and prefrontal cortex neural circuits, thereby leading to depression (Miller & Raison, 2016). Concurrently, the functioning of oxidative and nitrosative pathways (over-production of oxygen radicals and nitric oxide) may be elevated and DNA damage incurred, which may foster affective symptoms. The inflammation and altered oxygen and nitrosative functioning that promote depression could be exacerbated by psychosocial stressor experiences (Moylan et al., 2014). The behavioral and brain cytokine changes provoked by IFN-α in rodents were magnified if they had been stressed before the proinflammatory treatment (Anisman et al., 2007). Accordingly, in evaluating the actions of IFN-α therapy it ought to be considered that cancer patients or those with hepatitis C were already experiencing considerable distress, and thus the cytokine treatment and stressful experiences might collaborate to instigate depression.

As impressive as findings linking cytokine variations and depression might be, the actions of IFN-α might stem from other factors. Patients treated with IFN-α not only present with disturbed mood symptoms, but with a range of cognitive disturbances. They may experience fairly severe general malaise, impaired concentration and memory, together with features such as a confusional state, disorientation, psychotic-like features, irritability, anxiety, and disturbed vigilance. Predictably, elevated levels of inflammatory cytokines have been tied to a variety of psychiatric and neurological disturbances (Pape et al., 2019). Thus, the actions of IFN-α might reflect a nonspecific state stemming from toxicity engendered by the treatment, and the emergence of depression might represent one of several pathological outcomes. This said, to some extent the depressive actions of IFN-α can be prevented by antidepressant pretreatment (Sarkar & Schaefer, 2014), supporting the involvement of this cytokine in attenuating depression.

Poststroke depression

It can reasonably be expected that during a severe medical illness people are likely to become depressed. Especially high levels of depression are seen following a stroke, and this is often accompanied by suicidal ideation. As it turns out, proinflammatory cytokine levels are elevated following a stroke, just as they are following other neurological challenges, and owing to their excessive levels they might act in a neurodestructive fashion and hence promote pathology, including depression (Fang et al., 2019).

The occurrence of depression following stroke predicts a poor prognosis for functional recovery and future global functioning, and the early appearance of post-stroke depressive symptoms was associated with increased mortality over the ensuing few years. It is possible that specific inflammatory cytokines might constitute a clinical marker relevant to the persistence of depression, later functional recovery, and future incidence of stroke. Thus, it is especially significant that treatments that diminish the inflammatory response can reduce stroke-related pathophysiology (Jiang et al., 2021) and could thereby act against depression that might otherwise ensue.

Remember erythropoietin (EPO)? Here it is in a new context

Research concerning the cytokine-depression connection has focused on proinflammatory cytokines, and numerous other immune-related factors may be significant in this regard. One of these is erythropoietin (EPO) – yes, that's the same substance that has become (in)famous because of its involvement in blood doping (e.g., among professional cyclists). EPO is a cytokine that stimulates the production of red blood cells and acts to protect red blood cells from death that ordinarily occurs through apoptosis (programmed cell death). Beyond these effects, EPO could have beneficial actions in traumatic brain injury and stroke. As well, it promotes antidepressant-like effects in animal models and produced brain activity changes in humans like those associated with antidepressant treatments (Miskowiak et al., 2012). EPO might have such positive effects through its anti-inflammatory, anti-apoptotic, antioxidant, and neurotrophic actions, including increased synthesis and levels of BDNF. As such, EPO had been considered as a possible adjunctive treatment for depression. Unfortunately, EPO provokes numerous serious side effects, including those related to cardiovascular functioning and the development or progression of some forms of cancer, making its use in depression untenable.

Microbiota, anxiety, and depressive disorders

Psychogenic and neurogenic challenges can affect microbiota just as other biological processes are affected by these experiences. The psychological and physical insults that influence microbiota include environmental extremes (high altitude, heat, and cold), noise, disruption of sleep or circadian cycles, and diverse psychological stressors. Social defeat in rodents provoked changes in the diversity of microbiota and the genes regulating them, and these actions were more pronounced with repeated stressor challenges (Gautam et al., 2018). Stressors affected the expression of genes involved in the biosynthesis and metabolism of SCFAs, and influenced the levels of tryptophan and tyrosine, the precursors of serotonin and norepinephrine, respectively (Bharwani et al., 2016). Moreover, by affecting the translocation of microbiota from cutaneous and mucosal surfaces into regional lymph nodes, stressors could promote neuroendocrine and immune alterations (Maltz et al., 2019).

Stressors can cause the reductions of beneficial gut bacteria, such as *Lactobacillus and Bifidobacterium*, and supporting the causal role of microbiota in determining emotional responses, the impact of stressors could be attenuated by the restoration of *Lactobacillus* (Marin et al., 2017). Corticosterone levels were similarly elevated among germ-free mice (mice born and raised in an environment in which germs were absent), which could be exaggerated by a stressor (Crumeyrolle-Arias et al., 2014) and prevented by reconstitution with specific *Bifidobacteria* species.

Aside from linking gut bacteria and physical illnesses, considerable evidence has implicated imbalances between beneficial and harmful microbiota in affecting mood states and the promotion of mental health disturbances owing to numerous neurobiological changes that are engendered (Cryan et al., 2019). For that matter, gut microbiota can affect sociability and social behaviors (Sherwin et al., 2019) that are fundamental for coping with stressors and may thereby influence psychological disorders. These actions may come about through multiple processes that converge on brain neuronal functioning (Foster et al., 2017). Support for this position was derived from studies that entailed different experimental approaches. For instance, a genome-wide association study revealed multiple differences in genetic variants relevant to the abundance of specific microbiota among mouse strains that differed in anxiety levels (Jin et al., 2021). More to the point, manipulations of gut micro-biota can influence the production of various cytokines, hormones, and neuro-transmitters (e.g., GABA, serotonin, and dopamine), which have been implicated in anxiety and depressive disorders. Microbiota variations were likewise accompa-nied by alterations of newly born neurons within the hippocampus (Ogbonnaya et al., 2015), supporting the potential involvement of microbiota in modulating neurotrophin variations that have been linked to mood disorders. The relationship between microbiota and brain processes appears to be bidirectional as the antide-pressant fluoxetine that acts as a serotonin reuptake inhibitor affected gut bacterial colonization (Fung et al., 2019).

Speaking to the brain actions associated with microbial change, the transfer of microbiota (by fecal transplantation) from stress-sensitive animals (those that were most affected in a social defeat paradigm) to naïve animals was accompanied by elevated microglial density and elevated IL-1β in the ventral hippocampus together with the appearance of depressive symptoms. Similarly, transplantation of bacteria from depressed humans to naïve mice led to depressive-like behaviors in the recip-ient rodents (Kelly et al., 2015). Conversely, a probiotic treatment that promoted gut SCFAs diminished behavioral expression of anxiety and depression provoked by a chronic stressor regimen. For instance, probiotic treatments can diminish the emotion-related brain changes that occur following the separation of rat pups from their mother (Cowan et al., 2019). These actions may occur through altered sym-pathetic nervous system functioning, particularly the release of norepinephrine, diminished levels of inflammatory factors, and by alterations of oxidative stress. The microbial changes may promote activation of the vagus nerve, which affects brain processes (Fülling et al., 2019), or they may occur by influencing cytokine levels that affect brain functioning.

While the effects of stressors on microbiota were extensively assessed in rodents, far fewer studies assessed the effects of stressors and microbial manipulations in humans. Nevertheless, it was reported that academic exams among university stu-dents were associated with microbiota alterations, varying with students' perceived distress (Bastiaanssen et al., 2021). Gut microbiota diversity and richness was simi-larly reduced in individuals experiencing marital strife and indices of leaky gut (i.e., gaps in the intestinal wall that allow bacteria to pass into the bloodstream) and inflammation was observed (Kiecolt-Glaser et al., 2021). Even a relatively brief laboratory stressor that comprised participants feeling socially excluded was accompanied by neuronal activity changes within the prefrontal and the anterior cingulate cortex, which were diminished by a diet supplemented with *Bifidobacterium longum* but worsened by an antibiotic (H. Wang et al., 2019). As these brain regions are integral to executive functioning and mood states, the actions observed are consistent with the position that gut microbiota contribute to stressor elicited psychological disorders.

It is tempting to believe that studies of microbiota in rodents may be a suitable proxy for what occurs in humans. Considerable evidence in rodents revealed causal connections between stressor-provoked microbiota changes and elevated anxiety, and supplementation with a variety of microbes could diminish anxiety in several behavioral paradigms (Zou et al., 2021). However, these animal experiments did not uniformly translate well to human clinical studies as the anxiolytic effects of microbiota were not consistently observed (Yang et al., 2019). Prebiotic supplements (these stimulate the growth of gut bacteria) did not influence anxiety or depressive symptoms, and probiotics (i.e., those that feed microbiota or that comprise live bacteria) only elicited small effects, although these actions were more notable in clinical populations than in community samples (Liu et al., 2019). This does not exclude the possibility that a probiotic diet tailored to the individual's specific microbiota community would yield better effects, particularly if personalized treatments were combined with standard anti-anxiety therapies. Aside from the microbiota link to anxiety, powerful stressors that produce PTSD elicited diminished abundance of several microbiota phyla. It was considered that probiotic or prebiotic manipulations in combination with other treatments, might attenuate the signs of PTSD. There have been indications of this procedure having ameliorative actions, but this has not been widely assessed, and much more research is necessary to assess the therapeutic benefits of specific microbiota (Brenner et al., 2017).

The use of prebiotics and probiotics (in pill form) have become increasingly popular in attenuating various illnesses, but beneficial actions are much more likely to be generated when they are obtained through diet. The fact is that most individuals are entirely unaware whether or not they are deficient of specific bacteria, and positive effects might not be obtained when supplements are used indiscriminately. In the absence of microbial deficiencies, prebiotic and probiotic supplements may not result in elevated bacterial colonization and instead will be eliminated without having any benefits (Zmora et al., 2018). Foods, such as certain forms of yogurt may be a good source of probiotics, and fermented foods, such as sauerkraut, kefir, kombucha, fermented soy products (tempeh, natto, miso, kimchi), and sourdough bread, may have beneficial effects because they facilitate the growth of beneficial gut bacteria. In many instances, the value of specific nutrients on well-being has not been adequately assessed in human trials, or the studies conducted have been deemed to be of low quality (Dimidi et al., 2019). Of course, none of these foods are consumed in isolation of other nutrients, and if there is value to them, their best effects will be obtained as part of a broad diet containing plenty of foods containing diverse fibers.

The studies that have been conducted most often involved analyses of people within Western countries. As described in Chapter 6, considerable interindividual differences exist in the abundance and diversity of microbiota, and these differences are also apparent across cultures and geographical locations, which may be linked to health outcomes. In developing and underdeveloped countries benefits could be derived from the diversity of gut microbes, although these could be undermined by poverty-related stressors. There is still a paucity of data concerning gut microbiota across diverse populations and the implications for specific diseases. Limiting analyses regarding the cultural and geographical differences related to gut microbiota, much like those related to genetic diversity, may have squandered the opportunity to determine key variables that contribute to microbiota-related health disturbances and the factors that could limit their occurrence (Abdill et al., 2022).

Depression: what's it good for anyway?

Over the course of evolution, phenotypes that were useful and allowed for species to propagate should have been maintained, whereas those phenotypes that were disadvantageous should have been selected against and hence ought to have disappeared. And yet many phenotypes have persisted despite their apparent uselessness. How does this come about? As mentioned earlier, a gene can be altered by mutations, and thus genes that favor depression could occur simply by chance. Likewise, epigenetic changes could occur in germline cells and the resulting gene suppression can be passed on across generations. As well, although genetic factors can be associated with phenotypic effects that are apparent all the time, there are genetic factors that have negative consequences only under certain conditions (e.g., the presence of stressful experiences). Thus, the selection pressure against these characteristics might be diminished, allowing for the phenotype to persist.

There are instances in which a gene might have some sort of positive effect and hence there is selection for this characteristic, even though it might have some negative consequences. The classic example of this is sickle cell anemia, in which having a gene that codes for this disorder has the advantage of providing resistance to malaria, but also has the unfortunate effect of causing a change of red blood cells that can cause horrible pain as well as diminish the oxygen-carrying capacity of red blood cells. Inheriting genes for sickle cell anemia might be advantageous in some parts of Africa, but it won't be of much value for individuals living in Baltimore, London, or Paris. In addition to these processes, there are conditions in which a gene is passed on because the phenotype of the affected individual might not be apparent until later in life, long after they might have passed on their genes. Here, the classic example is Huntington's disease, which doesn't show up until an individual is about forty years of age and individuals might already have had children.

The same holds, incidentally, for several other genetic characteristics involved in pathologies, such as certain types of cancer.

Other characteristics present in humans that at first blush seem to be useless may be exceptionally common. Nausea and vomiting are highly aversive, but they help purge toxicants that have been consumed and inform us that something is amiss that needs to be looked after. Moreover, it tells us that whatever it was that was eaten shouldn't be consumed again. Likewise, feeling pain has positive attributes in that it lets us know when we've done something to harm ourselves and that care needs to be taken. Of course, there are severe pains that seem unnecessary, such as those associated with cancer or other diseases. Surely, nature could have been much kinder and given us some other sign that might have been just as effective.

Perhaps, as in these other situations, depression provides a signal that all isn't right and that actions need to be taken to change our situation. Most individuals who have been severely depressed will likely tell you about how bleak and difficult their lives had been, the dark dirty pool in which they had been submerged, and the endless days of rumination and thoughts of suicide. It's doubtful that many scientists would suggest that severe depression has positive value any more than severe, intractable pain may have benefits. But mild depression might, so long as it doesn't end up getting out of control and culminating in severe illness.

There is a school of thought (well, as there aren't a huge number in this camp, maybe we should call it a 'small class of thought' rather than a whole school) that suggests mild depression has some value. For some time, there has been an interest in the topic of self-regulation and goal pursuits in the context of depressive disorders. This essentially refers to an individual's ability to recognize and identify goals, and then to pursue and possibly attain these goals. In elementary school, children may be provided certain maxims as if they were absolute truths. The best known may be 'if at first you don't succeed, then try, try, try again'. Essentially, quitting isn't an option, and failure needs to be followed by greater efforts until success was achieved. But is it always the case? Simply because an individual has a certain goal doesn't mean they can attain it. Should the athletically challenged kid be pushed to the extent that she/he believes they can be a professional sports figure if they just tried hard enough, or is it realistic to believe that the kid who can't hold a tune might become the next American Idol? So, should they try, try, try again to reach unattainable goals? Alternatively, should they abandon the futility and move on to more productive endeavors?

From this perspective, mild depression might have positive effects as it was associated with goal disengagement and/or goal re-engagement. Finding some new more attainable goal was, in fact, accompanied by improved health and sleep efficiency, as well as more normal diurnal cortisol variations. Conversely, individuals who had trouble disengaging from the chase of unattainable goals exhibited elevated levels of the inflammatory marker CRP (Chat et al., 2021), which might be predictive of later health problems. In effect, the early signs of depression might be a harbinger that things aren't going well and might get still worse if the same path is followed. Mild depression might be a cogent signal for the individual to re-examine and perhaps regulate their goals more appropriately, thereby precluding the development of more severe depression.

Conclusion

Numerous factors likely contribute to the emergence of depression, and it is highly unlikely that any single neurotransmitter, neuropeptide, inflammatory factor, or hormone accounts for all of the symptoms observed. Likewise, the specific biological processes that lead to depression in one individual might differ from those that provoke depression in a second, just as the specific life events that led to this outcome differed among individuals. Figure 9.2 is a schematic representation of one neurochemical model of depression, and it is admittedly limited in the number of biochemical mechanisms proposed. You'll recognize that we have discussed each of these processes in this and in earlier chapters and at this point it is being brought up as an illustration of how biological processes can be linked to one another, ultimately resulting in depressive illness.

The figure caption largely explains.the sequence of events that could lead to depression, but there are several other messages embedded in it that should be considered. Placing enough strain on a structure will likely cause it to break at its weakest point, and the stressors encountered by an individual will likewise cause the most vulnerable component of biological defensive systems to crack. For one individual this might be their 5-HT responses, for another it may be BDNF or HPA functioning, and for still another it might involve GABA disturbances.

1. The fact that multiple routes exist in the evolution of depression might account for why the success rates for pharmacological treatments are as low as they are and why it takes several tries, using different remedies before success is realized in alleviating depressive symptoms. Thus, pharmacotherapy that involves multi-targeting might in many cases be preferential to monotherapies (single treatments).

2. A given therapy might not have fully 'cured' the illness, and as often as not the treated individual will still present with residual symptoms, attesting to the partial efficacy of the treatment. In addition, the treatment choice might not be getting to the root of the problem. By example, treatment with a 5-HT targeted manipulation might be effective in masking symptoms, but the original problem might still be present. Thus, while the symptoms of the illness may be eliminated for the moment, when the drug therapy stops, the adverse effects attributable to the causal biological processes may again emerge. Similarly, if the stressors experienced by an individual are responsible for the overload of neural circuits, hence leading to depression, the drug treatment might make things manageable for the moment, but once more, when the drug treatment is stopped, the system will crumble unless the root of the problem has been eliminated, including the presence of stressor

or how it is appraised and coped with. This said, it is certainly possible that when symptoms are attenuated by the drug treatment, the individual, being in a better place, might be more able or ready to rearrange the way they appraise and cope with their situation, and how they deal with future stressors. Thus, a combination of drug treatment and behavioral therapy or a change of socio-environmental context might be particularly efficacious.

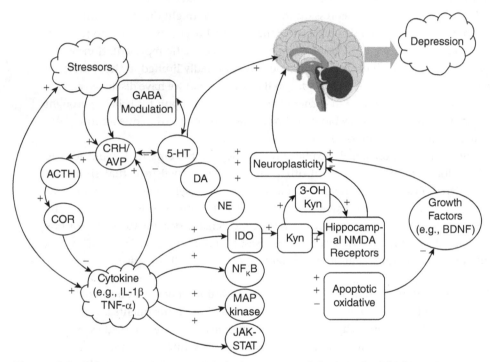

Figure 9.2   Schematic representation depicting potential routes by which stressors and cytokines could influence the depressive state. A stressor could potentially influence major depression through several interconnected loops. Stressors and cytokines can both increase hypothalamic (and extra-hypothalamic) CRH release. In addition to activating HPA functioning, CRH may influence 5-HT processes, and GABAA activity may act as a mediator in this regard. This, in turn, may influence depression directly or may do so by impairing neuroplastic processes. An alternative pathway involves cytokine/stress activation of either NFkB, MAP kinases, or JAK/STAT signaling, which serve to transmit information derived from chemical signals outside of a cell to gene promoters on DNA within the cell's nucleus. These processes influence oxidative or apoptotic mechanisms, leading to altered growth factor expression (e.g., BDNF), hence again favoring impaired neuroplastic processes, and culminating in major depression. As well, immune activation leading to cytokine changes might then affect IDO that could either reduce 5-HT availability or through several oxidative metabolites might disturb neuroplasticity, which would then favor the development of depression (adapted from Anisman et al., 2008).

More than anything, this chapter emphasized that depression is a complex disorder involving multiple neurochemical processes and that the mechanisms governing this illness in one individual might not be identical to that apparent in a second. Increasingly, the notion is being accepted that whether it's depression, heart disease, cancer, or a variety of other illnesses, the effectiveness of treatments will improve once an individualized (personalized) treatment approach is adopted. Once illnesses are diagnosed based on specific symptoms, genetic factors, etiological processes, biomarkers, and psychosocial determinants (including culture), it may be possible to tailor treatments more appropriately, and ought to provide better patient care and might limit the occurrence of comorbidities often associated with depression.

Suggested readings

Beck, A.T. & Haigh, E.A. (2014). Advances in cognitive theory and therapy: the generic cognitive model. *Annual Review in Clinical Psychology*, *10*, 1–24.

Miller, A.H. & Raison, C.L. (2016). The role of inflammation in depression: from evolutionary imperative to modern treatment target. *Nature Reviews in Immunology*, *16*, 22–34.

Price, R.B. & Duman, R. (2020). Neuroplasticity in cognitive and psychological mechanisms of depression: an integrative model. *Molecular Psychiatry*, *25*, 530–543.

10

ANXIETY DISORDERS AND PTSD

Is it a reality or an opinion?

In a recent episode of a television program, one of those that include the crime, the search for the bad guy, and then the trial, the defense's case was that the alleged perpetrator suffered from PTSD and as a result should not be found guilty. The prosecution lawyer, in cross-examining the expert witness, a psychiatrist, asks, 'How did you diagnose this illness?' The psychiatrist replied that he did this based on several interviews to see whether signs of PTSD were present. To this, the prosecutor replied with something like, 'So, I take it that you didn't perform any brain imaging analyses to see if there was a brain disturbance, or any blood tests or analyses of cerebrospinal fluid that could tell us whether there were chemical imbalances. So, really, this diagnosis of yours is nothing more than an opinion, a guess. Perhaps it was an educated guess, but still just a guess.'

Although psychological disorders are thought of as diseases of the brain and so should have some biological origin, identifying these underlying mechanisms hasn't been easy, and even finding markers for these illnesses has been difficult. Unlike diabetes, which can be detected based on blood sugar levels, or heart problems that can be seen through different tests of varying invasiveness, to assess the presence of mental disorders we're often reliant on behavioral, affective, or cognitive symptoms. With improved molecular, biochemical, and imaging technologies, sensitive biological indices of various illnesses could ultimately be determined. Yet, as most psychological illnesses represent an amalgam of multiple disturbed processes and biological mechanisms, this won't be simple or fast. This might be especially difficult as there are many subtypes of anxiety that differ from one another and may involve some common mechanisms and some that differ from one another. Likewise, posttraumatic stress disorder (PTSD) may involve diverse symptoms, including anxiety and depression, that vary over time after a traumatic or chronic stressor experience, which adds another level of complexity in determining biological processes.

Learning objectives

Most people have felt anxious at one time or another, usually in anticipation of something negative or uncertain (such as an exam, having to give an oral presentation to a group, or waiting for the results of a medical test). The anxiety is usually mild or moderate, but among some individuals, anxiety can be persistent and intense, to the extent that individuals describe themselves as 'just wanting to crawl out of their skin'. Some individuals who have suffered anxiety that was comorbid with severe depression have indicated that the anxiety was as bad as, or even more disturbing than, the depression. This chapter has several core objectives regarding what the reader should learn from it:

- Anxiety may be a component of several disorders that call for some sort of treatment. These comprise general anxiety disorder, panic disorder, phobias, social anxiety, and obsessive-compulsive disorder.
- Anxiety-related illnesses can be comorbid with other psychological illnesses, such as depressive disorders and PTSD.
- The causes for each of these disorders can be very different, and the social and biological processes associated with them may differ. Yet, this does not belie the possibility that these disorders share core underlying mechanisms.
- Despite the different characteristics of these disorders, they are amenable to some of the same treatments, although their long-term effectiveness has typically been lacking.

Subtypes of anxiety

Fear has generally been considered as apprehension that occurs rapidly in response to a threat, and then abates quickly once the threat is removed. In this sense, the 'fear' response may have significant adaptive value as it keeps individuals in a heightened state of alertness and readiness to respond. Anxiety, it seems, is more closely aligned with threats that are neither as specific nor as predictable as those that elicit fear. As well, the processes associated with current threats might be biologically distinct from those that are distal, and thus might require different ways to ameliorate their impact. Like fear, evolutionary pressures may have contributed to anxiety being a frequent emotion. After all, it would have been more advantageous to err on the side of elevated anxiety (and hence elevated caution) as the alternative might have been counterproductive for survival. In

essence, both anxiety and fear can have benefits in the sense that they may prepare an individual to deal with negative events that may be encountered. What
differentiates 'normal' anxiety from anxiety that requires treatment is the degree
of discomfort it creates and the extent to which it affects social and workplace
functioning or family interactions.

Several disorders that comprise anxiety and those that involve fear (e.g., phobias) are placed under the rubric of 'Anxiety Disorders', despite their many differences. Anxiety disorders affect about 20% of individuals in developed countries,
with women being about 50% more likely to experience an anxiety disorder.
Table 10.1 provides a summary of different anxiety-related disorders. We'll deal
with each independently, but as we move through these it should become clear
that even though profound differences exist between them, there are common
core symptoms, and in some instances the same treatments can provide a degree
of relief.

Table 10.1 Anxiety disorders.

Generalized anxiety disorder, the most common anxiety disorder among adults, is
characterized by persistent (at least six months) anxiety or worry that is not focused on
any single subject, object, or situation.

Panic disorder is diagnosed when individuals have discrete periods involving
sudden and unpredictable onset of intense apprehension or terror. These feelings
are accompanied by features, such as palpitations, accelerated heart rate, sweating,
trembling/shaking, shortness of breath (smothering), feelings of choking, nausea or
abdominal distress, dizziness, or light-headedness. As well, depersonalization (feeling
detached from oneself) or derealization (a feeling of unreality), and a fear of losing
control may be present.

Phobias are characterized by clinically significant anxiety (fear) elicited by certain
situations, activities, things, or people, in which individuals display an excessive and
unreasonable desire to avoid or escape from the feared object or situation.

Social anxiety disorder (social phobia) entails an intense fear of public embarrassment
or humiliation (negative public scrutiny). Most often this fear is evident across
situations, but can be specific to certain venues (e.g., public speaking). The severity of
symptoms can be sufficiently intense to provoke social isolation.

Obsessive-Compulsive Disorder (OCD) comprises obsessions or intrusive thoughts
that provoke anxiety and compulsions (e.g., hoarding, repeated checking, repeated
behavioral acts, such as hand washing or preoccupation with sexual, religious, or
aggressive impulses) that serve to alleviate the anxiety.

Separation anxiety disorder involves excessive and inappropriate levels of anxiety
in response to being separated from a person or place. Such feelings are common
in children but are only considered a disorder when these are excessive and
inappropriate.

Generalized anxiety disorder (GAD)

This relatively common illness, the symptoms of which are provided in Table 10.2, has a lifetime prevalence of about 5%. The appearance of GAD can occur in children, but onset is most common when individuals are in their twenties or early thirties and appears twice as often in women relative to men. The development of GAD is typically slow, but once present it may be persistent. It is frequently a comorbid feature of major depression or dysthymia, as well as other anxiety disorders, such as panic disorder and social phobia.

There appears to be a genetic link for this disorder as it often runs in families, although to a great extent vulnerability to GAD was tied to contextual (environmental) factors. Encountering a major life stressor (e.g., a car accident, a breast cancer diagnosis, as well as natural disasters such as earthquakes) has been implicated in the emergence of GAD. Likewise, GAD can occur through witnessing a trauma. For instance, this disorder appeared more frequently among individuals who knew someone at the 9/11 terrorist site than among those who did not. This is not to say that GAD occurs exclusively in those who have been traumatized. Individuals who experienced high psychological job demands (excessive workload, extreme time pressures) had a two-fold risk of GAD or depressive disorders relative to those with low job demands. Early-life stressors might contribute to the emergence of GAD, just as it may be a predisposing factor for depression and PTSD. Not unexpectedly, the incidence of GAD increased dramatically during the COVID-19 pandemic, even being elevated in countries, such as China, where the spread of the disease was largely contained.

Table 10.2 Generalized anxiety disorder (GAD) symptomatology.

According to the DSM-5, generalized anxiety disorder (GAD) is characterized by:
(1) excessive, uncontrollable, and often irrational worry about day-to-day things and events; the anxiety persists for at least six months, being present on more days than not;
(2) difficulty or inability in controlling these thoughts;
(3) three of the following symptoms must be present: restlessness (or feeling on edge), easily fatigued, difficulty concentrating, irritability, muscle tension, sleep disturbance typically involving difficulty falling asleep, or staying asleep (or restless sleep).

Excessive anxiety should not be related to the use of illicit drugs and is not limited to anxiety or worry about other psychological disorders. Beyond these core symptoms, GAD is often accompanied by physical signs that include sweating, cold clammy hands, dry mouth, headaches, nausea or diarrhea, numbness in the hands and feet, difficulty swallowing or the feeling of a lump in the throat, occasional bouts of breathing difficulty, trembling, and twitching.

Biological factors and treatment of GAD

In view of the considerable data suggesting that the amygdala and the bed nucleus of the stria terminalis are involved in anxiety and fear, it is thought that GAD might involve disturbed amygdala functioning or disturbed connectivity to other brain regions that might be fundamental in processing information related to anxiety-provoking stimuli. In this regard, top-down regulation through the prefrontal cortex and hippocampus are involved in anxiety and fear, contributing to the appraisal of fear-related events and the memory of these events. Anxiety has most often been related to variations of norepinephrine, serotonin, CRH, and GABA, but it might be more appropriate to consider anxiety from the perspective of intersecting neural circuits. Indeed, dopamine activity within the interpeduncular nucleus, through its connections to the VTA may contribute to anxiety (DeGroot et al., 2020), possibly by influencing the salience of threatening stimuli. Aside from these circuits, a connection exists between the amygdala and both the prefrontal and anterior cingulate cortex, specifically a white matter tract referred to as the uncinate fasciculus. Ordinarily, the anterior cingulate tells the amygdala to calm down in the face of non-threatening stimuli, but for those with GAD this might not occur and hence elevated anxiety persists (Kenwood et al., 2022).

To a significant extent strategies to treat the disorder have been based on knowledge of stressor effects on biological systems and founded on which drugs are effective in the treatment of other anxiety disorders. Anti-anxiety medications, such as diazepam (Valium), alprazolam (Xanax), or lorazepam (Ativan), each of which is fast-acting, may be an effective short-term remedy. However, these drugs are not recommended for long-term use as they may be associated with the development of tolerance, physical dependence, and withdrawal symptoms. Thus, GAD is more often treated with SSRIs as well as the serotonin-norepinephrine reuptake inhibitors (SNRIs), such as venlafaxine (Effexor) and duloxetine (Cymbalta). These agents may be more effective than benzodiazepines as they access comorbid depression that might be present, whereas benzodiazepines typically do not (Garakani et al., 2020). However, SSRIs may take several weeks to modify GAD, just as there is a delay in the alleviation of depression. As well, the remission may be incomplete, and SSRIs and SNRIs may have some unwanted side effects. An array of anti-anxiety medications are described in Chapter 13, so we won't deal with these in much detail here. Suffice it to say that several drugs that fall out of the usual anti-anxiety category have been used in the treatment of GAD. For instance, buspirone (BuSpar), a 5-HT$_{1A}$ receptor partial agonist (i.e., the drug only partially activates the receptor) that also acts as a dopamine D$_2$ and α-norepinephrine antagonist, may be effective in treating moderate GAD. Pregabalin (Lyrica), which is used in the treatment of neuropathic pain, may also be effective in the treatment of GAD, and the NE β-blocker propranolol, which is primarily used for hypertension, may act as an anti-anxiety treatment (Slee et al., 2019).

A meta-analysis indicated that although pharmacological treatment and CBT were both effective in attenuating GAD, the latter was more efficacious in several respects. Specifically, CBT was associated with greater effects on the depression that accompanied GAD, and therapeutic gains were maintained after the discontinuation of treatment (Kaczkurkin & Foa, 2015). In fact, CBT may have better long-term effects than pharmacological treatments, even if drugs may provide a more immediate fix. However, CBT is effective to some extent in just 50–60% of GAD patients, and other forms of behavioral therapy (e.g., relaxation or those treatments that enhance tolerance for uncertainty) were about as effective.

Panic disorder

In several ways, panic disorder is more unusual and puzzling than other anxiety disorders. Individuals may experience brief attacks of intense terror and apprehension as described in Table 10.2 that peak within a few minutes and typically last for only a brief period (1–20 minutes). The initial panic attack might seem to come out of the blue and it isn't certain what brought on the initial attack, although it is thought that stressful life events, or appraisals of events that promote embellished perceptions of potentially stressful stimuli, contribute to the development of panic disorder. This assumption is based on reports that panic attacks are first seen following such events, as well as after physical illnesses or certain drug treatments, including illicit drugs that might have engendered negative effects. Panic attacks are recurrent and, in some people (more so women than men), these attacks occur weekly or even daily. As a result, individuals often have ongoing concerns about having further attacks, especially as an attack may cause them embarrassment and promote social stigma.

Although panic disorder runs in families, occurring in 40% of first-degree relatives, it is not uncommon for panic attacks to develop among individuals with no family history of the disorder. Several genetic and epigenetic factors have been identified that confer susceptibility to panic disorder, but like many genes that have been identified in relation to other disorders, translating this knowledge into treatment strategies has been slow in materializing (Kim & Kim, 2018). It seems likely that the influence of genetic and epigenetic factors that have been tied to panic disorder may interact with stressful encounters, including adverse childhood experiences.

Behavioral and cognitive views of panic disorder

Diverse perspectives have been offered concerning the development of panic disorder. An emotion-based model suggested that some individuals may be disposed to overreact to stressors, possibly owing to genetic influences or adverse life events that had been encountered, including those that occurred early in life or during adolescence (Zhang et al., 2021). The panic response occurs most readily if individuals had the sense that events and emotions were uncontrollable and unpredictable.

It was suggested that through classical conditioning, anxiety-related arousal and panic may be associated with internal sensations (i.e., interoceptive cues), so that when these internal cues appear again, possibly as a response to reminder stimuli, a panic attack may be instigated. Relatedly, anxiety derived from the fear of symptoms re-emerging may contribute to panic episodes recurring (Van Diest, 2019). Another position held that feedback from the body is fundamental in the instigation of panic attacks. Specifically, certain sensations may be 'catastrophically' misinterpreted as being especially threatening, leading to high levels of arousal, which then promotes further bodily changes and still greater perceived threat. This recurrent cycle ultimately results in a panic attack.

Biological factors related to panic disorder

The neurobiological processes underlying panic disorder have yet to be fully defined but based on neuroimaging studies this condition may reflect a disturbance of an extensive fear network, including cortical brain regions and several limbic brain regions that respond to fear stimuli and anticipatory anxiety related to chronic stressful encounters (Goddard, 2017). Panic disorder is frequently associated with other anxiety disorders and phobias and may be comorbid with other illnesses, such as bipolar disorder and alcohol use disorder, and has been associated with elevated lifetime rates of cardiovascular, respiratory, and gastrointestinal illnesses.

Anxiety may emerge when the inhibitory signaling associated with GABA activity is diminished. Relative to healthy controls, patients with panic disorder exhibited lower GABA concentrations in the anterior cingulate cortex and basal ganglia. Moreover, cortical GABA concentrations were diminished in patients with a family history of mood and anxiety disorders, raising the possibility that genetic factors related to GABA functioning might be at play in determining vulnerability to panic disorder (Long et al., 2013).

In addition to GABA, it was maintained that the synergistic actions of 5-HT and endogenous opioids, through their actions on 5-HT$_{1A}$ and μ-opioid receptors diminish effective inhibitory mechanisms, thereby allowing activation of a fear network that may provoke panic disorder (Graeff, 2017). It has been known for some time that panic disorder is associated with altered 5-HT$_{1A}$ receptor availability, and the finding that SSRIs can diminish panic disorder is consistent with 5-HT involvement in this condition (although SSRIs may exacerbate panic disorder symptoms during the early stages of treatment). Commensurate with this view, a polymorphism of the gene coding for the serotonin transporter was associated with increased vulnerability to panic disorder and was predictive of the response to SSRI treatment (Zou et al., 2020). Although 5-HT regulation might contribute to panic disorder, there's certainly more behind this illness, such as the involvement of CRH, AVP, and a peptide that we hadn't discussed earlier, cholecystokinin (CCK). Although CCK is more often considered as one of several gut peptides involved in digestion, a low dose of CCK could induce a panic attack in individuals with this disorder.

One of the difficulties associated with determining the mechanisms underlying panic disorder is the wide range of brain regions that could potentially be involved in this illness. In response to a challenge that comprised emotionally salient cues (anxiety-provoking visual stimuli or threatening words), patients exhibited particularly elevated neuronal activity in brain regions involved in appraisal and executive processes, such as the anterior cingulate cortex, posterior cingulate cortex, orbital frontal cortex, as well as brain regions linked to anxiety, notably the amygdala and hippocampus (Oliva et al., 2020). As expected, following psychotherapy that diminished panic disorder symptoms, the activation patterns in some brain regions normalized. However, in remitted patients tested in paradigms that elicit negative emotional responses, elevated neuronal activity was still evident in the anterior cingulate cortex, dorsal medial prefrontal cortex, and amygdala. The persistence of the exaggerated brain responses to emotional stimuli might be taken to suggest that they are not involved in the disorder. Alternatively, the presence of the altered neuronal functioning might suggest that the root cause of the condition had not been altered so that the potential for relapse persisted, particularly in response to experiences with certain types of events.

Treatment of panic disorder

Both pharmacological and behavioral methods have been used to treat panic disorder, with moderate success being achieved in both cases. CBT was an effective treatment in about 60% of panic disorder patients, especially when treatments focused on the perceived likelihood of panic attacks occurring, the perceived consequences of such an event, and panic-coping efficacy. Antidepressant drugs, particularly SSRIs and SNRIs, can reduce panic disorder in some patients, but the doses required were well beyond those needed to treat depression, suggesting the involvement of different or additional processes in these disorders. The effectiveness of these agents on recurrence of the disorder is uncertain (Caldirola et al., 2020), although these treatments can be used concurrently with CBT. Despite the success of antidepressant drugs, it was suggested that CBT should still be considered the treatment of choice.

Phobias

A phobia refers to an intense and persistent fear of certain situations, activities, things, places, or people, and is typically characterized by an unreasonable avoidance of these stimuli. When the fear, which is typically seen as being uncontrollable, interferes with daily life, a diagnosis corresponding to this type of anxiety disorder can be applied. Estimates of the prevalence of phobias range from 8 to 18%, being more common in women than in men.

Development of phobias

For many phobic individuals the feared object or condition is not frequently encountered (e.g., fear of tarantulas if you live in northern climates) or is one that can readily be avoided. Other phobias, in contrast, might comprise frequent confrontations that need to be dealt with for a reasonable quality of life to be maintained. People with fears of public speaking know that this can become incapacitating, particularly when their job demands it. Being phobic about planes certainly cuts down on good times and might interfere with certain business ventures. Another fear that comprises the fear of leaving home or places where one feels safe (agoraphobia) is often tied to social phobias, making for multiple social problems.

Phobias might develop through simple conditioning processes in which an event or stimulus occurs in conjunction with a negative feeling or emotion. This pairing results in a classically conditioned anxiety response, so that future presentations of the conditioned stimulus will elicit the anxiety/fear response. As well, innate mechanisms may be related to the development of phobias making them resistant to extinction (Garcia, 2017). However, there may be a bit more to the development of phobias and the functioning of specific brain regions might be especially notable in promoting fear reactions based on visual cues and on experiences with threatening stimuli. Numerous processes related to appraisal processes have been tied to phobias, typically entailing circuits that comprise appraisal processes (e.g., anterior cingulate cortex) and those related to anxiety (e.g., amygdala) or disgust.

Social anxiety

Social anxiety, which has been viewed as a social phobia, is characterized by emotional discomfort, fear, apprehension, or worry about social situations, interactions with others, and about being evaluated or scrutinized by other people (walking into a room and worrying that everyone is watching them or making a public statement that results in attention being drawn to them). Many of us share characteristics of social anxiety and social evaluative threats (e.g., in relation to public speaking or other public performances) but this most often isn't incapacitating and doesn't necessarily imply a social phobia in a clinical sense.

Social anxiety frequently begins during childhood, typically waning with age, but it may persist into adolescence and adulthood. In children, the disorder can prove incapacitating, to the extent that they end up being fearful of playing with others or speaking to teachers. How the disorder comes about is uncertain, but it is not unlikely that negative experiences in social situations might have contributed to the development of this form of anxiety disorder. Once the anxiety is present, individuals may experience a confirmation bias in which they look for negative reactions from others (e.g., during public speaking the individual may focus on those in the audience who appear not to be receptive). It can be reinforced by the avoidance of social situations that is accompanied by relief. Genome-wide association studies have implicated genetic factors in conferring risk for social anxiety (Stein et al., 2017), presumably being furthered by negative social experiences.

Exaggerated neuronal activity in limbic regions (e.g., amygdala) and insular cortex might be associated with elevated attention to, and processing of, the social threats that accompany social anxiety. Additionally, social anxiety has been related to dysfunctional neuronal connectivity within several brain networks (Gellner et al., 2021). Thus, it would reasonably be expected that many neurochemical changes may be intimately involved in the production of social anxiety. In view of the role of oxytocin in relation to social behaviors and social stressors, attention has often focused on the possibility that disturbed functioning of this hormone or its receptor might contribute to the disorder and that manipulations of oxytocin could diminish signs of social anxiety disorder (Jones et al., 2017). Epigenetic influences, including those for oxytocin, have been linked to the development of social anxiety, and balances between oxytocin and vasopressin may contribute to this condition, which may account for sex differences that have been reported (Bredewold & Veenema, 2018). In this regard, manipulations of oxytocin and vasopressin were effective in diminishing symptoms of social anxiety.

Treatment of phobias

Several therapies for phobias, including prolonged exposure therapy and CBT have been used to diminish (extinguish) conditioned fear responses. Prolonged exposure therapy entails methods to *desensitize* the individual, typically in small steps in which the distress related to the feared situation or object is systematically reduced. This might include symbolic representation of the feared object, imagery, and virtual reality treatments, ultimately building up to exposure to the actual feared object or situation. Gradual desensitization treatment has a high success rate, provided that the individual is willing to endure the discomfort that comes with being exposed to the feared object or situation. CBT has been used to help individuals come to understand their negative thought patterns, and then to modify them. In some cases, CBT and exposure therapy may be given in conjunction with anti-anxiety agents or SSRIs, which have also been found effective.

─────**Case study 10.1**─────────────────────────────

Fear of flying

For years Joel had a fear of flying in airplanes. He doesn't anymore, but as he says, 'it may be gone but not forgotten'. This phobia was causing him problems since it often interfered with his job, so he chose to obtain therapy to overcome his phobia. During therapy, he

(Continued)

revealed that he may have understood the source of the problem, and why he was so resistant to overcoming this condition.

He thought that his phobia stemmed, in part, from not having control over the situation. 'I'm certain I would have been more comfortable if I had actually been flying the plane, even if it distressed other passengers.' He then added, 'Now that I think about this, it isn't the plane ride itself that gets to me, it's the days preceding the flight that are worst. Once I'm on the plane, and resigned to certain death, an odd calmness falls over me. Of course, this doesn't stop me from making deals with God. In my brain I'm saying to God that if I make it back alive I'm giving 10% of everything I have to charity... then I add, yeah, I know I said that before and then reneged, but this time I really, really, really mean it.'

Often, when friends tried to get him to abandon the phobia they would tell him that his fear was irrational and that more people died in car accidents within two miles of home, as if logical positions would get him to suddenly just change his mind about the phobia. In response, he would say, 'If fear of flying is so irrational, then why did so many people stop flying after 9/11?' He says that the second comment he would frequently hear is, 'Oh, it's all in your head', to which he would respond saying, 'Well that was helpful. I had thought it was in my bladder given the sensation that flying creates.'

Joel was treated through a combination of exposure therapy and an antidepressant. It was remarkably successful, as he had come to the point that he was ready to accept the therapy without his biases getting in the way. He now realizes that phobias aren't all that difficult to eliminate, but it takes commitment and the right mindset.

Obsessive-compulsive disorder (OCD)

Virtually everybody who's a fan of scary movies, and many who aren't, knows something about obsessive-compulsive disorder (OCD). Remember the scene in *Sleeping with the Enemy* when the woman (Julia Roberts) who runs away from her abusive husband (Patrick Bergin) opens her kitchen cabinet and sees the soup cans lined up neatly in rows facing forwards? Or do you recall your high school literature class where you were introduced to Lady Macbeth compulsively washing her hands? However, if you had been asked to classify these as OCD-like behaviors, you likely wouldn't have seen them as being an anxiety disorder.

Obsessive-compulsive disorder is considered an anxiety disorder that primarily involves repetitive obsessions (distressing, persistent, and intrusive thoughts or images) coupled with compulsions that entail urges to perform specific acts or rituals. Some individuals may primarily present with obsessions, but seemingly not the compulsive behaviors. This doesn't necessarily imply that they are independent components of the disorder (although they may be), since overt compulsive behaviors may be suppressed because of social opprobrium, but may still play out mentally. Although OCD sounds fairly unusual, its lifetime prevalence is about 2%. However, not everyone who exhibits obsessive or compulsive features should be considered to be suffering from the disorder. Some people may be just a little more obsessive or quirky (i.e., it's a personality style), but wouldn't be classified as being ill.

The behaviors that comprise OCD vary appreciably across individuals, but generally fall into several classes (Stein et al., 2019). These comprise (a) contamination symptoms in which individuals are obsessed about dirt and germs, leading to excessive washing or cleaning; (b) harm-related features so that individuals are constantly alert for potential harms, leading to repeated checking; (c) unacceptability symptoms (including 'forbidden thoughts') in which obsessions comprise aggressive, sexual, or religious thoughts that foster praying or mental rituals; (d) symmetry symptoms in which objects must appear in a precise fashion, wherein the person acts by ordering, straightening, repeating, or counting objects or acts; (e) hoarding may occur in which individuals obsessively collect items that they seem unable to let go of even if this undermines their ability to function. Some of these behaviors may appear abnormal to others, resulting in social alienation, which can aggravate an already bad situation.

Initially, obsessive thoughts may present weakly or are largely unformed, creating discomfort or anxiety until the obsession has been dealt with. The relief may be transient, and when obsessive thoughts again emerge, the behaviors that diminish anxiety will again be emitted and reinforced by the reduction of anxiety. As these thoughts become more formed, individuals might become preoccupied with specific notions, such as someone close to them becoming infected by a disease or dying, or that certain objects have important characteristics that are 'meaningful'. Still other obsessive thoughts can take the form of conspiracies or sexual characteristics, and in a severe form the obsessions may be delusional.

Is it really all that odd?

At first blush, obsessive-compulsive behaviors seem rather strange. Why would anyone engage in these behaviors? Is there anything even remotely rewarding about them that might promote their frequent repetition? For that matter, it might seem still stranger when the behavior involves self-injurious acts such as compulsive hair pulling (trichotillosis) or the repeated cutting of body parts? Many of us will have had the experience of being bugged by leaving something undone, and when we finally engage in behaviors to get rid of what had been gnawing at us, there's a sense of relief. Can you remember as a kid playing a game in which you touched every sign on the way to school (or had to step on every sidewalk crack)? If you missed one you had to go back and 'get it' since not doing so ate away at you. The relief was tangible when it was done, even though you knew it was dopey. Perhaps the person with OCD is taking this to an extreme and it's rewarding to 'scratch that itch'. In the case of self-injurious behaviors, other processes may be at play. Self-harm, for instance, may be a counterproductive way of dealing with emotional pain, intense anger, and frustration, but at the same time it allows the individual to feel that they have a semblance of control over their destiny. Relatedly, self-harm may cause the release of certain brain chemicals (e.g., dopamine, endorphins) that provide transient relief from emotional pain, thereby reinforcing the behavior.

(Continued)

Self-injurious behaviors aren't all that uncommon. It's frequently seen in animals under some conditions. Hair pulling, self-biting, or feather pulling are observed across many species. These behaviors often occur in animals that are kept in penned conditions, including caged zoo animals (they might exhibit OCD-like behaviors in the form of repeated pacing back and forth). It might be that isolation and loneliness trigger these behaviors if for no other reason than to create a degree of stimulation and relief from boredom or they may reflect frustration and emotional stress. Indeed, animals maintained in captivity exhibit signs of distress, including excessively elevated levels of glucocorticoids, immune disturbances, reduced fertility, and offspring death occurs frequently. Early death is not uncommon, especially in large-brained animals, such as elephants and orcas that have difficulties adapting to these restrictive environments. Appropriately, having animals penned has been described as 'neural cruelty' (Fischer & Romero, 2019).[1]

Biological factors related to OCD

Different views have been offered concerning the complex network of neural circuits involved in OCD (e.g., Stein, 2019). These often entailed complicated loops comprising many brain regions. Specifically, frontal cortical brain sites involved in executive functioning, decision-making, identifying cognitive conflict, and error monitoring (i.e., the anterior cingulate cortex, ventromedial, dorsolateral, and lateral-orbital cortex) may be fundamental components of the neural network involved in OCD. When individuals are in a situation where dual and inconsistent messages are received (e.g., where one signal tells them to 'go' and another tells them to 'stop'), the anterior cingulate cortex appears to be activated as it is necessary for decision-making. However, hyper-activation of the anterior cingulate cortex was evident when individuals presenting with OCD were placed in decision-making situations. This brain region might be having difficulty in making appropriate appraisals and decisions so that individuals end up with improper feedback that might lead to repeated behavioral responses. In addition, OCD may involve different aspects of the lateral and medial orbitofrontal cortex that are responsible for processing information with a negative or a positive valence, respectively. Thus, responding to punishment and escaping from danger might contribute to some of the repetitive or ritualized behaviors characteristic of OCD, as might appropriate inhibition of neuronal activity when situations were found to be safe. The brain regions related to executive functioning are linked to those associated with reward processes (the ventral tegmentum and nucleus accumbens) that culminate in certain behaviors being reinforced so that they're apt to be repeated. Neurons in these regions, in turn, activate the thalamus and the basal ganglia, which provide feedback

---

[1]There was a time when mental hospitals, such as the Bethlem Royal Hospital of London, which later became known as 'Bedlam', charged tourists to witness the ravings of patients (referred to as 'the beasts') who had been put on display. These patients typically were poor and powerless, whereas wealthier people with mental health difficulties were assigned to private facilities or maintained at home.

to several brain regions, including the cortex (Milad & Rauch, 2012). Other neural systems have been associated with this condition that may contribute to its different behavioral characteristics.

The features of OCD vary widely across individuals and, while it is likely that they involve overlapping processes, distinct mechanisms likely contribute to each. For instance, it was proposed that we ordinarily have a 'feeling of knowing' that is essential for us to end a task and move on to other activities. If the signal or its reception for this 'security motivation system' is not operating properly, then the OCD symptoms will persist (Szechtman et al., 2020). Many people exhibit these characteristics when faced with uncertainty. After leaving your home have you ever had the worry of 'Did I turn off the iron (or stove)?' or 'Did I shut the garage door?' This feeling might haunt you all day (some of us more than others) unless you go back and check. Perhaps the person with OCD might be affected in this way all or much of the time.

Treatment of OCD

It is difficult to determine a single best treatment of OCD as the features of the disorder may be different from one individual to the next, and the mechanisms involved may vary with characteristics of the illness (e.g., does repeated checking involve processes akin to those involved in hoarding?). Some success has been achieved with CBT and with exposure therapy in which patients learn, in gradual steps, to tolerate the anxiety that occurs when they do not engage in the compulsive behavior.

High doses of SSRIs have been used to treat OCD, although it may take some time for positive effects to appear, and side effects of high doses may create discomfort. The effectiveness of SSRIs can be enhanced by CBT as well as by antipsychotic medications. It seems that targeting glutamate, a neurotransmitter known to be involved in learning and memory, might also provide positive outcomes (Costa et al., 2017).

Posttraumatic stress disorder (PTSD)

Posttraumatic stress disorder (PTSD) has received growing attention, particularly as it affects a substantial portion of individuals who encounter traumatic experiences or chronic stressors, and because we have heard about it occurring so often among soldiers who served in combat missions. In the DSM-5, PTSD is no longer presented in the section dealing with anxiety, instead appearing in a category of 'Trauma and stressor-related disorders'. However, it has been included in this chapter because it shares many characteristics with anxiety disorders as well as depressive disorders, although as we'll see, it is quite different from either of these conditions.

───**Secrets from the front lines**─────────────────────────────

PTSD became widely known after its introduction in the DSM-III in 1980, but it has a very long history. For the most part, it was considered in the context of war-related injuries, and numerous reports of mental disturbances among soldiers who were not physically harmed had been described in conflicts during the early 1800s. Physicians at the time seemed perplexed by these occurrences but could offer little as to what caused this condition and offered still less for their patients.

It is unfortunate that in the early days of this disorder there was the belief in many circles that those who were suffering 'shell shock' were actually cowards who had either been feigning symptoms to avoid being at the front, or developed symptoms because of their personal weakness or lack of character. In fact, numerous soldiers that experienced shell shock were tried for military crimes, and in some instances were executed. In other instances, soldiers were treated brutally until they were ready to assume a heroic role at the front lines.

With the mounting toll of 'traumatic neurosis' during the early part of the twentieth century, particularly during World War I, greater attention was devoted to this condition. Affected individuals were hospitalized, although the treatments offered had little value, and the condition often worsened over time, frequently becoming a lifelong disorder. But several lessons had been learned from the experiences of soldiers, foremost was that treatment of what was then referred to as 'war neurosis' was best dealt with if individuals were treated soon after symptoms first appeared. Accordingly, patients were initially treated at the front lines or nearby, and in more than half the cases soldiers could eventually return to the battle. It was thought that keeping patients in the proximity of the front lines, in the din of war, produced positive effects. Perhaps being close to their comrades and the social support received may have been responsible for these actions, or because desensitization was inadvertently produced. It had similarly been assumed that nonintrusive psychotherapy (not digging deeply into the past) was beneficial. These approaches were adopted during World War II and continued to be used during the war in Vietnam with some success, but about 25% of soldiers developed incapacitating psychiatric infirmities.

The stigma that followed afflicted soldiers was intense, and self-stigma often developed, encouraged by self-blame for their perceived weaknesses. It was estimated that more than half of those individuals suffering from PTSD did so in silence rather than seeking help. In fact, the upper echelons of the armed forces seemed queasy about referring to the condition as a mental disorder and chose alternative names to describe it, such as 'operational fatigue'. Thanks to the bravery of individuals, such as Lieutenant-General The Honourable Roméo Dallaire, who developed PTSD while leading the UN Peacekeeping Mission during the Rwandan genocide, such mental illnesses began coming out of the shadows and were treated as they should have been years earlier.

───

Breadth of PTSD

Many people encounter traumatic events at one time or another, and the incidence of PTSD is as high as 7–8%, varying considerably across developed countries. The *DSM-IV* had described PTSD as occurring in response to an intense stressor that involves actual or threatened death, injury, or learning about an unexpected or violent death, and that the individual's response must comprise feelings of fear, helplessness, or horror. The *DSM-5* criteria for PTSD were changed to take into consideration nontraumatic stressors (i.e., those that didn't elicit fear, helplessness, and horror), and it also considered the timeline for the appearance of PTSD, and the expansion of the symptoms that comprise the disorder (see Table 10.3).

PTSD is usually considered in the context of individuals who experienced a natural disaster (earthquake, hurricane, tsunami), as well as experiences that many people unfortunately encounter in their daily lives. These include car accidents, medical complications, being told about a severe medical condition, rape, bullying, assault, and witnessing traumatic events (e.g., abuse). In fact, PTSD is not infrequent among women following childbirth even though it entailed a positive anticipatory component. In addition, PTSD symptoms can be instilled by chronic stressors, such as chronic racial discrimination (Matheson & Anisman, 2012), and symptoms of PTSD even developed when the stressor was a distal one (i.e., when individuals were not directly confronted with the trauma), as occurred among US residents following the 9/11 terrorist attacks.

Table 10.3 Posttraumatic stress disorder (DSM-5 criteria).

A diagnosis of PTSD comprises symptoms within several categories (criteria) being present for more than a month, the symptoms are perceived as being distressing and cause functional impairments, such as occupational or social disturbances. These symptoms should not be due to medications or substance use.

Criterion A. Exposure to actual or threatened death, serious injury, sexual violation, or witnessing others experience such a traumatic event. Trauma experiences can comprise learning of trauma experienced by a close friend/relative, or repeated exposure to details (consequences) regarding the traumatic event (e.g., first responders collecting human remains; police officers repeatedly exposed to details of child abuse), but not through exposure that occurs through electronic media, television, movies, or pictures.

Criterion B. Presence of one or more of the following *intrusion* symptoms:

1. intrusive, involuntary, distressing memories of the traumatic event(s) that occur spontaneously or in response to specific cues;

2. recurrent dreams in which the content or affect is related to the traumatic event(s);

3. dissociative reactions in which individuals feel as if the traumatic event(s) are recurring (flashbacks): in its extreme form individuals may experience loss of awareness of their current surroundings;

4. reminders of the trauma elicit intense or prolonged psychological distress or physiological reactions.

Criterion C. Persistent *avoidance* of stimuli associated with the trauma. These behaviors comprise either:

1. avoidance of distressing thoughts, or feelings associated with the traumatic event(s);

2. avoidance of reminders of the events (people, places, conversations, activities, objects) that promote distress.

(Continued)

Table 10.3   (Continued)

Criterion D. Disturbed cognitions and mood manifested by two or more of the following:

1.   disturbed recall of an important aspect of the event(s) for reasons other than head injury or drug intake;

2.   exaggerated, persistent negative perspectives or expectations about oneself, others, or the world;

3.   persistent and distorted self- or other-blame regarding the cause or consequences of the traumatic event(s);

4.   a strong, persistent negative emotional state (e.g., fear, horror, anger, guilt, or shame);

5.   anhedonia;

6.   feelings of detachment or estrangement from others;

7.   persistent failure to experience positive emotions (e.g., psychic numbing).

Criterion E. Marked *arousal* and reactivity associated with the traumatic event(s) that began or became worse following the traumatic event. Arousal and reactivity are reflected by two or more of the following:

2.   reckless or self-destructive behavior;

3.   hypervigilance;

4.   hyperarousal or an exaggerated startle response;

5.   concentration difficulties;

6.   sleep disturbance (e.g., difficulty falling or staying asleep or restless sleep).

In addition to these symptoms, dissociative features that comprise depersonalization or derealization may be present as they frequently are in acute stress disorder.

Acute stress disorder

It is not unusual for symptoms such as intense emotional reactions to appear soon after a catastrophic stressor, but they typically diminish with time. If the symptoms appear very soon after the trauma experience and are present for a period of 3–30 days, then it may be categorized as acute stress disorder (ASD). If symptoms persist beyond 30 days it is recategorized as PTSD. Many of the symptoms of ASD are the same as those of PTSD, accompanied by 'dissociative' symptoms. These comprise (a) a sense of numbing, absence of emotional responses or detachment; (b) reduced awareness of surroundings, or feeling as if in a daze; (c) derealization, wherein individuals experience altered perception or experience of the external world so that it seems unreal; (d) depersonalization, in which individuals have the feeling of watching themself act, but lack control over the situation – the world is dreamlike, less real, or lacking in significance; and (e) dissociative amnesia characterized by memory gaps in which individuals are unable to recall information concerning events of a traumatic or stressful nature (not due to head injury, drugs, or alcohol).

Individuals with ASD may repeatedly re-experience the event through either recurrent images, thoughts, dreams, illusions, flashbacks, as well as the feeling that they are reliving the traumatic experience, or distress that occurs in response to trauma reminders. They may display avoidance of stimuli that arouse recollections of the trauma, and symptoms of anxiety and/or arousal are present, characterized by poor sleep, irritability, impaired concentration, motor restlessness, hypervigilance, and hyper-reactivity.

Vulnerability to PTSD

Even moderately intense traumatic experiences may engender PTSD in some individuals, whereas others seem to be resilient after exceedingly traumatic events. What factors make individuals vulnerable to the effects of traumatic experiences, and which variables contribute to resilience? To a considerable extent, the vulnerability factors outlined earlier concerning other stressor-related pathologies are pertinent to the development of PTSD. Issues related to appraisals of the trauma (i.e., perceived level of threat) and some pretrauma features (psychiatric history, being abused, or experiencing trauma as a child, as well as being separated, divorced, or widowed) contributed to the emergence of PTSD. People who are deemed high in neuroticism (i.e., constant worriers who exhibit chronic anxiety and tend to overreact to daily negative experiences that most people take in their stride) were particularly likely to develop PTSD in response to trauma.

An important predictor of PTSD is that of having previously experienced multiple traumas or pre-existing mental health difficulties, such as anxiety (Kessler et al., 2018). The negative effects of traumatic events were pronounced among individuals with low social support, whereas having social support was associated with a reduction in avoidant coping that might otherwise favor PTSD symptoms. Variables that undermine coping effectiveness lend themselves to the development of PTSD; conversely, experiences that allow individuals to learn how to cope may act against the development of PTSD (Daskalakis et al., 2013). Thus, interventions that target maladaptive coping strategies (social avoidance), and those that encourage social support and understanding from others, might help in diminishing PTSD symptoms.

Traumatic experiences encountered during childhood were apt to increase the immediate reaction to trauma encountered during adulthood and the development of PTSD (Gould et al., 2021). Experiences such as abuse or neglect in childhood could have persistent effects on the ability to cope with stressors, sensitized neurobiological systems, and epigenetic changes that favor the development of PTSD in adulthood, and illness remission would take longer (Blacker et al., 2019).

PTSD in the context of physical illnesses

Traumatic experiences, such as the diagnosis of breast cancer, have been associated with the development of PTSD in more than 20% of survivors. One of the predictors of PTSD in these circumstances was whether individuals had experienced a psychological disorder, such as depression, prior to the cancer experience (De Padova et al., 2021). Likewise, PTSD was more likely to develop among individuals who had previously encountered traumatic or chronic stressor experiences. As such, PTSD might be less likely to develop and the cancer therapy might be more successful if steps were taken to deal with mental health issues related to the trauma rather than just focusing on the cancer. In fact, in women who had been surgically treated for breast cancer, those who received a psychological intervention to reduce distress exhibited improved mood, superior health behaviors, and adherence to cancer treatment and care. Among women who received the psychological intervention the probability of cancer recurrence and death within an 11-year window was reduced relative to women who had not received the intervention (Stagl et al., 2015). Irrespective of the processes that promote such outcomes, determining an individual's previous psychiatric history and coping abilities before beginning therapy could provide essential information for patient well-being.

Neuroanatomical underpinnings of PTSD

Stressors give rise to neuroanatomical and neurobiological changes that have been tied to PTSD. Among other brain changes, PTSD was accompanied by hippocampal atrophy, which led to the suggestion that a traumatic event produced the disorder by affecting hippocampal integrity. A study in twins demonstrated that reduced hippocampal size was not only apparent in individuals suffering PTSD following a war experience but was present in their co-twin who had neither been traumatized nor suffered PTSD (Pitman et al., 2006). Thus, it was thought that having a relatively small hippocampus might increase the vulnerability to PTSD rather than being a consequence of the disorder. However, further analyses revealed that the twin with combat experience who developed PTSD displayed diminished gray matter volume in several brain regions in addition to the hippocampus (e.g., anterior cingulate cortex and insula) relative to that of their co-twin who had not been in a war situation, as well as in other twin pairs who had been in war environments and had not developed PTSD (Kasai et al., 2008).

Major depression is also accompanied by altered brain volume, but changes were distinguishable from those apparent in PTSD, including the latter being accompanied by more pronounced volume of the insula and anterior cingulate cortex (Bromis et al., 2018). Thus, it is unlikely that the diminished brain volume associated with PTSD was secondary to actions related to comorbid depression. Based on genome-wide analyses that included more than 250,000 people, several gene loci were associated with PTSD that involved cortical and subcortical brain regions. Moreover, shared genetic variance was present with features of anxiety, depression, and what was described as an internalizing feature that comprised mood–anxiety–neuroticism. Yet, in several respects, the characteristics of PTSD were also distinct from anxiety disorders pointing to possible targets to deal with this disorder (Stein et al., 2021).

PTSD as a disturbance of memory processes

Is PTSD a disorder in which memory of the trauma is too strong or are other aspects of memory linked to this disorder? Understanding the link between memory and PTSD is complicated, not least because among some individuals who experienced trauma, memories are fragmented, whereas for others the memories are vivid and unrelenting. Furthermore, those who experienced trauma may ruminate incessantly, replaying events so that the memory might become progressively more strongly embedded within neural circuits.

Having been traumatized by a particular event it would be perfectly understandable to react strongly to stimuli subsequently experienced that were relevant to the trauma. For example, a woman who is assaulted in a dark parking lot might subsequently be afraid of dark parking lots, which certainly might be a highly adaptive response. But what if this response generalizes to all dark places, all parking lots (even in daylight), flat open spaces, or places where there are lots of cars? Obviously, this over-generalization might be maladaptive; PTSD-affected individuals not only react strongly to cues reminiscent of the original trauma but their behaviors can be triggered by relatively vague cues, even those distinct from the previously encountered experience (Ježek et al., 2010). Essentially, stressful stimuli might be capable of energizing memory processes related to a previous event not only because they are reminders of that event, but because they engage the same neural circuits that are activated by stressors. From this perspective, PTSD might be related to both focused memory and generalized behavioral and biological responses to stressors.

Another perspective that may be important for the development and treatment of PTSD has been based on the consolidation and reconsolidation of memory processes (Kida et al., 2019). Information that is meant to be remembered initially involves a 'short-term store' regulated by the hippocampus. At this time the memory is fragile and easily disrupted (for example, trying to remember a phone number and then having your thoughts interrupted, results in you having to look up the number again). The memory is then consolidated and transferred into what is referred to as long-term storage where the memory is much stronger and less readily disrupted. However, when this memory is recalled, it re-enters the hippocampal short-term store, where neuronal plasticity makes it susceptible to being altered. Thus, novel events and relevant cues can be incorporated into the original memory so that when it is re-consolidated and returns to long-term memory it may appear in a modified form (Lee et al., 2017). While this plasticity may result in embellishment and broadening of memories, it is possible to take advantage of this plasticity in treating PTSD. Specifically, if a person is asked to recall a trauma memory, manipulations can be undertaken through suggestions or by pharmacological treatments that can either alter the memory or dissociate it from the related emotional and cognitive responses (Kida et al., 2019). We'll consider this further when we discuss treatments for PTSD.

Most often, PTSD had been viewed as being tied to the development of strong memories, but the position emerged that this disorder ought to be seen as a failure of processes that lead to forgetting. Traditionally, forgetting had been thought to emanate from the decay of memory circuits ('engrams' that comprise the interconnections between particular neuronal connections). These engrams can be activated by cues that had been associated with specific events thereby encouraging retrieval of these memories. Forgetting may occur when these engrams are no longer accessible, which entails active processes in which neuroplasticity occurs owing to interference by experiential or environmental factors. From this vantage, PTSD may reflect the 'hijacking' of ordinary forgetting (or extinction) processes so that fear responses persist (Ryan & Frankland, 2022).

PTSD in relation to nonassociative processes

Aside from the influence of mechanisms related to memory and forgetting, the development of PTSD may involve neurocognitive processes that govern attention, information processing, and decision-making (Jacob et al., 2019). As already mentioned, the anterior cingulate cortex is reduced in size among patients with PTSD. This region plays an important role in the integration of neuroregulatory processes that involve emotional information from limbic brain regions and cognitive functioning related to prefrontal cortical functioning. The anterior cingulate cortex is exceptionally responsive to stressors and is important in the appraisal of events and decision-making. Accordingly, the suggestion that the anterior cingulate cortex might be involved in a syndrome such as PTSD is intuitively appealing.

Functional imaging studies indicated that among PTSD patients, activation of the medial PFC response, which is connected to the anterior cingulate cortex, was diminished upon the presentation of aversive stimuli. This included responses to pictures and the sound of combat, as well as narratives of a negative nature that were unrelated to the trauma experience, such as scripts containing traumatic imagery or depictions of fearful faces. In effect, among individuals with PTSD frontal cortical activity that ordinarily inhibits amygdala functioning was altered, not just in response to reminder stimuli, but to varied stressor images. These findings suggest that aberrant behavioral responses could be expected among these individuals in response to any number of stressor events that might be encountered (Dahlgren et al., 2018).

The involvement of the amygdala in PTSD was initially considered due to its sensitivity to stressors and the involvement in anxiety. In fact, vague cues that were related to a traumatic experience influenced amygdala functioning, suggesting that affected individuals were hyper-alert or hyper-responsive even to mild stimuli relevant to the trauma experience. Among veterans with PTSD excessive amygdala activity could be elicited by threatening faces to a greater extent than in veterans who had not developed PTSD (Badura-Brack et al., 2018). Evidently, the axis comprising the PFC, amygdala, and hippocampus, representing appraisal, emotional, and memory processes, respectively, is critically involved in PTSD, and this circuitry might define re-experiencing, emotional reactivity, and fear (avoidance), which comprise specific characteristics of the syndrome. In this context among rodents subjected to stressors that produce a PTSD-like syndrome, as well as in veterans with PTSD, the myelination of neurons is markedly elevated so that messages regarding trauma occur more quickly. As a result, fear responses and avoidant behaviors occur more readily, accompanied by diminished flexibility in the adoption of other behaviors (Long et al., 2021).

One further consideration should be emphasized that is related to the position concerning extinction (forgetting) of previously learned fear responses. A perspective that can be taken concerning PTSD is that the disorder might reflect a failure of recovery system(s) owing to repeated re-exposure to reminders of the trauma. Ordinarily, most individuals react strongly to traumatic events, but with the passage of time or the use of appropriate coping responses, the 'damage' created by trauma ought to diminish. However, if biological systems do not have the opportunity to recover, processes associated with PTSD may strengthen, becoming more resistant to their elimination. It has been maintained that to overcome trauma it is essential to have a 'safe place' to which an individual can retreat. In the face of some very negative events, including racial and cultural stigmatization as well as collective historical trauma that has been experienced by groups of people, finding these safe places can be exceptionally challenging (Matheson et al., 2020) rendering them at elevated risk for the emergence and maintenance of stress-related pathologies.

As described in Figure 10.1, numerous factors may contribute to the development of PTSD, including genetic factors and experiences that preceded a major trauma, and those that were related to the post-trauma period. PTSD has been linked to numerous neurobiological alterations and an array of behavioral alterations related to fear and anxiety processes together with multiple cognitive alterations.

Biochemical determinants of PTSD

Even though brain processes associated with PTSD can to some extent be distinguished from those of other illnesses, doing this in relation to neurochemical alterations can be a knotty problem. Given the limitations concerning what can be analyzed in human brain tissue, the conclusions that can be drawn regarding the neurochemical underpinnings of PTSD are limited. A good deal of evidence in this regard has been inferred from studies assessing the effectiveness of drug treatments, but it is uncertain whether the treatments are masking symptoms or getting at the root mechanisms responsible for the illness. Besides, given the array of symptoms associated with PTSD, different neurobiological processes may be aligned with the distinct features that characterize the syndrome.

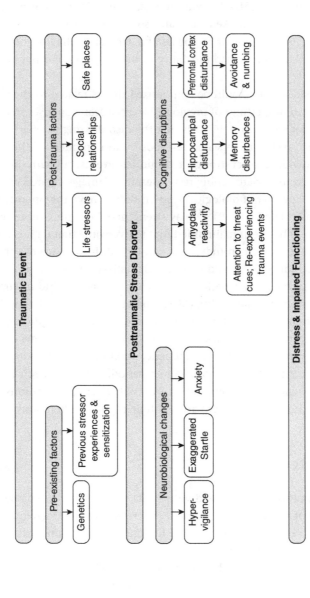

Figure 10.1 Vulnerability to PTSD may be related to genetic factors as well as earlier events that might have caused biological systems to be especially reactive to trauma encounters. At the same time, events that transpire during the post-trauma period may influence vulnerability or resilience to the disorder. Posttraumatic stress disorder may be affected by multiple neurobiological processes that influence fear and anxiety. As well, the trauma may be accompanied by neurobiological alterations within several brain regions that are linked to diverse features of the disorder, including the response to reminders of the trauma, memory processes and the inability to extinguish fear responses, as well as avoidant behaviors.

In assessing the biological processes related to PTSD, researchers have often relied on animal models, but as in other complex human diseases, there may be questions concerning their validity in recapitulating PTSD in humans. It is relatively simple to assess some behaviors that are characteristic of PTSD, such as hyperarousal (e.g., by evaluating startle responses to sudden noise) or the avoidance of specific stimuli. It is another matter to evaluate whether rodents are 're-experiencing' the trauma, although animals are certainly reactive to trauma-related cues, which can strengthen their emotional responses.

A second difficulty comes from the fact that stressors, especially those that are traumatic, might not only elicit PTSD but also produce general anxiety and depression. Indeed, the paradigms used in animal models to assess the behavioral changes taken to reflect PTSD are frequently the very same as those used to assess anxiety and depression. Because of this, it's uncertain whether the studies are actually tapping into PTSD or another condition. Likewise, the predictive validity of the models is compromised in pharmacological studies conducted to attenuate symptoms as the treatments used to diminish behavioral disturbances in PTSD (e.g., SSRIs) are effective for other anxiety disturbances and depression.

It isn't our intent to overstate inherent difficulties with these approaches. To be sure, several promising animal models of PTSD have been developed to simulate human experiences. But these models have not led to viable strategies to treat the disorder in humans. In part, this may reflect animal models not incorporating known risk factors for this disorder. Normally, only a subset of individuals who experience traumatic events develop PTSD. The goal in animal studies is typically to induce the symptoms in as many animals as possible, but without adequate consideration of the individual differences that ought to occur in a valid model of the disorder. In doing so, researchers forgo the opportunity of detecting individual differences linked to specific symptoms that could guide further experiments to determine causal connections between brain processes and the behavioral characteristics expressed in the model. Furthermore, effective models ought to consider the specific symptom profiles that experimental animals display and define the risk factors that favor (or act against) the development of a PTSD-like condition (e.g., Richter-Levin et al., 2019). This not only includes genetic and epigenetic factors but the animal's social environment and previous negative and positive experiences.

Norepinephrine

Stressor experiences in both animals and humans can influence neuronal activity within brain circuitry, such as the 'salience network' that includes the anterior insula and the anterior cingulate cortex, which is important for identifying and filtering stimuli that are fundamental for stress-related appraisal processes. Variations of NE functioning may be one of the neurotransmitters fundamental for the operation of this network and together with neurotransmitters in other brain regions may be important in learning, memory, and reactivity associated with stressful experiences (Ross & Van Bockstaele, 2020). As we'll see shortly, pharmacological treatments to alter NE receptors have been used to dampen PTSD symptoms.

Efforts have been made to determine the relationship between plasma NE and PTSD. A meta-analysis suggested that PTSD was accompanied by elevated circulating NE levels (Pan et al., 2018), but evaluating NE levels at a single point in time may not be an adequate representation concerning the link to a dynamic disorder, such as PTSD. Although it is possible that NE variations in cerebrospinal fluid may be associated with PTSD among individuals who had previously encountered stressors and subsequently experienced trauma (Hendrickson et al., 2018) the NE levels in urine or blood may have little to do with brain processes that subserve this condition.

CRH and corticoids

In view of the pronounced CRH and glucocorticoid changes elicited by stressors, it was reasonable to hypothesize that they might play a role in the development of PTSD. Manipulations of these hormones can influence features of PTSD to a modest extent, but the relationships between these hormones and PTSD are not straightforward. As cortisol release from the adrenal gland is a prototypical response to stressful situations, it might have been expected that PTSD would be accompanied by exceptionally elevated levels of this hormone. However, this frequently does not occur among individuals who experienced trauma or chronic stressors that led to PTSD. To the contrary, with the appearance of pronounced PTSD symptoms, cortisol levels are comparable or fall below those of individuals who show no symptoms, which may be related to elevated sensitivity of hippocampal glucocorticoid receptors that regulate HPA functioning (Szeszko et al., 2018). Furthermore, PTSD is associated with a change in the diurnal pattern of cortisol secretion, so that the normal daily fluctuations become flattened – the morning spike of cortisol levels that accompany increased life stressors are reduced, and evening cortisol levels are elevated. The more severe the PTSD symptoms, the flatter the morning cortisol response tended to be, particularly in the presence of arousal symptoms and to a lesser degree when emotional numbing was present (Garcia et al., 2020). Given the variations of HPA functioning, it was suggested that treatments that normalize glucocorticoid receptor sensitivity might have positive effects (Somvanshi et al., 2020).

It might be thought that once HPA functioning is down-regulated, glucocorticoid influences on varied target organs may be diminished and individuals might be at risk for pathology as they might not have the biological resources necessary to contend with further stressors. However, it will be recalled (Chapter 4) that even though cortisol levels are diminished among individuals with PTSD, a particularly exaggerated HPA response can be elicited in response to a meaningful stressor (Matheson & Anisman, 2012). It was maintained that down-regulated basal HPA reactivity among traumatized individuals may be an adaptive response to preclude the adverse effects generated by excessive cortisol release for a protracted period. However, this down-regulation might itself be maladaptive as the cortisol changes might be necessary to deal with certain stressors. As such, it might be advantageous for HPA functioning to be generally diminished, but in response to especially relevant stressor cues certain brain regions are activated (e.g., amygdala), which could override the otherwise down-regulated HPA response.

Like in many other spheres of research the cortisol response associated with severe stressors that led to PTSD and the exaggerated response to psychosocial stressors, such as the TSST, have not been uniform across studies (Metz et al., 2020). Numerous reasons might account for the diverse results obtained, including the nature of the trauma that led to PTSD, and the features of the laboratory stressor employed. Most of all, subgroups of PTSD may exist (e.g., those who do or do not display dissociative symptoms) in which HPA responses can be distinguished from one another (Zaba et al., 2015). In effect, it may be counterproductive to assume that all individuals with PTSD, even if they had experienced similar traumas, would exhibit comparable behavioral features or underlying biological processes. It follows that subgroups of individuals might likewise be differentially responsive to therapeutic interventions.

GABA and glutamate

When GABA levels in certain brain regions are low, the lack of inhibition allows for the persistence of neuronal functioning that is part of a fear or PTSD-like state (i.e., the stress response does not extinguish). Evidence for GABA involvement in PTSD has come from reports that a polymorphism on the gene that codes for the GABA transporter that removes GABA from the synaptic cleft was associated with PTSD irrespective of the presence of depression or substance use disorder (Bountress et al., 2017). Further support for GABA involvement in PTSD came from reports that this disorder was accompanied by reduced GABA in the prefrontal cortex and insula (Rosso et al., 2021), and the normal binding of benzodiazepine to GABA receptors was altered (Reuveni et al., 2018). As PTSD was accompanied by alterations of neuronal activity within the amygdala, anterior cingulate cortex, and insula, which are components of the brain network associated with the salience of environmental stimuli, these changes may underly several PTSD characteristics, notably hypervigilance, elevated attention toward potentially threatening stimuli, and failure to integrate sensory information and emotional processes (Szeszko & Yehuda, 2019).

In our discussion of depressive disorders, GABA and glutamate were considered to act conjointly in promoting this disorder. It similarly appeared that PTSD was accompanied by altered balances between glutamate and GABA within the anterior cingulate cortex, being most tightly linked to certain symptoms, such as poor sleep (Sheth et al., 2019). As glutamate is the most abundant excitatory neurotransmitter, it is not overly surprising that PTSD was accompanied by glutamate changes, although the nature of these changes varied across brain regions. In traumatized youth, glutamatergic functioning was diminished so that the connectivity between the prefrontal cortex and the amygdala was impaired (Ousdal et al., 2019). In other regions, such as the hippocampus, PTSD was accompanied by elevated glutamate varying with the trauma load and with re-experiencing symptoms (Rosso et al., 2017). Together, these findings indicate that glutamate links to PTSD are brain region-specific and may be related to different features of the disorder (e.g., those related to appraisal processes and those tied to memory).

Aside from the changes of glutamate concentrations, imaging analyses indicated that PTSD was accompanied by greater availability of certain glutamate receptors (mGluR5). This was especially apparent when avoidant symptoms were present. (Holmes et al., 2017). The links to mGluR5 were likely unrelated to comorbid depression given that this receptor was elevated in PTSD patients relative to that observed in depressed individuals and healthy controls, and the elevated levels of this receptor were especially notable among PTSD patients who reported suicidal ideation (Davis et al., 2019). It was further reported that elevated cortical mGluR5 was accompanied by avoidant symptoms, and in a parallel assessment of postmortem tissue cortical mGluR5 presence on cells was elevated, together with diminished FKBP5 expression that regulates cortisol receptor sensitivity. These findings point to potential conjoint glutamate and glucocorticoid actions in mediating PTSD (Holmes et al., 2017).

Neuropeptide Y

Neuropeptide Y (NPY), which is involved in eating processes, has been associated with the behavioral responses elicited by stressors. The anxiety and hyper-reactivity elicited by a stressor in rodents were accompanied by a reduction in the expression of NPY in the hippocampus and amygdala. Moreover, the greater vulnerability to PTSD among females than males in rodent models was associated with more pronounced reductions of NPY in females (Nahvi & Sabban, 2020). Of particular significance was that administration of NPY acting agents altered behavioral responses elicited by a stressor, pointing to this hormone engendering enhanced resilience. When NPY was administered intranasally to rats prior to prolonged stressor exposure, the subsequent development of PTSD-like symptoms was diminished (Sabban et al., 2016). It is unlikely that NPY acts alone in moderating PTSD symptoms, and it has been demonstrated that alterations of cannabinoid receptors (CB_1) and NPY within the amygdala could influence behavioral changes (Maymon et al., 2020). Similarly, NPY diminishes the effects of stressors in the promotion of CRH and NE release within the amygdala, and in this way may be the controller for the development of stress-related pathology, particularly fear-related symptoms, such as avoidance and hyper-reactivity.

The focus on NPY as a resilience factor in relation to PTSD began in earnest with the finding that this disorder was less common among trauma-exposed soldiers that had high levels of NPY (Sah & Geracioti, 2013). This was subsequently observed in association with stressors that could elicit PTSD in civilian populations (Schmeltzer et al., 2016). An impressive case was made that PTSD was most apt to occur in conjunction with low levels of NPY and that this outcome could be modified by treatments that altered NPY functioning, and thus could be a target to diminish PTSD in humans. However, human trials have fallen well behind the pre-clinical studies. Nonetheless, the preclinical studies demonstrating the efficacy of NPY administered by nasal spray during the post-trauma period to limit the development of PTSD may provide the impetus to assess NPY treatments in humans (Sabban et al., 2016).

Sensitized responses and epigenetic factors in PTSD

The features of PTSD in some individuals evolve and worsen with the passage of time and over-generalization may appear. It can be argued that the distress associated with trauma might result in persistent rumination and replaying of events that cumulatively have adverse consequences, much like chronic stressors can have such consequences. This view is in keeping with the position that stressors may result in permanent changes in the characteristics of neurons so that they are more readily triggered by certain stimuli, especially reminders of the adverse event. In effect, neurons might become sensitized, so that with repeated trauma or even reminders of the trauma, a progressively greater propensity toward pathology might develop. In discussing animal models of PTSD, it was pointed out that a single strong stressor followed by intermittent reminder cues resulted in behavioral changes, and that reminder cues were necessary for this long-lasting outcome to occur. These reminder cues might have their effects by strengthening the neuronal network associated with the emotional memories concerning the trauma, or alternatively they might prevent the time-related dissipation of emotional trauma memories that might otherwise occur.

Danger: brain at work

Individuals often make the mistake of assuming that once an exceptionally distressing event is over, so is the distress and the accompanying biological changes, and consequently recovery ought to follow. We even have expressions that speak to this, such as 'Time heals all wounds'. Time might allow for some wounds to heal in some individuals, whereas for others, time moves ever so slowly, and the trauma memories linger and so do their psychological and physical consequences. Parents who have lost a child, individuals who experienced the horrors of warfare, or survivors of genocidal efforts don't simply forget. Some might never speak about their experiences ('a conspiracy of silence'), whereas others can't stop speaking about them. Although the majority of individuals go on with life, their traumatic memories are often just below the surface, and their effects can re-emerge.

(Continued)

It's odd that so many people gain some sort of pleasure in deriding Sigmund Freud, despite the enormous contributions he made to psychology and psychiatry, including his thoughts on defense mechanisms and other processes that are still considered to be useful. He had postulated, among many other things, that early experiences might mark individuals for life, although he would have been unaware of how this came about from a biological perspective. After all, he didn't have the luxury of knowing about the workings of neurochemical systems. Nevertheless, Freud was sufficiently astute to recognize that a traumatic memory represented a causative 'agent still at work' in the development of pathology.

In addition to sensitized responses, stressful events encountered in childhood may engender epigenetic changes that influence responses to stressors in adulthood (Szyf, 2009), and might thus increase vulnerability to diseases, such as depression and PTSD (Torres-Berrío et al., 2019). Various epigenetic changes on genes that code for diverse neurobiological changes have been identified that could potentially act in this capacity. These have been identified in relation to processes involved in cortisol functioning, and trauma-related epigenetic effects could influence processes related to inflammation and cytotoxicity (Smith et al., 2020). These epigenetic changes may be associated with other mental illnesses and might account for the comorbidities that frequently appear with PTSD (Blacker et al., 2019). As we'll see in Chapter 12, epigenetic changes that are associated with pathologies, such as PTSD, can be passed across generations so that features of the illness can appear in the children (and perhaps grandchildren) of individuals who had encountered traumatizing events (Howie et al., 2019).

Complex PTSD (CPTSD)

In a subset of patients complex PTSD may develop, which comprises the usual symptoms of PTSD with several additional features being present. This entails difficulty regulating emotions in that persistent sadness or explosive anger may be present and dissociative features may be prominent. Individuals may become distrustful of others, maintain negative self-perceptions, including guilt and shame, and it is not unusual for relationships to be difficult so that social avoidance is maintained. Feelings of hopelessness regarding their situation may be accompanied by altered systems of meaning in which long-held beliefs (e.g., spirituality or religion) are abandoned.

CPTSD has only recently received much clinical attention and was included in the most recent International Classification of Diseases (ICD-11). The development of CPTSD has been associated with chronic, repeated, and prolonged exposure to trauma, such as childhood neglect or abuse as well as longstanding forms of interpersonal violence, such as forced sex work, being kidnapped or tortured, and repeated domestic violence. It is still unclear how CPTSD differs from PTSD from a neurochemical or neuroanatomical perspective, nor is it known whether CPTSD ought to be treated differently than PTSD (Cloitre, 2020).

Treatment of PTSD

An assortment of therapeutic methods has been used to treat PTSD, including family or interpersonal therapy, trauma management therapy, CBT, acceptance and commitment therapy, mindfulness training, prolonged exposure therapy, imagery training (rehearsal), and virtual reality treatments, as well as diverse pharmacological approaches. We'll limit our discussions here to some of the most prominent treatments. Other methods that can diminish features of PTSD are provided in Chapter 13.

Several forms of psychotherapy and behavioral therapy have been used to diminish symptoms of PTSD, with CBT being among the more effective treatments (Bisson et al., 2013). With the great number of individuals experiencing PTSD, it was desirable to apply group CBT. While the data comparing individual and group therapy are limited, it does appear that group CBT may be effective, having the built-in advantage of patients being able to gain from social support. Cognitive processing therapy (CPT), a form of CBT that was explicitly designed to treat PTSD and trauma-related disorders, has proven to be effective, although it has not been studied as well as more usual CBT procedures. A form of CBT was developed for people at risk in order to diminish the likelihood that PTSD would develop. Stress Inoculation Training (SIT), which facilitates ways of coping has been found to be relatively effective in treating people who develop PTSD, although it is usually considered as a second-line treatment. This procedure combines effective coping practice, muscle relaxation training, deep breathing, and role-playing so that individuals are more prepared to deal with actual triggers that can promote symptoms (Jackson et al., 2019). In contrast to CBT, procedures such as stress management/relaxation were less successful, and still other therapies (e.g., supportive therapy, nondirective counseling, psychodynamic therapies, and hypnotherapy) were generally reported to be largely ineffective.

Behavioral therapy that comprised prolonged exposure has been widely used in the treatment of PTSD. As described in diminishing phobias, this approach focuses on efforts to extinguish emotional and cognitive responses to danger cues that had not been properly extinguished previously. In the course of treatment, the danger cues are gradually reintroduced (using imagery or actual exposure to threatening cues), thereby resulting in the extinction of the fear response. Significantly, during the therapy sessions individuals also repeatedly retell their trauma experiences and engage emotionally with these. Eventually, the memories and cues that had elicited powerful emotional and physiological responses might no longer have such effects.

One form of therapy, eye movement desensitization and reprocessing (EMDR), is at first blush a bit flaky and, predictably, had not initially been accepted readily as a method of treatment. However, well-controlled trials have attested to its efficacy

(Khan et al., 2018), although the effectiveness of the procedure was considered to be moderate and many studies were reported to be of low quality (Morris et al., 2022). This procedure entails patients focusing on a vivid image of the traumatic event that they had encountered, during which the therapist has the patient conduct various eye movements (e.g., following a finger that moves across their visual field) or stimulating other senses. It is thought that the memory of the trauma (which has been activated during the session) will be associated with other less threatening stimuli so that the reconsolidation of traumatic memory and the emotions ordinarily elicited by these memories are dissociated from one another.

Given the profound neuronal changes that are elicited by stressors, and especially traumatic events, it would be expected that pharmacotherapy would be a first-line treatment to ameliorate the symptoms of PTSD, but the success obtained has been somewhat limited, thus it has often been relegated to a second-line treatment. A combination of CBT and an SSRI provoked a modest enhancement relative to either treatment alone (Mavranezouli et al., 2020). Somewhat surprisingly, in a randomized controlled trial exposure therapy combined with an SSRI was not more effective than that of either treatment administered alone. In contrast, exogenous corticoid treatments (hydrocortisone) augmented the action of prolonged exposure therapy (Lehrner et al., 2021).

Based on the findings that stressful experiences have significant autonomic effects and influenced brain NE activity, attention was devoted to the possibility that NE receptor antagonists might be useful in treating PTSD. While there had been reports that drugs that diminish NE release, such as those that block presynaptic receptors (e.g., clonidine and prazosin), modestly reduced some symptoms associated with PTSD, such as trauma-related nightmares and insomnia, this was not confirmed in a randomized controlled trial (Raskind et al., 2018). This does not rule out the possibility that such agents in combination with the β-NE antagonist propranolol, which might be efficacious in alleviating the emotional content associated with traumatic memories, would be more effective in treating PTSD.

It had been suggested that blocking NE activity soon after a trauma when memories were fresh would be effective in altering the course of PTSD. Like new memories, it was maintained that when previously established memories were being recalled, so that they appeared in a short-term hippocampal store (i.e., during memory reconsolidation), they would once again be susceptible to being altered. Thus, manipulations conducted during memory recall might allow for emotional responses and the traumatic memory to be dissociated from one another and then reconsolidated in a new form. Commensurate with perspective, if the β-adrenergic antagonist propranolol was administered soon after the trauma or when this treatment was combined with psychotherapy, PTSD symptoms were diminished (Giustino et al., 2016). Similarly, in a randomized controlled trial propranolol administered prior to memory recall on successive therapy sessions, PTSD symptoms were reduced (Brunet et al., 2018). The actions of propranolol treatment during memory recall appeared to be specific to the disruption of the reconsolidation of emotional memories, as the treatment did not affect declarative memory that entails personal information or general knowledge. The data supporting the use of propranolol in limiting the development of PTSD or reconsolidation has not uniformly been observed. Firm conclusions will have to await data that might be relevant to whether there are certain individuals or conditions that are amenable to this treatment approach, or whether β-blockers would be effective when combined with other therapeutic treatments.

Aside from norepinephrine manipulations, drug treatments that affect cortisol (e.g., hydrocortisone) administered during reconsolidation could reduce PTSD symptoms, just as they did when given early (within six hours) in the evolution of the illness (Astill Wright et al., 2021). Regardless of the mechanism by which glucocorticoids introduced their beneficial effects, these data point to the possibility that a 'window of opportunity' exists following a trauma experience, during which the protracted adverse effects can be diminished. This doesn't imply that the effects of corticoid manipulations are restricted to this brief window. The presence of specific epigenetic markers, including those related to glucocorticoid functioning, could be adopted to predict the subsequent efficacy of cortisol manipulations combined with exposure therapy to diminish PTSD symptoms (Yang et al., 2021).

Since glutamate changes are provoked by traumatic experiences, the possibility was assessed that glutamate manipulations could diminish PTSD features. Unfortunately, pharmacotherapy targeting glutamate did not provide impressive results. It is nevertheless exciting that the glutamate receptor antagonist ketamine, which has proven to be effective in ameliorating treatment resist depression, may be effective in ameliorating PTSD symptoms (Feder et al., 2020). This possibility needs to be confirmed more broadly, and it is important to determine whether the actions of ketamine operated on PTSD features rather than primarily affecting comorbid depression and whether the effects of this agent can be enhanced through concurrent psychotherapy.

A caveat concerning temporal changes in PTSD

One final point needs to be considered, which is applicable not just to PTSD, but also to anxiety disorders and depression, and in the development of substance use disorders. The evolution of PTSD seems to involve dynamic systems so the neurochemical systems activated soon after trauma might not be identical to those that are present during later phases of PTSD. Thus, the effectiveness of treatment strategies might similarly vary over the different phases of the disorder. While treatments that influence glucocorticoid functioning might be effective when administered soon after the traumatic experience, other treatments or treatment combinations (e.g., exposure therapy, CBT alone or in combination with an SSRI) might be more effective in ameliorating the symptoms once PTSD is firmly established. Still other treatments might be especially useful in limiting memory reconsolidation that is otherwise strengthened by reminder cues. Finally, if sensitization of neurochemical changes is fundamental in the development and strengthening of

PTSD symptoms, then it may be propitious to establish strategies that target mechanisms responsible for sensitization. This view is consistent with the suggestion that multi-targeted approaches may ultimately be needed to limit the emergence of PTSD or to treat the disorder once it is established and that the treatments need to be selected based on markers that might reflect these PTSD stages.

Conclusion

Several anxiety disorders have been identified that are not only distinguishable based on their overt symptoms but involve different etiological processes and lifetime trajectories. The various anxiety disorders likely involve both common and different brain processes and neural circuits. Particular attention in this regard has focused on 5-HT, NE, CRH, and GABA, but depending on the specific condition being considered, the involvement of these factors may vary over the course of the illness.

Anxiety disorders affect a large portion of individuals, but these disorders seem not to have received the attention that's needed. Having champions for various causes has been extremely helpful for the support of individuals with a particular pathology. Heart disease, juvenile diabetes, immune-related disorders, cancer of one sort or another, and Alzheimer's disease, have all received public and private support. Recent years have seen appreciable interest in PTSD, whereas to a great extent GAD, OCD, and phobias are still waiting their turn. Yet, anxiety-related disorders represent a considerable burden on individuals and their families as well as health systems. As with many of the illnesses we've discussed, anxiety is highly comorbid with other conditions, and thus its toll goes well beyond that attributed to the primary anxiety condition.

PTSD is among the most disabling mental health conditions, affecting a wide swath of society. At one time it was thought that PTSD developed from severe trauma outside of the usual human experiences (e.g., wars), but it became apparent that this condition could occur with chronic stressors and can even develop with common experiences (e.g., childbirth). Many interlinking neurobiological processes have been implicated in the development of this disorder, just as this is the case in various anxiety disorders. Perhaps for this reason, pharmacotherapies have not been particularly successful in ameliorating these disorders. The features of these disorders vary across people, and it would be reasonable to expect that there isn't any single treatment that would be best for all individuals. At the risk of being redundant, the development of effective treatments for anxiety disorders and PTSD may require individualized strategies based on identifiable biological markers and specific symptoms expressed.

Suggested readings

Kenwood, M.M., Kalin, N.H., & Barbas, H. (2022). The prefrontal cortex, pathological anxiety, and anxiety disorders. *Neuropsychopharmacology, 47*, 260–275.

Shalev, A., Liberzon, I., & Marmar, C. (2017). Post-traumatic stress disorder. *New England Journal of Medicine, 376*, 2459–2469.

Stein, M.B., Levey, D.F., Cheng, Z., et al. (2021). Genome-wide association analyses of post-traumatic stress disorder and its symptom subdomains in the Million Veteran Program. *Nature Genetics, 53*, 174–184.

11

ADDICTION

What's meant by addiction?

People most often think of addiction as physical and psychological dependence on substances (e.g., alcohol, cocaine, heroin, tobacco), and that over time the dose needed to maintain the pleasurable effects of these substances increases, whereas their discontinuation promotes highly aversive physical and psychological consequences. Addiction similarly occurs in relation to gambling, which can be as powerful as that associated with cocaine and heroin use and might be even harder to shake. One often hears the term 'addiction' being applied to sex, the internet, email, and pornography, but it isn't certain that these ought to be considered addictions like those that involve drugs or gambling and might more appropriately be assigned to categories related to compulsive behaviors. It is possible that at some point these behaviors will be examined more thoroughly and their status as addictions will be reconsidered.

Diseases like cancer and heart disease elicit empathetic responses from others, but this less often occurs for those who develop a drug addiction. Some people view addiction as a choice that individuals make, reflecting a moral failing or a character flaw, and considerable stigma is directed toward those experiencing these conditions. Yet, like so many psychological and physical disorders, addiction is a disease brought about by the unfortunate confluence of genetic and epigenetic factors related to neurobiological processes, coupled with the influence of numerous psychosocial factors, including poor or impoverished early-life experiences, stressors encountered in adulthood, some poor life choices, and the wrong social influences.

Learning objectives

Substance use disorders are a huge problem both for the individual and society and is a pathological condition facilitated and even encouraged by different levels of government (witness the proliferation of gambling venues, the paucity of attention given to limiting excessive alcohol consumption, and the weak response that existed for years in curtailing nicotine addiction). Addiction is a complex and multidimensional problem and there are several core issues that the reader should come away with after reading this chapter:

- Addiction comprises a process that might initally arise as a response to positive experiences that the individual might want to recreate, or it can stem from counterproductive efforts to cope with stressors, essentially serving as a self-medicating strategy.
- Factors that favor the development of a substance use disorder may be different from those involved in it being sustained, and these may differ yet again from those responsible for the recurrence of addiction after lengthy periods of abstinence.
- Most biological perspectives on substance use disorders have focused on the contribution of specific neurotransmitters that might be involved in reward or stress processes, and those that affect memory or habits. Environmental cues associated with earlier drug intake might instigate neurochemical changes that maintain the addiction and contribute to addiction recurrence.
- Many substance use disorders have common processes governing them, but clear differences exist between these conditions, and hence treatments that have positive effects for one substance use disorder may have few beneficial effects in the treatment of another.
- To some extent, substance use disorders can be diminished through psychosocial interventions, behavioral therapies, and pharmacological treatments. Optimal effects may be obtained when multiple approaches are adopted concurrently or sequentially.

Substance use disorder is characterized by the recurrent use of drugs that result in clinical and functional impairment, including the failure to meet responsibilities at work, school, or home. Substance use disorder falls on a continuum of severity based on the number of symptoms presented, as described in Table 11.1 (Hasin et al., 2013). Addiction is viewed as the most severe stage of substance use disorder in which individuals have lost self-control so that compulsive drug taking occurs despite their desire to eliminate their self-harming behaviors. Addictions most often involve the use of substances that are illicit (e.g., heroin, cocaine), those that can be obtained through prescriptions (e.g., oxycodone), and those over which there are no or few restrictions (e.g., alcohol, tobacco).

Addictions that do not involve drugs (e.g., gambling) are considered separately although their emergence and maintenance may comprise some similar antecedent events.

Table 11.1 Defining substance use disorder.

An individual is said to be experiencing substance use disorder when they exhibit impaired functioning or distress, reflected by at least two of the following in the preceding 12 months:

1. Tolerance should be evident, reflected by either (a) a need for greater quantities of the substance to obtain the desired outcome or for intoxication to occur; or (b) the use of a given amount (dose) of the substance induces progressively smaller effects with continued use.

2. Withdrawal occurs as reflected by (a) greater amounts of the drug being taken to limit withdrawal symptoms; or (b) closely related substances can be used to limit withdrawal.

3. The substance is not only taken in larger amounts but over longer periods than the individual had intended.

4. The individual was repeatedly unable to reduce substance use despite the desire to do so.

5. Considerable time and effort are expended to use or obtain the substance.

6. Social, occupational, or recreational activities are reduced owing to substance abuse.

7. The use of the substance continues even though the individual is aware the substance has created physical or psychological disturbances.

8. Social or interpersonal problems developed because of drug use.

In addition to the primary features of substance use disorder and addiction, it is not uncommon for any of several secondary characteristics to be present. Amphetamine and cocaine may induce symptoms that are virtually indistinguishable from those associated with schizophrenia, and alcohol has been associated with the emergence of depression. In the absence of physical damage, however, many of these features diminish with continued abstinence. Of course, once sufficient damage has occurred, as in the case of Korsakoff's syndrome (which involves damage to neurons and glial cells following chronic alcohol use), these disturbances cannot be undone. Similarly, after years of excessive alcohol use liver damage can occur, culminating in cirrhosis that if sufficiently profound leads to death unless a liver transplant can be performed. Furthermore, some drugs, such as alcohol intake can favor the occurrence of several forms of cancer, even with moderate levels of consumption.

Stress in relation to the addiction process

The initiation of drug intake and the development of a substance use disorder can come about for a variety of reasons. Both genetic and epigenetic factors may contribute to addictions as can a constellation of experiential and psychosocial factors. Being young (mid to late adolescence), for instance, may be associated with the initiation of drug use because of social pressures, the desire to experiment, the wish to have fun or the thrill of engaging in risky behaviors. These influences may be abetted by forebrain regions associated with executive functioning not being fully developed thus favoring impulsivity, whereas brain regions associated with reward develop sooner. Later, drug use might be repeated to re-experience positive feelings or to escape boredom. However, once an addiction has developed, drug use among some individuals might have continued to prevent the poor feelings that develop as the euphoric effects of the drug dissipate.

Several lines of evidence supported the view that stressors and traumatic events are linked to substance use. Substance use disorders were related to (a) recent stressful experiences, often involving fairly severe trauma, such as the loss of a child, unfaithfulness on the part of others, being the victim of violence, rape, or observing violent victimization; (b) early-life stressors, such as emotional and physical abuse or neglect, parental loss, divorce, or conflict; (c) cumulative stressor experiences, irrespective of whether they occurred in childhood or as an adult; (d) chronic psychiatric illnesses; (e) stress-related illnesses, such as PTSD; and (f) addiction frequently developed among individuals using prescription drugs to diminish chronic pain conditions or post-surgical pain. As more than 20% of individuals are beleaguered by chronic pain, many of whom received opioid treatments, the problem of opioid addiction and drug overdoses had reached critical levels some time ago.

The fact that stressors might contribute to substance use disorders isn't particularly surprising. Drug addiction might reflect a poor attempt at self-medication, wherein those who have experienced trauma might turn to alcohol or other drugs to help them deal with the emotional pain, bad memories, poor sleep, guilt, shame, anxiety, or terror. This might temporarily dampen the adverse effects of stressful or traumatic experiences, but this escape works only so well and for only so long. Individuals may find themselves in a cycle in which stressful events produce increased alcohol and drug use, which might then engender yet more stressful experiences (i.e., the drug use may act as a 'stress proliferator'), thereby encouraging further substance use. As the stressor likely persists, escalation of drug use can further undermine the motivation to cease drug use (Lijffijt et al., 2014).

As much as the stress–addiction link is well established, this begs the question as to why only some individuals are prone to developing substance use disorders in response to negative experiences. Essentially, what are the unique features that result in some individuals succumbing to an addiction whereas other individuals are not affected in this way? This likely involves many different processes and events, including genetic and epigenetic factors or personality traits that might dispose individuals to behave in certain ways to deal with stressors. It may also have to do with individual differences in neurochemical processes that are provoked by stressors actions and those related to drug actions.

The cycle of stressful experiences and drug intake gave rise to different perspectives concerning the processes that link them. According to the *susceptibility hypothesis*, some individuals who use alcohol and other drugs might be more disposed to encounter trauma, and when they do, they will be more vulnerable to psychopathology (such as PTSD), in part, because of poor coping, which may promote further drug use. Related to this, the *high-risk hypothesis* proposes that experiencing traumatic events and substance use is part of a broader tendency among some individuals to engage in high-risk behaviors. Finally, the *common factors hypothesis* suggests that addiction and other pathological conditions share common antecedents, such as stressful or traumatic experiences, hence favoring their co-occurrence.

Sex differences

Substance use disorders may be linked to sex-dependent characteristics. Specifically, in response to distress women often exhibit internalizing behaviors (e.g., rumination) that favor the development of mood and anxiety disorders, whereas men are more likely to display externalizing behaviors, such as impulsivity, and substance use. As a result, treatment protocols might benefit from the adoption of different approaches in the sexes. In women, for instance, coping and cognitive skills that limit rumination might be particularly effective, whereas the treatment for men might focus on limiting impulsive behaviors.

Historically, men had been more likely to experience substance use disorders, but for several years they have been on the rise in women, particularly prescription drugs, such as tranquilizers and sedatives. Indeed, women appear to experience a more rapid escalation in the transition from casual drug use to addiction, and withdrawal difficulties in women may be more intense than in men. The propensity for addiction in females may be related to variations of estrogen and that of dopamine functioning related to reward processes (Becker, 2016). Additional or alternative processes may be responsible for alcohol use disorder. Because women have less water in their bodies, alcohol isn't diluted as well as it is in men, thereby producing higher blood alcohol concentrations. Moreover, owing to greater adipose (fat) tissue in women, which can absorb alcohol, its effects take longer to dissipate. Thus, women may be in greater jeopardy for the development of alcohol use disorder.

Young people are generally susceptible to excessive alcohol consumption. Over the past few decades, the alcohol industry has made a concerted effort to woo young people to consume specific brands of alcohol. This has included advertising that targets youth, and the introduction of products having sweet fruity flavors and which successfully mask the typical taste of alcohol have been appealing to young women (Sudhinaraset et al., 2016). As women are more likely to experience anxiety and depression relative to men, the use of alcohol to self-medicate may also favor the development of alcohol use disorder in women.

Ethnicity and culture

Ethnic and cultural disparities have frequently been observed in relation to drug use. Genetic factors have been implicated in the development of addictions but identifying the specific genes that contribute to these outcomes have been difficult to identify. Among other things, genetic influences may interact with numerous other factors that figure into different addictions (Reed & Kreek, 2021) as well the differences that occur across countries. Moreover, the influence of genetic factors may vary with different substances even if they share some common processes.

Alcohol consumption and alcohol use disorder is far higher in Russia and former Soviet Bloc countries, such as Hungary and Ukraine than in the US, the UK, and Canada. Within Western countries the use of alcohol varies across diverse groups. Whereas whites reported the greatest use of alcohol, binge drinking was far more common in American Indians and Alaska Natives and was less common in African American and Hispanic people and was lowest among Asian people but has been increasing in these groups. Predictably, experiences of discrimination and stigmatization have been linked to alcohol use disorder (Desalu et al., 2019).

To an extent, opioid use disorders in the US have been more common in Hispanic and Native American youth, while African Americans have also experienced relatively high levels of opioid use. Owing to the criminalization of opioid use, many individuals are less likely to seek or obtain treatment for this disorder, and it is typical for community services that might be helpful to be lacking (Siddiqui & Urman, 2022). Likewise, opioid use disorder has for many years been exceptionally broad within Indigenous communities within Canada and elsewhere. This has been apparent among youth who frequently experienced loneliness, feelings of hopelessness, and discrimination, and there is reason to believe that intergenerational effects related to early-life stressor experiences may have contributed to these outcomes (Wilk et al., 2017).

For a time, opioid addiction had been viewed as a phenomenon that was restricted to certain groups and was widely believed to be tied to sociocultural factors, including poverty. However, as opioids have frequently been used in the treatment of pain, opioid use disorders have increased dramatically across all segments of society and in the US, death through overdose of synthetic opioids reached exceptionally high levels even in regions in which this had traditionally not been a problem.

Neuronal memories and addiction

The signal through which one neuron excites an adjacent neuron can be facilitated if these neurons are activated in synchrony. This phenomenon, known as long-term potentiation (LTP), has been viewed as a fundamental feature of memory wherein events that occurred in conjunction with one another are linked because synaptic strength is increased. The development of addiction may involve this sort of memory process in so far as synaptic connections that link a drug and feelings of euphoria are strengthened with repeated drug consumption. The network of neurons triggered by environmental cues that promote substance use may also widen with repeated drug experiences. As a result, the cues that instigate craving increase proportionately, and these feelings are more readily elicited in a wider set of situations. Some drugs, such as cocaine, may also promote epigenetic changes that favor long-lasting alterations of dopamine and glutamate functioning (Hamilton & Nestler, 2019), as well as that of growth factors such as BDNF and FGF-2 that affect synaptic plasticity. These processes, together with several intracellular changes, might be fundamental in accounting for the 'synaptic memory' associated with the drug and may thereby contribute to an addiction being maintained.

Supporting the view that some illicit drugs may affect brain processes that are involved in executive functioning and decision-making, long-term cocaine use was accompanied by altered integrity of neuronal functioning within several cortical regions so that the normal brain electrical response to rewarding stimuli was disturbed (Parvaz et al., 2011). This was apparent in brain electrophysiological responses measured when participants had the opportunity of earning varying amounts of money for making certain responses. Ordinarily, when the monetary value increases in such a task, the electrical response (termed 'the P300 response') increases commensurately. In contrast, the differential response to varying amounts of reward was not apparent in cocaine users even though participants indicated that with greater amounts of potential winnings, the task was more interesting and exciting. It seemed that the P300 response to reward was tied to the amount of gray matter present in several aspects of the prefrontal cortex. Thus, the altered brain functioning in cocaine users might undermine their ability to distinguish different levels of reward to obtain pleasure, particularly in high-risk situations (e.g., in response to stressors or in the presence of cravings), leading to increased drug intake.

FAILING TO LEARN FROM MISTAKES

Brain regions involved in reward processes may contribute to the initiation of substance use and its reinstatement after individuals had ceased drug intake. Other brain regions may contribute to recurrence of substance use through alternative processes. Once a certain behavior is well entrenched and runs on automatic pilot, these 'habits' are hard to break. But, even after these behaviors have been eliminated and replaced by others, they can re-emerge. Specific brain regions, such as the infralimbic cortex may play a critical role in modifying newly acquired behaviors. Turning off neuronal activity in this region may attenuate the expression of newly acquired behavioral response, but in doing so, counterproductive behaviors that had previously been eliminated may re-emerge. Evidently, even when habits might seem to have been suppressed, they can come to the surface under certain conditions, just as this occurs when a previously addicted individual takes just one hit of a substance or experiences certain stressors (Smith et al., 2012).

Besides the actions involving the infralimbic cortex, neurons of the lateral habenula, which is involved in communication between the forebrain and aspects of the midbrain, are activated in response to negative events, essentially transmitting an 'anti-reward signal'.

This process may counter the strength of reward processes that determine subjective preferences that otherwise favor drug intake, so that inactivation of the lateral habenula may disturb the ability to differentiate and select between actions that have different costs and outcomes (Stopper & Floresco, 2014). Thus, disturbed habenula functioning may produce decision biases that favor drug intake, despite the negative consequences of this choice. By influencing this brain region, chronic drug use may co-opt the brain's typical response to rewarding cues as well as disturbing judgment and decision-making concerning continued drug use. In conjunction with habenula disturbances, altered synaptic plasticity important for memory processes may undermine the inability to learn from past mistakes, thereby allowing for the recurrence of addictions when faced with temptation.

Dopamine and reward processes

To gain a better understanding of addiction processes, we ought to consider how stressors and stress-related neural circuits interact with the brain mechanism underlying feelings of reward. It will be recalled that several neurochemical mechanisms are involved in reward processes, but the activity of dopamine neurons within the mesolimbic dopamine system (the ventral tegmental area (VTA) and nucleus accumbens) is particularly relevant (Wise & Koob, 2014). If a drug stimulates dopamine activity, further reward-seeking behaviors may be promoted in the form of drug use. Dopamine activity in this brain circuit may also influence the salience of stimuli associated with specific rewards (i.e., the drug) so that these cues take on enhanced importance. Thus, upon subsequently encountering these cues, dopamine neuronal processes will be excited in *anticipation* of drug reward, resulting in cravings that promote further drug use even among individuals attempting to abandon their drug addiction (Volkow et al., 2016).

Other aspects of DA reward system functioning can encourage addiction. Although the effects of some drugs become less profound with repeated use (tolerance), one of the most prominent features of cocaine and amphetamine is that many of their behavioral effects become more pronounced with continued intake, as do brain DA changes. In fact, following repeated drug treatment DA cells in the VTA and in the prefrontal cortex undergo long-lasting molecular changes, possibly owing to the activation of growth factors, such as BDNF and FGF-2 (Flores & Stewart, 2000), which may promote functional changes of DA related processes that favor the propensity for substance use disorder.

━━━━━━━ FINDING INFORMATION IN ODD PLACES ━━━━━━━

Parkinson's disease, which occurs owing to degeneration of DA neurons within the substantia nigra (although other factors are also involved), is typically treated with drugs that increase DA functioning (e.g., l-DOPA). However, patients treated with l-DOPA may exhibit secondary effects that include compulsive shopping, computer gaming, binge

(Continued)

eating, hypersexuality, and gambling. Drugs, such as l-DOPA, don't just cause DA to increase in the substantia nigra, but also affect DA functioning in other brain regions, such as the nucleus accumbens. Accordingly, certain behaviors, such as gambling, may become more rewarding, suggesting a role for DA in compulsive behaviors.

Addiction in relation to stressor provoked dopamine changes

The mesolimbic DA system is not only essential in relation to natural reinforcers, such as food, social, and sexual interactions, it is an essential player in recognizing and responding to threatening situations. The importance of the nucleus accumbens in relation to stressor actions and addictions has come from studies showing that aversive experiences and the response to drugs with addiction potential share common mechanisms. Specifically, genes that can be transiently activated by diverse cellular stimuli (referred to as immediately early genes) are switched on by stressors. For instance, the immediate early gene deltaFosB (ΔFosB), which may be involved in the synthesis of proteins associated with addictions, is activated by a stressor in the form of social defeat. Likewise, chronic cocaine administration altered mRNA for ΔFosB in the nucleus accumbens (Larson et al., 2010) and similar effects were observed with other substances with abuse potential, such as morphine. This led to the suggestion that ΔFosB in reward-related brain regions might be a marker for addiction and may reflect the potential effects of stressors on addiction processes (Nestler, 2008). The ultimate understanding of the neuronal processes related to addiction might hinge on determining why addiction is as persistent as it is, particularly given the assumption that many stressor actions are usually relatively brief. It is thus significant that ΔFosB was elevated for protracted periods among mice that had been repeatedly treated with any of several drugs with abuse potential.

As much as stressors and drugs such as cocaine have overlapping effects, this doesn't imply that linking them is straightforward. The activation of some genes may comprise unique aspects of the stress response (e.g., those involved in the provocation of a depressive-like state), whereas activation of other genes might more directly govern drug addiction. There may be still other downstream factors that operate to influence both the stress and reward/addiction process, including variations in the functioning of particular dopamine receptors that ultimately differentiate between the effects of stressors and reward. As mentioned earlier, DA functioning associated with the VTA and the nucleus accumbens might serve to enhance the salience of stimuli related to motivational and emotional systems irrespective of their valence. In this way, mesolimbic DA activity could influence the response to cues that had been associated with either stressors or rewards (Berridge & Robinson, 2016).

While dopamine reward processes may be key in mediating addiction, neurochemical functioning in several brain regions may also contribute to this process. Although dopamine neuronal activity may contribute to the desire to re-experience the effects of a drug, this itself may not be sufficient to account for the detrimental behaviors displayed. Neuronal dysfunction within aspects of the prefrontal cortex that are related to executive functioning may be linked to decisions regarding drug use in that down-regulated serotonin and dopamine functioning in these regions may favor impulsivity. When the rewarding value of specific agents are exaggerated, and executive functioning is impaired so that impulsivity is elevated, the individual's desire for immediate gratification through drug use may not be thwarted by cognitive processes that might ordinarily give the individual pause to reconsider their decision to take the drug (Berridge & Robinson, 2016). Serotonin may thus be fundamental in casual drug use progressing to compulsive behavior and ultimately to addiction. By increasing serotonin functioning in mice the propensity for cocaine use was diminished, which may be attributable to serotonin acting as a brake to attenuate compulsive drug seeking and use (Li et al., 2021)

Epigenetic factors related to substance use disorder

Over somewhat more than a decade, epigenetic processes have come to the foreground as a possible way by which addictions are maintained. Much like stressors, cocaine can engender epigenetic changes of genes that code for the regulation of dendritic plasticity within the nucleus accumbens (Feng et al., 2014). As already described, epigenetic actions at the promoter region for the FosB gene may be integral to cocaine addiction and since epigenetic changes can be long lasting they might contribute to the persistence of addictions (Browne et al., 2020). These epigenetic changes may also account for the effectiveness of stressors or cues related to certain drugs being as effective as they are in reinstating an addiction following a period of abstention. While we have focused here on the FosB, a vast number of epigenetic changes occur in response to stressor and drug challenges. Identifying specific epigenetic changes in diverse brain regions that are relevant to addiction and withdrawal may be difficult but could eventually be used to identify targets to treat addictions (Hamilton & Nestler, 2019). At the same time, it is important to recognize that the epigenetic changes that occur may vary across individuals, and the drivers of addiction may differ accordingly (Lüscher & Janak, 2021).

Cross-sensitization in relation to addiction

Just as a stressor enhances the response to a later challenge comprising a similar stressor, cross-sensitization effects have been demonstrated in which a stressor experience influences responses subsequently elicited by amphetamine or cocaine (Koob, 2008). This was reflected by elevated mesolimbic DA activity, which was accompanied by potentiated behavioral responses to drugs. Likewise, cocaine and amphetamine provoked synaptic remodeling in VTA dopamine neurons that could affect the later stress response as well as the reinforcing properties of drugs, thereby influencing the propensity for their intake. For that matter, adverse early events may set the stage so that adult responses to drugs such as cocaine are increased, thereby contributing to cocaine use disorder (Vannan et al., 2018). In fact, among individuals with a substance use disorder the occurrence of early-life trauma is disproportionately high. The downstream effects of early trauma could, of course, occur for any number of reasons, including altered behavioral and psychological functioning, and could likewise stem from these events affecting the rewarding actions of some drugs (Carlyle et al., 2021).

Corticotropin hormone in relation to stress and addiction

Given that CRH functioning is markedly affected by stressors and is involved in anxiety, it was posited that this neuropeptide might contribute to the addiction process (Koob & Le Moal, 2008). The anxiety or poor mood associated with stressor-provoked CRH elevations may encourage drug intake, and as expected, manipulations of CRH and CRH_1 receptor functioning in rodents influenced the self-administration of cocaine, heroin, and alcohol (Zorrilla et al., 2014). But the involvement of CRH in addiction needs to be considered from a broader perspective, which we will now address.

Linking reward and aversion in addiction

Most theoretical constructs related to addiction have included both reward and aversion processes, and typically their contribution has involved complex neural circuits whose functions vary over the course of the addiction (Volkow et al., 2016). The neural circuits involved in the addiction processes may become increasingly broader and better entrenched as drug taking moves from simply obtaining reward, the development of a drug-seeking habit, and eventually to an established compulsion (Lüscher et al., 2021). As described in Figure 11.1, an individual might initially consume a drug to diminish the distress they may be feeling. During this initial stage (binge and intoxication) of the addiction process, the drug activates DA and opioid peptide receptor functioning within brain regions that subserve reward, together with glutamate systems that are involved in learning and memory. Thus, individuals might again use the drug to gain the rewarding feelings that the drug provides. As the substance use disorder progresses and the related neural circuits expand and gain functioning, the strength of the disorder increases commensurately (Lüscher & Janak, 2021).

In a later phase (termed withdrawal and negative affect in Figure 11.1), as the euphoric effects of the drug diminish over time or during periods of withdrawal, changes of CRH and dynorphin in brain regions associated with emotions (amygdala, basal nucleus of the stria terminalis) lead to negative mood and elevated stress reactivity. With the diminished euphoria, individuals may seek the drug to ward off the negative feelings that have arisen. During the final phase of addiction (the preoccupation and anticipation phase), the profound drug craving is elevated and individuals become preoccupied with ways of obtaining it. It is especially significant that prefrontal cortex functioning (notably within the orbital and anterior cingulate cortex) may be impaired so that individuals are unable to regulate the conflicting craving for the drug and their desire to abstain (i.e., self-control has been hijacked). Thus, among individuals who had stopped using the drug, relapse ('reinstatement') can be promoted by the reintroduction of the cues associated with the drug or by some types of stressors (Mantsch et al., 2016). From this perspective, the addiction process involves sequential neurobiological variations, including activation of the nucleus accumbens involved in reward effects, hippocampal functioning to process contextual information related to obtaining the drug, and craving determined by aspects of appraisal that involve activation of the orbital and anterior cingulate cortex, together with the amygdala.

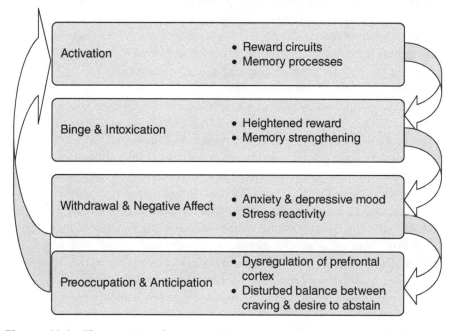

Figure 11.1   The transition from casual drug use to addiction: As described in the text, the initial intake of a drug may stem from a desire to experiment, peer pressure, or misguided attempts to diminish ongoing distress. Afterward, drug use may occur to re-experience the drug's euphoric actions (binge and intoxication phase). During the next phase (withdrawal and negative affect) drug intake may occur to diminish the negative emotions that appear as the drug actions dissipate (or those that occur during withdrawal). Finally, during the preoccupation and anticipation (craving) phase, the strong addiction leads to individuals focusing on obtaining the drug, which may be accompanied by prefrontal cortex dysfunction. At this point, self-control has been hijacked so that the person is unable to regulate the balance between the intense craving for the drug and their desire to abstain (i.e., self-control has been hijacked). Even after individuals have received some sort of therapy so that they have ceased their drug use, cues associated with the drug or stressors can instigate reinstatement of the substance use disorder.

Source: based on Koob & Volkow (2016).

An opponent process perspective

Homeostatic-like processes ordinarily assure that excessive biological changes in response to intrinsic and extrinsic challenges are countered by the functioning of other systems. For instance, sympathetic activation is met by elevated parasympathetic responses, and proinflammatory responses are regulated by anti-inflammatory responses. An 'opponent process theory' has similarly been incorporated in perspectives of addiction. In particular, a drug that elicits a state of euphoria involving dopamine or opioid functioning provokes homeostatic changes that entail activation of an anti-reward system that includes CRH activation (Koob & LeMoal, 2008). As the drug's euphoric effects wear off with the passage of time, the opponent responses persist, and so the feelings of euphoria are replaced by dysphoria. With repeated drug use the countervailing dysphoria grows, thereby necessitating greater drug doses to promote the positive state again. Ultimately, the 'set point' responsible for the positive state is altered. The processes responsible for reward and those that subserve the dysphoric effects are reset so that the desire (need) for drug occurs earlier and greater drug doses are required to limit negative affect.

A similar view had previously been offered based on the classical conditioning of compensatory responses to account for the processes involved in addiction (Siegel & Ramos, 2002). By assuming that compensatory responses were classically conditioned and could be instigated by situational cues, this model provided a way to explain how tolerance developed toward drugs, and perhaps how drug overdose could occur. Specifically, the net effect of a drug might reflect its direct physiological action coupled with a classically conditioned opposing response in which cues associated with drug intake elicited this compensatory response. These conditioned responses become stronger with repeated drug use, hence progressively greater drug doses are needed for a euphoric effect to be obtained. If on a particular occasion, the drug (now at a high dose) is taken in a novel context, the classically conditioned compensatory response would not be provoked as readily, and hence the action to oppose the drug's physiological effects would be absent, thus leading to an overdose.

Different drugs, different reinstatement processes

Drugs such as cocaine, heroin, and alcohol have several common actions and their effects are influenced by some of the same manipulations (e.g., being influenced by a CRH_1 antagonist), but the development of substance use disorders involving different drugs likely do not involve all of the same underlying processes and might not follow the same temporal trajectory. It follows that those treatments effective in attenuating one form of addiction might be ineffective or less effective in modifying a second type of drug addiction. As well, the mechanisms associated with drug reinstatement after a period of abstinence may involve different mechanisms.

One of the greatest challenges in dealing with addiction is that even after quitting, individuals are so readily drawn back. Thus, they will often say that they are still addicted, but have it under control (at least for the moment). They might at some point feel as if they have 'beaten the habit' but temptation is a hard beast to defeat, and given the right (wrong) circumstances, relapse can occur. The factors that contribute to relapse may involve different processes or brain networks and may be dependent on the nature of the reinstating stimulus (i.e., a drug or drug cues versus stressors). Relapse of cocaine or heroin use elicited by priming with these drugs may be produced by activation of mesolimbic DA processes, whereas reinstatement by stressors might be related to CRH and NE activation (Stewart, 2000). Similarly, the reinstatement of alcohol intake by relevant cues could be attenuated by naltrexone, an opioid receptor antagonist that has been used in the treatment of alcoholism, whereas this treatment did not affect stressor-provoked reinstatement (Burattini et al., 2006). Commensurately, stressor-elicited reinstatement could be attenuated by a CRH antagonist, but this treatment did not have such an effect on cue-elicited reinstatement. It likewise appeared that drug-induced reinstatement might involve a reward circuit entailing glutamate activity that is modulated by DA functioning within the prefrontal cortex and nucleus accumbens. Cue-elicited craving, in contrast, may be determined by projections between the basolateral amygdala and the nucleus accumbens, although these actions might similarly be modulated by cortical DA activity.

There is ample reason to believe that CRH–DA interactions that contribute to addiction can be affected by NE and 5-HT processes. For instance, social defeat in mice, which has been used to elicit depressive-like symptoms, also reliably elicited the reinstatement of cocaine preference, which could be prevented by disturbing the functioning of serotonin-producing neurons of the dorsal raphe nucleus. Pharmacological studies similarly implicated glutamate, dynorphin, and several other peptides in moderating stress-induced mesocorticolimbic dopamine functioning, thereby promoting substance use. It has been maintained that 'liking' and 'wanting' should be distinguished from one another. Whereas liking, which refers to the hedonic (pleasureful) aspects of positive events or stimuli, may involve DA functioning within limbic brain regions, wanting is governed by cues linked to reward that produce craving (referred to as incentive salience) may involve additional factors, including opioid-related processes (Castro & Berridge, 2014). Again, from this perspective the reinstatement of different types of rewards might involve different mechanisms and hence not subject to the same triggering stimuli.

Given the diversity of factors that might contribute to addiction, and the possibility of their involvement in reinstatement processes, it isn't surprising that treatments to diminish substance use and relapse has been exceptionally difficult. In view of the powerful actions of drug-related cues and stressors in promoting relapse, therapeutic interventions may need to continue even after individuals have successfully abstained from drug use for extended periods.

CANNABIS USE DISORDER

The use of cannabis has increased dramatically over the past few decades, and common views within the general population concerning the potential risks associated with cannabis use seem to have diminished, perhaps being abetted by the legalization of this compound in several places. Although cannabis may have medicinal properties, in vulnerable individuals it can promote psychosis and other mental disorders. It can likewise progress to a substance use disorder that in many ways has the characteristics described in relation to other drugs with addiction potential. This includes the preoccupation with the drug, negative affect and withdrawal signs upon drug discontinuation, and a high propensity to relapse. Among users, fully 22% were deemed to have a cannabis use disorder and it was still higher among young people who engaged in daily or weekly use (Leung et al., 2020).

A detailed review concerning the effects of cannabis has pointed to the great number of behavioral and physiological changes associated with chronic cannabis use, making it clear that both short- and long-term adverse effects can be engendered (Zehra et al., 2018). To be sure, the behavioral risks and brain changes provoked by chronic cannabis use are unlike those produced by other substances (e.g., opioids) but these are hardly benign. Chronic cannabis use in humans, particularly among adolescents, can promote dysphoria, anhedonia, and anxiety. As well, functional changes occur in several brain regions (e.g., amygdala) as was the connectivity between prefrontal cortical areas that govern cognitive and emotional functioning. There aren't many pharmacological treatments that have enduring effects in limiting cannabis use disorder, although treatments that increase endocannabinoid system functioning without producing the rewarding effects or cognitive impairments (e.g., by differentially influencing CB_1 and CB_2 receptors) could diminish cannabis withdrawal and relapse (Volkow & Boyle, 2018).

The FDA has indicated their interest in cannabis in relation to health, but they have not made any explicit statements as to their position on its use other than to provide consumer information.

Gambling addiction

Gambling addiction has been around for ages, but it was only included alongside substance use disorders in the DSM-5. Prior to this, it was considered as an impulse control disorder, not unlike pyromania, kleptomania, and trichotillomania (hair-pulling). In several ways it is reminiscent of drug addictions; individuals with a gambling addiction may exhibit features such as preoccupation with gambling and needing to gamble with increasingly greater amounts of money to obtain the same thrill, and as they lose, they often bet more to recoup their losses (chasing their losses). Those with gambling issues may have started down this road to escape problems or to counter feelings of helplessness, guilt, anxiety, or depression. It is not unusual for individuals with the disorder to encounter family problems owing to their losses and lying to cover up their gambling, and in some instances, they may resort to fraud or theft to meet their needs. Health may suffer owing to the distress experienced and other mental health conditions may occur, such as depression, and comorbid conditions are frequently present, such as anxiety, bipolar disorder, and OCD. Moreover, suicidal ideation and suicide occurrence are elevated. In fact, death by suicide is 15 times greater among problem gamblers than among non-gamblers.

Understanding the biochemical processes associated with gambling had been difficult owing to the absence of appropriate animal models, but in recent years increasingly more methods of studying risky choices have appeared, although in most instances these can be challenged based on whether they capture the complexities inherent in the human disorder. Nevertheless, these animal models have pointed to the involvement of specific dopamine receptors as being involved in risky choices (Barrus & Winstanley, 2016). As in the case of substance use disorders, dopamine and serotonin may affect gambling through their actions on impulsivity. As well, GABA and glutamate functioning within prefrontal cortical regions have been implicated in gambling disorder (Weidacker et al., 2020).

Analyses in humans based on imaging studies have pointed to specific brain changes, including those associated with decision-making, among individuals with gambling problems. To some extent, these changes shared features with those that accompany substance use disorders. Individuals with a gambling disorder exhibited dysfunctions that spanned multiple brain regions linked to impulsivity and networks related to top-down control of reward processes (Balodis & Potenza, 2020). Gambling addiction has also been associated with personality characteristics (high levels of disinhibition) that may be related or interact with genetic factors that influence neurotransmitter functioning.

Studies in humans have considered remedial actions that can be undertaken to diminish gambling addiction. While some procedures were grounded in 12-step programs or focused on other psychosocial factors, others seemed trivial and ineffective, such as instructing gamblers to bet within their limits (imagine the reaction of a problem gambler paying attention to this message while immersed in chasing their losses). Likewise, educational approaches were attempted to diminish gambling, even though these methods are most often ineffective in producing behavioral change in other contexts. Furthermore, even when educational procedures had any discernible effects, they weren't lasting.

Attempts to treat problem gambling through drug therapies, such as mood stabilizers, had few positive effects and when they did, their actions were relatively transient (Di Nicola et al., 2020). CBT has been reported to provide a measure of success, but these were limited, and it is uncertain how lasting the effects are (Di Nicola et al., 2020). Having adequate social support may be associated with diminished likelihood of problem gambling appearing, and it may be that the combination of improved social support (e.g., through group interventions, such as Gamblers Anonymous) and CBT may produce better outcomes.

BETTING ON GAMBLING: HENS IN THE FOX'S LAIR

The prevalence of problem gambling in the US and UK is about 3% and is comparable in EU countries and only slightly higher in China. Gambling addiction is far less frequent than tobacco and alcohol use disorder but still ranks well above other substances, although it is not unusual for those with problem gambling to also develop substance use disorders. Gambling addiction, which has frequently been state-sponsored (and even encouraged), has had devastating effects on individuals and families. Because problem gamblers don't stagger down the street in a haze, aren't incoherent, don't attack others in a gambling-fueled rage, it's often assumed that the problem isn't as acute or as problematic as that of drug addiction. In fact, however, in several respects, a gambling addiction can be more devastating than a drug addiction. In the case of drugs, there's only so much that can be used before the need is sated. In contrast, for gambling there may not be anything like satiety. Moreover, gambling opportunities are everywhere. A person can bet on horses, football, baseball, and any other sport; they can bet at the track, at the casino, at bars (in some cities), and at their buddy's house, lottery tickets can be obtained at the corner store, and of course, there is always internet betting. In essence, gamblers suffer from a double whammy: the natural 'stop' mechanisms that apply to other forms of addiction seem not to apply to gambling (at least not in the same way), and this problem is compounded by the remarkable availability of gambling venues.

It's likely that an effective treatment will be found for most drug addictions. But what are the odds that a cure for gambling addiction is found anytime soon? The difficulties in diminishing gambling include the extensive research dedicated to having gambling continue. The research is sponsored or undertaken by the people who own casinos or build the equipment that is used for gambling purposes. Their aim is that of increasing their profits, which amounts to getting more customers and having them bet for a longer duration and greater amounts. Unlike researchers at universities, they don't require external grants to do their research. They simply apply some of their profits to 'market research' and then pay less tax as this was a legitimate expense. They don't have to receive ethics approval to do their research, and they don't need to search for participants and then obtain their informed consent. Plenty of participants show up without being asked to do so, but if a push is needed, their hotel rooms can be offered as freebies, and this ought to do the trick. Ultimately, the lighting, oxygen circulation, drinks being consumed, the nature of the gaming (e.g., slots vs. cards or craps), and the presence of high-quality restaurants are thoroughly examined to determine if they support gambling. The biggest problem these operators might encounter is the desire not to share the loot with their partners – no, not the mob, the government that takes a cut of the action in the form of federal, state/provincial, and municipal taxes. In some places, governments even build casinos, operate lotteries, and provide the amenities to facilitate gambling. Unlike everyone else, they don't pay taxes, and remarkably they're not in the least bit ashamed of their behaviors.

A different perspective on addiction: eating-related processes

Opposing effects of stress and eating systems

Eating and substance use disorders involve overlapping processes. Activation of neurons of the VTA that drive the appetite for drugs such as cocaine may also promote overeating by affecting the rewarding value of food (Volkow et al., 2013). It has long been known based on animal studies that the propensity to prefer sugar is predictive of drug intake, possibly because the desire for both involve common mechanisms.

For some individuals eating serves as a means of attenuating distress, essentially serving as a form of self-medication to diminish negative mood, just as drug-taking may operate in this way. Given the neurobiological similarities associated with consummatory processes and substance use, the notion took hold that the processes related to eating and regulation of energy balance may be linked to substance use disorders. This linkage was supported by the finding that fasting and chronic food restrictions, like traditional stressors, are associated with HPA axis activation and increased mesolimbic DA activity. In addition, chronic food restriction potentiates drug-seeking behaviors, engenders behavioral sensitization to psychostimulants (e.g., cocaine and amphetamine), and increases relapse to drug self-administration. In fact, it is often said that for individuals abstaining from drug use it's a very bad idea to allow themselves to become too hungry.

The tie between eating and drug addictions led to the evaluation of several hormones associated with consummatory behaviors that could influence substance use disorders. The hormone orexin, which influences arousal and increases food intake, affects the neural mechanisms associated with stress responses, and stressors stimulate the activity of orexin cells through the actions of CRH processes. Furthermore, stimulation of orexin receptors located at the VTA promoted the release of DA and glutamate at terminal sites within the prefrontal cortex and the nucleus accumbens, which then influence the motivation to engage in behaviors that support addiction (James et al., 2017). Thus, it was proposed that blocking different orexin receptors could potentially be useful in diminishing addictions (Hopf, 2020).

Neuropeptide Y (NPY), which was discussed earlier in relation to anxiety disorders, PTSD, and eating processes, has also been implicated in substance use disorders. NPY elevations were accompanied by increased heroin and cocaine self-administration and facilitated the reinstatement of heroin intake in rats (Reiner et al., 2019). Furthermore, manipulations of NPY receptors within the extended amygdala influenced alcohol intake (Robinson & Thiele, 2017), perhaps by modulating anxiety or threat appraisals. Whatever the case, these data again indicate that NPY might be fundamentally related to voluntary drug consumption, and could thus be a suitable target for the treatment of alcohol and cocaine use disorders.

As we learned earlier, ghrelin is involved in the initiation of consummatory responses and may influence dopamine reward processes as well as being affected by stressors, but this hormone has been a relative stranger in the stress and addiction domain. Ghrelin levels ordinarily increase in anticipation of a meal and then decline after eating. In some individuals who had been exposed to a stressor, ghrelin levels remained elevated after food consumption, possibly reflecting the inability of the normal message of 'go ahead and eat' to be turned off as it normally should. In effect, the stressor promotes continued eating, but as genuine hunger is not present, individuals will resort to feel-good foods, rather than those that fulfill their nutritional needs. It is possible that the absence of this shut-down mechanism might also render individuals vulnerable to obtaining reward through other means, including drug intake.

Aside from affecting eating processes, ghrelin binds to DA receptors at sites associated with reward processes, including the VTA (Abizaid et al., 2009). Thus, the rise of ghrelin could potentiate the positive effects obtained from rewarding stimuli. Beyond affecting the consumption of desirable foods, when administered directly to the VTA, ghrelin enhanced the rewarding value of cocaine and alcohol intake, whereas a ghrelin antagonist reduced alcohol consumption (Zallar et al., 2017). Similarly, in heavy alcohol drinkers, alcohol cravings could be instigated by intravenous ghrelin administration (Leggio et al., 2014). The available data are still sparse and it's too soon to determine whether ghrelin and other hormones associated with eating processes underlie addictions. However, it's also premature to dismiss a role for eating circuitry in the addiction process and the data at hand are sufficiently compelling to prompt further research on this issue.

The involvement of serotonin in eating processes was recognized long ago, and remedies for weight loss had included drugs that affect serotonin functioning. The serotonin and norepinephrine reuptake inhibitor sibutramine had been used to this end but was withdrawn from the market in 2010 owing to side effects that emerged. Another agent, lorcaserin (Belviq), which stimulates 5-HT_{2C} receptors, was used for weight loss, but in 2020 the FDA recommended its removal owing to the potential for this agent to cause pancreatic, colorectal, and lung cancer. While this drug probably won't be seen on the market any time soon, it is notable that it has positive effects on various forms of addiction. In rodents, this compound reduced the rewarding feelings obtained from nicotine and reduced impulsivity. Moreover, in a small 12-week trial in humans, lorcaserin reduced smoking and could diminish cocaine and alcohol use. From a theoretical perspective, these findings point to the interrelations between eating processes and addictions, raising the possibility that manipulations that influence 5-HT_{2C} receptors may affect substance use disorder by acting on craving-related processes (Higgins et al., 2020).

Treatments of addictions

Addictions are difficult to treat, and there is no magic pill that resolves the problem in most individuals. Many pharmacological compounds have been developed to treat different addictions (Volkow & Boyle, 2018) and diverse behavioral treatment approaches have been used to curtail substance use disorders. The choice of treatment depends on the nature of the addiction and its severity, as well as a constellation of factors related to the individual, including their readiness for treatment and their belief that certain treatments will be effective.

Behavioral and cognitive therapies

The most widely known behavioral strategies to diminish addictions include 12-step programs (e.g., Alcoholics Anonymous, Narcotics Anonymous). As social support is a fundamental component of these programs, they take advantage of one of the most important ways of coping, thereby facilitating abstinence. Another approach is to check into 'rehab' (more formally referred to as 'substance-abuse rehabilitation') that allows individuals to be away from the cues related to their addiction, and at the same time to engage in therapy that facilitates the active elimination of the addiction. Reiterating our earlier comment, rehab will only be effective if the individual accepts that they have a problem, wants to get better, and believes that they can beat the problem. We're reminded of Amy Winehouse singing, 'They tried to make me go to rehab, but I said no, no, no'. For individuals with this mindset, rehab would probably not be useful.

Even if the individuals are in rehab for all the right reasons and the treatment produces positive effects, relapse rates are high, and returning to the same old environment may be counterproductive. A change of venue is often necessary and continued social support from the right people may facilitate recovery. The rehabilitation programs that provide the best results are those that offer continuity of therapy rather than abandoning individuals once they have reached specific goals. To be sure, rehabilitation centers have the potential to provide effective treatment, but too often they are unregulated and unaccountable, staff may not be fully qualified, procedures are sometimes outdated, supervision to deal with problems associated with abstinence may be lacking, and follow-up care may be non-existent.

Several behavioral methods of dealing with addictions are available. One of these, the Transtheoretical Model (TTM) of behavior change, is an approach in which individuals go through five stages beginning with disinterest in changing (precontemplation stage), a contemplation stage in which individuals are thinking about quitting their behaviors, a preparation stage in which they place themselves in a position for change (obtain needed resources and remove themselves from cues that could promote craving). Thereafter, individuals enter the change stage where active efforts are made to cease the unwanted behavior, followed by the maintenence stage in which individuals make efforts not to succumb to temptations that will invariably arise. It is common for people to relapse and thus they are encouraged to return to the program – it often takes several such episodes before recovery occurs.

The TTM approach has not been universally accepted, especially since this intervention to eliminate smoking and eating disorders was no more effective than non-stage-based approaches. Predictably, vociferous defense of this method has been provided by those who use it in clinical practice and researchers who have found positive results. The last word on this topic hasn't been uttered yet, but as we've indicated repeatedly in the context of other disorders, no treatment will be effective in treating all individuals. Accordingly, methods ought to be established to determine for whom this approach is most likely to be effective.

Cognitive behavioral therapy (CBT) that has been used to diminish distress and alleviate depressive disorders has been used to treat substance use disorders and relapse. Through CBT individuals with a substance use disorder may acquire skills to perceive events from a more realistic perspective and develop effective coping strategies so that negative events won't promote drug intake or trigger relapse. As well, individuals may recognize when cravings first emerge and are able to deal with these situations effectively. Speaking to the efficacy of cognitive interventions, these procedures were accompanied by the normalization of neuronal functioning within brain reward circuitry and enhanced inhibitory control networks needed to diminish substance use (Zilverstand et al., 2016). As CBT allows for the inclusion of other approaches to yield optimal effects, the incorporation of procedures to enhance motivation as well as drug therapies can enhance the effectiveness of this procedure.

Mindfulness training has been reported to act against substance use disorders and drug relapse (Korecki et al., 2020). When individuals were trained to focus on positive experiences at the moment, the need to use opioids to diminish chronic pain was reduced, as was the propensity to respond to cues that might otherwise promote opioid intake. Mindfulness training approaches can influence diverse processes associated with addiction, including altered connectivity between prefrontal cortical networks and limbic circuitry tied to reward processes. Thus, mindfulness training may be effective in usurping the influence of stressors on reward-related substance use and concurrently influence executive functioning that may promote self-control, decision-making, and response inhibitory processes that are so essential for abstinence being maintained (Garland & Howard, 2018).

The effectiveness of mindfulness, like that of CBT, especially when provided in a group format, has been apparent in relation to the use of a variety of substances, but the question arose as to whether mindfulness or CBT were the best approaches. For instance, strategies that included community reinforcement could yield better outcomes than CBT itself (De Crescenzo et al., 2018). Furthermore, it needs to be determined to what extent mindfulness and CBT, alone or in combination with other strategies, is effective for different addictions, whether this varies with the severity of the addiction, and critically the extent to which treatments are effective over the long run.

Yet another approach to deal with substance use disorders is Self Management and Recovery Training (SMART) which borrows from TTM and CBT. This program considers an individual's readiness to act to gain new healthier behaviors and provides strategies to maintain motivation, as well as to identify and cope with cravings. The procedure also helps individuals identify and modify their irrational thinking and to focus on both their short- and long-term goals. A major advantage of the approach is that it encourages self-empowerment. The SMART approach is still relatively new and thus insufficient data are available concerning its effectiveness, who is most likely to gain from it, and whether it is more effective for some addictions than others.

Pharmacological therapies

One of the most common approaches in the treatment of opioid addictions has been the use of methadone or buprenorphine as opioid replacement therapies. Specifically, buprenorphine produces a weak euphoric effect but causes relatively long-lasting actions in attenuating the distress of opioid withdrawal and diminishing cravings. More commonly, a combination of buprenorphine and naloxone (Suboxone) is used to this end, which provides individuals the opportunity of eliminating their addiction (Volkow et al., 2019). For a variety of reasons, these treatments have had their share of critics. In part, this may have stemmed from the compounds being given in outpatient clinics, which has resulted in communities not wanting them in their backyards. Beyond this, it was maintained that replacement therapies don't reduce addiction, but simply provide a short-term solution for a chronic condition. Others have argued that the treatments keep addicted individuals compliant but do not provide a cure. Perhaps so, but when opioid replacement therapy incorporates behaviorally based strategies, it often provides long-term benefits.

A considerable number of pharmacological agents have been developed (or are being assessed) to limit different aspects of addiction (Volkow & Boyle, 2018). For instance, manipulation of mu-opioid receptors has some positive effects as have α_2-adrenergic receptor agonists. Manipulations of oxytocin have also been found to have beneficial effects, perhaps owing to the actions of this hormone on social behaviors and by affecting dopamine reward processes. Likewise, therapies that influence glutamate processes have been evaluated to treat stimulant use disorders that are notoriously resistant to therapies (e.g., cocaine, methamphetamine).

Several unconventional treatments have been used to diminish addictions. Repetitive transcranial magnetic stimulation that has been used to diminish depressive illness was helpful in the treatment of addictions (Diana et al., 2017). Likewise, although limited attention has been been given to the influence of inflammatory factors in relation to addiction, there is reason to believe that manipulations that affect these processes could be useful in treating substance use disorders. Several drugs with addictive potential (alcohol, cocaine, methamphetamine, cannabinoids) promote marked cytokine variations peripherally and may influence brain microglia. Preclinical studies have supported the possibility that agents that diminish inflammation may have benefits as adjunctive therapies in diminishing additions (Kohno et al., 2019). For the moment, however, limited research has been conducted assessing the influence of anti-inflammatory treatments in abating substance use disorders in humans.

In addition to alleviating depression, PTSD, and the fear of death associated with severe illnesses, psychedelic compounds have been used to diminish substance use disorders, presumably through the reorganization of neural processes of the mesolimbic reward system (Nutt et al., 2020). Agents such as LSD, MDMA, and ketamine have been used to this end, typically being administered with a trained therapist present in an environment conducive for therapy. It has been suggested that drugs, such as ketamine, may be effective because of the neurotrophic effects produced, such as enhanced neuroplasticity, which can enhance the efficacy of psychotherapy (McAndrew et al., 2017).

The notion that such compounds can have beneficial effects in relation to addiction is often thought to be a new revelation, but it had actually been advanced five decades ago. In more recent times, attention to such compounds came from reports that *Ibogaine*, a psychoactive compound derived from Tabernanthe iboga, a plant used in some rituals in West Central Africa, could be effective in treating addictions. The anecdotal reports indicating that it markedly diminished substance use disorders, were confirmed in experimental studies showing that its administration at a safe dose diminished cravings and opioid withdrawal symptoms for at least one month (Mash et al., 2018). Ibogaine found its way into clinics as part of an alternative medicine strategy, but inherent risks associated with its use have made it less than the ideal agent to attenuate addictions. To overcome these issues, it was possible to engineer a non-hallucinogenic, non-toxic analogue of ibogaine. In rodents, this agent reduced alcohol- and heroin-seeking behavior in conjunction with altered neural plasticity. It hasn't yet been used in clinical trials, but for the moment it appears to be a safe non-hallucinogenic alternative to Ibogaine itself (Cameron et al., 2021).

Conclusion

While genetic factors have been associated with several forms of addiction, these account for only a modest portion of the variance. To a significant extent, vulnerability to substance use disorders may be dictated by socioeconomic factors, prenatal and early-life stressful experiences, the presence of some psychological pathologies, and the way in which individuals appraise and cope with stressful experiences. Similarly, personality factors, such as traits comprising negative emotionality, especially when it occurs together with elevated sensitivity to drug-based reward, might make individuals at elevated risk for addiction.

It has been maintained that the development of addiction moves through several phases that may involve diverse neurochemical processes (e.g., Koob & Volkow, 2016; Lüscher & Janak, 2021). Drugs that activate DA reward pathways or opioid functioning promote euphoric effects that encourage drug intake. However, with continued drug use the neurochemical changes that elicit positive feelings are countered by naturally occurring homeostatic changes, such as elevated CRH functioning. This compensatory (anti-reward) response becomes progressively stronger so that as the euphoric effects of the drug wane over time following its intake, the dysphoria becomes predominant, and thus the drug is again needed to counter these ill feelings.

As substance use continues, brain regions associated with executive functioning may become impaired so that mechanisms that might otherwise inhibit drug intake will no longer be operating as they should. Essentially, by hijacking these neural circuits and especially if impulsivity is elevated, control of processes that ordinarily limit compulsive drug consumption may be overwhelmed (Volkow et al., 2010). In essence, individuals may be incapable of controlling their behavior so that the short-term reward obtained from the drug take precedence over the long-term negative consequences that will occur (Volkow & Boyle, 2018). Even when individuals make efforts to cease their drug habit, and have done so for an extended period, recurrence of drug consumption can be promoted by stressors or by cues that elicit drug cravings. Like a taste of the drug, these experiences may reactivate 'memory circuits' associated with drug expectancy and reward.

Research to uncover the biological processes of addictions has focused on those involved in reward processes (dopamine), stress responses (CRH), and impulsivity (serotonin), but increasingly it has been considered that neurotrophins involved in neuronal plasticity and learning/habits might also be contributing factors. Likewise, microbiota have been implicated in the regulation of reward processes and may contribute to eating and alcohol use disorders and may be related to opioid use (e.g., Reb & Lotfipour, 2020).

Given that different mechanisms may be operative over the phases of addiction, it follows that certain therapies might be more effective at specific phases of the addiction cycle. Whereas DA or CRH acting agents might be effective in earlier phases of the addiction, treatments that influence cravings might be best at the later stages. Likewise, psychedelic agents, such as psilocybin, may diminish cravings and might also be effective in limiting recurrence. At the same time, as aberrant cognitive functioning, impaired stressor appraisal processes, and the use of ineffective coping strategies may contribute to substance use disorders being maintained and in the reinstatement of addiction, a first line of defense might include the use of behavioral therapies to quell cravings, diminish impulsive behaviors, and training to use effective appraisal and coping methods to deal with stressors.

Suggested readings

Koob, G.F. & Volkow, N.D. (2016). Neurobiology of addiction: A neurocircuitry analysis. *The Lancet Psychiatry, 3*, 760–773.

Lüscher, C. & Janak, P.H. (2021). Consolidating the circuit model for addiction. *Annual Review of Neuroscience, 44*, 173–195.

Volkow, N.D. & Boyle, M. (2018). Neuroscience of addiction: relevance to prevention and treatment. *American Journal of Psychiatry, 175*, 729–740.

12

TRANSMISSION OF TRAUMA ACROSS GENERATIONS

─A brief walk through a collective, historical trauma─

Colonization of many regions of North Africa dates back more than two millennia, successively being occupied by the Phoenicians and Greeks and later the Gothic Vandals and then the Romans and Arabs; everyone it seems saw the value of the territories. Initially, colonization occurred primarily in coastal regions, but inevitably the practice moved inland and to the south, with Britain, France, Spain, Belgium, and Portugal setting up their cruel fiefdoms.

The Americas similarly experienced colonization by European countries beginning early in the sixteenth century. Prior to colonization by Europeans, Indigenous Peoples had established their own political, cultural, and economic institutions, maintained a close connection to the land, and kinship and socialization customs were well-entrenched. Australia and New Zealand had been spared for a time, but colonization began in earnest during the later part of the eighteenth century.

The subjugation of Indigenous Peoples was largely possible due to the availability of armaments that the European colonizers had, but this was facilitated by the spread of smallpox and influenza that the settlers had brought with them from Europe (Diamond, 1997). Indeed, 500 years ago the Spanish conquistador Hernán Cortés was able to overwhelm the Aztecs in what is now Mexico by using his secret weapon, smallpox, to decimate them before a single shot was fired. Later Spanish 'explorers' went further inland where they spread the disease, thereby eradicating small and large communities. Throughout the 1600 to 1800s Indigenous Peoples across North America suffered the same fate, and beginning in 1789 smallpox brought to Australia by the British colonizers killed 50-70% of Indigenous Peoples.

First contact between the Indigenous People and Europeans in North America, which occurred in the sixteenth century, seemed to begin on fairly good terms. The Indigenous People within what is now the United States and Canada served the settlers well, providing them with food and they were essential for the profitable fur trade in Canada. They were considered valued allies - until they weren't. This occurred for political reasons, land and economic gains, as well as to promote Christianization either by violent or non-violent means.

With their growing population the settlers within North America were more desirous of land and appropriated it by whatever means they felt was necessary. Eventually, treaties were made (e.g., following the Royal Proclamation in 1763 in Canada) entrenching the creation of Indian reserve lands and inherent rights (e.g., hunting and fishing rights). By the early 1800s, these provisions were no longer comfortable for the European expansion, and the settler governments reneged on earlier treaties, and progressively diminished the rights of Indigenous Peoples (Royal Commission on Aboriginal Peoples, 1996). The period that followed involved unrelenting government and church interventions in the lives of Indigenous Peoples, and the institution of racist and assimilationist policies. The hubris of European settlers in North America went so far as to create Acts that dictated who could consider themselves First Nations.) .

Learning objectives

Powerful chronic stressful experiences can have enduring effects that may even be transmitted across generations. The generational interchange from parent to child ('intergenerational') and then to their children ('transgenerational') depends on a variety of psychosocial and socioeconomic factors. Although studies of intergenerational trauma typically consider the impact of events that are especially severe (e.g., genocide, famine, earthquake, tsunami), in some instances, stressors that are usually considered to be 'non-traumatic', such as financial problems or work-related distress, especially if these occur on a chronic basis, can have disturbing consequences. When combined with traumatic stressors, non-traumatic events can have additive or synergistic effects on health outcomes. Thus, in discussing the intergenerational transmission of health and social outcomes it would be negligent not to consider both traumatic and apparently non-traumatic stressors, and to assess their effects from varied perspectives. There are several take-home messages that this chapter offers:

- Trauma may have long-lasting effects on a society or culture, but to a significant extent the long-term ramifications are dependent on what occurred after the traumatic event, including the support resources available and the individual's ability to maintain their group identity.

- Trauma effects are especially notable when survivors and their children are raised under toxic conditions stemming from poverty.
- The effects of trauma are particularly poignant if the initial stressor was experienced in childhood, and intergenerational effects are similarly evident when the initial stressor was experienced prenatally (i.e., the mother experienced the trauma), which elicit biological changes that affect the fetus.
- Stressful experiences, especially when they occurred during childhood, can lead to variations in gene expression. These epigenetic alterations can be passed across generations, thereby producing intergenerational phenotypic effects.
- For some groups, the impact of trauma should be viewed in the context of collective and historical events that can either promote vulnerability or resilience to further adverse experiences.

A voyage across generations

To fully appreciate the intergenerational and transgenerational effects of stressors, it is essential to consider the multiple routes, both direct and indirect, by which traumatic events can have these consequences. It won't be surprising to be told that trauma experienced by a pregnant mother may influence the fetus and thereby have health consequences on offspring, many of which last throughout their lifetime. Likewise, the trauma-elicited behaviors of a parent might directly affect their children. These effects can be still more dramatic when these parent–child interactions are superimposed on a negative environment (e.g., poverty), which might be secondary to the trauma individuals had endured (e.g., witness the financial and social consequences of many recent or ongoing civil and international wars). Having experienced poor parenting themselves, the parenting skills of the next generation of children might likewise be affected, which may influence the emotional stability and behaviors of their children.

In addition to the effects brought about through disturbed parenting, stressful events could promote epigenetic changes that can influence psychological and physical well-being. These epigenetic changes can be transmitted to offspring, and then passed on to the ensuing generation. Such intergenerational and transgenerational effects have been repeatedly demonstrated in rodents, whereas the data in humans are still limited and often difficult to dissociate from other effects brought about by historic traumatic encounters. In this respect, socioeconomic and cultural factors together with collective and historical memories might play a significant role in promoting the intergenerational effects of traumatic events. In this chapter, we'll cover each of these topics, and so the journey we'll be taking will range from situations in which stressors affect individuals to those that affect whole societies.

Intergenerational effects of trauma

Let's begin our analyses of trauma consequences with a view of two (not so) hypothetical groups who were the victims of genocide. After the trauma, one of these groups received considerable intragroup and intergroup support, so that they had the potential to rebuild their lives, and they and their children had the opportunity to achieve remarkable goals. Essentially, these individuals had found 'safe places' that allowed them to flourish and grow. In contrast, following trauma, members of a second group lived in horrid conditions, lost their network of ingroup support, were denigrated by outsiders, were robbed of their cultural values, and possessed limited opportunities to flourish. Both groups might share some of the biological consequences associated with the original trauma (such as epigenetic changes). For the latter group, however, there were no safe places (Matheson et al., 2020) and therefore the impact on a variety of health and social outcomes is likely to be more dramatic.

When we consider the influence of trauma, both within and across generations, it is essential to consider aspects of the trauma itself as well as the events that constitute the posttrauma period. The influences of traumatic experiences on intergenerational behavioral processes also ought to be viewed within the context of other cultural and historical traumas. Among other things, was the trauma unique to an individual or small group, or was a collective affected? As we've seen, social identity and social support (and unsupportive interactions) may have critical ramifications for dealing with stressors and in promoting personal resilience, particularly as social identity in the face of trauma may encourage a collective resilience that favors survival and recovery (Haslam et al., 2012). While the impact of traumatic events might never be entirely eliminated, their adverse effects across generations might be diminished by encouraging the development of effective social networks and the ability to derive meaning from the events.

Psychological and physical sequelae of trauma

The transmission of trauma effects (both within individuals and within communities) has been evaluated in several specific populations. Data collected from Jewish survivors of the Holocaust and their families have implicated biological changes, as well as the influence of parenting and attachment styles, as being fundamental in mediating the intergenerational effects of trauma. In fact, however, survivors don't fit neatly into a package in which characteristics are readily identified. Some survivors may show few symptoms, whereas others may display a wide range of psychological symptoms, such as survivor guilt, denial, and mistrust. There are those who might experience intrusive thoughts, nightmares, anxiety, and depression, although in most instances these had been at subsyndromal levels (Bar-On & Rottgardt, 1998).

It has often been maintained that, as a group, Holocaust survivors and their children were more vulnerable to the negative effects of stressors and were at elevated risk of developing PTSD and depression when faced with subsequent traumatic events. However, this perspective is overly simplistic. In a large cohort that comprised more than 38,500 Holocaust survivors and almost 35,000 control participants, the survivors experienced many more serious illnesses, but they also lived longer (Fund et al., 2019). It seemed that there were two sets of individuals. In one, the Holocaust was aligned with future adverse outcomes as might be expected in response to severe trauma. The second may have represented a group that was uniquely hardy, perhaps reflecting their greater resilience, which had allowed them to survive the Holocaust. As we'll see, the children of survivors probably should not be viewed as being more vulnerable to pathology. Some might be, but others may have been or become more resilient.

Although considerable data were collected regarding the intergenerational consequences of the trauma experienced by second- and third-generation survivors of the Holocaust, for a variety of reasons much less information is available regarding the intergenerational effects of trauma in other groups. Collective trauma occurred in Japanese Americans subjected by the US government to internment during World War II, and among survivors of the Armenian genocide conducted by the Ottomans. More recently, there's Syria, Somalia, Darfur, Bosnia, the mass killing of Tutsis by Hutus in Rwanda in 1994, and the deaths of Hutus at the hands of Tutsis in Burundi after 1973, the violent persecution of people of the Bahá'í faith in Iran, the experiences of Uyghur people in China, and that of the Rohingya minority in Myanmar are still playing out. Likewise, the purposeful killing of 3.5 – 5 million Ukrainian people by starvation between 1932 and 1933 (the Holodomor) instigated by the ruthless Russian leader Stalin may have promoted intergenerational consequences, which could potentially be exacerbated by Putin's treacherous attack on Ukraine in 2022. The intergenerational consequences of these tragedies remain to be assessed.

The experience of survivors across different collective traumas cannot, of course, be compared to one another given the differences in the magnitude, ferocity, and duration of the events, the hatreds and motivations that gave rise to these, and the conditions that prevailed in the post-trauma period. As well, in some cases, the genocide focused on the intentional eradication of a people, whereas in others the goal was cultural and spiritual genocide. Nevertheless, based on the data available related to other collective tragedies, it's a fair assumption that multiple consequences will be experienced, perhaps appearing across generations.

Impact of trauma on later responses to challenges

Persistent negative influences of early-life stressors

Several factors may feed into the way that traumatic experiences, especially those encountered in childhood, can affect later behaviors. Just as depressive illness has been associated with stress generation (stress proliferation), adverse childhood experiences have been associated with an increased risk of re-victimization experiences, including rape or being the victim of domestic violence. In addition, owing to the sensitization of biological systems, the effects of later trauma experiences may be amplified and sustained, making pathological outcomes more likely to occur. In fact, among children exposed to family violence and discord, but who had normal levels of anxiety, the depiction of angry faces (but not sad faces) was accompanied by increased neuronal activity in the amygdala and anterior cortex, likely reflecting threat responses (McCrory et al., 2011). Although elevated reactivity to threat cues might be a normal response, the extent of the excitation might represent a neurobiological marker indicative of elevated risk for pathology.

Children are greatly affected by collective traumatic events even if they might not fully comprehend the cause of these experiences. Indeed, it is widely documented that adverse childhood experiences (short of collective trauma), including abuse and neglect, may disrupt school performance, decision-making processes, and the ability to form and maintain close relationships. These disturbances might then directly and indirectly increase the risk of stressor experiences in adulthood. Thus, in assessing the influence of childhood stressors in relation to the subsequent emergence of pathology, analyses should not be limited to particularly severe stressors, but also to the cumulative effects of multiple stressors that might have been endured. Indeed, individuals who reported a large number of adverse early-life experiences (i.e., those related to childhood maltreatment and disturbed home environments) were at especially high risk for adult psychopathology, such as depression, PTSD, suicidality, and substance use disorders. Such adverse experiences have similarly been linked to a wide assortment of physical illnesses, including type 2 diabetes, heart disease, and numerous immune-related disorders, likely operating through hormonal, immune, and inflammatory alterations (Anisman & Kusnecov, 2022). As depicted in Figure 12.1, stressful encounters (e.g., childhood abuse) often don't occur in isolation from other trauma encounters and hence the way things play out is determined by the constellation of adverse events that might be experienced. In this regard, victimization is not simply an 'event' but is a 'condition' that entails ongoing distress (e.g., Pratchett & Yehuda, 2011), although such experiences might, in some cases, also form the basis of resilience.

Poor appraisal and coping methods associated with adverse childhood experiences

Traumatic events experienced early in life might disturb the way individuals appraise the world around them as well as the way they interpret subsequently encountered stressful events. These new stressor experiences might be accompanied by negative cognitive styles, warped internal attributions (i.e., self-blaming and self-criticizing), and other cognitive distortions, including those associated with safety or a preoccupation with danger, as well as issues related to having

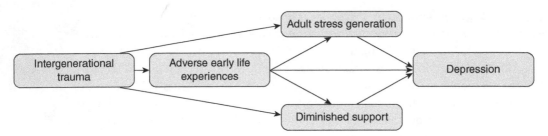

Figure 12.1   Trauma experienced in an earlier generation may increase the occurrence of further trauma (e.g., poor parenting, poverty) as well as the likelihood of further trauma being experienced throughout life. Adverse early-life experiences may also undermine the individual's ability to cope effectively, accompanied by impoverished social support and social connectivity. Together, these factors increase the likelihood of psychological disorders evolving.

control over their own lives. Exaggerated concerns of future harm and maintaining this sense of threat and unpredictability about the future may contribute to the development of anxiety, depression, and PTSD following a subsequent traumatic experience.

Appraisal and coping go hand-in-hand and, as described earlier, the coping strategies available to children are typically not well formed, and their resources to deal with stressors are limited. Chronic or repeated childhood adversities may give rise to an inferential process wherein children attempt to understand why abusive or neglectful experiences are happening to them. These children might come to believe that these adverse events are stable and pervasive, with the effect of undermining individuals' coping development and their ability to engage in new and more effective strategies. While some children may internalize the cause of these experiences believing them to reflect their own inadequacies, others might externalize their behaviors in a manner that reflects a lack of trust and openness to relationships with others. Children who have experienced traumatic events are apt to use inappropriate coping strategies, such as avoidant coping or strategies characterized by risk-taking, confrontation, and the release of frustration that may extend into adulthood (Gruhn & Compas, 2020). As a result, adverse childhood stressors may be fundamental in the subsequent development of numerous psychological and physical disorders – it has been said in relation to these pathologies that early-life trauma is the root of all roots.

Transmission of trauma from parent to child: the case of poor parenting

Adverse childhood experiences may set in motion biological and psychosocial factors that comprise the (im)perfect ingredients that foster marked and long-lasting repercussions on children. It is predictable that high levels of parental stress and trauma, as well as parental mental health conditions (including substance use disorders) can have enormous impacts on a range of parenting abilities, manifested as disengagement and disorganized attachment styles, hostility, coercion, abusive or neglectful behaviors, and low positive parent–child interactions. Regrettably, poor parenting begets later poor parenting (Lomanowska et al., 2017) and it was estimated that child maltreatment occurs in about 30% of children whose parents had themselves been maltreated. Aside from these psychosocial influences, it is likely that genetic and epigenetic factors interact with adverse early experiences in determining the wide array of psychological and physical health outcomes that frequently occur (Jiang et al., 2019). Evidently, the many consequences of adverse experiences of one generation might foster the recapitulation of negative events in the next generation.

CONSPIRACY OF SILENCE

The children of survivors of the Holocaust have recounted that some parents talked about their experiences over and over. Conversely, many survivors withheld any communication about their experiences, an intergenerational communication pattern that was termed the 'conspiracy of silence' (Danieli, 1998). A similar but less common profile has been apparent in the survivors of Indian Residential Schools (Matheson, Bombay, Dixon & Anisman, 2020).

The messages embedded within this silence were at one level ambiguous, but at another they were very clear, and perhaps not surprisingly, children of Holocaust survivors who experienced this silence generally seemed to be more vulnerable to the intergenerational transmission of trauma (Wiseman et al., 2002). Children often grew up in families in which there was no outright communication regarding the parents' trauma, but the trauma was still 'silently present in the home'. In a remarkably powerful book regarding the Holocaust, *After Such Knowledge*, Eva Hoffman, states, 'A few survivors were determined never to talk about what they had lived through; but others wanted to give expression to the horror, or perhaps couldn't help doing so ... to their immediate intimates, to spouses and siblings, and yes, to their children. There, they spoke in the language of family – a form of expression that is both more direct and more ruthless than social and public speech ...'

In her discussion related to genocide and its impact across generations, Hirsch (2001) discussed what is referred to as 'postmemory' or a 'reclaiming of memory'. She viewed postmemory as the relationship of children of 'survivors of cultural or collective trauma to the experiences of their parents, experiences that they "remember" only as the narratives and images with which they grew up, but that are so powerful, so monumental, as to constitute memories in their own right' (p. 16). The consequences of trauma experiences can wane over generations, but they might not be far from the surface.

Early-life stressors influence biological processes

Aside from affecting the child's psychological and cognitive development through their parenting styles, biological processes can also be affected. These might influence the child's ability to cope with further stressors, thereby affecting their psychological development as well as their vulnerability to several physical illnesses. In the section that follows we will consider the influence of stressors and immunological insults on later neurobiological and psychological processes.

We learned earlier that stressors experienced during early life or during the juvenile period could provoke the reprogramming of biological signals, such as those related to hormonal, inflammatory, neurotrophin, and immunological processes that, in turn, could disturb behavioral, emotional, and cognitive functioning (e.g., high threat vigilance, mistrust of others, disrupted social relations, and disturbed self-regulation). These early-life stressors (including maternal neglect) may likewise influence developmental trajectories that culminate in adult anxiety, depression, metabolic disorders, cardiovascular disease, stroke, and autoimmune disorders.

The early-life stressors that elicit these protracted effects in animals were frequently assessed in the context of mother–pup interactions in which poor maternal care was associated with numerous negative outcomes. Similar long-term consequences were observed in rodents that experienced other types of stressors and in response to systemic insults, such as bacterial infection during the first few days after birth. Particular attention had been devoted to the analysis of early-life stressors on HPA hormones, but challenges likewise have marked actions that go well beyond these hormones. In fact, such stressors influence varied neurotrophins and neurotransmitters, such as serotonin, dopamine, GABA, glutamate, and oxytocin, and their receptors (Mumtaz et al., 2018; Onaka & Takayanagi, 2021). With so many biological changes potentially being affected by negative early-life experiences, it is understandable that a wide assortment of pathological outcomes may emerge.

Genetic factors that code for hormones and neurotrophins may play a significant role in moderating the actions of stressful events. However, a gene mutation or epigenetic change might not invariably cause psychological disorders. Instead, the presence of certain polymorphisms, as in the case of those related to oxytocin and BDNF, might influence an individual's malleability (or at least make their biological systems more or less plastic), so that environmental events could, for better or for worse, differentially shape behavioral outcomes (Belsky et al., 2009). Ordinarily, negative early-life events may result in a greater likelihood of subsequent negative outcomes, whereas positive events might similarly increase the probability of positive outcomes emerging. However, in the presence of polymorphisms related to oxytocin and BDNF, the effects of positive and nurturing early-life experiences may not emerge, but equally, the impact of adversity might be less marked (McQuaid et al., 2013). The essential point is that adverse early-life events may have profound implications for later pathology, but this might depend on the presence of other factors, the individual's genetic disposition being among them. As well, epigenetic changes elicited by adverse early experiences may contribute to the array of psychological and physical health outcomes that frequently occur (Jiang et al., 2019).

STRESS MAKES YOU OLD
BEFORE YOUR YEARS

The DNA sequences found at the tips of chromosomes, which serve to prevent the DNA from unraveling, are referred to as 'telomeres'. With each replication of the DNA strand these telomeres become shorter, and at a certain point the cell will not be able to replicate. This is part of our aging process and telomere length may be predictive of age-related diseases (Blackburn et al., 2015). Interestingly, stressful events have the effect of reducing the length of these telomeres, which may tell us about the cumulative effects attributable to stressors, much like rings on a tree can inform us about its age and past weather conditions. In this regard, stressful experiences in children, including parental violence, emotional or physical assaults, or even witnessing domestic disputes, resulted in the shortening of telomere length. It similarly appeared that adverse childhood experiences among women may subsequently be associated with accelerated aging in their children reflected by shortened telomere length (Nwanaji-Enwerem et al., 2021). Moreover, prenatal stressors may promote shorter telomere length in offspring measured in later adulthood (Shalev et al., 2013). The diverse processes that come to affect these actions haven't been fully identified, but it has been reported that shortened telomere length was accompanied by poorer physical and psychological health. Thus, telomere length or levels of the enzyme telomerase involved in this process may be useful in predicting the development of such disorders (Lindqvist et al., 2015).

Impact of prenatal insults

As we consider whether and how the effects of stressors can be passed from one generation to the next, we probably shouldn't limit ourselves to events that occurred early in childhood, but also consider what occurs when stressors are encountered during pregnancy. We'll now take a closer look at the ramifications of psychogenic and systemic stressors experienced during pregnancy on the well-being of offspring across their life span.

Biological effects of prenatal stressors: animal studies

A great number of studies have shown that stressors experienced by a pregnant rodent can increase the propensity for behavioral and emotional disturbances in her offspring. In mice, strong prenatal stressors disrupted offspring DA neuronal functioning and altered the response to drugs (e.g., amphetamines) that affect DA activity. Thus, in addition to promoting anxiety and depressive-like states, these changes might serve as a link to substance use disorder in offspring (Pastor et al., 2017). Aside from these effects, stressors encountered prenatally disrupted BDNF functioning (Badihian et al., 2020) and promoted brain-region specific variations of basic fibroblast growth factor (FGF-2), which are key regulators of neurodevelopment and plasticity related to depression. Physical and psychological challenges experienced prenatally or during early life can promote epigenetic changes that may affect offspring vulnerability to pathology, and the alterations of gene expression can be transmitted to the next generation (Cao-Lei et al., 2020).

Simply witnessing other rodents experience stressors may have negative effects on observer animals. Ordinarily, when an animal is stressed, observers will exhibit stress reactions even though they are not directly stressed. If pregnant rats are bystanders to another rat being stressed, epigenetic changes occur in their offspring who subsequently exhibit altered behavioral responses. These bystander effects can be dramatic, in that the offspring of rats that had witnessed another animal being stressed also displayed several brain morphological changes. The complexity and extent of dendritic arborization (the branching and connections characteristic of well-formed dendrites) were reduced and glial cells were diminished in the prefrontal cortex and hippocampus. These biological alterations were accompanied by depressive-like behaviors and cognitive deficits (Mychasiuk et al., 2011).

Impact of prenatal stressors: human studies

Premature birth and diminished birth weight

Stressors experienced by pregnant women have been associated with numerous adverse effects in offspring. Shortened gestation periods and reduced birth weight are among the best documented effects of prenatal stressors. Chronic maternal distress increases circulating CRH, probably of placental origin, and together with other hormones (e.g., cortisol and the endogenous opioid met-enkephalin) that pass into the placenta, might precipitate preterm labor and reduced birth weight. The stressors that induce these actions are fairly ubiquitous, ranging from domestic violence and work-related psychosocial distress, to experiences of racial discrimination and wartime conditions. As well, the birth weights of offspring of mothers who had experienced PTSD during pregnancy were lower than that of the offspring of non-stressed mothers or that of mothers who experienced trauma but did not develop PTSD (Seng et al., 2011).

Prenatal stressors, like treatments that increased endogenous glucocorticoid levels late in gestation (e.g., synthetic glucocorticoids, such as betamethasone, used to promote lung maturation in fetuses at risk of preterm delivery) may influence neurotransmitter systems and RNA transcriptional machinery. Consequently, later corticoid responses to stressful stimuli may be increased, and infant behavioral reactivity might be elevated. The hormonal changes produced by prenatal stressors have been associated with delayed fetal nervous system maturation, including diminished grey matter volume and impaired mental development (Reynolds, 2013). The consequences of prenatal stressors are also apparent in relation to immune and inflammatory processes that may not only promote negative effects on the developing embryo but may have cascading effects that are realized throughout postnatal development (Entringer et al., 2015).

There is some debate about the gestational stage at which stressors might have their greatest impact. Pronounced offspring psychopathology occurred among individuals whose mothers were stressed during late pregnancy, and other studies indicated that distress during the first trimester of pregnancy, and to a lesser extent the second trimester, were associated with reduced birth weight. Furthermore, reduced birth weight and shorter gestation periods were reported among women who experienced a moderately strong stressor prior to pregnancy. In this regard, chronic stressors experienced in advance of pregnancy may have profound ramifications on fetal brain development and hence the appearance of psychological disorders (Lafortune et al., 2021). Given that stressful experiences may promote negative rumination, the adverse events experienced prior to pregnancy might have influenced the fetus owing to the distress related to continued rumination.

Neurocognitive disturbances related to prenatal stress

Stressful maternal experiences that comprised emotional, psychological, physical, or sexual violence gave rise to developmental disturbances in offspring (Toso et al., 2020). Epidemiological studies similarly indicated that the risk of neurodevelopmental disorders, such as schizophrenia and autism spectrum disorders, was elevated in association with prenatal stressors (Van den Bergh et al., 2020). Like the impact of other stressors encountered during pregnancy, the distress associated with relationship strain predicted later emotional and cognitive disturbances among offspring. Such effects have been associated with numerous brain changes and variations of limbic and frontotemporal networks (Lautarescu et al., 2020).

A broad overview of the effects of prenatal challenges revealed that offspring of mothers who had been stressed while pregnant exhibited functional and structural brain connectivity disturbances. These comprised functional and morphological variations of the amygdala, prefrontal cortex, and hippocampus, and changes in HPA and autonomic nervous system processes. These were accompanied by poor neurocognitive functioning and social-emotional development (Moog et al., 2021; Van den Bergh et al., 2020).

Inflammatory and hormonal changes associated with prenatal stressors

Prenatal stressors were related to increased risk of immune-related disorders in offspring, having been linked to increased occurrence of allergies and asthma, altered reactions to immunological challenges, and an increase in the probability of contracting infectious diseases (e.g., Robinson et al., 2021). The prenatal experiences were associated with elevated production of inflammatory factors, notably C-reactive protein (CRP) and IL-6 (Pedersen et al., 2018), which together with hormonal changes favor the development of chronic diseases (Anisman & Kusnecov, 2022).

Markers of inflammation were apparent in women who had been depressed during pregnancy, or who had a history of earlier depression but were not depressed during pregnancy. The indices of inflammation predicted poor social-interactive behaviors in neonates (Osborne et al., 2022). Similarly, the experience of multiple stressful events and their timing rather than just the severity of a given prenatal stressor was most closely aligned with negative outcomes that were monitored in offspring from 2 to 14 years of age (Robinson et al., 2011). While the findings might point to direct actions of prenatal stressors on disturbances in offspring, it is equally possible that these actions stemmed from the mother's psychological or physical responses to these events.

Prenatal stress and epigenetic changes

The actions of prenatal stressors can engender the reprogramming of gene expression within the fetus, which may lead to increased risk of later disorders, such as attention deficit hyperactivity disorder (ADHD), schizophrenia, anxiety, depression, and illnesses comorbid with these conditions. These actions may be related to epigenetic changes that can be transmitted to ensuing generations (Babenko et al., 2015). A longitudinal assessment in the offspring of women who were pregnant during Hurricane Sandy in 2012 revealed elevated cortisol levels measured in hair samples of their children when they were 3–4 years of age, which were accompanied by increased anxiety and aggressive behaviors. These variations were linked to broad placental mRNA changes, including within genes associated with endocrine and immune processes that may have influenced the later biological and behavioral changes observed (Nomura et al., 2021).

Intense lifetime psychosocial stressor experiences (e.g., sexual assault, domestic violence, family hardships) have been related to epigenetic changes that code for diverse biological factors. These experiences were associated with the elevated occurrence of placental mitochondrial mutations (these are distinct from DNA mutations that appear in the nucleus of cells) that can be passed down from a mother to her offspring (Brunst et al., 2021). While most analyses have focused on mutations of DNA within the nucleus, mitochondrial DNA mutations were linked to several inherited diseases.

As much as behavioral changes stemming from prenatal stressors may be due to epigenetic actions, the impact of prenatal trauma may be confounded with other factors, including postnatal maternal anxiety and poor rearing conditions. Likewise, genetic factors may have interacted with the prenatal stressors to produce effects on offspring. To assess this possibility, an analysis was undertaken to evaluate prenatal stress in which pregnant mothers were either genetically related or unrelated to their child based on assessments of offspring conceived through in vitro fertilization. Using this approach, offspring birth weight and antisocial behavior were shown to be associated with prenatal stressors regardless of whether the offspring were genetically related or unrelated to the mothers. In contrast, the relation between prenatal stress and offspring anxiety was more closely aligned with postnatal maternal anxiety/depression, whereas subsequent ADHD in the offspring was uniquely present in mother–offspring pairs who were genetically related. Evidently, genetic and environmental factors may both have effects on offspring, but their relative contributions vary with the specific phenotypes of interest (Rice et al., 2010).

In view of the breadth of biological and behavioral changes associated with prenatal stressors, these insults may create a 'general susceptibility' to pathology, rather than one that is related to specific pathological states (Huizink et al., 2004). Importantly, as strong as the effects of prenatal stressors might be on numerous physiological processes, the expression of some of these effects can be moderated by postnatal experiences. While prenatal stressors might affect later emotional, cognitive, and neuroendocrine functioning, these events don't necessarily doom the offspring to disturbances in adulthood. Although depression in pregnant women can have multiple adverse effects on their offspring, these outcomes could be diminished if the mother provided an infant with a high degree of contact comfort during the initial weeks of life. This emphasizes the importance of engaging in stress interventions in pregnant women, and failing this, assuring that the offspring's postnatal environment is a positive one that could potentially antagonize the adverse effects that had already been created or act against the negative trajectory that would otherwise evolve.

Sex-dependent effects of prenatal stressors

A persistent question that has emerged in relation to various pathologies is why females are more prone to certain illnesses than are males, especially stress-related psychological disturbances and autoimmune disorders. In part, this might be related to the fact that males and females exhibit markedly different biological and behavioral responses to stressors (e.g., Rainville et al., 2018). As well, the sexual dimorphism (i.e., sex-specific effects) appeared in response to prenatal stressors, reflected by differences in later behavioral outcomes, as well as brain morphology and gene expression profiles. Given the sex differences that exist during embryonic development, it might not be altogether surprising that stressors that affect hormones and inflammatory factors in a pregnant woman would differentially influence the male and female fetus. Among other things, the female fetus might be better able to adapt to stressors and may be in an advantageous position to withstand intrauterine challenges that favor enhanced viability (e.g., diminished nutrient availability). The male fetus, in contrast, seems to prioritize growth and physical development in the context of prenatal adversity. The net result of these differences could manifest as greater neuroendocrine and emotional reactivity in females (Sutherland & Brunwasser, 2018).

Although the effects of stressors can be realized at any phase of pregnancy, it was suggested that during a particularly sensitive period of prenatal development a surge in gonadal hormones may be elicited by stressors that might be responsible for the brain being biased in a sexually dimorphic manner. With subsequent postnatal development, these gonadal hormones contribute to further neuronal changes that promote the expression of sex-specific phenotypes. Thus, the greater anxiety and depression evident in female offspring were attributed to estrogen changes and elevated HPA responsiveness, whereas learning disturbances that occurred preferentially in prenatally stressed males were attributed to sex-dependent reductions of hippocampal neurogenesis and dendritic spine density in the prefrontal cortex. In effect, prenatal stressors may have adverse effects in both sexes, but the specific negative outcomes that develop might be related to the prenatal hormonal changes that occur.

Consequences of prenatal infection

Systemic stressors that comprise biological challenges, such as infection, can produce hormonal and neurotransmitter changes that in many ways resemble those produced by psychological and physical stressors. Thus, in evaluating the intergenerational changes that occur, it is important to consider the impact of systemic stressors especially as women from disadvantaged groups have been found to be more likely to contract some forms of viral infection, such as influenza (Hadler et al., 2016). Pregnant women who develop viral or bacterial illnesses may, understandably, be concerned about the consequences to their offspring. There is good reason for this concern given that fetal exposure to such illnesses, as well as parasites, may elicit neuropsychiatric disturbances. It has long been known that pregnant women who contract rubella are at elevated risk of miscarriage and stillbirth, and their offspring are more likely to present with birth defects, such as deafness. Other fetal bacterial and viral infections may similarly elicit neuropsychiatric disturbances.

Prenatal infection and schizophrenia

Prenatal viral challenges have been associated with varied behavioral and physiological disturbances that can manifest years later. Prenatal infection in rodents may influence the neurodevelopment and behavioral dysfunctions in offspring, some of which have been used to model schizophrenia. The effects of prenatal infection were not evident in offspring when they were assessed soon after birth but, rather, emerged during the juvenile period (Meyer, 2019), just as schizophrenia in humans typically emerges during this time (i.e., during the late teens). It had been maintained that prenatal infection, through its effects on DA neuronal activity, might contribute to the later emergence of schizophrenia. As the DA changes elicited by prenatal infection were apparent regardless of whether pups were raised by a dam that had experienced the infection or a surrogate dam that had not been infected, postnatal factors were ruled out. In addition to the involvement of DA processes, the offspring of dams exposed to infection exhibited glutamate alterations that have been linked to schizophrenia (Meyer, 2019). Moreover, the schizophrenia-like behaviors associated with prenatal infections co-occurred with elevated expression of genes linked to inflammatory factors, reduced expression of genes tied to BDNF and diminished antioxidant defense processes (Talukdar et al., 2020).

Epidemiological findings have pointed to ties between infectious illness in pregnant women and the later occurrence of schizophrenia in their offspring (Davies et al., 2020). The risk of schizophrenia was elevated by 700% in the offspring of mothers exposed to influenza during the first trimester of pregnancy. Furthermore, following a rubella pandemic in 1964, *in utero* exposure to the virus was accompanied by a 500% increase of non-affective psychosis, and at mid-adulthood over 20% of those individuals who had been exposed to rubella had a diagnosis of either schizophrenia or a schizophrenia spectrum disorder (Brown & Derkits, 2010). Exposure to Toxoplasma gondii, an intracellular parasite, was likewise associated with various CNS abnormalities, as well as neuropsychiatric consequences, including a 200% increase of schizophrenia.

The impact of viral infections might have stemmed from cytokine changes commonly produced by these illnesses, perhaps interacting with genetic or epigenetic factors (Allswede et al., 2020). Relatedly, fever produced by cytokines and fetal/neonatal hypoxia secondary to infection may have led to pathological outcomes. Moreover, the possibility exists that prenatal inflammation could disrupt maternal gut microbiota thereby affecting the offspring.

Data from pandemics prior to COVID-19 had suggested that viral infection during pregnancy was related to neuropsychiatric disturbances in offspring, although the findings were often inconsistent (Zimmer et al., 2021). Varied obstetrical complications arose during pandemics over the past decades (e.g., during MERS and SARS-CoV-1) and this has similarly been seen among pregnant women who had contracted COVID-19 (SARS-CoV-2) infection. The risk of stillbirth was markedly elevated and unvaccinated pregnant women were more likely to develop severe symptoms and death (Stock et al., 2022). Moreover, COVID-19 may produce an inflammatory immune response in the fetus (Garcia-Flores et al., 2022). The consequences on offspring aren't known yet, but given the long-term effects associated with other infections, this will no doubt be monitored carefully.

In an interesting review of the literature related to prenatal infection, Harvey and Boksa (2012) indicated that in addition to schizophrenia, such events have been associated with numerous pathological conditions, such as autism, cerebral palsy, epilepsy, and Parkinson's disease. Thus, they suggested that prenatal and early postnatal infection might reflect a general vulnerability factor for diverse neurodevelopmental disorders. The nature of the pathology that emerges may be related to the time of prenatal infections as well as other vulnerability factors that might be present.

━━━━━━━━━━━━━━━ **AUTISM AND IMMUNITY** ━━━━━━━━━━━━━━━

Vaccine hesitancy is not a new phenomenon having been around as long as vaccines have been available. In the context of COVID-19, this hesitancy has been influenced by political factors and veritable floods of misinformation obtained through social media. Today's hesitancy concerning vaccination of children has a shady history that largely stemmed from a discredited report by Wakefield suggesting that vaccination with MMR (mumps, measles, rubella) led to autism. *The Lancet*, where it was published, described this work as being the greatest scientific fraud in one hundred years. Based on this paper many parents stopped immunizing their children, thus leaving them vulnerable to these diseases. Although it has been almost two decades since Wakefield's fraud was uncovered, the damage he created is still being felt, exacerbated by parental anxiety concerning their children's well-being and reinforced by public figures with limited knowledge.

A credible view of autism has emerged in relation to immune functioning, although this perspective will need to go through well-controlled experimental evaluations. Among women who had experienced a viral infection during the first trimester of pregnancy a 300% increase of autism was later detected, and when the infection occurred in the second trimester, a 40% increase of later autism occurred. It was proposed that inflammatory-related disturbances might be at the root of autism in more than a third of cases. Brain samples of those with autism exhibited elevated microglia and astroglia that might be associated with chronic inflammation (Matta et al., 2019), and genes coding for inflammation were switched on continuously and cytokine levels elevated. It appeared that mothers of autistic children often have antibodies of a unique nature that can bind to fetal brain proteins, thereby causing damage. Regardless of the perspectives, the common denominator in these studies is that neuroinflammatory responses during pregnancy or in early life can have effects that will become apparent during later development. It has repeatedly been reported that vaccination in children has not been associated with autism, nor is it accompanied by developmental delays, ADHD, or type 1 diabetes, but too often myths trump reality (Geoghegan et al., 2020).

Epigenetic changes

Intergenerational transmission

The last two decades have seen exponential growth in the analysis of epigenetic changes in relation to the progression of the aging process and the emergence of diseases (Cavalli & Heard, 2019). Early-life experiences, including environmental factors, stressors, endocrine challenges, and impoverished nutrient intake, can instigate epigenetic changes that influence biological processes and hence might have long-term health repercussions. What was especially significant from the perspective of the current discussion is that stress reactivity and health outcomes that stemmed from epigenetic effects can be transmitted across generations (Cavalli & Heard, 2019). Specifically, if the epigenetic changes occur on germline cells (i.e., sperm or ova), these can be passed down from parent to offspring (intergenerational effect) and possibly across several generations (transgenerational effects) even if further stressors or other experience-dependent changes had not been encountered.

Just as epigenetic changes are readily introduced during early life when neuronal growth and plasticity is at their peak, epigenetic variations can be promoted in the fetus by environmental challenges experienced by the mother. This was provoked by a range of toxicants, such as pesticides, fungicides (e.g., the androgenic fungicide vinclozolin), the endocrine disruptor bisphenol-A, and estrogenic peptides. Being exposed to pollutants (e.g., dioxins) while the mother was pregnant resulted in offspring mice showing impaired immunity against influenza virus, which was likewise evident in ensuing generations (Post et al., 2019). Consistent with these findings, exposure to pesticides, such as methoxychlor (which, ironically, replaced DDT owing to the health problems it created), promoted epigenetic actions that were recapitulated over several generations (Manikkam et al., 2014). Likewise, stressful challenges during pregnancy can produce epigenetic changes that affected HPA functioning in offspring and similarly influenced their emotionality (Bale, 2015).

The epigenetic changes introduced by stressful experiences have been apparent in genes that code for neurotrophins and several immune factors that have been implicated in the provocation of psychological and physical disturbances (e.g., Nilsson et al., 2018). Lifestyle factors, particularly diet and exercise, can similarly influence the expression of genes that can affect well-being. The actions of poor diets may come about because they influence microbiota that affect microRNAs, which then favor the appearance of psychological disorders. This relationship is bidirectional, in that microbial changes can affect brain processes, and conversely, changes of neuronal activity in specific brain regions can influence microbiota abundance (Moloney et al., 2019). The essential point is that diverse environmental events and experiences can influence the expression of genes, and thus have phenotypic consequences that can be transmitted from one generation to the next. Increasingly frequent reports that toxicants and both prenatal or early-life stressors may have effects that extend beyond a single generation have been fundamental in changing our views about the transmission of traits and abilities, as well as the processes that are linked to trauma-related pathologies (Szyf, 2019).

Epigenetic changes in rodents related to maternal behaviors

The neglectful behavior of a dam toward her pups during early development may cause the silencing of particular genes. Specifically, poor maternal care during early postnatal development may influence the methylation of the promoter for the gene that regulates glucocorticoid receptors, thereby leading to altered hippocampal glucocorticoid receptor expression and elevated stressor reactivity that persists into adulthood (Szyf, 2019). Aside from epigenetic changes related to the glucocorticoid receptor, stressful events influence DNA methylation of many other neurobiological processes. Stressors experienced during early life can influence serotonin-associated genes, which can affect behavior (Soga et al., 2021). Moreover, poor maternal care resulted in the methylation of the gene promoter of estrogen receptor alpha (ERa) in the hypothalamus of female rodents (Champagne & Curley, 2009). As ERa is important for the functioning of estrogen and oxytocin, both of which may contribute to maternal behaviors, the silencing of this gene might be responsible for the transmission of poor maternal behaviors.

Variations of BDNF functioning in several brain regions are also subject to epigenetic changes that were implicated in psychopathology (Miao et al., 2020). To simulate the experiences of abuse or neglect among children from poor homes, Roth et al. (2009) raised rat pups for the first postnatal week with adult caretakers that had been stressed, and thus displayed abusive behaviors. When the abused pups were subsequently assessed in adulthood, methylation of BDNF DNA gene expression was apparent, leading to altered BDNF protein in the prefrontal cortex. When this generation of rats had their own litters, this profile of BDNF methylation was apparent in the offspring. These data not only point to epigenetic changes in controlling this trophic factor but also implicate it in the intergenerational effects of early-life stressors.

As much as early life is a time in which epigenetic change can readily be induced by stressful events, this period is not uniquely sensitive to these effects. Rodents stressed during the juvenile period (the equivalent of adolescence in humans) subsequently displayed increased reactivity and anxiety, and this effect was apparent in their offspring, possibly reflecting an epigenetic change. Similarly, strong stressors encountered in adulthood have been associated with epigenetic effects and diminished transcription of BDNF, accompanied by the emergence of depressive-like features (e.g., Park et al., 2019).

It is of considerable relevance that although many epigenetic changes can be permanent, some of these are modifiable. For instance, epigenetic changes introduced by early-life stressors could be reversed by treating rats with a methyl donor (methionine) or a histone deacetylase inhibitor that limits gene transcription (Weaver et al., 2005). Similarly, a histone deacetylase inhibitor administered directly into the nucleus accumbens acted like an antidepressant agent in modifying behavioral disturbances (Covington et al., 2009). Aside from such intrusive manipulations, environmental enrichment (e.g., providing rodents with a larger cage, toys) could reverse the epigenetic changes introduced by early-life adversity in the form of maternal separation (Borba et al., 2021). Significantly, negative intergenerational stressor effects were attenuated among rats that had been exposed to a juvenile stressor but subsequently raised in an enriched environment, possibly operating through effects on BDNF (Taouk & Schulkin, 2016). Likewise, the epigenetic changes stemming from prenatal stressors that influenced neuronal density within the prefrontal cortex, glucocorticoid receptor sensitivity, and early development of anxiety-related behaviors could be attenuated by environmental enrichment during adolescence, again seemingly occurring through increased expression of genes linked to BDNF (McCreary et al., 2016). It may be especially consequential from an intervention perspective that the epigenetic effects of toxicants and inflammatory processes might be modifiable by lifestyle changes, including exercise and nutritional changes (Ramos-Lopez et al., 2021).

Even though analyses of epigenetic effects, such as those that occurred in response to prenatal or early-life challenges have typically considered the negative effects that may evolve, some actions of seemingly negative prenatal experiences can have beneficial actions in offspring. For example, among mice that had experienced a prenatal bacterial or inflammatory challenge, epigenetic changes related to immune functioning appeared to provide them with improved protection in response to bacterial threats that were subsequently encountered (Katzmarski et al., 2021). The typical view of natural selection is that certain mutations will be selected because they offer survival advantages, which allow for the relevant genes to be passed across generations. It is similarly possible epigenetic changes that provide survival benefits could drive natural selection and could be transmitted across generations (Sarkies, 2020).

Maternal and paternal behaviors in intergenerational epigenetic transmission

Is it just the female parent who passes on epigenetic changes that affect offspring, or does paternal transmission also occur? There is evidence consistent with the transmission of stressor effects through paternal lineage. Male pups that experienced chronic maternal separation later exhibited depressive-like behaviors and altered behavioral responses to aversive stimuli when subsequently assessed as adults. In the offspring of these males, epigenetically related behavioral and neuroendocrine disturbances were apparent even though these animals had not been in contact with their male parent (Franklin et al., 2010; Gapp & Bohacek., 2018). Actions such as these may vary with the characteristics of the parent. Differential epigenetic actions were more readily produced by chronic stressors among mice that were deemed stress-sensitive than in those that were stress-resilient, supporting the importance of considering individual characteristics in the transmission of stressor effects over generations (Cunningham et al., 2021).

The possibility was considered that paternal epigenetic transmission may have occurred because stressed male mice had caused the females to become distressed, which then directly or indirectly influenced their pups. To assess this, females were impregnated through *in vitro* fertilization using sperm from a stressed mouse. When this was done, the behavioral effects otherwise passed down from parent to offspring were largely absent (Dietz et al., 2011). Hence, it seems as if the transmission might not actually be linked to epigenetic changes in the sire being passed on to the offspring. It is conceivable, however, that stressors experienced by a male might affect sperm quality, including sperm motility, and these actions might be particularly notable when *in vitro* fertilization was adopted, hence precluding intergenerational actions.

While there have been questions concerning the paternal transmission of epigenetic effects related to stressors, the data overall seem to suggest that such actions can occur. In fact, it seems that diseases in offspring can be epigenetically transmitted by the paternal diet that comprises high fat or low protein (Klastrup et al., 2019). More broadly, epigenetic changes have been tied to lifestyles endorsed and by deficiencies of folic acid, which is involved in red blood cell production (Ly et al., 2017). Inasmuch as stressful experiences may affect lifestyles and folic acid deficiencies can influence anxiety, it is conceivable that the effects of stressors may have indirect actions on epigenetic changes.

Not unexpectedly, determining the epigenetic effects of stressors and the transmission of these actions across generations necessarily consider multiple factors beyond those already mentioned. Among other things, intergenerational effects may be determined by the characteristics of the stressor used (e.g., social versus non-social stressors; acute versus chronic stressors) and the age of the animals at which stressors were encountered (Cunningham et al., 2021). Yet, it was demonstrated that chronic stress experienced during puberty or adulthood could instigate paternal transmission of epigenetic changes (Rodgers et al., 2013) and such effects differed between male and female offspring (Manners et al., 2019). Most studies assessed these actions in rodents, but there have been indications that paternal transmission of epigenetic changes associated with ACEs was tied to attention problems apparent in offspring at 3 years of age (Merrill et al., 2021).

Epigenetic changes associated with stressors in humans

Owing to the length of time for each generation to come to the age of having children, there have been relatively few studies in humans that assessed the role of epigenetic factors in mediating the transgenerational effects of stressful experiences on behavioral disturbances. Nonetheless, an array of factors related to stressors have been identified that are subject to epigenetic changes, some of which may be relevant to intergenerational effects.

Among individuals who died by suicide and had a history of early childhood neglect/abuse, hippocampal hypermethylation within the promoter region of the gene for the glucocorticoid receptor was apparent, accompanied by reduced glucocorticoid receptor mRNA expression (McGowan et al., 2009). In infants at three months of age, increased methylation of the genes for glucocorticoid receptors along with increased salivary cortisol stress responses were apparent if mothers had been depressed/anxious during the third trimester of pregnancy. This outcome was evident even after controlling for antidepressant use among mothers as well as their postnatal maternal mood (Oberlander et al., 2008).

In the children of individuals who encountered intense trauma, such as that experienced by Holocaust survivors, epigenetic changes were present within the FKBP5 gene, which is associated with glucocorticoid functioning and has been tied to depressive illnesses and PTSD (Yehuda et al., 2016). Effects such as these were more pronounced among individuals if both parents had been Holocaust survivors. While some of the observed effects might have been related to epigenetic changes, they could also be linked to parenting style, attachments, and the presence of parental mental health conditions (Dashorst et al., 2019). These investigators made the point that offspring might not have exhibited disturbed behaviors on a day-to-day basis, but the actions of epigenetic changes were primarily apparent when adverse events were encountered.

Although these findings are consistent with the view that early experiences are accompanied by glucocorticoid receptor functioning that can be affected through epigenetic processes, causal conclusions concerning the epigenetic changes and depression are unwarranted. Indeed, other neurobiological processes were associated with epigenetic changes in depressed individuals who died by suicide. Specifically, among these individuals, epigenetic changes were observed in $GABA_A$ subunit expression (Poulter et al., 2008). Women's trauma history, including early-life abuse, was likewise associated with elevated methylation of genes coding for BDNF in her male, but not female children. In fact, among mothers who reported increased fear, methylation of these genes was reduced in female offspring (Pilkay et al., 2020). It is uncertain which epigenetic changes, if any, causally contribute to pathological outcomes. Ultimately, strong inferential conclusions will be possible when studies are conducted using a larger number of participants and when more detailed longitudinal analyses linking early experiences and adult pathology are undertaken that include whole epigenome analyses.

Epigenetic changes that influenced health were observed among the children of individuals exposed to famine. The offspring born during or immediately after the Great Chinese Famine that occurred from 1959 to 1961 were more likely to display type 2 diabetes in adulthood, which could be transmitted across generations (Li et al., 2017). When comparisons were made between two regions of China in which famine conditions differed, specific epigenetic changes were restricted to regions where the famine occurred. Epigenetic changes were observed in the gene coding for insulin-like growth factor 2 that contributes to elevated cholesterol levels and the occurrence of type 2 diabetes (Shen et al., 2019). The current high levels of type 2 diabetes has, in fact, been attributed to transgenerational epigenetic effects that originated with the famine (Zimmet et al., 2018). As well, epigenetic changes were observed that were related to the ability of the kidneys to filter excess waste (glomerular filtration rate) and these actions were evident across two generations (Jiang et al., 2020).

Consistent with these actions, famine-related intergenerational outcomes have been reported in other situations. Toward the end of World War II, the Nazi regime prevented towns in western parts of the Netherlands from obtaining food or fuel. The resulting famine, which came to be known as the Dutch Hunger Winter, not only affected those who were present at the time but were apparent in offspring that were born during that time. Offspring born during this period displayed epigenetic changes within genes that influence birth weight as well as later LDL cholesterol levels (Tobi et al., 2014).

Decades after this famine, individuals that had been prenatally exposed to this condition expressed epigenetic changes related to insulin-like growth factor 2 (IGF2), which is important for cell growth and development (Heijmans et al., 2008). Actions such as these were linked to the development of type 2 diabetes, being more evident in offspring that had experienced prenatal hunger through pregnancy than during later periods (Yohannes, 2015). In addition to the physical disorders, children of the Dutch Hunger Winter were subsequently at elevated risk of poor cognitive function as well as the development of depression and schizophrenia (Roseboom et al., 2011).

━━━━━━━━━ EVOLUTION AND RE-EVOLUTION ━━━━━━━━━

Before Darwinian theory made its mark, one way that evolution was thought to occur was by Lamarckian inheritance. The view expounded by Lamarck was that an organism could pass on physical characteristics to its offspring based on their use or disuse. Essentially, if a person was a blacksmith and developed huge muscles, then his children would inherit these large muscles and might themselves become blacksmiths. As a result, instead of inheritance being passed on through genes that had been selected based on environmental pressures, traits were deemed to be inherited simply because a parent acquired them through experience.

The Darwinian perspective was eventually adopted because it had greater explanatory power, but die-hards existed who were reluctant to abandon the Lamarckian perspective. Lysenko, a Russian agronomist and politician, drove the agricultural productivity of the Soviet Union into the ground, literally and figuratively, based on counterfactual thinking and a nonscientific basis for his views (largely reflecting Lamarckian propositions). The story of Lysenko highlights how the ignorance of one individual can have remarkably wide-ranging consequences. More relevant to the present point is that the Lamarckian view, which was largely discarded, might not have been entirely wrong. Phenotypes might not only be determined by inherited genes but also from genes that are turned off or on based on parental experiences, although these inherited characteristics might be unrelated to the specific experiences of the parent.

Collective and historic trauma

Indigenous Peoples in numerous countries experienced assaults on their cultures, and these occurred over many generations. The 'collective historical trauma', which is described as cumulative emotional and psychological wounding over the life span and across generations, may profoundly contribute to the current well-being of Indigenous Peoples. Such traumas have unique social and psychological trajectories, and their consequences may be aligned with collective responses and interpretations at the family and community levels that result in changes in social dynamics, processes, structures, and functioning (Bombay et al., 2014). For these groups, recent assaults on their lives and dignity in the form of poverty and racial discrimination reflect just one chapter of a very long book. As William Faulkner stated in *Requiem for a Nun*, 'The past is never dead. It's not even past.'

When considering the intergenerational transmission of trauma, it would be profitable to evaluate current challenges in the context of historical and collective traumas endured by that group. The children and grandchildren of survivors of such experiences recognize that they were not the victims of a historically isolated event, as numerous indignities experienced had persisted for generations. Assaults on their culture, language, and identity, and experiences of discrimination and disputed land claims, act as reminders of the transgressions committed against their group that was part of an historical pattern of abuse (Bombay et al., 2014). This has not only been documented amongst Indigenous Peoples in the US, Canada, and Australia, having been seen in other cultural groups. Among Iraqi Kurds who have a long history of trauma, the occurrence of negative mental health has been substantial. But among individuals who strongly identified with their group the negative mental health that was otherwise present was diminished (Skrodzka et al., 2021). Holocaust survivors and their children similarly recognize that this event was one of a series of cumulative traumas that dated back to the pre-Christian era. Thus, when subsequent stressors are encountered, the behaviors of members of these groups will be influenced by their collective historical experiences. In fact, collectively experienced traumas might instigate unique social and psychological trajectories, and their consequences may be aligned with collective responses and interpretations of past indignities.

Trauma on a backdrop of trauma

Following colonization by Europeans, Native Americans and First Nations Peoples in Canada were frequently confined to reserves where they experienced poverty, inadequate education, and exceptionally poor health. It is tempting to view the treatment of Indigenous Peoples as ancient history. However, one of the most egregious actions undertaken within the US and Canada was that conducted from the mid-1800s until 1996 in which Indigenous children were forcibly removed from their families with the goal of assimilating them, effectively 'taking the Indian out of the child'. The First Nations children in Canada were placed in Indian Residential Schools (IRSs) while Native American children in the US were placed in Indian Boarding Schools, where they were targets for missionaries who were intent on saving the souls of the 'savages' through religious conversion.

Children placed in the IRSs experienced a regimen of strict discipline and suffered neglect and abuse, a loss of identity, and feelings of shame and isolation. Cultural expressions through language, dress, food, or beliefs were suppressed, and children were taught to be ashamed of their culture. Children experienced harsh and denigrating conditions, not only perpetrated by the clerics and administrators of these IRSs, but also by other children (inmates) who followed the encouragement of their malevolent custodians. Multiple 'medical' experiments were conducted using these children, including assessment of whether supplements of vitamins, notably riboflavin, thiamine, and/or ascorbic acid would attenuate the influence of purposeful malnourishment or starvation. Predictably, health declined and mortality rates increased among those attending these schools (Mosby, 2013).[1]

When these children subsequently returned to devastated communities, they were often seen as or felt like strangers, and frequently displayed the abusive behaviors modeled after those who had punished them at the IRSs. In fact, the individual conflicts that had been created at the IRSs were brought home so that conflicts between groups of individuals persisted (Matheson et al., 2016). The large-scale removal of Indigenous children from their homes resulted in deeply painful effects on the parents and extended families left behind. Familial bonds were disrupted and often irreparably broken, and many parents were beset by feelings of powerlessness, guilt, and shame, for not saving their children from being taken, and there were often feelings of no longer being needed by their children. Indigenous Peoples in Canada have gone through many traumas since their first contact with white Europeans. The IRSs not only affected those who were directly exposed to the trauma, having impacted individual communities, and Indigenous Peoples, in general. It became a reminder of the poor relationship that existed between the government of Canada and Indigenous Peoples.

The First Nations Regional Longitudinal Health Survey, which was the most extensive analysis of the impact of IRSs, revealed that Indigenous youth who had one or both parents, or even grandparents, attend an IRS experienced relatively poor quality of parenting. It was subsequently reported that those First Nations adults who had a parent who attended an IRS experienced more frequent adverse childhood experiences and adult traumas, as well as greater depressive symptoms often accompanied by thoughts of suicide relative to adults whose parents did not attend these schools (Bombay et al., 2010). Similar effects were apparent even in third-generation survivors of the IRSs, and the magnitude of the transmitted effects was greater for those who had both a parent and grandparent attend IRSs than among those who had either a parent or a grandparent in this circumstance.

This issue is especially acute since individuals who experienced collective traumatic events ultimately end up living at or below the poverty line. The children of survivors, who likewise lived in these same impoverished conditions, might therefore be at an increased risk of encountering stressful experiences, and their psychological and physical health was duly diminished. These effects were apparent among individuals who were living in urban centers, indicating that the second-generation consequences of IRSs were not simply a result of living on reserve. For

---

[1]The number of children who died at the IRSs was greatly underestimated by the Truth and Reconciliation Commission, and unmarked graves were still being found in 2020 and 2021.

the IRS survivors, the conditions experienced in the period following their institutionalization were grim, and consequently a period of recuperation and healing was not possible, especially given the racial discrimination that was so often experienced.

Much like the experiences of First Nations Peoples in Canada and Australia's First Peoples, historical loss among contemporary Native Americans is part of a schema or cognitive framework that has been linked to the development of diverse pathologies (Whitbeck et al., 2004). Individuals one generation removed from the era of American Indian Boarding Schools, and several generations removed from many earlier collective traumas, experienced lasting effects. They frequently had thoughts about historical losses, including the loss of language and culture, the loss of respect for traditional ways, the loss of land, and the loss stemming from broken promises. These feelings were often accompanied by disturbed concentration, feeling isolated, and sleep problems, as well as anxiety or nervousness and other harmful emotions (e.g., anger, rage, shame, fear/distrust of white people, and avoidance of places that served as reminders of losses). Like Indigenous Peoples in Canada, they were twice as likely to experience type 2 diabetes and 50% more likely to develop heart disease. Suicide occurrences vary across Indigenous communities, but the overall frequency of suicide among Alaskan and Native Americans was about 2.5 times that of other groups. In Canada, the frequency of suicide among First Nations Peoples and Inuit varied across communities, ranging from 2 to 11 times that of non-Indigenous people. Alarmingly, the frequency of suicide increased in the last two decades and was prominent among young people. Clearly, the numerous assaults against Indigenous Peoples not only affected those who directly experienced the transgressions but continued to affect the experiences of current group members and influence their psychological and physical health.

With these considerations in mind, we can better understand some of the consequences of collective and historical abuses. Beyond the impact of individual traumas, multiple effects of collective trauma were apparent at the family and community levels. Changes in the aftermath of shared collective trauma included erosion of basic trust, and the deterioration of social norms and values (Bombay et al., 2010, 2011). The retelling of these experiences over generations may result in sensitized responses to subsequently encountered stressful events. As Brave Heart (2011) suggested, the cumulative consequences of the many traumas experienced by Indigenous Peoples engendered a 'soul wound', which profoundly affects individuals across generations.

The growing recognition concerning the potential actions of epigenetic changes experienced prenatally or during the early postnatal period in promoting health risks that could be transmitted across generations led to the view that epigenetic effects stemming from cumulative historical trauma could contribute to poor health experienced by Indigenous Peoples (Bombay et al., 2014). Data are currently unavailable concerning the involvement of epigenetic changes in relation to the experiences of Indigenous Peoples. Having been used in unsolicited experiments in the past, Indigenous Peoples have been reluctant to participate in such studies, although several groups have expressed interest in uncovering the role of epigenetic factors in determining the influence of trauma. Of course, as mentioned earlier, trauma experiences encountered across generations are often accompanied by many individual and societal hardships, making it exceedingly difficult to identify the specific processes that render individuals susceptible to health disturbances. On the positive side, through actions on epigenetic processes, the adoption of healthy lifestyles could engender health benefits that could be transmitted across generations (Denham, 2018), making it that much more important today for concerted efforts to be made to enhance living conditions of Indigenous Peoples. Of particular significance, the adoption of traditional ways, together with cultural autonomy and self-determination may provide the agency to shape their own destinies.

INTERGROUP APOLOGIES

Much like the apology offered by one individual to another, apologies offered by one group to a second can have beneficial actions and may allow both groups to move forward. In acknowledgment of harms done to Indigenous Peoples by colonizers, in 2008 and 2009, respectively, the governments of Australia and of Canada offered an apology for the behavior of their forebears. A First Nations-led Truth and Reconciliation Commission (TRC) was established in Canada that focused on uncovering information regarding years of abuse in Indian Residential Schools without prosecuting individuals who were guilty of transgressions. The TRC provided a series of calls to action to the Canadians and the government of Canada to achieve equity for Indigenous Peoples.

Even with the best intentions, apologies cannot undo the horrors that had previously been created, and some individuals will not readily forgive. In 1951, the West German government acknowledged the unspeakable crimes that had been committed against the Jewish people during the Holocaust and provided compensation to help individuals who were directly affected. Many Jews were virulently opposed to accepting this 'blood money' to assuage the guilt of descendants of their tormentors who were viewed as 'angels with dirty faces'. Still, positive effects can emerge if the apology is meant in earnest and followed by concrete actions. Unfortunately, the Canadian government has been slow in enacting the recommendations provided by the Truth and Reconciliation Commission. For Indigenous Peoples in Canada, the apology offered and the acceptance of the Truth and Reconciliation Commission calls to action represented a *first step* to facilitate improved relations. This said, hope for this was modest, particularly amongst First Nations individuals who had experienced repeated racial discrimination (Bombay et al., 2013). For many government officials (and for many non-Indigenous people), the apology was not the first step toward healing but instead seemed to be seen as a handshake indicating that all was now well and good and that everyone could move on.

In light of the collective memory and the postmemories among those whose forebears suffered the abuses of others, it is no wonder that the reaction toward those who deny that past events had even occurred is as great as it is (witness the response by Jews and others toward Holocaust deniers). Make no mistake, however, these deniers have their following, and if the lie is repeated often enough it can seem to be a truth, and over generations it will be as if it never happened. But it did! How many people know about the Armenian genocide conducted by the Ottomans during World War I, known as Medz Yeghern, which resulted in the deaths of about a million people? Successive Turkish governments, including the current one, have been successful in their denial, even though some countries have made a point of recognizing this genocide. For the perpetrators of genocides, more so in their descendants, the denial of history may serve to minimize their culpability. Closing the door on history may be a convenient short-term solution but acknowledging the crimes may facilitate the endorsement of positive actions that can help the victimized group and in so doing they may help themselves (Hirschberger, 2018).

Identity in the context of cumulative trauma

To understand the impact of collective assaults, it is necessary to appreciate group processes that may serve to buffer against negative outcomes. As we've discussed repeatedly (see Chapter 3), a sense of self, or identity, is derived from group memberships. Having a particular identity and affiliation with a group serves multiple functions, including support from ingroup members, and markedly influences well-being in numerous domains (Haslam et al., 2018). These identities often take on considerable importance for the individual's and the group's well-being, particularly when the group is challenged. If the challenge threatens the viability of the group (i.e., the threat entails the group's extinction), then collective distress and anxiety may be instigated. The nature of the threat, as well as the contextual factors surrounding it, largely influence the emotions elicited (e.g., collective shame or guilt vs. anger), and will determine individual or group behaviors (Branscombe & Doosje, 2004).

Members of a group (e.g., a religious group) might view their own lives as being impermanent, but they might also believe that the values, morals, beliefs, traditions, and symbols representing the group itself will be passed on from one generation to the next. The more group members invest themselves in the group, or the more they identify with it, exposure to threats may yield greater individual distress but concurrently might promote increased cohesion among group members. In the same fashion, if the group had experienced previous (historical) traumatic incidents that threatened their survival, then greater collective distress will be engendered by threats to generations of descendants even if they had not directly experienced the trauma. Given a history of collective abuse and threats of extermination, group members might become especially sensitive to the perceived malign intent of others (Paez & Liu, 2011).

A component of healing processes in response to traumatic events may involve the capacity to find meaning from these experiences. In this regard, collective trauma may encourage a sense of 'collective self' that is transmitted across generations. This may foster group cohesion and identification, and in this way may create a sense of meaning that could diminish existential threats. To be sure, the constant reminders of collective historical trauma may be seen as possibly having negative health ramifications. At the same time, the collective response to historical trauma may become 'the epicenter of group identity' so that individuals will clearly understand the risks inherent in their social environment (Hirschberger, 2018). Heightened vigilance towards potential threats that may develop should not be misconstrued as reflecting heightened paranoia; if history is a teacher, then elevated vigilance might be perfectly reasonable and adaptive.

It is essential to underscore that it is likely inappropriate to draw parallels between the collective historical trauma experienced by different groups. Each is unique, each involves its own series of events, and each has its own consequences. For many groups, collective historical trauma may reflect much more than a loss of life. The point has often been made, for instance, that historical trauma is reflected by the loss of cultural and ancestral, sacred lands, which promotes a sense of grief. To Indigenous Peoples, lands are not objects to be possessed – the plants, animals, and waters harbored within lands are 'members of the larger other-than-human community' (Brave Heart & DeBruyn, 1998).

With time, attitudes amongst the victims of historical trauma have changed. It is not unusual for the children of survivors of collective historical trauma to feel negatively toward the notion that they were diminished by the horrid experiences of their forebears. This is perfectly reasonable; those that directly experienced the cruelties of others might have been shamed by their victimization. But attitudes adopted in ensuing generations have often been very different. They frequently do not share feelings of shame. Instead, when they think of past egregious behaviors towards their group they might feel outraged and take on what outgroup members will perceive as 'militant' behaviors when they loudly say 'Never again'. We've seen exactly this attitude from survivors of IRSs and of the Holocaust, and among Black people in the US and in European countries. Anger catalyzes active resistance and unifies the group to take strong actions. So, when Indigenous Peoples block a road because it traverses ancestral lands, consider that this behavior is coming from a history of abusive behaviors, and they're simply saying 'Enough'.

Unfortunately, time and again we've seen that the response of the outgroup is often unsupportive: 'Here we go again', 'Now what do they want?', or 'Playing the race card' are comments that are not uncommon from outgroup members. Perhaps it would be useful for outgroup individuals to consider the behaviors they witness as a response to collective injustices. Collective anger can be a powerful motivating force, and it's not likely that they'll 'just get over it'. Instead, it may have imbued individuals with resilience, although they may still need supportive allies.

Conclusion

It is predictable that the collective trauma experienced by individuals of a particular generation would influence the behavior and attitudes of the next generation. In fact, it is hard to imagine that it wouldn't, particularly if it were part of cumulative historical trauma. Would it be surprising to find that such experiences influenced their collective conscious and unconscious and that parents would pass such experiences on to their children?

Reminders of collective trauma are potent in eliciting emotional responses such as shame, depression, and despair in those who highly identify with the group, but as the injustice of the situation becomes more pronounced, anger and social activism may become prominent. Those who are now dealing with collective trauma might not be inclined to once again be herded into IRSs or ghettos or to remain silent in the face of blatant discrimination. But generations pass quickly and so might ancestral memories, unless symbols are provided to remind us not to become complacent (e.g., Veterans' Day, Armistice Day, Orange Shirt Day, Passover).

Past egregious actions do not only affect individuals through collective memories, but also through biological processes, such as epigenetic mechanisms, whereby the response to stressors may be altered over successive generations. The epigenome is dynamic, and epigenetic changes are alterable. Indeed, in the case of prenatal and postnatal stressor effects, the behavioral disturbances can be attenuated to some extent by later positive experiences. If the social environment is improved, then the sequence leading to adverse outcomes might be interrupted. Essentially, it seems that in the case of epigenetic changes the 'bell can be unrung' but postmemories will remain. Based on the Haudenosaunee (Iroquois) Seventh Generation Principle, the decay of Indigenous Peoples' way of life developed over many generations and healing will likewise require seven generations to pass.

Suggested readings

Bombay, A., Matheson, K., & Anisman, H. (2014). The intergenerational effects of Indian Residential Schools: Implications for the concept of historical trauma. *Transcultural Psychiatry*, 51, 320–338.

Gone, J.P. & Kirmayer, L.J. (2020). Advancing Indigenous mental health research: Ethical, conceptual and methodological challenges. *Transcultural Psychiatry*, 57, 235–249.

Hirsch, M. (2001). Surviving images: Holocaust photographs and the work of postmemory. *Yale Journal of Criticism*, 14, 5–37.

13

STRESS BUSTING
Treatment Strategies

─╸Snake oil╺───

There's a huge industry offering new approaches to dealing with stressors. Magazine articles found at the supermarket checkout relentlessly promote 'Eleven ways to beat stress', 'The five most important lessons to avoid stress', 'The ten most stressful jobs', or 'Getting rid of bad karma in 24 easy steps'. Two different tea companies were advertising their wares (green tea or green tea plus other stuff added) to help you become mellow or to reduce stress. And an enormous cabal exists offering 'alternative medicines' to treat virtually any illness imaginable. Because of lax policies regarding the validity of claims they keep appearing and mutating like viruses.

Given the alleged expertise about stress and how to de-stress, we checked out stress management through the internet. One well-known website provided the following de-stressing methods: cognitive therapy, autogenic training (a relaxation technique that involves a set of visualizations to induce calmness), conflict resolution, exercise, taking up a hobby, meditation, deep breathing, yoga, nootropics, nutraceuticals, and foods that improve mental functions, reading novels, prayer, relaxation techniques, artistic expression, spas, somatic training, spending time in nature, stress balls (those squishy rubber things), natural medicine, clinically validated alternative treatments, time management, listening to certain types of relaxing music (e.g., new age music, classical music, psychedelic music, sleep music), and spending quality time with pets. In going through the list, some of these methods are pretty loopy but others appear to be reasonable. For instance, for some of us meditation or yoga simply isn't in the cards, whereas for others they sound ideal. Likewise, for some people spending quality time with a pet sounds, well, goofy. However, if you're a dog (or any animal) lover, then you'll appreciate what your pet can do for you.

Earlier chapters outlined the influence of stressors on pathology and the many factors that moderate the impact of stressors. So, the obvious question now is: what can reliably be done to diminish the negative impact of stressors? To a certain extent there isn't always an easy solution. In some instances, the stressor might be fairly mild to which we might be overreacting because that's just part of our personality, or because we simply don't know how to deal with it. In other instances, it might not be a simple matter to rid ourselves of a stressor as it may be outside of our control. Even in the worst scenario, where it seems that there's not a thing that can be done and coping might feel near impossible (and we accept that 'it just is what it is'), there may be ways of diminishing distress, even if just a little. This chapter should provide readers with the understanding that:

- Individuals react differently to stressors, and other things being equal, they might not respond in the same way to a particular stress-reducing technique. Furthermore, the effectiveness of any particular way of dealing with distress varies across situations and over time.
- Several methods are available to deal with stressors, including cognitive behavioral and pharmacological approaches as well as some that fall outside of the recognized treatments.
- Drug therapies have been used extensively to diminish distress or stress-related psychological disturbances, including a variety of antidepressants and anti-anxiety agents that act on varied neurochemical processes. These agents are only moderately effective, although newer therapies have been developed that diminish symptoms even among patients who had not responded positively to other treatments.
- Ultimately, treatments to reduce distress, like treatments to address mental illness, might be best served by an individualized treatment approach based on the symptoms expressed, the resources to sustain them in individuals' daily lives, and the presence of biomarkers related to underlying processes.

Despite the many approaches available to alleviate stress-related disorders, it seems that a significant portion of individuals experiencing signs of distress or clinical levels of a psychological disorder do not seek or obtain professional treatment. As we noted in Chapter 3, this may occur because some people feel that they can get through it on their own, the belief that the treatments won't be effective, or because of the stigma related to mental health conditions. As well, older individuals are less likely to seek help, and for a variety of reasons, members of some cultural groups may not find a route to therapy (e.g., cultural views related to mental health, lack of access to care, as well as lack of insurance in countries where universal health care is unavailable). Perhaps not surprisingly, reports from different countries indicated that during the early days of the COVID-19 pandemic, when individuals were isolated, the occurrence of mental health issues increased, whereas help-seeking declined. With the burden of psychological illnesses being as pronounced as they have been, getting individuals to obtain treatment ought to be the first line of defence. To an extent, this can be encouraged on an individual basis, but to a considerable degree, this is a societal problem related to structural stigma and effective prevention programs not being in place.

In too many countries the severe shortage of clinicians to treat mental illness has resulted in lengthy waitlists, sometimes exceeding a year, making it clear that much more is needed to facilitate access to treatment. In countries within Africa, such as Zimbabwe, where psychiatrists (and other health workers) are exceptionally rare, alternative strategies have been adopted, including having kindly 'grandmothers' sitting on wooden benches to offer advice to those in distress (Cavanaugh, 2017). These grandmothers have been receiving basic training in identifying mental health difficulties and behavioral therapy and this will hopefully be effective and concurrently reduce the burden on the health system. A similar approach may not be viable within Western countries, but a friendly ear at times of crisis may be better than no treatment for lengthy periods.

It is apparent that strategies need to be developed within Western countries to identify the presence of mental illness and then to provide early interventions. The improved abilities of artificial intelligence have prompted efforts to develop novel algorithms to detect the presence of mental illnesses. Several studies revealed that elevated depression among youth was accompanied by greater use of social media (Lin et al., 2016). Moreover, through clever machine learning approaches early signs of depression could be identified based on semantic characteristics within social media texts, even when these messages did not explicitly contain words such as 'depression' (Chiong et al., 2021). The possibility of identifying depression, and doing so early, is very exciting. However, to what extent will this facilitate people receiving treatment given issues related to individual privacy and confidentiality? Moreover, even when individuals who need help are identified, will this be translated to better care?

Individualized treatments: precision medicine

Whether it's depression, heart disease or cancer, therapies effective in one individual may be ineffective in a second even if they exhibit comparable symptoms. Conversely, individuals may present with somewhat different symptoms but respond similarly to a given treatment. It will be recalled that this led to the view that instead of treating patients based on a diagnosed syndrome, therapies should be administered based on the characteristics of the individual, including the specific symptoms displayed, the biological correlates that are present, and the presence of specific genes and epigenetic factors. To an extent, this approach has been used in determining specific cancer therapies, but the psychiatric community hasn't yet been successful in broadly adopting this strategy. This said, it has become increasingly apparent that the incorporation of genetic information in developing therapeutic strategies was useful in the treatment of depression. The predictive ability of drug therapies, even among treatment resistant patients, was further enhanced using algorithms that determined how genes might influence how individuals are affected by a drug (pharmacodynamics) and how characteristics of the individual influence the drug's functioning (pharmacokinetics) (Tiwari et al., 2022).

The National Institutes of Health developed a platform, the Research Domain Criteria (RDoC), to achieve this goal (Cuthbert & Insel, 2013). This framework considers psychopathologies on the basis of the behavioral, motivational, cognitive, social, and regulatory/arousal characteristics presented by patients. These features are matched to biological substrates that might be tied to these symptom domains, notably genes, molecules, cells, neural circuits, and physiological processes. Thus, a profile can be obtained to determine the linkages between overt symptoms and specific biological factors, which, in turn, can be tied to the effectiveness of specific treatment strategies. Making this functional 'roadmap' will require the evaluation of thousands of individuals who present with diverse symptoms. Once it is created it might be possible to select the therapeutic strategies that will have the best effects for individual patients.

The RDoC was widely praised, but it has also had its share of detractors. Among other things, given the heterogeneous characteristics of mental illnesses and the comorbidities that are so often present, there is no a priori reason to believe that the biological measures will comfortably map on to the diverse behavioral phenotypes. Likewise, it is unclear whether this paradigm would be sufficiently sensitive to predict therapeutic efficacy. This is especially problematic as specific behavioral and biological measures may not be stable, varying over time and across diverse contexts, thus requiring multiple assessments of individuals. As well, the RDoC does not adequately consider the influences of cultural factors that may define what is considered normal versus abnormal as well as the therapies appropriate (and acceptable) across different cultural groups (Kirmayer & Crafa, 2014). Relatedly, even if effective therapeutic approaches are identified for individuals, are these remedies lasting or do they wane over time. Many mental illnesses may be lifelong conditions so that they frequently recur, thus patients would be best served by identifying or creating therapies (including after care) that have long-term benefits. Finally, ambitious projects, such as the RDoC, may not be feasible given the number of participants that would have to be recruited to create a reliable platform and the financial costs might be untenable. Ultimately, hard choices will have to be made. But, the present situation, which has largely been unchanged for decades, simply isn't working well enough.

Therapeutic approaches

Relaxation training

Relaxation training encompasses a variety of methods that, as indicated by the name, are aimed at getting a person to relax (i.e., 'destress'). There's nothing inherently wrong with this, although it needs to be put into a proper perspective. A limited treatment strategy, as this is, won't go all that far if it is used in isolation from other methods. To obtain a genuinely positive response in dealing with stressors, the actual problem needs to be tackled rather than relying on just masking a few symptoms. At the same time, some individuals are wired so that they are in a perpetually reactive state, and so they need to relax before they can adequately tackle tough problems. Thus, for a subset of individuals, a simple relaxation protocol can have some benefits.

Guided imagery is a procedure in which a person takes advantage of their ability to use their imagination to take them to a place that is comforting and soothing ('their happy place'). This may diminish signs of distress (e.g., autonomic hyper-reactivity) and could break the loop by which physical and brain reactions feed on one another to promote distress. This procedure was found to provide benefits across a range of stress-related conditions, such as diminishing pre-operative anxiety and coping with pain (Pile et al., 2021). While it may not be ideal for every individual, it could be an asset when combined with other therapeutic approaches.

Progressive muscle relaxation procedures have been widely used to diminish anxiety and have been included in relaxation programs. The view had been adopted that anxiety and muscle tension often appear together and through feedback processes, muscle tension might influence brain processes that support stress reactions. Thus, it was considered that alternately tensing and relaxing muscles might disturb this feedback process. Progressive muscle relaxation procedures involve a mental component in which one focuses and feels the difference between the sensations associated with tension and relaxation. This feedback helps the individual distinguish between these states and facilitates achieving somatic calmness. In the long run, especially when dealing with strong stressful experiences and their consequences, progressive muscle relaxation might have limited positive effects on their own but can be incorporated with other stress-reducing methods.

Cognitive behavioral therapy (CBT)

The goal of CBT, which comes from Beck's theorizing concerning hopelessness, is to diminish dysfunctional behaviors, cognitions, and emotions through a goal-oriented, systematic procedure that employs behavioral and cognitive approaches to change maladaptive thinking. To this end, CBT techniques help individuals challenge inappropriate and counterproductive patterns and beliefs, and replace cognitive errors (e.g., overgeneralizing, magnification of negatives, minimization of positives, and catastrophizing) with thoughts that are both realistic and effective, thereby limiting self-defeating behavior and emotional distress. Replacing inappropriate appraisals, coping, cognitions, emotions, and behaviors occurs through a series of steps that challenge an individual's way of thinking and their reactions to entrenched habits and behaviors.

Cognitive distortions

Negative cognitions are frequently experienced automatically and do not seem to arise through reasoning. Instead, these automatic thoughts have an involuntary quality such that they invade the conscious experience of the depressed or anxious individual, and too often these thoughts reflect the individual's negative appraisal style rather than an objective determination. According to the hopelessness view of depression, the cognitive system consists of components that are primitive and others that are mature. Primitive systems comprise idiosyncratic and unrealistic thoughts and while they typically have limited influence, they seem to predominate in the presence of psychopathology. The ways in which these primitive cognitions are expressed vary across pathologies. For example, depressed individuals may report cognitive distortions, as well as automatic thoughts or images concerned with deprivation, hopelessness, or self-debasement. Anxious individuals, in contrast, may report cognitions or imagery concerned with imminent danger related to a specific or generalized stimulus. Cognitive distortions associated with illnesses, described in Table 13.1, govern appraisals and hence the coping methods used.

Table 13.1   Common cognitive distortions.

Arbitrary inference, in which the individual arrives at a particular conclusion when there is, in fact, limited (or opposite) evidence that would predict a particular outcome.
Dichotomous thinking, in which the individual considers one or both of two extreme positions without consideration of the multiple shades of grey that exist in between.
Selective abstraction, where only certain aspects of a situation (typically negative) are recalled or emphasized, and positive aspects are ignored.
Mind reading, where inferences are made regarding another individual's state of mind or thoughts without having evidence to support the conclusions.
Overgeneralization is characteristic of situations in which the individual applies the negative results of an event to a broader set of events or to all events.
Magnification refers to a situation in which the individual exaggerates the importance or meaning of a particular event.
Cognitive deficiency comprises a global pattern of thinking in which individuals fail to integrate pieces of information or when they ignore bits of information about a given situation that could inform them about the likelihood of particular outcomes.

Therapeutic change and cognitive therapy

As negative automatic thoughts are considered fundamental to the poor appraisals and coping methods that promote pathology, a primary goal of cognitive therapy is to have patients gain symptomatic relief by noticing and challenging these automatic thoughts (Beck et al., 1979). Later, the attitudes and dysfunctional belief systems (i.e., 'schemas') that generate automatic thoughts can be dealt with systematically. Among other things, a therapeutic change may arise by providing an opportunity for 'quieting' the hyperactive primitive (automatic) cognitive system. This can be achieved, in part, through Socratic questioning, wherein the therapist helps the patient identify these thoughts and then generate alternatives that are more likely and more favorable. Along with this, the patient might practice identifying cognitive distortions in their thinking. Using these methods, changes in thoughts might precipitate a change in both feelings (affect) and actions, and fundamentally alter the individual's beliefs surrounding the situations in which they find themselves. Added to this, the therapeutic environment affords the individual the opportunity to 'reality-test' their verbal and visual automatic thoughts so that they can assess whether these thoughts have some validity in fact.

Early in their treatment, patients might recognize that their appraisals are generally impractical and counter-productive, but knowing such things is only a first step. Replacing disturbed processes with those that are functionally effective is more difficult and may take weeks to achieve. To this end, individuals are asked to question and test their appraisals (assumptions, evaluations, and beliefs) that might be counterproductive and likely incorrect. Moreover, they are encouraged to deal directly with uncomfortable issues and find new approaches to dealing with them. Generally, the procedures used are not set in stone, and it is not uncommon for other methods to be incorporated into a CBT program, including distraction techniques and relaxation training.

Cognitive behavioral therapy or variants of the basic procedure that are tailored for specific conditions can be highly effective in the treatment of numerous illnesses beyond that of depressive disorders and anxiety. These include eating disorders, obsessive-compulsive disorder, and substance abuse, as well as psychotic disorders, and could diminish the distress associated with illnesses, such as multiple sclerosis, cancer, epilepsy, and HIV. It is effective when applied on a one-on-one basis and for some illnesses a group therapy approach can be used. It has been used in a guided self-help approach, although the usefulness of this method has been questioned. Different pathological states call for variants of the CBT procedure, but regardless of the disorder considered, a degree of flexibility is often needed in applying the treatment, and the odds are that a clinician's preferences and experiences influence where the greatest emphasis is placed over the course of therapy. It is of practical significance that in some illnesses (but not all) CBT acts additively with standard antidepressant medications as well as with other behavioral and cognitive techniques.

A potential limitation of CBT is that it works primarily among individuals who have the belief that this procedure can help them and are prepared to invest themselves in this approach. CBT is sometimes rejected by patients as a mode of treatment owing to the length of the therapy or simply because they don't like talk therapy. The preferences that individuals have might reflect aspects of their personality, their beliefs about treatments, and their views as to what brought on the depression (biological vs. experience-related factors). Irrespective of the cause for individuals preferring one therapy over another, for CBT to be effective patients need to accept the treatment and believe that it can help them. When the treatment and the individual's preferences were aligned with one another, the initiation of treatment, adherence rates, and attrition were improved, often producing better effects than alternative approaches (McHugh et al., 2013). Even when patients expressly indicate a preference for CBT and are fully committed to the process, the outcomes may depend on the abilities of the therapist and the development of a patient–therapist alliance.

Case study 13.1

The insidious illness

It was slow and changed subtly over time. First, she primarily felt annoyed by the many day-to-day hassles that she encountered. Later, she experienced some pretty strong stressors that seemed to knock her for a loop, which were aggravated by the continuous hassles, one after another when she was least capable of dealing with them. She and her friends seemed tight, at least until she had a falling-out with her two best buds. Her rumination seemed to be an almost constant companion; she began to wake very early, spending her time ruminating. She did this in relation to her traitorous now ex-friends, anybody who had wronged her in the past, the advantages that others had – she seemed to look for things that were negative.

It was only when she noticed that she wasn't eating well and lost a significant amount of weight from her thin frame that she considered that she might have a serious problem. Then again, she thought that most people had ups and downs, and this was just one of those things. Besides, there was no way she was going to seek professional help. That was too embarrassing, and people would find out, and she would be labeled and face the stigmatization that followed. It was only after she confided in her younger sister who let their parents know that she was encouraged to obtain therapy, and she opted for cognitive behavioral therapy through an online forum that protected her privacy. After multiple sessions she came to the realization that she was not seeing things in a proper perspective, and she learned to appraise situations more objectively and how to cope effectively. She began to feel better about herself and she viewed the world more positively.

(Continued)

In hindsight she understood what led to depression and promised herself that she would never allow herself to reach those lows again. She knew how to handle things before they became too great a problem. For about five years depression did not raise its horrid head, but then it snuck up on her again. Fortunately, the ice had been broken based on her previous experience and she sought help that entailed a combination of a drug treatment and psychotherapy. She might not ever be entirely free of this wretched illness, but she also realized that the situation wasn't hopeless, and remedies were available to help her.

Meditation

Meditation refers to a practice wherein individuals train their mind or body so that they reach an alternative level of consciousness that might bring them a sense of calmness. Although meditation is usually thought to come from Buddhism and Hinduism, forms of meditation are, in fact, evident in numerous religions. Whether the individual uses prayer beads, repetitive sounds or body movements, or attends to a focal point, these are, in a sense, related to meditation, and ought to have the effect of creating a positive internal state. Indeed, various forms of meditation (e.g., transcendental meditation, spiritual meditation, visualization medication, focused meditation, among others), as well as progressive relaxation, yoga, and tai chi, have been used to achieve awareness of the present moment, acceptance of difficult emotions, and to diminish distress.

A vast amount of information has accumulated concerning the calming effects of meditation as well as the physiological repercussions associated with the diminished stress engendered. The broadness of the topic, unfortunately, precludes a proper review of the literature. Suffice it that meditation practices have been associated with diminished cortisol levels, and brain network changes that have been associated with cognitive and emotional control (Afonso et al., 2020). Meditation was accompanied by reduced blood pressure and attenuation of the inflammatory immune response that was ordinarily evident in stressful situations (e.g., among caregivers). Unfortunately, not all studies have been well controlled, and many were affected by confounding variables that were not adequately considered. For example, meditation practices are often accompanied by other lifestyle factors (in relation to sleep, eating, smoking, and exercise) that affect well-being, and the personality of individuals who seek out meditation might be distinguishable from those who don't, which may influence well-being.

Mindfulness

Mindfulness as a way of coping was derived from both meditation-centered practices and traditions and cognitive behavior therapy (Kabat-Zinn, 1990; Brown &

Ryan, 2003). Within some cultural and religious practices, meditation can be used to draw attention away from unpleasant external thoughts and distractions (i.e., recent stresses, conflicts, etc.) and redirect the individual's focus towards moment-to-moment internal processes. To an extent, mindfulness adopts this strategy insofar as it involves a focus on being attentive, aware, and non-judgmental regarding events in the present moment. As such, individuals will be less likely to ruminate or fixate on non-productive or counterproductive thoughts. This permits them to observe events as they are unfolding, and to experience physical and emotional responses to these situations without attributing blame, judgment, or motivation to them (Segal et al., 2002; Brown & Ryan, 2003).

Sadness and negative rumination form a loop whereby one feeds into the other. Thinking in the moment in a non-judgmental manner may disturb this loop by which negative appraisals come to affect anxiety and depressive symptoms. Through a process that has been described as 'reperceiving', a shift in perspective occurs wherein self-regulation, cognitive and behavioral flexibility, and a clarification of values, may limit negative outcomes. Kabat-Zinn (1990) has expressed this as follows: 'By watching your thoughts without being drawn into them, you can learn something profoundly liberating... which may help you to be less of a prisoner of those thought patterns – often so strong in us – which are narrow, inaccurate, self-involved, [and] habitual to the point of being imprisoning...'

Although mindfulness in a clinical context is considered to be a method for dealing with stressors (or particular moods) that can be taught, fairly pronounced differences exist in the degree of mindfulness that individuals exhibit in the absence of training. Just as some people are described as having one trait or another that can influence the way in which stressors affect them (or are dealt with), individuals may exhibit high (or low) trait mindfulness characteristics. The degree of mindfulness an individual has can be measured through the Mindful Attention Awareness Scale (MAAS; Brown & Ryan, 2003). An alternative to this scale is the Five Facet Mindfulness Questionnaire (FFMQ), which divides mindfulness into several components and thus is sometimes preferred as a research tool (Baer et al., 2006). Using such instruments, trait mindfulness was found to be associated with optimism, the endorsement of positive self-views, and engagement in effective problem-oriented coping strategies.

MBSR and MBCT

The extent to which mindfulness-based stress reduction (MBSR; Kabat-Zinn, 1990) and mindfulness-based cognitive therapy (MBCT; Segal et al., 2002) has caught on as a therapeutic strategy to deal with stress and stress-related illnesses has been impressive. In addition to the benefits of mindfulness already described, some of the positive effects of these procedures may develop by increasing attention control, self-acceptance, and mood regulation that facilitate appraisal of stressors in a focused and objective manner. Besides terminating the cycle of negative appraisals, mindfulness might have the benefit of individuals becoming more aware of the positive events that they experience. Moreover, by promoting acceptance, mindfulness might come to diminish feelings of guilt and self-criticism that might otherwise evolve in association with some stressors or pathological conditions. This is not to say that guilt reduction is always beneficial and may be counterproductive when it diminishes reparative behaviors toward a person they had wronged. As described earlier, some forms of meditation, such as kindness meditation, which concerns feelings of others, may be most effective in these situations (Hafenbrack et al., 2022).

Current moment awareness associated with mindfulness might facilitate the individual's focus on pertinent aspects of a stressful situation, rather than being overwhelmed by extraneous factors, including past or future concerns. In a sense, mindfulness might produce its effects through a process of 'disidentification', which essentially entails the banishment of automatic thoughts and their replacement with momentary events without judgment or cognitive elaboration. This might result in diminished dysfunctional thinking patterns that lead to maladaptive appraisals and hence ineffective coping methods. Essentially, awareness of thoughts and emotions, in concert with the appraisals of stressors as they unfold, might help individuals tailor their coping strategies to suit specific situations, allowing creative problem solving, persistence in dealing with difficult tasks, and maintaining flexible coping strategies. Mindfulness procedures have been found to reduce distress and produce positive effects in relation to a number of conditions, such as substance abuse, chronic pain, binge eating, anxiety, loneliness in the elderly, recurrent depression, OCD, distress related to cancer, and may improve cardiovascular health.

Neurobiological correlates of mindfulness

Mindfulness has been reported to impact physiological indices associated with diminished distress. For instance, in patients with psychiatric disorders (e.g., anxiety, depression) mindfulness interventions have been accompanied by altered HPA functioning and lower levels of inflammatory cytokines (Sanada et al., 2020). Further, mindfulness interventions diminished the inflammatory response associated with early-life adverse events and thus could potentially act against the pathological outcomes associated with such experiences (Lindsay, 2021). Likewise, the use of MBSR to diminish loneliness was accompanied by reduced levels of C-reactive protein and the transcription factor NFkB that is associated with cytokine production (Creswell et al., 2012). When individuals engaged in an intensive three-day mindfulness retreat, their anxiety and perceived stress levels were reduced, accompanied by reduced cortisol levels and that of proinflammatory cytokine (e.g., IL-6) and elevated levels of the anti-inflammatory cytokine IL-10 (Concetta et al., 2022). Clearly, mindfulness training has positive effects that go beyond psychological well-being, affecting biological processes that are ordinarily affected by stressors, which can influence the development of multiple physical illnesses.

The default mode network and mindfulness

It might be thought that when individuals are at rest, or seemingly not thinking purposefully (mind wandering), brain functioning might be relatively quiescent. However, neuroimaging studies revealed that during quiet states when attention was not focused on environmental stimuli, an assembly of interconnected brain regions dubbed the default mode network (DMN) was active (Raichle et al., 2015). The DMN includes several cortical regions (the medial prefrontal cortex, posterior cingulate cortex and precuneus, posterior inferior parietal regions, lateral temporal cortex) and the hippocampal formation is active during passive thinking or what is referred to as stimulus-independent thought. DMN functioning has been considered to be a critical component of creativity and may be fundamental for our understanding of the mechanisms associated with consciousness, and may play a pivotal role in the development and maintenance of psychological disorders

In contrast to the brain activity pattern seen at rest, the DMN is deactivated during goal-oriented activity (during tasks that are attention-demanding and involve a focus on external stimuli), and neuronal activity predominates in a different network comprising the lateral PFC, premotor cortex, lateral parietal regions, anterior cingulate cortex, insula and occipital regions, which comprise the 'task-positive network' (TPN). To some degree, the TPN and DMN act in an opposing fashion in that the latter corresponds to task-independent self-referential thought or introspection, whereas the TPN is associated with action. Activation of the TPN generally suppresses activity in the DMN but when these processes are out of sync, difficulties can be encountered in focusing attention, making decisions, and solving problems, which can ultimately affect the development of mood disturbances.

For complex cognitive activities, it is not only necessary that the TPN become engaged, but it is important for the DMN to be deactivated or tuned down. For instance, neurocognitive disturbances, such as those evident in association with schizophrenia, are accompanied by the failure of DMN suppression when individuals are performing complicated tasks. Variations within the DMN have been associated with dementia, autism, and attention deficit/hyperactivity disorder. Disturbances of the DMN predicted the development of PTSD in acutely traumatized individuals and were related to acute or early-life trauma associated with later PTSD (Zeev-Wolf et al., 2019). Moreover, DMN alterations were associated with clinical levels of depression as well as recurrent depressive disorders (Yan et al., 2019) and components of the DMN, notably the dorsal medial prefrontal cortex subsystem, has been tied to greater maladaptive, depressive rumination and lower levels of more adaptive, reflective rumination (Zhou et al., 2020). Of particular interest was that mindfulness training could act against depressive illness by affecting DMN functioning (Barnhofer et al., 2016), and a variant of mindfulness training that affected DMN functioning was similarly effective in diminishing

PTSD features in combat veterans (King et al., 2016). If mindfulness can modify the activity within networks engaged in rumination and self-focus and influences an individual's method of appraising and coping with stressors, then this might turn out to be a useful long-term strategy to deal with stressors that might otherwise encourage psychopathology.

The third wave of behavioral therapies

As with most scientific endeavors, therapeutic approaches to treat psychological disorders are constantly modified and new approaches may evolve. These generally adopt the best of earlier conceptualizations and add improvements. A third wave of behavioral therapies emerged, such as Acceptance and Commitment Therapy (ACT), which adopted the perspective that psychopathology arises when long-standing beliefs or views that an individual holds limits or precludes behavioral flexibility. Thus, ACT is geared to having people become open to unpleasant feelings, and then learn to neither overreact to them, nor avoid situations that instigate these feelings. With a greater understanding of their own emotions, individuals will eventually be able to take the steps needed to reach specific goals (Hayes et al., 2006).

Unlike CBT, ACT does not entail training to control their cognitions, feelings, and memories, and other private events, but instead focuses on having people 'just notice', accept, and embrace their private experiences, even those that may be unwanted. From the ACT perspective, cognitive rigidity and experiential avoidance impedes movement toward valued goals, and thus the function of therapy is to develop psychological flexibility that will facilitate this movement. This entails six core constructs and processes: acceptance, defusion, mindfulness, self-as-context (observing the self), values, and committed action (Hayes et al., 2006).

Acceptance comprises the active embrace of feelings such as anxiety, distress, and sadness, as well as the uncomfortable bodily sensations that might accompany these states. Having accepted this feature of the self, the second component, cognitive defusion, encourages the reduction of the negative impact of certain thoughts and sensations. This entails the facilitation of processes that promote a critical analysis of the content of thoughts relative to actual experience, with the goal of the individual being able to reduce their attachment to their thoughts as reflecting reality. The third component, mindfulness, involves an on-going, non-judgmental perception of both internal (e.g., psychological) and external (e.g., environmental) events as they occur. By non-judgmentally evaluating internal and external events, the aim is to reduce the extent to which *cognitive fusion* limits psychological and behavioral flexibility that otherwise prevents movement toward valued goals. As already indicated, a central component of ACT comprises the self as context (sometimes referred to as observing the self) in which individuals are not their thoughts, experiences, worries, and bodily sensations. These experiences come and go, but there is a self that remains that can rise above these moment-to-moment experiences. Portraying the self in this way de-emphasizes the importance or attachment to internal and external events, thereby allowing cognitive *defusion* to occur. Along with these components, individuals are prompted to live on the basis of their personal *values*, which entails not being driven by avoidance of distress and the expectations created by others.

Finally, and this is of particular significance, ACT promotes *committed action* that moves the individual towards identified values (i.e., what is important to the person). Once these values have been defined, committed action can be undertaken through activities, such as exposure to particular events, skills acquisition, shaping methods, and goal setting. Through committed action, the individual can build a larger and more flexible repertoire of psychological and behavioral responses, and simultaneously mitigate the ability of cognitive fusion and experiential avoidance to promote poor well-being. Therapeutic change can occur quickly because ACT focuses on the purpose of the actions or feelings that are the individual's central difficulty. For example, anxiety or depression is not viewed to be the problematic aspect of these disorders, but instead it is the actions undertaken to manage negative feelings that are problematic, especially as they limit the time and energy needed to pursue appropriate actions that are aligned with their identified goals.

Although ACT is not especially new, it has only recently been gaining a substantial number of adherents. A meta-analysis revealed that relative to treatment as usual, a waitlist, or placebo treatment, those in an ACT condition fared considerably better (Bai et al., 2020) and was as effective as CBT in the treatment of several psychological disorders, but there has been bitter debate on this issue. Indeed, there had been questions concerning whether the data supporting the usefulness of ACT were as reliable and untainted as originally purported (Coyne, 2012). Aside from these difficulties, ACT has other shortcomings. Among other things, it implicitly requires individuals to be psychologically minded, able to think abstractly, and to have strong verbal abilities for the various metaphors and demonstrations employed, and for some individuals this approach might simply be too nebulous.

An offshoot of CBT, dialectical behavior therapy (DBT) also borrows from ACT and mindfulness in promoting strategies to alleviate mental health conditions. This procedure was initially established as a way of treating borderline personality disorder but found its way into the treatment of a broad array of conditions, including depressive disorders, anxiety disorders, PTSD, various eating disorders, and substance use disorders. DBT seeks to have individuals acquire ways of regulating their emotions, cope effectively with stressors, live in the moment, and enhance social relations. While this procedure has been found to be effective for many patients, it requires a substantial time commitment, including homework assignments outside of regular therapy sessions. As well, some patients find it difficult to confront emotionally painful memories as well as to explore their traumatic experiences.

No treatment is effective for all individuals, and most strategies are effective for some individuals. Determining which strategy is best would require head-to-head comparisons between treatments for diverse conditions, which is not often done. This said, a large meta-analysis that assessed the influence of a large array of approaches indicated that mindfulness-based strategies, as well as multi-component positive psychological interventions generally had the most beneficial effects, whereas cognitive and behavioural therapies, as well ACT led to somewhat lower positive actions (van Agteren et al., 2021). This should not be taken to suggest that patients uncertain as to which therapeutic strategy to select should base such a decision on which treatments are alleged to have the best overall outcomes. The choice of therapeutic strategy ought to consider the features of the illness together with characteristics of the individuals and the likelihood that they will complete the therapy, as well as the match (alliance) between the patient and the therapist.

Pharmacotherapy

Numerous pharmacological agents have been developed to diminish the psychological ramifications of stressors. In the sections that follow we'll consider the influence of a variety of drug treatments that can serve in this capacity. To a considerable degree, responses to stressors are governed by how events are appraised and the expectancies established that can move individuals in one direction or another. These psychological factors also apply to responses to medications to deal with a variety of illnesses (e.g., pain, psychological disturbances, and Parkinson's disease). If a person is primed to believe (expect) that a treatment will be beneficial, then it's more likely that it will have positive effects. So, before we deal with the efficacy of various pharmacological treatments on stress-related psychological disturbances, we'll first examine how expectancies can affect illness amelioration in response to drug therapies.

The placebo response

Placebo effects refer to the positive outcomes that are obtained in response to a treatment that cannot have direct effects on the physiological processes associated with a disorder – the treatment is an inert one that should, from a physiological perspective, have no effect on the pathology. Placebo treatments, as most people know, can have very powerful effects and are used in some drug studies to distinguish between the 'real' effect of the drug being tested versus those that are due to the patient's expectancies.

It is generally thought that placebo effects arise because of verbal and observational cues, and classically conditioned responses, which give rise to expectancies, which then promote behavioral and clinical changes. When individuals believe they have control over medications they receive it is more likely that they will report a positive treatment response. Just as the expectancy of positive responses can assist the healing process, patients who believe that a treatment will be ineffective may experience no benefits from a genuine therapeutic agent, which is referred to as a *nocebo* effect (Damien et al., 2018).

Placebos come in a variety of guises. Aside from inert medications, they may comprise mechanical or electrical devices to reduce pain or muscle aches, acupuncture needles inserted into inappropriate locations, or even faith healing. The key element is that the patient believes that the treatment will work. Physicians may themselves be part of the placebo treatment, and trust in a physician may contribute to whether a prescribed treatment will be followed and whether positive effects will be realized.

Placebo effects are often seen in relation to procedures to diminish pain. Patients told that they will receive morphine treatment through an automated infusion pump to alleviate pain associated with a surgical procedure, reported greater pain relief than did patients who weren't told when the treatment began. Conversely, when patients were led to believe that their pain medication had been stopped, they reported increased pain perception. The motivation and expectancies of the patient are so fundamental in producing a positive response that when a patient sees another person receiving pain medicine that works, they too will be more likely to show a similar response.

As in the case of pain treatments, it is not unusual for depressed patients treated with antidepressants to show a positive response within a few days, after which the depression resumes until (and if) the full effects of the drug develop over the ensuing two to four weeks. Ordinarily, antidepressants require several weeks before their positive effects are significant, but the early response might be predictive of later treatment effects, perhaps because these patients are the 'true believers'. In fact, some of the positive effects attributable to antidepressants drugs in treating moderate depression might come from the placebo effect that accompanies the treatment, and the biological effects of drug treatments are primarily effective in the treatment of severe depression (Fournier et al., 2010).

As powerful as placebos might be, only a minority of patients show a sustained positive response to them. Placebo responses vary with the nature of the condition being treated. In the case of pain relief, where placebo effects are fairly high (ranging from 25 to 50%, depending on the nature of the condition associated with the pain), the effectiveness of the placebo treatments may approach that of low doses of morphine. Furthermore, personality factors, such as optimism and altruism, as well as being introverted versus extroverted, contribute to whether and to what extent a placebo treatment will be associated with diminished pain perception (Shi et al., 2021). There are, to be sure, limits to the effects of placebo treatments, generally being absent when the illness involves severe physical diseases or viral illnesses, but they nevertheless might diminish the anxiety that accompanies these conditions. Given the important role of psychological factors, including expectancies, in determining pain perception, psychological interventions (CBT, mindfulness, supportive psychotherapy, and psychologically informed physical therapy that combines physical therapy and CBT) have been recommended as a component of chronic pain that can be especially difficult to manage through drugs alone (Driscoll et al., 2021).

Placebo effects are so common, and expectancies of health improvement so dramatic, the case was made forty years ago that placebos ought to be considered as a part of the efficacy of many drug treatments. Hence, it is a bit surprising to find that there are those who view patients who show a placebo response as either being a bit 'off', malingerers, or individuals who hadn't really been ill from the start. The fact is that placebo treatments influence biological processes and might thereby affect a variety of illnesses or the perception of their symptoms (Colagiuri et al., 2015).

It's all very well to say that the placebo response emerges because of expectancies, and that factors that influence these expectancies will affect the strength of this response, but what are the brain processes that govern these effects? Placebo analgesic treatments are accompanied by variations of hypothalamic and amygdala activity, which are fundamental in stress responses as well as the midbrain periaqueductal gray, a brain region fundamental in pain perception and the elicitation of defensive behaviors. Placebo responses are accompanied by elevated thalamic activity that is involved in the integration of information relevant to pain perception as well as portions of the somatosensory cortex that is essential for the processing of experiences associated with pain. Studies in humans revealed that placebo and nocebo responses were associated with differential neuronal activity within pain modulatory nuclei within the pathway comprising the periaqueductal gray – rostral ventromedial pathway (Crawford et al., 2021).

More than these changes, the placebo effect was accompanied by changes in the neuronal activity within aspects of the brain that govern how pain is construed (e.g., posterior insula) and in brain regions associated with the motivation to take action (Zunhammer et al., 2021). Placebo responses varied with the functional coupling of prefrontal regions, anterior cingulate, and periaqueductal gray (Vachon-Presseau et al., 2018), thereby affecting emotional and cognitive processes as well as those associated with executive functioning and reward processes. Several neurobiological and genetic processes have also been implicated in the expression of a placebo response, including those tied to dopamine, serotonin, opioid, and endocannabinoid functioning (Cai & He, 2019).

━━━━━━━━━━ WALKS LIKE A DUCK ━━━━━━━━━━

Many people, when they see television clips of faith healers placing their hands on the forehead of a person wishing to become well, might perform an eye roll and mutter something disparaging about these people. Yet, if this isn't preventing sick people from seeking more traditional methods of healing that could have some benefit, then there's really nothing wrong with it. It might be 'just' a placebo effect, but if it reduces symptoms, even for the moment, it can be a boon for patients.

Deng Xiaoping, who served as the leader of the People's Republic of China from 1978 to 1992, in attempting to alter the course of China's development by dragging it into a market economy, famously stated, 'No matter if it is a white cat or a black cat; as long as it can catch mice, it is a good cat'. Such beliefs ultimately caused him immense political problems and he was sent off for rehabilitation. After Mao died in 1976, however, Deng was able to attain the position of de facto head of state.

The comment Deng Xiaoping made regarding white and black cats applies to placebo effects. It might not matter why placebos work - if they do the job then they are a good treatment.

Caveats concerning drug treatments

Before we get into the specific treatments that are used to deal with distress, anxiety, and depression, several fundamental issues should be addressed. Psychiatric illnesses are biochemically and behaviorally heterogeneous, involving complex neural circuits. Accordingly, it ought to be expected that no drug treatment will be effective for every person. The sad fact is that antidepressants are not as effective as originally hoped. In published studies the positive response rates are usually moderate; in the unpublished studies the efficacy hovers just above placebo rates, which in the case of depression can be as low as 20 to 35%. Moreover, even when therapies are effective, some symptoms persist, and the relapse rate is high. This information has become more widely disseminated, which might have diminished trust in the treatments and those who prescribe it. Given what we know about nocebo effects, the negative information regarding these drugs may also have undermined their effectiveness.

A second caveat concerns what the drugs are actually doing for patients. It has been maintained that drugs to treat psychiatric disorders might not be getting to the underlying processes but might simply be 'masking' the symptoms. Of course, it would be preferable to get to the specific processes that are disturbed and repair them. Unfortunately, in many instances it is uncertain what mechanisms are responsible for a disorder, let alone what would mend them using some yet to be discovered tools. Mental illnesses are often considered to be lifelong disorders and hence current drug treatments often need to be continued for protracted periods. Even if a drug therapy did not cure the illness, it is significant that among patients who were doing well with treatment, when they stopped taking their meds, they often fell back into a schizophrenic, bipolar, or depressed condition.

It is important to address the question of how effective treatment for a given illness is defined. After patients had been treated, many exhibited better than a 50% decline of symptom severity and no longer reported the number of symptoms required for a formal diagnosis of depression. However, if they reach these criteria, does this mean that they are now better even though residual symptoms may be present and predictive of illness recurrence?

No doubt patients and their families would like a more complete fix so that all the residual symptoms would be eliminated. But consider this from a slightly different perspective. An individual with a migraine headache is relieved that a drug alleviates the pain. They likely will get a migraine headache again at some later time as the painkiller didn't fix the underlying problem, but the person is happy to have gained some relief, at least for the moment. They hope for better treatments to prevent headaches entirely, but in the interim, the medication provided must be good enough.

Given the number of treatment choices that are available, how does a physician decide which drugs to administer? Some physicians understand what certain drugs and drug combinations do to specific symptoms, considering a host of variables, and thus are selective in the drugs that they prescribe. For these physicians, their success rates are likely well above the average. Others may have their favorite drug (based on various criteria or inclinations) and hence prescribe this treatment to anyone who seems depressed or anxious, irrespective of the specific symptom profile presented. As a result, the effectiveness of a pharmacological treatment to diminish the depressed mood would yield highly variable outcomes across patients. This might sound like a crude approach that doesn't inspire confidence, but the fact is that in many randomized controlled trials to evaluate drug efficacy this is exactly what happens. Patients who meet certain criteria (regarding their basic health and particular symptoms) may be enrolled in a trial in which they receive either a drug or a placebo treatment, sometimes in a single- or a double-blind protocol (or in an open-label trial comparing different drugs), and their symptoms and outcomes are monitored over a set period. Even though the symptoms of a particular illness may vary across individuals, and might even differ in subtypes of depression (e.g., typical versus atypical depression), they still might appear in the same study having been conscripted based on a syndrome rather than the specific constellation of symptoms. Thus, strictly speaking the negative perspectives concerning the effects of antidepressant drugs may be misplaced or excessive, but there may be ways of enhancing the effectiveness of therapies.

Selecting the right treatment

It is not unusual to find that patients may not be responsive to a particular drug, and a second or third drug may be tried before some success is achieved, although a subset of patients might be deemed to be 'treatment resistant' (also referred to as treatment refractory depression) when three or more drugs of different classes were found not to be effective. Often, when a drug isn't successful in reducing depression, a second drug can be included as an adjunct treatment based on the symptoms that the patient presents. For instance, it isn't unusual for patients to receive a particular antidepressant together with trazodone, which is a 5-HT acting antidepressant that also has strong sedative effects and may facilitate sleep. Likewise, mirtazapine (Remeron), an antidepressant that helps alleviate sleep disturbances, can be used in conjunction with venlafaxine (Effexor). In some instances, quetiapine (Seroquel) and risperidone (Risperidal), which are primarily used in the treatment of schizophrenia and bipolar disorder, may be used as adjunctive treatment with an antidepressant, especially when the depression is accompanied by high anxiety or high levels of irritability. Some antidepressant agents are also used in conjunction with augmenter drugs that, as the name implies, have an augmenting action. The judicious use of drug combinations may provide better therapeutic outcomes and may limit side effects that might otherwise occur (Blier, 2016).

Antidepressant agents

Selective serotonin reuptake inhibitors (SSRIs)

The class of drugs that had become especially popular in combating depression, the 'selective serotonin reuptake inhibitors' (SSRIs), was at first thought to have their beneficial effects by diminishing the reuptake of serotonin, thereby increasing the availability of serotonin within the synaptic cleft (5-HT). When these agents first appeared they were heralded as a panacea that would eliminate depression in most people. The SSRIs never lived up to the hype concerning the degree of relief obtained or the proportion of people that experienced diminished symptoms (Jakobson et al., 2017). Nevertheless, with appropriate drug combinations, antidepressant effects may be obtained well beyond those of monotherapies, and could be effective in the treatment of OCD, GAD, and PTSD. Likewise, in combination with CBT, the effects SSRIs on depression and OCD may be significantly improved and could provide improved outcomes among youth (Strawn et al., 2022).

An advantage of SSRIs over earlier treatments (e.g., tricyclic antidepressants) is that their side effects are less pronounced. Still, these agents may produce unpleasant consequences, such as a loss of appetite, weight loss (or gain), nausea, sleep disturbance, and reduced libido or ability to reach orgasm. Sexual dysfunction of some form is a relatively common side effect of SSRI treatment, varying with the specific drug used, and has been reported to be the most bothersome side effect of treatment. To maintain the therapeutic effects of the SSRIs and yet diminish the sexual side effects, several strategies have been used with varying levels of success. Increasing DA ordinarily enhances sexual responses, and some DA-acting agents improved sexual functioning among individuals taking SSRIs. There has also been success by prescribing adjunctive treatments that affect 5-HT receptors. Many of these treatments have their own side effects (e.g., sedation) or provide only limited diminution of the side effects of the SSRIs. The good news, as we'll see, is that some drugs have little, if any, sexual side effects, and thus might be the preferred treatments for some individuals.

One of the shortcomings of SSRI treatments, like those of other 5-HT acting antidepressants, is that it usually takes several weeks (usually between two and four) before effects of SSRIs are evident. This itself leads to the possibility that the effectiveness of these drugs is not simply due to increasing the availability of 5-HT but instead may reflect changes in one or more processes downstream of altered 5-HT levels. These could entail gradual changes of certain receptors, changes of second messenger systems (i.e., molecules responsible for relaying signals from cell surface receptors to targets that reside within the cell), or cumulative indirect effects on other systems, particularly growth factors, such as BDNF.

Serotonin-norepinephrine reuptake inhibitors (SNRIs)

The serotonin-norepinephrine reuptake inhibitors (SNRIs), a newer class of antidepressant drugs, have their effect by inhibiting the reuptake of both 5-HT and NE. These agents (e.g., Effexor, Cymbalta) have been used to treat depression and various anxiety disorders, including generalized anxiety disorder, social anxiety disorder, and OCD (Bandelow, 2020). Moreover, these agents have been used in the treatment of attention deficit hyperactivity disorder (ADHD), chronic neuropathic pain, fibromyalgia, and in diminishing menopausal symptoms. To a considerable extent, these agents have side effects like those elicited by the SSRIs, and upon withdrawal some symptoms can potentially worsen (e.g., anxiety) and thus their discontinuation is usually done by gradually tapering the daily dosage.

Norepinephrine and specific serotonergic antidepressants (NaSSAs), referred to as 'tetracyclic antidepressants', influence mood disturbances by increasing NE and 5-HT neurotransmission. Unlike the SNRIs, these agents do so by blocking presynaptic α2-adrenergic receptors, which results in a greater synthesis of NE, while the drug concurrently blocks certain 5-HT receptors. Drugs in this group (e.g., mianserin, mirtazapine) are as effective as SSRIs (Watanabe et al., 2011).

DRUG REPURPOSING

Many compounds that had been developed for one purpose are subsequently found to be effective in other conditions. Probably the best known of these is Viagra, which was initially developed to diminish hypertension and angina but turned out to be ineffective for these conditions. They were, however, effective in diminishing erectile dysfunction, and an analysis of more than 7 million individuals revealed that Viagra was associated with a 69% reduction in the occurrence of Alzheimer's disease (Fang et al., 2021). Warfarin, which was initially developed as a rat poison, has been used since the 1950s as an anticoagulant (blood thinner), and proved essential to prevent blood clots (Coumadin is one of the brand names under which it is marketed). Likewise, thalidomide, which was initially used to quell morning sickness during early pregnancy, induced a vast number of birth deformities before it was removed from the market. Since then, it has resurfaced (administered together with the synthetic corticoid dexamethasone) in the treatment of multiple myeloma. The anti-malarial agent hydroxychloroquine has been adopted to reduce symptoms of lupus erythematosus and rheumatoid arthritis, diminishing disease flares, joint pain, mouth sores, and fatigue (the suggestion that it could be used in limiting COVID-19 symptoms was entirely incorrect). Compounds that are used in the treatment of diabetes have been found to be exceptionally useful in other conditions. Metformin, a first line treatment to reduce blood sugar levels in type 2 diabetes acted against some forms of cancer, and GLP-1 agonists that help in the regulation of insulin release from the pancreas and diminish release of glucose from the liver, has proven to be a way of reducing weight, possibly through their actions on hypothalamic processes. More than most other drugs,

SSRIs have been repurposed in the treatment of a variety of conditions other than those for which they were first developed. As already described, these have included attenuation of anxiety, as well as eating disorders and migraine headaches, and one of these agents, fluvoxamine, diminishes health deterioration in symptomatic COVID-19 patients (Lenze et al., 2020).

Drug repurposing not only reduces the cost and time of bringing drugs to market, but as these agents have already been around the block, their side effects and potential long-term adverse actions might already be well known. Through drug repurposing, pharmaceutical companies gain by their costs being reduced (they might even pass the gain on to patients), and patients may gain by having effective treatments available sooner.

Norepinephrine-dopamine reuptake inhibitors

As DA plays a pivotal role in reward processes, it was thought that dysfunction of this neurotransmitter in certain brain regions might contribute to the anhedonia that is a primary symptom of depression. It was reasoned that targeting dopamine functioning ought to diminish depressive disorders. However, increasing DA availability through treatment with l-DOPA did not act as an antidepressant so the focus on this neurotransmitter had largely been abandoned. Since then, a resurgence of interest developed with evidence pointing to antidepressant actions occurring with alternative ways of increasing DA availability. As with the other reuptake inhibitors that affect more than a single system, bupropion (Wellbutrin, Zyban) inhibits the reuptake of both DA and NE, and it may indirectly affect 5-HT activity as well. In general, bupropion is about as effective as the SSRIs but is not accompanied by sex-related side effects or weight changes (Patel et al., 2016). As it has been associated with increased blood pressure and the provocation of seizure, it is not prescribed for individuals with risk factors for seizure, such as those withdrawing from alcohol or benzodiazepines, anorexia nervosa, bulimia, or those with a brain tumor.

Although bupropion was established as an antidepressant, like many other agents it has been found to be effective for other conditions, including social phobia and anxiety comorbid with depression, as well as hyposexuality, obesity, and adult attention deficit disorder. It has been effective in reducing smoking in about 20% of individuals and was used to diminish symptoms of Crohn's disease, likely by reducing the inflammatory mediators TNF-α and IFN-γ.

Monoamine oxidase inhibitors (MAOIs)

One route for the degradation of 5-HT, NE, and DA is through the enzyme monoamine oxidase (MAO). Thus, increasing the levels of these neurotransmitters through monoamine oxidase inhibitors (MAOIs) should provide antidepressant effects, but this class of drug seemed to have only modest effects when administered by itself. As well, MAO ordinarily degrades tyramine, an amino acid important in regulating blood pressure, increases of this amino acid by MAOIs, which were further elevated by some foods (e.g., certain cheeses, cured meats), thus producing deadly heart consequences. A new generation of MAOIs has seen increased use when other drugs were found to be ineffective. This includes moclobemide (Manerix), which is known as a reversible inhibitor of monoamine oxidase A (RIMA) that serves in a relatively short-lived and selective manner, and unlike the older MAOIs its use does not require a special diet.

Glutamate receptor antagonists

Glutamate has taken on increasing allure as a target to treat depressive disorders. Chronic stressor exposure diminishes glutamate levels within the prefrontal cortex of rodents and diminished glutamate levels have been observed within the prefrontal cortex of depressed patients (Moriguchi et al., 2019). The focus on this excitatory neurotransmitter was reinforced by the findings that drugs that antagonize N-methyl-D-aspartate (NMDA) glutamate receptors may have antidepressant actions, although the therapeutic effects of these agents may occur owing to actions on downstream neurobiological changes or by diminishing inflammation.

Several drugs in this class can promote antidepressant-like actions, but the effect of ketamine has received particular attention. Ketamine was best known as a general anaesthetic and analgesic (e.g., in veterinary practice), but it found its way into the street drug culture (where it is known as Special K) because it produces dissociative and hallucinogenic-like effects. When patients were treated with ketamine for chronic pain, it was noted that the frequent comorbid depressive symptoms disappeared. This occurred within a few hours after treatment, rather than the two to three weeks usually required for antidepressants to have positive effects. Subsequent clinical trials confirmed that intravenous ketamine administered over a 40-minute period could be effective as an antidepressant (Phillips et al., 2019). However, these effects typically lasted for only about three to five days, and the poor mood fully returned within one to two weeks. Later studies produced equally impressive results, and a rapid response was even obtained in treatment-resistant patients, and somewhat more sustained effects could be obtained with repeated treatments. Significantly, ketamine could diminish suicidality even when depressive mood was not alleviated (Grunebaum et al., 2018). The FDA approved a form of ketamine as a nasal spray (esketamine) that can be used at a clinic or doctor's office for treatment-resistant depression, although the efficacy of the treatment was appreciably lower than ketamine administered intravenously (Bahji et al., 2021).

The effects of ketamine in alleviating depression may come about by altering synaptic plasticity and by attenuating the synaptic disturbances ordinarily provoked by stressors. But these actions occur rapidly so that a lag does not occur between treatment and the antidepressant action (Duman et al., 2016). It has been suggested that its antidepressant effects are due to an increase of the neurotrophic BDNF, which rapidly causes synaptogenesis and spine formation in frontal cortical regions. Consistent with this suggestion, ketamine can reverse the atrophy of cortical neurons ordinarily produced by chronic stressors (Duman et al., 2016). Beyond these relatively specific actions, ketamine affected the default mode network that accompanies depression, which could influence the inflexible ruminative features of depression. In effect, ketamine might have allowed individuals to break out of the negative cognitive rut that frequently accompanies depression.

TREATING DEPRESSION AND PTSD THROUGH PSYCHEDELICS

Although psychedelic compounds have been banned for years, they may have powerful therapeutic actions. Increasing evidence has shown that several psychedelic compounds, including psilocybin, MDMA, LSD, and ayahuasca, may be effective in alleviating PTSD, intense anxiety, treatment-resistant depression, and addictions. Typically, these treatments are administered in clinical settings with the guidance of a therapist so that patients don't travel down the wrong path during their psychedelic experience.

The number of trials supporting the benefits of these agents has increased exponentially in recent years and may be a game changer in the treatment of some disorders. When administered along with supportive therapy psilocybin (magic mushrooms) there were marked reductions of depressive symptoms in 71% of depressed patients, lasting for at least four weeks (Davis et al., 2021). In fact, psilocybin could promote pronounced, rapid, and lasting action for treatment-resistant depressive illness and may diminish depressive symptoms present among individuals with life-threatening diseases (Vargas et al., 2020). Lysergic acid diethylamide (LSD) and MDMA (ecstasy, molly) have similarly been used to treat depressive disorders, and like psilocybin, they could diminish distress among cancer patients, and MDMA-assisted psychotherapy was effective in diminishing features of severe PTSD (Mitchell et al., 2021). The actions of compounds such as psilocybin may have positive effects by increasing serotonin and dopamine activity, by altering glutamate functioning or through a rapid increase in the interconnections between neurons (Shao et al., 2021). To be sure, we've been fooled before when novel therapies didn't turn out to be as effective as first reported, but this time we might be seeing the development of a new generation of therapeutic agents.

Transcranial magnetic stimulation (TMS)

As electroconvulsive shock had positive effects in reducing depression, attention began to focus on the possibility that other ways of stimulating the brain could have positive effects. Noninvasive transcranial direct current stimulation (tDCS), which entails the delivery of low direct currents through electrodes placed on the head can diminish depressive symptoms. Instead of a direct current application, repeated bursts of transcranial magnetic stimulation (rTMS) applied through an electromagnetic coil placed against the skull (near the forehead) can successfully diminish symptoms of OCD and depression. In general, rTMS has been studied more extensively and seems to be used clinically more often, although both procedures were found to moderately reduce depressive symptoms (H. Li et al., 2021).

A meta-analysis indicated that repeated TMS (rTMS) elicited positive effects and has even been effective in treatment-resistant patients and could be used to prevent depression relapse (Rachid et al., 2018). In addition, TMS found a berth in the treatment of anxiety disorders, neurodegenerative diseases, pain syndromes, and the auditory hallucinations associated with schizophrenia. How TMS comes to produce its beneficial effects isn't certain, but it may do so by affecting glutamate functioning and by increasing BDNF related signaling processes that influence dendritic growth and synaptic sprouting, as well as by affecting glial cell functioning (Chervyakov et al., 2015).

DEEP BRAIN STIMULATION

Electrical stimulation of neurons deep in the brain, a procedure referred to as deep brain stimulation (DBS), attenuated the symptoms of Parkinson's disease that are due to a loss of neurons within the substantia nigra, the site of cell bodies for a major dopamine pathway (Lang & Lozano, 1998). Considering the success achieved in Parkinson's patients, clinical studies were done to assess whether deep brain stimulation would be effective in alleviating psychiatric conditions. Indeed, when electrodes targeted aspects of the brain involving reward processes, this treatment frequently alleviated features of OCD (Alonso et al., 2015).

Initial reports indicated that DBS was effective in depressed patients for whom no other treatment seemed to be effective. Depression involves complex neural circuits and it was considered that activity of the subgenual cingulate cortex (CG25 or area 25) was particularly relevant in the development of depression. This region is reciprocally linked to other sites deemed significant for depression, such as the medial prefrontal, orbital, and aspects of the anterior and posterior cingulate cortices. Stimulation of the CG25 had marked effects in four out of six depressed patients who had been treatment-resistant (Mayberg et al. 2005). The efficacy of the treatment declined over time, but when lasting stimulation was provided by a battery pack implanted just beneath the collar bone, more than half the patients reported symptom reduction (and 36% reported complete relief) even after two years. Unfortunately, in randomized controlled trials the effects of DBS were limited (e.g., Holtzheimer et al., 2017), although longer-term follow-up analyses revealed that positive effects were apparent in some patients (Hitti et al., 2021). With improved technologies and by stimulating other nearby brain sites, early indications are that further positive effects may emerge.

Anti-anxiety agents

Benzodiazepines

A large arsenal of anti-anxiety medications is available that have their effects by influencing GABA receptor activity. The anti-anxiety medications that likely come to mind are those such as diazepam (Valium), alprazolam (Xanax), chlordiazepoxide (Librium), clonazepam (Klonopin), and lorazepam (Ativan), each of which is fast acting and may be an effective short-term remedy to diminish anxiety, insomnia, and some benzodiazepines (e.g., chlordiazepoxide) have been used to manage alcohol withdrawal syndrome. As effective as they might be, benzodiazepines are not recommended for long-term use as they are associated with the development of tolerance, physical dependence, and withdrawal symptoms (Balon & Starcevic, 2020). Thus, SSRIs have generally become the first-line choice of drug treatment for chronic anxiety, whereas benzodiazepines are primarily prescribed for their short-term actions.

Treatments such as pregabalin and gabapentin, which increase GABA functioning, may be effective as anxiolytics (Frampton, 2014) and are most often used among patients with moderate/severe anxiety, in those with subsyndromal depression, and in older people. Consequently, in some individuals these compounds might be preferable to benzodiazepines in the treatment of anxiety disorders. Together with SSRIs or SNRIs, pregabalin might be effective in the treatment of generalized anxiety disorder. However, these compounds may produce a variety of side effects (e.g., blurred vision, tremor, constipation, dizziness, drowsiness, fatigue, headache, peripheral edema, weight gain) so that some patients discontinue their use.

Norepinephrine β-blockers

The activity of NE in several brain regions is markedly influenced by stressors, and this neurotransmitter has been implicated in the provocation of anxiety. Although it is technically not an anti-anxiety medication, the β-adrenergic antagonist propranolol has been used to diminish anxiety, particularly the autonomic change that accompanies anxiety (e.g., reducing heart rate and blood pressure). Because of these actions, it is frequently used off-label to diminish performance anxiety. However, for the most part, the efficacy of propranolol and similar compounds has not been found to be particularly effective in the treatment of chronic anxiety disorders (Steenen et al., 2016).

Nutrients, exercise, and sleep as medicines

As described in earlier chapters, lifestyles may profoundly influence multiple diseases, and this has been apparent in relation to anxiety and depression. The adoption of certain diets (e.g., Mediterranean diet) can have numerous beneficial effects in the prevention of diseases and in limiting their progression. This said, a veritable quagmire developed in determining which specific diets are best in preventing some illnesses (e.g., cancer), with experts disagreeing with one another concerning the best regimens, and which foods can have harmful effects on health. This area of research has been encumbered by poor experimental procedures as well as 'findings that were too good to be true' (Schoenfeld & Ioannidis, 2013). These caveats notwithstanding, it is generally agreed that diets that promote obesity, those that promote elevated inflammation, and those comprising highly processed foods and containing trans fats are likely harmful. Conversely, foods that favor high abundance and diversity of gut microbiota may be aligned with effective immune functioning, diminished inflammation, better responses to medical treatments, and generally improved health (Anisman & Kusnecov, 2022). Considerable data have amassed indicating that gut microbiota have significant sway in relation to psychiatric conditions, particularly anxiety and depression (Cryan et al., 2019).

Exercise may produce multiple health benefits. Most often, this has been reported in relation to enhanced heart health, limiting diabetes, and cancer occurrence and progression; broad analyses revealed that exercise can positively affect 26 independent diseases. The benefits of exercise being as extensive as they are, sports physiologists and others frequently refer to 'Exercise as Medicine' (Pedersen & Saltin, 2015). The actions of exercise may come about through diverse physiological processes, such a reduced proinflammatory cytokine levels, enhanced microbial abundance and diversity, and attenuation of the normal age-related decline of immune functioning (Simpson et al., 2015). It appeared that exercise was associated with epigenetic variations in several genes that code for immune and inflammatory processes (Ferioli et al., 2019). Not surprisingly, when coupled with healthy eating, the effects of exercise on inflammatory processes were still more pronounced (Campbell et al., 2018).

Because exercise is beneficial to well-being, it shouldn't be misinterpreted to mean 'the more the better'. To the contrary, excessive exercise can have detrimental effects. Be this as it may, there is little doubt that moderate levels of exercise, such as brisk walking for 30 minutes a day, has enormous health benefits that may come about through altered levels of inflammatory factors, improved gut microbiota presence, and the production of short chain fatty acids (Simpson et al., 2015). Of course, numerous roadblocks can be encountered in obtaining proper exercise, such as situational factors (e.g., living in an area that is not conducive to exercise and lacks gyms or green space or is subject to high levels of air pollution) as well as individual factors ('I'm too tired after a full day of work'; 'I'm so bogged down with work I just don't have the time'). These can be overcome by selecting appropriate exercise regimens so that they become a fun activity and developing effective exercise routines can be enhanced when activities are conducted in groups (e.g., Stevens et al., 2017).

While the benefits related to exercise have most often been considered in the context of physical health, it has become ever more certain that exercise influences cognitive and emotional processes and can diminish moderate symptoms of anxiety and depressed mood (Morres et al., 2019). Based on an 11-year prospective study it was estimated that depression could be curtailed by about 12% through a regular exercise regimen (Harvey et al., 2018). While exercise may be less effective in relation to severe depression, particularly as affected individuals often resist strenuous activity, benefits can be achieved by gradually introducing exercise over the course of standard treatments. Unfortunately, severely depressed individuals who don't seek help will likely not obtain the value of this natural antidepressant therapy.

Aside from attenuating anxiety and depression, moderate exercise can enhance brain functioning reflected by improved executive functioning, attention, information processing speed, executive functioning, and memory ability. Moreover, exercise might limit the cognitive decline otherwise associated with aging. These changes may be linked to enhanced brain neuroplasticity through changes of several neurotrophic factors (Fernandes et al., 2017) as well as by functional reorganization of neural circuits relevant to dealing with stressful experiences, enhanced microbial diversity, and by limiting inflammation (Mailing et al., 2019).

Like other lifestyle factors, sleep plays a prominent role in maintaining good health, whereas sleep disturbances can promote ill-health. Among its other actions, sleep acts in a recuperative capacity allowing for the replenishment of resources stemming from the wear and tear that was incurred during the preceding day. Sleep is accompanied by restoration of glycogen energy stores that had declined over the day, thereby rejuvenating skeletal and muscular systems, hormone and neurotransmitter functioning, repair of damaged tissue can be facilitated, and accumulating DNA damage within neurons can be diminished (Zada et al., 2019). In addition, waste and toxins that had built up during the day can be flushed out of the brain during sleep. This is particularly relevant for individuals who had experienced traumatic brain injuries in whom appreciable waste accumulates (Hablitz et al., 2020).

Just as obtaining sufficient sleep is essential for well-being, sleep loss and disturbed circadian regulation have been linked to immune and inflammatory cytokine disturbances and hormonal dysregulation (Besedovsky et al., 2019; Irwin, 2019), thereby favoring the development of physical disturbances, such as heart disease and cancer progression, as well as mood disorders. Variations of inflammatory cytokines have been observed with too little sleep (< 5 hours a night) as well as too much sleep (> 9 hours), and could be engendered by sleep disorders (e.g., sleep apnea) as well as by jobs that entail altered circadian rhythms (e.g., chronic or variable night shift work). Gut microbiota imbalances may similarly be generated by sleep disturbances, which can foster the development of illnesses (Nobs et al., 2019).

Stressful experiences may undermine sleep, and conversely sleep loss influences reactivity to stressors, thereby affecting biological processes that cause varied illnesses. As well, sleep disturbances have been associated with altered eating, including consumption of comfort foods, possibly reflecting an effort to self-medicate. In combination with immune alterations, the resulting metabolic changes favor the development of varied inflammatory-related illnesses. In view of the wide-ranging negative effects of sleep and circadian disturbances, it is significant that behavioral change strategies and altering lifestyles might be effective in modifying sleep patterns and sleep quality and may thereby limit or prevent the development of pathology.

═══════ SUPPORT FROM COMPANION ANIMALS ═══════

Service dogs have facilitated the lives of their human partners, acting as guide dogs for the visually impaired, assisting those with hearing impairments, facilitating mobility, doing chores for people with movement-related disorders, and their keen olfactory abilities can sense the presence of allergens and excessively elevated or reduced blood sugar levels among those with diabetes. Companion dogs can also sense changes in anxiety and mood and have been used to help individuals with depressive and anxiety disorders. Indeed, several universities have provided access to trained therapy dogs so that student anxiety could be reduced by interacting with these animals. Companion animals can have multiple benefits for those with PTSD. Not only do they help diminish symptoms of PTSD (Hediger et al., 2021) they serve as a barrier between the affected individuals and potential threats, and those with PTSD frequently reported that their service dog provided them with a sense of safety. Aside from the multiple abilities of companion animals they provide social support and unconditional love to their human partners – one may not be able to count on support from friends, but our dogs are always there for us.

Herbal (naturopathic) treatments

An array of treatments for an enormous number of ailments has included a wide assortment of natural products. Some natural products are undeniably important in the armamentarium of therapeutic agents for diverse illnesses. Among many other functions, these have included treatments for breast cancer (tamoxifen), aloe vera for the treatment of burns, opium to reduce pain, digitalis as a heart stimulant, and aspirin as an anti-inflammatory and pain suppressant. There have been indications that some natural products may have psychological benefits. A systematic review had indicated that St John's Wort (extracts of the plant *Hypericum perforatum* L) had antidepressant effects with fewer side effects than SSRIs (Linde et al., 2008). Curiously, the effects were most notable in Germany (and German-speaking countries) where it has been used for some time, and where there seems to be a great deal of confidence in its effectiveness (is this a culturally dependent placebo effect?). Subsequent studies indicated that it was ineffective in the treatment of chronic low-grade depression (dysthymia), and a study conducted through the National Center for Complementary and Alternative Medicine (NCCAM) indicated its efficacy in the treatment of depression was no greater than that of placebo.

As with herbal medicines, specific nutrients have long been recognized as important to our psychological well-being. Polyunsaturated fatty acids (PUFAs), such as those present in fatty fish and fish oils, notably omega 3 fatty acids, have been associated with the prevention of depressive illness owing to its ability to diminish inflammation (Grosso et al., 2016), but the findings concerning the effectiveness of omega 3 fatty acids in the treatment of existent depression have been inconsistent. To be sure, PUFAs have been implicated in the prevention of a variety of diseases, including those related to neuronal degeneration and immunological disturbances, but findings have been inconsistent. Consequently, it's hard to know what's hype and what's real. A safe presumption might be that eating certain foods, such as those containing omega-3 might have benefits and it is unlikely that they'll have any negative effects.

Several natural products have been assessed in legitimate experimental trials. Curcumin, a component of turmeric that has antioxidant and anti-inflammatory actions has repeatedly been experimentally assessed to determine its effectiveness in moderating several illnesses, often showing moderate benefits. Treatment with kava, a South Pacific plant, has been assessed to determine whether it has anti-anxiety effects. While anecdotal reports had supported its efficacy in this regard, inconsistent results were reported in controlled experimental analyses. Other natural compounds, such as passion flower (*Passiflora incarnata* L) and lavender consumed as an oil were thought to have anti-anxiety actions, but mixed results were observed in experimental analyses. Many other natural products have been offered as anxiolytics. By and large, the number of studies conducted to assess these and other products with purported benefits have involved a small number of participants and have been deemed to be of low quality. Thus, it's often difficult to determine whether genuine anti-anxiety effects are produced.

Given the interest in natural products, it isn't overly surprising that an enormous number of herbal products with dubious efficacy have been pushed to treat virtually any disease imaginable. These supplementary medicines often appear as a component of complementary and alternative medicine (CAM) despite their uncertain value. These supplements aren't marketed as drugs and consequently haven't had to undergo scrupulous and rigorous testing ordinarily required before they can be sold as medicines. Typically, the labels on supplements do not provide information about the contents, their purity, or even how much to consume to achieve particular effects, and they rarely provide information of the possible risks inherent in the use of these substances. It might be tempting to believe that most of these agents don't create any harm. However, most substances that are peddled are not inert and some of them can affect biological processes that could have adverse effects or interact negatively with medications that an individual may be using. In fact, some supplements have been found to be laced with substances, such as stimulants, so that consumers will come to believe that the compound is producing some sort of effect. Far too often people with serious illnesses may select these as alternatives to well-tested medicines, typically leading to poor outcomes.

While we're on this topic, something should be said about the attention that has been given to prebiotic and probiotic supplements. As we've seen, microbial communities can influence immune system functioning and having appreciable diversity of microbiota can have important health benefits. Thus, transplanting microbiota (through fecal transplants) from a healthy individual to individuals with certain illnesses can be therapeutic, including in alleviating *C. difficile* that produces intestinal inflammation and in the treatment of Crohn's disease. There have similarly been reports that fecal transplants may be effective in diminishing anxiety and depression (Chinna Meyyappan et al., 2020).

Can microbiota obtained through other means likewise favor good health? Beneficial bacteria found in many foods (e.g., yogurt, cheese, sauerkraut, and kimchi) might act in this way. However, it's less likely that probiotic supplements (in pill form) can reliably have these actions. There have been reports showing positive actions amongst individuals with specific health conditions, and among individuals with known microbiota disturbances. However, very different microbial communities exist across people, and it is questionable whether probiotics are useful as a preventative measure for otherwise healthy people. Even if an individual's microbial balance was disturbed, they likely wouldn't be aware of this, and certainly wouldn't know what bacterial supplements they needed. While some illnesses may be associated with diminished microbiota abundance and diversity, off-the-shelf probiotics may not contain the right mix to remedy this. Among healthy individuals, the microbes obtained through supplements might not colonize the gut and would be eliminated with other undigested substances. Ultimately, formulations may be developed that are effective for individuals with specific microbial disturbances, but at the moment the value of these supplements as they're currently marketed is questionable (Suez et al., 2019).

Conclusion

One message that has been emphasized repeatedly in this book has been that appreciable differences exist across individuals with respect to the behavioral and neurochemical changes that are induced by stressors. It is reasonable to expect that there will be differences in the efficacy of various treatments in diminishing these effects and in attenuating pathological states. Not all individuals are equally responsive to various SSRIs or SNRIs, and therapy often involves a hit-and-miss process. Likewise, some individuals respond positively to CBT or mindfulness training, whereas others seem not to respond well at all. For some, depressive disorders combined drug and cognitive therapy may have positive effects beyond those of a single treatment.

After being certain of a diagnosis, the big trick for therapists is to decide on the proper treatment. As indicated earlier, the specific symptoms presented will often guide the way, but this is not always the case. Just as there is a need for measurable biological substrates that are tied to disease states (biomarkers) to predict who is vulnerable to an illness, it would be profitable to identify behavioral or biological markers that could inform which treatment will be most effective for a particular patient. This is especially the case when treatments have moderate success rates, and it takes weeks to find out whether the drug is actually doing the job. It can't be said often enough, individualized treatments will ultimately be necessary wherein treatments are determined by genetic factors, the presence of certain blood or cerebrospinal fluid (CSF) markers, the individual symptoms presented, and a constellation of psychosocial factors, such as the way individuals deal with stressors and their capacity to sustain treatments. Unlike the simplicity inherent in buying new socks, in the treatment of stress-related illness there's currently no such thing as 'one size fits all'.

Suggested readings

Beck, A.T. & Haigh, E.A. (2014). Advances in cognitive theory and therapy: The generic cognitive model. *Annual Review in Clinical Psychology, 10*, 1–24.

Duman, R.S., Aghajanian, G.K., Sanacora, G., & Krystal, J.H. (2016). Synaptic plasticity and depression: New insights from stress and rapid-acting antidepressants. *Nature Medicine, 22*, 238–249.

Topol, E. (2019). *Deep Medicine: How Artificial Intelligence Can Make Healthcare Human Again*. New York: Basic Books.

REFERENCES

Abdill, R.J., Adamowicz, E.M., & Blekhman, R. (2022). Public human microbiome data are dominated by highly developed countries. *PLOS Biology, 20*, e3001536

Abel, A.M., Yang, C., Thakar, M.S., & Malarkannan, S. (2018). Natural killer cells: Development, maturation, and clinical utilization. *Frontiers in Immunology, 9*, 1869.

Abid, M.B., Shah, N.N., Maatman, T.C., & Hari, P.N. (2019). Gut microbiome and CAR-T therapy. *Experimental Hematology & Oncology, 8*, 31.

Abizaid A. (2019). Stress and obesity: The ghrelin connection. *Journal of Neuroendocrinology, 31*, e12693.

Abizaid, A. (2009). Ghrelin and dopamine: New insights on the peripheral regulation of appetite. *Journal of Neuroendocrinology, 21*, 787–793.

Abizaid, A. & Horvath, T.L. (2008). Brain circuits regulating energy homeostasis. *Regulatory Peptides, 149*, 3–10.

Abizaid, A., Luheshi, G., & Woodside, B.C. (2013). Interaction between immune and energy balance signals in the regulation of feeding and metabolism. In A. Kusnecov and H. Anisman (eds.), *Handbook of Psychoneuroimmunology*. London: Wiley-Blackwell.

Abramson, L.Y., Seligman, M.E., & Teasdale, J.D. (1978). Learned helplessness in humans: Critique and reformulation. *Journal of Abnormal Psychology, 87*, 49–74.

Adamczyk-Sowa, M., Medrek, A., Madej, P., Michlicka, W., & Dobrakowski, P. (2017). Does the gut microbiota influence immunity and inflammation in multiple sclerosis pathophysiology? *Journal of Immunology Research, 2017*, 7904821.

Adiamah, A., Skořepa, P., Weimann, A., & Lobo, D.N. (2019). The impact of preoperative immune modulating nutrition on outcomes in patients undergoing surgery for gastrointestinal cancer: A systematic review and meta-analysis. *Annals of Surgery, 270*, 247–256.

Afonso, R.F., Kraft, I., Aratanha, M.A., & Kozasa, E.H. (2020). Neural correlates of meditation: A review of structural and functional MRI studies. *Frontiers in Bioscience, 12*, 92–115.

Ahrends, T., Aydin, B., Matheis, F., Classon, C.H., Marchildon, F., et al. (2021). Enteric pathogens induce tissue tolerance and prevent neuronal loss from subsequent infections. *Cell, 184*, 5715–5727.e12.

Aizer, A.A., Chen, M.H., McCarthy, E.P., Mendu, M.L., Koo, S., et al. (2013). Marital status and survival in patients with cancer. *Journal of Clinical Oncology, 31*, 3869–3876.

Aknin, L.B., Sandstrom, G.M., Dunn, E.W., & Norton, M.I. (2011). It's the recipient that counts: Spending money on strong social ties leads to greater happiness than spending on weak social ties. *PLoS One, 6*, e17018.

Akondy, R.S., Fitch, M., Edupuganti, S., Yang, S., Kissick, H.T., et al. (2017). Origin and differentiation of human memory CD8 T cells after vaccination. *Nature, 552*, 362–367.

Albert, M.A., Durazo, E.M. & Slopen, N., Zaslavsky, A.M., Buring, J.E., et al. (2017). Cumulative psychological stress and cardiovascular disease risk in middle aged and older women: Rationale, design, and baseline characteristics. *American Heart Journal, 192*, 1–12.

Albert, P.R., Le François, B., & Vahid-Ansari, F. (2019). Genetic, epigenetic and posttranscriptional mechanisms for treatment of major depression: The 5-HT1A receptor gene as a paradigm. *Journal of Psychiatry & Neuroscience, 44*, 164–176.

Albrecht, A., Müller, I., Ardi, Z., Çalışkan, G., Gruber, D., et al. (2017). Neurobiological consequences of juvenile stress: A GABAergic perspective on risk and resilience. *Neuroscience & Biobehavioral Reviews, 74*, 21–43.

Allen, M.C., Clinchy, M., & Zanette, L.Y. (2022). Fear of predators in free-living wildlife reduces population growth over generations. *Proceedings of the National Academy of Sciences, 119*, e2112404119.

Alloy, L.B., Abramson, K.Y., Keyser, J., Gerstein, R.K., & Sylvia, L.G. (2008). Negative cognitive style. In K.S. Dobson & D.J.A. Dozois (eds.), *Risk Factors in Depression* (pp. 237–263). New York: Academic.

Allswede, D.M., Yolken, R.H., Buka, S.L. & Cannon, T.D. (2020). Cytokine concentrations throughout pregnancy and risk for psychosis in adult offspring: a longitudinal case-control study. *The Lancet Psychiatry, 7*, 254–261.

Al Mamun A.A.., Lombardo, M.J., Shee, C., Lisewski, A.M., Gonzalez, C., et al. (2012). Identity and function of a large gene network underlying mutagenic repair of DNA breaks. *Science, 338*, 1344–1348.

Alonso, P., Cuadras, D., Gabriëls, L., Denys, D., Goodman, W., et al. (2015). Deep brain stimulation for obsessive-compulsive disorder: A meta-analysis of treatment outcome and predictors of response. *PLoS One, 10*, e0133591.

Amato, K.R., Arrieta, M.C., Azad, M.B., Bailey, M.T., Broussard, J.L., et al. (2021). The human gut microbiome and health inequities. *Proceedings of the National Academy of Sciences, 118*, e2017947118.

Amitay, E.L. & Keinan-Boker, L. (2015). Breastfeeding and childhood leukemia incidence: A meta-analysis and systematic review. *JAMA Pediatrics, 169*, e151025.

Amuasi, J.H., Lucas, T., Horton, R., & Winkler, A.S. (2020). Reconnecting for our future: The Lancet One Health Commission. *The Lancet, 395*, 1469–1471.

Ananth, A.A., Tai, L.H., Lansdell, C., Alkayyal, A.A., Baxter, K.E., et al. (2016). Surgical stress abrogates pre-existing protective T cell mediated anti-tumor immunity leading to postoperative cancer recurrence. *PLoS One, 11*, e0155947.

Andersen, B.L., Goyal, N.G., Westbrook, T.D., Bishop, B., & Carson, W.E. 3rd. (2017). Trajectories of stress, depressive symptoms, and immunity in cancer survivors: Diagnosis to 5 years. *Clinical Cancer Research, 23*, 52–61.

Anisman, H. (2021). *Health Psychology: A Biopsychosocial Approach*. London: Sage Publications.

Anisman, H. (2011). Sensitization in relation to posttraumatic stress disorder. *Biological Psychiatry, 70,* 404–405.

Anisman, H. (2009). Cascading effects of stressors and inflammatory immune system activation: implications for major depressive disorder. *Journal of Psychiatry & Neuroscience, 34,* 4–20.

Anisman, H. & Hayley, S. (2012). Illness comorbidity as a biomarker? *Journal of Psychiatry & Neuroscience, 37,* 221–223.

Anisman, H., Hayley, S., & Kusnecov, A. (2018). *The Immune System and Mental Health.* London: Academic Press.

Anisman, H., Hayley, S., & Merali, Z. (2003). Cytokines and stress: Sensitization and cross-sensitization. *Brain, Behavior, and Immunity, 17,* 86–93.

Anisman, H. & Kusnecov, A. (2022). *Cancer: How Lifestyles May Impact Disease Development, Progression and Treatment.* London: Elsevier.

Anisman, H. & Matheson, K. (2005). Stress, anhedonia and depression: Caveats concerning animal models. *Neuroscience & Biobehavioral Reviews, 29,* 525–546.

Anisman, H., Merali, Z., & Hayley, S. (2008). Neurotransmitter, peptide and cytokine processes in relation to depressive disorder: Comorbidity of depression with neurodegenerative disorders. *Progress in Neurobiology, 85,* 1–74.

Anisman, H., Merali, Z., & Poulter, M. (2012). Gamma-aminobutyric acid involvement in depressive illness: Interactions with corticotropin-releasing hormone and serotonin. In Y. Dwivedi (ed.), *The Neurobiological Basis of Suicide.* New York: Taylor & Francis.

Anisman, H., Poulter, M.O., Gandhi, R., Merali, Z., & Hayley, S. (2007). Interferon-alpha effects are exaggerated when administered on a psychosocial stressor backdrop: Cytokine, corticosterone and brain monoamine variations. *Journal of Neuroimmunology, 186,* 45–53.

Annane, D. (2016). The role of ACTH and corticosteroids for sepsis and septic shock: An update. *Frontiers in Endocrinology, 7,* 70.

Antoni, M.H. & Dhabhar, F.S. (2019). The impact of psychosocial stress and stress management on immune responses in patients with cancer. *Cancer, 125,* 1417–1431.

Antoniuk, S., Bijata, M., Ponimaskin, E., & Wlodarczyk, J. (2019). Chronic unpredictable mild stress for modeling depression in rodents: Meta-analysis of model reliability. *Neuroscience & Biobehavioral Reviews, 99,* 101–116.

Apfel, B.A., Ross, J., Hlavin, J., Meyerhoff, D.J., Metzler, T.J., et al. (2011). Hippocampal volume differences in Gulf War veterans with current versus lifetime posttraumatic stress disorder symptoms. *Biological Psychiatry, 69,* 541–548.

Arnold, C. (2022). Is precision public health the future — or a contradiction? *Nature, 601,* 18–20.

Arnone, D., Mumuni, A.N., Jauhar, S., Condon, B., & Cavanagh, J. (2015). Indirect evidence of selective glial involvement in glutamate-based mechanisms of mood regulation in depression: meta-analysis of absolute prefrontal neuro-metabolic concentrations. *European Neuropsychopharmacology, 25,* 1109–1117.

Astill Wright, L., Horstmann, L., Holmes, E.A., & Bisson, J.I. (2021). Consolidation/reconsolidation therapies for the prevention and treatment of PTSD and re-experiencing: a systematic review and meta-analysis. *Translational Psychiatry, 11*, 453.

Audet, M.C. (2019). Stress-induced disturbances along the gut microbiota–immune–brain axis and implications for mental health: Does sex matter? *Frontiers in Neuroendocrinology, 54*, 100772.

Audet, M.C., Jacobson-Pick, S., Wann, B.P., & Anisman, H. (2011). Social defeat promotes specific cytokine variations within the prefrontal cortex upon subsequent aggressive or endotoxin challenges. *Brain, Behavior, and Immunity, 25*, 1197–1205.

Austenfeld, J.L. & Stanton, A.L. (2004). Coping through emotional approach: A new look at emotion, coping, and health-related outcomes. *Journal of Personality, 72*, 1335–1363.

Averill, L.A., Abdallah, C.G., Fenton, L.R., Fasula, M.K., Jiang, L., et al. (2020). Early life stress and glutamate neurotransmission in major depressive disorder. *European Neuropsychopharmacology, 35*, 71–80.

Aversa, Z., Atkinson, E.J., Schafer, M.J., Theiler, R.N., & Rocca, W.A. (2021). Association of infant antibiotic exposure with childhood health outcomes. *Mayo Clinic Proceedings, 96*, 66–77.

Aydillo, T., Rombauts, A., Stadlbauer, D., Aslam, S., Abelenda-Alonso, G., et al. (2021). Immunological imprinting of the antibody response in COVID-19 patients. *Nature Communications, 12*, 3781.

Ayling, K., Jia, R., Coupland, C., Chalder, T., Massey, A., et al. (2022). Psychological predictors of self-reported COVID-19 outcomes: Results from a prospective cohort study. *Annals of Behavioral Medicine, 56*, 484–497.

Azevedo, C.A. & Mammis, A. (2018). Neuromodulation therapies for alcohol addiction: A literature review. *Neuromodulation, 21*, 144–148.

Babenko, O., Kovalchuk, I., & Metz, G.A. (2015). Stress-induced perinatal and transgenerational epigenetic programming of brain development and mental health. *Neuroscience & Biobehavioral Reviews, 48*, 70–91.

Bach, D.R., Seymour, B., & Dolan, R.J. (2009). Neural activity associated with the passive prediction of ambiguity and risk for aversive events. *Journal of Neuroscience, 29*, 1648–1656.

Bachtiar, M., Ooi, B.N.S., Wang, J., Jin, Y., Tan, T.W., et al. (2019). Towards precision medicine: Interrogating the human genome to identify drug pathways associated with potentially functional, population-differentiated polymorphisms. *Pharmacogenomics Journal, 19*, 516–527.

Badura-Brack, A., McDermott. T.J., Heinrichs-Graham. E., Ryan. T.J., Khanna, M.M., et al. (2018). Veterans with PTSD demonstrate amygdala hyperactivity while viewing threatening faces: A MEG study. *Biological Psychology, 132*, 228–232.

Bachiller, S., Jiménez-Ferrer, I., Paulus, A., Yang,Y., Swanberg, M., et al. (2018). Microglia in neurological diseases: A road map to brain-disease dependent-inflammatory response. *Frontiers in Cellular Neuroscience, 12*, 488.

Badihian, N., Daniali, S.S., & Kelishadi, R. (2020). Transcriptional and epigenetic changes of brain derived neurotrophic factor following prenatal stress: A systematic review of animal studies. *Neuroscience & Biobehavioral Reviews, 117*, 211–231.

Baer, R., Smith, G., Hopkins, J., Krietemeyer, J., & Toney, L. (2006). Using self-report assessment methods to explore facets of mindfulness. *Assessment, 13*, 27–45.

Bahji, A., Vazquez, G.H., & Zarate Jr, C.A. (2021). Comparative efficacy of racemic ketamine and esketamine for depression: A systematic review and meta-analysis. *Journal of Affective Disorders, 278*, 542–555.

Bai, M., Zhu, X., Zhang, L., Zhang, Y., Xue, L., et al. (2017). Divergent anomaly in mesocorticolimbic dopaminergic circuits might be associated with different depressive behaviors, an animal study. *Brain & Behavior, 7*, e00808.

Bai, Z., Luo, S., Zhang, L., Wu, S., & Chi, I. (2020). Acceptance and Commitment Therapy (ACT) to reduce depression: A systematic review and meta-analysis. *Journal of Affective Disorders, 260*, 728–737.

Baik, J.H. (2021). Dopaminergic control of the feeding circuit. *Endocrinology & Metabolism (Seoul), 36*, 229–239.

Bakkalci, D., Jia, Y., Winter, J. R., Lewis, J.E., Taylor, G.S., et al. (2020). Risk factors for Epstein Barr virus-associated cancers: A systematic review, critical appraisal, and mapping of the epidemiological evidence. *Journal of Global Health, 10*, 010405.

Bale, T.L. (2015). Epigenetic and transgenerational reprogramming of brain development. *Nature Reviews in Neuroscience, 16*, 332–344.

Bale, T.L. & Epperson, C.N. (2015). Sex differences and stress across the lifespan. *Nature Neuroscience, 18*, 1413–1420.

Balodis, I.M. & Potenza, M.N. (2020). Common neurobiological and psychological underpinnings of gambling and substance-use disorders. *Progress in Neuropsychopharmacology & Biological Psychiatry, 99*, 109847.

Balog, P. & Konkolÿ Thege, B. (2019). The role of vital exhaustion in predicting the recurrence of vascular events: A longitudinal study. *International Journal of Clinical Health Psychology, 19*, 75–79.

Balon, R. & Starcevic, V. (2020). Role of benzodiazepines in anxiety disorders. *Advanvces in Experimental Medicine & Biology, 119*, 367–388.

Banack, H. & Stokes, A. (2017). The 'obesity paradox' may not be a paradox at all. *International Journal of Obesity, 41*, 1162–1163.

Bandelow, B. (2020). Current and novel psychopharmacological drugs for anxiety disorders. *Advances in Experimental Medicine & Biology, 1191*, 347–365.

Bandinelli, L.P., Levandowski, M.L., & Grassi-Oliveira, R. (2017). The childhood maltreatment influences on breast cancer patients: A second wave hit model hypothesis for distinct biological and behavioral response. *Medical Hypotheses, 108*, 86–93.

Banks, W. (2019). The blood–brain barrier as an endocrine tissue. *Nature Review in Endocrinology, 15*, 444–455.

Baratta, M.V., Gruene, T.M., Dolzani, S.D., Chun, L.E., Maier, S.F., & Shansky, R.M. (2019). Controllable stress elicits circuit-specific patterns of prefrontal plasticity in males, but not females. *Brain Structure and Function, 224*, 1831–1843.

Barbhaiya, M. & Costenbader, K.H. (2016). Environmental exposures and the development of systemic lupus erythematosus. *Current Opinions in Rheumatology*, *28*, 497–505.

Barker, B., Goodman, A., & DeBeck, K. (2017). Reclaiming Indigenous identities: Culture as strength against suicide among Indigenous youth in Canada. *Canadian Journal of Public Health*, *108*, e208–e210.

Barnes, H.A., Hurley, R.A., & Taber, K.H. (2019). Moral injury and PTSD: Often co-occurring yet mechanistically different. *The Journal of Neuropsychiatry and Clinical Neurosciences*, *31*, A4–103.

Barnhofer, T., Huntenburg, J.M., Lifshitz, M., Wild, J., Antonova, E., et al. (2016). How mindfulness training may help to reduce vulnerability for recurrent depression: A neuroscientific perspective. *Clinical Psychological Science*, *4*, 328–343.

Bar-On, D. & Rottgardt, E. (1998). Reconstructing silenced biographical issues through feeling-facts. *Psychiatry*, *61*, 61–83.

Barrere-Cain, R. & Allard, P. (2020). An understudied dimension: Why age needs to be considered when studying epigenetic-environment interactions. *Epigenetics Insights*, *13*, 2516865720947014.

Barrus, M.M. & Winstanley, C.A. (2016). Dopamine D3 receptors modulate the ability of win-paired cues to increase risky choice in a rat gambling task. *Journal of Neuroscience*, *36*, 785–794.

Bar-Sela, G., Zalman, D., Semenysty, V., & Ballan, E. (2019). The effects of dosage-controlled cannabis capsules on cancer-related cachexia and anorexia syndrome in advanced cancer patients: pilot study. *Integrative Cancer Therapy*, *18*, 1534735419881498.

Bastiaanssen, T.F.S., Gururajanab, A., de Wouwab, M., Moloney, G.M., Ritzab, N.L., et al. (2021). Volatility as a concept to understand the impact of stress on the microbiome. *Psychoneuroendocrinology*, *124*, 105047.

Batty, G.D., Russ, T.C., Stamatakis, E., & Kivimäki, M. (2017). Psychological distress in relation to site specific cancer mortality: Pooling of unpublished data from 16 prospective cohort studies. *BMJ*, *356*, j108.

Baudon, P. & Jachens, L. (2021). A scoping review of interventions for the treatment of eco-anxiety. *International Journal of Environmental Research & Public Health*, *18*, 9636.

Beasley, J.M., Newcomb, P.A., Trentham-Dietz, A., Hampton, J.M., Ceballos, R.M., et al. (2010). Social networks and survival after breast cancer diagnosis. *Journal of Cancer Survivorship*, *4*, 372–380.

Beck, A.T. (2008). The evolution of the cognitive model of depression and its neurobiological correlates. *American Journal of Psychiatry*, *165*, 969–977.

Beck, A.T. & Dozois, D.J. (2011). Cognitive therapy: Current status and future directions. *Annual Review of Medicine*, *62*, 397–409.

Beck, A.T. & Haigh, E.A. (2014). Advances in cognitive theory and therapy: The generic cognitive model. *Annual Review in Clinical Psychology*, *10*, 1–24.

Beck, A.T., Rush, A.J., Shaw, B.F., & Emery, G. (1979). *Cognitive Therapy of Depression*. New York: Guilford.

Becker, J.B. (2016). Sex differences in addiction. *Dialogues in Clinical Neuroscience*, *18*, 395–402.

Beis, D., von Känel, R., Heimgartner, N., Zuccarella-Hackl, C., Bürkle, A., et al. (2018). The role of norepinephrine and α-adrenergic receptors in acute stress-induced changes in granulocytes and monocytes. *Psychosomatic Medicine, 80*, 649–658.

Bekhbat, M. & Neigh, G.N. (2018). Sex differences in the neuro-immune consequences of stress: Focus on depression and anxiety. *Brain, Behavior, and Immunity, 67*, 1–12.

Bekkar, B., Pacheco, S., Basu, R., & DeNicola, N. (2020). Association of air pollution and heat exposure with preterm birth, low birth weight, and stillbirth in the US: A systematic review. *JAMA Network Open, 3*, e208243.

Belda, X., Nadal, R., & Armario, A. (2016). Critical features of acute stress-induced cross-sensitization identified through the hypothalamic–pituitary–adrenal axis output. *Science Reports, 6*, 31244.

Bell, J.A., Hamer, M., Sabia, S., Singh-Manoux, A., Batty, G.D., & Kivimaki, M. (2015). The natural course of healthy obesity over 20 years. *Journal of the American College of Cardiology, 65*, 101–102.

Belleau, E.L., Treadway, M.T., & Pizzagalli, D.A. (2019). The impact of stress and major depressive disorder on hippocampal and medial prefrontal cortex morphology. *Biological Psychiatry, 85*, 443–453.

Bellis, M.A., Hughes, K., Ford, K., Ramos Rodriguez, G., Sethi, D., & Passmore, J. (2019). Life course health consequences and associated annual costs of adverse childhood experiences across Europe and North America: A systematic review and meta-analysis. *The Lancet Public Health, 4*, e517–e528.

Belsky, D.W., Caspi, A., Arseneault, L., Corcoran, D.L., & Domingue, B.W. (2019). Genetics and the geography of health, behaviour and attainment. *Nature Human Behaviour, 3*, 576–586.

Belsky, J., Jonassaint, C., Pluess, M., Stanton, M., Brummett, B., & Williams, R. (2009). Vulnerability genes or plasticity genes? *Molecular Psychiatry, 14*, 746–754.

Belujon, P. & Grace, A.A. (2017). Dopamine system dysregulation in major depressive disorders. *International Journal of Neuropsychopharmacology, 20*, 1036–1046.

Bergman, K., Sarkar, P., O'Connor, T.G., Modi, N., & Glover, V. (2007). Maternal stress during pregnancy predicts cognitive ability and fearfulness in infancy. *Journal of the American Academy of Child & Adolescent Psychiatry, 46*, 1454–1463.

Berkessel, J.B., Gebauer, J.E., Joshanloo, M., Bleidorn, W., Rentfrow, P.J., et al. (2021). National religiosity eases the psychological burden of poverty. *Proceedings of the National Academy of Sciences, 118*, e2103913118.

Berkman, L.F., Glass, T., Brissette, I., & Seeman, T.E. (2000). From social integration to health: Durkheim in the new millennium. *Social Science & Medicine, 51*, 843–d57.

Berridge, K.C. & Robinson, T.E. (2016). Liking, wanting, and the incentive-sensitization theory of addiction. *American Psychologist, 71*, 670–679.

Besedovsky, L., Lange, T., & Haack, M. (2019). The sleep-immune crosstalk in health and disease. *Physiological Reviews, 99*, 1325–1380.

Bharwani, A., Mian, M.F., Foster, J.A., Surette, M.G., Bienenstock, J., & Forsythe, P. (2016). Structural & functional consequences of chronic psychosocial stress on the microbiome & host. *Psychoneuroendocrinology, 63*, 217–227.

Bian, G., Gloor, G.B., Gong, A., Jia, C., Zhang, W., et al. (2017). The gut microbiota of healthy aged Chinese is similar to that of the healthy young. *mSphere, 2*, e00327-17.

Bisht, K., Sharma, K., & Tremblay, M.È. (2018). Chronic stress as a risk factor for Alzheimer's disease: Roles of microglia-mediated synaptic remodeling, inflammation, and oxidative stress. *Neurobiology of Stress, 9*, 9–21.

Bisson, J.I., Roberts, N.P., Andrew, M., Cooper, R., & Lewis, C. (2013). Psychological therapies for chronic post-traumatic stress disorder (PTSD) in adults. *Cochrane Database of Systematic Reviews, 12*.

Bjornevik, K., Cortese, M., Healy, B.C., Kuhle, J., Mina, M.J., et al. (2022). Longitudinal analysis reveals high prevalence of Epstein–Barr virus associated with multiple sclerosis. *Science, 375*, 296–301.

Black, N., Stockings, E., Campbell, G., Tran, L.T., Zagic, D., et al. (2019). Cannabinoids for the treatment of mental disorders and symptoms of mental disorders: A systematic review and meta-analysis. *The Lancet Psychiatry, 6*, 995–1010.

Black, P.H. (2006). The inflammatory consequences of psychologic stress: Relationship to insulin resistance, obesity, atherosclerosis and diabetes mellitus, type II. *Medical Hypotheses, 67*, 879–891.

Blackburn, E.H., Epel, E.S., & Lin, J. (2015). Human telomere biology: A contributory and interactive factor in aging, disease risks, and protection. *Science, 350*, 1193–1198.

Blacker, C.J, Frye, M.A., Morava, E., Kozicz, T., & Veldic, M. (2019). A review of epigenetics of PTSD in comorbid psychiatric conditions. *Genes, 10*, 140.

Blackhart, G.C., Eckel, L.A., & Tice, D.M. (2007). Salivary cortisol in response to acute social rejection and acceptance by peers. *Biological Psychology, 75*, 267–276.

Blanc-Lapierre, A., Rousseau, M.C., Weiss, D., El-Zein, M., Siemiatycki, J., et al. (2017). Lifetime report of perceived stress at work and cancer among men: A case-control study in Montreal, Canada. *Preventive Medicine, 96*, 28–35.

Bland, S.T., Tamlyn, J.P., Barrientos, R.M., Greenwood, B.N., Watkins, L.R. et al. (2007). Expression of fibroblast growth factor-2 and brain-derived neurotrophic factor mRNA in the medial prefrontal cortex and hippocampus after uncontrollable or controllable stress. *Neuroscience, 144*, 1219–1228.

Blankenstein, N.E., Peper, J.S., Crone, E.A., & van Duijvenvoorde, A.C.K. (2017). Neural mechanisms underlying risk and ambiguity attitudes. *Journal of Cognitive Neuroscience, 29*, 1845–1859.

Blier, P. (2016). Neurobiology of depression and mechanism of action of depression treatments. *Journal of Clinical Psychiatry, 77*, e319.

Blüher, M. (2020). Metabolically healthy obesity. *Endocrine Reviews, 41*, 405–420.

Bodden, C., van den Hove, D., Lesch, K.P., & Sachser, N. (2017). Impact of varying social experiences during life history on behaviour, gene expression, and vasopressin receptor gene methylation in mice. *Scientific Reports, 7*, 8719.

Boehm, J.K., Chen, Y., Williams, D.R., Ryff, C.D., & Kubzansky, L.D. (2016). Subjective well-being and cardiometabolic health: An 8–11 year study of midlife adults. *Journal of Psychosomatic Research, 85*, 1–8.

Bombay, A., Matheson, K., & Anisman, H. (2010). Decomposing identity: Differential relationships between several aspects of ethnic identity and the negative effects of perceived discrimination among First Nations adults in Canada. *Cultural Diversity and Ethnic Minority Psychology, 16*, 507–516.

Bombay, A., Matheson, K., & Anisman, H. (2011). The impact of stressors on second generation Indian Residential School survivors. *Transcultural Psychiatry, 48*, 367–391.

Bombay, A., Matheson, K., and Anisman, H. (2013). Expectations among Aboriginal Peoples in Canada regarding the potential impacts of a government apology. *Political Psychology, 34*, 443–460.

Bombay, A., Matheson, K., & Anisman H. (2014). The intergenerational effects of Indian Residential Schools: Implications for the concept of historical trauma. *Transcultural Psychiatry, 51*, 320–338.

Borba, L.A., Broseghini, L.D., Manosso, L.M., de Moura, A.B., Botelho, M.E.M. (2021). Environmental enrichment improves lifelong persistent behavioral and epigenetic changes induced by early-life stress. *Journal of Psychiatric Research, 138*, 107–116.

Borgi, M., Collacch, B., Ortona, E., & Cirulli, F. (2020). Stress and coping in women with breast cancer: Unravelling the mechanisms to improve resilience. *Neuroscience & Biobehavioral Reviews, 119*, 406–421.

Boroughs, L.K. & DeBerardinis, R.J. (2015). Metabolic pathways promoting cancer cell survival and growth. *Nature Cell Biology, 17*, 351–359.

Bountress, K.E., Wei, W., Sheerin, C., Chung, D., Amstadter, A.B., et al. (2017). Relationships between GAT1 and PTSD, depression, and substance use disorder. *Brain Science, 7*, 6.

Bowman, J.D., Surani, S., & Horseman, M.A. (2017). Endotoxin, toll-like receptor-4, and atherosclerotic heart disease. *Current Cardiology Review, 13*, 86–93.

Brady, K.T., Dansky, B.S., Sonne, S.C., & Saladin, M.E. (1998). Posttraumatic stress disorder and cocaine dependence – order of onset. *American Journal of Addictions, 7*, 128–135.

Branscombe, N. & Doosje, B. (2004). International perspectives on the experience of collective guilt. In N. Branscombe and B. Doosje (eds.), *Collective Guilt: International Perspectives.* Cambridge: Cambridge University Press.

Bratman, G.N., Anderson, C.B., Berman, M.G., Cochran, B., De Vries, S., et al. (2019). Nature and mental health: An ecosystem service perspective. *Science Advances, 5*, eaax0903.

Brave Heart, M.Y. & DeBruyn, L.M. (1998). The American Indian Holocaust: Healing historical unresolved grief. *American Indian & Alsaskan Native Mental Health Research, 8*, 56–78.

Brave Heart, M.Y.H., Chase, J., Elkins, J., & Altschul, D.B. (2011). Historical trauma among indigenous peoples of the Americas: Concepts, research, and clinical considerations. *Journal of Psychoactive Drugs, 43*, 282–290.

Bredewold, R. & Veenema, A.H. (2018). Sex differences in the regulation of social and anxiety-related behaviors: Insights from vasopressin and oxytocin brain systems. *Current Opinions in Neurobiology*, *49*, 132–140.

Brenner, L.A., Stearns-Yoder, K.A., Hoffberg, A.S., Penzenik, M.E., Starosta, A.J., et al. (2017). Growing literature but limited evidence: A systematic review regarding prebiotic and probiotic interventions for those with traumatic brain injury and/ or posttraumatic stress disorder. *Brain, Behavior, and Immunity*, *65*, 57–67.

Briones-Buixassa, L., Milà, R.M., Aragonès, J., Bufill, E., Olaya, B., & Arrufat, F.X. (2015). Stress and multiple sclerosis: A systematic review considering potential moderating and mediating factors and methods of assessing stress. *Health Psychology Open*, *2*, 2055102915612271.

Brives, C. & Pourraz, J. (2020). Phage therapy as a potential solution in the fight against AMR: Obstacles and possible futures. *Palgrave Communications*, *6*, 100.

Brivio, B., Lopez, J.P., & Chen, A. (2020). Sex differences: Transcriptional signatures of stress exposure in male and female brains. *Genes, Brain and Behavior*, *19*, e12643.

Bromis, K., Calem, M., Reinders, A.A.T.S., Williams, S.C.R., & Kempton, M.J. (2018). Meta-Analysis of 89 Structural MRI studies in posttraumatic stress disorder and comparison with major depressive disorder. *American Journal of Psychiatry*, *175*, 989–998.

Brosseron, F., Maass, A., Kleineidam, L., Ravichandran, K.A., González, P.G., et al. (2022). Soluble TAM receptors sAXL and sTyro3 predict structural and functional protection in Alzheimer's disease. *Neuron*, *110*, 1009–1022.

Brown, A.S., Davis, J.M., Murphy, E.A., Carmichael, M.D., Carson, J.A., et al. (2007). Susceptibility to HSV-1 infection and exercise stress in female mice: Role of estrogen. *Journal of Applied Physiology*, *103*, 1592–1597.

Brown, A.S. & Derkits, E.J. (2010). Prenatal infection and schizophrenia: a review of epidemiologic and translational studies. *American Journal of Psychiatry*, *167*, 261–280.

Brown, K.W. & Ryan, R. (2003). The benefits of being present: Mindfulness and its role in psychological well-being. *Journal of Personality and Social Psychology*, *84*, 822–848.

Brown, R.P. & Phillips, A. (2005). Letting bygones be bygones: Further evidence for the validity of the tendency to forgive scale. *Personality and Individual Differences*, *38*, 627–638.

Browne, C. & Winkelman, C. (2007). The effect of childhood trauma on later psychological adjustment. *Journal of Interpersonal Violence*, *22*, 684–697.

Browne, C.J., Godino, A., Salery, M., & Nestler, E.J. (2020). Epigenetic mechanisms of opioid addiction. *Biological Psychiatry*, *87*, 22–33.

Brunet, A., Saumier, D., Liu, A., Streiner, D.L., Tremblay, J., & Pitman, R.K. (2018). Reduction of PTSD symptoms with pre-reactivation propranolol therapy: A randomized controlled trial. *American Journal of Psychiatry*, *175*, 427–433.

Brunst, K.J., Zhang, L., Zhang, X., Baccarelli, A.A., Bloomquist, T., & Wright, R.J. (2021). Associations between maternal lifetime stress and placental mitochondrial DNA mutations in an urban multiethnic cohort. *Biological Psychiatry, 89*, 570–578.

Brydon, L., Walker, C., Wawrzyniak, A.J., Chart, H., & Steptoe, A. (2009). Dispositional optimism and stress-induced changes in immunity and negative mood. *Brain, Behavior, and Immunity, 23*, 810–816.

Bu, F., Zaninotto, P., & Fancourt, D. (2020). Longitudinal associations between loneliness, social isolation and cardiovascular events. *Heart, 106*, 1394–1399.

Budiu, R.A., Vlad, A.M., Nazario, L., Bathula, C., Cooper, K.L., et al. (2017). Restraint and social isolation stressors differentially regulate adaptive immunity and tumor angiogenesis in a breast cancer mouse model. *Cancer & Clinical Oncology, 6*, 12–24.

Bufill, E., Olaya, B., & Arrufat, F.X. (2015). Stress and multiple sclerosis: A systematic review considering potential moderating and mediating factors and methods of assessing stress. *Health Psychology Open, 2*, 2055102915612271.

Burattini, C., Gill, T.M., Aicardi, G., & Janak, P.H. (2006). The ethanol self-administration context as a reinstatement cue: Acute effects of naltrexone. *Neuroscience, 139*, 877–887.

Burgess, R.A., Osborne, R.H., Yongabi, K.A., Greenhalgh, T., & Gurdasani, D. (2021). The COVID-19 vaccines rush: Participatory community engagement matters more than ever. *The Lancet, 397*, 8–10.

Burnett, F.M. (1970). The concept of immunological surveillance. *Progress in Experimental Tumor Research, 13*, 1–27.

Busch, E.L., Whitsel, E.A., Kroenke, C.H., & Yang, Y.C. (2018). Social relationships, inflammation markers, and breast cancer incidence in the women's health initiative. *Breast, 39*, 63–69.

Cacioppo, J.T., Cacioppo, S., & Boomsma, D.I. (2014). Evolutionary mechanisms for loneliness. *Cognition & Emotion, 28*, 3–21.

Cacioppo, S., Grippo, A.J., London, S., Goossens, L., & Cacioppo, J.T. (2015). Loneliness: Clinical import and interventions. *Perspectives on Psychological Science, 10*, 238–249.

Cadamuro, A., Birtel, M.D., Di Bernardo, G.A., Crapolicchio, E., Vezzali, L., & Drury, J. (2021). Resilience in children in the aftermath of disasters: A systematic review and a new perspective on individual, interpersonal, group, and intergroup level factors. *Journal of Community & Applied Social Psychology, 31*, 259–275.

Cai, L. & He, L. (2019). Placebo effects and the molecular biological components involved. *General Psychiatry, 32*, e100089.

Cain, D.W. & Cidlowski, J.A. (2017). Immune regulation by glucocorticoids. *Nature Reviews in Immunology, 17*, 233–247.

Caldirola, D., Alciati, A., Daccò, S., Micieli, W., & Perna, G. (2020). Relapse prevention in panic disorder with pharmacotherapy: where are we now? *Expert Opinion on Pharmacotherapy, 21*, 1699–1711.

Cameron, L.P., Tombari, R.J., Lu, J., Pell, A.J., Hurley, Z.Q., et al. (2021). A non-hallucinogenic psychedelic analogue with therapeutic potential. *Nature, 589*, 474–479.

Campbell, K.L., Landells, C.E., Fan. J., & Brenner, D.R. (2018). A systematic review of the effect of lifestyle interventions on adipose tissue gene expression: Implications for carcinogenesis. *Nature Communications, 9*, 5379.

Cantoni, C., Lin, Q., Dorsett, Y., Ghezzi, L., Liu, Z., et al. (2022). Alterations of host-gut microbiome interactions in multiple sclerosis. *eBioMedicine, 76*, 103798.

Cao-Lei, L., De Rooij, S.R., King, S., Matthews, S.G., Metz, G.A.S., et al. (2020). Prenatal stress and epigenetics. *Neuroscience & Biobehavioral Reviews, 117*, 198–210.

Capistrant, B.D., Moon, J.R., Berkman, L.F., & Glymour, M.M. (2012). Current and long-term spousal caregiving and onset of cardiovascular disease. *Journal of Epidemiology and Community Health, 66*, 951–956.

Cardoso, C., Kingdon, D., & Ellenbogen, M.A. (2014). A meta-analytic review of the impact of intranasal oxytocin administration on cortisol concentrations during laboratory tasks: Moderation by method and mental health. *Psychoneuroendocrinology, 49*, 161–170.

Carhart-Harris, R.L. & Nutt, D.J. (2017). Serotonin and brain function: A tale of two receptors. *Journal of Psychopharmacology, 31*, 1091–1120.

Carlyle, M., Broomby, R., Simpson, G., Hannon, R., Fawaz, L., et al. (2021). A randomised, double-blind study investigating the relationship between early childhood trauma and the rewarding effects of morphine. *Addiction Biology, 26*, e13047.

Carney, R.M. & Freedland, K.E. (2017). Depression and coronary heart disease. *Nature Reviews in Cardiology, 14*, 145–155.

Carter, E.E., Barr, S.G., & Clarke, A.E. (2016). The global burden of SLE: Prevalence, health disparities and socioeconomic impact. *Nature Reviews in Rheumatology, 12*, 605–620.

Carver, C.S. & Connor-Smith, J. (2010). Personality and coping. *Annual Review of Psychology, 61*, 679–704.

Carver, C.S., Scheier, M.F., & Weintraub, J.K. (1989). Assessing coping strategies: A theoretically based approach. *Journal of Personality and Social Psychology, 56*, 267–283.

Caspi, A., Sugden, K., Moffitt, T.E., Taylor, A., Craig, I.W., et al. (2003). Influence of life stress on depression: Moderation by a polymorphism in the 5-HTT gene. *Science, 301*, 386–389.

Castro, D.C. & Berridge, K.C. (2014). Opioid hedonic hotspot in nucleus accumbens shell: Mu, delta, and kappa maps for enhancement of sweetness "liking" and "wanting". *Journal of Neuroscience, 34*, 4239–4250.

Cavalli, G. & Heard, E. (2019). Advances in epigenetics link genetics to the environment and disease. *Nature, 571*, 489–499.

Cavanaugh, R. (2017). Dixon Chibanda – "Taking mental health to the community". *The Lancet Psychiatry, 4*, 833.

Chaby, L.E., Sadik, N., Burson, N.A., Lloyd, S., O'Donnel, K., et al. (2020). Repeated stress exposure in mid-adolescence attenuates behavioral, noradrenergic, and epigenetic effects of trauma-like stress in early adult male rats. *Science Reports, 10*, 17935.

Chaki, S. (2021). Vasopressin V1B receptor antagonists as potential antidepressants. *International Journal of Neuropsychopharmacology*, *24*, 450–463.

Champagne, F.A. & Curley, J.P. (2009). Epigenetic mechanisms mediating the long-term effects of maternal care on development. *Neuroscience & Biobehavioral Reviews*, *33*, 593–600.

Chan, J.C., Nugent, B.M., & Bale, T.L. (2018). Parental advisory: Maternal and paternal stress can impact offspring neurodevelopment. *Biological Psychiatry*, *83*, 886–894.

Chan, K., Nestor, J., Huerta, T.S., Certain, N., Moody, G., et al. (2020). Lupus autoantibodies act as positive allosteric modulators at GluN2A-containing NMDA receptors and impair spatial memory. *Nature Communications*, *11*, 1403.

Chang, S.H., Yu, Y.H., He, A., Ou, C.Y., Shyu, B.C., & Huang, A.C.W. (2021). BDNF protein and BDNF mRNA expression of the medial prefrontal cortex, amygdala, and hippocampus during situational reminder in the PTSD animal model. *Behavioral Neurology*, *2021*, 6657716.

Charmchi, E., Zendehdel, M., & Haghparast, A. (2016). The effect of forced swim stress on morphine sensitization: Involvement of D1/D2-like dopamine receptors within the nucleus accumbens. *Progress in Neuropsychopharmacology & Biological Psychiatry*, *70*, 92–99.

Chat, I.K.Y., Nusslock, R., Moriarity, D.P., Bart, C.P., Mac Giollabhui, N., et al. (2021). Goal-striving tendencies moderate the relationship between reward-related brain function and peripheral inflammation. *Brain, Behavior, and Immunity*, *94*, 60–70.

Chaudhury, D., Walsh, J.J., Friedman, A.K., Juarez, B., Ku, S.M., et al. (2013). Rapid regulation of depression-related behaviours by control of midbrain dopamine neurons. *Nature*, *493*, 532–536.

Chee, M.J., Koziel Ly, N.K., Anisman, H., & Matheson, K. (2020). Piece of cake: Coping with COVID-19. *Nutrients*, *12*, 3803.

Chen, Y. & Baram, T.Z. (2016). Toward understanding how early-life stress reprograms cognitive and emotional brain networks. *Neuropsychopharmacology*, *41*, 197–206.

Chervyakov, A.V., Chernyavsky, A.Y., Sinitsyn, D.O., & Piradov, M.A. (2015). Possible mechanisms underlying the therapeutic effects of transcranial magnetic stimulation. *Frontiers in Human Neuroscience*, *9*, 303.

Chida, Y. & Mao, X. (2009). Does psychosocial stress predict symptomatic herpes simplex virus recurrence? A meta-analytic investigation on prospective studies. *Brain, Behavior, and Immunity*, *23*, 917–925.

Chida, Y. & Steptoe, A. (2010). The association of anger and hostility with future coronary heart disease: A meta-analytic review of prospective evidence. *Journal of the American College of Cardiology*, *53*, 936–946.

Chinna Meyyappan, A., Forth, E., Wallace, C.J.K. & Milev, R. (2020). Effect of fecal microbiota transplant on symptoms of psychiatric disorders: a systematic review. *BMC Psychiatry*, *20*, 299.

Chiong, R., Budhi, G.S., Dhakal, S., & Chiong, F. (2021). A textual-based featuring approach for depression detection using machine learning classifiers and social media texts. *Computers in Biology & Medicine*, *135*, 104499.

Chiriac, V.F., Baban, A., & Dumitrascu, D.L. (2018). Psychological stress and breast cancer incidence: a systematic review. *Clujul Medical, 91*, 18–26.

Choudhury, A., Aron, S., Botigué, L.R., Sengupta, D., Botha, et al. (2020). High-depth African genomes inform human migration and health. *Nature, 586*, 741–748.

Chu, D.M., Ma, J., Prince, A.L., Antony, K.M., Seferovic, M.D., & Aagaard, K.M. (2017). Maturation of the infant microbiome community structure and function across multiple body sites and in relation to mode of delivery. *Nature Medicine, 23*, 314–326.

Churchwell, K., Elkind, M.S.V., Benjamin, R.M., Carson, A.P., Chang, E.K., et al. (2020). American Heart Association. Call to action: structural racism as a fundamental driver of health disparities: A presidential advisory from the American Heart Association. *Circulation, 142*, e454–e468.

Ciavarra, R.P., Machida, M., Lundberg, P.S., Gauronskas, P., Wellman, L.L., et al. (2018). Controllable and uncontrollable stress differentially impact pathogenicity and survival in a mouse model of viral encephalitis. *Journal of Neuroimmunology, 319*, 130–141.

Cipponi, A., Goode, D.L., Bedo, J., McCabe, M.J., & Pajic, M. (2020). MTOR signaling orchestrates stress-induced mutagenesis, facilitating adaptive evolution in cancer. *Science, 368*, 1127–1131.

Clement, S., Schauman, O., Graham, T., Maggioni, F., & Evans-Lacko, S. (2015). What is the impact of mental health-related stigma on help-seeking? A systematic review of quantitative and qualitative studies. *Psychological Medicine, 45*, 11–27.

Cloitre, M. (2020). ICD-11 complex post-traumatic stress disorder: simplifying diagnosis in trauma populations. *British Journal of Psychiatry, 216*, 129–131.

Cohen, F., Kemeny, M.E., Zegans, L.S, Johnson, P., Kearney, K.A., & Stites, D.P. (2007). Immune function declines with unemployment and recovers after stressor termination. *Psychosomatic Medicine, 69*, 225–234.

Cohen, R., Bavishi, C., Haider, S., Thankachen, J., & Rozanski, A. (2017). Meta-analysis of relation of vital exhaustion to cardiovascular disease events. *American Journal of Cardiology, 119*, 1211–1216.

Cohen, S. (2021). Psychosocial vulnerabilities to upper respiratory infectious illness: implications for susceptibility to coronavirus disease 2019 (COVID-19). *Perspectives in Psychological Science, 16*, 161–174.

Cohen, S., Evans, G.W., Stokols, D., & Krantz, D.S. (1986). *Behavior, Health, and Environmental Stress*. New York: Plenum.

Cohen, S., Janicki-Deverts, D., Doyle, W.J., Miller, G.E., Frank, E., et al. (2012). Chronic stress, glucocorticoid receptor resistance, inflammation, and disease risk. *PNAS, 109*, 5995–5999.

Cohen, S., Kamarck, T., & Mermelstein, R. (1983). A global measure of perceived stress. *Journal of Health and Social Behavior, 24*, 385–396.

Cohen, S., Miller, G.E., & Rabin, B.S. (2001). Psychological stress and antibody response to immunization: A critical review of the human literature. *Psychosomatic Medicine, 63*, 7–18.

Cohen, S., Tyrrel, D.A.G., & Smith, A.P. (1991). Psychological stress and susceptibility to the common cold. *New England Journal of Medicine, 325,* 606–612.

Colagiuri, B., Schenk, L.A., Kessler, M.D., Dorsey, S.G. & Colloca, L. (2015). The placebo effect: From concepts to genes. *Neuroscience, 307,* 171–190.

Colonna, M. & Butovsky, O. (2017). Microglia function in the central nervous system during health and neurodegeneration. *Annual Review of Immunology, 35,* 441–468.

Colpaert, R.M.W. & Calore, M. (2021). Epigenetics and microRNAs in cardiovascular diseases. *Genomics, 113,* 540–551.

Concetta, G., Teresa, F., Blerta, S., & Fabio, G., (2022). A short Mindfulness retreat can improve biological markers of stress and inflammation. *Psychoneuroendocrinology, 135,* 105579.

Corrigan, P.W., Rafacz, J., & Rüsch, N. (2011). Examining a progressive model of self-stigma and its impact on people with serious mental illness. *Psychiatry Research, 189,* 339–343.

Costa, D.L.C., Diniz, J.B., Requena, G., Joaquim, M.A., Pittenger, C. et al., (2017). Randomized, double-blind, placebo-controlled trial of N-Acetylcysteine augmentation for treatment-resistant obsessive-compulsive disorder. *Journal of Clinical Psychiatry, 78,* e766–e773.

Costa, P. & McCrae, R. (1992). *Revised NEO Personality Inventory (NEO-PI-R) and NEO Five-Factor Inventory (NEO-FFI) Manual.* Odessa, FL: Psychological Assessment Resources.

Costi, S., Morris, L.S., Collins, A., Fernandez, N.F., Patel, M., et al. (2021). Peripheral immune cell reactivity and neural response to reward in patients with depression and anhedonia. *Translational Psychiatry, 11,* 565.

Cottagiri, S.A., Villeneuve, P.J., Raina, P., Griffith, L.E., & Rainham, D. (2022). Increased urban greenness associated with improved mental health among middle-aged and older adults of the Canadian Longitudinal Study on Aging (CLSA). *Environmental Research, 206,* 112587.

Coulon, M., Nowak, R., Andanson, S., Ravel, C., Marnet, P.G., et al. (2013). Human–lamb bonding: oxytocin, cortisol and behavioural responses of lambs to human contacts and social separation. *Psychoneuroendocrinology, 38,* 499–508.

Covington, H.E., Maze, I., LaPlant, Q.C., Vialou, V.F., Ohnishi, Y.N., et al. (2009). Antidepressant actions of histone deacetylase inhibitors. *The Journal of Neuroscience, 29,* 11451–11460.

Covington, H.E., Maze, I., Sun, H., Bomze, H.M., DeMaio, K.D., et al. (2011). A role for repressive histone methylation in cocaine-induced vulnerability to stress. *Neuron, 71,* 656–670.

Cowan, C.S.M., Stylianakis, A.A., & Richardson, R. (2019). Early-life stress, microbiota, and brain development: Probiotics reverse the effects of maternal separation on neural circuits underpinning fear expression and extinction in infant rats. *Developmental & Cognitive Neuroscience, 37,* 100627.

Coyne, J. (2012). Troubles in the branding of psychotherapies as "evidence supported". PLoS Blogs. https://web.archive.org/web/20160304014203/http://blogs.plos.org/mindthebrain/2012/10/22/troubles-in-the-branding-of-psychotherapies-as-evidence-supported/. Accessed August 2021.

Crawford, L.S., Mills, E.P., Hanson, T., Macey, P.M., Glarin, R., et al. (2021). Brainstem mechanisms of pain modulation: A within-subjects 7T fMRI study of Placebo Analgesic and Nocebo Hyperalgesic Responses. *Journal of Neuroscience, 41*, 9794–9806.

Creswell, J.D., Irwin, M.R., Burklund, L.J., Lieberman, M.D., Arevalo, J.M., et al. (2012). Mindfulness-based stress reduction training reduces loneliness and pro-inflammatory gene expression in older adults: A small randomized controlled trial. *Brain, Behavior, and Immunity, 26*, 1095–1101.

Crumeyrolle-Arias, M., Jaglin, M., Bruneau, A., Vancassel, S., Cardona, A., et al. (2014). Absence of the gut microbiota enhances anxiety-like behavior and neuroendocrine response to acute stress in rats. *Psychoneuroendocrinology, 42*, 207–217.

Cruwys, T., Haslam, S.A., Dingle, G.A., Jetten, J., Hornsey, M.J., et al. (2014). Feeling connected again: Interventions that increase social identification reduce depression symptoms in community and clinical settings. *Jourrnal of Affective Disorders, 159*, 139–146.

Cryan, J.F., O'Riordan, K.J., Cowan, C.S.M., Sandhu, K.V., Bastiaanssen, T.F.S., et al. (2019). The microbiota-gut-brain axis. *Physiological Reviews, 99*, 1877–2013.

Cui, B., Peng, F., Lu, J., He, B., Su, Q., et al. (2021). Cancer and stress: NextGen strategies. *Brain, Behavior, and Immunity, 93*, 368–383.

Cui, B., Su, D., Li, W., She, X., Zhang, M. et al. (2018). Effects of chronic noise exposure on the microbiome-gut-brain axis in senescence-accelerated prone mice: Implications for Alzheimer's disease. *Journal of Neuroinflammation, 15*, 190.

Culverhouse, R.C., Saccone, N.L., Horton, A.C., Ma, Y., Anstey, K.J., et al. (2018). Collaborative meta-analysis finds no evidence of a strong interaction between stress and 5-mediating stress phenotypes of offspring. *European Journal of Neuroscience, 53*, 271–280.

Cunningham, A.M., Walker, D.M., & Nestler, E.J. (2021). Paternal transgenerational epigenetic mechanisms mediating stress phenotypes of offspring. *European Journal of Neuroscience, 53*, 271–280.

Cunsolo, A. & Ellis, N.R. (2018). Ecological grief as a mental health response to climate change-related loss. *Nature Climate Change, 8*, 275–281.

Curry, O.S., Alfano, M., Brandt, M.J., & Pelican, C. (2021). Moral molecules: Morality as a combinatorial system. *Review of Philosophy and Psychology*, 1–20.

Cuthbert, B.N. & Insel, T.R. (2013). Toward the future of psychiatric diagnosis: the seven pillars of RDoC. *BMC Medicine, 11*, 126.

Czéh, B., Vardya, I., Varga, Z., Febbraro, F., Csabai, D., et al. (2018). Long-term stress disrupts the structural and functional integrity of GABAergic neuronal networks in the medial prefrontal cortex of rats. *Frontiers in Cellular Neuroscience, 12*, 148.

Dahlgren, M.K., Laifer, L.M., VanElzakker, M.B., Offringa, R., & Hughes, K.C. (2018). Diminished medial prefrontal cortex activation during the recollection of stressful events is an acquired characteristic of PTSD. *Psychological Medicine, 48*, 1128–1138.

Dallman, M.F. (2010). Stress-induced obesity and the emotional nervous system. *Trends in Endocrinology and Metabolism, 21*, 159–165.

Damien, J., Colloca, L., Bellei-Rodriguez, C.É., & Marchand, S. (2018). Pain modulation: From conditioned pain modulation to placebo and nocebo effects in experimental and clinical pain. *International Review of Neurobiology, 139*, 255–296.

Dan, R., Canetti, L., Keadan, T., Segman, R., Weinstock, M. et al. (2019). Sex differences during emotion processing are dependent on the menstrual cycle phase. *Psychoneuroendocrinology, 100*, 85–95.

Dane, E., Rockmann, K.W., & Pratt, M.G. (2012). When should I trust my gut? Linking domain expertise to intuitive decision-making effectiveness. *Organizational Behavior and Human Decision Processes, 119*, 187–194.

Danieli, Y. (1998). *International Handbook of Multigenerational Legacies of Trauma.* New York: Plenum.

Daniels, S., Lemaire, D., Lapointe, T., Limebeer, C., Parker, L., & Leri, F. (2021). Effects of inescapable stress on responses to social incentive stimuli and modulation by escitalopram. *Psychopharmacology, 238*, 32398–33247.

Danielson, A.M., Matheson, K., & Anisman, H. (2011). Cytokine levels at a single time point following a reminder stimulus among women in abusive dating relationships: Relationship to emotional states. *Psychoneuroendocrinology, 36*, 40–50.

Dantzer, R., O'Connor, J.C., Lawson, M.A., & Kelley, K.W. (2011). Inflammation-associated depression: From serotonin to kynurenine. *Psychoneuroendocrinology, 36*, 426–436.

Dashorst, P., Mooren, T.M., Kleber, R.J., de Jong, P.J., & Huntjens, R.J.C. (2019). Intergenerational consequences of the Holocaust on offspring mental health: A systematic review of associated factors and mechanisms. *European Journal of Psychotraumatology, 10*, 1654065.

Daskalakis, N.P., Bagot, R.C., Parker, K.J., Vinkers, C.H., & de Kloet, E.R. (2013). The three-hit concept of vulnerability and resilience: Toward understanding adaptation to early-life adversity outcome. *Psychoneuroendocrinology, 38*, 1858–1873.

Davies, C., Segre, G., Estradé, A., Radua, J., De Micheli, A., et al. (2020). Prenatal and perinatal risk and protective factors for psychosis: A systematic review and meta-analysis. *The Lancet Psychiatry, 7*, 399–410.

Davis, A.K., Barrett, F.S., May, D.G., Cosimano, M.P., & Sepeda, N.D. (2021). Effects of psilocybin-assisted therapy on major depressive disorder: A randomized clinical trial. *JAMA Psychiatry, 78*, 481–489.

Davis, M.T., Hillmer, A., Holmes, S.E., Pietrzak, R.H., DellaGioia, N., et al. (2019). In vivo evidence for dysregulation of mGluR5 as a biomarker of suicidal ideation. *PNAS, 116*, 11490–11495.

de Agüero, M.G., Ganal-Vonarburg, S.C., Fuhrer, T., Rupp, S., Uchimura, Y., et al. (2016). The maternal microbiota drives early postnatal innate immune development. *Science, 351*, 1296–1302.

Declerck, C.H., Boone, C., Pauwels, L. Vogt, B., & Fehr, E. (2020). A registered replication study on oxytocin and trust. *Nature Human Behavior, 4*, 646–655.

De Crescenzo, F., Ciabattini, M., D'Alò, G.L., De Giorgi, R., & Del Giovane, C. (2018). Comparative efficacy and acceptability of psychosocial interventions for individuals with cocaine and amphetamine addiction: A systematic review and network meta-analysis. *PLoS Medicine, 15*, e1002715.

Dedic, N., Chen, A., & Deussing, J.M. (2018). The CRF family of neuropeptides and their receptors – mediators of the central stress response. *Current Molecular Pharmacology, 11*, 4–31.

Dedic, N., Kühne, C., Gomes, K.S., Hartmann, J., Ressler, K.J., et al. (2019). Deletion of CRH from GABAergic forebrain neurons promotes stress resilience and dampens stress-induced changes in neuronal activity. *Frontiers in Neuroscience, 12*, 986.

De Dreu, C.K. (2012). Oxytocin modulates cooperation within and competition between groups: An integrative review and research agenda. *Hormones and Behavior, 61*, 419–428.

DeGroot, S.R., Zhao-Shea, R., Chung, L., Klenowski, P.M., Sun, F., et al. (2020). Midbrain dopamine controls anxiety-like behavior by engaging unique interpeduncular nucleus microcircuitry. *Biological Psychiatry, 88*, 855–866.

De Hert, M., Detraux, J., & Vancampfort, D. (2018). The intriguing relationship between coronary heart disease and mental disorders. *Dialogues in Clinical Neuroscience, 20*, 31–40.

Deijns, S.J., Broen, J.C.A., Kruyt, N.D., Schubart. C.D., Andreoli, L., et al. (2020). The immunologic etiology of psychiatric manifestations in systemic lupus erythematosus: A narrative review on the role of the blood brain barrier, antibodies, cytokines and chemokines. *Autoimmunity Reviews, 19*, 102592.

Del Giudice, M. & Gangestad, S.W. (2018). Rethinking IL-6 and CRP: Why they are more than inflammatory biomarkers, and why it matters. *Brain, Behavior, and Immunity, 70*, 61–75.

DelFattore, J. (2019). Death by stereotype? Cancer treatment in unmarried patients. *New Englnd Journal of Medicine, 381*, 982–985.

Del-Pino-Casado, R., Rodríguez Cardosa, M., López-Martínez, C., & Orgeta, V. (2019). The association between subjective caregiver burden and depressive symptoms in carers of older relatives: A systematic review and meta-analysis. *PLoS One, 14*, e0217648.

DeLongis, A. & Holtzman, S. (2005). Coping in context: The role of stress, social support, and personality in coping. *Journal of Personality, 73*, 1633–1656.

Demaria, O., Cornen, S., Daëron, M., Morel, Y., Medzhitov, R., & Vivier, E. (2019). Harnessing innate immunity in cancer therapy. *Nature, 574*, 45–56.

Den, H., Dong, X., Chen, M., & Zou, Z. (2020). Efficacy of probiotics on cognition, and biomarkers of inflammation and oxidative stress in adults with Alzheimer's disease or mild cognitive impairment – a meta-analysis of randomized controlled trials. *Aging, 12*, 4010–4039.

Denham, J. (2018). Exercise and epigenetic inheritance of disease risk. *Acta Physiologica, 222*.

Denollet, J., Schiffer, A.A., & Spek, V. (2010). A general propensity to psychological distress affects cardiovascular outcomes: Evidence from research on the type D (distressed) personality profile. *Circulation: Cardiovascular Quality and Outcomes*, *3*, 546–557.

De Padova, S., Grassi, L., Vagheggini, A., Belvederi Murri, M., Folesani, F., et al. (2021). Post-traumatic stress symptoms in long-term disease-free cancer survivors and their family caregivers. *Cancer Medicine*, *10*, 3974–3985.

De Palma, G., Blennerhassett, P., Lu, J., Deng, Y., Park, A.J., et al. (2015). Microbiota and host determinants of behavioural phenotype in maternally separated mice. *Nature Communications*, *6*, 7735.

DiRenzo, D., Crespo-Bosque, M., Gould, N., Finan, P., Nanavati, J., & Bingham, C.O. (2018). Systematic review and meta-analysis: mindfulness-based interventions for rheumatoid arthritis. *Current Rheumatology Reports*, *20*, 75.

Desalu, J.M., Goodhines, P.A., & Park, A. (2019). Racial discrimination and alcohol use and negative drinking consequences among Black Americans: A meta-analytical review. *Addiction*, *114*, 957–967.

Deshpande, R.P., Sharma, S., & Watabe, K. (2020). The confounders of cancer immunotherapy: Roles of lifestyle, metabolic disorders and sociological factors. *Cancers (Basel)*, *12*, 2983.

Destoumieux-Garzón, D., Mavingui, P., Boetsch, G., Boissier, J., & Darriet, F. (2018). The one health concept: 10 years old and a long road ahead. *Frontiers in Veterinary Science*, *5*, 14.

De Vita, M.J., Maisto, S.A., Gilmour, C.E., McGuire, L., Tarvin, E., & Moskal, D. (2021). The effects of cannabidiol and analgesic expectancies on experimental pain reactivity in healthy adults: A balanced placebo design trial. *Experimental and Clinical Psychopharmacology*, *10*.1037.

Dewall, C.N., Macdonald, G., Webster, G.D., Masten, C.L., Baumeister, R.F., et al. (2010). Acetaminophen reduces social pain: Behavioral and neural evidence. *Psychological Science*, *21*, 931–937.

Deyama, S., Bang, E., Kato, T., Li, X.Y., & Duman, R.S. (2019). Neurotrophic and antidepressant actions of brain-derived neurotrophic factor require vascular endothelial growth factor. *Biological Psychiatry*, *86*, 143–152.

Dhabhar, F.S. (2018). The short-term stress response – Mother Nature's mechanism for enhancing protection and performance under conditions of threat, challenge, and opportunity. *Frontiers in Neuroendocrinology*, *49*, 175–192.

Dhabhar, F.S. (2014). Effects of stress on immune function: The good, the bad, and the beautiful. *Immunology Research*, *58*, 193–210.

Dhabhar, F.S. (2009). Enhancing versus suppressive effects of stress on immune function: Implications for immunoprotection and immunopathology. *Neuroimmunomodulation*, *16*, 300–317.

Dhakan, D., Maji, A., Sharma, A., Saxena, R., Pulikkan, J., et al. (2019). The unique composition of Indian gut microbiome, gene catalogue, and associated fecal metabolome deciphered using multi-omics approaches. *GigaScience*, *8*, 1–20.

Diamond, J. (1997). *Guns, Germs, and Steel*. New York: W.W. Norton.

Diana, M., Raij, T., Melis, M., Nummenmaa, A., Leggio, L., & Bonci, A. (2017). Rehabilitating the addicted brain with transcranial magnetic stimulation. *Nature Reviews in Neuroscience*, *18*, 685–693.

Dich, N., Rozing, M.P., Kivimäki, M., & Doan, S.N. (2020). Life events, emotions, and immune function: Evidence from Whitehall II cohort study. *Behavioral Medicine, 46*, 153–160.

Dickens, L.R. (2017). Using gratitude to promote positive change: A series of meta-analyses investigating the effectiveness of gratitude interventions. *Basic and Applied Social Psychology, 39*, 193–208.

Dickerson, S. & Kemeny, M. (2004). Acute stressors and cortisol responses: A theoretical integration and synthesis of laboratory research. *Psychological Bulletin, 130*, 355–391.

Dietz, D.M., Laplant, Q., Watts, E.L., Hodes, G.E., Russo, S.J., et al. (2011). Paternal transmission of stress-induced pathologies. *Biological Psychiatry, 70*, 408–414.

Di Forti, M., Quattrone, D., Freeman, T.P., Tripoli, G., Gayer-Anderson, C., et al. (2019). Disorder across Europe (EU-GEI): A multicentre case-control study. *The Lancet Psychiatry, 6*, 427–436.

Dimidi, E., Cox, S.R., Rossi, M., & Whelan, K. (2019). Fermented foods: Definitions and characteristics, impact on the gut microbiota and effects on gastrointestinal health and disease. *Nutrients, 11*, 1806.

Dinan, T.G. & Cryan, J.F. (2017). Gut instincts: Microbiota as a key regulator of brain development, ageing and neurodegeneration. *Journal of Physiology, 595*, 489–503.

Dingle, G.A., Sharman, L.S., Haslam, C., Donald, M., Turner, C., et al. (2020). The effects of social group interventions for depression: Systematic review. *Journal of Affective Disorders, 281*, 67–81.

Di Nicola, M., De Crescenzo, F., D'Alò, G.L., Remondi, C., Panaccione, I., et al. (2020). Pharmacological and psychosocial treatment of adults with gambling disorder: A meta-review. *Journal of Addiction Medicine, 14*, e15–e23.

DiSabato, D.J., Nemeth, D.P., Liu, X., Witcher, K.G., & O'Neil, S.M. (2021). Interleukin-1 receptor on hippocampal neurons drives social withdrawal and cognitive deficits after chronic social stress. *Molecular Psychiatry, 26*, 4770–4782.

Disner, S.G., Beevers, C.G., Haigh, E.A., & Beck, A.T. (2011). Neural mechanisms of the cognitive model of depression. *Nature Reviews Neuroscience, 12*, 467–477.

Douma, E.H. & de Kloet, E.R. (2020). Stress-induced plasticity and functioning of ventral tegmental dopamine neurons. *Neuroscience & Biobehavioral Reviews, 108*, 48–77.

Dourado, E., Ferro, M., Sousa Guerreirom C., & Fonsecam, J.E. (2020). Diet as a modulator of intestinal microbiota in rheumatoid arthritis. *Nutrients, 12*, 3504.

Driscoll, M.A., Edwards, R.R., Becker, W.C., Kaptchuk, T.J., & Kerns, R.D. (2021). Psychological interventions for the treatment of chronic pain in adults. *Psychological Science in the Public Interest, 22*, 52–95.

Drury, J., Carter, H., Cocking, C., Ntontis, E., & Guven, S.K. (2019). Facilitating collective psychosocial resilience in the public in emergencies: Twelve recommendations based on the social identity approach. *Frontiers in Public Health, 7*, 141.

Drysdale, A.T., Grosenick, L., Downar, J., Dunlop, K., Mansouri, F., et al. (2017). Resting-state connectivity biomarkers define neurophysiological subtypes of depression. *Nature Medicine, 23*, 28–38.

Duman, R.S., Aghajanian, G.K., Sanacora, G., & Krystal, J.H. (2016). Synaptic plasticity and depression: new insights from stress and rapid-acting antidepressants. *Nature Medicine, 22*, 238–249.

Duman, R.S. & Monteggia, L.M. (2006). A neurotrophic model for stress-related mood disorders. *Biological Psychiatry, 59*, 1116–1127.

Duman, R.S., Sanacora, G., & Krystal, J.H. (2019). Altered connectivity in depression: GABA and glutamate neurotransmitter deficits and reversal by novel treatments. *Neuron, 102*, 75–90.

Egecioglu, E., Skibicka, K.P., Hansson, C., Alvarez-Crespo, M., Friberg, P.A., et al. (2011). Hedonic and incentive signals for body weight control. *Reviews in Endocrine and Metabolic Disorders, 12*, 141–151.

Eidelman, S. & Biernat, M. (2003). Derogating black sheep: Individual or group protection? *Journal of Experimental Social Psychology, 39*, 602–609.

Einvik, G., Dammen, T., Namtvedt, S.K., Hrubos-Strøm, H., Randby, A., et al. (2014). Type D personality is associated with increased prevalence of ventricular arrhythmias in community-residing persons without coronary heart disease. *European Journal of Preventive Cardiology, 21*, 592–600.

Eisenberger, N.I., Inagaki, T.K., Mashal, N.M., & Irwin, M.R. (2010). Inflammation and social experience: An inflammatory challenge induces feelings of social disconnection in addition to depressed mood. *Brain, Behavior, and Immunity, 24*, 558–563.

Eisenberger, N.I., Moieni, M., Inagaki, T.K., Muscatell, K.A., & Irwin, M.R. (2017). In sickness and in health: The co-regulation of inflammation and social behavior. *Neuropsychopharmacology, 42*, 242–253.

Eisenberger, N.I., Taylor, S.E., Gable, S.L., Hilmert, C.J., & Lieberman, M.D. (2007). Neural pathways link social support to attenuated neuroendocrine stress responses. *NeuroImage, 35*, 1601–1612.

Elftman, M.D., Hunzeker, J.T., Mellinger, J.C., Bonneau, R.H., Norbury, C.C., & Truckenmiller, M.E. (2010). Stress-induced glucocorticoids at the earliest stages of herpes simplex virus-1 infection suppress subsequent antiviral immunity, implicating impaired dendritic cell function. *Journal of Immunology, 184*, 1867–1875.

Elhussiny, M.E.A., Carini, G., Mingardi, J., Tornese, P., Sala, N., et al. (2021). Modulation by chronic stress and ketamine of ionotropic AMPA/NMDA and metabotropic glutamate receptors in the rat hippocampus. *Progress in Neuropsychopharmacology & Biological Psychiatry, 104*, 110033.

Elsayed, M., Banasr, M., Duric, V., Fournier, N.M., Licznerski, P., & Duman, R.S. (2012). Antidepressant effects of fibroblast growth factor-2 in behavioral and cellular models of depression. *Biological Psychiatry, 72*, 258–265.

Emon, M.P.Z., Das, R., Nishuty, N.L., Shalahuddin Qusar, M.M.A., Bhuiyan, M.A., & Islam, M.R. (2020). Reduced serum BDNF levels are associated with the increased risk for developing MDD: A case-control study with or without antidepressant therapy. *BMC Research Notes, 13*, 83.

Engemann, K., Pedersen, C.B., Arge, L., Tsirogiannis, C., Mortensen, P.B., & Svenning, J.C. (2019). Residential green space in childhood is associated with lower risk of psychiatric disorders from adolescence into adulthood. *Proceedings of the National Academy of Sciences, 116*, 5188–5193.

Entringer, S., Buss. C., & Wadhwa, P.D. (2015). Prenatal stress, development, health and disease risk: A psychobiological perspective – 2015 Curt Richter Award Paper. *Psychoneuroendocrinology, 62*, 366–375.

Fali, T., Vallet, H., & Sauce, D. (2018). Impact of stress on aged immune system compartments: Overview from fundamental to clinical data. *Experimental Gerontology, 105*, 19–26.

Fang, J., Zhang, P., Zhou, Y., Chiang, C.W., Tan, J., et al. (2021). Endophenotype-based in silico network medicine discovery combined with insurance record data mining identifies sildenafil as a candidate drug for Alzheimer's disease. *Nature Aging, 1*, 1175–1188.

Fang, M., Zhong, L., Jin, X., Cui, R., Yang, W., et al. (2019). Effect of inflammation on the process of stroke rehabilitation and poststroke depression. *Frontiers in Psychiatry, 10*, 184.

Farhat, M.M., Morell-Dubois, S., Le Gouellec, N., Launay, D., & Maillard, H., et al. (2020). Consideration of coping strategies for patients suffering from systemic lupus erythematosus: Reflection for a personalised practice of patient education. *Clinical & Experimental Rheumatology, 38*, 705–712.

Faught, E. & Vijayan, M.M. (2018). The mineralocorticoid receptor is essential for stress axis regulation in zebrafish larvae. *Science Reports, 8*, 18081.

Fede, S.J., Pearson, E.E., Kerich, M., & Momenan, R., (2021). Charity preferences and perceived impact moderate charitable giving and associated neural response. *Neuropsychologia, 160*, 107957.

Feder, A., Rutter, S.B., Schiller, D., & Charney, D.S. (2020). The emergence of ketamine as a novel treatment for posttraumatic stress disorder. *Advances in Pharmacology, 89*, 261–286.

Feduccia, A.A. & Mithoefer, M.C. (2018). MDMA-assisted psychotherapy for PTSD: Are memory reconsolidation and fear extinction underlying mechanisms? *Progress in Neuropsychopharmacology & Biological Psychiatry, 84*, 221–228.

Fellows Yates, J.A., Velsko, I.M., Aron, F., Posth, C., Hofman, C.A., et al. (2021). The evolution and changing ecology of the African hominid oral microbiome. *Proceedings of the National Academy of Science, 118*, e2021655118.

Feng, J., Wilkinson, M., Liu, X., Purushothaman. I, Ferguson, D., et al., (2014). Chronic cocaine-regulated epigenomic changes in mouse nucleus accumbens. *Genome Biology, 15*, R65.

Ferioli, M., Zauli, G., Maiorano, P., Milani, D., Mirandola, P., & Neri, L.M. (2019). Role of physical exercise in the regulation of epigenetic mechanisms in inflammation, cancer, neurodegenerative diseases, and aging process. *Journal of Cell Physiology, 10*, 1002.

Fernandes, J., Arida, R.M., & Gomez-Pinilla, F. (2017). Physical exercise as an epigenetic modulator of brain plasticity and cognition. *Neuroscience & Biobehavioral Reviews, 80*, 443–456.

Finnell, J.E., Muniz, B.L., Padi, A.R., Lombard, C.M., Moffitt, C.M., et al. (2018). Essential role of ovarian hormones in susceptibility to the consequences of witnessing social defeat in female rats. *Biological Psychiatry, 84*, 372–382.

Fioranelli, M., Bottaccioli, A.G., Bottaccioli, F., Bianchi, M., Rovesti, M.G, et al. (2018). Stress and inflammation in coronary artery disease: A review psychoneuroendocrineimmunology-based. *Frontiers in Immunology*, *9*, 2031.

Fischer, C.P. & Romero, L.M. (2019). Chronic captivity stress in wild animals is highly species-specific. *Conservation Physiology*, *7*, p.coz093.

Flack, J.M., Ference, B.A., & Levy, P. (2014). Should African Americans with hypertension be treated differently than non-African Americans? *Current Hypertension Reports*, *16*, 409.

Flegal, K.M., Kit, B.K., Orpana, H., & Graubard, B.I. (2013). Association of all-cause mortality with overweight and obesity using standard body mass index categories: A systematic review and meta-analysis. *JAMA*, *309*, 71–82.

Fleshner, M. & Crane, C.R. (2017). Exosomes, DAMPs and miRNA: Features of stress physiology and immune homeostasis. *Trends in Immunology*, *38*, 768–776.

Flores, C. & Stewart, J. (2000). Basic fibroblast growth factor as a mediator of the effects of glutamate in the development of long-lasting sensitization to stimulant drugs: Studies in the rat. *Psychopharmacology (Berl)*, *151*, 152–165.

Fogaça, M.V. & Duman, R.S. (2019). Cortical GABAergic dysfunction in stress and depression: New insights for therapeutic interventions. *Frontiers in Cellular Neuroscience*, *13*, 87.

Foley, P. & Kirschbaum, C. (2010). Human hypothalamus–pituitary–adrenal axis responses to acute psychosocial stress in laboratory settings. *Neuroscience and Biobehavioral Reviews*, *35*, 91–96.

Folkman, S. & Lazarus, R.S. (1988). *Manual of the Ways of Coping Questionnaire*. Palo Alto, CA: Consulting Psychologists Press.

Forslund, S.K., Chakaroun, R., Zimmermann-Kogadeeva, M., Markó, L., Aron-Wisnewsky, J., et al. (2021). Combinatorial, additive and dose-dependent drug–microbiome associations. *Nature*, *600*, 500–505.

Foster, J.A., Rinaman, L., & Cryan, J.F. (2017). Stress & the gut–brain axis: Regulation by the microbiome. *Neurobiology of Stress*, *7*, 124–136.

Fournier, J.C., DeRubeis, R.J., Hollon, S.D., Dimidjian, S., Amsterdam, J.D., et al. (2010). Antidepressant drug effects and depression severity: A patient-level meta-analysis. *Journal of the American Medical Association*, *303*, 47–53.

Frampton, J.E. (2014). Pregabalin: A review of its use in adults with generalized anxiety disorder. *CNS Drugs*, *28*, 835–854.

Frank, M.G., Baratta, M.V., Zhang, K., Fallon, I.P., & Pearson, M.A. (2020). Acute stress induces the rapid and transient induction of caspase-1, gasdermin D and release of constitutive IL-1β protein in dorsal hippocampus. *Brain, Behavior, and Immunity*, *90*, 70–80.

Franklin, T.B., Russig, H., Weiss, I.C., Gräff, J., Linder, N., et al. (2010). Epigenetic transmission of the impact of early stress across generations. *Biological Psychiatry*, *68*, 408–415.

Fransen, F., van Beek, A.A., Borghuis, T., Aidy, S.E., Hugenholtz. F., et al. (2017). Aged gut microbiota contributes to systemical inflammaging after transfer to germ-free mice. *Frontiers in Immunology*, *8*, 1385.

Fredrickson, B.L. (2001). The role of positive emotions in positive psychology: The broaden-and-build theory of positive emotions. *American Psychologist, 56,* 218–226.

Frestad, D. & Prescott, E. (2017). Vital exhaustion and coronary heart disease risk: A systematic review and meta-analysis. *Psychosomatic Medicine, 79,* 260–272.

Frøbert, O., Götberg, M., Erlinge, D., Akhtar, Z., Christiansen, E.H., et al. (2021). Influenza vaccination after myocardial infarction: A randomized, double-blind, placebo-controlled, multicenter trial. *Circulation, 144,* 1476–1484.

Fromentin, S., Forslund, S.K., Chechi, K., Aron-Wisnewsky, J., Chakaroun, R., et al. (2022). Microbiome and metabolome features of the cardiometabolic disease spectrum. *Nature Medicine, 28,* 303–314.

Frumkin, H., Bratman, G.N., Breslow, S.J., Cochran, B., Kahn Jr, P.H. et al. (2017). Nature contact and human health: A research agenda. *Environmental Health Perspectives, 125,* 075001.

Fu, W.W., Popovic, M., Agarwal, A., Milakovic, M., Fu, T.S., et al. (2016). The impact of psychosocial intervention on survival in cancer: A meta-analysis. *Annals of Palliative Medicine, 5,* 93–106.

Fu, Y., Wu, Y., & Liu, E. (2020). C-reactive protein and cardiovascular disease: From animal studies to the clinic. *Experimental & Therapeutic Medicine, 20,* 1211–1219.

Fu, Z., Brouwer, M., Kennis, M., Williams, A., Cuijpers, P., & Bockting, C. (2021). Psychological factors for the onset of depression: A meta-analysis of prospective studies. *BMJ Open, 11,* e050129.

Fülling, C., Dinan, T.G., & Cryan, J.F. (2019). Gut microbe to brain signaling: What happens in vagus ... *Neuron, 101,* 998–1002.

Fulton, S., Pissios, P., Manchon, R.P., Stiles, L., Frank, L., et al. (2006). Leptin regulation of the mesoaccumbens dopamine pathway. *Neuron, 51,* 811–822.

Fumagalli, F., Bedogni, F., Slotkin, T.A., Racagni, G., & Riva, M.A. (2005). Prenatal stress elicits regionally selective changes in basal FGF-2 gene expression in adulthood and alters the adult response to acute or chronic stress. *Neurobiology of Disease, 20,* 731–737.

Fumagalli, M., Moltke, I., Grarup, N., Racimo, F., Bjerregaard, P., et al. (2015). Greenlandic Inuit show genetic signatures of diet and climate adaptation. *Science, 349,* 1343–1347.

Fund, N., Ash, N., Porath, A., Shalev, V., & Koren, G. (2019). Comparison of mortality and comorbidity rates between Holocaust survivors and individuals in the general population in Israel. *JAMA Network Open, 2,* e186643–e186643.

Fung, T.C., Vuong, H.E., Luna, C.D.G., Pronovost, G.N., Aleksandrova, A.A., et al. (2019). Intestinal serotonin and fluoxetine exposure modulate bacterial colonization in the gut. *Nat Microbiol, 4,* 2064–2073.

Furman, D., Campisi, J., Verdin, E., Carrera-Bastos, P., Targ, S., et al. (2019). Chronic inflammation in the etiology of disease across the life span. *Nature Medicine, 25,* 1822–1832.

Gabbay, V., Bradley, K.A., Mao, X., Ostrover, R., Kang, G., & Shungu, D.C. (2017). Anterior cingulate cortex γ-aminobutyric acid deficits in youth with depression. *Translational Psychiatry, 7,* e1216.

Gabriele, L., Fragale, A., Romagnoli, G., Parlato, S., Lapenta, C., et al. (2021). Type I IFN-dependent antibody response at the basis of sex dimorphism in the outcome of COVID-19. *Cytokine & Growth Factor Reviews, 58*, 66–74.

Gabrys, R.L., Tabri, N., Anisman, H., & Matheson, K. (2018). Cognitive control and flexibility in the context of stress and depressive symptoms: The cognitive control and flexibility questionnaire. *Frontiers in Psychology, 9*, 2219.

Gapp, K., & Bohacek, J. (2018). Epigenetic germline inheritance in mammals: Looking to the past to understand the future. *Genes Brain & Behavior, 17*, e12407.

Garakani, A., Murrough, J.W., Freire, R.C., Thom, R.P., Larkin. K., et al. (2020). Pharmacotherapy of anxiety disorders: Current and emerging treatment options. *Frontiers in Psychiatry, 11*, 595584.

Garcia, M., Almuwaqqat, Z., Moazzami, K., Young, A., & Lima, B.B. (2021). Racial disparities in adverse cardiovascular outcomes after a myocardial infarction in young or middle-aged patients. *Journal of the American Heart Association, 10*, e020828.

Garcia, M.A., Junglen, A., Ceroni, T., Johnson, D., Ciesla, J., & Delahanty, D.L. (2020). The mediating impact of PTSD symptoms on cortisol awakening response in the context of intimate partner violence. *Biological Psychology, 152*, 107873.

Garcia, R. (2017). Neurobiology of fear and specific phobias. *Learning & Memory, 24*, 462–471.

Garcia-Flores, V., Romero, R., Xu, Y., Theis, K.R., & Arenas-Hernandez, M. (2022). Maternal-fetal immune responses in pregnant women infected with SARS-CoV-2. *Nature Communications, 13*, 320.

Garland, E.L. & Howard, M.O. (2018). Mindfulness-based treatment of addiction: Current state of the field and envisioning the next wave of research. *Addiction Science & Clinical Practice, 13*, 14.

Garssen, B. (2004). Psychological factors and cancer development: Evidence after 30 years of research. *Clinical Psychology Review, 24*, 315–338.

Gatenby, R. & Brown, J. (2018). The evolution and ecology of resistance in cancer therapy. *Cold Spring Harbor Perspectives in Medicine, 8*, pii: a033415.

Gatenby, R., Zhang, J., & Brown, J. (2019). First strike-second strike strategies in metastatic cancer: Lessons from the evolutionary dynamics of extinction. *Cancer Research, 79*, 3174–3177.

Gautam, A., Kumar, R., Chakraborty, N., Muhie, S., Hoke, A., et al. (2018). Altered fecal microbiota composition in all male aggressor-exposed rodent model simulating features of post-traumatic stress disorder. *Journal of Neuroscience Research, 96*, 1311–1323.

Gellner, A.K., Voelter, J., Schmidt, U., Beins, E.C., Stein, V., et al. (2021). Molecular and neurocircuitry mechanisms of social avoidance. *Cellular & Molecular Life Sciences, 78*, 1163–1189.

Gentile, C.L. & Weir, T.L. (2018). The gut microbiota at the intersection of diet and human health. *Science, 362*, 776–780.

Geoghegan, S., O'Callaghan, K.P., & Offit, P.A. (2020). Vaccine safety: Myths and misinformation. *Frontiers in Microbiology, 11*, 372.

Gerritsen, L., Tendolkar, I., Franke, B., Vasquez, A.A., Kooijman, S., et al. (2011). BDNF Val66Met genotype modulates the effect of childhood adversity on subgenual anterior cingulate cortex volume in healthy subjects. *Molecular Psychiatry*, *17*, 597–603.

Geva-Zatorsky, N., Sefik, E., Kua, L., Pasman, L., Tan, T.G., et al. (2017). Mining the human gut microbiota for immunomodulatory organisms. *Cell*, *168*, 928–943.e11.

Gibb, J., Al-Yawer, F., & Anisman, H. (2013). Synergistic and antagonistic actions of acute or chronic social stressors and an endotoxin challenge vary over time following the challenge. *Brain, Behavior, and Immunity*, *28*, 149–158.

Gibb, J., Hayley, S., Poulter, M.O., & Anisman, H. (2011). Effects of stressors and immune activating agents on peripheral and central cytokines in mouse strains that differ in stressor responsivity. *Brain, Behavior, and Immunity*, *25*, 468–482.

Gilman, J.M., Schuster, R.M., Potter, K.W., Schmitt, W., Wheeler, G., et al. (2022). Effect of medical marijuana card ownership on pain, insomnia, and affective disorder symptoms in adults: a randomized clinical trial. *JAMA Network Open*, *5*, e222106.

Gimbrone Jr, M.A. & García-Cardeña, G. (2016). Endothelial cell dysfunction and the pathobiology of atherosclerosis. *Circulation Research*, *118*, 620–636.

Ginting, H., van de Ven, M., Becker, E.S., & Näring, G. (2014). Type D personality is associated with health behaviors and perceived social support in individuals with coronary heart disease. *Journal of Health Psychology*, *19*, 1–11.

Ginty, A.T., Kraynak, T.E., Fisher, J.P., & Gianaros, P.J. (2017). Cardiovascular and autonomic reactivity to psychological stress: Neurophysiological substrates and links to cardiovascular disease. *Autonomic Neuroscience*, *207*, 2–9.

Giustino, T.F., Fitzgerald, P.J., & Maren, S. (2016). Revisiting propranolol and PTSD: Memory erasure or extinction enhancement? *Neurobiology of Learning & Memory*, *130*, 26–33.

Glaser, R. (2005). Stress-associated immune dysregulation and its importance for human health: A personal history of psychoneuroimmunology. *Brain, Behavior, and Immunology*, *17*, 321–328.

Glaser, R. & Kiecolt-Glaser, J.K. (2005). Stress-induced immune dysfunction: Implications for health. *Nature Reviews in Immunology*, *5*, 243–251.

Glaser, R., MacCallum, R.C., Laskowski, B.F., Malarkey, W.B., Sheridan, J.F., & Kiecolt-Glaser, J.K. (2001). Evidence for a shift in the Th-1 to Th-2 cytokine response associated with chronic stress and aging. *Journals of Gerontology Series A: Biological Sciences and Medical Sciences*, *56*, M477–M482.

Glover, V. (2011). Annual research review: Prenatal stress and the origins of psychopathology: An evolutionary perspective. *Journal of Child Psychology and Psychiatry*, *52*, 356–367.

Gluzman, M., Scott, J.G., & Vladimirsky, A. (2020). Optimizing adaptive cancer therapy: Dynamic programming and evolutionary game theory. *Proceedings of Biological Science*, *287*, 20192454.

Goddard, A.W. (2017). The neurobiology of panic: A chronic stress disorder. *Chronic Stress*, *1*, 2470547017736038.

Goldstein, D.S. (2011). Stress, allostatic load, catecholamines, and other neurotransmitters in neurodegenerative diseases. *Endocrine Regulations, 45,* 91–98.

Gonçalves, V., Jayson, G., & Tarrier, N. (2011). A longitudinal investigation of posttraumatic stress disorder in patients with ovarian cancer. *Journal of Psychosomatic Research, 70,* 422–431.

Gone, J.P. & Kirmayer, L.J. (2020). Advancing Indigenous mental health research: Ethical, conceptual and methodological challenges. *Transcultural Psychiatry, 57,* 235–249.

Goodyer, I.M., Croudace, T., Dudbridge, F., Ban, M., & Herbert, J. (2010). Polymorphisms in BDNF (Val66Met) and 5-HTTLPR, morning cortisol and subsequent depression in at-risk adolescents. *British Journal of Psychiatry, 197,* 365–371.

Goshen, I., Kreisel, T., Ben-Menachem-Zidon, O., Licht, T., Weidenfeld, J., et al. (2008). Brain interleukin-1 mediates chronic stress-induced depression in mice via adrenocortical activation and hippocampal neurogenesis suppression. *Molecular Psychiatry, 13,* 717–728.

Gostic, K.M., Ambrose, M., Worobey, M., & Lloyd-Smith, J.O. (2016). Potent protection against H5N1 and H7N9 influenza via childhood hemagglutinin imprinting. *Science, 354,* 722–726.

Gouin, J.P., Hantsoo, L., & Kiecolt-Glaser, J.K. (2008). Immune dysregulation and chronic stress among older adults: A review. *Neuroimmunomodulation, 15,* 251–259.

Gould, F., Harvey, P.D., Hodgins, G., Jones, M.T., Michopoulos, V., et al. (2021). Prior trauma-related experiences predict the development of posttraumatic stress disorder after a new traumatic event. *Depression & Anxiety, 38,* 40–47.

Grace, P.M., Tawfik, V.L., Svensson, C.I., Burton, M,D., Loggia, M.L., & Hutchinson, M.R. (2021). The neuroimmunology of chronic pain: From rodents to humans. *Journal of Neuroscience, 41,* 855–865.

Gradus, J.L., Farkas, D.K., Svensson, E., Ehrenstein, V., Lash, T.L., et al. (2015). Posttraumatic stress disorder and cancer risk: A nationwide cohort study. *European Journal of Epidemiology, 30,* 563–568.

Graeff, F.G. (2017). Translational approach to the pathophysiology of panic disorder: Focus on serotonin and endogenous opioids. *Neuroscience & Biobehavioral Reviews, 76,* 48–55.

Grønli, J., Bramham, C., Murison, R., Kanhema, T., Fiske, E., et al. (2006). Chronic mild stress inhibits BDNF protein expression and CREB activation in the dentate gyrus but not in the hippocampus proper. *Pharmacology Biochemistry and Behavior, 85,* 842–849.

Grosso, G., Micek, A., Marventano, S., Castellano, S., Mi Pajak, A., & Galvano, F. (2016). Dietary n-3 PUFA, fish consumption and depression: A systematic review and meta-analysis of observational studies. *Journal of Affective Disorders, 205,* 269–281.

Gruhn, M.A. & Compas, B.E. (2020). Effects of maltreatment on coping and emotion regulation in childhood and adolescence: A meta-analytic review. *Child Abuse & Neglect, 103,* 104446.

Grundwald, N.J. & Brunton, P.J. (2015). Prenatal stress programs neuroendocrine stress responses and affective behaviors in second generation rats in a sex-dependent manner. *Psychoneuroendocrinology, 62,* 204–216.

Grunebaum, M.F., Galfalvy, H.C., Choo, T.H., Keilp, J.G., & Moitra, V.K. (2018). Ketamine for rapid reduction of suicidal thoughts in major depression: A midazolam-controlled randomized clinical trial. *American Journal of Psychiatry, 175,* 327–335.

Guo, J., Wang, J., Sun, W., & Liu, X. (2021). The advances of post-stroke depression: 2021 update. *Journal of Neurology, 269,* 1236–1249.

Guo, M., Hao, Y., Feng, Y., Li, H., Mao, Y., et al. (2021). microglial exosomes in neurodegenerative disease. *Frontiers in Molecular Neuroscience, 14,* 630808.

Gurdasani, D., Barroso, I., Zaeggini, E., & Sandhu, M.S. (2019). Genomics of disease risk in globally diverse populations. *Nature Review in Genetics, 20,* 520–535.

Hablitz, L.M., Pla, V., Giannetto, M., Vinitsky, H.S., Staeger, F.F., et al. (2020). Circadian control of brain glymphatic and lymphatic fluid flow. *Nature Communications, 11,* 4411.

Hackett, R.A. & Steptoe, A. (2017). Type 2 diabetes mellitus and psychological stress – a modifiable risk factor. *Nature Reviews in Endocrinology, 13,* 547–560.

Hackett, R.A., Hamer, M., Endrighi, R., Brydon, L., & Steptoe, A. (2012). Loneliness and stress-related inflammatory and neuroendocrine responses in older men and women. *Psychoneuroendocrinology, 37,* 1801–1809.

Hadler, J.L., Yousey-Hindes, K., Pérez, A., Anderson, E.J., Bargsten, M., et al. (2016). Influenza-related hospitalizations and poverty levels—United States, 2010–2012. *Morbidity and Mortality Weekly Report, 65,* 101–105.

Hafenbrack, A.C., LaPalme, M.L., & Solal, I. (2022). Mindfulness meditation reduces guilt and prosocial reparation. *Journal of Personality and Social Psychology,* ePub ahead of print.

Halaris, A. (2017). Inflammation-associated co-morbidity between depression and cardiovascular disease. *Current Topics in Behavioral Neuroscience, 31,* 45–70.

Hamer, M., Chida, Y., & Molloy, G.J. (2009). Psychological distress and cancer mortality. *Journal of Psychosomatic Research, 66,* 255–258.

Hamilton, P.J. & Nestler, E.J. (2019). Epigenetics and addiction. *Current Opinions in Neurobiology, 59,* 128–136.

Haney, M. (2020). Perspectives on cannabis research-barriers and recommendations. *JAMA Psychiatry, 77,* 994–995.

Hanson, J.L., Nacewicz, B.M., Sutterer, M.J., et al. (2015). Behavioral problems after early life stress: contributions of the hippocampus and amygdala. *Biological Psychiatry, 77,* 314–323.

Harrison, N.A., Brydon, L., Walker, C., Gray, M.A., Steptoe, A., & Critchley, H.D. (2009). Inflammation causes mood changes through alterations in subgenual cingulated activity and mesolimbic connectivity. *Biological Psychiatry, 66,* 407–414.

Harvey, L. & Boksa, P. (2012). Prenatal and postnatal animal models of immune activation: relevance to a range of neurodevelopmental disorders. *Developmental Neurobiology, 72,* 1335–1348.

Harvey, S.B., Øverland, S., Hatch, S.L., Wessely, S., Mykletun, A., & Hotopf, M. (2018). Exercise and the prevention of depression: Results of the HUNT cohort study. *American Journal of Psychiatry, 175*, 28–36.

Hasin, D.S., O'Brien, C.P., Auriacombe, M., Borges, G., Bucholz, K., et al. (2013). DSM-5 criteria for substance use disorders: Recommendations and rationale. *American Journal of Psychiatry, 170*, 834–851.

Haslam, C., Cruwys, T., Haslam, S.A., Dingle, G., & Chang, M.X. (2016). Groups 4 Health: Evidence that a social-identity intervention that builds and strengthens social group membership improves mental health. *Journal of Affective Disorders, 194*, 188–195.

Haslam, S.A., Haslam, C., Cruwys, T., Jetten, J., Bentley, S.V., et al. (2022). Social identity makes group-based social connection possible: Implications for loneliness and mental health. *Current Opinion in Psychology, 43*, 161–165.

Haslam, C., Jetten, J., Cruwys, T., Dingle, G.A., & Haslam, S.A. (2018). *The New Psychology of Health: Unlocking the Social Cure*. Abingdon, UK: Routledge.

Haslam, S.A. & Reicher, S.D. (2012). Contesting the 'nature' of conformity: What Milgram and Zimbardo's studies really show. *PLoS Biology, 10*, e1001426.

Haslam, S.A., Reicher, S.D., & Levine, M. (2012). When other people are heaven, when other people are hell: How social identity determines the nature and impact of social support. In J. Jetten, C. Haslam, & S. A. Haslam (eds.), *The Social Cure: Identity, Health and Well-Being* (pp. 157–174). New York: Psychology Press.

Hasler, G., van der Veen, J.W., Grillon, C., Drevets, W.C., & Shen, J. (2010). Effect of acute psychological stress on prefrontal GABA concentration determined by proton magnetic resonance spectroscopy. *American Journal of Psychiatry, 167*, 1226–1231.

Hayes, S.C., Luoma, J., Bond, F., Masuda, A., & Lillis, J. (2006). Acceptance and commitment therapy: Model, processes, and outcomes. *Behaviour Research and Therapy, 44*, 1–25.

Healey, N. (2021). Is there more to a healthy-heart diet than cholesterol? *Nature, 594*, S12–S13.

Hediger, K., Wagner, J., Künzi, P., Haefeli, A., & Theis, F. (2021). Effectiveness of animal-assisted interventions for children and adults with post-traumatic stress disorder symptoms: A systematic review and meta-analysis. *European Journal of Psychotraumatology, 12*, 1879713.

Heijmans, B.T., Tobi, E.W., Stein, A.D., Putter, H., Blauw, G.J., et al. (2008). Persistent epigenetic differences associated with prenatal exposure to famine in humans. *Proceedings of the National Academy of Science, 105*, 17046–17049.

Heilig, M. & Koob, G.F. (2007). A key role for corticotropin-releasing factor in alcohol dependence. *Trends in Neuroscience, 30*, 399–406.

Heim, C. & Nemeroff, C.B. (2002). Neurobiology of early life stress: Clinical studies. *Seminars in Clinical Neuropsychiatry, 7*, 147–159.

Heim, C., Newport, D.J., Mletzko, T., Miller, A.H., & Nemeroff, C.B. (2008). The link between childhood trauma and depression: Insights from HPA axis studies in humans. *Psychoneuroendocrinology, 33*, 693–710.

Heim, C., Shugart, M., Craighead, W.E., & Nemeroff, C.B. (2010). Neurobiological and psychiatric consequences of child abuse and neglect. *Developmental Psychobiology, 52*, 671–690.

Heinlein, M., Gandolfo, L.C., Zhao, K., Teh, C.E., Nguyen, N., et al. (2022). The acetyltransferase KAT7 is required for thymic epithelial cell expansion, expression of AIRE target genes, and thymic tolerance. *Science Immunology, 7*, eabb6032.

Helliwell, J. F., Huang, H., & Putnam, R. D. (2009). How's the job? Are trust and social capital neglected workplace investments? In V.O. Bartkus and J.H. Davis (eds.), *Social Capital: Reaching Out, Reaching In* (pp. 87–144). Cheltenham, UK: Edward Elgar.

Hendrickson, R.C., Raskind, M.A., Millard, S.P., Sikkema, C., & Terry, G.E. (2018). Evidence for altered brain reactivity to norepinephrine in Veterans with a history of traumatic stress. *Neurobiology of Stress, 8*, 103–111.

Heneka, M.T., Golenbock, D.T. & Latz, E. (2015). Innate immunity in Alzheimer's disease. *Nature Immunology, 16*, 229–236.

Hermes, G., Fogelman, N., Seo, D., & Sinha, R. (2021). Differential effects of recent versus past traumas on mood, social support, binge drinking, emotional eating and BMI, and on neural responses to acute stress. *Stress, 17*, 1–10.

Herrmann, M., Scholmerich, J., & Straub, R.H. (2000). Stress and rheumatic diseases. *Rheumatic Disease Clinics of North America, 26*, 737–763.

Hersman, S., Hoffman, A.N., Hodgins, L., Shieh, S., & Lam, J. (2019). Cholinergic signaling alters stress-induced sensitization of hippocampal contextual learning. *Frontiers in Neuroscience, 13*, 251.

Hetrick, S. E., Purcell, R., Garner, B., & Parslow, R. (2010). Combined pharmacotherapy and psychological therapies for post traumatic stress disorder (PTSD). *Cochrane Database of Systematic Reviews, 7*, CD007316.

Hickman, C., Marks, E., Pihkala, P., Clayton, S., Lewandowski, E.R., et al. (2021). Young people's voices on climate anxiety, government betrayal and moral injury: A global phenomenon. *The Lancet Public Health, 5*, e863–e873.

Higgins, G.A., Fletcher, P.J., & Shanahan, W.R. (2020). Lorcaserin: A review of its preclinical and clinical pharmacology and therapeutic potential. *Pharmacology & Therapeutics, 205*, 107417.

Hill, L.K. & Thayer, J.F. (2019). The autonomic nervous system and hypertension: Ethnic differences and psychosocial factors. *Current Cardiology Reports, 21*, 15.

Hill, M.N. & McEwen, B.S. (2010). Involvement of the endocannabinoid system in the neurobehavioural effects of stress and glucocorticoids. *Progress in Neuropsychopharmacology & Biological Psychiatry, 34*, 791–797.

Hill, M.N., Campolongo, P., Yehuda, R., & Patel, S. (2018). Integrating endocannabinoid signaling and cannabinoids into the biology and treatment of posttraumatic stress disorder. *Neuropsychopharmacology, 43*, 80–102.

Hill, M.N. & Tasker, J.G. (2012). Endocannabinoid signaling, glucocorticoid-mediated negative feedback, and regulation of the hypothalamic-pituitary-adrenal axis. *Neuroscience, 204*, 5–16.

Hinton, D.E. & Kirmayer, L.J. (2017). The flexibility hypothesis of healing. *Culture, Medicine & Psychiatry, 41*, 3–34.

Hirsch, M. (2001). Surviving images: Holocaust photographs and the work of postmemory. *Yale Journal of Criticism, 14*, 5–37.

Hirschberger, G. (2018). Collective trauma and the social construction of meaning. *Frontiers in Psychology, 9*, 1441.

Hitti, F.L., Cristancho, M.A., Yang, A.I., O'Reardon, J.P., Bhati, M.T., & Baltuch, G.H. (2021). Deep brain stimulation of the ventral capsule/ventral striatum for treatment-resistant depression: a decade of clinical follow-up. *Journal of Clinical Psychiatry, 82*, 21m13973.

Hodes, G.E. & Epperson, C.N. (2019). Sex differences in vulnerability and resilience to stress across the life span. *Biological Psychiatry, 86*, 421–432.

Hodes, G.E., Pfau, M.L., Leboeuf, M., Golden, S.A., Christoffel, D.J., et al. (2014). Individual differences in the peripheral immune system promote resilience versus susceptibility to social stress. *Proceedings of the National Academy of Sciences, 111*, 16136–16141.

Hoen, P.W., Denollet, J., de Jonge, P., & Whooley, M.A. (2013). Positive affect and survival in patients with stable coronary heart disease: Findings from the Heart and Soul Study. *Journal of Clinical Psychiatry, 74*, 716–722.

Hoffman-Goetz, L. & Quadrilatero, J. (2003). Treadmill exercise in mice increases intestinal lymphocyte loss via apoptosis. *Acta Physiologica Scandinavica, 179*, 289–297.

Hogan, B.V., Peter, M.B., Shenoy, H.G., Horgan, K., & Hughes, T.A. (2011). Surgery induced immunosuppression. *Surgeon, 9*, 38–43.

Holmes, S.E., Girgenti, M.J., Davis, M.T., Pietrzak, R.H., & DellaGioia, N. (2017). Altered metabotropic glutamate receptor 5 markers in PTSD: In vivo and postmortem evidence. *PNAS, 114*, 8390–8395.

Holmes, T.H. & Rahe, R.H. (1967). The social readjustment rating scale. *Journal of Psychosomatic Research, 11*, 213–218.

Holsboer, F. & Ising, M. (2010). Stress hormone regulation: Biological role and translation into therapy. *Annual Review of Psychology, 61*, 81–109.

Holt-Lunstad, J., Robles, T.F., & Sbarra, D.A. (2017). Advancing social connection as a public health priority in the United States. *American Psychologist, 72*, 517.

Holtzheimer, P.E., Husain, M.M., Lisanby, S.H., Taylor, S.F., & Whitworth, L.A. (2017). Subcallosal cingulate deep brain stimulation for treatment-resistant depression: A multisite, randomised, sham-controlled trial. *The Lancet Psychiatry, 4*, 839–849.

Hooper, L.V., Littman, D.R., & Macpherson, A.J. (2012). Interactions between the microbiota and the immune system. *Science, 336*, 1268–1273.

Hopf, F.W. (2020). Recent perspectives on orexin/hypocretin promotion of addiction-related behaviors. *Neuropharmacology, 168*, 108013.

Horovitz, O., Ardi, Z., Ashkenazi, S.K., Ritov, G., Anunu, R., & Richter-Levin, G. (2020). Network neuromodulation of opioid and GABAergic receptors following a combination of "juvenile" and "adult stress" in rats. *International Journal of Molecular Science, 21*, 5422.

Howie, H., Rijal, C.M., & Ressler, K.J. (2019). A review of epigenetic contributions to post-traumatic stress disorder. *Dialogues in Clinical Neuroscience, 21*, 417–428.

Hsu, T.Y., Liu, T.L., Cheng, P.Z., Lee, H.C., Lane, T.J., & Duncan, N.W. (2021). Depressive rumination is correlated with brain responses during self-related processing. *Journal of Psychiatry & Neuroscience, 46*, E518–E527.

Hu, S.C., Tsai, Y.H., Li, D.C., Hsu, W.C., & Huang, N.C. (2021). Social-economic environments and depressive symptoms in community-dwelling adults: A multi-level analysis for two nationwide datasets in Taiwan. *International Journal of Environmental Research and Public Health, 18*, 7487.

Huffman, J.C., Legler, S.R., & Boehm, J.K. (2017). Positive psychological well-being and health in patients with heart disease: A brief review. *Future Cardiology, 13*, 443–450.

Hughes, J. & Scholer, A.A. (2017). When wanting the best goes right or wrong: Distinguishing between adaptive and maladaptive maximization. *Personality and Social Psychology Bulletin, 43*, 570–583.

Hughes, K., Ford, K., Bellis, M.A., Glendinning, F., Harrison, E., & Passmore, J. (2021). Health and financial costs of adverse childhood experiences in 28 European countries: A systematic review and meta-analysis. *The Lancet Public Health, 6*, e848–e857.

Huizink, A.C., Mulder, E.J.H., & Buitelaar, J.K. (2004). Prenatal stress and risk for psychopathology: Specific effects or induction of general susceptibility? *Psychological Bulletin, 130*, 115–142.

Hur, J., Smith, J.F., DeYoung, K.A., Anderson, A.S., Kuang, J., et al. (2020). Anxiety and the neurobiology of temporally uncertain threat anticipation. *Journal of Neuroscience, 40*, 7949–7964.

Hwang, B., Moser, D.K., Pelter, M.M., Nesbitt, T.S., & Dracup, K. (2015). Changes in depressive symptoms and mortality in patients with heart failure: Effects of cognitive-affective and somatic symptoms. *Psychosomatic Medicine, 77*, 798–807.

Ilchmann-Diounou, H. & Menard, S. (2020). Psychological stress, intestinal barrier dysfunctions, and autoimmune disorders: An overview. *Frontiers in Immunology, 11*, 1823.

Illescas-Montes, R., Corona-Castro, C.C., Melguizo-Rodríguez, L., Ruiz, C., & Costela-Ruiz, V.J. (2019). Infectious processes and systemic lupus erythematosus. *Immunology, 158*, 153–160.

Ingram, K.M., Betz, N.E., Mindes, E.J., Schmitt, M.M., & Smith, N.G. (2001). Unsupportive responses from others concerning a stressful life event: Development of the unsupportive social interactions inventory. *Journal of Social and Clinical Psychology, 20*, 173–207.

Iñiguez, S.D., Flores-Ramirez, F.J., Riggs, L.M., Alipio, J.B., & Garcia-Carachure, I. (2018). Vicarious social defeat stress induces depression-related outcomes in female mice. *Biological Psychiatry, 83*, 9–17.

Insel, T., Cuthbert, B., Garvey, M., Heinssen, R., Pine, D.S., et al. (2010). Research domain criteria (RDoC): Toward a new classification framework for research on mental disorder. *American Journal of Psychiatry, 167*, 748–751.

Insel, T.R. & Young, L.J. (2001). The neurobiology of attachment. *Nature Reviews Neuroscience, 2*, 129–136.

Ioannidis, J.P. (2013). Implausible results in human nutrition research. *British Medical Journal, 347*, f6698.

IPCC Sixth Assessment Report (2022). Climate Change 2022: Impacts, Adaptation, and Vulnerability. https://www.ipcc.ch/report/ar6/wg2/, Accessed March, 2022.

Irwin, M.R. (2019). Sleep and inflammation: partners in sickness and in health. *Nature Review in Immunology, 19*, 702–715.

Irwin, M. (1999). Immune correlates of depression. *Advances in Experimental Medicine and Biology, 461*, 1–24.

Isaevska, E., Moccia, C., Asta, F., Cibella, F., Gagliardi, L., et al. (2021). Exposure to ambient air pollution in the first 1000 days of life and alterations in the DNA methylome and telomere length in children: A systematic review. *Environmental Research, 193*, 110504.

Ito, Y., Gotoh, K., Hirota, K., Matsushita, M., Furuta, Y., et al. (2016). Dysbiosis contributes to arthritis development via activation of autoreactive T cells in the intestine. *Arthritis & Rheumatology, 68*, 2646–2661.

Iwata, M., Ota, K.T., & Duman, R.S. (2013). The inflammasome: Pathways linking psychological stress, depression, and systemic illnesses. *Brain, Behavior, and Immunity, 31*, 105–114.

Jackson, S., Baity, M.R., Bobb, K., Swick, D., & Giorgio, J. (2019). Stress inoculation training outcomes among veterans with PTSD and TBI. *Psychological Trauma, 11*, 842–850.

Jacob, S.N., Dodge, C.P., & Vasterling, J.J. (2019). Posttraumatic stress disorder and neurocognition: A bidirectional relationship? *Clinical Psychology Review, 72*, 101747.

Jacobs, R., Pawlak, C.R., Mikeska, E., Meyer-Olson, D., Martin, M., et al. (2001). Systemic lupus erythematosus and rheumatoid arthritis patients differ from healthy controls in their cytokine pattern after stress exposure. *Rheumatology, 40*, 868–875.

Jaén, R.I., Val-Blasco, A., Prieto, P., Gil-Fernández, M., Smani, T., et al. (2020). Innate immune receptors, key actors in cardiovascular diseases. *JACC Basic Translational Science, 5*, 735–749.

Jakobsen, J.C., Katakam, K.K., Schou, A., Hellmuth, S.G., Stallknecht, S.E., et al. (2017). Selective serotonin reuptake inhibitors versus placebo in patients with major depressive disorder: A systematic review with meta-analysis and Trial Sequential Analysis. *BMC Psychiatry, 17*, 1–28.

James, M.H., Mahler, S.V., Moorman, D.E., & Aston-Jones, G. (2017). A decade of orexin/hypocretin and addiction: Where are we now? *Current Topics in Behavioral Neuroscience, 33*, 247–281.

Janicki-Deverts, D., Cohen, S., & Doyle, W.J. (2017). Dispositional affect moderates the stress-buffering effect of social support on risk for developing the common cold. *Journal of Personality, 85*, 675–686.

Javadi, P., Rezayof, A., Sardari, M., & Ghasemzadeh, Z. (2017). Brain nicotinic acetylcholine receptors are involved in stress-induced potentiation of nicotine reward in rats. *Journal of Psychopharmacology, 31*, 945–955.

Jbaily, A., Zhou, X., Liu, J., Lee, T.H., Kamareddine, L., et al. (2022). Air pollution exposure disparities across US population and income groups. *Nature, 601,* 228–233.

Jetten, J., Haslam, C., & Haslam, S. A. (2012). *The Social Cure: Identity, Health and Well-being.* New York: Psychology Press, Taylor & Francis.

Ježek, K., Lee, B.B., Kelemen, E., McCarthy, K.M., McEwen, B.S., & Fenton, A.A. (2010). Stress-induced out-of-context activation of memory. *PLoS Biology, 8,* e1000570.

Jia, Q., Li, H., Zhou, H., Zhang, X., Zhang, A., et al. (2019). Role and effective therapeutic target of gut microbiota in heart failure. *Cardiovascular Therapy, 2019,* 5164298.

Jiang, Q., Stone, C.R., Elkin, K., Geng, X., & Ding, Y. (2021). Immunosuppression and neuroinflammation in stroke pathobiology. *Experimental Neurobiology, 30,* 101–112.

Jiang, S., Postovit, L., Cattaneo, A., Binder, E.B., & Aitchison, K.J. (2019). Epigenetic modifications in stress response genes associated with childhood trauma. *Frontiers in Psychiatry, 10,* 808.

Jiang, T., Yakin, S., Crocker, J., & Way, B.M. (2021). Perceived social support-giving moderates the association between social relationships and interleukin-6. *Brain, Behavior, and Immunity, 100,* 25–28.

Jiang, W., Han, T., Duan, W., Dong, Q., Hou, W., et al. (2020). Prenatal famine exposure and estimated glomerular filtration rate across consecutive generations: Association and epigenetic mediation in a population-based cohort study in Suihua China. *Aging (Albany NY), 12,* 12206–12221.

Jin, X., Zhang, Y., Celniker, S.E., Xia, Y., Mao, J.H., et al. (2021). Gut microbiome partially mediates and coordinates the effects of genetics on anxiety-like behavior in Collaborative Cross mice. *Scientific Reports, 11,* 270.

Jinek, M., Chylinski, K., Fonfara, I., Hauer, M., Doudna, J.A., & Charpentier, E. (2012). A programmable dual-RNA-guided DNA endonuclease in adaptive bacterial immunity. *Science, 337,* 816–821.

Joëls, M., Karst, H., & Sarabdjitsingh, R.A. (2018). The stressed brain of humans and rodents. *Acta Physiologica (Oxf), 223,* e13066.

John, A., Glendenning, A.C., Marchant, A., Montgomery, P., Stewart, A., et al. (2018). Self-harm, suicidal behaviours, and cyberbullying in children and young people: Systematic review. *Journal of Medical Internet Research, 20,* e9044.

Johnson, J.A., Rash, J.A., Campbell, T.S., Savard, J., Gehrman, P.R., et al. (2016). A systematic review and meta-analysis of randomized controlled trials of cognitive behavior therapy for insomnia (CBT-I) in cancer survivors. *Sleep Medicine Review, 27,* 20–28.

Jones, C., Barrera, I., Brothers, S., Ring, R., & Wahlestedt, C. (2017). Oxytocin and social functioning. *Dialogues in Clinical Neuroscience, 19,* 193–201.

Jones, J.L., Esber, G.R., McDannald, M.A., Gruber, A.J., Hernandez, A., Mirenzi, A., & Schoenbaum, G. (2012). Orbitofrontal cortex supports behavior and learning using inferred but not cached values. *Science, 338,* 953–956.

Joseph, D.N. & Whirledge, S. (2017). Stress and the HPA Axis: Balancing homeostasis and fertility. *International Journal of Molecular Science, 18,* 2224.

Juster, R.P., Raymond, C., Desrochers, A.B., Bourdon, O., Durand, N., et al. (2016). Sex hormones adjust "sex-specific" reactive and diurnal cortisol profiles. *Psychoneuroendocrinology, 63,* 282–290.

Jutagir, D.R., Blomberg, B.B., Carver, C.S., Lechner, S.C., Timpano, K.R., et al. (2017). Social well-being is associated with less pro-inflammatory and pro-metastatic leukocyte gene expression in women after surgery for breast cancer. *Breast Cancer Research & Treatment, 165,* 169–180.

Kabat-Zinn, J. (1990). *Full Catastrophe Living: Using the Wisdom of Your Body and Mind to Face Stress, Pain, and Illness.* New York: Delacorte.

Kaczkurkin, A.N. & Foa, E.B. (2015). Cognitive-behavioral therapy for anxiety disorders: an update on the empirical evidence. *Dialogues in Clinical Neuroscience, 17,* 337–346.

Kaffman, A. & Meaney, M.J. (2007). Neurodevelopmental sequelae of postnatal maternal care in rodents: Clinical and research implications of molecular insights. *Journal of Child Psychology and Psychiatry, 48,* 224–244.

Kahneman, D. (2011). *Thinking, Fast and Slow.* New York: Farrar, Straus and Giroux.

Kahneman, D. & Tversky, A. (1979). Prospect theory: An analysis of decision under risk. *Econometrica, 47,* 263–292.

Kalichman, S.C., Eaton, L.A., Earnshaw, V.A., & Brousseau, N. (2022). Faster than warp speed: Early attention to COVID-19 by anti-vaccine groups on Facebook. *Journal of Public Health, 44,* e96–e105.

Kanner, A.D., Coyne, J.C., Schaefer, C., & Lazarus, R.S. (1981). Comparison of two modes of stress measurement: Daily hassles and uplifts versus major life events. *Journal of Behavioral Medicine, 4,* 239–249.

Kasai, K., Yamasue, H., Gilbertson, M.W., Shenton, M.E., Rauch, S.L., & Pitman, R.K. (2008). Evidence for acquired pregenual anterior cingulate gray matter loss from a twin study of combat-related posttraumatic stress disorder. *Biological Psychiatry, 63,* 550–556.

Katsi, V., Didagelos, M., Skevofilax, S., Armenis, I., Kartalis, A., et al. (2019). GUT Microbiome – GUT Dysbiosis-Arterial Hypertension: New horizons. *Current Hypertension Reviews, 15,* 40–46.

Katzmarski, N., Domínguez-Andrés, J., Cirovic, B., Renieris, G., Ciarlo, E., et al. (2021). Transmission of trained immunity and heterologous resistance to infections across generations. *Nature Immunology, 22,* 1382–1390.

Kaufman, S.B. (2020). Post-traumatic growth: Finding meaning and creativity in adversity. *Scientific American.* https://blogs.scientificamerican.com/beautiful-minds/post-traumatic-growth-finding-meaning-and-creativity-in-adversity/. Accessed June 2021.

Kaushik, A., Kostaki, E., & Kyriakopoulos, M. (2016). The stigma of mental illness in children and adolescents: A systematic review. *Psychiatry Research, 243,* 469–494.

Kekow, J., Moots, R., Khandker, R., Melin, J., Freundlich, B., & Singh, A. (2011). Improvements in patient-reported outcomes, symptoms of depression and anxiety, and their association with clinical remission among patients with moderate-to-severe active early rheumatoid arthritis. *Rheumatology, 50,* 401–409.

Kelly, J.R., Borre, Y., O'Brien, C., Patterson, E., El Aidy, S., et al. (2016). Transferring the blues: Depression-associated gut microbiota induces neurobehavioural changes in the rat. *Journal of Psychiatric Research, 82,* 109–118.

Kelly, O., Matheson, K., Ravindran, A., Merali, Z., & Anisman, H. (2007). Ruminative coping among patients with dysthymia before and after pharmacotherapy. *Depression and Anxiety, 24,* 233–243.

Kempter, E., Amoroso, M., Duffner, H.L., Werner, A.M., Langgartner, D., et al. (2021). Changes in functional glucocorticoid sensitivity of isolated splenocytes induced by chronic psychosocial stress – a time course study. *Frontiers in Immunology, 12,* 753822.

Kendall, M.M. & Sperandio, V. (2021). Gut microbes regroup to aid defence after infection. *Nature, 592,* 29–31.

Kenwood, M.M., Kalin, N.H., & Barbas, H. (2022). The prefrontal cortex, pathological anxiety, and anxiety disorders. *Neuropsychopharmacology, 47,* 260–275.

Kessler, R.C. & Bromet, E.J. (2013). The epidemiology of depression across cultures. *Annual Review of Public Health, 34,* 119–138.

Kessler, R.C., Aguilar-Gaxiola, S., Alonso, J., Bromet, E.J., Gureje, O., et al. (2018). The associations of earlier trauma exposures and history of mental disorders with PTSD after subsequent traumas. *Molecular Psychiatry, 23,* 1892–1899.

Khan, A.M., Dar, S., Ahmed, R., Bachu, R., Adnan, M., & Kotapati, V.P. (2018). Cognitive behavioral therapy versus eye movement desensitization and reprocessing in patients with post-traumatic stress disorder: Systematic review and meta-analysis of randomized clinical trials. *Cureus, 10,* e3250.

Khera, A.V. & Kathiresan, S. (2017). Genetics of coronary artery disease: discovery, biology and clinical translation. *Nature Review in Genetics, 18,* 331–344.

Khoury, J.E., Bosquet Enlow, M., Plamondon, A., & Lyons-Ruth, K. (2019). The association between adversity and hair cortisol levels in humans: A meta-analysis. *Psychoneuroendocrinology, 103,* 104–117.

Kiank, C., Zeden, J.P., Drude, S., Domanska, G., Fusch, G., Otten, W., & Schuett, C. (2010). Psychological stress-induced, IDO1-dependent tryptophan catabolism: Implications on immunosuppression in mice and humans. *PLoS One, 5,* e11825.

Kida, S. (2019). Reconsolidation/destabilization, extinction and forgetting of fear memory as therapeutic targets for PTSD. *Psychopharmacology, 236,* 49–57.

Kiecolt-Glaser, J.K., Wilson, S.J., Shrout, M.R., Madison, A.A., Andridge, R., Peng, J., et al. (2021). The gut reaction to couples' relationship troubles: A route to gut dysbiosis through changes in depressive symptoms. *Psychoneuroendocrinology, 125,* 105132.

Kim, E.J. & Kim, Y.K. (2018). Panic disorders: The role of genetics and epigenetics. *AIMS Genetics, 5,* 177–190.

Kim, T.Y., Kim, S.J., Chung, H.G., Choi, J.H., Kim, S.H., & Kang, J.I. (2017). Epigenetic alterations of the BDNF gene in combat-related post-traumatic stress disorder. *Acta Psychiatrica Scandinavica, 135,* 170–179.

Kim-Fuchs, C., Le, C.P., Pimentel, M.A., Shackleford, D., Ferrari, D., et al. (2014). Chronic stress accelerates pancreatic cancer growth and invasion: A critical role for beta-adrenergic signaling in the pancreatic microenvironment. *Brain, Behavior, and Immunity, 40,* 40–47.

King, A.P., Block, S.R., Sripada, R.K., Rauch, S., Giardino, N., et al. (2016). Altered default mode network (DMN) resting state functional connectivity following a mindfulness-based exposure therapy for posttraumatic stress disorder (PTSD) in combat veterans of Afghanistan and Iraq. *Depression & Anxiety, 33,* 289–299.

King, M.L. Jr. (1967). *The Trumpet of Conscience.* Boston: Beacon Press.

Kirby (2006). Standing Senate Committee on Social Affairs, Science and Technology (May 2006). *Out of the Shadows at Last: Transforming Mental Health, Mental Illness and Addiction Services in Canada. Final Report of the Standing Senate Committee on Social Affairs, Science and Technology.* Ottawa.

Kirmayer, L.J. & Crafa, D. (2014). What kind of science for psychiatry? *Frontiers in Human Neuroscience, 8,* 435.

Kirschbaum, C., Pirke, K.-M., & Hellhammer, D.H. (1993). The "Trier Social Stress Test" – a tool for investigating psychobiological stress responses in a laboratory setting. *Neuropsychobiology, 28,* 76–81.

Kivimäki, M., Nyberg, S.T., Batty, G.D., Fransson, E.I., Heikkilä, K., et al. (2012). Job strain as a risk factor for coronary heart disease: A collaborative meta-analysis of individual participant data. *The Lancet, 380,* 1491–1497.

Klastrup, L.K., Bak, S.T., & Nielsen, A.L. (2019). The influence of paternal diet on sncRNA-mediated epigenetic inheritance. *Molecular Genetics & Genomics, 294,* 1–11.

Klein, S.L. & Flanagan, K.L. (2016). Sex differences in immune responses. *Nature Reviews in Immunology, 16,* 626–638.

Klumpers, F., Kroes, M.C.W., Baas, J.M.P., & Fernández, G. (2017). How human amygdala and bed nucleus of the stria terminalis may drive distinct defensive responses. *Journal of Neuroscience, 37,* 9645–9656.

Knight, L.K. & Depue, B.E. (2019). New frontiers in anxiety research: The translational potential of the bed nucleus of the stria terminalis. *Frontiers in Psychiatry, 10,* 510.

Kohler, O., Krogh, J., Mors, O., & Benros, M.E. (2016). Inflammation in depression and the potential for anti-inflammatory treatment. *Current Neuropharmacology, 14,* 732–742.

Kohno, M., Link, J., Dennis, L.E., McCready, H., Huckans, M., et al. (2019). Neuroinflammation in addiction: A review of neuroimaging studies and potential immunotherapies. *Pharmacology Biochemistry & Behavior, 179,* 34–42.

Koo, J.W., Chaudhury, D., Han, M.H., & Nestler, E.J. (2019). Role of mesolimbic brain-derived neurotrophic factor in depression. *Biological Psychiatry, 86,* 738–748.

Koob, G.F. (2008). A role for brain stress systems in addiction. *Neuron, 59,* 11–34.

Koob, G.F. & Le Moal, M. (2008b). Review: Neurobiological mechanisms for opponent motivational processes in addiction. *Philosophical Transactions of the Royal Society B: Biological Sciences, 363,* 3113–3123.

Koob, G.F. & Volkow, N.D. (2016). Neurobiology of addiction: A neurocircuitry analysis. *The Lancet Psychiatry, 3,* 760–773.

Kop, W.J. & Mommersteeg, P.M.C. (2013). Psychoneuroimmunological processes in coronary artery disease and heart failure. In A. Kusnecov and H. Anisman (eds.), *Handbook of Psychoneuroimmunology*. London: Wiley-Blackwell.

Korecki, J.R., Schwebel, F.J., Votaw, V.R., & Witkiewitz, K. (2020). Mindfulness-based programs for substance use disorders: A systematic review of manualized treatments. *Substance Abuse Treatment, Prevention, & Policy*, *15*, 51.

Koroma, D., Pestalozzi, M.I., & Znoj, H. (2022). How social exclusion, embitterment, and conspiracy beliefs mediate individual's intention to vaccination against COVID-19: Results from a moderated serial mediation analysis. *Psychopathology*, *55*, 93–103.

Krishnan, S.M., Sobey, C.G., Latz, E., Mansell, A., & Drummond, G.R. (2014). IL-1β and IL-18: Inflammatory markers or mediators of hypertension? *British Journal of Pharmacology*, *171*, 5589–5602.

Kroenke, C.H., Michael, Y.L., Poole, E.M., Kwan, M.L., Nechuta, S., et al. (2017). Postdiagnosis social networks and breast cancer mortality in the After Breast Cancer Pooling Project. *Cancer*, *123*, 1228–1237.

Kroenke, C.H., Paskett, E.D., Cene, C.W., Caan, B.J., Luo, J., et al. (2020). Prediagnosis social support, social integration, living status, and colorectal cancer mortality in postmenopausal women from the women's health initiative. *Cancer*, *126*, 1766–1775.

Kubany, E.S., Haynes, S.N., Leisen, M.B., Owens, J.A., Kaplan, A.S., et al. (2000). Development and preliminary validation of a brief broad-spectrum measure of trauma exposure: The traumatic life events questionnaire. *Psychological Assessment*, *12*, 210–224.

Kupper, N. & Denollet, J. (2018). Type D Personality as a risk factor in coronary heart disease: A review of current evidence. *Current Cardiology Reports*, *20*, 104.

Kushner, S.H. (1981). *When Bad Things Happen to Good People*. New York: Schocken Publishing.

Labonté, B., Engmann, O., Purushothaman, I., Menard, C., Wang, J., et al. (2017). Sex-specific transcriptional signatures in human depression. *Nature Medicine*, *23*, 1102–1111.

Lafortune, S., Laplante, D.P., Elgbeili, G., Li, X., Lebel, S., et al. (2021). Effect of natural disaster-related prenatal maternal stress on child development and health: A meta-analytic review. *International Journal of Environmental Research & Public Health*, *18*, 8332.

Lancet Planetary Health, The (2018). Environmental racism: Time to tackle social injustice. *The Lancet Planetary Health*, *2*, e462.

Lang, A.E., & Lozano, A.M. (1998). Parkinson's disease: First of two parts. *New England Journal of Medicine*, *339*, 1044–1053.

Langford, D.J., Bailey, A.L., Chanda, M.L., Clarke, S.E., Drummond, T.E., et al. (2010). Coding of facial expressions of pain in the laboratory mouse. *Nature Methods*, *7*, 447–449.

La Rosa, F., Clerici, M., Ratto, D., Occhinegro, A., Licito, A., et al. (2018). The gut–brain axis in alzheimer's disease and omega-3. A critical overview of clinical trials. *Nutrients*, *10*, 1267.

Larson, E.B., Akkentli, F., Edwards, S., Graham, D.L., Simmons, D.L., et al. (2010). Striatal regulation of ΔFosB, FosB, and cFos during cocaine self-administration and withdrawal. *Journal of Neurochemistry*, *115*, 112–122.

Larson, J.E. & Corrigan, P. (2008). The stigma of families with mental illness. *Academic Psychiatry*, *32*, 87–91.

Lautarescu, A., Craig, M.C., & Glover, V. (2020). Prenatal stress: Effects on fetal and child brain development. *International Review of Neurobiology*, *50*, 17–40.

Lawler, P.R., Bhatt, D.L., Godoy, L.C., Lüscher, T.F., Bonow, R.O., et al. (2020). Targeting cardiovascular inflammation: next steps in clinical translation. *European Heart Journal*, *42*, 113–131.

Lazarus, R. S. & Folkman, S. (1984). *Stress, Appraisal, and Coping*. New York: Springer.

Lebowitz, E.R., Orbach, M., Marin, C.E., Salmaso, N., Vaccarino, F.M., & Silverman, W.K. (2021). Fibroblast growth factor 2 implicated in childhood anxiety and depression symptoms. *Journal of Affective Disorders*, *282*, 611–616.

LeDoux, J.E. (2000). Emotion circuits in the brain. *Annual Review of Neuroscience*, *23*, 155–184.

LeDoux, J.E. & Brown, R. (2017). A higher-order theory of emotional consciousness. *Proceedings of the National Academy of Sciences*, *114*, E2016–E2025.

Lee, A.S., de Lencastre, H., Garau, J., Kluytmans, J., Malhotra-Kumar, S., et al. (2018). Methicillin-resistant Staphylococcus aureus. *Nature Reviews Disease Primers*, *4*, 18033.

Lee, H.Y. & Kim, Y.K. (2008). Plasma brain-derived neurotrophic factor as a peripheral marker for the action mechanism of antidepressants. *Neuropsychobiology*, *57*, 194–199.

Lee, J.L.C., Nader, K., & Schiller, D. (2017). An update on memory reconsolidation updating. *Trends in Cognitive Science*, *21*, 531–545.

Lee, P., Le Saux, M., Siegel, R., Goyal, M., Chen, C., et al. (2019). Racial and ethnic disparities in the management of acute pain in US emergency departments: meta-analysis and systematic review. *The American Journal of Emergency Medicine*, *37*, 1770–1777.

Leggio, L., Zywiak, W.H., Fricchione, S.R., Edwards, S.M., de la Monte, S.M., et al. (2014). Intravenous ghrelin administration increases alcohol craving in alcohol-dependent heavy drinkers: A preliminary investigation. *Biological Psychiatry*, *76*, 734–741.

Lehrer, S. & Rheinstein, P.H. (2019). Nonsteroidal anti-inflammatory drugs (NSAIDs) reduce suicidal ideation and depression. *Discovery Medicine*, *28*, 205–212.

Lehrner, A., Hildebrandt, T., Bierer, L.M., Flory, J.D., Bader, H.N., et al. (2021). A randomized, double-blind, placebo-controlled trial of hydrocortisone augmentation of Prolonged Exposure for PTSD in US combat veterans. *Behaviour Research and Therapy*, *144*, 103924.

Lenze, E.J., Mattar, C., Zorumski, C.F., Stevens, A., Schweiger, J., et al. (2020). Fluvoxamine vs placebo and Clinical deterioration in outpatients with symptomatic COVID-19: A randomized clinical trial. *JAMA*, *324*, 2292–2300.

Leon, L.J., Doyle, R., Diez-Benavente, E., Clark, T.G., Klein, N., et al. (2018). Enrichment of clinically relevant organisms in spontaneous preterm-delivered placentas and reagent contamination across all clinical groups in a large pregnancy cohort in the United Kingdom. *Applied & Environmental Microbiology, 84*, pii: e00483-18.

Leone, R.D., Zhao, L., Englert, J.M., Sun, I.M., Oh, M.H., et al. (2019). Glutamine blockade induces divergent metabolic programs to overcome tumor immune evasion. *Science, 366*, 1013–1021.

Leor, J., Poole, W.K., & Kloner, R.A. (1996). Sudden cardiac death triggered by an earthquake. *New England Journal of Medicine, 334*, 413–419.

LeRoy, A.S., Murdock, K.W., Jaremka, L.M., Loya, A., Fagundes. C.P. (2017). Loneliness predicts self-reported cold symptoms after a viral challenge. *Health Psychology, 36*, 512–520.

Leschak, C.J. & Eisenberger, N.I. (2019). Two distinct immune pathways linking social relationships with health: Inflammatory and antiviral processes. *Psychosomatic Medicine, 81*, 711–719.

Leuchter, A.F., Cook, I.A., Hunter, A.M., Cai, C., & Horvath, S. (2012). Resting-state quantitative electroencephalography reveals increased neurophysiologic connectivity in depression. *PlosOne, 7*, e32508.

Leung, J., Chan, G.C.K., Hides, L., & Hall, W.D. (2020). What is the prevalence and risk of cannabis use disorders among people who use cannabis? A systematic review and meta-analysis. *Addictive Behaviors, 109*, 106479.

Levenson, R.W. (2019). Stress and illness: A role for specific emotions. *Psychosomatic Medicine, 81*, 720–730.

Levy, M., Thaiss, C.A., & Elinav, E. (2015). Taming the inflammasome. *Nature Medicine, 21*, 213–215.

Lewis, A.C. & Sherman, S.J. (2010). Perceived entitativity and the black-sheep effect: When will we denigrate negative ingroup members? *Journal of Social Psychology, 150*, 211–225.

Li, C.T., Yang, K.C., & Lin, W.C. (2019). Glutamatergic dysfunction and glutamatergic compounds for major psychiatric disorders: Evidence from clinical neuroimaging studies. *Frontiers in Psychiatry, 9*, 767.

Li, H., Cui, L., Li, J., Liu, Y., & Chen, Y. (2021). Comparative efficacy and acceptability of neuromodulation procedures in the treatment of treatment-resistant depression: A network meta-analysis of randomized controlled trials. *Journal of Affective Disorders, 287*, 115–124.

Li, J., Liu, S., Li, S., Feng, R., Na, L., et al. (2017). Prenatal exposure to famine and the development of hyperglycemia and type 2 diabetes in adulthood across consecutive generations: a population-based cohort study of families in Suihua, China. *American Journal of Clinical Nutrition, 105*, 221–227.

Li, Y., Simmler, L.D., Van Zessen, R., Flakowski, J., Wan, J.X., et al. (2021). Synaptic mechanism underlying serotonin modulation of transition to cocaine addiction. *Science, 37*, 1252–1256.

Li, Z., Yan, H., Zhang, X., Shah, S., & Yang, G. (2021). Air pollution interacts with genetic risk to influence cortical networks implicated in depression. *Proceedings of the National Academy of Sciences, 118*, e2109310118.

Liang, G., Zhao, C., Zhang, H., Mattei, L., Sherrill-Mix, S., et al. (2020). The stepwise assembly of the neonatal virome is modulated by breastfeeding. *Nature, 581*, 470–474.

Liao, L.M. & Carey, M.G. (2015). Laboratory-induced mental stress, cardiovascular response, and psychological characteristics. *Reviews in Cardiovascular Medicine, 16*, 28–35.

Liebenberg, L., Ikeda, J., & Wood, M. (2015). "It's just part of my culture": Understanding language and land in the resilience processes of Aboriginal youth. In L. Theron, L. Liebenberg, & M. Ungar (eds.), *Youth Resilience and Culture* (pp. 105–116). Dordrecht: Springer.

Lieberman, M.D. & Eisenberger, N.I. (2015). The dorsal anterior cingulate cortex is selective for pain: Results from large-scale reverse inference. *Proceedings of the National Academy of Sciences, 112*, 15250–15255.

Lijffijt, M., Hu, K., & Swann, A.C. (2014). Stress modulates illness-course of substance use disorders: a translational review. *Frontiers in Psychiatry, 5*, 83.

Lin, L.Y., Sidani, J.E., Shensa, A., Radovic, A., Miller, E. et al. (2016). Association between social media use and depression among US young adults. *Depression and Anxiety, 33*, 323–331.

Linde, K., Berner, M.M., & Kriston, L. (2008). St John's wort for major depression. *Cochrane Database Systematic Reviews, 4*, CD000448.

Lindqvist, D., Epel, E.S., Mellon, S.H., Penninx, B.W., Révész, D., et al. (2015). Psychiatric disorders and leukocyte telomere length: Underlying mechanisms linking mental illness with cellular aging. *Neuroscience & Biobehavioral Reviews, 55*, 333–364.

Lindsay, E.K. (2021). Mindfulness interventions for offsetting health risk following early life stress: Promising directions. *Behavior, and Immunity – Health, 17*, 100338.

Liossis, S.N. & Staveri, C. (2021). What's new in the treatment of systemic lupus erythematosus. *Frontiers in Medicine, 8*, 655100.

Liotti, M., Mayberg, H.S., McGinnis, S., Brannan, S.L., Jerabek, P. (2002). Unmasking disease-specific cerebral blood flow abnormalities: Mood challenge in patients with remitted unipolar depression. *American Journal of Psychiatry, 159*, 1830–1840.

Lismer, A., Dumeaux, V., Lafleur, C., Lambrot, R., Brind'Amour, J., et al. (2021). Histone H3 lysine 4 trimethylation in sperm is transmitted to the embryo and associated with diet-induced phenotypes in the offspring. *Developmental Cell, 56*, 671–686.e676.

Liu, Q.S., Pu, L., & Poo, M.M. (2005). Repeated cocaine exposure in vivo facilitates LTP induction in midbrain dopamine neurons. *Nature, 437*, 1027–1031.

Liu, R.T. & Alloy, L.B. (2010). Stress generation in depression: A systematic review of the empirical literature and recommendations for future study. *Clinical Psychology Review, 30*, 582–593.

Liu, R.T., Walsh, R.F., & Sheehan, A.E. (2019). Prebiotics and probiotics for depression and anxiety: A systematic review and meta-analysis of controlled clinical trials. *Neuroscience & Biobehavioral Reviews, 102*, 13–23.

Loftus, E. (2003). Our changeable memories: Legal and practical implications. *Nature Reviews Neuroscience, 4*, 231–234.

Lomanowska, A.M., Boivin, M., Hertzman, C., & Fleming, A.S. (2017). Parenting begets parenting: A neurobiological perspective on early adversity and the transmission of parenting styles across generations. *Neuroscience, 342*, 120–139.

Long, K.L., Chao, L.L., Kazama, Y., An, A., & Hu, K.Y. (2021). Regional gray matter oligodendrocyte- and myelin-related measures are associated with differential susceptibility to stress-induced behavior in rats and humans. *Translational Psychiatry, 11*, 631.

Long, Z., Medlock, C., Dzemidzic, M., Shin, Y.W., Goddard, A.W., & Dydak, U. (2013). Decreased GABA levels in anterior cingulate cortex/medial prefrontal cortex in panic disorder. *Progress in Neuropsychopharmacology & Biological Psychiatry, 44*, 131–135.

Loucks, E.B., Britton, W.B., Howe, C.J., Eaton, C.B., & Buka, S.L. (2015). Positive associations of dispositional mindfulness with cardiovascular health: The New England Family Study. *International Journal of Behavioral Medicine, 22*, 540–550.

Lu, A., Steiner, M.A., Whittle, N., Vogl, A.M., Walser, S.M., et al. (2008). Conditional mouse mutants highlight mechanisms of corticotropin-releasing hormone effects on stress-coping behavior. *Molecular Psychiatry, 13*, 1028–1042.

Lu, H.C. & Mackie, K. (2016). An introduction to the endogenous cannabinoid system. *Biological Psychiatry, 79*, 516–525.

Luby, J.L. Barch, D.M., Belden, A., Gaffrey, M.S., Tillman, R., et al. (2012). Maternal support in early childhood predicts larger hippocampal volumes at school age. *Proceedings of the National Academy of Sciences, 109*, 2854–2859.

Lukkes, J.L., Meda, S., Norman, K.J., & Andersen, S.L. (2018). Anhedonic behavior and γ-amino butyric acid during a sensitive period in female rats exposed to early adversity. *Journal of Psychiatry Research, 100*, 8–15.

Luo, F.F., Han, F., & Shi, Y.X. (2011). Changes in 5-HT1A receptor in the dorsal raphe nucleus in a rat model of post-traumatic stress disorder. *Molecular Medicine Reports, 4*, 843–847.

Luo, J., Zhu, X., Jian, J., Chen, X., & Yin, K. (2021). Cardiovascular disease in patients with COVID-19: Evidence from cardiovascular pathology to treatment. *Acta Biochimica et Biophysica Sinica, 53*, 273–282.

Lupien, S.J., McEwen, B.S., Gunnar, M.R., & Heim, C. (2009). Effects of stress throughout the lifespan on the brain, behaviour and cognition. *Nature Reviews Neuroscience, 10*, 434–445.

Lupien, S.J., Ouellet-Morin, I., Herba, C.M., Juster, R., & McEwen, B.S. (2016). From vulnerability to neurotoxicity: A developmental approach to the effects of stress on the brain and behavior. *Epigenetics and Neuroendocrinology*, 3–48.

Lüscher, C. & Janak, P.H. (2021). Consolidating the circuit model for addiction. *Annual Review of Neuroscience, 44*, 173–195.

Lüscher, C., Robbins, T.W., & Everitt, B.J. (2020). The transition to compulsion in addiction. *Nature Reviews in Neuroscience, 21*, 247–263.

Lussier, D.M. & Schreiber, R.D. (2016). Cancer immunosurveillance: Immunoediting. *Encyclopedia of Immunobiology, 4,* 396–405.

Lutgendorf, S.K., Weinrib, A.Z., Penedo, F., Russell, D., DeGeest, K., et al. (2008). Interleukin-6, cortisol, and depressive symptoms in ovarian cancer patients. *Journal of Clinical Oncology, 26,* 4820–4827.

Lutz, B., Marsicano, G., Maldonado, R., & Hillard, C.J. (2015). The endocannabinoid system in guarding against fear, anxiety and stress. *Nature Reviews in Neuroscience, 16,* 705–718.

Luu, M., Riester, Z., Baldrich, A., Reichardt, N., & Yuille, S. (2021). Microbial short-chain fatty acids modulate CD8 T cell responses and improve adoptive immunotherapy for cancer. *Nature Communications, 12,* 4077.

Ly, L., Chan, D., Aarabi, M., Landry, M., Behan, N.A., et al. (2017). Intergenerational impact of paternal lifetime exposures to both folic acid deficiency and supplementation on reproductive outcomes and imprinted gene methylation. *Molecular Human Reproduction, 23,* 461–477.

Lyons, C., Hopley, P., & Horrocks, J. (2009). A decade of stigma and discrimination in mental health: *plus ça change, plus c'est la même chose* (the more things change, the more they stay the same). *Journal of Psychiatric and Mental Health Nursing, 16,* 501–507.

MacCormack, J.K., Gaudier-Diaz, M.M., Armstrong-Carter, E.L., Arevalo, J.M.G., Meltzer-Brody, S. et al. (2021). Beta-adrenergic blockade blunts inflammatory and antiviral/antibody gene expression responses to acute psychosocial stress. *Neuropsychopharmacology, 46,* 756–762.

MacIntyre, C.R., Mahimbo, A., Moa, A.M., & Barnes, M. (2016). Influenza vaccine as a coronary intervention for prevention of myocardial infarction. *Heart, 102,* 1953–1956.

Mackenzie, J.S. & Jeggo, M. (2019). The One Health approach—Why is it so important? *Tropical Medicine and Infectious Disease, 4,* 88.

Madison, A.A., Shrout, M.R., Renna, M.E., & Kiecolt-Glaser, J.K. (2021). Psychological and behavioral predictors of vaccine efficacy: Considerations for COVID-19. *Perspectives on Psychological Science, 16,* 191–203.

Maier, S.F. & Seligman, M.E. (2016). Learned helplessness at fifty: Insights from neuroscience. *Psychological Review, 123,* 349–367.

Mailing, L.J., Allen, J.M., Buford, T.W., Fields, C.J., & Woods J.A. (2019). Exercise and the gut microbiome: A review of the evidence, potential mechanisms, and implications for human health. *Exercise Sports Science Review, 47,* 75–85.

Maltz, R.M., Keirsey, J., Kim, S.C., Mackos, A.R., Gharaibeh, R.Z., et al. (2019). Social stress affects colonic inflammation, the gut microbiome, and short-chain fatty acid levels and receptors. *Journal of Pediatric Gastroenterology & Nutrition, 68,* 533–540.

Mamdani, M., Gomes, T., Greaves, S., Manji, S., Juurlink, D.N., et al. (2019). Association between angiotensin-converting enzyme inhibitors, angiotensin receptor blockers, and suicide. *JAMA Network Open, 2,* e1913304-e1913304.

Manikkam, M., Haque, M.M., Guerrero-Bosagna, C., Nilsson, E.E., & Skinner, M.K. (2014). Pesticide methoxychlor promotes the epigenetic transgenerational inheritance of adult-onset disease through the female germline. *PLoS One, 9,* e102091.

Manners, M.T., Yohn, N.L., Lahens, N.F., Grant, G.R., Bartolomei, M.S., & Blendy, J.A. (2019). Transgenerational inheritance of chronic adolescent stress: Effects of stress response and the amygdala transcriptome. *Genes, Brain and Behavior, 18,* e12493.

Mantsch, J.R., Baker, D.A., Funk, D., Lê, A.D., & Shaham, Y. (2016). Stress-induced reinstatement of drug seeking: 20 years of progress. *Neuropsychopharmacology, 41,* 335–356.

Marano, R.J. & Ben-Jonathan, N. (2014). Minireview: Extrapituitary prolactin: An update on the distribution, regulation, and functions. *Molecular Endocrinology, 28,* 622–633.

Marin, I.A., Goertz, J.E., Ren, T., Rich, S.S., Onengut-Gumuscu, S., et al. (2017). Microbiota alteration is associated with the development of stress-induced despair behavior. *Science Reports, 7,* 43859.

Marmot, M.G., Rose, G., Shipley, M., & Hamilton, P.J. (1978). Employment grade and coronary heart disease in British civil servants. *Journal of Epidemiology and Community Health, 32,* 244–249.

Marmot, M.G., Shipley, M.J., Hemingway, H., Head, J., & Brunner, E.J. (2008). Biological and behavioural explanations of social inequalities in coronary heart disease: the Whitehall II study. *Diabetologia, 51,* 1980–1988.

Marshall, B.J. & Warren, J.R. (1984). Unidentified curved bacilli in the stomach of patients with gastritis and peptic ulceration. *The Lancet, 323,* 1311–1315.

Martin, M.D. & Badovinac, V.P. (2018). Defining Memory CD8 T Cell. *Frontiers in Immunology, 9,* 2692.

Martínez, P., Gloger, S., Diez de Medina, D., González, A., Carrasco, M.I., et al. (2021). Early adverse stress and depressive and bipolar disorders: A systematic review and meta-analysis of treatment interventions. *Frontiers in Psychiatry, 12,* 650706.

Martinez-Muniz, G.A. & Wood, S.K. (2020). Sex differences in the inflammatory consequences of stress: Implications for pharmacotherapy. *Journal of Pharmacology & Experimental Therapy, 375,* 161–174.

Mash, D.C., Duque, L., Page, B., & Allen-Ferdinand, K. (2018). Ibogaine detoxification transitions opioid and cocaine abusers between dependence and abstinence: Clinical observations and treatment outcomes. *Frontiers in Pharmacology, 9,* 529.

Maslanik, T., Bernstein-Hanley, I., Helwig, B., & Fleshner, M. (2012). The impact of acute-stressor exposure on splenic innate immunity: A gene expression analysis. *Brain, Behavior, and Immunity, 26,* 142–149.

Masten, C.L., Telzer, E.H., Fuligni, A.J., Lieberman, M.D., & Eisenberger, N.I. (2011). Time spent with friends in adolescence relates to less neural sensitivity to later peer rejection. *Social Cognition and Affective Neuroscience, 7,* 106–114.

Matejuk, A. & Ransohoff, R.M. (2020). Crosstalk between astrocytes and microglia: An overview. *Frontiers in Immunology*, *11*, 1416.

Matheson, K. & Anisman, H. (2003). Systems of coping associated with dysphoria, anxiety and depressive illness: A multivariate profile perspective. *Stress*, *6*, 223–234.

Matheson, K. & Anisman, H. (2012). Biological and psychosocial responses to discrimination. In J. Jetten, C. Haslam, and S.A. Haslam (eds.), *The Social Cure* (pp. 133–154). New York: Psychology Press.

Matheson, K., Asokumar, A., & Anisman, H. (2020). Resilience: Safety in the aftermath of traumatic stressor experiences. *Frontiers in Behavioral Neuroscience*, *14*, 596919.

Matheson, K., Bombay, A., Dixon, K., & Anisman, H. (2020). Intergenerational communication regarding Indian Residential Schools: Implications for cultural identity, perceived discrimination, and depressive symptoms. *Transcultural Psychiatry*, *57*, 304–332.

Matheson, K., Bombay, A., Haslam, S.A., & Anisman, H. (2016). Indigenous identity transformations: The pivotal role of student-to-student abuse in Indian Residential Schools. *Transcultural Psychiatry*, *53*, 551–573.

Matheson, K., Foster, M.D., Bombay, A., McQuaid, R.J., & Anisman, H. (2019). Traumatic experiences, perceived discrimination, and psychological distress among members of various socially marginalized groups. *Frontiers in Psychology*, *10*, 416.

Matheson, K., Skomorovsky, A., Fiocco, A., & Anisman, H. (2007). The limits of 'adaptive' coping: Well-being and affective reactions to stressors among women in abusive dating relationships. *Stress*, *10*, 75–92.

Matta, S.M., Hill-Yardin, E., & Crack, P.J. (2019). The influence of neuroinflammation in Autism Spectrum Disorder. *Brain, Behavior, and Immunity*, *79*, 75–90.

Matzrafi, M. (2019). Climate change exacerbates pest damage through reduced pesticide efficacy. *Pest Management Science*, *75*, 9–13.

Mavranezouli, I., Megnin-Viggars, O., Daly, C., Dias, S., Welton, N.J., et al. (2020). Psychological treatments for post-traumatic stress disorder in adults: A network meta-analysis. *Psychological Medicine*, *50*, 542–555.

Mayberg, H.S., Lozano, A.M., Voon, V., McNeely, H.E., Seminowicz, D., Hamani, C., & Kennedy, S.H. (2005). Deep brain stimulation for depression. *Neuron*, *45*, 651–660.

Maymon, N., Mizrachi Zer-Aviv, T., Sabban, E.L., & Akirav, I. (2020). Neuropeptide Y and cannabinoids interaction in the amygdala after exposure to shock and reminders model of PTSD. *Neuropharmacology*, *162*, 107804.

Mays, J.W., Bailey, M.T., Hunzeker, J.T., Powell. N.D., Papenfuss, T., et al. (2010). Influenza virus-specific immunological memory is enhanced by repeated social defeat. *Journal of Immunology*, *184*, 2014–2025.

McAndrew, A., Lawn, W., Stevens, T., Porffy, L., Brandner, B., & Morgan, C.J. (2017). A proof-of-concept investigation into ketamine as a pharmacological treatment for alcohol dependence: study protocol for a randomised controlled trial. *Trials*, *18*, 159.

McAuley, P.A., Artero, E.G., Sui, X., Lee, D.C., Church, T.S., et al. (2012). The obesity paradox, cardiorespiratory fitness, and coronary heart disease. *Mayo Clinic Proceedings*, *87*, 443–451.

McCarthy, A.H., Peck, L.S., & Aldridge, D.C. (2022). Ship traffic connects Antarctica's fragile coasts to worldwide ecosystems. *Proceedings of the National Academy of Sciences, 119,* e2110303118.

McCreary, J.K., Erickson, Z.T., Hao, Y., Ilnytskyy, Y., Kovalchuk, I., & Metz, G.A. (2016). Environmental intervention as a therapy for adverse programming by ancestral stress. *Science Reports, 6,* 37814.

McCrory, E.J., De Brito, S.A., Sebastian, C.L., Mechelli, A., Bird, G., Kelly, P.A., & Viding, E. (2011). Heightened neural reactivity to threat in child victims of family violence. *Current Biology, 21,* R947–R948.

McCullough, M.E. (2000). Forgiveness as human strength: Theory, measurement, and links to well-being. *Journal of Social and Clinical Psychology, 19,* 43–55.

McDaniel, M.M., Chawla, A.S., Jain, A., Meibers, H.E., Saha, I., et al. (2022). Effector memory CD4+ T cells induce damaging innate inflammation and autoimmune pathology by engaging CD40 and TNFR on myeloid cells. *Science Immunology, 7,* eabk0182.

McDonald, B. & McCoy, K.D. (2019). Maternal microbiota in pregnancy and early life. *Science, 365,* 984–985.

McEwen, B.S. & Akil, H. (2020). Revisiting the stress concept: Implications for affective disorders. *Journal of Neuroscience, 40,* 12–21.

McEwen, B.S., Bowles, N.P., Gray, J.D., Hill, M.N., & Hunter, R.G. (2015). Mechanisms of stress in the brain. *Nature Neuroscience, 18,* 1353–1363.

McEwen, B.S. & Gianaros, P.J. (2011). Stress- and allostasis-induced brain plasticity. *Annual Review of Medicine, 62,* 431–445.

McEwen, B.S. & Wingfield, J.C. (2003). The concept of allostasis in biology and biomedicine. *Hormones and Behavior, 43,* 2–15.

McEwen, C.A. & McEwen, B.S. (2017). Social structure, adversity, toxic stress, and intergenerational poverty: An early childhood model. *Annual Review of Sociology, 43,* 445–472

McEwen, S.A. & Collignon, P.J. (2018). Antimicrobial resistance: A one health perspective. *Microbiology Spectrum, 6.*

McGowan, P.O., Sasaki, A., D'Alessio, A.C., Dymov, S., Labonté, B., et al. (2009). Epigenetic regulation of the glucocorticoid receptor in human brain associates with childhood abuse. *Nature Neuroscience, 12,* 342–348.

McGowan, P.O. & Szyf, M. (2010). The epigenetics of social adversity in early life: Implications for mental health outcomes. *Neurobiology of Disease, 39,* 66–72.

McHugh, R.K., Whitton, S.W., Peckham, A.D., Welge, J.A., & Otto, M.W. (2013). Patient preference for psychological vs pharmacologic treatment of psychiatric disorders: A meta-analytic review. *Journal of Clinical Psychiatry, 74,* 595–602.

McInnes, I.B., Buckley, C.D., & Isaacs, J.D. (2016). Cytokines in rheumatoid arthritis – shaping the immunological landscape. *Nature Reviews in Rheumatology, 12,* 63–68.

McInnes, I.B., & Schett, G. (2017). Pathogenetic insights from the treatment of rheumatoid arthritis. *The Lancet, 389,* 2328–2337.

McNamara, N., Stevenson, C., Costa, S., Bowe, M., Wakefield, J., et al. (2021). Community identification, social support, and loneliness: The benefits of social identification for personal well-being. *British Journal of Social Psychology, 60,* 1379–1402.

McQuaid, R.J., McInnis, O.A., Abizaid, A., & Anisman, H. (2014). Making room for oxytocin in understanding depression. *Neuroscience & Biobehavioral Reviews, 45,* 305–322.

McQuaid, R.J., McInnis, O.A., Matheson, K., & Anisman, H. (2015). Distress of ostracism: Oxytocin receptor gene polymorphism confers sensitivity to social exclusion. *Social Cognitive & Affective Neuroscience, 10,* 1153–1159.

McQuaid, R.J., McInnis, O.A., Stead, J.D., Matheson, K., & Anisman, H. (2013). A paradoxical association of an oxytocin receptor gene polymorphism: Early-life adversity and vulnerability to depression. *Frontiers in Neuroscience, 7,* 128.

Mechoulam, R., Hanuš, L.O., Pertwee, R., & Howlett, A.C. (2014). Early phytocannabinoid chemistry to endocannabinoids and beyond. *Nature Reviews in Neuroscience, 15,* 757–764.

Merali, Z., Anisman, H., James, J.S., Kent, P., & Schulkin, J. (2008). Effects of corticosterone on corticotrophin-releasing hormone and gastrin-releasing peptide release in response to an aversive stimulus in two regions of the forebrain (central nucleus of the amygdala and prefrontal cortex). *European Journal of Neuroscience, 28,* 165–172.

Merali, Z., Du, L., Hrdina, P., Palkovits, M., Faludi, G., et al. (2004). Dysregulation in the suicide brain: mRNA expression of corticotropin releasing hormone receptors and GABAA receptor subunits in frontal cortical brain region. *Journal of Neuroscience, 24,* 1478–1485.

Merali, Z., Graitson, S., Mackay, J.C. & Kent, P. (2013). Stress and eating: A dual role for bombesin-like peptides. *Frontiers in Neuroscience, 7,* 193.

Merali, Z., Kent, P., Du, L., Hrdina, P., Palkovits, M., et al. (2006). Corticotropin-releasing hormone, arginine vasopressin, gastrin-releasing peptide, and neuromedin B alterations in stress-relevant brain regions of suicides and control subjects. *Biological Psychiatry, 59,* 594–602.

Merali, Z., Khan, S., Michaud, D. S., Shippy, S.A., & Anisman, H. (2004). Does amygdaloid corticotropin-releasing hormone (CRH) mediate anxiety-like behaviors? Dissociation of anxiogenic effects and CRH release. *European Journal of Neuroscience, 20,* 229–239.

Merrill, S.M., Moore, S.R., Gladish, N., Giesbrecht, G.F., Dewey, D. (2021). Paternal adverse childhood experiences: Associations with infant DNA methylation. *Developmental Psychobiology, 63,* e22174.

Metz, S., Duesenberg, M., Hellmann-Regen, J., Wolf, O.T., Roepke, S., et al. (2020). Blunted salivary cortisol response to psychosocial stress in women with posttraumatic stress disorder. *Journal of Psychiatry Research, 130,* 112–119.

Meyer, U. (2019). Neurodevelopmental resilience and susceptibility to maternal immune activation. *Trends in Neuroscience, 42,* 793–806.

Miao, Z., Wang, Y., & Sun, Z. (2020). The relationships between stress, mental disorders, and epigenetic regulation of BDNF. *International Journal of Molecular Science, 21,* 1375.

Michaud, K., Matheson, K., Kelly, O. & Anisman, H. (2008). Impact of stressors in a natural context on release of cortisol in healthy adult humans: a meta-analysis. *Stress, 11*, 177–197.

Mika, A., Day, H.E.W., Martinez, A., Rumian, N.L., Greenwood, B.N., et al. (2017). Early life diets with prebiotics and bioactive milk fractions attenuate the impact of stress on learned helplessness behaviours and alter gene expression within neural circuits important for stress resistance. *European Journal of Neuroscience, 45*, 342–357.

Mikton, C., de la Fuente-Núñez, V., Officer, A., & Krug, E. (2021). Ageism: A social determinant of health that has come of age. *The Lancet, 397*, 1333–1334.

Milad, M.R. & Rauch, S.L. (2012). Obsessive-compulsive disorder: Beyond segregated cortico-striatal pathways. *Trends in Cognitive Sciences, 16*, 43–51.

Milgram, S. (1963). Behavioral study of obedience. *The Journal of Abnormal and Social Psychology, 67*, 371–378.

Miller, A.H., Maletic, V., & Raison, C.L. (2009). Inflammation and its discontents: The role of cytokines in the pathophysiology of major depression. *Biological Psychiatry, 65*, 732–741.

Miller, A.H. & Raison, C.L. (2016). The role of inflammation in depression: From evolutionary imperative to modern treatment target. *Nature Reviews in Immunology, 16*, 22–34.

Miller, G.E., Chen, E., & Parker, K.J. (2011). Psychological stress in childhood and susceptibility to the chronic diseases of aging: Moving toward a model of behavioural and biological mechanisms. *Psychological Bulletin, 137*, 959–997.

Mineur, Y.S. & Picciotto, M.R. (2021). The role of acetylcholine in negative encoding bias: Too much of a good thing? *European Journal of Neuroscience, 53*, 114–125.

Mishra, A., Lai, G.C., Yao, L.J., Aung, T.T., Shental N., et al. (2021). Microbial exposure during early human development primes fetal immune cells. *Cell, 25*, S0092-8674(21)00574-2.

Miskowiak, K.W., Vinberg, M., Harmer, C.J., Ehrenreich, H., & Kessing, L.V. (2012). Erythropoietin: A candidate treatment for mood symptoms and memory dysfunction in depression. *Psychopharmacology, 219*, 687–698.

Mitchell, J.M., Bogenschutz, M., Lilienstein, A., Harrison, C., Kleiman, S., Parker-Guilbert, K., et al. (2021). MDMA-assisted therapy for severe PTSD: A randomized, double-blind, placebo-controlled phase 3 study. *Nature Medicine, 27*, 1025–1033.

Mody, I. & Maguire, J. (2012). The reciprocal regulation of stress hormones and GABA(A) receptors. *Frontiers in Cellular Neuroscience, 6*, 4.

Mogil, J.S. (2020). Qualitative sex differences in pain processing: Emerging evidence of a biased literature. *Nature Reviews in Neuroscience, 21*, 353–365.

Mohr, D.C. (2007). Stress and multiple sclerosis. *Journal of Neurology, 254*, Suppl. 2: II65–8.

Moisan, M.P. (2021). Sexual dimorphism in glucocorticoid stress response. *International Journal of Molecular Science, 22*, 3139.

Molla, M.D., Akalu, Y., Geto, Z., Dagnew, B., Ayelign, B., & Shibabaw, T. (2020). Role of caspase-1 in the pathogenesis of inflammatory-associated chronic noncommunicable diseases. *Journal of Inflammatory Research, 13*, 749–764.

Moloney, G.M., Dinan, T.G., Clarke, G., & Cryan, J.F. (2019). Microbial regulation of microRNA expression in the brain–gut axis. *Current Opinions in Pharmacology, 48*, 120–126.

Monteggia, L.M., Luikart, B., Barrot, M., Theobold, D., Malkovska, I., et al. (2007). Brain-derived neurotrophic factor conditional knockouts show gender differences in depression-related behaviors. *Biological Psychiatry, 61*, 187–197.

Moody, T.W. & Merali, Z. (2004). Bombesin-like peptides and associated receptors within the brain: Distribution and behavioral implications. *Peptides, 25*, 511–520.

Moog, N.K., Nolvi, S., Kleih, T.S., Styner, M., Gilmore, J.H., et al. (2021). Prospective association of maternal psychosocial stress in pregnancy with newborn hippocampal volume and implications for infant social-emotional development. *Neurobiology of Stress, 15*, 100368.

Morales, M.E. & Yong, R.J. (2021). Racial and ethnic disparities in the treatment of chronic pain. *Pain Medicine, 22*(1), 75–90.

Morena, M., Patel, S., Bains, J.S., & Hill, M.N. (2016). Neurobiological interactions between stress and the endocannabinoid system. *Neuropsychopharmacology, 41*, 80–102.

Morewedge, C.K. & Kahneman, D. (2010). Associative processes in intuitive judgment. *Trends in Cognitive Sciences, 14*, 435–440.

Moriguchi, S., Takamiya, A., Noda, Y., Horita, N., Wada, M., et al. (2019). Glutamatergic neurometabolite levels in major depressive disorder: a systematic review and meta-analysis of proton magnetic resonance spectroscopy studies. *Molecular Psychiatry, 24*, 952–964.

Morres, I.D., Hatzigeorgiadis, A., Stathi, A., Comoutos, N., Arpin-Cribbie, C., et al. (2019). Aerobic exercise for adult patients with major depressive disorder in mental health services: A systematic review and meta-analysis. *Depression & Anxiety, 36*, 39–53.

Morris, H., Hatzikiriakidis, K., Savaglio, M., Dwyer, J., Lewis, C., et al. (2022). Eye movement desensitization and reprocessing for the treatment and early intervention of trauma among first responders: A systematic review. *Journal of Traumatic Stress, 35*, 778–790.

Mosby, I. (2013). Administering colonial science: Nutrition research and human biomedical experimentation in Aboriginal communities and residential schools, 1942–1952. *Histoire sociale/Social History, 46*, 145–172.

Moylan, S., Berk, M., Dean, O.M., Samuni, Y., Williams, L.J., et al. (2014). Oxidative & nitrosative stress in depression: Why so much stress? *Neuroscience & Biobehavioral Reviews, 45*, 46–62.

Mrkobrada, M., Chan, M.T.V., Cowan, D., Campbell, D., Wang, C.Y., et al. (2019). Perioperative covert stroke in patients undergoing non-cardiac surgery (NeuroVISION): A prospective cohort study. *The Lancet, 394*, 1022–1029.

Mumtaz, F., Khan, M.I., Zubair, M., & Dehpour, A.R. (2018). Neurobiology and consequences of social isolation stress in animal model—A comprehensive review. *Biomedicine & Pharmacotherapy, 105*, 1205–1222.

Muncan, B. (2018). Cardiovascular disease in racial/ethnic minority populations: Illness burden and overview of community-based interventions. *Public Health Review, 39*, 32.

Murnane, K.S. (2019). Serotonin 2A receptors are a stress response system: Implications for post-traumatic stress disorder. *Behavioral Pharmacology, 30,* 151–162.

Murphy, M.L., Slavich, G.M., Rohleder, N., & Miller, G.E. (2013). Targeted rejection triggers differential pro- and anti-inflammatory gene expression in adolescents as a function of social status. *Clinical Psychological Science, 1,* 30–40.

Musazzi, L., Treccani, G., & Popoli, M. (2015). Functional and structural remodeling of glutamate synapses in prefrontal and frontal cortex induced by behavioral stress. *Frontiers in Psychiatry, 6,* 60.

Muscatell, K.A., Eisenberger, N.I., Dutcher, J.M., Cole, S.W., & Bower, J.E. (2016). Links between inflammation, amygdala reactivity, and social support in breast cancer survivors. *Brain, Behavior, and Immunity, 53,* 34–38.

Muthuswamy, R., Okada, N.J., Jenkins, F.J., McGuire, K., McAuliffe, H.J., et al. (2017). Epinephrine promotes COX-2-dependent immune suppression in myeloid cells and cancer tissues. *Brain, Behavior, and Immunity, 62,* 78–86.

Mychasiuk, R., Schmold, N., Ilnytskyy, S., Kovalchuk, O., Kolb, B., & Gibb, R. (2011). Prenatal bystander stress alters brain, behavior, and the epigenome of developing rat offspring. *Developmental Neuroscience, 33,* 159–169.

Nackenoff, A.G., Moussa-Tooks, A.B., McMeekin, A.M., Veenstra-VanderWeele, J. & Blakely, R.D. (2016). Essential contributions of serotonin transporter inhibition to the acute and chronic actions of fluoxetine and citalopram in the SERT Met172 mouse. *Neuropsychopharmacology, 41,* 1733–1741.

Nagasawa, M., Mitsui, S., En, S., Ohtani, N., Ohta, M., et al. (2015). Social evolution: Oxytocin-gaze positive loop and the coevolution of human-dog bonds. *Science, 348,* 333–336.

Nahvi, R.J. & Sabban, E.L. (2020). Sex differences in the neuropeptide Y system and implications for stress related disorders. *Biomolecules, 10,* 1248.

Nautiyal, K.M. & Hen, R. (2017). Serotonin receptors in depression: from A to B. *F1000Res, 6,* 123.

Negi, S., Das, D.K., Pahari, S., Nadeem, S., & Agrewala, J.N. (2019). Potential role of gut microbiota in induction and regulation of innate immune memory. *Frontiers in Immunology, 10,* 2441.

Nejad, A.B., Rotgé, J.Y., Valabregue, R., Guérin-Langlois, C., & Hoertel, N. (2019). Medial prefrontal disengagement during self-focus in formerly depressed patients prone to rumination. *Journal of Affective Disorders, 247,* 36–44.

Nestler, E.J. (2008). Transcriptional mechanisms of addiction: Role of DeltaFosB. *Philosophical Transactions of the Royal Society of London, Series B: Biological Sciences, 363,* 3245–3255.

Neufeld-Cohen, A., Kelly, P.A., Paul, E.D., Carter, R.N., Skinner, E., et al. (2012). Chronic activation of corticotropin-releasing factor type 2 receptors reveals a key role for 5-HT1A receptor responsiveness in mediating behavioral and serotonergic responses to stressful challenge. *Biological Psychiatry, 72,* 437–447.

Nicolopoulou-Stamati, P., Maipas, S., Kotampasi, C., Stamatis, P., & Hens, L. (2016). Chemical pesticides and human health: The urgent need for a new concept in agriculture. *Frontiers in Public Health, 4,* 148.

Nie, X., Kitaoka, S., Tanaka, K., Segi-Nishida, E., Imoto, Y., et al. (2018). The innate immune receptors TLR2/4 mediate repeated social defeat stress-induced social avoidance through prefrontal microglial activation. *Neuron, 99,* 464–479.

Nikzad, R., Angelo, L.S., Aviles-Padilla, K., Le, D.T., Singh, V.K., et al. (2019). Human natural killer cells mediate adaptive immunity to viral antigens. *Science Immunology, 4,* pii: eaat8116.

Nilsson, E.E., Sadler-Riggleman, I., & Skinner, M.K. (2018). Environmentally induced epigenetic transgenerational inheritance of disease. *Environmental Epigenetics, 4,* dvy016.

Nobs, S.P., Tuganbaev, T., & Elinav, E. (2019). Microbiome diurnal rhythmicity and its impact on host physiology and disease risk. *EMBO Reports, 20,* e47129.

Nolan, M., Roman, E., Nasa, A., Levins, K.J., O'Hanlon, E., et al. (2020). Hippocampal and amygdalar volume changes in major depressive disorder: A targeted review and focus on stress. *Chronic Stress, 4,* p.2470547020944553.

Nolen-Hoeksema, S. (2000). The role of rumination in depressive disorders and mixed anxiety/depressive symptoms. *Journal of Abnormal Psychology, 109,* 504–511.

Nolen-Hoeksema, S. (1998). Ruminative coping with depression. In J. Heckhausen & C.S. Dweck (eds.), *Motivation and Self-Regulation Across the Life Span* (pp. 237–256). Cambridge: Cambridge University Press.

Nomura, Y., Rompala, G., Pritchett, L., Aushev, V., Chen, J., & Hurd, Y.L. (2021). Natural disaster stress during pregnancy is linked to reprogramming of the placenta transcriptome in relation to anxiety and stress hormones in young offspring. *Molecular Psychiatry, 26,* 6520–6530.

Nowacka-Chmielewska, M.M., Paul-Samojedny, M., Bielecka-Wajdman, A.M., Barski, J.J., & Obuchowicz, E. (2017). Alterations in VEGF expression induced by antidepressant drugs in female rats under chronic social stress. *Experimental & Therapeutic Medicine, 13,* 723–730.

Nuss, P. (2015). Anxiety disorders and GABA neurotransmission: A disturbance of modulation. *Neuropsychiatric Disease & Treatment, 11,* 165–175.

Nutt, D., Erritzoe, D., & Carhart-Harris, R. (2020). Psychedelic psychiatry's brave new world. *Cell, 181,* 24–28.

Nwanaji-Enwerem, J.C., Van Der Laan, L., Kogut, K., Eskenazi, B., Holland, N., et al. (2021). Maternal adverse childhood experiences before pregnancy are associated with epigenetic aging changes in their children. *Aging, 13,* 25653.

Oberlander, T.F., Weinberg, J., Papsdorf, M., Grunau, R., Misri, S., & Devlin, A.M. (2008). Prenatal exposure to maternal depression, neonatal methylation of human glucocorticoid receptor gene (NR3C1) and infant cortisol stress responses. *Epigenetics, 3,* 97–106.

Obradovich, N., Migliorini, R., Paulus, M.P., & Rahwan, I. (2018). Empirical evidence of mental health risks posed by climate change. *Proceedings of the National Academy of Sciences, 115,* 10953–10958.

Ochoa Arnedo, C., Sánchez, N., Sumalla, E.C., & Casellas-Grau, A. (2019). Stress and growth in cancer: mechanisms and psychotherapeutic interventions to facilitate a constructive balance. *Frontiers in Psychology, 10,* 177.

O'Connell, C.P., Goldstein-Piekarski, A.N., Nemeroff, C.B., Schatzberg, A.F., Debattista, C., et al. (2018). Antidepressant outcomes predicted by genetic variation in corticotropin-releasing hormone binding protein. *American Journal of Psychiatry, 175*, 251–261.

O'Donnell, K., Brydon, L., Wright, C.E., & Steptoe, A. (2008). Self-esteem levels and cardiovascular and inflammatory responses to acute stress. *Brain, Behavior, and Immunity, 22*, 1241–1247.

Offer, D. & Spiro, R.P. (1987). The disturbed adolescent goes to college. *Journal of American College Health, 35*, 209–214.

Ogbonnaya, E.S., Clarke, G., Shanahan, F., Dinan, T.G., Cryan, J.F., & O'Leary, O.F. (2015). Adult hippocampal neurogenesis is regulated by the microbiome. *Biological Psychiatry, 78*, e7–e9.

Ojard, C., Donnelly, J.P., Safford, M.M., Griffin, R., & Wang, H.E. (2015). Psychosocial stress as a risk factor for sepsis: a population-based cohort study. *Psychosomatic Medicine, 77*, 93–100.

Oliva, A., Torre, S., Taranto, P., Delvecchio, G., & Brambilla, P. (2020). Neural correlates of emotional processing in panic disorder: A mini review of functional magnetic resonance imaging studies. *Journal of Affective Disorders, 282*, 906–914.

O'Mahony, S.M., McVey Neufeld, K., Waworuntu, R.V., Pusceddu, M.M., Manurung, S., et al. (2020). The enduring effects of early-life stress on the microbiota-gut-brain axis are buffered by dietary supplementation with milk fat globule membrane and a prebiotic blend. *European Journal of Neuroscience, 51*, 1042–1058.

Onaka, T. & Takayanagi, Y. (2021). The oxytocin system and early-life experience-dependent plastic changes. *Journal of Neuroendocrinology, 33*, e13049.

Onasanya, O., Iyer, G., Lucas, E., Lin, D., Singh, S., & Alexander, G.C. (2016). Association between exogenous testosterone and cardiovascular events: an overview of systematic reviews. *The Lancet Diabetes & Endocrinology, 4*, 943–956.

Opacka-Juffry, J. & Mohiyeddini, C. (2012). Experience of stress in childhood negatively correlates with plasma oxytocin concentration in adult men. *Stress, 15*, 1–10.

Orri, M., Scardera, S., Perret, L.C., Bolanis, D., Temcheff, C., et al. (2020). Mental health problems and risk of suicidal ideation and attempts in adolescents. *Pediatrics, 146*, e20193823.

Ortiz-Ospina, E. & Beltekian, D. (2018). Why do women live longer than men. Our World in Data. Available online: https://ourworldindata.org/why-do-women-live-longer-than-men (accessed April 26, 2022).

Ortiz-Ospina, E. & Roser, M. (2016). Global health. Our World in Data. https://ourworldindata.org/health-meta

Osborne, S., Biaggi, A., Hazelgrove, K., Du Preez, A., & Nikkheslat, N. (2022). Increased maternal inflammation and poorer infant neurobehavioural competencies in women with a history of major depressive disorder from the psychiatry research and motherhood–Depression (PRAM-D) study. *Brain, Behavior, and Immunity, 99*, 223–230.

Ost, K.S. & Round, J.L. (2018). Communication between the microbiota and mammalian immunity. *Annual Review in Microbiology, 72*, 399–422.

Ostendorf, B.N., Bilanovic, J., Adaku, N., Tafreshian, K.N., Tavora, B., Vaughan, R.D., et al. (2020). Common germline variants of the human APOE gene modulate melanoma progression and survival. *Nature Medicine, 26*, 1048–1053.

Ousdal, O.T., Milde, A.M., Craven, A.R., Ersland, L., Endestad, T. et al. (2019). Prefrontal glutamate levels predict altered amygdala-prefrontal connectivity in traumatized youths. *Psychological Medicine, 49*, 1822–1830.

Oyola, M.G. & Handa, R.J. (2017). Hypothalamic–pituitary–adrenal and hypothalamic–pituitary–gonadal axes: Sex differences in regulation of stress responsivity. *Stress, 20*, 476–494.

Pace, T.W., Mletzko, T.C., Alagbe, O., Musselman, D. L., Nemeroff, C.B., et al. (2006). Increased stress-induced inflammatory responses in male patients with major depression and increased early life stress. *American Journal of Psychiatry, 163*, 1630–1633.

Paez, D.R. & Liu, J.H.-F. (2011). Collective memory of conflicts. In D. Bar-Tal (ed.), *Intergroup Conflicts and their Resolution: A Social Psychological Perspective* (pp. 105–124). New York: Psychology Press.

Pan, Q., Chen, X., Liao, S., Chen, X., Zhao, C., et al. (2019). Updated advances of linking psychosocial factors and sex hormones with systemic lupus erythematosus susceptibility and development. *PeerJ, 7*, e7179.

Pan, X., Kaminga, A.C., Wen, S.W., & Liu, A. (2018). Catecholamines in post-traumatic stress disorder: A systematic review and meta-analysis. *Frontiers in Molecular Neuroscience, 11*, 450.

Pandey, G.N., Rizavi, H.S., Ren, X., Fareed, J., Hoppensteadt, D.A., et al. (2011). Proinflammatory cytokines in the prefrontal cortex of teenage suicide victims. *Journal of Psychiatric Research, 46*, 57–63.

Panza, G.A., Puhl, R.M., Taylor, B.A., Zaleski, A.L., Livingston, J., & Pescatello, L.S. (2019). Links between discrimination and cardiovascular health among socially stigmatized groups: A systematic review. *PLoS One, 14*, e0217623.

Pape, K., Tamouza, R., Leboyer, M., & Zipp, F. (2019). Immunoneuropsychiatry – novel perspectives on brain disorders. *Nature Reviews Neurology, 15*, 317–328.

Paradies, Y., Ben, J., Denson, N., Elias. A., Priest, N., et al. (2015). Racism as a determinant of health: A systematic review and meta-analysis. *PLoS One, 10*, e0138511.

Park, C., Rosenblat, J.D., Brietzke, E., Pan, Z., Lee, Y., et al. (2019). Stress, epigenetics and depression: A systematic review. *Neuroscience & Biobehavioral Reviews, 102*, 139–152.

Park, C.L. (2010). Making sense of the meaning literature: An integrative review of meaning making and its effects on adjustment to stressful life events. *Psychological Bulletin, 136*, 257–301.

Park, J.E., Kim, K.I., Yoon, S.S., Hahm, B.J., Lee, S.M., et al. (2010). Psychological distress as a negative survival factor for patients with hematologic malignancies who underwent allogeneic hematopoietic stem cell transplantation. *Pharmacotherapy, 30*, 1239–1246.

Park, S.G., Kim, H.C., Min, J.Y., Hwang, S.H., Park, Y.S., & Min, K.B. (2011). A prospective study of work stressors and the common cold. *Occupational Medicine, 61*, 53–56.

Parker, L. (2017). *Cannabinoids and the Brain*. Cambridge, MA: MIT Press.

Parvaz, M.A., Konova, A.B., Tomasi, D., Volkow, N.D., & Goldstein, R.Z. (2011). Structural integrity of the prefrontal cortex modulates electrocortical sensitivity to reward. *Journal of Cognitive Neuroscience, 24*, 1560–1570.

Pastor, V., Antonelli, M.C., & Pallarés, M.E. (2017). Unravelling the link between prenatal stress, dopamine and substance use disorder. *Neurotoxicity Research, 31*, 169–186.

Pastushenko, I., Brisebarre, A., Sifrim, A., Fioramonti, M., Revenco, T., et al. (2018). Identification of the tumour transition states occurring during EMT. *Nature, 556*, 463–468.

Patel, K., Allen, S., Haque, M.N., Angelescu, I., Baumeister, D., & Tracy, D.K. (2016). Bupropion: A systematic review and meta-analysis of effectiveness as an antidepressant. *Therapeutic Advances in Psychopharmacology, 6*, 99–144.

Paykel, E.S., Prusoff, B.A., & Uhlenhuth, E.H. (1971). Scaling of life events. *Archives of General Psychiatry, 25*, 340–347.

Peacock, E.J. & Wong, P.T. (1990). The Stress Appraisal Measure (SAM): A multidimensional approach to cognitive appraisal. *Stress Medicine, 6*, 227–236.

Pedersen, A.F., Zachariae, R., & Bovbjerg, D.H. (2009). Psychological stress and antibody response to influenza vaccination: A meta-analysis. *Brain, Behavior, and Immunity, 23*, 427–433.

Pedersen, B.K. & Saltin, B. (2015). Exercise as medicine – evidence for prescribing exercise as therapy in 26 different chronic diseases. *Scandinavian Journal of Medicine Science, 25*, Suppl. 3, 1–72.

Pedersen, J.M., Mortensen, E.L., Christensen, D.S., Rozing, M., & Brunsgaard, H. (2018). Prenatal and early postnatal stress and later life inflammation. *Psychoneuroendocrinology, 88*, 158–166.

Peralta-Ramírez, M.I., Jiménez-Alonso, J., Godoy-García, J.F., & Pérez-García, M. (2004). The effects of daily stress and stressful life events on the clinical symptomatology of patients with lupus erythematosus. *Psychosomatic Medicine, 66*, 788–794.

Perlis, R.H., Ognyanova, K., Santillana, M., Lin, J., & Druckman, J. (2022). Association of major depressive symptoms with endorsement of COVID-19 vaccine misinformation among US adults. *JAMA Network Open, 5*, e2145697–e2145697.

Perry, M., Baumbauer, K., Young, E.E., Dorsey, S.G., Taylor, J.Y., & Starkweather, A.R. (2019). The influence of race, ethnicity and genetic variants on postoperative pain intensity: An integrative literature review. *Pain Management Nursing, 20*, 198–206.

Phillips, J.L., Norris, S., Talbot, J., Birmingham, M., Hatchard, T., et al. (2019). Single, repeated, and maintenance ketamine infusions for treatment-resistant depression: A randomized controlled trial. *American Journal of Psychiatry, 176*, 401–409.

Piazza, J.R., Stawski, R.S., & Sheffler, J.L. (2019). Age, daily stress processes, and allostatic load: A longitudinal study. *Journal of Aging Health, 31*, 1671–1691.

Pierrehumbert, B., Torrisi, R., Laufer, D., Halfon, O., Ansermet, F., & Beck Popovic, M. (2010). Oxytocin response to an experimental psychosocial challenge in adults exposed to traumatic experiences during childhood or adolescence. *Neuroscience, 166*, 168–177.

Pile, V., Williamson, G., Saunders, A., Holmes, E.A., & Lau, J.Y.F. (2021). Harnessing emotional mental imagery to reduce anxiety and depression in young people: An integrative review of progress and promise. *The Lancet Psychiatry, 8*, 836–852.

Pilkay, S.R., Combs-Orme, T., Tylavsky, F., Bush. N., & Smith, A.K. (2020). Maternal trauma and fear history predict *BDNF* methylation and gene expression in newborns. *PeerJ, 22*, e8858.

Pimple, P., Lima, B.B., Hammadah, M., Wilmot, K., Ramadan, R., et al. (2019). Psychological distress and subsequent cardiovascular events in individuals with coronary artery disease. *Journal of the American Heart Association, 8*, e011866.

Pinquart, M. & Duberstein, P.R. (2010). Associations of social networks with cancer mortality: A meta-analysis. *Critical Reviews in Oncology & Hematology, 75*, 122–137.

Pitman, R.K., Gilbertson, M.W., Gurvits, T.V., May, F.S., Lasko, N.B., & Orr, S.P. (2006). Harvard/VA PTSD twin study investigators. *Annals of the New York Academy of Sciences, 1071*, 242–254.

Popoli, M., Yan, Z., McEwen, B.S., & Sanacora, G. (2012). The stressed synapse: the impact of stress and glucocorticoids on glutamate transmission. *Nature Reviews Neuroscience, 13*, 22–37.

Post, C.M., Boule, L.A., Burke, C.G., O'Dell, C.T., Winans, B., et al. (2019). The ancestral environment shapes antiviral CD8+ T cell responses across generations. *iScience, 20*, 168–183.

Post, R.M. (2021). The kindling/sensitization model and early life stress. *Current Topics in Behavioral Neuroscience, 48*, 255–275.

Poštuvan, V., Podlogar, T., Zadravec Šedivy, N., & De Leo, D. (2019). Suicidal behaviour among sexual-minority youth: a review of the role of acceptance and support. *The Lancet Child & Adolescent Health, 3*, 190–198.

Poulter, M.O., Du, L., Weaver, I.C.G., Palkovits, M., Faludi, G., et al. (2008). GABAA receptor promoter hypermethylation in suicide brain: Implications for the involvement of epigenetic processes. *Biological Psychiatry, 64*, 645–652.

Poulter, M.O., Du, L., Zhurov, V., Merali, Z., & Anisman, H. (2010). Plasticity of the GABAA receptor subunit cassette in response to stressors in reactive versus resilient mice. *Neuroscience, 165*, 1039–1051.

Poulter, M.O., Du, L., Zhurov, V., Palkovits, M., Faludi, G., Merali, Z., & Anisman, H. (2010). Altered organization of GABAA receptor mRNA expression in the depressed suicide brain. *Frontiers in Neuroscience, 3*, 3–11.

Powell, N.D., Mays, J.W., Bailey, M.T., Hanke, M.L., & Sheridan, J.F. (2011). Immunogenic dendritic cells primed by social defeat enhance adaptive immunity to influenza A virus. *Brain, Behavior, and Immunity, 25*, 46–52.

Prabhu, S.D. & Frangogiannis, N.G. (2016). The biological basis for cardiac repair after myocardial infarction: From inflammation to fibrosis. *Circulation Research, 119*, 91–112.

Pratchett, L.C. & Yehuda, R. (2011). Foundations of posttraumatic stress disorder: Does early life trauma lead to adult posttraumatic stress disorder? *Development and Psychopathology, 23,* 477–491.

Pretorius, C., Chambers, D., & Coyle, D. (2019). Young people's online help-seeking and mental health difficulties: Systematic narrative review. *Journal of Medical Internet Research, 21,* e13873.

Prévot, T. & Sibille, E. (2021). Altered GABA-mediated information processing and cognitive dysfunctions in depression and other brain disorders. *Molecular Psychiatry, 26,* 151–167.

Price, R.B. & Duman, R. (2020). Neuroplasticity in cognitive and psychological mechanisms of depression: an integrative model. *Molecular Psychiatry, 25,* 530–543.

Pulopulos, M.M., Baeken, C., & De Raedt, R. (2020). Cortisol response to stress: The role of expectancy and anticipatory stress regulation. *Hormones & Behavior, 117,* 104587.

Pyter, L.M., McKim, D.B., Husain, Y., Calero, H., Godbout, J.P., et al. (2018). Effects of dermal wounding on distal primary tumor immunobiology in mice. *Journal of Surgical Research, 221,* 328–335.

Quaglia, M., Merlotti, G., De Andrea, M., Borgogna, C., & Cantaluppi, V. (2021). Viral infections and systemic lupus erythematosus: New players in an old story. *Viruses, 13,* 277.

Rachid, F. (2018). Maintenance repetitive transcranial magnetic stimulation (rTMS) for relapse prevention in with depression: A review. *Psychiatry Research, 262,* 363–372.

Raggi, P., Genest, J., Giles, J.T., Rayner, K.J., Dwivedi, G., et al. (2018). Role of inflammation in the pathogenesis of atherosclerosis and therapeutic interventions. *Atherosclerosis, 276,* 98–108.

Raichle, M.E. (2015). The brain's default mode network. *Annual Review of Neuroscience, 38,* 433–447.

Rainville, J.R., Tsyglakova, M., & Hodes, G.E. (2018). Deciphering sex differences in the immune system and depression. *Frontiers in Neuroendocrinology, 50,* 67–90.

Raison, C.L., Rutherford, R.E., Woolwine, B.J., Shuo, C., Schettler, P., et al. (2013). A randomized controlled trial of the tumor necrosis factor antagonist infliximab for treatment-resistant depression: the role of baseline inflammatory biomarkers. *JAMA Psychiatry, 70,* 31–41.

Ramirez, K., Fornaguera-Trías, J., & Sheridan, J.F. (2017). Stress-induced microglia activation and monocyte trafficking to the brain underlie the development of anxiety and depression. *Current Topics in Behavioral Neuroscience, 31,* 155–172.

Ramos-Lopez, O., Milagro, F.I., Riezu-Boj, J.I., & Martinez, J.A. (2021). Epigenetic signatures underlying inflammation: An interplay of nutrition, physical activity, metabolic diseases, and environmental factors for personalized nutrition. *Inflammation Research, 70,* 29–49.

Ransohoff, R.M. (2016). How neuroinflammation contributes to neurodegeneration. *Science, 353,* 777–783.

Raposa, E.B., Laws, H.B., & Ansell, E.B. (2016). Prosocial behavior mitigates the negative effects of stress in everyday life. *Clinical Psychological Science, 4,* 691–698.

Raskind, M.A., Peskind, E.R., Chow, B., Harris, C., Davis-Karim, A., et al. (2018). Trial of Prazosin for post-traumatic stress disorder in military veterans. *New England Journal of Medicine, 378,* 507–517.

Rauch, S.A.M., King, A.P., Liberzon, I., & Sripada, R.K. (2017). Changes in salivary cortisol during psychotherapy for posttraumatic stress disorder: A pilot study in 30 veterans. *Journal of Clinical Psychiatry, 78,* 599–603.

Read, R.W., Schlauch, K.A., Neveux, I., Lipp, B., Slonim, A., & Grzymski, J. (2022). The impact of ACEs on BMI: An investigation of the genotype-environment effects of BMI. *Frontiers in Genetics, 13,* 331.

Reece, J.C., Neal, E.F.G., Nguyen, P., McIntosh, J.G., & Emery, J.D. (2021). Delayed or failure to follow-up abnormal breast cancer screening mammograms in primary care: A systematic review. *BMC Cancer, 21,* 373.

Reed, B. & Kreek, M.J. (2021). Genetic vulnerability to opioid addiction. *Cold Spring Harbor Perspectives in Medicine, 11,* a039735.

Reed, R.G., Presnell, S.R., Al-Attar, A., Lutz, C.T., & Segerstrom, S.C. (2019). Perceived stress, cytomegalovirus titers, and late-differentiated T and NK cells: Between-, within-person associations in a longitudinal study of older adults. *Brain, Behavior, and Immunity, 80,* 266–274.

Regitz-Zagrosek, V. & Kararigas, G. (2017). Mechanistic pathways of sex differences in cardiovascular disease. *Physiological Reviews, 97,* 1–37.

Reiner, D.J., Fredriksson, I., Lofaro, O.M., Bossert, J.M., & Shaham, Y. (2019). Relapse to opioid seeking in rat models: Behavior, pharmacology and circuits. *Neuropsychopharmacology, 44,* 465–477.

Rempelos, L., Wang, J., Barański, M., Watson, A., Volakakis, N., et al. (2021). Diet and food type affect urinary pesticide residue excretion profiles in healthy individuals: Results of a randomized controlled dietary intervention trial. *The American Journal of Clinical Nutrition, 115,* 364–377.

Ren, M. & Lotfipour, S. (2020). The role of the gut microbiome in opioid use. *Behavioral Pharmacology, 31,* 113–121.

Renard, J., Rushlow, W.J., & Laviolette, S.R. (2018). Effects of adolescent THC exposure on the prefrontal GABAergic system: Implications for schizophrenia-related psychopathology. *Frontiers in Psychiatry, 9,* 281.

Reuveni, I., Nugent, A.C., Gill, J., Vythilingam, M., Carlson, P.J., et al. (2018). Altered cerebral benzodiazepine receptor binding in post-traumatic stress disorder. *Translational Psychiatry, 8,* 206.

Reynolds, R.M. (2013). Glucocorticoid excess and the developmental origins of disease: Two decades of testing the hypothesis – 2012 Curt Richter Award Winner. *Psychoneuroendocrinology, 38,* 1–11.

Rice, F., Harold, G.T., Boivin, J., van den Bree, M., Hay, D.F., & Thapar, A. (2010). The links between prenatal stress and offspring development and psychopathology: Disentangling environmental and inherited influences. *Psychological Medicine, 40,* 335–345.

Richards, S.H., Anderson, L., Jenkinson, C.E., Whalley, B., Rees, K., et al. (2018). Psychological interventions for coronary heart disease: Cochrane systematic review and meta-analysis. *European Journal of Preventive Cardiology, 25,* 247–259.

Richter-Levin, G., Stork, O., & Schmidt, M.V. (2019). Animal models of PTSD: A challenge to be met. *Molecular Psychiatry, 24*, 1135–1156.

Ricon, I., Hanalis-Miller, T., Haldar, R., Jacoby, R., & Ben-Eliyahu, S. (2019). Perioperative biobehavioral interventions to prevent cancer recurrence through combined inhibition of β-adrenergic and cyclooxygenase 2 signaling. *Cancer, 125*, 45–56.

Ridker, P.M., Everett, B.M., Thuren, T., MacFadyen, J.G., & Chang, W.H. (2017). Antiinflammatory therapy with canakinumab for atherosclerotic disease. *New England Journal of Medicine, 377*, 1119–1131.

Ridley, M., Rao, G., Schilbach, F., & Patel, V. (2020). Poverty, depression, and anxiety: Causal evidence and mechanisms. *Science*, 370, eaay0214.

Riera Romo, M., Perez-Martinez, D., & Castillo Ferrer, C. (2016). Innate immunity in vertebrates: An overview. *Immunology, 148*, 125–139.

Riley, V. (1981). Psychoneuroendocrine influences on immunocompetence and neoplasia. *Science, 212*, 1100–1109.

Rinaldi, S., Ghissi, M., Iaccarino, L., Zampieri, S., Ghirardello, A., et al. (2006). Influence of coping skills on health-related quality of life in patients with systemic lupus erythematosus. *Arthritis Care & Research, 55*, 427–433.

Rincel, M., Aubert, P., Chevalier, J., Chevalier, G., Grohard, P., et al. (2019). Multi-hit early life adversity affects gut microbiota, brain and behavior in a sex-dependent manner. *Brain, Behavior, and Immunity, 80*, 179–192.

Roberts, A.L., Huang, T., Koenen, K.C., Kim, Y., Kubzansky, L.D., & Tworoger, S.S. (2019). Posttraumatic stress disorder is associated with increased risk of ovarian cancer: A prospective and retrospective longitudinal cohort study. *Cancer Research, 79*, 5113–5120.

Roberts, A.L., Malspeis, S., Kubzansky, L.D., Feldman, C.H., Chang, S.C., et al. (2017). Association of trauma and posttraumatic stress disorder with incident systemic lupus erythematosus in a longitudinal cohort of women. *Arthritis & Rheumatology, 69*, 2162–2169.

Robinson, D.R., Wu, Y.M., Lonigro, R.J., Vats, P., Cobain, E., et al. (2017). Integrative clinical genomics of metastatic cancer. *Nature, 548*, 297–303.

Robinson, M., Carter, K.W., Pennell, C.E., Jacoby, P., Moore, H.C., et al. (2021). Maternal prenatal stress exposure and sex-specific risk of severe infection in offspring. *PLoS One, 16*, e0245747.

Robinson, M., Mattes, E., Oddy, W.H., Pennell, C.E. van Eekelen, A., et al. (2011). Prenatal stress and risk of behavioral morbidity from age 2 to 14 years: The influence of the number, type, and timing of stressful life events. *Development and Psychopathology, 23*, 155–168.

Robinson, S.L. & Thiele, T.E. (2017). The role of neuropeptide Y (NPY) in alcohol and drug abuse disorders. *International Review in Neurobiology, 136*, 177–197.

Rod, N.H., Bengtsson, J., Budtz-Jørgensen, E., Clipet-Jensen, C., Taylor-Robinson, D., et al. (2020). Trajectories of childhood adversity and mortality in early adulthood: A population-based cohort study. *The Lancet, 396*, 489–497.

Rodgers, A.B., Morgan, C.P., Bronson, S.L., Revello, S., & Bale, T.L. (2013). Paternal stress exposure alters sperm microRNA content and reprograms offspring HPA stress axis regulation. *Journal of Neuroscience, 33*, 9003–9012.

Rook, G.A., Lowry, C.A., & Raison, C.L. (2013). Microbial 'Old Friends', immunoregulation and stress resilience. *Evolution, Medicine, and Public Health, 2013*, 46–64.

Roseboom, T.J., Painter, R.C., van Abeelen, A.F., Veenendaal, M.V., & de Rooij, S.R. (2011). Hungry in the womb: What are the consequences? Lessons from the Dutch famine. *Maturitas, 70*, 141–145.

Rosen, N., Knäuper, B., & Sammut, J. (2007). Do individual differences in intolerance of uncertainty affect health monitoring? *Psychology and Health, 22*, 413–430.

Rosenman, R.H., Brand, R.J., Jenkins, D., Friedman, M., Straus, R., & Wurm, M. (1975). Coronary heart disease in Western Collaborative Group Study: Final follow-up experience of 8 1/2 years. *Journal of the American Medical Association, 233*, 872–877.

Ross, J.A. & Van Bockstaele, E.J. (2020). The role of catecholamines in modulating responses to stress: Sex-specific patterns, implications, and therapeutic potential for post-traumatic stress disorder and opiate withdrawal. *European Journal of Neuroscience, 52*, 2429–2465.

Rosso, I.M., Crowley, D.J., Silveri, M.M., Rauch, S.L., & Jensen, J.E. (2017). Hippocampus glutamate and N-acetyl aspartate markers of excitotoxic neuronal compromise in posttraumatic stress disorder. *Neuropsychopharmacology, 42*, 1698–1705.

Rosso, I.M., Silveri, M.M., Olson, E.A., Eric Jensen, J., & Ren, B. (2021). Regional specificity and clinical correlates of cortical GABA alterations in posttraumatic stress disorder. *Neuropsychopharmacology, 47*, 1055–1062.

Rosso, I.M., Weiner, M.R., Crowley, D.J., Silveri, M.M., Rauch, S.L., & Jensen, J.E. (2014). Insula and anterior cingulate GABA levels in posttraumatic stress disorder: preliminary findings using magnetic resonance spectroscopy. *Depression & Anxiety, 31*, 115–123.

Roth, D.L., Sheehan, O.C., Haley, W.E., Jenny, N.S., Cushman, M., & Walston, J.D. (2019). Is family caregiving associated with inflammation or compromised immunity? A meta-analysis. *Gerontologist, 59*, e521–e534.

Roth, T.L., Lubin, F.D., Funk, A.J., & Sweatt, J.D. (2009). Lasting epigenetic influence of early-life adversity on the BDNF gene. *Biological Psychiatry, 65*, 760–769.

Rottenberg, J., Yaroslavsky, I., Carney, R.M., Freedland, K.E., George, C.J., et al. (2014). The association between major depressive disorder in childhood and risk factors for cardiovascular disease in adolescence. *Psychosomatic Medicine, 76*, 122–127.

Royal Commission on Aboriginal Peoples. (1996). *Looking Forward, Looking Back – Report of the Royal Commission on Aboriginal Peoples, Volume 1*. Ottawa: Communication Group Publishing.

Rudd, K.E., Johnson, S.C., Agesa, K.M., Shackelford, K.A., & Tsoi, D. (2020). Global, regional, and national sepsis incidence and mortality, 1990–2017: Analysis for the Global Burden of Disease Study. *The Lancet, 395*, 200–211.

Rudes, G. & Fantuzzi, C. (2021). The association between racism and suicidality among young minority groups: A systematic review. *Journal of Transcultural Nursing, 33,* 228–238.

Rudolph, B., Wunsch, A., Herschbach, P., & Dinkel, A. (2018). Cognitive-behavioral group therapy addressing fear of progression in cancer out-patients. *Psychotherapie Psychosomatik Medizinische Psychologie, 68,* 38–43.

Rudolph, K.D., Davis, M.M., Skymba, H.V., Modi, H.H., & Telzer, E.H. (2021). Social experience calibrates neural sensitivity to social feedback during adolescence: A functional connectivity approach. *Developmental Cognitive Neuroscience, 47,* 100903.

Rüsch, N., Corrigan, P.W., Powell, K., Rajah, A., Olschewski, M., Wilkniss, S., & Batia, K. (2009). A stress-coping model of mental illness stigma: II. Emotional stress responses, coping behavior and outcome. *Schizophrenia Research, 110,* 65–71.

Russo, E., Nannini, G., Dinu, M., Pagliai, G., Sofi, F., et al. (2020). Exploring the food–gut axis in immunotherapy response of cancer patients. *World Journal of Gastroenterology, 26,* 4919–4932.

Russo, M., Crisafulli, G., Sogari, A., Reilly, N.M., Arena, S., et al. (2019). Adaptive mutability of colorectal cancers in response to targeted therapies. *Science, 366,* 1473–1480.

Ryan, M.K. & Haslam, S.A. (2005). The glass cliff: Evidence that women are over-represented in precarious leadership positions. *British Journal of Management, 16,* 81–90.

Ryan, T.J. & Frankland, P.W. (2022). Forgetting as a form of adaptive engram cell plasticity. *Nature Reviews Neuroscience, 23,* 173–186.

Sabban, E.L., Alaluf, L.G., & Serova, L.I. (2016). Potential of neuropeptide Y for preventing or treating post-traumatic stress disorder. *Neuropeptides, 56,* 19–24.

Sacchet, M.D., Levy, B.J., Hamilton, J.P., Maksimovskiy, A., Hertel, P.T., et al. (2017). Cognitive and neural consequences of memory suppression in major depressive disorder. *Cognitive & Affective Behavioral Neuroscience, 17,* 77–93.

Sadetzki, S., Chetrit, A., Freedman, L.S., Hakak, N., Barchana, M., et al. (2017). Cancer risk among Holocaust survivors in Israel – A nationwide study. *Cancer, 123,* 3335–3345.

Safi, S., Sethi, N.J., Korang, S.K., Nielsen, E.E., Feinberg, J., et al. (2022). Beta-blockers in patients without heart failure after myocardial infarction. *Cochrane Database Systematic Reviews, 11,* CD012565.

Sah, R. & Geracioti, T.D. (2013). Neuropeptide Y and posttraumatic stress disorder. *Molecular Psychiatry, 18,* 646–655.

Salosensaari, A., Laitinen, V., Havulinna, A.S., Meric, G., Cheng, S., et al. (2021). Taxonomic signatures of cause-specific mortality risk in human gut microbiome. *Nature Communications, 12,* 2671.

Salovey, P. & Mayer, J.D. (1990). Emotional intelligence. *Imagination, Cognition, and Personality, 9,* 185–211.

Salvestrini, V., Sell, C., & Lorenzini, A. (2019). Obesity may accelerate the aging process. *Frontiers in Endocrinology, 10,* 266.

Sampathkumar, N.K., Bravo, J.I., Chen, Y., Danthi, P.S., Donahue, E.K., et al. (2020). Widespread sex dimorphism in aging and age-related diseases. *Human Genetics, 139*, 333–356.

Sanada, K., Montero-Marin, J., Barceló-Soler, A., Ikuse, D., & Ota, M. (2020). Effects of mindfulness-based interventions on biomarkers and low-grade inflammation in patients with psychiatric disorders: a meta-analytic review. *International Journal of Molecular Sciences, 21*, 2484.

Sapolsky, R.M. (2017). *Behave: The Biology of Humans at Our Best and Worst.* New York: Penguin Press.

Sapolsky, R.M., Romero, L.M., & Munck, A.U. (2000). How do glucocorticoids influence stress responses? Integrating permissive, suppressive, stimulatory, and preparative actions. *Endocrine Reviews, 21*, 55–89.

Sarkar, S. & Schaefer, M. (2014). Antidepressant pretreatment for the prevention of interferon alfa-associated depression: A systematic review and meta-analysis. *Psychosomatics, 55*, 221–234.

Sarkies, P. (2020). Molecular mechanisms of epigenetic inheritance: Possible evolutionary implications. *Seminars in Cell Development & Biology, 97*, 106–115.

Scaini, S., Palmieri, S., Caselli, G., & Nobile, M. (2021). Rumination thinking in childhood and adolescence: a brief review of candidate genes. *Journal of Affective Disorders, 280*, 197–202.

Scheier, M.F. & Carver, C.S. (1985). Optimism, coping, and health: Assessment and implications of generalized outcome expectancies. *Health Psychology, 4*, 219–247.

Schell, L.K., Monsef, I., Wöckel, A., & Skoetz, N. (2019). Mindfulness-based stress reduction for women diagnosed with breast cancer. *Cochrane Database of Systematic Reviews, 3*, CD011518.

Schiweck, C., Piette, D., Berckmans, D., Claes, S., & Vrieze, E. (2019). Heart rate and high frequency heart rate variability during stress as biomarker for clinical depression: A systematic review. *Psychological Medicine, 49*, 200–211.

Schlotz, W., Hellhammer, J., Schulz, P., & Stone, A.A. (2004). Perceived work overload and chronic worrying predict weekend–weekday differences in the cortisol awakening response. *Psychosomatic Medicine, 66*, 207–214.

Schmeltzer, S.N., Herman, J.P., & Sah, R. (2016). Neuropeptide Y (NPY) and posttraumatic stress disorder (PTSD): A translational update. *Experimental Neurology, 284*, 196–210.

Schmidt, K., Cowen, P.J., Harmer, C.J., Tzortzis, G., Errington, S., & Burnet, P.W. (2015). Prebiotic intake reduces the waking cortisol response and alters emotional bias in healthy volunteers. *Psychopharmacology, 232*, 1793–1801.

Schmidt-Reinwald, A., Pruessner, J.C., Hellhammer, D.H., Federenko, I., Rohleder, N., Schurmeyer, T.H., & Kirschbaum, C. (1999). The cortisol response to awakening in relation to different challenge tests and a 12-hour cortisol rhythm. *Life Sciences, 64*, 1653–1660.

Schoemaker, M.J., Jones, M.E., Wright, L.B., Griffin, J., McFadden, E., Ashworth, A., & Swerdlow, A.J. (2016). Psychological stress, adverse life events and breast cancer incidence: A cohort investigation in 106,000 women in the United Kingdom. *Breast Cancer Research, 18*, 72.

Schoenfeld, J.D. & Ioannidis, J.P. (2013). Is everything we eat associated with cancer? A systematic cookbook review. *The American Journal of Clinical Nutrition, 97,* 127–134.

Schraufnagel, D.E., Balmes, J.R., Cowl, C.T., De, Matteis, S., Jung, S.H., et al. (2019). Air pollution and noncommunicable diseases: A review by the forum of international respiratory societies' environmental committee, part 1: The damaging effects of air pollution. *Chest, 155,* 409–416.

Schueller, S.M. & Seligman, M.E.P. (2008). Optimism and pessimism. In K.S. Dobson and D.J. A. Dozois (eds.), *Risk Factors in Depression* (pp. 171–194). San Diego, CA: Academic Press.

Schuler, L.A. & Auger, A.P. (2010). Psychosocially influenced cancer: Diverse early-life stress experiences and links to breast cancer. *Cancer Prevention Research, 3,* 1365–1370.

Schultz, W.M., Kelli, H.M., Lisko, J.C., Varghese, T., Shen, J., et al. (2018). Socioeconomic status and cardiovascular outcomes: Challenges and interventions. *Circulation, 137,* 2166–2178.

Schür, R.R., Draisma, L.W., Wijnen, J.P., Boks, M.P., Koevoets, M.G., et al. (2016). Brain GABA levels across psychiatric disorders: A systematic literature review and meta-analysis of (1) H-MRS studies. *Human Brain Mapping, 37,* 3337–3352.

Schuster, M.A., Stein, B.D., Jaycox, L.H., Collins, R.L., Marshall, G.N., et al. (2001). A national survey of stress reactions after the September 11, 2001, terrorist attacks. *New England Journal of Medicine, 345,* 1507–1512.

Schwartz, B. (2004). *The Paradox of Choice: Why More Is Less.* New York: HarperPerennial.

Schwarz-Bart, A. (1959). *The Last of the Just.* Woodstock & New York: Overlook.

Segal, Z.V., Williams, J.M.G., & Teasdale, J. (2002). *Mindfulness-based Cognitive Therapy for Depression: A New Approach to Preventing Relapse.* New York: Guilford.

Segovia, G., del Arco, A., & Mora, F. (2009). Environmental enrichment, prefrontal cortex, stress, and aging of the brain. *Journal of Neural Transmission, 116,* 1007–1016.

Selak, V., Jackson, R., Poppe, K., Wu, B., Harwood, M., Grey, C., et al. (2019). Personalized prediction of cardiovascular benefits and bleeding harms from aspirin for primary prevention: A benefit-harm analysis. *Annals of Internal Medicine, 15,* 529–539.

Seligman, M.E. & Csikszentmihalyi, M. (2000). Positive psychology: An introduction. *American Psychologist, 55,* 5–14.

Seligman, M.E.P. (2019). Positive psychology: A personal history. *Annual Review of Clinical Psychology, 15,* 1–23.

Senders, A., Hanes, D., Bourdette, D., Carson, K., Marshall, L.M., & Shinto, L. (2019). Impact of mindfulness-based stress reduction for people with multiple sclerosis at 8 weeks and 12 months: A randomized clinical trial. *Multiple Sclerosis, 25,* 1178–1188.

Seng, J., Low, L., Sperlich, M., Ronis, D., & Liberzon, I. (2011). Post-traumatic stress disorder, child abuse history, birthweight and gestational age: A prospective cohort study. *BJOG: An International Journal of Obstetrics & Gynecology, 118,* 1329–1339.

Sequeira, A., Mamdani, F., Ernst, C., Vawter, M.P., Bunney, W.E., et al. (2009). Global brain gene expression analysis links glutamatergic and GABAergic alterations to suicide and major depression. *PLoS One, 4*, e6585.

Shah, A. J., Veledar, E., Hong, Y., Bremner, J. D., & Vaccarino, V. (2011). Depression and history of attempted suicide as risk factors for heart disease mortality in young individuals. *Archives of General Psychiatry, 68*, 1135–1142.

Shalaby, A.M. & Kamal, S.M. (2012). Effect of rolipram, a phosphodiesterase enzyme type-4 inhibitor, on γ-amino butyric acid content of the frontal cortex in mice exposed to chronic mild stress. *Journal of Pharmacology and Pharmacotherapeutics, 3*, 132–137.

Shalev, I., Entringer, S., Wadhwa, P.D., Wolkowitz, O.M., & Puterman, E. (2013). Stress and telomere biology: A lifespan perspective. *Psychoneuroendocrinology, 201*, 38, 1835–1842.

Shalev, A., Liberzon, I., & Marmar, C. (2017). Post-traumatic stress disorder. *New England Journal of Medicine, 376*, 2459–2469.

Shao, L.X., Liao, C., Gregg, I., Davoudian, P.A., Savalia, N.K., et al. (2021). Psilocybin induces rapid and persistent growth of dendritic spines in frontal cortex in vivo. *Neuron, 109*, 2535–2544.e4.

Sharif, K., Sharif, A., Jumah, F., Oskouian, R., & Tubbs, R.S. (2018). Rheumatoid arthritis in review: Clinical, anatomical, cellular and molecular points of view. *Clinical Anatomy, 31*, 216–223.

Sharma, V.K. & Singh, T.G. (2020). Chronic stress and diabetes mellitus: Interwoven pathologies. *Current Diabetes Review, 16*, 546–556.

Sharpe, L., Sinclair, J., Kramer, A., de Manincor, M., & Sarris, J. (2020). Cannabis, a cause for anxiety? A critical appraisal of the anxiogenic and anxiolytic properties. *Journal of Translation Medicine, 18*, 374.

Shaw, J.M., Sekelja, N., Frasca, D., Dhillon, H.M., & Price, M.A. (2018). Being mindful of mindfulness interventions in cancer: A systematic review of intervention reporting and study methodology. *Psychooncology, 27*, 1162–1171.

She, Z., Li, D., Zhang, W., Zhou, N., Xi, J., & Ju, K. (2021). Three versions of the perceived stress scale: Psychometric evaluation in a nationally representative sample of Chinese adults during the covid-19 pandemic. *International Journal of Environmental Research and Public Health, 18*, 8312.

Shelton, R.C. & Miller, A.H. (2011). Inflammation in depression: Is adiposity a cause? *Dialogues in Clinical Neuroscience, 13*, 41–53.

Shen, L., Li, C., Wang, Z., Zhang, R., Shen, Y., et al. (2019). Early-life exposure to severe famine is associated with higher methylation level in the IGF2 gene and higher total cholesterol in late adulthood: The Genomic Research of the Chinese Famine (GRECF) study. *Clinical Epigenetics, 11*, 88.

Shepherd, R., Cheung, A.S., Pang, K., Saffery, R., & Novakovic, B. (2021). Sexual dimorphism in innate immunity: The role of sex hormones and epigenetics. *Frontiers in Immunology, 11*, 604000.

Sherwin, E., Bordenstein, S.R., Quinn, J.L., Dinan, T.G., & Cryan, J.F. (2019). Microbiota and the social brain. *Science, 366*, pii: eaar2016.

Sheth, C., Prescot, A.P., Legarreta, M., Renshaw, P.F., McGlade, E., et al. (2019). Reduced gamma-amino butyric acid (GABA) and glutamine in the anterior cingulate cortex (ACC) of veterans exposed to trauma. *Journal of Affective Disorders, 248,* 166–174.

Shi, Y., Wang, Y., Zeng, Y., Zhan, H., Huang, S., et al. (2021). Personality differences in brain network mechanisms for placebo analgesia and nocebo hyperalgesia in experimental pain: a functional magnetic resonance imaging study. *Annals of Translational Medicine, 9,* 371.

Shields, G.S., Sazma, M.A., & Yonelinas, A.P. (2016). The effects of acute stress on core executive functions: A meta-analysis and comparison with cortisol. *Neuroscience & Biobehavioral Reviews, 68,* 651–668.

Shonkoff, J.P., Boyce, W.T., & McEwen, B.S. (2009). Neuroscience, molecular biology, and the childhood roots of health disparities: Building a new framework for health promotion and disease prevention. *Journal of the American Medical Association, 301,* 2252–2259.

Siddiqui, N. & Urman, R.D. (2022). Opioid use disorder and racial/ethnic health Disparities: Prevention and management. *Current Pain Headache Reports, 26,* 129–137.

Siegel, S. & Ramos, B.M. (2002). Applying laboratory research: Drug anticipation and the treatment of drug addiction. *Experimental & Clinical Psychopharmacology, 10,* 162–183.

Silberstein, S., Liberman, A.C., Dos Santos Claro, P.A., Ugo, M.B., Deussing, J.M., & Arzt, E. (2021). Stress-related brain neuroinflammation impact in depression: Role of the corticotropin-releasing hormone system and P2X7 receptor. *Neuroimmunomodulation, 28,* 52–60.

Silver, R.C. (2011). An introduction to "9/11: Ten years later". *American Psychologist, 66,* 427–428.

Simard, S., Shail, P., MacGregor, J., El Sayed, M., Duman, R.S., et al. (2018). Fibroblast growth factor 2 is necessary for the antidepressant effects of fluoxetine. *PLoS One, 13,* e0204980.

Simpson, R.J., Kunz, H., Agha, N., & Graff, R. (2015). Exercise and the regulation of immune functions. *Progress in Molecular & Biological Translation Science, 135,* 355–380.

Sims, M., Glover, L.S.M., Gebreab, S.Y., & Spruill, T.M. (2020). Cumulative psychosocial factors are associated with cardiovascular disease risk factors and management among African Americans in the Jackson Heart Study. *BMC Public Health, 20,* 556.

Sin, N.L. (2016). The protective role of positive well-being in cardiovascular disease: Review of current evidence, mechanisms, and clinical implications. *Current Cardiology Reports, 18,* 106.

Skilbeck, K.J., Johnston, G.A., & Hinton, T. (2010). Stress and GABA receptors. *Journal of Neurochemistry, 112,* 1115–1130.

Skrodzka, M., Sosnowski, P., Bilewicz, M., & Stefaniak, A. (2021). Group identification attenuates the effect of historical trauma on mental health: A study of Iraqi Kurds. *American Journal of Orthopsychiatry, 91,* 693–702.

Slavich, G.M., O'Donovan, A., Epel, E.S., & Kemeny, M.E. (2010). Black sheep get the blues: A psychobiological model of social rejection and depression. *Neuroscience & Biobehavioral Reviews, 35,* 39–45.

Slavich, G.M., Shields, G.S., Deal, B.D., Gregory, A., & Toussaint, L.L. (2019). Alleviating social pain: A double-blind, randomized, placebo-controlled trial of forgiveness and acetaminophen. *Annals of Behavioral Medicine, 53*, 1045–1054.

Slavich, G.M., Way, B.M., Eisenberger, N.I., & Taylor, S.E. (2010). Neural sensitivity to social rejection is associated with inflammatory responses to social stress. *Proceedings of the National Academy of Sciences, 107*, 14817–14822.

Slee, A., Nazareth, I., Bondaronek, P., Liu, Y., Cheng, Z., & Freemantle, N. (2019). Pharmacological treatments for generalised anxiety disorder: A systematic review and network meta-analysis. *The Lancet, 393*, 768–777.

Smith, A.K., Ratanatharathorn, A., Maihofer, A.X., Naviaux, R.K., Aiello, A.E., et al. (2020). Epigenome-wide meta-analysis of PTSD across 10 military and civilian cohorts identifies methylation changes in AHRR. *Nature Communications, 11*, 5965.

Smith, K.S., Virkud, A., Deisseroth, K., & Graybiel, A.M. (2012). Reversible online control of habitual behavior by optogenetic perturbation of medial prefrontal cortex. *Proceedings of the National Academy of Sciences, 109*, 18932–18937.

Snyder-Mackler, N., Burger, J.R., Gaydosh, L., Belsky, D.W., & Noppert, G.A. (2020). Social determinants of health and survival in humans and other animals. *Science, 368*, eaax9553.

Sochocka, M., Donskow-Łysoniewska, K., Diniz, B.S., Kurpas, D., Brzozowska, E. & Leszek, J. (2019). The gut microbiome alterations and inflammation-driven pathogenesis of Alzheimer's disease – a critical review. *Molecular Neurobiology, 56*, 1841–1851.

Soga, T., Teo, C.H., & Parhar, I. (2021). Genetic and epigenetic consequence of early-life social stress on depression: Role of serotonin-associated genes. *Frontiers in Genetics, 11*, 601868.

Sominsky, L. & Spencer, S.J. (2014). Eating behavior and stress: A pathway to obesity. *Frontiers in Psychology, 5*, 434.

Sommershof, A., Scheuermann, L., Körner, J., & Groettrup, M. (2017). Chronic stress suppresses anti-tumor TCD8+ responses and tumor regression following cancer immunotherapy in a mouse model of melanoma. *Brain, Behavior, and Immunity, 65*, 140–149.

Somvanshi, P.R., Mellon, S.H., Yehuda, R., Flory, J.D., Makotkine, I., et al. (2020). Role of enhanced glucocorticoid receptor sensitivity in inflammation in PTSD: Insights from computational model for circadian-neuroendocrine-immune interactions. *American Journal of Physiology, Endocrinology & Metabolism, 319*, E48–E66.

Song, H., Fall, K., Fang, F., Erlendsdóttir, H., Lu, D., et al. (2019). Stress related disorders and subsequent risk of life threatening infections: Population based sibling controlled cohort study. *British Medical Journal, 367*, l5784.

Song, P., Zhang, Y., Yu, J., Zha, M., Zhu, Y., et al. (2019). Global prevalence of hypertension in children: a systematic review and meta-analysis. *JAMA Pediatrics, 173*, 1154–1163.

Song, S.J., Wang, J., Martino, C., Jiang, L., Wesley K., et al. (2021). Naturalization of the microbiota developmental trajectory of Cesarean-born neonates after vaginal seeding. *Med, 13*, 951–964.e1.

Sonnenburg, E.D. & Sonnenburg, J.L. (2019). The ancestral and industrialized gut microbiota and implications for human health. *Nature Reviews in Microbiology, 17*, 383–390.

Sorrells, S.F., Caso, J.R., Munhoz, C.D., & Sapolsky, R.M. (2009). The stressed CNS: When glucocorticoids aggravate inflammation. *Neuron, 64*, 33–39.

Sotiropoulos, I. & Sousa, N. (2016). Tau as the converging protein between chronic stress and Alzheimer's disease synaptic pathology. *Neurodegenerative Disorders, 16*, 22–25.

Southwick, S.M. & Charney, D.D. (2018). *Resilience: The Science of Mastering Life's Greatest Challenges*. Cambridge, UK: Cambridge University Press.

Speer, M.E. & Delgado, M.R. (2017). Reminiscing about positive memories buffers acute stress responses. *Nature Human Behavior, 1*, 0093.

Spencer, C.N., McQuade, J.L., Gopalakrishnan, V., McCulloch, J.A., Vetizou, M., et al. (2021). Dietary fiber and probiotics influence the gut microbiome and melanoma immunotherapy response. *Science, 374*, 1632–1640.

Spierling, S.R. & Zorrilla, E.P. (2017). Don't stress about CRF: Assessing the translational failures of CRF1 antagonists. *Psychopharmacology, 234*, 1467–1481.

Stagl, J.M., Lechner, S.C., Carver, C.S., Bouchard, L.C., Gudenkauf, L.M., et al. (2015). A randomized controlled trial of cognitive-behavioral stress management in breast cancer: Survival and recurrence at 11-year follow-up. *Breast Cancer Research & Treatment, 154*, 319–328.

Stanková, K., Brown, J.S., Dalton, W.S., & Gatenby, R.A. (2019). Optimizing cancer treatment using game theory: A review. *JAMA Oncology, 5*, 96–103.

Starcke, K. & Brand, M. (2016). Effects of stress on decisions under uncertainty: A meta-analysis. *Psychological Bulletin, 142*, 909–933.

Steel, J.L., Antoni, M., Pathak, R., Butterfield, L.H., & Vodovotz, Y. (2020). Adverse childhood experiences (ACEs), cell-mediated immunity, and survival in the context of cancer. *Brain, Behavior, and Immunity, 88*, 566–572.

Stein, D.J., Costa, D.L.C., Lochner, C., Miguel, E.C., Reddy, Y.C.J., et al. (2019). Obsessive-compulsive disorder. *Nature Reviews Disease Primers, 5*, 52.

Stein, M.B., Chen, C.Y., Jain, S., Jensen, K.P., & He, F. (2017). Genetic risk variants for social anxiety. *American Journal of Medical Genetics Part B: Neuropsychiatric Genetics, 174*, 120–131.

Stein, M.B., Levey, D.F., Cheng, Z., Wendt, F.R., Harrington, K., Pathak, G.A., et al. (2021). Genome-wide association analyses of post-traumatic stress disorder and its symptom subdomains in the Million Veteran Program. *Nature Genetics, 53*, 174–184.

Steinman, R.M. & Cohn, Z.A. (1973). Identification of a novel cell type in peripheral lymphoid organs of mice. I. Morphology, quantitation, tissue distribution. *Journal of Experimental Medicine, 137*, 1142–1162.

Steptoe, A., Kivimäki, M., Lowe, G. Rumley, A., & Hamer, M. (2016). Blood pressure and fibrinogen responses to mental stress as predictors of incident hypertension over an 8-year period. *Annals of Behavioral Medicine, 50*, 898–906.

Stevens, M., Rees, T., Coffee, P., Steffens, N.K., Haslam, S.A., & Polman, R.A (2017). A social identity approach to understanding and promoting physical activity. *Sports Medicine, 47*, 1911–1918.

Stewart, J. (2000). Pathways to relapse: The neurobiology of drug- and stress-induced relapse to drug-taking. *Journal of Psychiatry and Neuroscience, 25,* 125–136.

Stinson, L.F., Boyce, M.C., Payne, M.S., & Keelan, J.A. (2019). The not-so-sterile womb: Evidence that the human fetus is exposed to bacteria prior to birth. *Frontiers in Microbiology, 10,* 1124.

Stock, S.J., Carruthers, J., Calvert, C., Denny, C., Donaghy, J., et al. (2022). SARS-CoV-2 infection and COVID-19 vaccination rates in pregnant women in Scotland. *Nature Medicine 28,* 504–512.

Stopper, C.M. & Floresco, S.B. (2014). What's better for me? Fundamental role for lateral habenula in promoting subjective decision biases. *Nature Neuroscience, 17,* 33–35.

Strachan, D.P. (2000). Family size, infection and atopy: The first decade of the 'hygiene hypothesis'. *Thorax, 55,* S2.

Strawn, J.R., Mills, J.A., Suresh, V., Peris, T.S., Walkup, J.T., & Croarkin, P.E. (2022). Combining selective serotonin reuptake inhibitors and cognitive behavioral therapy in youth with depression and anxiety. *Journal of Affective Disorders, 298,* 292–300.

Steenen, S.A., van Wijk, A.J., Van Der Heijden, G.J., van Westrhenen, R., de Lange, J., & de Jongh, A. (2016). Propranolol for the treatment of anxiety disorders: Systematic review and meta-analysis. *Journal of Psychopharmacology, 30,* 128–139.

Sturgeon, J.A., Finan, P.H., & Zautra, A.J. (2016). Affective disturbance in rheumatoid arthritis: Psychological and disease-related pathways. *Nature Reviews in Rheumatology, 12,* 532–542.

Sturgis, P., Brunton-Smith, I., & Jackson, J. (2021). Trust in science, social consensus and vaccine confidence. *Nature Human Behavior, 5,* 1528–1534.

Sudhinaraset, M., Wigglesworth, C., & Takeuchi, D.T. (2016). Social and cultural contexts of alcohol use: Influences in a social-ecological framework. *Alcohol Research: Current Reviews, 38,* 35–45.

Suez, J., Zmora, N., Segal, E., & Elinav, E. (2019). The pros, cons, and many unknowns of probiotics. *Nature Medicine, 25,* 716–729.

Sukhato, K., Akksilp, K., Dellow, A., Vathesatogkit, P., & Anothaisintawee, T. (2020). Efficacy of different dietary patterns on lowering of blood pressure level: An umbrella review. *American Journal of Clinical Nutrition, 112,* 1584–1598.

Sumis, A., Cook, K.L., Andrade, F.O., Hu, R., Kidney, E., et al. (2016). Social isolation induces autophagy in the mouse mammary gland: Link to increased mammary cancer risk. *Endocrine-Related Cancer, 23,* 839–856.

Sun, D., Phillips, R.D., Mulready, H.L., Zablonski, S.T., Turner, J.A. et al. (2019). Resting-state brain fluctuation and functional connectivity dissociate moral injury from posttraumatic stress disorder. *Depression and Anxiety, 36,* 442–452.

Sun, H., Zhang, X., Kong, Y., Gou, L., Lian, B., et al. (2021). Maternal separation-induced histone acetylation correlates with BDNF-programmed synaptic changes in an animal model of PTSD with sex differences. *Molecular Neurobiology, 58,* 1738–1754.

Sunstein, C.R. (2009). *Going to Extremes: How Like Minds Unite and Divide.* New York: Oxford University Press.

Sutherland, S. & Brunwasser, S.M. (2018). Sex differences in vulnerability to prenatal stress: A review of the recent literature. *Current Psychiatry Reports, 20*, 102.

Szechtman, H., Harvey, B.H., Woody, E.Z., & Hoffman, K.L. (2020). The psychopharmacology of obsessive-compulsive disorder: A preclinical roadmap. *Pharmacological Reviews, 72*, 80–151.

Szeszko, P.R., Lehrner, A., & Yehuda, R. (2018). Glucocorticoids and hippocampal structure and function in PTSD. *Harvard Review in Psychiatry, 26*, 142–157.

Szeszko, P.R. & Yehuda, R. (2019). Magnetic resonance imaging predictors of psychotherapy treatment response in post-traumatic stress disorder: A role for the salience network. *Psychiatry Research, 277*, 52–57.

Szyf, M. (2009). Epigenetics, DNA methylation, and chromatin modifying drugs. *Annual Review of Pharmacology and Toxicology, 49*, 243–263.

Szyf, M. (2011). The early life social environment and DNA methylation: DNA methylation mediating the long-term impact of social environments early in life. *Epigenetics, 6*, 971–978.

Szyf, M. (2019). The epigenetics of perinatal stress. *Dialogues in Clinical Neuroscience, 21*, 369–378.

Szyf, M., Tang, Y.Y., Hill, K.G., & Musci, R. (2016). The dynamic epigenome and its implications for behavioral interventions: A role for epigenetics to inform disorder prevention and health promotion. *Translational Behavioral Medicine, 6*, 55–62.

Taha, S.A., Matheson, K., & Anisman, H. (2013). The 2009 H1N1 Influenza Pandemic: The role of threat, coping, and media trust on vaccination intentions in Canada. *Journal of Health Communications, 18*, 278–290.

Takizawa, R., Danese, A., Maughan, B., & Arseneault, L. (2015). Bullying victimization in childhood predicts inflammation and obesity at mid-life: A five-decade birth cohort study. *Psychological Medicine, 45*, 2705–2715.

Takkouche, B., Regueira, C., & Gestal-Otero, J.J. (2001). A cohort study of stress and the common cold. *Epidemiology, 12*, 345–349.

Taleb, N.N. (2007). *The Black Swan.* New York: Random House.

Talukdar, P.M., Abdul, F., Maes, M., Binu, V.S., Venkatasubramanian, G., et al. (2020). Maternal immune activation causes schizophrenia-like behaviors in the offspring through activation of immune-inflammatory, oxidative and apoptotic pathways, and lowered antioxidant defenses and neuroprotection. *Molecular Neurobiology, 57*, 4345–4361.

Tang, M.M., Lin, W.J., Pan, Y.Q., & Li, Y.C. (2018). Fibroblast growth factor 2 modulates hippocampal microglia activation in a neuroinflammation induced model of depression. *Frontiers in Cellular Neuroscience, 12*, 255.

Tang, W.H.W., Li, D.Y., & Hazen, S.L. (2019). Dietary metabolism, the gut microbiome, and heart failure. *Nature Reviews in Cardiology, 16*, 137–154.

Taouk, L. & Schulkin, J. (2016). Transgenerational transmission of pregestational and prenatal experience: Maternal adversity, enrichment, and underlying epigenetic and environmental mechanisms. *Journal of Developmental Origins of Health & Disease, 7*, 588–601.

Taylor, S.E., Klein, L.C., Lewis, B.P., Gruenewald, T.L., Gurung, R.A., et al. (2000). Biobehavioral responses to stress in females: Tend-and-befriend, not fight-or-flight. *Psychological Review, 107*, 411–429.

Teo, K.K. & Rafiq, T. (2021). Cardiovascular risk factors and prevention: A perspective from developing countries. *Canadian Journal of Cardiology, 37*, 733–743.

ter Heegde, F., De Rijk, R.H., & Vinkers, C.H. (2015). The brain mineralocorticoid receptor and stress resilience. *Psychoneuroendocrinology, 52*, 92–110.

Tetz, G. & Tetz, V. (2018). Bacteriophages as new human viral pathogens. *Microorganisms, 6*, 54, pii: E54.

Tetzlaff, F., Epping, J., Sperlich, S., & Tetzlaff, J. (2020). Widening income inequalities in life expectancy? Analysing time trends based on German health insurance data. *Journal of Epidemiology & Community Health, 74*, 592–597.

Thaker, P., Han, L.Y., Kamat, A.A., Arevalo, J.M., Takahashi, R., et al. (2006). Chronic stress promotes tumor growth and angiogenesis in a mouse model of ovarian carcinoma. *Nature Medicine, 12*, 939–944.

Thayer, J.F., Åhs, F., Fredrikson, M., Sollers III, J.J., & Wager, T.D. (2012). A meta-analysis of heart rate variability and neuroimaging studies: implications for heart rate variability as a marker of stress and health. *Neuroscience & Biobehavioral Reviews, 36*, 747–756.

Thoits, P.A. (2010). Stress and health: major findings and policy implications. *Journal of Health and Social Behavior, 51*, S41–S53.

Thong, M.S.Y., Wolschon, E.M., Koch-Gallenkamp, L., Waldmann, A., Waldeyer-Sauerland, M., et al. (2018). "Still a Cancer Patient" – Associations of cancer identity with patient-reported outcomes and health care use among cancer survivors. *JNCI Cancer Spectrum, 2*, pky031.

Thornicroft, G., Mehta, N., Clement, S., Evans-Lacko, S., & Doherty, M. (2016). Evidence for effective interventions to reduce mental-health-related stigma and discrimination. *The Lancet, 387*, 1123–1132.

Thornton, J. (2019). WHO report shows that women outlive men worldwide. *British Medical Journal (Online), 365*.

Tian, W., Liu, Y., Cao, C., Zeng, Y., Pan, Y., et al. (2021). Chronic stress: Impacts on tumor microenvironment and implications for anti-cancer treatments. *Frontiers in Cell and Developmental Biology, 9*, 777018.

Tilders, F.J.H. & Schmidt, E.D. (1999). Cross-sensitization between immune and non-immune stressors: A role in the etiology of depression? *Advances in Experimental Medicine, 461*, 179–197.

Tiwari, A.K., Zai, C.C., Altar, C.A., Tanner, J.A., Davies, P.E., et al. (2022). Clinical utility of combinatorial pharmacogenomic testing in depression: A Canadian patient- and rater-blinded, randomized, controlled trial. *Translational Psychiatry, 12*, 101.

Tobi, E.W., Goeman, J.J., Monajemi, R., Gu, H., & Putter, H. (2014). DNA methylation signatures link prenatal famine exposure to growth and metabolism. *Nature Communications, 5*, 5592.

Todd, B.L., Moskowitz, M.C., Ottati, A., & Feuerstein, M. (2014). Stressors, stress response, and cancer recurrence: A systematic review. *Cancer Nursing, 37*, 114–125.

Toenders, Y.J., Laskaris, L., Davey, C.G., Berk, M., Milaneschi, Y., et al. (2021). Inflammation and depression in young people: A systematic review and proposed inflammatory pathways. *Molecular Psychiatry, 27*, 315–327.

Tomaz, V., Chaves Filho, A.J.M., Cordeiro, R.C., Jucá, P.M., Soares, M.V.R., et al. (2020). Antidepressants of different classes cause distinct behavioral and brain pro- and anti-inflammatory changes in mice submitted to an inflammatory model of depression. *Journal of Affective Disorders, 268*, 188–200.

Tomova, L., Tye, K., & Saxe, R. (2021). The neuroscience of unmet social needs. *Social Neuroscience, 16*, 221–231.

Topol, E. (2019). *Deep Medicine: How Artificial Intelligence Can Make Healthcare Human Again*. New York: Basic Books.

Torres-Berrío, A., Issler, O., Parise, E.M., & Nestler, E.J. (2019). Unraveling the epigenetic landscape of depression: Focus on early life stress. *Dialogues in Clinical Neuroscience, 21*, 341–357.

Toso, K., de Cock, P., & Leavey, G. (2020). Maternal exposure to violence and offspring neurodevelopment: A systematic review. *Paediatric & Perinatal Epidemiology, 34*, 190–203.

Tsao, C.W., Aday, A.W., Almarzooq, Z.I., Alonso, A., Beaton, A.Z., et al. (2022). Heart disease and stroke statistics—2022 update: A report from the American Heart Association. *Circulation, 145*, e153–e639.

Tseng, R.J., Padgett, D.A., Dhabhar, F.S., Engler, H., & Sheridan, J.F. (2005). Stress-induced modulation of NK activity during influenza viral infection: Role of glucocorticoids and opioids. *Brain, Behavior, and Immunity, 19*, 153–164.

Tumurkhuu, G., Montano, E., & Jefferies, C. (2019). Innate immune dysregulation in the development of cardiovascular disease in lupus. *Current Rheumatology Reports, 21*, 46.

Turbitt, W.J., Demark-Wahnefried, W., Peterson, C.M., & Norian, L.A. (2019). Targeting glucose metabolism to enhance immunotherapy: Emerging evidence on intermittent fasting and calorie restriction mimetics. *Frontiers in Immunology, 10*, 1402.

Turecki, G. & Meaney, M.J. (2016). Effects of the social environment and stress on glucocorticoid receptor gene methylation: A systematic review. *Biological Psychiatry, 79*, 87–96.

Turner, C.A., Watson, S.J., & Akil, H. (2012). The fibroblast growth factor family: Neuromodulation of affective behavior. *Neuron, 76*, 160–174.

Tversky, A. & Kahneman, D. (1974). Judgment under uncertainty: Heuristics and biases. *Science, 185*, 1124–1131.

Twenge, J.M., Haidt, J., Blake, A.B., McAllister, C., Lemon, H., & Le Roy, A. (2021). Worldwide increases in adolescent loneliness. *Journal of Adolescence, 93*, 257–269.

Tye, K.M., Mirzabekov, J.J., Warden, M.R., Ferenczi, E.A., Tsai, H.C., et al. (2013). Dopamine neurons modulate neural encoding and expression of depression-related behaviour. *Nature, 493*, 537–541.

Uchida, S., Hara, K., Kobayashi, A., Otsuki, K., Yamagata, H., et al. (2011). Epigenetic status of Gdnf in the ventral striatum determines susceptibility and adaptation to daily stressful events. *Neuron, 69*, 359–372.

Uffelmann, E., Huang, Q.Q., Munung, N.S., de Vries, J., Okada, Y., et al. (2021). Genome-wide association studies. *Nature Reviews Methods Primers, 1*, 11–21.

Ungar, M. (2021). Modeling multisystem resilience: Connecting biological, psychological, social, and ecological adaptations in the context of adversity (pp. 6–34). In M. Ungar (ed.), *Multisystemic Resilience.* New York: Oxford University Press.

UN Women. (2022). Facts and figures: Ending violence against women. www.unwomen.org/en/what-we-do/ending-violence-against-women/facts-and-figures. Accessed April 2022.

Ury, W. (1993). *Getting Past No.* New York: Bantam.

Ushakov, A.V., Ivanchenko, V.S., & Gagarina, A.A. (2016). Psychological stress in pathogenesis of essential hypertension. *Current Hypertension Review, 12*, 203–214.

Vaccarino, V., Almuwaqqat, Z., Kim, J.H., Hammadah, M., & Shah, A.J. (2021). Association of mental stress–induced myocardial ischemia with cardiovascular events in patients with coronary heart disease. *JAMA, 326*, 1818–1828.

Vachon-Presseau, E., Berger, S.E., Abdullah, T.B., Huang, L., Cecchi, G.A., et al. (2018). Brain and psychological determinants of placebo pill response in chronic pain patients. *Nature Communications, 9*, 1–15.

Valsamakis, G., Chrousos, G., & Mastorakos, G. (2019). Stress, female reproduction and pregnancy. *Psychoneuroendocrinology, 100*, 48–57.

Valtorta, N.K., Kanaan, M., Gilbody, S., Ronzi, S., & Hanratty, B. (2016). Loneliness and social isolation as risk factors for coronary heart disease and stroke: Systematic review and meta-analysis of longitudinal observational studies. *Heart, 102*, 1009–1016.

van Agteren, J., Iasiello, M., Lo, L., Bartholomaeus, J., Kopsaftis, Z., et al. (2021). A systematic review and meta-analysis of psychological interventions to improve mental wellbeing. *Nature Human Behavior, 5*, 631–652.

Van Boven, L., Loewenstein, G., Welch, E., & Dunning, D. (2012). The illusion of courage in self-predictions: Mispredicting one's own behavior in embarrassing situations. *Journal of Behavioral Decision Making, 25*, 1–12.

Van den Bergh, B.R.H., van den Heuvel, M.I., Lahti, M., Braeken, M., de Rooij, S.R., et al. (2020). Prenatal developmental origins of behavior and mental health: The influence of maternal stress in pregnancy. *Neuroscience & Biobehavioral Reviews, 117*, 26–64.

van der Wal, J.M., van Borkulo, C.D., Deserno, M.K., Breedvelt, J.J., Lees, M., et al. (2021). Advancing urban mental health research: From complexity science to actionable targets for intervention. *The Lancet Psychiatry, 8*, 991–1000.

Van Diest, I. (2019). Interoception, conditioning, and fear: The panic threesome. *Psychophysiology, 56*, e13421.

Vannan, A., Powell, G.L., Scott, S.N., Pagni, B.A., & Neisewander, J.L. (2018). Animal models of the impact of social stress on cocaine use disorders. *International Review of Neurobiology, 140*, 131–169.

Vargas, A.S., Luis, A., Barroso, M., Gallardo, E., & Pereira, L. (2020). Psilocybin as a new approach to treat depression and anxiety in the context of life-threatening diseases: A systematic review and meta-analysis of clinical trials. *Biomedicines, 8*, 331.

Varker, K. A., Terrell, C. E., Welt, M., Suleiman, S., Thornton, L., et al. (2007). Impaired natural killer cell lysis in breast cancer patients with high levels of psychological stress is associated with altered expression of killer immunoglobin-like receptors. *Journal of Surgical Research, 139*, 36–44.

Vasefi, M., Hudson, M., & Ghaboolian-Zare, E. (2019). Diet associated with inflammation and Alzheimer's disease. *Journal of Alzheimer's Disease Reports, 16*, 299–309.

Vaverková, Z., Milton, A.L., & Merlo, E. (2020). Retrieval-dependent mechanisms affecting emotional memory persistence: Reconsolidation, extinction, and the space in between. *Frontiers in Behavioral Neuroscience, 14*, 574358.

Verdura, S., Cuyàs, E., Martin-Castillo, B., & Menendez, J.A. (2019). Metformin as an archetype immuno-metabolic adjuvant for cancer immunotherapy. *Oncoimmunology, 8*, e1633235.

Victora, C.G., Bahl, R., Barros, A.J.D., França, G.V.A., Horton, S., et al. (2016). Breastfeeding in the 21st century: epidemiology, mechanisms, and lifelong effect. *The Lancet, 387*, 475.

Vladoiu, M.C., El-Hamamy, I., Donovan, L.K., Farooq, H., Holgado, B.L., et al. (2019). Childhood cerebellar tumours mirror conserved fetal transcriptional programs. *Nature, 572*, 67–73.

Vohra, K., Vodonos, A., Schwartz, J., Marais, E.A., Sulprizio, M.P., & Mickley, L.J. (2021). Global mortality from outdoor fine particle pollution generated by fossil fuel combustion: Results from GEOS-Chem. *Environmental Research, 195*, 11075.

Volkow, N.D. & Boyle, M. (2018). Neuroscience of addiction: Relevance to prevention and treatment. *American Journal of Psychiatry, 175*, 729–740.

Volkow, N.D., Koob, G.F., & McLellan, A.T. (2016). Neurobiologic advances from the brain disease model of addiction. *New England Journal of Medicine, 374*, 363–371.

Volkow, N.D., Wang, G.J., Fowler, J.S., Tomasi, D., Telang, F., & Baler, R. (2010). Addiction: Decreased reward sensitivity and increased expectation sensitivity conspire to overwhelm the brain's control circuit. *Bioessays, 32*, 748–755.

Volkow, N.D., Wang, G.J., Tomasi, D., & Baler, R.D. (2013). Obesity and addiction: Neurobiological overlaps. *Obesity Reviews, 14*, 2–18.

Vollrath, M. (2001). Personality and stress. *Scandinavian Journal of Psychology, 42*, 335–347.

Votinov, M., Wagels, L., Hoffstaedter, F., Kellermann, T., Goerlich, K.S., et al. (2020). Effects of exogenous testosterone application on network connectivity within emotion regulation systems. *Science Reports, 10*, 2352.

Vyas, D.A., Eisenstein, L.G., & Jones, D.S. (2020). Hidden in plain sight—reconsidering the use of race correction in clinical algorithms. *New England Journal of Medicine, 383*, 874–882.

Vyas, S., Rodrigues, A.J., Silva, J.M., Tronche, F., Almeida, O.F., et al. (2016). Chronic stress and glucocorticoids: From neuronal plasticity to neurodegeneration. *Neural Plasticity, 2016*:6391686.

Walker, C.D. (2010). Maternal touch and feed as critical regulators of behavioral and stress responses in the offspring. *Developmental Psychobiology, 52*, 638–650.

Walker, E., Ploubidis, G., & Fancourt, D. (2019). Social engagement and loneliness are differentially associated with neuro-immune markers in older age: Time-varying associations from the English Longitudinal Study of Ageing. *Brain, Behavior, and Immunity, 82*, 224–229.

Wallace-Wells, D. (2019). *The Uninhabitable Earth*. New York: Tim Guggan Books.

Wang, H., Braun, C., Murphy, E.F., & Enck, P. (2019). Bifidobacterium longum 1714™ strain modulates brain activity of healthy volunteers during social stress. *American Journal of Gastroenterology, 114*, 1152–1162.

Wang, H.L., Sun, Y.X., Liu, X., Wang, H., Ma, Y.N., et al. (2019). Adolescent stress increases depression-like behaviors and alters the excitatory–inhibitory balance in aged mice. *Chinese Medical Journal, 132*, 1689–1699.

Wang, W., Zeng, F., Hu, Y., & Li, X. (2019). A mini-review of the role of glutamate transporter in drug addiction. *Frontiers in Neurology, 10*, 1123.

Wang, X., Wang, N., Zhong, L., Wang, S., Zheng, Y., Yang, B., et al. (2020). Prognostic value of depression and anxiety on breast cancer recurrence and mortality: A systematic review and meta-analysis of 282,203 patients. *Molecular Psychiatry, 25*, 3186–3197.

Wang, X., Zhang, H., & Chen, X. (2019). Drug resistance and combating drug resistance in cancer. *Cancer Drug Resistance, 2*, 141–160.

Wang, X.B., Zhang, Y.Q., Xue, R.R., Yang, Z.Z., & Zhang, X.F. (2020). Corticotropin-releasing hormone 1 receptor antagonism attenuates chronic unpredictable mild stress-induced depressive-like behaviors in rats. *Neuroreport, 31*, 1–8.

Wann, B.P., Audet, M.C., Gibb, J., & Anisman, H. (2010). Anhedonia and altered cardiac atrial natriuretic peptide following chronic stressor and endotoxin treatment in mice. *Psychoneuroendocrinology, 35*, 233–240.

Warburg, O. (1956). On the origin of cancer cells. *Science, 123*, 309–314.

Ward, S., Womick, J., Titova, L., & King, L. (2022). Meaning in life and coping with everyday stressors. *Personality and Social Psychology Bulletin*, ePub ahead of print.

Warth, M., Zöller, J., Köhler, F., Aguilar-Raab, C., Kessler, J., & Ditzen, B. (2020). Psychosocial interventions for pain management in advanced cancer patients: A systematic review and meta-analysis. *Current Oncology Reports, 21*, 3.

Wassmann, C.S., Højrup, P., & Klitgaard, J.K. (2020). Cannabidiol is an effective helper compound in combination with bacitracin to kill Gram-positive bacteria. *Scientific Reports, 10*, 4112.

Watanabe, N., Omori, I.M., Nakagawa, A., Cipriani, A., Barbui, C., et al. (2011). Mirtazapine versus other antidepressive agents for depression. *Cochrane Database Systematic Reviews*, CD006528.

Watts, N., Amann, M., Arnell, N., Ayeb-Karlsson, S., Beagley, J. (2021). The 2020 report of the Lancet Countdown on health and climate change: responding to converging crises. *The Lancet, 397*, 129–170.

Weaver, I.C., Champagne, F.A., Brown, S.E., Dymov, S., Sharma, S., Meaney, M.J., & Szyf, M. (2005). Reversal of maternal programming of stress responses in adult offspring through methyl supplementation: Altering epigenetic marking later in life. *Journal of Neuroscience, 25*, 11045–11054.

Wedervang-Resell, K., Friis, S., Lonning, V., Smelror, R.E., Johannessen, C., et al. (2020). Increased interleukin 18 activity in adolescents with early-onset psychosis is associated with cortisol and depressive symptoms. *Psychoneuroendocrinology, 112*, 104513.

Wei, D., Janszky, I., Fang, F., Chen, H., & Ljung, R. (2021). Death of an offspring and parental risk of ischemic heart diseases: A population-based cohort study. *PLoS Medicine, 18*, e1003790.

Weidacker, K., Johnston, S.J., Mullins, P.G., Boy, F., & Dymond, S. (2020). Impulsive decision-making and gambling severity: The influence of γ-amino-butyric acid (GABA) and glutamate-glutamine (Glx). *European Journal of Neuropsychopharmacology, 32*, 36–46.

Weinrib, A.Z., Sephton, S.E., Degeest, K., Penedo, F., Bender, D., et al. (2010). Diurnal cortisol dysregulation, functional disability, and depression in women with ovarian cancer. *Cancer, 116*, 4410–4419.

Weiss, D.S. & Marmar, C.R. (1997). The impact of event scale–revised. In J.P. Wilson & T.M. Keane (eds.), *Assessing Psychological Trauma and PTSD* (pp. 399–411). New York: Guilford.

Whitbeck, L.B., Adams, G.W., Hoyt, D.R., & Chen, X. (2004). Conceptualizing and measuring historical trauma among American Indian people. *American Journal of Community Psychology, 33*, 119–130.

White, C.A., Uttl, B., & Holder, M.D. (2019). Meta-analyses of positive psychology interventions: The effects are much smaller than previously reported. *PLoS One, 14*, e0216588.

Wibral, M., Dohmen, T., Klingmüller, D., Weber, B., & Falk, A. (2012). Testosterone administration reduces lying in men. *PLoS One, 7*, e46774.

Wiesel, E. (1958). *Night*. New York: Hill & Wang.

Wiles, T.J. & Guillemin, K. (2019). The other side of the coin: What beneficial microbes can teach us about pathogenic potential. *Journal of Molecular Biology, 431*, 2946–2956.

Wilk, P., Maltby, A., & Cooke, M. (2017). Residential schools and the effects on Indigenous health and well-being in Canada—a scoping review. *Public Health Reviews, 38*, 1–23.

Willner, P. (2016). The chronic mild stress (CMS) model of depression: History, evaluation and usage. *Neurobiology of Stress, 6*, 78–93.

Willner, P., Gruca, P., Lason, M., Tota-Glowczyk, K., & Litwa, E. (2019). Validation of chronic mild stress in the Wistar-Kyoto rat as an animal model of treatment-resistant depression. *Behavioural Pharmacology, 30*, 239–250.

Wilmanski, T., Diener, C., Rappaport, N., Patwardhan, S., Wiedrick, J., et al. (2021). Gut microbiome pattern reflects healthy ageing and predicts survival in humans. *Nature Metabolism, 3*, 274–286.

Wingfield, J.C. & Sapolsky, R.M. (2003). Reproduction and resistance to stress: When and how. *Journal of Neuroendocrinology, 15*, 711–724.

Wise, R.A. & Koob, G.F. (2014). The development and maintenance of drug addiction. *Neuropsychopharmacology, 39*, 254–262.

Wiseman, H., Barber, P., Raz, A., Yam, I., Foltz, C., & Livne-Snir, S. (2002). Parental communication of Holocaust experiences and interpersonal patterns in offspring of Holocaust survivors. *International Journal of Behavioral Development, 26,* 371–381.

Wiysonge, C.S., Bradley, H.A., Volmink, J., Mayosi, B.M., & Opie, L.H (2017). Beta-blockers for hypertension. *Cochrane Database of Systematic Reviews,* CD002003.

Wodtke, G.T., Harding, D.J., & Elwert, F. (2011). Neighborhood effects in temporal perspective: the impact of long-term exposure to concentrated disadvantage on high school graduation. *American Sociology Reviews, 76,* 713–736.

Wong, P.T.P. & Roy, S. (2017). Critique of positive psychology and positive interventions. In N.J.L. Brown, T. Lomas, & F.J. Eiroa-Orosa (eds.), *The Routledge International Handbook of Critical Positive Psychology* (pp. 142–160). London: Routledge.

Wright, N.D., Bahrami, B., Johnson, E., Di Malta, G., Rees, G., et al. (2012). Testosterone disrupts human collaboration by increasing egocentric choices. *Proceedings of the Royal Society B: Biological Sciences, 279,* 2275–2280.

Xia, C., Canela-Xandri, O., Rawlik, K., & Tenesa, A. (2021). Evidence of horizontal indirect genetic effects in humans. *Nature Human Behaviour, 5,* 399–406.

Xiang, Y., Yan, H., Zhou, J., Zhang, Q., Hanley, G., et al. (2015). The role of toll-like receptor 9 in chronic stress-induced apoptosis in macrophage. *PLoS One, 10,* e0123447.

Xie, W., Zheng, F., Yan, L., & Zhong, B. (2019). Cognitive decline before and after incident coronary events. *Journal of the American College of Cardiology, 73,* 3041–3050.

Yan, C., Luo, Z., Li, W., Li, X., Dallmann, R., et al. (2020). Disturbed Yin–Yang balance: Stress increases the susceptibility to primary and recurrent infections of herpes simplex virus type 1. *Acta Pharmaceutica Sinica B, 10,* 383–398.

Yan, C.G., Chen, X., Li, L., Castellano, F.X., Bai, T.J., et al. (2019). Reduced default mode network functional connectivity in patients with recurrent major depressive disorder. *Proceedings of the National Academy of Sciences, 116,* 9078–9083.

Yang, A., Xin, X., Yang, W., Li, M., Li, L., & Liu, X. (2019). Etanercept reduces anxiety and depression in psoriasis patients, and sustained depression correlates with reduced therapeutic response to etanercept. *Annales de Dermatologie et de Vénéréologie, 146,* 363–371.

Yang, B., Wei, J., Ju, P., & Chen, J. (2019). Effects of regulating intestinal microbiota on anxiety symptoms: A systematic review. *General Psychiatry, 2,* e100056.

Yang, R., Xu, C., Bierer, L.M., Flory, J.D., Gautam, A., et al. (2021). Longitudinal genome-wide methylation study of PTSD treatment using prolonged exposure and hydrocortisone. *Translational Psychiatry, 11,* 398.

Yao, S., Zhao, W., Cheng, R., Geng, Y., Luo, L., et al. (2014). Oxytocin makes females, but not males, less forgiving following betrayal of trust. *International Journal of Neuropsychopharmacology, 17,* 1785–1792.

Yehuda, R., Daskalakis, N.P., Bierer, L.M., Bader, H.N., Klengel, T., et al. (2016). Holocaust exposure induced intergenerational effects on FKBP5 methylation. *Biological Psychiatry, 80,* 372–380.

Ying, Z., Huang, X.F., Xiang, X., Liu, Y., Kang, X., et al. (2019). A safe and potent anti-CD19 CAR T cell therapy. *Nature Medicine, 25,* 947–953.

Yohannes, S. (2015). Dermatoglyphic meta-analysis indicates early epigenetic outcomes & possible implications on genomic zygosity in type-2 diabetes. *F1000Research, 4,* 617.

Yohn, C.N., Gergues, M.M., & Samuels, B.A. (2017). The role of 5-HT receptors in depression. *Molecular Brain, 10,* 28.

Youngblood, B., Hale, J.S., Kissick, H.T., Ahn, E., Xu, X., et al. (2017). Effector CD8 T cells dedifferentiate into long-lived memory cells. *Nature, 552,* 404–409.

Younge, N., McCann, J.R., Ballard, J., Plunkett, C., Akhtar, S., et al. (2019). Fetal exposure to the maternal microbiota in humans and mice. *JCI Insight, 4,* pii: 127806.

Ysseldyk, R., Matheson, K., & Anisman, H. (2019). Revenge is sour, but is forgiveness sweet? Psychological health and cortisol reactivity among women with experiences of abuse. *Journal of Health Psychology, 24,* 2003–2021.

Ysseldyk, R., Matheson, K., & Anisman, H. (2010). Religiosity as identity: Toward an understanding of religion from a social identity perspective. *Personality and Social Psychology Review, 14,* 60–71.

Yusuf, S., Joseph, P., Rangarajan, S., Islam, S., Mente, A., et al. (2020). Modifiable risk factors, cardiovascular disease, and mortality in 155 722 individuals from 21 high-income, middle-income, and low-income countries (PURE): a prospective cohort study. *The Lancet, 395,* 795–808.

Zaba, M., Kirmeier, T., Ionescu, I.A., Wollweber, B., & Buell, D.R. (2015). Identification and characterization of HPA-axis reactivity endophenotypes in a cohort of female PTSD patients. *Psychoneuroendocrinology, 55,* 102–115.

Zada, D., Bronshtein, I., Lerer-Goldshtein, T., Garini, Y., & Appelbaum, L. (2019). Sleep increases chromosome dynamics to enable reduction of accumulating DNA damage in single neurons. *Nature Communications, 10,* 895.

Zallar, L.J., Farokhnia, M., Tunstall, B.J., et al. (2017). The role of the ghrelin system in drug addiction. *International Review of Neurobiology, 136,* 89–119.

Zanchi, D., Depoorter, A., Egloff, L., Haller, S., Mählmann, L., et al. (2017). The impact of gut hormones on the neural circuit of appetite and satiety: A systematic review. *Neuroscience & Biobehavioral Reviews, 80,* 457–475.

Zeev-Wolf, M., Levy, J., Goldstein, A., Zagoory-Sharon, O., & Feldman, R. (2019). Chronic early stress impairs default mode network connectivity in preadolescents and their mothers. *Biological Psychiatry: Cognitive Neuroscience & Neuroimaging, 4,* 72–80.

Zehra, A., Burns, J., Liu, C.K., Manza, P., Wiers, C.E., et al. (2018). Cannabis addiction and the brain: a review. *Journal of Neuroimmune Pharmacology, 13,* 438–452.

Zelenski, J.M. (2020). *Positive Psychology: The Science of Well-Being.* London: Sage Publishing.

Zhang, J., Wiecaszek, P., Sami, S., & Meiser-Stedman, R. (2021). Association between panic disorder and childhood adversities: A systematic review and meta-analysis. *Psychological Medicine,* ePub ahead of print.

Zhang, L., Bao, Y., Wang, X., Zhou, Y., Tao, S., et al. (2020). A meta-analysis on the prevalence, associated factors and diagnostic methods of mental stress induced myocardial ischemia. *Journal of Translational Medicine, 18,* 218.

Zhang, L., Pan, J., Chen, W., Jiang, J., & Huang, J. (2020). Chronic stress-induced immune dysregulation in cancer: Implications for initiation, progression, metastasis, and treatment. *American Journal of Cancer Research, 10,* 1294–1307.

Zhang, Y., Wang, L., Wang, X., Wang, Y., Li, C., & Zhu, X. (2019). Alterations of DNA methylation at GDNF gene promoter in the ventral tegmental area of adult depression-like rats induced by maternal deprivation. *Frontiers in Psychiatry, 9,* 732.

Zhao, L., Xu, J., Liang, F., Li, A., Zhang, Y., & Sun, J. (2015). Effect of chronic psychological stress on liver metastasis of colon cancer in mice. *PLoS One, 10,* e0139978.

Zhao, M., Chen, L., Yang, J., Han, D., & Fang, D. (2018). BDNF Val66Met polymorphism, life stress and depression: A meta-analysis of gene-environment interaction. *Journal of Affective Disorders, 227,* 226–235.

Zhao, S., Zhu, Y., Schultz, R.D., Li, N., He, Z., et al. (2019). Partial leptin reduction as an insulin sensitization and weight loss strategy. *Cell Metabolism, 30,* 706–719.e6.

Zheng, H., Echave, P., Mehta, N., & Myrskylä, M. (2021). Life-long body mass index trajectories and mortality in two generations. *Annals of Epidemiology, 56,* 18–25.

Zhou, H.X., Chen, X., Shen, Y.Q., Li, L., Chen, N.X., et al. (2020). Rumination and the default mode network: Meta-analysis of brain imaging studies and implications for depression. *Neuroimage, 206,* 116287.

Zilverstand, A., Parvaz, M.A., Moeller, S.J., & Goldstein, R.Z. (2016). Cognitive interventions for addiction medicine: Understanding the underlying neurobiological mechanisms. *Progress in Brain Research, 224,* 285–304.

Zimmer, A., Youngblood, A., Adnane, A., Miller, B.J., & Goldsmith, D.R. (2021). Prenatal exposure to viral infection and neuropsychiatric disorders in offspring: a review of the literature and recommendations for the COVID-19 pandemic. *Brain, Behavior, and Immunity, 91,* 756–770.

Zimmet, P., Shi, Z., El-Osta, A., & Ji, L. (2018). Epidemic T2DM, early development and epigenetics: implications of the Chinese Famine. *Nature Reviews Endocrinology, 14,* 738–746.

Zitvogel, L., Daillère, R., Roberti, M.P., Routy, B., & Kroemer, G. (2017). Anticancer effects of the microbiome and its products *Nature Review in Microbiology, 15,* 465–478.

Zmora, N., Zilberman-Schapira, G., Suez, J., Mor, U., Dori-Bachash, M., et al. (2018). Personalized gut mucosal colonization resistance to empiric probiotics is associated with unique host and microbiome features. *Cell, 174,* 1388–1405.e21.

Zohar, J., Juven-Wetzler, A., Sonnino, R., Cwikel-Hamzany, S., Balaban, E., & Cohen, H. (2011). New insights into secondary prevention in post-traumatic stress disorder. *Dialogues in Clinical Neuroscience, 13,* 301–309.

Zorrilla, E.P., Logrip, M.L., & Koob, G.F. (2014). Corticotropin-releasing factor: A key role in the neurobiology of addiction. *Frontiers in Neuroendocrinology, 35,* 234–244.

Zou, R., Tian, P., Xu, M., Zhu, H., Zhao, J., et al. (2021). Psychobiotics as a novel strategy for alleviating anxiety and depression. *Journal of Functional Foods, 86,* 104718.

Zou, Z., Huang, Y., Wang, J., Min, W., & Zhou, B. (2020). The association between serotonin-related gene polymorphisms and susceptibility and early sertraline response in patients with panic disorder. *BMC Psychiatry, 20,* 388.

Zuma, B.Z., Parizo, J.T., Valencia, A., Spencer-Bonilla, G., Blum, M.R., et al. (2021). County-level factors associated with cardiovascular mortality by race/ethnicity. *Journal of the American Heart Association, 10,* e018835.

Zunhammer, M., Spisák, T., Wager, T.D., & Bingel, U. (2021). Meta-analysis of neural systems underlying placebo analgesia from individual participant fMRI data. *Nature Communications, 12,* 1391.

INDEX

References in **bold** are to tables and in *italic* are to figures.